THE

LITERATURE

AND

THE LITERARY MEN

OF

Great Britain and Ireland.

BY

ABRAHAM MILLS, A.M.,

AUTHOR OF LECTURES ON RHETORIC AND BELLES LETTRES, ETC. ETC. ETC.

IN TWO VOLUMES.

VOLUME THE FIRST.

NEW YORK:

HARPER & BROTHERS, PUBLISHERS,

Nos. 329 AND 331 PEARL STREET,

FRANKLIN SQUARE.

1856.

TO

HON. THEODORE FRELINGHUYSEN,

LATE

Chancellor of the University

OF THE CITY OF NEW YORK,

NOW

PRESIDENT OF RUTGER'S COLLEGE,

NEW JERSEY,

THESE VOLUMES

ARE, AS A MARK OF GREAT RESPECT,

INSCRIBED,

BY THE AUTHOR.

PREFACE.

More than twenty years ago the author of this work was invited to deliver, professionally, a Course of Lectures on English Literature. The lectures then prepared, with such additions and corrections as successive years of investigation and study naturally suggested, have since been annually repeated. In preparing them for the press the author has availed himself of every assistance that other publications on kindred subjects afford. In investigating the literature of the Saxons he has derived much assistance from *Wright's Anglo-Saxon Period of British Literature*, and *Thorp's Edition of Cædmon;* and in the period that immediately follows the Saxon, *Ellis's Metrical Romances*, and *Wright's Lyric Poetry and Political Songs of the Reign of Edward I.* have been of equal service. To *Godwin's Life of Chaucer* he also acknowledges himself particularly indebted.

After the age of Chaucer the exposition of English Literature is so full, and the expositors are so numerous, that in the selection of authorities, both judgment and discretion were required. The works to which the author is here most indebted, are *Warton's History of English Poetry*, *Percy's Reliques of English Poetry*, *Hazlitt's Lectures on the Age of Elizabeth*, the *Lectures of Dr. Drake*, *Bale's Account of the Lives of Eminent Writers of Great Britain*, *Burnett's Specimens of English Prose Writers*, *Hallam's Literature of the Fifteenth, Sixteenth, and Seventeenth Centuries*, and *Chambers' Cyclopædia of English Literature;* from the last of which a number of the illustrations and minor criticisms were taken. He has also made liberal use of various articles in the *Edinburgh* and other *Reviews*, and has, as occasion required, freely consulted the *Biographia Britannica*,

Literaria. With aids so abundant, the author has still, in no instance, sacrificed his own judgment to the opinion of others; but has endeavored, in all cases, to present such views of the Literature and Literary Men of Great Britain and Ireland, as truth and justice seemed to require: aiming, throughout, to leave a correct impression of the *moral* influence which the life of each author, and each work noticed, is calculated to produce. He can not, however, withhold an expression of the deep solicitude with which he offers so important a production to the public; and in the language used by Burke under similar circumstances, he would 'desire one favor, that no part of this work may be judged of by itself, and independently of the rest; for he is sensible he has not disposed his materials to abide the test of a captious controversy, but of a sober and even forgiving examination; that they are not armed at all points for battle, but dressed to visit those who are willing to give a peaceful entrance to truth.'

GLOBE HOTEL, BROOKLYN,
AUGUST, 1851.

AUTHORS' NAMES,

IN VOLUME THE FIRST,

ALPHABETICALLY ARRANGED.

CONTENTS OF VOLUME THE FIRST.

LECTURE THE FIRST.

LECTURE THE SECOND.

LECTURE THE THIRD.

LECTURE THE FOURTH.

LECTURE THE FIFTH.

LECTURE THE SIXTH.

LECTURE THE SEVENTH.

LECTURE THE EIGHTH.

LECTURE THE NINTH.

LECTURE THE TENTH.

LECTURE THE ELEVENTH.

LECTURE THE TWELFTH.

LECTURE THE THIRTEENTH.

LECTURE THE FOURTEENTH.

LECTURE THE FIFTEENTH.

LECTURE THE SIXTEENTH.

LECTURE THE SEVENTEENTH.

LECTURE THE EIGHTEENTH.

LECTURE THE NINETEENTH.

LECTURE THE TWENTIETH.

LECTURE THE TWENTY-FIRST.

LECTURE THE TWENTY-SECOND.

LECTURE THE TWENTY-THIRD.

LECTURE THE TWENTY-FOURTH.

Lecture the First.

THE CELTIC LANGUAGE—THE ORIGIN AND FORMATION OF THE ANGLO-SAXON—OSSIAN, THE CELTIC POET—GILDAS—NENNIUS—ST. COLUMBANUS—CÆDMON—JOHN OF BEVERLY—BEDE—KING ALFRED—ALFRIC, ARCHBISHOP OF CANTERBURY—NORMAN FRENCH WRITERS—MAISTRE WACE—THE ORIGIN OF THE ENGLISH LANGUAGE—RHYMING CHRONICLES—LAYAMON—ROBERT OF GLOUCESTER—METRICAL ROMANCES—MINSTRELS OR JONGLEURS—RICHARD THE FIRST—ROGER BACON.

THE English language, now so rich in its literature, is essentially based upon the Teutonic, a dialect spoken by the inhabitants of Central Europe at the dawn of history, and which also constitutes the basis of the language of Germany, of Holland, and of Denmark. It was introduced from the continent by the Anglo-Saxons in the latter part of the fifth century of the Christian era, and gradually spread with the people who spoke it, over nearly the whole of Southern Britain; the Celtic, the language of the Aborigines of the country, soon shrinking before it into Caledonia, Wales, Cornwall, and other remote parts of the island.

During the first five centuries after its introduction into the country now called England, the Anglo-Saxon language underwent little change farther than that which resulted from the occasional introduction of Latin words by Christian missionaries from the continent; and its literature, meantime, was cultivated, chiefly, by members of the different religious orders, some of whom were evidently men of more than ordinary genius. This early age presents us with many valuable historical chronicles, and theological treatises, together with occasional poetical effusions that well deserve to be carefully preserved.

But before we proceed to speak of these writers more particularly, we can not forbear to pause for a moment on the Celtic age, and briefly notice Ossian, its brightest, and perhaps its only ornament. Without concerning ourselves with those perplexing questions which respect Ossian's identity, we shall assume, according to Dr. Blair and Lord Kames, that he really lived, and actually composed the poems attributed to him by Macpherson.

The era assigned to Ossian is the beginning of the fourth Christian century, which places him two centuries at least anterior to any Southern British writer. He was the son of Fingal, a Caledonian chief, and having survived all the companions of his youth, under the influence of the "Joy of Grief"—his own luminous expression, looked back upon the scenes of his early life, and breathed forth in strains of melancholy tenderness, and deep pathos, all those chastening recollections which now burthened his memory.

The principal poems of Ossian are *Fingal*, and *Temora*, both of which are regular epics, though they are comparatively limited in extent. Of these poems, as well as of the minor productions of his muse, the principal characteristics are sublimity and tenderness. They breathe nothing of the gay and cheerful kind, but an air of solemnity and seriousness is diffused over the whole. Ossian is, perhaps, the only poet who never relaxes, or lets himself down into the light or amusing strain: he moves perpetually in the high region of the grand and the pathetic. One key-note is struck at the beginning, and supported to the end; nor is any ornament introduced that is not perfectly concordant with the general tone of the melody. The events recorded are all serious and grave, and the scenery throughout is wild and romantic. The extended heath by the sea-shore; the mountains shaded with mist; the torrent rushing through a silent valley; the scattered oaks, and the tombs of warriors overgrown with moss; all produce a solemn attention in the mind, and prepare it for great and extraordinary events.

We find not in Ossian an imagination that supports itself, and dresses out gay trifles to please the fancy. His poetry, to a greater extent, perhaps, than that of any other writer, deserves to be styled the poetry of the heart —a heart penetrated with noble sentiments, and with sublime and tender passions; a heart that glows and kindles the fancy; a heart that is full to overflowing, and pours its gushing feelings forth unrestrained.

Ossian, like Homer, did not write as modern poets write, to please readers and critics: he sang from the pure love of poetry and song. His delight was to think of the heroes among whom he had flourished; to recall the affecting incidents of his life; to dwell upon his past wars, and loves, and friendships; till, as he himself expresses it,

> There comes a voice to Ossian, and awakes his soul. It is the voice of years that are gone; they roll before me with all their deeds;

and under this true poetic inspiration, giving vent to genius, it is no wonder that we should so often hear and acknowledge, in his strains, the powerful and ever-pleasing voice of humanity.

It is necessary to remark, however, that the beauties of the poems of Ossian can not be felt by those who give them only a single or hasty perusal. They require to be taken up at intervals, and to be frequently reviewed; and then it is impossible that his beauties should not develop themselves to every reader who is capable of sensibility. Those indeed who have the highest degree of it, will relish him the most. In the absence of religion, and religious sentiment of every kind, Ossian has created a machinery for himself out of the departed spirits of heroes and friends; and these properly constitute his mythology. The aspect of these spirits, and their breathing tones, are frequently wrought up to a height of sublimity wonderfully great; such passages therefore as the following abound in every part of his poems:

A dark red stream of fire comes down from the hill. Crugal sat upon the beam; he that lately fell by the hand of Suaran, striving in the battle of heroes. His face is like the beam of the setting moon. His robes are of the cloud of the hill. His eyes are like two decaying flames. Dark is the wound of his breast. The stars dim twinkle through his form; and his voice was like the sound of a distant stream.

The attitude in which the spirit of Crugal is afterward placed, and the speech which he utters, are full of that solemn and awful sublimity, which is so peculiarly suited to the subject.

Dim, and in tears he stood, and he outstretched his pale hand over the hero. Faintly he raised his feeble voice, like the gale of the reedy Sego. My ghost, Oh Conal! is on my native hills; but my course is on the sands of Ulla. Thou shalt never talk with Crugal, or find his lonely steps in the heath. I am light as the blast of Cromla; and I move like the shadow of mist. Conal, son of Colga! I see the dark cloud of death; it hovers over the plains of Lena. The sons of green Erin shall fall. Remove from the field of ghosts ——— Like the darkened moon, he retired in the midst of the whistling blast.

With scenes of exquisite painting also Ossian abounds. Such is the scenery with which Temora opens, and the attitude in which Caibar is there presented; the description of the young prince Cormac in the same book, and the ruins of Balclutha in Cartho.

I have seen the walls of Balclutha, but they were desolate. The fire had resounded in the halls; and the voice of the people is heard no more. The stream of Clutha was removed from its place by the fall of the walls. The thistle shook there its lonely head; the moss whistled to the wind. The fox looked out from the windows; the rank grass of the wall waved round his head. Desolate is the dwelling of Moina, silence is in the house of her fathers.

But Ossian's genius, though chiefly turned toward the sublime and the pathetic, was by no means confined to it. In subjects also of grace and delicacy, he discovers the hand of a master. As an instance of this, we may notice the following exquisite description of Agandecca, the tenderness of which is, perhaps, unsurpassed.

The daughter of the snow overheard, and left the hall of her secret sigh. She came in all her beauty; like the moon from the cloud of the east. Loveliness was around her as light. Her steps were like the music of songs. She saw the youth and loved him. He was the stolen sigh of her soul. Her blue eyes rolled on him in secret; and she blessed the chief of Morven.

The metaphors of Ossian, such as,

In peace thou art the gale of spring—in war, the mountain storm,

and his similes, such as,

The music of Carol was like the memory of joys that are past,—pleasant, and mournful to the soul,

are of the most delicate kind, and adorn almost every page of his poetry; but we are constrained here to close our notice of this venerable poet, and we shall do so with that noble 'Address to the Sun,' found in Carthon, and his 'Last Song,' at the close of his poems.

Oh thou that rollest above, round as the shield of my fathers. Whence are thy beams, Oh sun! thy everlasting light! Thou comest forth in thy awful beauty; the stars hide themselves in the sky; the moon, cold and pale, sinks in the western way; but thou thyself movest alone. Who can be a companion of thy course? The oaks of the mountains fall; the mountains themselves decay with years; the ocean shrinks and grows again; the moon herself is lost in heaven: but thou art forever the same, rejoicing in the brightness of thy course. When the world is dark with tempests, when thunder rolls and lightning flies, thou lookest in thy beauty from the clouds, and laughest at the storm. But to Ossian thou lookest in vain, for he beholds thy beams no more: whether thy yellow hair flows on the eastern clouds, or thou tremblest at the gates of the west. But thou art, perhaps, like me, for a season; thy years will have an end. Thou shalt sleep in thy clouds, careless of the voice of the morning. Exult, then, oh Sun, in the strength of thy youth! Age is dark and unlovely; it is like the glimmering light of the moon when it shines through broken clouds, and the mist is on the hills: the blast of the north is on the plain, the traveller shrinks in the midst of his journey.

The tenderness and pathos of the close of the 'Last Song' strikingly re mind us of a similar passage in the Roman poet Ovid.

My harp hangs on a blasted branch. The sound of its strings is mournful. Does the wind touch thee, Oh harp, or is it some passing ghost? It is the hand of Malvina! Bring me the harp, son of Alpin. Another song shall rise. My soul shall depart in the sound. My fathers shall hear it in their airy hall. Their dim faces shall hang, with joy, from their clouds; and their hands receive their son. The aged oak bends over the stream. It sighs with all its moss. The withered fern whistles near, and mixes, as it waves, with Ossian's hair.

Strike the harp, and raise the song; be near, with all your wings, ye winds. Bear the mournful sound away to Fingal's airy hall. Bear it to Fingal's hall, that he may hear the voice of his son; the voice of him that praised the mighty.

The blast of the north opens thy gates, Oh king! I behold thee sitting on mists dimly gleaming in all thine arms. Thy form now is not the terror of the valiant. It is like the watery cloud when we see the stars behind it with their weeping eyes. Thy shield is the aged moon: thy sword, a vapor half kindled with fire. Dim and feeble is the chief who travelled in brightness before! But thy steps are on the winds of the desert. Thy storms are darkening in thy hand. Thou takest the sun in thy wrath, and hidest him in thy clouds. The sons of little men are afraid. A thousand showers descend. But when thou comest forth in thy mildness, the gate of the morning is near thy course. The sun laughs in his blue fields. The gray stream winds in its vale. The bushes shake their green heads in the wind. The roes bound toward the desert.

There is a murmur in the heath! The stormy winds abate! I hear the voice of Fingal. Long has it been absent from mine ear! 'Come, Ossian, come away,' he says. Fingal has received his fame. We passed away like flames that shone for a season. Our departure was in renown. Though the plains of our battles are dark and silent, our fame is in the four gray stones. The voice of Ossian has been heard. The harp has been strung in Selma! 'Come, Ossian, come away,' he says; 'come, fly with thy fathers on clouds.' I come, I come, thou king of men! The life of Ossian fails. I begin to vanish on Cona. My steps are not seen in Selma. Beside the stone of Mora I shall fall asleep. The winds whistling in my gray hair, shall not awaken me. Depart on thy wings, O wind, thou canst not disturb the rest of the bard. The night is long, but his eyes are heavy. Depart, thou rustling blast.

But why art thou sad, son of Fingal? Why glows the cloud of thy soul? The chiefs of other times are departed. They have gone without their fame. The sons of future years shall pass away. Another race shall arise. The people are like the waves of the ocean; like the leaves of woody Morven they pass away in the rustling blast, and other leaves lift their green heads on high.

Did thy beauty last, O Ryno? Stood the strength of car-borne Oscar! Fingal himself departed! The halls of his fathers forgot his steps. Shalt thou then remain, thou aged bard, when the mighty have failed? But my fame shall remain, and grow like the oak of Morven; which lifts its broad head to the storm, and rejoices in the course of the wind!

From this brief notice of the poetic genius of Ossian, we return to those early Anglo-Saxon writers to whom we have already referred.

GILDAS, the first of these, in the order of time, was a native of the north of England, and his residence was in the vicinity of the wall of Severus; but at what precise period he lived, is uncertain. His calling seems to have been that of a Christian missionary, but of his life nothing farther is known. As a writer, Gildas is to be gratefully remembered for being the author of an *Historical Epistle*, containing an account of all the important events in the history of his native country, from the earliest period of that history down to the year 560. This epistle, though inelegantly written in the Latin language, is of the utmost importance, as it is the only reliable source whence our knowledge of the period of which it treats is to be drawn. This important work remained for many centuries comparatively neglected, but during the reign of Charles the Second it was translated into English, and has since been more generally known.

NENNIUS, a contemporary of Gildas, was the reputed author of some comparatively unimportant tracts; but with regard to this writer himself, and also of the productions of his pen, so much uncertainty prevails that no farther notice of him is deemed necessary.

ST. COLUMBANUS, another writer of the same period, and also a man of much greater genius and wider celebrity than either of his contemporaries, was a native of Ireland, and his name is still embalmed in that country in the sweetest recollections, for his vigorous and continuous efforts toward the advancement of Christianity throughout his native island. He was also a devoted patron of learning, and was the author of various religious tracts, and some Latin poems, the merit of which was very unusual when we consider the period at which the author wrote. Neither of the three writers just mentioned, can, however, justly be considered as Anglo-Saxon authors, for they all wrote in the Latin language.

CÆDMON, the next author to be noticed, may, therefore, properly be considered the first writer who distinguished himself among the British Anglo-Saxons.

Cædmon was a monk of Whitby, and was originally of so comparatively low and obscure circumstances, as to be a menial in public service. In this capacity he was engaged when his talents were first developed, according to the narrative of the venerable Bede, in the following marvelous and extraordinary manner.

'Cædmon,' we are told by this author, 'was so much less instructed than most of his equals, that he had not even learned any poetry; so that he was frequently obliged to retire, in order to hide his shame, when the harp was moved toward him in the hall, where at supper it was customary for each person to sing in turn. On one of these occasions, it happened to be Cædmon's turn to keep guard at the stable during the night, and overcome with vexation, he quitted the table, and retired to his post of duty, where, laying himself down, he fell into a sound slumber. In the midst of his sleep, a stranger appeared to him, and saluting him by his name, said, 'Cædmon, sing me something.' Cædmon answered, 'I know nothing to sing, for my incapacity in this respect was the cause of my leaving the hall to come hither.' 'Nay,' said the stranger, 'but thou hast something to sing.' 'What must I sing?' said Cædmon. 'Sing the creation,' was the reply,—and thereupon Cædmon began to sing verses 'which he had never heard before,' and which are said to have been as follows:—

Now we shall praise
the guardian of heaven,
the might of the Creator,
and his council,
the glory—father of men!
how he of all wonders,
the eternal lord,
formed the beginning.
He first created
for the children of men
heaven as a roof,
the holy Creator!
then the world
the guardian of mankind,
the eternal lord
produced afterward,
the earth for men,
the Almighty master.

Cædmon then awoke; and he was not only able to repeat the lines which he had made in his sleep, but he continued them in a strain of admirable versification. In the morning, he hastened to the bailiff of Whitby, who carried him before the abbess Hilda; and there, in the presence of some of the learned men of the place, he told his story, and they were all of opinion that he had received the gift of song from heaven. They then expounded to him, in his mother tongue, a portion of Scripture, which he was required to repeat in verse. Cædmon went home with his task, and the next morning he produced a poem which excelled in beauty, all that they were accustomed to hear. He afterward yielded to the earnest solicitation of the abbess Hilda, and became a monk of her house; and she ordered him to transfer into verse the whole of the sacred history. We are told that he was continually occupied in repeating to himself what he heard, and, 'like a clean animal, ruminating it, he turned it into most sweet verse.'

Cædmon thus composed many poems on the Bible histories, and on miscellaneous religious subjects, and some of these have been preserved. His account of the *Fall of Man* is not unlike that which is given in 'Paradise Lost,' and the following passage in it might almost be supposed to have been the foundation of a corresponding passage in Milton's sublime Epic. It is that in which Satan is described as reviving from the consternation of his overthrow, and in English is as follows:

SATAN'S SPEECH.

Boiled within him
his thoughts about his heart;
Hot was without him
his dire punishment.
Then spake he words:
This narrow place is most unlike
that other that we formerly knew,
high in heaven's kingdom,
Which my master bestowed on me,
though we it, for the All-powerful,
may not possess.
We must cede our realm;
yet hath he not done rightly,
that he hath struck us down
to the fiery abyss
of the hot hell,
bereft us of heaven's kingdom,
hath decreed
to people it
with mankind.
That is to me of sorrows the greatest,
that Adam
who was wrought of earth,
shall possess
my strong seat;
that it shall be to him in delight,
and we endure this torment,
misery in this hell.
Oh! had I the power of my hands,
then with this host I——
But round me lie
iron bonds;
presseth this cord of chain;
I am powerless!
me have so hard
the clasps of hell
so firmly grasped!

Here is a vast fire
above and underneath;
never did I see
a loathier landskip;
the flame abateth not,
hot over hell.
Me hath the clasping of these rings
this hard polished band,
impeded in my course,
debarred me from my way.
My feet are bound,
my hands manacled;
Of these hell doors are
the ways obstructed;
so that with aught I can not
from these limb-bonds escape.
About me lie
huge gratings
of hard iron,
forged with heat,
with which me God
hath fastened by the neck.
Thus perceive I that he knoweth my mind,
and that he knew also,
the Lord of hosts,
that should us through Adam
evil befall,
About the realm of heaven,
where I had power of my hands.

The specimen of Cædmon's writing here given, may serve as a general one of Anglo-Saxon poetry. It will be observed that it is neither in measured feet, like Latin verse, nor rhymed, but that the only peculiarity which distinguishes it from prose, is a regular alliteration in the original, so arranged that in every couplet there should be two principal words in the line beginning with the same letter, and that this letter must also be the initial of the first word on which the stress of the voice falls in the second line.

A few more names of inferior order, such as Aldhelm, Abbot of Malmsberry, Coilfrid, Abbot of Wearmouth, and Felix of Croyland, bring down the list of Anglo-Saxon writers to the celebrated John of Beverly, and the venerable Bede.

JOHN OF BEVERLY was descended from a noble family, and was born at Harpham, in Northumberland, near the middle of the seventh century. The evidence of genius which he early evinced, attracting the attention of the Archbishop of Canterbury, he was instructed in the learned languages by that prelate in person; and such was the rapidity of his attainments, that he soon came to be esteemed one of the first scholars of the age. On his return to his native country, in 685, he was preferred by Alfred, king of Northumberland, to the see of Haxam; and in 687, two years after ward, he was translated by the same prince to the Archbishopric of York. In this exalted position, Beverly continued for many years to exert all the energies of his capacious and accomplished mind toward the improvement of the see over which he presided, and the clergy who were under his control.

In 704, Beverly, in order that he might the more effectually further the great objects of instruction which he had in view, founded, in the town of Beverly, a college for secular priests, which soon rose to great importance, and was endowed with unusual immunities. Among other privileges attached to this college, was an asylum or sanctuary for debtors, and for persons suspected of capital crimes. Within this sanctuary was placed a stone chair, which contained upon it the following inscription:—'The chair of peace, to which what criminal soever flies, has full protection.'

After having governed the see of York during thirty-four successive years, he divested himself of his Episcopal character, and died four years after on the seventh of May, 721.

Many years after Beverly's death, Alfric, Archbishop of York, caused his body to be disinterred, and placed in a new shrine, richly adorned with silver, gold, and precious stones; and such was the respect which the place of his repose universally inspired, that when William the Conqueror desolated Northumberland with a numerous army, he spared Beverly alone—out of veneration for the memory of the eminent prelate.

Bede, and many other monkish writers, unhesitatingly attribute to Beverly the performance of many miracles; but this, when we consider the superstition of the times, is not at all to be wondered at, as the extreme sanctity of his life and character must have elevated him far above all his contemporaries.

Beverly was the author of several literary productions, many of which were works of much merit, but as they were all written in the Latin language, a more particular notice of them does not fall within our present province.

Bede, the next writer of this period, in the order of time, was born in 672, at Wearmouth, on a family estate, situated near the mouth of the Tyne. His precocious intellect induced his parents to send him in 679, when he was only seven years of age, to the monastery of St. Peters, to receive his education. He remained at this monastery twelve years; and during that period his literary attainments were so remarkable, that attracting the attention of Beverly, now Archbishop of York, he was ordained by that prelate into the order of deacon at the early age of nineteen.

Bede did not, however, immediately enter upon his religious functions, but still remained attached to his monastery, prosecuting his literary studies with such ardor, that within comparatively a few years, he became one of the most eminent scholars of the age.

In the thirtieth year of his age, Bede was elevated to the priestly office;

and his scholastic fame having already spread over the continent, a mandate was sent by Pope Sergius from Rome, ordering him immediately to repair to the papal see, in order that his opinion and advice might be obtained upon some critical and important subjects, which at that period required the attention of the Pope's counsellors. Bede, however, resisted an order so flattering to his fame, and still remained in his cell for many years, ardently prosecuting his studies, until he had rendered himself master of every branch of learning then cultivated. His whole life was that of a religious recluse; and at his death, which occurred on the 26th of May, 735, he was buried in his own monastery, but his remains were afterward removed to Durham, where they were allowed in uninterrupted quiet to repose.

The literary productions of Bede were very numerous, comprising no less than forty-four distinct works, among which were a translation of the Gospel by John into the Saxon language, Scriptural Commentaries, Religious Treatises, Biographies, and an *Ecclesiastical History of the Anglo-Saxons*, which is the only history of the subject of which it treats, at all useful at the present time. In the collecting of the materials for this work, Bede occupied many laborious years, drawing them from the lives of eminent saints, from the annals of convents, and from religious chronicles written before his own time. The work was presented to the public in 731, when the author was in the fifty-ninth year of his age, and its reception among the learned was such, as at once to place the writer upon a parallel with the early fathers of the church. The last literary performance of Bede was a letter to the Archbishop of York, which contains a very singular and interesting account of the state of the church at that time, and which was finished by an amanuensis at the moment of the venerable author's death.

Of this interesting author Camden remarks, that, 'for his profound learning, in a most barbarous age, we may more easily admire than sufficiently praise him;' and Bale also says, 'that there is scarcely any thing in all antiquity worthy to be read, which is not to be found in Bede, though he travelled not out of his own country; and that if he had flourished in the times of St. Augustine, Jerome, or Chrysostom, he would undoubtedly have equalled them, since even in the midst of a superstitious age, he wrote so many excellent treatises.' Testimonials equally flattering might also be drawn from the learned Seldon, the great antiquarian Spelman, and the famous Stillingfleet.

The two centuries which followed the death of Bede, were perhaps, with regard to literature, the darkest period that ever shrouded the British Isles, and the amiable and intrepid king Alfred, to whom our remarks have now brought us down, must therefore be emphatically regarded as a bright light in the midst of the surrounding gloom. In this prince, learning and authorship graced the royal state, without interfering with its proper duties.

ALFRED was the sixth king of the Saxon dynasty, and was born in 848,

After a life of fifty-three years in extent, the early part of which was spent in the most severe conflicts with the enemies of his country for the national existence of his very kingdom, and the latter, covered with glory and honor, he died in 901, and left his kingdom perhaps more formidable and prosperous than any other cotemporary monarchy.

Alfred is represented to have attained the fifteenth year of his age without having learned to read even his native language. But about that period his mind was aroused, through the assiduous care of his mother, by the recitation of simple Saxon poems, to the subject of learning; and in the course of a few years, he made those wonderful attainments in literature which rendered him both an able and accomplished scholar. When he became quietly seated on his throne, he, through anxiety for the improvement of his subjects, translated the historical works of Bede, and some religious and moral treatises, perhaps also Æsop's Fables and the Psalms of David, into the Anglo-Saxon language. These translations are accompanied with frequent and appropriate reflections, some of which have much point and beauty. Alfred's poems are based chiefly on Boethius; but the original writer often merely suggests the thought, which the royal bard expands into symmetrical beauty. This is peculiarly the case in the odes that follow, the first and second of which were composed during his exile from his throne, and the third at some after-period.

A SONG OF SORROW.

Lo! I sang cheerily
  In my bright days,
But now all wearily
  Chant I my lays;
Sorrowing tearfully,
  Saddest of men,
Can I sing cheerfully,
  As I could then?

Many a verity
  In those glad times
Of my prosperity
  Taught I in rhymes;
Now from forgetfulness
  Wanders my tongue,
Wasting in fretfulness
  Metres unsung.

Worldliness brought me here
  Foolishly blind,
Riches have wrought me here
  Sadness of mind;
When I rely on them,
  Lo! they depart,—
Bitterly, fie on them!
  Rend they my heart.

Why did your songs to me,
  World-loving men,
Sad joy belongs to me
  Even as then?
Why did ye lyingly
  Think such a thing,
Seeing how flyingly
  Wealth may take wing?

A SONG OF DESPAIR.

Alas! in how grim
  A gulf of despair,
Dreary and dim
  For sorrow and care,
My mind toils along
  When the waves of the world,
Stormy and strong,
  Against it are hurl'd.

When in such strife,
  My mind will forget
Its light and its life
  In worldly regret;
And through the night
  Of this world doth grope,
Lost to the light
  Of heavenly hope.

Thus it hath now
  Befallen my mind,
I know no more how
  God's goodness to find;
But groan in my grief,
  Troubled and tost,
Needing relief
  For the world I have lost.

A PSALM TO GOD.

O Thou, that art Maker of heaven and earth,
Who steerest the stars and hast given them birth,
Forever Thou reignest upon Thy high throne,
And turnest all swiftly the heavenly zone.

Thou, by Thy strong holiness, drivest from far
In the way that Thou willest each worshiping star;
And through thy great power, the sun from the night
Drags darkness away by the might of her light.

The moon, at Thy word, with his pale-shining rays
Softens and shadows the stars as they blaze,
And even the sun of her brightness bereaves
Whenever upon her too closely he cleaves.

So also the Morning and Evening Star
Thou makest to follow the Sun from afar,

To keep in her pathway each year evermore,
And go as she goeth in guidance before.

Behold, too, O Father, Thou workest aright
To summer hot day-times of long-living light,
To winter all wondrously orderest wise
Short seasons of sunshine with frost on the skies.

Thou givest the trees a south-westerly breeze,
Whose leaves the swart storm in its fury did seize
By winds flying forth from the east and the north
And scattered and shattered all over the earth.

On earth and in heaven each creature and kind
Hears Thy behest with might and with mind;
But Man, and Man only, who oftenest still
Wickedly worketh against Thy wise will.

Forever, Almighty One, Maker and Lord,
On us, wretched earth-worms, Thy pity be poured;
Why wilt Thou that welfare to sinners should wend,
But lettest weird ill the unguilty ones rend?

Evil men sit, each on earth's highest seat,
Trampling the holy ones under their feet;
Why good should go crookedly no man can say,
And bright deeds in crowds should lie hidden away.

The sinner at all times is scorning the just,
The wiser in right, and the worthier of trust;
Their leasing for long while with fraud is beclad;
And oaths that are lies do no harm to the bad.

O Guide, if Thou wilt not steer fortune amain
But lettest her rush so self-will'd and so vain,
I know that the worldly will doubt of Thy might,
And few among men in Thy rule will delight.

My Lord, overseeing all things from on high
Look down on mankind with mercy's mild eye;
In wild waves of trouble they struggle and strive,
Then spare the poor earth-worms, and save them alive![1]

The character of this monarch, embracing so much gentleness, together with such manly vigor and dignity, and displaying, at the same time, so pure a taste, seems sufficient to have graced the most civilized age, nearly as much as it did the rude one in which he lived.

Alfric, Archbishop of Canterbury, is the next important name after Alfred, that graces British literature. This learned prelate was a voluminous writer, and, like Alfred, entertained a strong desire to enlighten the common people. He therefore wrote much in his native tongue, particularly a collection of homilies, a translation of the first seven books of the

[1] For the translation of these poems we are indebted to the recent publication of King Alfred's Poems in English Metres by Martin F. Tupper, the author of 'Proverbial Philosophy.' They were kindly communicated to us by C. Edwards Lester, Esq.

Bible, and some religious treatises. He was also the author of a grammar of the Latin tongue, in consequence of which he is usually called 'the Grammarian.' Alfric himself declares that he wrote in Anglo-Saxon, and that he might be understood by the unlettered people, avoided the use of all obscure words. This interesting writer died in 1006.

. CYNEWULF, Bishop of Winchester, Wulfstan, Archbishop of York, and some others of less note, bring down the list of Anglo-Saxon authors to the Conquest, giving to this period of English literature a duration of nearly five hundred years. During this time there were many seats of learning in England, many writers, and many books; although these have now chiefly become matter of curiosity to the antiquary only. Saxon literature may, indeed, be said to have had a protracted existence, till the breaking up of the language in the latter part of the twelfth century; but during that whole period it was graced by no names of distinction. We must here, however, advert to the historical productions usually called the *Anglo-Saxon Chroncle*, which consists of a view of early English history, written it is believed by a series of authors, commencing soon after the time of Alfred, and continued to the reign of Henry the Second, the first prince of the house of Plantagenet. This Chronicle is chiefly valuable as the basis of our historical knowledge of the period of which it treats.

The Conquest, by which a Norman government and nobility were imposed upon England, led to a very great change in the language. Norman French, one of those modifications of Latin which arose in the middle ages, now became the language of education, of the courts of law, and of the higher classes of society generally, while Saxon shared in the degradation which the mass of the people experienced under their Conquerors. Though depressed, yet as the speech of the great body of the nation, it could not, however, be extinguished; but it was destined, in the course of the twelfth century, to undergo very essential grammatical changes. Its sounds were greatly altered, syllables were shortened in the pronunciation, and the termination, and inflections of words were softened down until they were entirely lost. Indeed, in the opinion of Dr. Johnson, the Normans affected the Anglo-Saxon language more in this manner than by the introduction of new words. The language which resulted from this change, was the commencement of the present English.

The first literary productions that call for attention after the Conquest, are a class which may, in a great measure, be considered foreign both to the country and to its language. Before the Conqueror's invasion of England, poetical literature had begun to be cultivated in France, with a considerable degree of spirit and taste. The language, which, from its origin, was called *Romane*, was separated into two great divisions—that of the South, which is represented popularly by the Provençal, and that of the North, which was subdivided into French and Anglo-Norman, the latter dialect being the one which was chiefly confined to England. The poets of the South were called in their native dialect Troubadours, and those of the North were distinguished by the same title, though written in their language Trouvères. In Provence arose a series of elegant versifiers who employed their talents in composing romantic and complimentary poems, full of warlike and amatory sentiments, of the recitation of which, before assemblies of the great, many of them made a regular business. Norman poets writing with more plainness and simplicity, were celebrated even earlier than those of Provence; and one of them named Taillefer, was the first man to break the English ranks at the battle of Hastings. From the preference which the Norman kings of England gave to the poets of their own country, and from the general depression of the Anglo-Saxon language, the natural result was that the distinguished literary names of the first two centuries after the Conquest, should be those of Norman poets—men who are as frequently natives of France as of England.

Philippe de Thaun, author of treatises on popular sciences in verse; Thorold, who wrote the fine romance of *Roland;* Sampson de Nanteuil, who translated the Proverbs of Solomon into French verse; Geoffroi Gaimar, author of a chronicle of the Anglo-Saxon kings; and David, a trouvere of eminence, whose works are lost, were the most noted predecessors of one of much greater celebrity, named Maistre Wace, a native of Jersey.

About 1160, Wace wrote, in his native French, a narrative poem called *Brutus of England.* The principal hero of this poem was an imaginary son of Æneas of Troy, who was represented as having founded the state of Britain many centuries before the Christian era. This, however, was no creation of the fancy of the Norman poet, as he only translated a serious history, written in Latin a few years before, by a monk named Jeoffrey of Monmouth, in which the affairs of Britain were traced, with all possible gravity, through a series of imaginary kings, beginning with Brutus of Troy, and ending with Cadwalader, who was said to have lived in the year 689 of the Christian era.

This history is, on account of its origin and its influence on subsequent literature, a very remarkable work. The Britons settled in Wales, Cornwall, and Bretagne, were distinguished at this time for the numberless fanciful and fabulous legends which they possessed—a traditionary kind of literature resembling that which has since been found among a kindred people of the Scottish highlands. Walter Calenius, archdeacon of Oxford, collected some of these of a professedly historical kind relating to England, and communicated them to Jeoffrey, by whom they were put into the form of a regular historical work, and introduced, for the first time, to the then existing learned world. As little else than a mass of incredible stories, some of which may be slightly founded on fact, this production is of small value; but it formed a basis for Wace's poem, and proved an unfailing resource for the writers of romantic narrative for the ensuing two centuries. Nor even in a later age was its influence exhausted; for from it Shakspeare drew the story of Lear, and Sackville that of Ferrax and Porrex, while Drayton reproduced much of it in his Polyolbion; and it has also given occasion to many allusions in the poems of Milton and other writers.

Maistre Wace also composed a history of the Normans, under the title of the *Romance of Rolla, first duke of Normandy*, and some other works. Henry the Second, through admiration of his writings, rewarded Wace for the efforts of his genius, by bestowing upon him a canonry in the Cathedral of Bayeux.

BENOIT, a contemporary of Wace, and author of a History of the Dukes of Normandy, and Guernes, an ecclesiastic of Pont St. Maxence, in Picardy, who wrote a metrical life of Thomas à Becket, are the other two Norman poets of most eminence, whose genius or whose writings can be connected with the history of English literature.

Besides the productions of these romancers, the century following the Conquest presents some compositions of a different kind, the principal of which were written in Latin by learned ecclesiastics, the most prominent of whom were John of Salisbury, Peter of Blois, Joseph of Exeter, and Geoffrey of Monmouth, the last being the author of the History of England, already alluded to, and which is supposed to have been written about 1138. About the year 1154, according to Dr. Johnson, the Saxon began to take a form in which the beginning of the present English may plainly be discovered. It does not, as already hinted, contain many Norman words, but its grammatical structure is considerably altered. There is a metrical Saxon or English translation, by one Layamon, a priest of Erenly on the Severn, from the 'Brutus of England' of Wace. Its date is not ascertained; but if it be as supposed by some writers, a composition of the latter part of the twelfth century, we must consider it as throwing a valuable light on the history of the English language at, perhaps, the most important period of its existence. Of an extract from this work Mr. Ellis remarks, 'As it does not contain any word which we are under the necessity of referring to a French origin, we can not but consider it as simple and unmixed, though very barbarous Saxon. At the same time its orthography seems to prove that the pronunciation of the language had already undergone a very considerable change. Layamon's versification is also no less remarkable than his language. Sometimes he seems anxious to imitate the rhymes, and to adopt the regular number of syllables which he had observed in his original; at other times he disregards both, either because he did not consider the laws of metre, or the consonance of final sounds as essential to the gratification of his readers, or because he was unable to adopt them throughout so long a work, from the want of models.'

LAYAMON, therefore, may be regarded as the first of a series of writers, who, about the end of the thirteenth century, began to be conspicuous in English literary history, which usually recognizes them under the general appellation of *Rhyming Chronicles*. The first writer of this class after Layamon, though at a considerable distance, was Robert of Gloucester. He wrote in Alexandrian lines a history of England from the time of the imaginary 'Brutus' to his own time. Though cold and prosaic, Robert is not deficient in the valuable talent of arresting the attention. The orations with which he occasionally diversifies the thread of his story, are, in general, appropriate and dramatic, and not only prove his good sense, but exhibit no unfavorable specimen of his eloquence.

ROBERT MANNING is the next Rhyming Chronicler after Robert of Gloucester. He was a Gilbertine canon in the monastery of Brunne, in Lincolnshire, and he is hence usually called Robert de Brunne. The verse, however, adopted in his chronicles is shorter than that of the Gloucester monk, making an approach to the octo-syllabic stanza of modern times. Of this writer we present the following brief specimen, in reduced spelling :—

PRAISE OF GOOD WOMAN.

Nothing is to man so dear
As woman's love in good mannér;
A good woman is man's bliss,
When her love right and steadfast is.
There is no solace under heaven
Of all that a man may neven,[1]
That should a man so much glew,[2]
As a good woman that loveth true:
Ne dearer is none in God's hurd[3]
Than a chast woman with lovely wurd.

Besides these Chroniclers, the period of which we are now speaking abounded with *Metrical Romances*, of which the 'Life of Alexander the Great,' 'Sir Guy,' 'King Robert of Sicily,' and 'The Death of Arthur,' were the principal; but these we can not farther notice. Another class of poets, called *Minstrels* or *Jongleurs*, at this time filled all western Europe. They wandered from mansion to mansion, and from court to court; and such was the general favor in which they were held, that even kings were frequently their companions, and often vied with them in their own favorite strains. Of the poetry of these minstrels, Sismondi has given many specimens; but of these our time and space will allow us to present but one. This, however, from the exalted source whence it emanated, should command special attention. It is the production of Richard the First, the second prince of the house of Plantagenet, and is supposed to have been written during his imprisonment in the Black Tower in Austria. It is thus sweetly rendered into modern English verse by Roscoe.

No wretched captive of his prison speaks
  Unless with pain and bitterness of soul;
Yet consolation from the muse he seeks
  Whose voice alone misfortune can control.

[1] Know. [2] Delight. [3] Family.

Where now is each ally, each baron, friend,
  Whose face I ne'er beheld without a smile?
Will none, his sovereign to redeem, expend
  The smallest portion of his treasures vile.

Though none may blush that, ne'er two tedious years,
  Without relief my bondage has endured,
Yet know my English, Norman, Gascon Peers,
  Not one of you should thus remain immur'd:
The meanest subject of my wide domains
  Had I been free a ransom should have found:
I mean not to reproach you with my chains,
  Yet still I wear them on a foreign ground.

Too true it is —— so selfish human race!
  'Nor dead, nor captive, friend or kindred find!'
Since here I pine in bondage and disgrace,
  For lack of gold my fetters to unbind;
Much for myself I feel, yet ah! still more
  That no compassion from my subjects flows:
What can from infamy their names restore,
  If, while a prisoner, death my eyes should close?

But small is my surprise, though great my grief,
  To find, in spite of all his solemn vows,
My lands are ravaged by the Gallic chief,
  While none my cause has courage to espouse.
Though lofty towers obscure the cheerful day,
  Yet through the dungeon's melancholy gloom,
Kind Hope, in gentle whispers, seems to say,
  'Perpetual thraldom is not yet thy doom.'

Ye dear companions of my happy days,
  Of Chail and Pausavin, aloud declare
Throughout the earth, in everlasting lays,
  My foes against me wage inglorious war.
Oh, tell them, too, that ne'er among my crimes,
  Did breach of faith, deceit, or fraud, appear;
That infamy will brand, to latest times,
  The insults I receive, while captive here.

Know, all ye men of Anjou and Touraine,
  And every bach'lor knight, robust and brave,
That duty, now, and love alike are vain
  From bonds your sovereign and your friend to save.
Remote from consolation, here I lie,
  The wretched captive of a powerful foe,
Who all your zeal and ardor can defy,
  Nor leaves you aught but pity to bestow.

Our remarks upon the period of English literature of which we are now speaking, have thus brought us down to Roger Bacon, a man of genius so extraordinary, that he would have splendidly adorned any age or country.

ROGER BACON was descended from an ancient and honorable family, and was born at Ilchester, Somersetshire, in 1214, four years before the amiable but weak Henry the Third ascended the throne. His early education appears to have been carefully attended to in the midst of domestic relations, and after he had made thorough preparation for college, he entered the University of Oxford, intending there to complete his studies. But the passion for studying upon the continent had already become very general with the sons of English gentlemen, and Bacon, with others, removed from Oxford to the University of Paris, at that time the most celebrated seat of learning in Europe, there to complete his collegiate course. At Paris he became acquainted with many English students whom he had not hitherto known, and many of whom afterward rose to eminence in their own country. With some of these he there formed an intimacy which continued through life.

Having obtained his doctor's degree at the University, Bacon returned to England, and soon after, in 1240, he entered the Franciscan order of monks, though some writers suppose he had assumed the religious habit before he left France.

At the time of his return to Oxford, Bacon was regarded by the most learned and accomplished scholars of that University, as so able and indefatigable an inquirer after knowledge, that they willingly defrayed the expenses of advancing science by experiments—the method of investigation which he had determined to follow. His discoveries, however, were little understood by the mass even of his own order; and because, by the aid of mathematical knowledge, he performed things above the comprehension of the common people, he was suspected of magic. Even his own fraternity finally rose against him, and not only persecuted him, and refused to admit his works into their library, but finally had interest enough with the general of their order to obtain his apprehension and imprisonment. Clement the Fourth at that time occupied the papal chair, and having received information respecting the character of Bacon's works, he requested him to transmit a copy of them to Rome for inspection. Bacon, in compliance with the request, in 1267, collected and enlarged his various productions, and sent a copy of them thither. This collection is still extant, and is known as the Author's *Opus Majus*, or *Great Work*. Dr. Jebb, its learned and accomplished editor remarks, in his preface to the folio edition which he published of it, that 'Bacon seems in it to have principally proposed two things—either by laying down a good scheme for philosophy to excite the pope to reform the errors which had then crept into the church; or, if he could not effect this, to propose such expedients as might break the power of Antichrist, and retard his progress. For he appears to have been firmly persuaded that the church would soon be reformed, either by means of the pope himself, who was a man of integrity, or because the exorbitant dominion of Antichrist would become obnoxious to mankind, and so fall to destruction.'

When Bacon had been confined ten years in prison, Jerome d'Ascoli, general of the Franciscan order, and who had condemned his doctrines, was chosen pope, and assumed the name of Nicholas the Fourth. As he was reputed to be a person of great abilities, and one who had turned his thoughts much to philosophical subjects, Bacon resolved to apply to him for his release; and in order to show that his studies had been both innocent and useful, he addressed to him a treatise 'On the means of avoiding the infirmities of old age.' This important work was afterward translated into English, by Dr. Richard Browne, under the title of 'The cure of old age, and preservation of youth,' and was, by the learned translator, regarded as one of the most important works ever written.

Whether this treatise produced any immediate effect upon the mind of the pope or not, does not appear; but toward the latter part of Nicholas' reign, Bacon, through the influence of some of those English noblemen with whom he had formed an intimacy while pursuing his studies at Paris, obtained his liberty, and returned to Oxford, where he passed the remainder of his life in peace, and died in the college of his order on the eleventh of June, 1294, and in the eighty-first year of his age.

Bacon, in the opinion of Dr. Peter Shaw, a very competent judge of merit, was, 'beyond all comparison, the greatest man of his time, and might perhaps stand in competition with the greatest that have appeared since. It is wonderful, considering the ignorant age in which he lived, how he came to such a knowledge on all subjects. His writings are composed with such elegance, conciseness, and strength, and adorned with such just and exquisite observation on nature, that among all the chemists, we do not know his equal.' 'From a repeated perusal of his works,' the same skillful chemist proceeds to remark, 'we find that Bacon was no stranger to many of the most important discoveries of the present and of past ages. Gunpowder he certainly knew: thunder and lightning, he tells us, may be produced by art; for that sulphur, nitre, and charcoal, which, when separate, have no sensible effect, yet when mixed together in a due proportion, and closely confined and fired, they yield a loud report. A more precise description of gunpowder could not be given in language.'

Dr. Freind unhesitatingly ascribes to Bacon the honor of first introducing chemistry into Europe; and observes that in different parts of his works, he speaks of almost every operation now made in that science. That he was entirely familiar with the science of Optics also, is perfectly evident from the accuracy with which he described the use of reading-glasses, and gave directions for making them. He also describes the camera obscura, and all sorts of glasses which magnify or diminish objects, bring them near to the eye, or remove them farther from it. A passage in his writings indicates a knowledge of the telescope also; for he expressly says, 'that he was able to form glasses in such a manner with respect to our sight and the object, that the rays shall be refracted and reflected wherever we please, so that we may see a thing under whatever angle we think proper, either near by or far off, and be able to read the smallest letters at an incredible distance, and to count even the grains of dust and sand, in consequence of the greatness of the angle under which these objects shall be seen.'

Bacon's skill in astronomy too, when we consider the disadvantages under which he, in his investigations, must have labored, was amazingly great. He discovered the error in the computation of time, which resulted in the reformation of the calendar; one of the greatest efforts, in the opinion of Dr. Jebb, of human industry; and his plan for correcting it was followed by pope Gregory the Thirteenth, only varying from it in that Bacon would have had the correction reach back to the birth of Christ, while Gregory carried it only as far as the Nicene council.

All these mighty efforts of mind, it must not be forgotten, were made centuries before Schwarts developed, to the public, the composition of gunpowder, or Newton reduced to a science the principles of Optics, or Galileo constructed his telescope.

We are, however, admonished that our time will not permit us longer to dwell upon this important character in English literature; and we shall therefore here bring our remarks upon him, and upon the period which we have thus far contemplated, to a close—simply observing that its literary developments do great credit to the five or six centuries which it embraces. The immediate predecessors of Chaucer, that great poet himself, and his contemporaries, will next occupy our attention. We must, however, first briefly notice John Wickliffe; for, perhaps no man ever exerted a more powerful influence over his age, than did that learned ecclesiastic.

Lecture the Second.

THE ERA OF EDWARD THE THIRD—JOHN WICKLIFFE—THE PRECURSORS OF CHAUCER—GEOFFREY CHAUCER—JOHN GOWER—SIR JOHN MANDEVILLE.

THE entire annals of English history do not, perhaps, present another period more splendid, in all respects, than the age of Edward the Third. Besides that illustrious monarch himself, than whom a superior never occupied the English throne, it was the era of Wickliffe, emphatically the Father of the Reformation, and of Chaucer, the Father of English poetry.

JOHN WICKLIFFE, certainly not the least brilliant of the great lights of this remarkable period, was born at Wickliffe, Yorkshire, in 1324. He early entered Queen's College, Oxford, but soon after removed to Merton College in the same university, because the scholastic theology which at that time prevailed in the latter institution was better calculated to display the acuteness of his intellect, and enable him to distinguish himself above his fellows. After having successfully graduated at the college to which he was attached, he, for some years, turned his exclusive attention toward theological studies, and finally obtained the divinity professorship. He had not long discharged the important duties which this new position imposed upon him, before he was made doctor in divinity, and raised, in 1361, to the position of master of Baliol College in the same university. His reputation now advanced so rapidly, that in 1365, he was elevated to the head of Canterbury Hall, a new Oxford College just at that time founded. His election to this important office was made by the students of the college themselves, and as the tenets which he now entertained in opposition to the Church of Rome, began to undisguisedly manifest themselves, he was strenuously opposed by a number of monks who had gained admission to the college, and who wished a head of their own order. Wickliffe and his secular associates, however, gained the ascendency in the contest which followed; and the monks were, accordingly, expelled from the college. From this sentence of expulsion, they immediately appealed to Cardinal Langham, Archbishop of Canterbury, under whose control the college then was. The

Archbishop at once espoused their cause, and immediately ordered Wickliffe to resign his office; but as Wickliffe refused to submit to this order, Langham had recourse to a sequestration of the revenues of the college, and thus left it without support. Wickliffe and his secular associates now appealed from the decision of the Archbishop to Pope Urban the Fifth. The Pope, however, having been well advised of all the circumstances connected with this contest between Wickliffe and the monks, confirmed the decree of the archbishop, and Wickliffe having no alternative left him, resigned his position, and retired to a small living which he had previously secured at Lutterworth in Leicestershire.

Being now released from all obligation to the court of Rome, Wickliffe began more seriously to inquire into its impositions. The authority of the pope, and the temporalities of the church, were at that time very firmly established in England, and the jurisdiction of the bishops was of vast extent. Wickliffe resolved to oppose both; and he had scarcely entered upon the course of opposition which he had determined to pursue, before he found many able associates and protectors; for the doctrine which he inculcated was favorable to the king, whose authority was weakened by that of the pope and the bishops; to the great lords, who were in possession of the revenues of the church; and to the people, to whom the tax of Peter-pence and other impositions of the Church of Rome were very burthensome.

Wickliffe's doctrines having now become a matter of public notoriety, Simon Sudbury, who had recently succeeded to the Archbishopric of Canterbury, assembled in 1377, a council at Lambeth, before which he cited Wickliffe to appear and defend himself against the charge of heresy preferred against him by the monks. This summons he unhesitatingly obeyed; and being accompanied by the duke of Lancaster, who, at that time, exercised an important share in the government, and by other noble lords, he was honorably acquitted.

Pope Gregory the Eleventh, however, being advised of the doctrines which Wickliffe was inculcating, and of the protection which he received from those who were able to screen him from condemnation, wrote to the bishops of England, and directed that if they could not have him apprehended, they should cite him to repair to Rome, and there defend himself before the pope. But Wickliffe, now the favorite both of the lords and of the people, refused to obey the pontiff's summons, in consequence of which another council was held at Lambeth, before which Wickliffe unhesitatingly appeared, and in the event as signally triumphed as he had in the former case.

Strengthened by these recurring discomfitures of his opponents, Wickliffe now proclaimed his new doctrines boldly and without reserve; and as he drew after him great numbers of disciples, William Courteney, the new Archbishop of Canterbury, called a council in 1382, and condemned the Reformer's doctrines by public decree. Unfortunately the weak and pusillanimous Richard the Second now occupied the English throne, and through feai of the power of the Romish church, gave to this decree his royal sanction; in consequence of which the followers of Wickliffe were severely persecuted, though he himself remained undaunted: and such was the respect in which he was held, that the reformation, which he had so boldly commenced, was rapidly advancing, when he unfortunately died, just at the time when nothing but a leader equal to the exigency was needed to carry the work to a successful consummation. His death occurred 1384, in the sixty-first year of his age; but the good seed which he had already sown, continued, though slowly, yet surely, to geminate in the heart of the whole nation, until it burst forth in the full bloom of the Reformation, perfected more than two centuries afterward under the auspicious reign of Queen Elizabeth.

More than forty years after his death, by decree of the same council of Constance which condemned John Huss and Jerome of Prague to be burned, Wickliffe's bones were ordered to be disinterred, and burnt, and the ashes thrown into a brook. 'This brook,' says Fuller, the church historian, in a passage which brings quaintness to the borders of sublimity, 'hath conveyed his ashes into Avon, Avon into Severn, Severn into the narrow seas, they into the main ocean: and thus the ashes of Wickliffe are the emblem of his doctrine, which is now dispersed all over the world.'

The principles of the Romish church against which Wickliffe particularly inveighed, were the supremacy of the pope, his infallibility, and the corruptions to which these unfounded pretensions necessarily lead; and in his controversy with his antagonists, he wrote many works on those subjects, the principal of which was the *Trialogus*, a dialogue, the three speakers in which were *Truth*, *Lye*, and *Wisdom*. But by far his most important literary performance was a translation of the Bible into his native language. This important work he accompanied by explanatory notes, the value of which is still very generally acknowledged. A single passage from this translation will close our notice of this important character in English literature. It is given in the original spelling, that it may serve as a specimen of the language at that period.

And Marye seyde, My soul magnifieth the Lord,
And my spiryt hath gladid in God myn helthe.
For he hath behulden the mekenesse of his handmayden: for
lo for this alle generatiouns schulen seye that I am blessid.
For he that is mighti hath don to me grete thingis, and his
name is holy.
And his mercy is fro kyndrede into kyndredis to men that
dreden him.
He hath made myght in his arm, he scatteride proude men
with the thoughte of his herte.
He sette doun myghty men fro seete, and enhaunside meke men. He
hath fulfillid hungry men with goodis, and he has left riche men voide.
He heuynge mynde of his mercy took up Israel his child.
As he hath spokun to oure fadris, to Abraham, and to his seed
into worlds.

Chaucer, the remaining member of this bright trio, next demands our attention; but before we proceed to investigate his life and genius, we must glance at those of his predecessors who immediately preceded him; for until that time, English poetry assumed no other form than that of the Chronicle, and the Romance. Henceforward, however, we shall be called upon to regard it under all those varied and interesting aspects under which it has been employed to point a moral lesson, to describe natural scenery, to convey satiric reflections, and to give expression to refined and delicate sentiment. The dawn of miscellaneous poetry, as these poems may be comprehensively called, is to be faintly discovered about the middle of the thirteenth century, during the reign of Henry the Third. The earliest of these poems which can be said to possess any literary merit, is an *Elegy*, written in 1307, on the death of king Edward the First. This poem is executed in musical and energetic stanzas, of which the following may be taken as a fair specimen:

Jerusalem, thou hast i-lore,
The flour of all chivalerie,
Nou kyng Edward liveth na more,
Alas! that he yet shulde deye!
He wolde ha rered up ful heyge[1]
Our baners that bueth broht to grounde;
Wel longe we mowe clepe[2] and crie,
Er we such a kyng han y-founde!

The first name that occurs in this department of English literature, is that of Lawrence Minot, who about 1350 composed a series of short poems on the victories of Edward the Third, beginning with the battle of Halidon Hill, and ending with the Siege of Guines Castle. At about the same time flourished Richard Rolle, a hermit of the order of St. Augustine, who lived a solitary life in the vicinity of the nunnery of Hampole, near Doncaster. He wrote paraphrases of various parts of the Scriptures, and an original poem of a moral and religious nature, entitled, *The Precke of Conscience.* From this long and generally tedious poem, we select the following agreeable passage, and present it in the original spelling.

WHAT IS IN HEAVEN.

Ther is lyf withoute ony deth,
And ther is youthe without ony elde;[3]
And ther is alle manner welthe to welde:
And ther is rest without ony travaille;
And ther is pees without ony strife,
And ther is alle manner lykinge of lyf:—
And ther is bright somer ever to se,
And ther is nevere wynter in that countrie:—
And ther is more worshipe and honour,
Then evere hade kynge other emperour.

---

[1] High. [2] Call. [3] Age.

And ther is grete melodie of aungeles songe,
And ther is preysing hem amonge.
And ther is alle manner frendshipe that may be,
And ther is evere perfect love and charite;
And ther is wisdom without folye,
And ther is honeste without vileneye.
Al these a man may joyes of hevene call:
Ac yutte the most sovereyn joye of alle
Is the sighte of Goddes bright face,
In wham resteth alle mannere grace.

The Vision of Pierce Ploughman, a satirical poem of the same period, ascribed to Robert Langlande, a secular priest, also shows very clearly and expressively the progress which was made about the middle of the fourteenth century, toward a literary style. This poem is, in many respects, one of the most important works that appeared in England previous to the invention of printing. It is the popular representative of the doctrines which were even then silently bringing about the Reformation; and it is also a peculiarly national poem, not only as being a purer specimen of the English language than even Chaucer's poetry presents, but as exhibiting the revival of the same system of alliteration to which we have already alluded as characterizing the Anglo-Saxon poetry. It is, in fact, both in this particular, and in its political character, characteristic of a great literary and political revolution, in which the language as well as the independence of the Anglo-Saxons had at last gained the ascendency over those of the Normans.

Pierce is represented as falling asleep on the Melvern hills, and as seeing, in his sleep, a series of visions. In describing these, he exposes the corruptions of society, and particularly the dissolute lives of the religious orders, with much bitterness. From this poem we present the allegory of Mercy and Truth, as fairly indicating the spirit of the entire work.

MERCY AND TRUTH ALLEGORIZED.

Out of the west coast, a wench, as me thought,
Came walking in the way, to hell-ward she looked;
Mercy hight that maid, a meek thing withal,
A full benign burd,[1] and buxom of speech;
Her sister, as it seemed, came soothly walking,
Even out of the east, and westward she looked,
A full comely creature, Truth she hight,
For the virtue that her followed afeard was she never.
When these maidens mette, Mercy and Truth,
Either axed other of this great wonder,
Of the din and of the darkness.

With these imperfect models before him as his only native guides, arose the great Father of English poetry, Geoffrey Chaucer. Though the English language had risen into importance with the rise of the Commons in the time of Edward the First, yet the French long kept possession of the court,

[1] Maiden.

the schools, and the higher circles; and it required a genius like that of Chaucer—familiar with different modes of life both at home and abroad, and openly patronized by his sovereign—to give literary permanence and consistency to the language and poetry of England. From that period his native style, which Spencer terms 'the pure well of English undefiled,' formed a standard for composition, though the national distractions which followed, and the absence of any striking poetical genius for at least a century and a half after his death, too truly exemplified the fine simile of Warton, that 'Chaucer was like a genial day in an English spring, when a brilliant sun enlivens the face of nature with unusual warmth and lustre, but is succeeded by the redoubled horrors of winter, and those tender buds and early blossoms which were called forth by the transient gleams of a temporary sunshine, are nipped by frosts and torn by tempests.'

GEOFFREY CHAUCER was born in the city of London, in 1328, one year after that eminent monarch, Edward the Third, ascended the English throne. He entered the university of Cambridge in the sixteenth year of his age, and during that part of his collegiate course which he there pursued, though he did not neglect his more important duties, yet much of his attention was devoted to poetry. Before he reached the eighteenth year of his age, and while he was still a student at Cambridge, he wrote and published the *Court of Love*, and some other minor poems, all of which gave promise of the future poetic eminence to which he was destined to attain.

From Cambridge Chaucer removed, according to Warton and others, to the university of Oxford; and having there completed his collegiate studies, he thence returned to London, and soon after left his native country for the purpose of travelling upon the continent, that he might thus, by freely intermingling with other nations, increase his accomplishments both of mind and manners. Having travelled through France, Holland, and some other countries, and critically regarded whatever fell under his observation, he returned to London, and soon after entered the Inner Temple as a student of law. He, however, was not permitted long to remain in the obscurity of a law student; for the beauty of his person, and his distinguished accomplishments, attracting the attention of the court, he was invited to leave his prospective profession, and enter into the service of the king. Assenting without hesitation to this proposition, Edward the Third at once appointed him one of his pages, with an annuity of twenty marks per annum—a sum equal to about two hundred pounds sterling.

From the office of king's page, Chaucer was elevated to the position of 'Gentleman of the King's Privy Chamber,' with twenty additional marks to his annual income. From the position of 'Gentleman of the King's Privy Chamber,' he became shield-bearer to his majesty, and in that capacity attended the king during his celebrated invasion of France, which terminated in the prostration of that nation by the victory obtained upon the field of Cressy, and the siege and capture of Calais

In 1372, in preparation for that invasion, Chaucer was sent by the king on an embassy to the Duke of Genoa, the object of which was to hire ships to aid him in transporting his army across the English Channel; and having successfully closed his mission, he improved a brief period of leisure which followed, by visiting the famous Italian poet Petrarch, then residing at Padua. For this incident in the life of Chaucer, we are entirely indebted to the following lines found in the tale of the Oxford Clerk, in Canterbury Tales.

Learned at Padua of a worthy clerk—
Francis Petrarch, the laureat poet
Hight this clerk, whose rhetoric sweet
Enlumined all Italy of poetry.

During the whole of this rapid advancement of Chaucer's fortunes, John of Ghent, Duke of Lancaster, had been his professed patron and personal friend; and at the duke's suggestion, he married Philippa Pyckard, sister to lady Swainford, governess in the duke's family. As both Philippa and lady Swainford were very great favorites of the Duke and the Duchess of Lancaster, this marriage contributed greatly to Chaucer's advantage; and as an expression of his personal regard for him, the duke obtained from the king as his residence, a delightful mansion in Woodstock Park. The scenery surrounding this park was beautiful in the extreme, and it is thus described by the poet in *The Dream*, one of his minor poems:

And right anon as I the day espied,
No longer would I in my bed abide,
I went forth myself alone and boldely,
And held the way down by a brook side,
Till I came to a land of white and green,
So fair a one had I never in been.
The ground was green y-powdered with daisy,
The flowers and the groves alike high,
All green and white was nothing else seen.

Immediately after the return of Edward from the invasion of France, that monarch appointed Chaucer to the important and responsible post of collector of the customs of the port of London; and such were the emoluments arising from this new post, that Chaucer's income now amounted to a thousand pounds sterling per annum—a sum so great as to place his revenue upon an equality with that of the princes of the royal family.

Surrounded now by affluence, and with daily occupation, Chaucer's time glided smoothly and happily on until the close of the reign of his munificent monarch, and the accession of Richard the Second to the throne. But henceforth we are to contemplate his whole career under a very different aspect. He had early imbibed many of the tenets of Wickliffe, and in the second year of Richard the Second's reign, he used all his influence to aid Camberton, usually known as John of Northampton, mayor of London, to promote the doctrines of the Reformer in that city. These measures were resented by the clergy, who had meantime gained an ascendency over the mind of their weak king, with such earnestness and severity that the mayor was apprehended and cast into prison, and Chaucer, in order to escape a similar fate, sought safety in flight from his country. He repaired to Flanders, and as he there spent some years before he dared venture to return to London, many writers suppose that during his exile he conceived the design of his *Canterbury Tales*, and partially executed it. Wearied, however, with his long absence from his native home, and his early associations, Chaucer, at length, ventured to return to London; but he had scarcely arrived in that city before he was apprehended and cast into prison. And here a shade rests upon his hitherto pure and unsullied fame; for he is more than suspected of having obtained his release from imprisonment by revealing the names of many eminent individuals who were associated with himself and the lord mayor in the project which had terminated so fatally to their temporal interests.

From this period Chaucer resumed his residence in Woodstock Park, and there passed the remainder of his life in that quiet retirement, and in those literary pursuits for the enjoyment of which his previous life had so eminently qualified him; and though the duke of Lancaster had meantime married lady Swainford, and thus become Chaucer's brother-in-law, no consideration could induce the venerable poet to leave his quiet retirement, notwithstanding the most flattering offers of court favor were extended to him. It was during this period that he completed his 'Canterbury Tales,' and composed many other works, the last of which was the *Testament of Love*, an allegory in prose.

Upon the death of the duke of Lancaster, Chaucer left Woodstock Park, and retired to Dunnington Castle, where he passed the last two years of his life. Upon the accession of Henry the Fourth, son of the late duke of Lancaster, in 1399, the new king granted to Chaucer an annuity of forty marks, or four hundred pounds sterling. The aged poet did not, however, long live to enjoy his new monarch's munificence, but died in the following year, on the twenty-fifth of October, 1400, in the seventy-third year of his age, and was the first of the illustrious band of English poets buried in Westminster Abbey.

Chaucer's genius was vast, versatile, and original. He was evidently thoroughly familiar with classical, with French, and with Italian literature, with the sciences so far as they were at that time known, and with the polemical and theological questions, which were then the favorite and fashionable studies of all the higher classes of society. His knowledge of human nature was really profound. Though the knights, the monks, the Reves, and the prioresses, which he has painted, have long since passed away, yet wherever we look we still recognize the same passions, and feelings, and characters, which he has so faithfully exhibited; for the poet who 'dips his pencil in the human heart,' as Garrick said of Shakspeare, will produce forms and colors, the truth and beauty of which will be recognized wherever such a heart beats. His versatility, too, was extraordinary. No other

English poet, if we except Shakspeare, ever exhibited such striking instances of comic and tragic powers united in the same mind. His humor and wit were also of the brightest and keenest character; his pathos too was tremendous, and his descriptive powers were of the highest order of excellence.

Of Chaucer's minor poems, after the Court of Love, the principal are, *The Flower and Leaf*, a spirited and graceful allegorical poem, *The House of Fame*, and *Troilas and Cresseide;* from the latter of which we quote the following passages chiefly for the sake of the delicate and beautiful similes which they contain.

But right as floures through the cold night
  Inclosed stoupen in hir stalke lowe,
Redressen hem ayen the sunne bright,
  And spreden in hir kindlie course by rowe;
  Right so began his eyen up to throw
This Troilas, and seth, O Venus dere,
Thy might, thy grace, yheried be it here.

But right as when the sunne shineth bright
  In Marche that changeth ofttimes his face,
And that a cloud is put with winde to flight
  Which oversprad the sunne, as for a space
  A cloudy thought gan through her soule to pace,
That overspread her bright thoughts all,
So that for fear almost she gan to fall.

And as the new-abashed nightingale,
  That stinteth first when she beginneth sing,
When that she heareth any herdes tale,
  Or in the hedges any wright stirring.
  And after sicker, doth her voice outring;
Right so Cresseide, when that her dread slent,
Opened her heart, and told him her intent.

Have ye not seen some time a pale face
  (Emong a prus) of him that hath been lad
Toward his deth, wher as him get no grace,
  And soch a colour in his face hath had
  That men might know his face that was bestad
Emonges all the faces in that rout;
So standeth Custance, and loketh her about.

But the best and most durable monument of Chaucer's genius is the *Canterbury Tales.* This is clearly a narrative poem, and the model upon which it was constructed was evidently the *Decameron* of Bocaccio, though our poet greatly improved upon the original. He supposes a company of pilgrims, consisting of twenty-nine 'sundry folk,' to meet together in fellowship at Tabard Inn, Southwark, all being bent upon a pilgrimage to the shrine of Thomas-à-Becket at Canterbury. The poet himself is one of the party. They all sup together in the large room of the hostelrie, and after great cheer, the landlord proposes that they shall travel together to Canter bury; and to shorten the way, that each shall tell a tale, both in going and returning, and whoever told the best should have a supper at the expense of the rest. The company assent, and 'mine host' who was both

> Bold of his speech, and wise and well taught,

is appointed judge and reporter of the stories. The characters composing this social party, are inimitably drawn and discriminated. We have a knight, a mirror of chivalry, who had fought against the Heathenesse in Palestine; his son a gallant young squire with curled locks, laid in presse, and all manner of debonnair accomplishments; a nun, or prioresse, beautifully drawn in her arch simplicity and coy reserve; and a jolly monk, who boasted a dainty, well-caparisoned horse:

> And when he rode, men might his bridle hear
> Jingling in a whistling wind as clear
> And eke as loud as doth the chapel bell.

A wanton prior is also of the party,—full of sly and solemn mirth, and well beloved for his accommodating disposition:

> Full sweetly heard he confession,
> And pleasant was his absolution.

We have a pardoner from Rome with some sacred relics, such as a part of the sail of St. Peter's ship, and who is also

> Brim full of pardons come from Rome all hot.

In satirical contrast to these merry and interested churchmen, we have a poor parson of a town,

> Rich in holy thought and work,

and a clerk of Oxford also, who was skilled in logic:

> Sounding in moral virtue was his speech,
> And gladly would he learn, and gladly teach.

Among the other characters are a doctor of physic, a great astronomer and student, 'whose study was but little on the Bible;' a purse-proud merchant; a sergeant-at-law, who was always busy, yet seemed busier than he was; and a jolly Franklin, a freeholder, who had been a lord of sessions, and who was fond of good eating:

> Withouten baked meat never was his house,
> Of fish and flesh, and that so plenteous;
> It snowed in his house of meat and drink.

This character is a fine picture of the wealthy rural Englishman, and it shows how much of enjoyment and hospitality was even then associated with this station of life. The Wife of Bath is another lively national portrait: she is shrewd and witty, has abundant means, and is always first with her offering at church.

Besides these, there are many humbler characters, which, combined with those already noticed, form so genuine a Hogarthian picture that we may well exclaim with Campbell, 'What an intimate scene of English life in the fourteenth century do we enjoy in these tales, beyond what history displays by glimpses through the stormy atmosphere of her scenes, or the antiquary can discover by the cold light of his researches.' Yet with all the inimitable description and truth to nature with which the Canterbury Tales abound, we are constrained to confess that we have looked in vain throughout the entire poem for any thing that inculcates an important moral lesson.

The following brief extracts are all that our space will allow us to introduce from this great work, the last extract, the Good Parson, being somewhat modernized:—

DESCRIPTION OF A POOR COUNTRY WIDOW.

A poore widow, somedeal stoop'n in age,
Was whilom dwelling in a narwé cottage
Beside a grove standing in a dale.
This widow, which I tell you of my Tale,
Since thilke day that she was last a wife,
In patience led a full simple life,
For little was her cattle and her rent,
By husbandry[1] of such as God her sent
She found herself and eke her daughters two.
Three large sowes had she, and no mo,
Three kine, and eke a sheep that highte[2] Mall:
Full sooty was her bower and eke her hall,
In which she ate many a slender meal,
Of poignant sauce ne knew she never a deal;[3]
No dainty morsel passed through her throat;
Her diet was accordant to her cote:[4]
Repletion ne made her never sick;
Attemper[5] diet was all her physic,
And exercise, and heartes suffisance:
The goute let[6] her nothing for to dance,
Ne apoplexy shente[7] not her head,
No wine ne drank she neither white nor red;
Her board was served most with white and black,
Milk and brown bread, in which she found no lack
Seinde[8] bacon, and sometime an egg or tway,
For she was as it were a manner dey.[9]

THE DEATH OF ARCITE.

Swelleth the breast of Arcite, and the sore
Encreaseth at his hearte more and more.
The clottered blood for any leche-craft[10]
Corrupteth, and is in his bouk[11] ylaft,
That neither veine-blood ne ventousing,[12]
Ne drink of herbes may be his helping.

---

[1] Thrift, economy. [2] Called. [3] Not a bit. [4] Cot, cottage.
[5] Temperate. [6] Prevented. [7] Injured. [8] Singed.
[9] Mr. Tyrwhitt supposes the word 'dey' to refer to the management of a dairy; and that it originally signified a hind. 'Manner dey' may therefore be interpreted 'a species of hired or day laborer.'
[10] Medical skill. [11] Body.
[12] Ventousing, (Fr.) cupping; hence the term, 'breathing a vein.'

The virtue expulsive or animal,
From thilke virtue cleped[1] natural,
Ne may the venom voiden ne expell;
The pipes of his lungs 'gan to swell,
And every lacert[2] in his breast adown
Is shent[3] with venom and corruption.
He gaineth neither,[4] for to get his life,
Vomit upward ne downward laxative:
All is to-bursten thilke region;
Nature hath now no domination:
And certainly where nature will not werche,[5]
Farewell physic; go bear the man to church.
This is all and some, that Arcite muste die;
For which he sendeth after Emily,
And Palamon, that was his cousin dear;
Then said he thus, as ye shall after hear:
'Naught may the woful spirit in mine heart
Declare one point of all my sorrows' smart
To you my lady, that I love most,
But I bequeath the service of my ghost
To you aboven every creature,
Since that my life ne may no longer dure.
'Alas the woe! alas the paines strong,
That I for you have suffered, and so long!
Alas the death! alas mine Emily!
Alas departing of our company!
Alas mine hearte's queen! alas my wife!
Mine hearte's lady, ender of my life!
What is this world?—What asken men to have?
Now with his love, now in his colde grave—
Alone—withouten any company.
Farewell my sweet—farewell mine Emily!
And softe take me in your armes tway
For love of God, and hearkeneth what I say.
'I have here with my cousin Palamon
Had strife and rancour many a day agone
For love of you, and for my jealousy;
And Jupiter so wis[6] my soule gie,[7]
To speaken of a servant properly,
With alle circumstances truely;
That is to say, truth, honour, and knighthead,
Wisdom, humbless, estate, and high kindred,
Freedom, and all that 'longeth to that art,
So Jupiter have of my soule part,
As in this world right now ne know I none
So worthy to be loved as Palamon,
That serveth you, and will do all his life;
And if that ever ye shall be a wife,
Forget not Palamon, the gentle man.'
And with that word his speeche fail began;
For from his feet up to his breast was come

[1] Called. [2] Muscle. [3] Ruined, destroyed. [4] He is able for.
[5] Work. [6] Surely. [7] Guide.

The cold of death that had him overnome;[1]
And yet, moreover, in his armes two,
The vital strength is lost and all ago;[2]
Only the intellect, withouten more,
That dwelled in his hearte sick and sore,
'Gan faillen when the hearte felte death;
Dusked his eyen two, and fail'd his breath:
But on his lady yet cast he his eye;
His laste word was, 'Mercy Emily!'

DEPARTURE OF CUSTANCE.

Custance is banished from her husband, Alla, king of Northumberland, in consequence of the treachery of the king's mother. Her behaviour in embarking at sea, in a rudderless ship, is thus described:

Weepen both young and old in all that place,
When that the king this cursed letter sent;
And Custance with a deadly pale face
The fourthe day toward the ship she went;
But natheless,[3] she tak'th in good intent
The will of Christ, and kneeling on the strond,
She saide, 'Lord, aye welcome be thy sond.[4]
'He that me kepte from the false blame,
While I was in the land amonges you,
He can me keep from harm and eke from shame
In the salt sea, although I see not how:
As strong as ever he was, he is yet now:
In him trust I, and in his mother dear,
That is to me my sail and eke my steer.'[5]
Her little child lay weeping in her arms;
And kneeling piteously to him she said—
'Peace, little son, I will do thee no harm:'
With that her kerchief off her head she braid,[6]
And over his little eyen she it laid,
And in her arm she lulleth it full fast,
And into th' heaven her eyen up she cast.
'Mother, quod she, and maiden bright, Mary!
Soth is, that through womannes eggement,[7]
Mankind was lorn,[8] and damned aye to die,
For which thy child was on a cross yrent:[9]
Thy blissful eyen saw all his torment;
Then is there no comparison between
Thy woe and any woe man may sustain.
'Thou saw'st thy child y-slain before thine eyen,
And yet now liveth my little child parfay:[10]
Now, lady bright! to whom all woful crien,
Thou glory of womanhood, thou faire May!
Thou haven of refute,[11] bright star of day!
Rue[12] on my child, that of thy gentleness
Ruest on every rueful in distress.

---

1 Overtaken. 2 Agone. 3 Nevertheless. 4 Message.
5 Guide, helm. 6 Took. 7 Incitement. 8 Undone.
9 Torn. 10 By my faith. 11 Refuge. 12 Have Pity.

'O little child, alas! what is thy guilt,
That never wroughtest sin as yet, pardie?
Why will thine hardé father have thee spilt?[1]
O mercy, deare Constable! (quod she,)
As let my little child dwell here with thee;
And if thou dar'st not saven him from blame,
So kiss him one's in his father's name.'
Therewith she looketh backward to the land,
And saide, 'Farewell, husband rutheless!'[2]
And up she rose, and walketh down the strand
Toward the ship; her followeth all the press:[3]
And ever she prayeth her child to hold his peace,
And tak'th her leave, and with a holy intent
She blesseth her, and into the ship she went.
Victailled was the ship, it is no drede,[4]
Abundantly for her a full long space;
And other necessaries that should need
She had enow, heried[5] be Goddes grace:
The wind and weather, Almighty God purchase,[6]
And bring her home, I can no better say,
But in the sea she driveth forth her way.

THE GOOD PARSON.

A true good man there was, there of religion,
Pious and poor ——— the parson of a town.
But rich he was in holy thought and work;
And thereto a right learned man; a clerk
That Christ's pure gospel would sincerely preach,
And his parishioners devoutly teach.
Benign he was, and wondrous diligent,
And in adversity full patient,
As proven oft; to all who lack'd a friend.
Loth for his tithes to ban or to contend,
At every need much rather was he found
Unto his poor parishioners around
Of his own substance and his dues to give:—
Content on little, for himself, to live.
Wide was his cure; the houses far asunder,
Yet never fail'd he, or for rain or thunder,
Whenever sickness or mischance might call
The most remote to visit, great or small,
And, staff in hand, on foot, the storm to brave.
This noble ensample to his flock he gave,
That first he wrought, and afterward he taught.
The word of life he from the gospel caught;
And well this comment added he thereto,
If that gold rusteth, what should iron do?
And if the priest be foul on whom we trust,
What wonder if the unletter'd layman lust?
And shame it were in him the flock should keep,
To see a sullied shepherd, and clean sheep.

---

[1] Destroyed. [2] Pitiless. [3] Crowd.
[4] Doubt. [5] Praised. [6] Procure, provide.

For sure a priest the sample ought to give
By his own cleanness how his sheep should live.
  He never set his benefice to hire,
Leaving his flock acomber'd in the mire,
And ran to London cogging at St. Paul's,
To seek himself a chauntery for souls,
Or with a brotherhood to be enroll'd;
But dwelt at home, and guarded well his fold,
So that it should not by the wolf miscarry.
He was a shepherd, and no mercenary.
  Tho holy in himself, and virtuous,
He still to sinful men was mild and piteous:
Not of reproach imperious or malign;
But in his teaching soothing and benign.
To draw them on to heaven, by reason fair
And good example, was his daily care.
But were there one perverse and obstinate,
Were he of lofty or of low estate,
Him would he sharply with reproof astound.
A better priest is no where to be found.
  He waited not on pomp or reverence,
Nor made himself a spiced conscience.
The lore of Christ and his apostles twelve
He taught: but, first, he followed it himselve.

The following poem was the last production that emanated from Chaucer's prolific pen. It was written on his death-bed, and may properly close these extracts :—

Fly from the press,[1] and dwell with sothfastness;[2]
  Suffice unto thy good[3] though it be small;
For hoard hath hate, and climbing tickleness,
  Press[4] hath envy, and weal is blent[5] o'er all;
  Savour[6] no more than thee behoven shall;
Rede[7] well thyself, that other folk can'st rede,
And truth thee shall deliver 't is no drede.[8]

Pain thee not each croocked to redress
  In trust of her that turneth as a ball;
Great rest standeth in little baseness;
  Beware also to spurn against a nalle;[9]
  Strive not as doth a crocke[10] with a wall;
Deemeth[11] thyself that deemest other's deed;
And truth thee shall deliver 't is no drede.

That[12] thee is sent receive in buxomness;[13]
  The wrestling of this world asketh a fall;
Here is no home, here is but wilderness;
  Forth, pilgrim, forth, O beast out of thy stall;
  Look up on high, and thank thy God of all;
Waiveth thy lust and let thy ghost[14] thee lead,
And truth thee shall deliver 't is no drede.

---

[1] Crowd. [2] Truth. [3] Be satisfied with thy wealth. [4] Striving.
[5] Prosperity has ceased. [6] Taste. [7] Counsel. [8] Without fear.
[9] Nail. [10] Earthen pitcher. [11] Judge. [12] That (which).
[13] Humility, obedience. [14] Spirit.

Though Chaucer was eminent chiefly as a poet, yet he deserves a passing notice as a writer in prose also. His longest unversified production is The 'Testament of Love,' to which we have already alluded. This is an allegorical and meditative work, and was written chiefly for the purpose of defending his character against certain imputations which had been cast upon it. Two of the 'Canterbury Tales,' also, are in prose; in one of which, the Tale of Melibeus, is found a passage on Riches, not less remarkable for the great amount of ancient wisdom which it contains, than for the clearness and simplicity of its diction. We have, however, already afforded to Chaucer so much space that we have not room to introduce this interesting passage, but must at once pass briefly to notice Gower, his illustrious contemporary.

Though the genius of Chaucer far transcended that of all preceding writers in England, yet he was not the solitary light of the age. The national mind, and the national language had now arrived at a certain degree of maturity favorable for the production of able writers in both prose and verse. Besides Wickliffe, Gower and Mandeville also belong to the same period.

JOHN GOWER was born of an illustrious family at Stitenham, Yorkshire, in 1320. He was educated at Merton College, Oxford, and at the time at which he was graduated, his eminence as a scholar was extensively known. Being designated by his parents for the legal profession, he removed to London immediately after he left the university, and entered the Middle Temple as a student at law; and though devoted to his profession, yet he did not permit it to engross his entire attention, but gave much of his leisure time to poetry and other literary pursuits. While thus occupied, and soon after he had completed his preparatory legal studies, he formed an acquaintance with Chaucer, who had just then returned from his travels on the continent, and the similarity of their tastes soon created a very close intimacy between them. Poetry, however, with Gower, was a pastime, while to his profession he devoted himself with such untiring industry, that before the close of the reign of Edward the Third, his position as a lawyer had become so commanding that when Richard the Second succeeded to the crown, that unfortunate monarch first selected him as his legal adviser, and Chancellor in Commons, and soon after raised him to the office of Chief Justice of the Court of Common Pleas.

In this imposing position Gower remained until his royal patron was dethroned by the duke of Lancaster, afterward Henry the Fourth, when he being far advanced in age, and having also recently had the misfortune to lose his eyesight, retired from the busy scenes of life, and took leave at the same time, both of the muses and of the world, in his pathetic poem *The Commendation of Peace*. In this sweet production he plainly and affectingly indicates a full sense of his consciousness of an approaching death, which accordingly happened soon after at Southwark, where he then resided, in 1402. His remains were interred in St. John's Chapel, and to his memory a monument of unparalleled magnificence, for that age, was erected, upon which was inscribed a Latin Epitaph, that may be thus rendered into English.

His shield henceforth is useless grown,
To pay death's tribute slain,
His soul with joyous freedom flown,
Where spotless spirits reign.

Gower was a man of very extensive literary and legal attainments, and his poems, therefore, were rather the offspring of his learning than of his genius. His spirit was bold and uncompromising, and he accordingly inveighed in clear and energetic language against the debaucheries of the times, the immorality of the clergy, the wickedness of corrupt judges, and the vices of an abandoned court.

His principal poetic work was a poem in three parts, which were respectively entitled, *Speculum Meditantis*, *Vox Clamantis*, and *Confessio Amantis;* the last of which, the 'Confession of a Lover,' was written in English, and was so pure and elevated in tone and sentiment, that Chaucer, upon reading it, immediately called its author, in spontaneous admiration, the Moral Gower—an encomium, to deserve which in that corrupt age, certainly argues very exalted merit. From this poem we select the following specimen, as it fully indicates the character of the author's poetic genius.

THE ENVIOUS MAN AND THE MISER.

Of Jupiter thus I find y-writ,
How whilom that he would wit,
Upon the plaints which he heard
Among the men, how it fared,
As of the wrong condition
To do justification;
And for that cause down he sent
An angel, that about went,
That he the sooth know may.

So it befel upon a day,
This angel which him should inform
Was clothed in a man's form,
And overtook, I understand,
Two men that wenten over lond;
Through which he thought to aspy
His cause, and go'th in company.

This angel with his words wise
Opposeth them in sundry wise;
Now loud words and now soft,
That made them to disputen oft;
And each his reason had,
And thus with tales he them led,
With good examination,
Till he knew the condition,

What men they were both two;
And saw well at last tho,[1]
That one of them was covetous,
And his fellow was envious.
And thus when he hath knowledging,
Anon he feigned departing,
And said he mote algate wend;
But hearken now what fell at end!
For than he made them understond
That he was there of God's sond,
And said them for the kindship,
He would do them some grace again,
And bade that one of them should sain,[2]
What thing is him levest to crave,[3]
And he it shall of gift have.
And over that ke forth with all
He saith, that other have shall
The double of that his fellow axeth;
And thus to them his grace he taxeth.

The Covetous was wonder glad;
And to that other man he bade,
And saith, that he first ax should;
For he supposeth that he would
Make his axing of world's good;
For then he knew well how it stood;
If that himself by double weight
Shall after take, and thus by sleight
Because that he would win,
He bade his fellow first begin.

This Envious, though it be late,
When that he saw he mote, algate,
Make his axing first, he thought,
If he his worship and profit sought
It shall be double to his fere,
That he would chuse in no manner.
But then he showeth what he was
Toward envy, and in this case,
Unto this angel thus he said,
And for his gift thus he prayed,
To make him blind on his one ee,
So that his fellow nothing see.

This word was not so soon spoke,
That his one ee anon was loke:
And his fellow forthwith also
Was blind on both his eyes two.
Tho was that other glad enough:
That one wept, that other lough.
He set his one ee at no cost,
Whereof that other two hath lost.

Sir John Mandeville, the last writer to whom our attention will at present be directed, was born at St. Albans, Hertfordshire, in the begin-

[1] Then. [2] Say. [3] What thing he was most disposed to crave.

ning of the fourteenth century. He was liberally educated, and was designed for the medical profession; but early conceiving an unconquerable desire to visit foreign countries, he left England when in the twenty-third year of his age, and passed thirty-four years in travelling through various parts of Europe, Asia, and Africa, visiting Cythia, the Greater and the Lesser Armenia, Arabia, Syria, Media, Mesopotamia, Persia, Chaldea, Greece, Dalmatia, and Egypt, dwelling a sufficient length of time in each of these countries to acquire a thorough knowledge of their respective languages, and closely to inspect the habits and manners of the people.

On his return to his native country, Mandeville wrote an *Iteniary*, or account of his travels, in the Latin, the French, and the English languages respectively; but his absence had been so prolonged by his various journeyings in foreign lands, that when he returned home he could not be recognized even by his relatives and friends. This circumstance, together with the vices with which his native country then abounded, induced him again to leave his home, to pass the remainder of his life among strangers. He, accordingly, embarked once more for the continent, but soon after died at Liege, in Holland, on the seventeenth of November, 1372, and in the seventy-third year of his age.

The travels of Mandeville contain little information that is important at the present time, farther than as they contribute to furnish us with another specimen of the English language in the fourteenth century. The following extract, however, presents a moral lesson which should not be neglected:—

A MOHAMMEDAN'S LECTURE ON CHRISTIAN VICES.

And therefore I shall tell you what the Soudan told me upon a day, in his chamber. He let voiden out of his chamber all manner of men, lords, and other; for he would speak to me in counsel. And there he asked me how the Christian men governed 'em in our country. And I said [to] him, 'Right well, thonked be God.' 'And he said [to] me, 'Truly nay, for ye Christian men ne reckon right not how untruly to serve God. Ye should given ensample to the lewed people for to do well, and ye given 'em ensample to don evil. For the commons, upon festival days, when they shoulden go to church to serve God, then gon they to taverns, and ben there in gluttony all the day and all night, and eaten and drinken, as beasts that have no reason, and wit not when they have enow. And therewithal they ben so proud, that they knowen not how to ben clothed; now long, now short, now strait, now large, now sworded, now daggered, and in all manner guises. They shoulden ben simple, meek, and true, and full of alms-deeds, as Jesu was, in whom they trow; but they been all the contrary, and ever inclined to the evil, and to don evil. And they been so covetous, that for a little silver they sellen 'eir daughters, 'eir sisters, and 'eir own wives, to putten 'em to lechery. And one withdraweth the wife of another; and none of 'em holdeth faith to another, but they defoulen 'eir law, that Jesu Christ betook 'em keep for 'eir salvation. And thus for 'eir sins, han, [have] they lost all this lond that we holden. For 'eir sins here, hath God taken 'em in our honds, not only by strength of ourself, but for 'eir sins. For we knowen well in very sooth, that when ye serve God, God will help you; and when he is with you, no man may be against you. And that know we well by our prophecies, that Christian men shall winnen this lond again out of our honds, when they serve God more devoutly. But as long as they ben of foul and unclean living, (as they ben now) we have no dread of 'em in no kind; for here God will not helpen 'em in no wise.'

And then I asked him how he knew the state of Christian men. And he answered me, when he knew all the states of the commons also by his messengers, that he sent to all londs, in manner as they were merchants of precious stones, of cloths of gold, and of other things, for to knowen the manner of every country amongs Christian men. And then he let clepe[1] in all the lords, that he made voiden first out of his chamber; and there he showed me four that were great lords in the country, that tolden me of my country, and of many other Christian countries, as well as if they had been of the same country; and they spak French right well, and the Soudan also, whereof I had great marvel. Alas, that it is great slander to our faith and to our laws, when folk that ben withouten law shall reproven us, and undernemen[2] us of our sins. And they that shoulden ben converted to Christ, and to the law of Jesu, by our good example, and by our acceptable life to God, ben through our wickedness and evil living, far fro us; and strangers fro the holy and very[3] belief shall thus appallen us and holden us for wicked livirs and cursed. And truly they say sooth. For the Saracens ben good and faithful. For they keepen entirely the commandment of the holy book Alcoran, that God sent 'em by his messager Mahomet; to the which, as they sayen, St. Gabriel, the angel, oftentimes told the will of God.

---

[1] Call. [2] Remind. [3] True.

Lecture the Third.

CAUSES OF THE DEARTH IN LITERATURE THAT FOLLOWED THE AGE OF EDWARD THE THIRD—THE FORMATION OF THE LANGUAGE OF THE LOWLANDS OF SCOTLAND—SCOTTISH POETS—JOHN BARBOUR—ANDREW WYNTOUN—BLIND HARRY—JAMES THE FIRST—ROBERT HENRYSON—WILLIAM DUNBAR—GAVIN DOUGLAS—SIR DAVID LYNDSAY—SIR PATRICK SPENS.

THE light of genius which spread such lustre over the English nation during the reign of Edward the Third, and that of his successor Richard the Second, when Wickliffe was shaking the papal power of Rome to its very center, and Chaucer was chanting forth his sweet poetic strains, and Gower was clothing his severe moral and didactic lessons in harmonious numbers, was succeeded by a long period of literary darkness and gloom; for, from that time until toward the close of the reign of Henry the Eighth—embracing a period of more than a century and a half—only an occasional literary star glimmered through the surrounding darkness. The civil disturbances by which the kingdom was then convulsed, was probably the principal reason why this was the state of the national mind; for while men were trembling for their lives, they were not likely to occupy themselves very greatly, either in the production, or the perusal of literary works.

The sceptre first passed from the strenuous grasp of Edward the Third into the feeble hands of his grandson Richard the Second. Then came the usurpation of the Duke of Lancaster, which was soon followed by the rebellion of the Earl of Northumberland, and afterward the long and bloody war of the Roses. Henry the Seventh of the House of Lancaster, however, after triumphing over Richard the Third of the opposite faction, by marrying Elizabeth, heiress of the House of York, united the interest of the contending parties; but it occupied the whole of that monarch's long and vigorous reign to raise the kingdom from the exhausted state in which he found it, to happiness and prosperity. His son and successor, Henry the Eighth, succeeded to an undisputed crown; and as he had been carefully educated, and possessed some small degree of literary taste, he made some pretensions to the patronage of learning. This dark period was, it is true, occasionally relieved by some light of genius twinkling through its murky gloom. To a brief notice of the writers who afforded this relief, we shall, therefore, now proceed; but as we shall have occasion first to mention some of the early authors of Scotland, we may remark, in passing, that the language used at this time in the lowland district of that country, was, like that of England, based upon the Teutonic, and had, like the cotemporary English, a Norman admixture.

To account for these circumstances, some writers have supposed that the language of England, in its various shades of improvement, reached the North through the settlers who are known to have flocked thither from England during the eleventh, twelfth, and thirteenth centuries; while others suggest that the great body of the Scottish people, apart from the Highlanders, must have been of Teutonic origin; and they point to the very probable theory as to the Picts having been a German race. They farther suggest that a Norman admixture might readily have come to the national tongue, through the long intercourse between the two countries during the three centuries just mentioned. Thus it is presumed, 'one common language was separately formed in the two countries, and owed its identity to its being constructed out of similar materials, by similar gradations, and by nations in the same state of society.'

Whatever might have been the cause, there can be no doubt that the language used by the first Scottish vernacular writers in the fourteenth century, greatly resembled that which was used cotemporaneously in England. Of these writers, John Barbour is the first of whom we possess any certain knowledge.

JOHN BARBOUR was born in 1320, but at what precise place is unknown. His early education, and the development of his genius must have been, for the age in which he lived, very remarkable; as we find him in 1357, when he was in the thirty-seventh year of his age, exercising the duties of the important office of archdeacon of Aberdeen. Besides his clerical attainments, Barbour was distinguished for political abilities also; and was, accordingly, chosen by the Bishop of Aberdeen to act as his commissioner at Edinburgh, when the ransom of David the Second was there debated. His learning too was such that on several occasions he accompanied men of rank to study at Oxford. His death occurred in 1396, when he was in the seventy-seventh year of his age.

Barbour, in all probability, formed his taste upon the Romance writers who preceded him in England, as his first poem was founded upon *The Brute*—a subject made famous, as already observed, by Geoffrey of Monmouth and other writers. *The Bruce*, his great poem, is conducted upon a similar plan; but unlike the former work, the principal incidents which it narrates, are founded on authenticated facts. It is, therefore, a very important production, and may be considered as a complete history of the memorable transactions in which king Robert the First, asserted the independence of Scotland, and obtained its crown for himself and his family. At the same time it is far from being destitute of poetical spirit or rhythmical sweetness and harmony. It contains many vividly descriptive passages, and abounds in dignified and even pathetic sentiment.

In the opening of this important poem, the author, contemplating the enslaved condition of his country, breaks forth in the following animated

APOSTROPHE TO FREEDOM.

A! fredome is a nobill thing!
Fredome mayse man to haiff liking!
Fredome all solace to man giffis:
He levys at ese that frely levys!
A noble hart may haiff nane ese,
Na ellys nocht that may him plese,
Gyff fredome failythe: for fre liking
Is yearnyt our all other thing
Na he, that ay hase levyt fre,
May nocht knaw weill the propyrte,
The angyr, na the wrechyt dome,
That is cowplyt to foule thyrldome.
Bot gyff he had assayit it,
Then all perquer he suld it wyt;
And suld think fredome mar to pryse
Than all the gold in warld that is.

From this poem we might select many other passages fraught with deep interest; particularly that which describes the death of Sir Henry De Bohun —an event which took place on the eve of the battle of Bannockburn; but our space will permit us to introduce a single extract only from the description of that important battle itself.

THE BATTLE OF BANNOCKBURN.

When this was said——
The Scottismen commonally
Kneelit all doun, to God to pray.
And a short prayer there made they
To God, to help them in that ficht.
And when the English king had sicht
Of them kneeland, he said, in hy,
'Yon folk kneel to ask mercy.'
Sir Ingram[1] said, 'Ye say sooth now—
They ask mercy, but not of you;
For their trespass to God they cry:
I tell you a thing sickerly,
That yon men will all win or die;
For doubt of deid[2] they sall not flee.'
'Now be it sae then!' said the king.
And then, but langer delaying,
They gart trump till the assembly
On either side men micht then see
Mony a wicht man and worthy,
Ready to do chivalry.

[1] Sir Ingram L'Umphraville.

[2] Fear of death.

* * * * * *
Almighty God! how douchtily
Sir Edward the Bruce and his men
Amang their facs conteinit them than!
Fechting in sae gude covine,[1]
Sae hardy, worthy, and sae fine,
That their vaward frushit was. * *
Almighty God! wha then micht see
That Stewart Walter, and his rout,
And the gude Douglas, that was sae stout,
Fechting into that stalwart stour,
He sould say that till all honour
They were worthy. * * *
There micht men see mony a steed
Flying astray, that lord had nane. * *
Their micht men hear ensenzies cry:
And Scottismen cry hardily,
'On them! On them! On them! They fail!'
With that sae hard they gan assail,
And slew all that they micht o'erta'.
And the Scots archers alsua[2]
Shot amang them so deliverly,
Engrieving them sae greatumly,
That what for them, that with them faucht,
That sae great routs to them raucht,
And pressit them full eagerly;
And what for arrows, that fellonly
Mony great wounds gan them ma',
And slew fast off their horse alsua,
That they vandist[3] a little weel.
* * * * *

The appearance of a mock host, composed of the servants of the Scottish camp, completes the panic of the English army; the king flies, and Sir Giles D'Argentine is slain. The narrative then proceeds :—

They were, to say sooth, sae aghast,
And fled sae fast, richt effrayitly,
That of them a full great party
Fled to the water of Forth, and there
The maist part of them drownit were.
And Bannockburn, betwixt the braes,
Of men, of horse, sae steckit[4] was,
That, upon drownit horse and men,
Men micht pass dry out—ower it then.
And lads, swains, and rangle,[5]
When they saw vanquished the battle,
Ran amang them, and sae gan slay,
As folk that nae defence micht ma'.
* * * * * *

---

1 Company. 2 Also. 3 Failed, gave way.
4 Shut up. 5 Rabble. 6 Slime, mud.

On ane side, they their faes had,
That slew them down, without mercy:
And they had, on the tother party,
Bannockburn, that sae cumbersome was,
For slike[1] and deepness for to pass,
That they micht nane out-ower it ride:
Them worthies, maugre theirs, abide;
Sae that some slain, some drownit were:
Micht nane escape that ever came there.

Andrew Wyntoun, the next important poet that the Scottish literature of this period presents, lived some time after the age of Barbour, but neither the place nor the period of his birth is now known. He was Prior of St. Serf's monastery at Lochleven, and about the year 1420, he completed an *Orygynale Cronykil of Scotland*, including much universal history, and extending down to his own time. The genius of this author was inferior to that of Barbour; but his versification is easy, his language pure, and his style often animated. His Chronicle is valuable as a picture of ancient manners, as a repository of historical anecdotes, and as a specimen of the literary attainments of that age in Scotland. It contains a considerable number of fabulous legends, such as we may suppose to have been told beside the parlor fire of the monasteries of those days, and which convey a curious idea of the credulity of the age. From this Chronicle we extract the following singular imaginary interview between St. Serf and Sathanas. St. Serf lived in the sixth century, and was the founder of the monastery f which Wyntoun was Prior:[2]

NTERVIEW OF ST. SERF WITH SATHANAS.

While St. Serf, intil a stead,
Lay after matins in his bed,
The devil came, in foul intent
For til found him with argument,
And said, 'St. Serf, by thy werk
I ken thou art a cunning clerck.'
St. Serf said, 'Gif I sae be,
Foul wretch, what is that for thee?'
The devil said, 'This question
I ask in our collation,—
Say where was God, wit ye oucht,
Before that heaven and erd was wroucht?'
St. Serf said, 'In himself steadless
His Godhead hampered never was.'
The devil then askit, 'What cause he had
To make the creatures that he made?'
To that St. Serf answered there,
'Of creatures made he was maker.
A maker micht he never be,
But gif creatures made had he.'

---

[1] Slime, mud. [2] Ellis

The devil askit him, 'Why God of noucht
His werkis all full gude had wroucht.'
St. Serf answered, 'That Goddis will
Was never to make his werkis ill,
And as envious he had been seen,
Gif nought but he full gude had been.'
St. Serf the devil askit than,
'Where God made Adam, the first man?'
'In Ebron Adam formit was,'
St. Serf said. And til him Sathanas,
'Where was he, eft that, for his vice,
He was put out of Paradise?'
St. Serf said, 'Where he was made.'
The devil askit, 'How lang he bade
In Paradise, after his sin.'
'Seven hours,' Serf said, 'bade he therein.'
'When was Eve made?' said Sathanas.
'In Paradise,' Serf said, 'she was.' * *
The devil askit, 'Why that ye
Men, are quite delivered free,
Through Christ's passion precious boucht,
And we devils sae are noucht?'
St. Serf said, 'For that ye
Fell through your awn iniquity;
And through ourselves we never fell,
But through your fellon false counsell.' * *
Then saw the devil that he could noucht,
With all the wiles that he wrought,
Overcome St. Serf. He said than
He kenned him for a wise man.
Forthy there he gave him quit,
For he wan at him na profit.
St. Serf said, 'Thou wretch, gae
Frae this stead, and 'noy nae mae
Into this stead, I bid ye.'
Suddenly then passed he;
Frae that stead he held his way,
And never was seen there to this day.

Besides Wyntoun there were a few other Scottish writers of the same period, such as Hutcheon of the Hall Royal, who wrote a metrical Romance entitled the *Gest of Arthur;* and Clerk of Tranent, who wrote a Romance entitled *The Adventure of Sir Gawain.* In the narrative of what remains of this latter poem, there is a sort of wildness which is very striking, though the language is often so obsolete, as to be quite unintelligible. *The Howlate*, an allegorical, satirical poem written about the same time by a poet named Howland, but of whom nothing more is known, strikingly reminds us of The 'Pricke of Conscience,' and 'Pierce Ploughman's Vision.'

The last of the romantic or minstrel class of compositions in Scotland of this period was *The Adventures of Sir William Wallace*, written about the middle of the fifteenth century by a wandering poet usually called Blind Harry. Of the author, however, nothing is farther known than that he was blind from his infancy, that he wrote this poem, and that he supported himself by reciting it before company. The work abounds with marvellous stories respecting the prowess of its hero, and in one or two places, grossly outrages real history: its value has, perhaps, on this account been generally understated. But within a very few years past, several of the transactions attributed by the blind minstrel to Wallace, and hitherto supposed to be fictitious—such as his expeditions to France—have been confirmed by the discovery of authentic evidence. The poem is in ten-syllable lines, and is not deficient in poetical effect, and elevated sentiment. A paraphrase of it into modern Scotch, by William Hamilton of Gilbertfield, has long been a favorite volume among the Scotch peasantry; and it was the study of this book which had so great an effect in kindling the genius of Robert Burns.[1] Perhaps the most striking passages in this poem are the Adventures of Wallace while fishing in Irvine Water—The Escape of Wallace from Perth—and Wallace's Death: the last of which follows:

THE DEATH OF WALLACE.

On Wednesday the false Southron furth brocht
To martyr him, as they before had wrocht.[2]
Of men in arms led him a full great rout.
With a bauld sprite guid Wallace blent about:
A priest he asked, for God that died on tree.
King Edward then commanded his clergy,
And said, 'I charge you, upon loss of life,
Nane be sae bauld yon tyrant for to shrive.
He has reigned long in contrar my highness.'
A blyth bishop soon, present in that place.
Of Canterbury he then was righteous lord;
Again the king he made this richt record,
And said, 'Myself shall hear his confession,
If I have micht in contrar of thy crown.
An thou through force will stop me of this thing,
I vow to God, who is my righteous king,
That all England I shall her interdite,
And make it known thou art a heretic.
The sacrament of kirk I shall him give:
Syne take thy choice, to starve[3] or let him live.
It were mair weil, in worship of thy crown,
To keep sic ane in life in thy bandoun,
Than all the land and good that thou hast reived,
But cowardice thee ay fra honour dreived,
Thou has thy life rougin[4] in wrangeous deed;
That shall be seen on thee or on thy seed.'
The king gart[5] charge they should the bishop ta,
But sad lords counsellit to let him ga.
All Englishmen said that his desire was richt.
To Wallace then he rakit in their sicht

[1] Burn's life by Dr. Currie.
[2] Contrived.
[3] The necessary consequence of an interdict.
[4] Spent.
[5] Caused.

And sadly heard his confession till ane end:
Humbly to God his sprite he there commend
Lowly him served with hearty devotion
Upon his knees and said ane orison.
A psalter-book Wallace had on him ever
Fra his childheid—fra it wald nocht dissever;
Better he trowit in wyage[1] for to speed.
But then he was despalyed of his weed.[2]
This grace he asked at Lord Clifford, that knicht,
To let him have his psalter-book in sicht.
He gart a priest it open before him hald,
While they till him had done all that they wald.
Stedfast he read for ought they did him there;
Feil[3] Southrons said that Wallace felt na sair.
Guid devotion, sae, was his beginning,
Conteined therewith, and fair was his ending.
While speech and sprite at anis all can fare
To lasting bliss, we trow, for evermair.

From these romantic writers of Scotland, we proceed to notice a few of a different class, the first of whom, in the order of time, is the Scottish king, James the First.

JAMES THE FIRST was the son of Robert the Third, king of Scotland, and was born in 1395. His father being of a weak mind and easy disposition, allowed his brother, the Duke of Albany, to gain a complete ascendency over him. The reins of government consequently passed entirely into the duke's hands; and as he was the next heir to the crown after Robert and his issue, he soon entertained the ambitious and criminal design of securing the kingdom for himself. With this view, he so misrepresented the conduct of the king's eldest son, the Duke of Rothsay, that the weak monarch committed the prince to the care of the regent Albany, by whom he was immediately imprisoned in Falkland Castle, and soon after starved to death. The king, too weak to punish the man to whom he had foolishly committed the administration of the government, had still sufficient discernment to perceive the necessity of preserving his remaining son from a similar fate. With this view he, in 1404, caused the prince to embark, attended by a large retinue, for the court of his ally, Charles the Sixth of France, there to be educated. The vessel in which the prince sailed, had the misfortune to be captured on its way thither by an English ship-of-war, and James and his attendants were immediately conveyed to London as prisoners. This event occurred in the sixth year of the reign of Henry the Fourth; and during the remaining eight years of that monarch's reign, throughout the whole of the reign of Henry the Fifth, and until the commencement of the fourth year of the reign of Henry the Sixth, James remained a prisoner in England. Though Windsor Castle was his prison-house during the eighteen years of his captivity, yet his captors treated him

[1] Expedition. [2] Clothes. [3] Many.

with every mark of respect and kindness, and bestowed upon him an education far superior to what he could, in that age, have received in his own country.

The captivity of the young prince so deeply affected his father's mind, that he soon sunk under the weight of the affliction, and James was, accordingly, in 1405, declared king by an assembly of the Scottish states, though the Duke of Albany still retained the regency.

In 1424, when James was set at liberty, and assumed the reins of the government of his country, he found his kingdom in such disorder that the most rigorous measures were required to curb the existing abuses. These measures bore very severely upon the usurpations of the crown lands by the nobility, in consequence of which a conspiracy was formed against the king, at the head of which was his uncle, the Earl of Athole. James received timely intelligence of the designs of the conspirators, but his natural intrepidity led him to treat the threatened danger with contempt; 'and while in the Dominican Convent, near Perth, attended by his queen and a very few of his courtiers, he was murdered in the most cruel manner, in the forty-fourth year of his age, and the thirteenth of his reign.'[1]

While James was a prisoner in Windsor Castle, and pining for his liberty, he accidentally saw, in an adjacent garden, a young princess, Jane Beaufort, daughter of the Duke of Somerset. This incident exerted a most remarkable influence over the captive, and induced him to seek the hand of the princess, which he eventually obtained. To the Lady Jane, James was most ardently attached, and her praises elicited his finest poetic strains.

The only unquestioned production of this youthful monarch, is a long poem entitled *The King's Quhair, or Book.* This poem, which embraces the relation of various particulars in his own life, and a full development of his passion for the Lady Jane, abounds in simplicity and pathos, and contains poetry superior to any other, with the exception of that of Chaucer, produced in England previous to the reign of Elizabeth. To sustain this remark, we need only present the following stanzas :—

THE FIRST SIGHT OF LADY JANE BEAUFORT AS SEEN FROM WINDSOR CASTLE.

Bewailing in my chamber, thus alone,
Despaired of all joy and remedy,
For-tired of my thought, and woe-begone,
And to the window gan I walk in hy[2]
To see the world and folk that went forbye,[3]
As, for the time, though I of mirthis food
Might have no more, to look it did me good.

Now was there made, fast by the towris wall,
A garden fair; and in the corners set
Ane arbour green, with wandis long and small
Railed about, and so with trees set

[1] Pinkerton. [2] Haste. [3] Past.

Was all the place, and hawthorn hedges knet,
That lyf was none walking there forbye,
That might within scarce any wight espy.

So thick the boughis and the leavis green
Beshaded all the alleys that there were,
And mids of every arbour might be seen
The sharpe greene sweete juniper,
Growing so fair with branches here and there,
That as it seemed to a lyf without,
The boughis spread the arbour all about.
And on the smalle greene twistis[1] sat,
The little sweete nightingale, and sung
So loud and clear, the hymnis consecrat
Of lovis use, now soft, now loud among,
That all the gardens and the wallis rung
Right of their song. * *

—— Cast I down mine eyes again,
Where as I saw, walking under the tower,
Full secretly, new comen here to plain,
The fairest or the freshest younge flower
That ever I saw, methought, before that hour,
For which sudden abate, anon astart,[2]
The blood of all my body to my heart.

And though I stood abasit tho a lite [3]
No wonder was; for why? my wittis all
Were so overcome with pleasance and delight,
Only through letting of my eyen fall,
That suddenly my heart became her thrall,
Forever of free will,—for of menace
There was no token in her sweete face.

And in my head I drew right hastily,
And eftesoons I leant it out again,
And saw her walk that very womanly,
With no wight mo', but only women twain.
Then gan I study in myself, and sayn,[4]
'Ah, sweet! are ye a worldly creature,
Or heavenly thing in likeness of nature?

Or are ye god Cupidis own princess,
And comin are to loose me out of band?
Or are ye very Nature the goddess,
That have depainted with your heavenly hand,
This garden full of flowers as they stand?
What shall I think, alas! what reverence
Shall I mister[5] unto your excellence?

If ye a goddess be, and that ye like
To do me pain, I may it not astart:[6]
If ye be warldly wight, that doth me sike,[7]

---

[1] Twigs. [2] Went and came. [3] Confounded for a little while.
[4] Say. [5] Minister. [6] Fly.
[7] Makes me sigh.

Why list[1] God make you so, my dearest heart,
To do a seely[2] prisoner this smart,
That loves you all, and wot of nought but woe?
And therefore mercy, sweet! sin' it is so.' * *

Of her array the form if I shall write,
Towards her golden hair and rich attire,
In fretwise couchit[3] with pearlis white
And great balas[4] leaming[5] as the fire,
With mony ane emeraut and fair sapphire;
And on her head a chaplet fresh of hue,
Of plumis parted red, and white, and blue.

Full of quaking spangis bright as gold,
Forged of shape like to the amorets,
So new, so fresh, so pleasant to behold,
The plumis eke like to the flower jonets,[6]
And other of shape, like to the flower jonets;
And above all this, there was, well I wot,
Beauty enough to make a world to doat.

About her neck, white as the fire amail,[7]
A goodly chain of small orfevory,[8]
Whereby there hung a ruby, without fail,
Like to ane heart shapen verily,
That as a spark, of low,[9] so wantonly
Seemed burning upon her white throat,
Now if there was good party,[10] God it wot.

And for to walk that fresh May's morrow,
Ane hook she had upon her tissue white,
That goodlier had not been seen to-forow,[11]
As I suppose; and girt she was alite,[12]
Thus halflings loose for haste, to such delight
It was to see her youth in goodlihede,
That for rudeness to speak thereof I dread.

In her was youth, beauty, with humble aport,
Bounty, richess, and womanly feature,
God better wot than my pen can report:
Wisdom, largess, estate, and cunning[13] sure,
In every point so guided her measure,
In word, in deed, in shape, in countenance,
That nature might no more her child avance!
* * * * * *
And when she walked had a little thraw
Under the sweete greene boughis bent,
Her fair fresh face, as white as any snaw,

---

1 Pleased. 2 Wretched. 3 Inlaid like fretwork.
4 A kind of precious stone. 5 Glittering.
6 A kind of lily. It is conjectured that the royal poet may here allude covertly to the name of his mistress, which, in the diminutive, was Janet or Jonet.—*Thompson's Edition of King's Quhair, Ayr*, 1824. 7 Enamel.
8 Gold work. 9 Flame. 10 Match.
11 Before. 12 Slightly. 13 Knowledge.

She turned has, and furth her wayis went;
But tho began mine aches and torment,
To see her part and follow I na might;
Methought the day was turned into night.

The 'King's Quhair' was written while James was confined in Windsor Castle, and it is supposed that he wrote several poems descriptive of humorous rustic scenes after he ascended the Scottish throne; none of these, however, can be identified.

James was followed in comparatively rapid succession by such writers as Henryson, Dunbar, Douglass and Lyndsay, of whom Warton remarks that 'they displayed a degree of sentiment and spirit, a command of phraseology, and a fertility of imagination not to be found in any contemporary English poets.'

ROBERT HENRYSON, the first of these writers, followed king James after an interval of about a half a century. Of this poet there are no personal memorials farther than that he was a schoolmaster of Dunfermlane, and that he died about 1508. His principal poem is *The Testament of Cresseid*, being a sequel to Chaucer's romantic poem Troilus and Cresseide. Henryson also wrote a series of fables, thirteen in number, and some miscellaneous poems chiefly of a moral character. One of his fables is the common story of the *Town Mouse and the Country Mouse*, which he treats with much humor and characteristic description, and concludes with the following beautifully expressed moral:—

Blissed be simple life, withouten dreid;
Blissed be sober feast in quieté;
Wha has eneuch of no more has he neid,
Though it be little into quantity.
Grit abundance, and blind prosperity,
Oft timis make ane evil conclusion;
The sweetest life, theirfor, in this country,
Is of sickerness, with small possession.

To these lines we may add the following pointed though fanciful description of

THE GARMENT OF GOOD LADIES.

Would my good lady love me best,
  And work after my will,
I should a garment goodliest
  Gar make her body till.[1]

Of high honoùr should be her hood,
  Upon her head to wear,
Garnish'd with governance, so good
  Na deeming should her deir.[2]

---

[1] Cause to be made to her shape.

[2] No opinion should injure her.

Her sark[1] should be her body next,
  Of chastity so white:
With shame and dread together mixt,
  The same should be perfyte.[2]

Her kirtle should be of clean constance,
  Lacit with lesum[3] love;
The mailies[4] of continuance,
  For never to remove.

Her gown should be of goodliness,
  Well ribbon'd with renown;
Purfill'd[5] with pleasure in ilk[6] place,
  Furrit with fine fashioùn.

Her belt should be of benignity,
  About her middle meet;
Her mantle of humility
  To thole[7] both wind and weit.[8]

Her hat should be of fair having,
  And her tippet of truth;
Her patelet of good pansing,[9]
  Her hals-ribbon of ruth.[10]

Her sleeves should be of esperance,
  To keep her fra despair:
Her glovis of good governance,
  To hide her fingers fair.

Her shoen should be of sickerness,
  In sign that she not slide;
Her hose of honesty, I guess,
  I should for her provide.

Would she put on this garment gay,
  I durst swear by my seill,[11]
That she wore never green nor gray
  That set[12] her half so weel.

William Dunbar, the poet who follows Henryson, was born at Salton, in 1465. Of his early life little is farther known than that, though poor, he was educated at the university of St. Andrews, where he is represented to have taken the degree of master of arts in 1479, when not yet fifteen years of age. Having, soon after he closed his studies, entered the Franciscan Order of Friars, he travelled for a number of years in Scotland, England, and France, as a novitiate of that Order, preaching, and living by the alms of the pious—a mode of life which he himself afterward acknowledged involved him in the constant exercise of falsehood, deceit, and flattery.

In 1490, Dunbar, when in the twenty-fifth year of his age, returned to

[1] Shift.
[2] Perfect.
[3] Lawful.
[4] Eyelet-holes for lacing her kirtle.
[5] Parfilé (French), fringed or bordered.
[6] Each.
[7] Endure.
[8] Wet.
[9] Thinking.
[10] Her neck—ribbon of pity.
[11] Salvation.
[12] Became.

his own country, and having soon after renounced his sordid profession, entered into the service of the king. He was employed from that time until 1500, in some subordinate, though not unimportant capacity, in connection with various foreign embassies, and thus visited Germany, Italy, Spain, and France, besides England and Ireland. He could not, in such a mode of life, fail to acquire much of that knowledge of mankind which forms so important a part of the education of a poet.

For these various services, 'Dunbar, in 1500, received from the king an annual pension of ten pounds, soon afterward increased to twenty, and eventually to eighty.'[1] He is supposed to have been employed by James about this time, in some of the negotiations preparatory to the marriage of that prince with the princess Margaret, daughter of Henry the Seventh of England, which took place in 1503. It was on this occasion that Dunbar wrote the *Thistle and the Rose*, one of his allegorical poems.

For a number of years after this important marriage, Dunbar continued to reside at court, regaling his royal master with various poetic compositions, and probably also with his conversation, the charms of which, if we may judge from his writings, must have been very great. His situation, however, was far from being happy; for he seems constantly to have repined at the servile course of life which he was condemned to lead, and to have anxiously longed for some more independent means of subsistence. But he sadly realized that while the great listen with delight to the flattering compliments of the learned, they seldom adequately reward their merit. He died in 1530, in the sixty-sixth year of his age.

The poetic genius of Dunbar, in the judgment of Sir Walter Scott, and also of Mr. Ellis, was superior to that of any other poet that Scotland ever produced; and it is a matter of great surprise, therefore, that, with few exceptions, his poems should have remained in the obscurity of manuscript for nearly two centuries after they were written. 'These poems may be divided into three classes, the Allegorical, the Moral, and the Comic; besides which there is a vast number of productions composed on occasions affecting himself alone, and which may, therefore, be called Personal poems.'[2] His principal Allegorical poems are the *Thistle and the Rose*, a Nuptial Song to celebrate the union of King James with the princess Margaret, *The Dance*, and *The Golden Terge*. Perhaps the most remarkable of all his poems is 'The Dance.' It describes a procession of the seven deadly sins in the infernal regions, and for strength and vividness of painting, would bear a comparison with any other poem in the language. From this great poem we offer the following brief extract:—

Let see, quoth he, who now begins—
With that the foul Seven Deadly Sins
  Begoud to leap at anes.
And first in all the Dance was Pride,
With hair wiled back, and bonnet on side,

[1] Pinkerton.

Like to mak vaistie wanes;[1]
And round about him as a wheel,
Hang all in rumples[2] to the heel
His kethat[3] for the nanes.[4]
Mony proud trumpour with him trippit;
Through scaldand fire aye as they skippit,
They grinned with hideous granes.
Then Ire came in with sturt and strife;
His hand was aye upon his knife,
He brandished like a bear,
Boasters, braggarts, and bargainers,
After him, passit in to pairs,
All boden in 'feir of weir,'[5]
In jacks, and scrips, and bonnets of steel;
Their legs were chained down to the heel;
Froward was their effeir:
Some upon other with brands beft,[6]
Some jaggit others, to the heft,
With knives that sharp could shear.

Next in the Dance followed Envy,
Filled full of feid and felony,
Hid malice and despite:
For privy hatred that traitor trembled;
Him followed mony freik[7] dissembled,
With feigned wordis white:
And flatterers into men's faces;
And backbiters in secret places,
To lee that had delight;
And rouners of fals lesings,
Alas! that courts of noble kings
Of them can never be quit.

Next him in Dance came Covetice,
Root of all evil and grund of vice,
That never could be content:
Caitiffs, wretches, and ockerars,[8]
Hood-pykes,[9] hoarders, and gatherers,
All with that warlock went:
Out of their throats they shot on other
Het molten gold, methought, a fother,[10]
As fire-flaught maist fervent;
Ay as they toomit them of shot,
Fiends filled them new up to the throat
With gold of all kind prent.[11]

Of Dunbar's moral poems the most solemn and impressive is the one in which he represents a Thrush and a Nightingale taking opposite sides in a debate upon earthly and spiritual affections, the Thrush ending

[1] Something touching puffed-up manners appears to be hinted at in this obscure line. [2] Large folds. [3] Robe.
[4] For the occasion. [5] Arrayed in the accoutrements of war.
[6] Gave blows. [7] Contentious persons. [8] Usurers.
[9] Misers. [10] Great quantity. [11] Every coinage.

every stanza with a recommendation of 'A lusty life in Love's service,' and the Nightingale with the more melodious declaration that 'All love is lost but upon God alone.' From this poem we present, with much pleasure, the following stanzas:—

THE MERLE AND THE NIGHTINGALE.

In May, as that Aurora did upspring,
With crystal een chasing the cluddes sable,
I heard a Merle with merry notis sing
A sang of love, with voice right comfortable,
Again' the orient beamis, amiable,
Upon a blissful branch of laurel green;
This was her sentence sweet and delectable,
A lusty life in Lovis service been.

Under this branch ran down a river bright,
Of balmy liquor, crystalline of hue,
Again' the heavenly azure skyis light,
Where did upon the tother side pursue
A Nightingale, with sugared notis new,
Whose angel feathers as the peacock shone;
This was her song, and of a sentence true,
All love is lost but upon God alone.

With notis glad, and glorious harmony,
This joyful Merle, so salust she the day,
While rung the woodis of her melody,
Saying, Awake ye lovers of this May;
Lo, fresh Flora has flourished every spray,
As nature has her taught, the noble queen,
The field been clothit in a new array;
A lusty life in Lovis service been.

Ne'er sweeter noise was heard with living man,
Na made this merry gentle Nightingale;
Her sound went with the river as it ran,
Out through the fresh and flourished lusty vale;
O Merle! quoth she, O fool! stint of thy tale,
For in thy song good sentence is there none,
For both is tint, the time and the travail
Of every love but upon God alone.

Cease, quoth the Merle, thy preaching, Nightingale:
Shall folk their youth spend into holiness?
Of young sanctis, grows auld feindis, but fable;
Fye, hypocrite, in yeiris tenderness,
Again' the law of kind thou goes express,
That crookit age makes one with youth serene,
Whom nature of conditions made diverse:
A lusty life in Lovis service been.

The Nightingale said, Fool, remember thee,
That both in youth and eild,[1] and every hour,
The love of God most dear to man suld be;
That him, of nought, wrought like his own figour,

[1] Age.

And died himself fro' dead him to succour;
O, whether was kythit[1] there true love or none?
He is most true and stedfast paramour,
And love is lost but upon him alone.

The Merle said, Why put God so great beauty
In ladies, with sic womanly having,
But gif he would that they suld lovit be?
To love eke nature gave them inclining,
And He of nature that worker was and king,
Would nothing frustir put, nor let be seen,
Into his creature of his own making;
A lusty life in Lovis service been.

The Nightingale said, Not to that behoof
Put God sic beauty in a lady's face,
That she suld have the thank therefor or luve,
But He, the worker, that put in her sic grace;
Of beauty, bounty, riches, time, or space,
And every gudeness that been to come or gone
The thank redounds to him in every place:
All love is lost, but upon God alone.

O Nightingale! it were a story nice,
That love suld not depend on charity;
And, gif that virtue contrar be to vice,
Then love maun be a virtue, as thinks me;
For, aye, to love envy maun contrar' be:
God bade eke love thy neighbour fro the spleen,[2]
And who than ladies sweeter neighbours be?
A lusty life in Lovis service been.

The Nightingale said, Bird, why does thou rave?
Man may take in his lady sic delight,
Him to forget that her sic virtue gave,
And for his heaven receive her colour white:
Her golden tressit hairis redomite,[3]
Like to Opollo's beamis tho' they shone,
Suld not him blind fro' love that is perfite;
All love is lost but upon God alone.

The Merle said, Love is cause of honour aye,
Love makis cowards manhood to purchase,
Love makis knichtis hardy at essay,
Love makis wretches full of largeness,
Love makis sweir[4] folks full of business,
Love makis sluggards fresh and well be seen,
Love changes vice in virtuous nobleness;
A lusty life in Lovis service been.

The Nightingale said, True is the contrary;
Sic frustis love it blindis men so far,
Into their minds it makis them to vary;
In false vain glory they so drunken are,

[1] Shown.
[2] Equivalent to the modern phrase, from the heart.
[3] Bound, encircled.
[4] Slothful.

Their wit is went, of woe they are not waur,
While that all worship away be fro' them gone,
Fame, goods, and strength; wherefore well say I daur,
All love is lost but upon God alone.

Then said the Merle, mine error I confess.
This frustis love is all but vanity:
Blind ignorance me gave sic hardiness,
To argue so again the verity;
Wherefore I counsel every man that he
With love not in the feindis net be tone,[1]
But love the love that did for his love die:
All love is lost but upon God alone.

Then sang they both with voices loud and clear,
The Merle sang, Man, love God that has thee wrought.
The Nightingale sang, Man, love the Lord most dear,
That thee and all this world made of nought.
The Merle said, love him that thy love has sought
Fro' heaven to earth, and here took flesh and bone.
The Nightingale sang, And with his dead thee bought:
All love is lost, but upon him alone.

Then flew thir birdis o'er the boughis sheen,
Singing of love amang the leavis small;
Whose eidant plead yet made my thoughtis grein,[2]
Both sleeping, waking, in rest, and in travail:
Me to recomfort most it does avail,
Again for love, when love I can find none,
To think how sung this Merle and Nightingale;
All love is lost but upon God alone.

To most readers there is something more touching in those less labored verses in which the poet moralizes on the brevity of existence, the shortness and uncertainty of all ordinary enjoyments, and the wickedness and woes of mankind, than in his more elaborate productions. From these poems we select the following specimen :—

This wavering warld's wretchedness
The failing and fruitless business,
The misspent time, the service vain
    For to consider is ane pain.

The sliding joy, the gladness short,
The feigned love, the false comfort,
The sweir abade,[3] the slightful train,[4]
    For to consider is ane pain

The suggared mouths, with minds therefra,
The figured speech, with faces tway;
The pleasing tongues with hearts in plain,
    For to consider is ane pain.

Dunbar was, however, by no means disposed habitually to take gloomy

[1] Ta'en, taken.
[2] Whose close disputation yet moved my thoughts.
[3] Delay.
[4] Snare.

or desponding views of life. He has one poem each stanza of which ends with

For to be blythe methinks it best;

and in another poem he advises, since life is so uncertain, that the good things of this world be rationally enjoyed while it is yet possible. In a third, these maxims are still more forcibly expressed; and from this we extract the following stanzas, the philosophy of which is excellent.

Be merry, man, and tak not sair in mind
  The wavering of this wretched world of sorrow;
To God be humble, to thy friend be kind,
  And with thy neighbours gladly lend and borrow;
  His chance to-night, it may be thine to-morrow;
Be blyth in hearte for my aventure,
  For oft with wise men it has been said aforow,
Without Gladness availes no Treasure.

Make thee gude cheer of it that God thee sends,
  For warld's wrak but welfare[1] nought avails;
Nae gude is thine save only that thou spends,
  Remanant all thou bruikes but with bails;[2]
  Seek to solace when sadness thee assails;
In dolour lang thy life may not endure.
  Wherefore of comfort set up all thy sails;
Without gladness availes no Treasure.

Follow on pity, flee trouble and debate,
  With famous folkis hald thy company;
Be charitable and hum'le in thine estate,
  For warldly honour lastes but a cry.
  For trouble in earth tak no melancholy;
Be rich in patience, if thou in gudes be poor;
  Who lives merrily he lives mightily;
Without gladness availes no Treasure.

Dunbar was as great in the Comic as in the solemn strain, but unfortunately not so pure. Among his Comic poems there is one piece of peculiar humor, descriptive of an imaginary tournament between a Tailor and a Shoemaker in the same low regions where he places 'The Dance' of 'The Seven Deadly Sins.' It is written in the style of the broadest farce, and though the language is very often offensive, yet it is as droll as any thing in Smollett.

We have dwelt longer upon the life, genius, and writings of Dunbar than we had intended; but the greatest of Scotland's poets required something more than a mere passing notice.

GAVIN DOUGLAS, a contemporary of Dunbar was the youngest son of the sixth earl of Angus, and was born at Brechin in 1471. He was educated at the university of St. Andrews, after which he travelled in Germany and

[1] World's trash without health. [2] Injuries.

Italy, where he cultivated the muses so successfully as to merit the acquaintance and commendation of the learned wherever he went. On his return to Scotland in 1496, having previously taken orders, he was made provost of St. Giles's church, Edinburgh, and in 1515, was elevated to the office of bishop of Dunkeld, to which the rich Abbey of Aberbrothin was soon after added. The purity of his life and character, however, exposed him to the virulent persecutions of the times, and having retired to London he there soon after died, in April 1522, and in the fifty second year of his age.

Douglas shines both as an allegorical and a descriptive poet. He wants the vigorous sense, and also the graphic force of Dunbar; for while the latter is always close and nervous, Douglas is often soft aud verbose. The genius of Dunbar is so powerful that manner sinks beneath it; that of Douglas is so much matter of culture, that manner is frequently its most striking peculiarity.

The principal original composition of Douglas is a long poem entitled *The Palace of Honor*. It was intended as an apology for the conduct of a king, and was therefore addressed to James the Fourth. The poet represents himself as seeing, in a vision, a large company travelling toward the Palace of Honor. He joins them and narrates the particulars of the pilgrimages. The celebrated 'Pilgrim's Progress' bears, in its design, so striking a resemblance to this poem, that we can hardly conceive it possible that Bunyan could have been ignorant of it. *King Hart*, the only other long poem of Douglas, presents a metaphorical view of human life.

But by far the most able production of this author is a translation of Virgil's Æneid into Scottish verse. This work was executed in 1513, and is remarkable for being the first version of a Latin classic into any British tongue. It is generally allowed to be a masterly performance, though in too obsolete a language ever to regain its popularity. The original poems styled *Prologues*, which the translator prefixes to each book, are esteemed among his happiest pieces. From the Prologue to the twelfth book we select the following passage :—

MORNING IN MAY.

As fresh Aurore, to mighty Tithon spouse
Ished of[1] her saffron bed and ivor house,
In cram'sy clad and grained violate,
With sanguine cape, and selvage purpurate,
Unshet[2] the windows of her large hall,
Spread all with roses, and full of balm royal,
And eke the heavenly portis chrystalline
Unwarps braid, the warld till illumine;
The twinkling streamers of the orient
Shed purpour spraings with gold and azure ment;[3]
Eous, the steed, with ruby harness red,
Above the seas liftis furth his head,

---

[1] Issued from.
[2] Opened.
[3] Purple streaks mingled with gold and azure.

Of colour sore,[1] and some deal brown as berry,
For to alichten and glad our emispery;
The flame out-bursten at the neisthirls,[2]
So fast Phaeton with the whip him whirls.
While shortly, with the bleezand torch of day,
Abulyit in his lemand[3] fresh array,
Furth of his palace royal ishit Phœbus,
With golden crown and visage glorious,
Crisp hairs, bricht as chrysolite or topaz;
For whase hue micht nane behald his face.
The auriate vanes of his throne soverane
With glitter and glance o'erspread the oceane;[4]
The large fludes, lemand all of licht,
But with ane blink of his supernal sicht.
For to behald, it was ane glore to see
The stabled windis, and calmed sea,
The soft season, the fermanent serene,
The loune illuminate air and ferth amene.
And lusty Flora did her bloomis spread
Under the feet of Phœbus' sulyart[5] steed;
The swarded soil embrode with selcouth[6] hues,
Wood and forests obnumbrate with bews.[7]
* * * * * * * *
Dame Nature's menstrals, on that other part,
Their blissful lay intoning every art,
And all small fowlis singis on the spray,
Welcome the lord of licht, and lampe of day,
Welcome fosterer of tender herbis green,
Welcome quickener of flourist flouirs sheen,
Welcome support of every rute and vein,
Welcome comfort of all kind fruit and grain,
Welcome the birdis beild[8] upon the brier,
Welcome master and ruler of the year,
Welcome weelfare of husbands at the plews,
Welcome repairer of woods, trees, and bews,
Welcome depainter of the bloomit meads,
Welcome the life of every thing that spreads,
Welcome storer of all kind bestial,
Welcome be thy bricht beamis, gladdand all.

Sir David Lyndsay, another Scottish poet of the period of which we are now treating, and the last that we shall at present notice, was born at the Mount, Fifeshire, in 1496, and was educated at the university of St. Andrews. He early entered upon a court life, and during the childhood of James the Fifth, he officiated as his carver, his cupbearer, his purse-master, and even as his nurse, bearing him as an infant upon his back, and dancing antics for his amusement as a boy. When James assumed the reins of government, he amply rewarded the companion of his childish sports, by elevating him to the important office of *Lord Lyon King at arms;* but after the fatal battle of Flodden-field, Lyndsay went to France, and

[1] Yellowish brown. [2] Nostrils. [3] Glittering. [4] Ocean.
[5] Sultry. [6] Uncommon. [7] Boughs. [8] Shelter.

greatly distinguished himself at the battle of Pavia. He afterward returned again to Scotland, resumed his position at court, and was employed by his sovereign on various important foreign embassies. He died in 1557, in the sixty-first year of his age.

Lyndsay chiefly shone as a satirical and humorous writer, and his great fault is a total absence of all refinement. The principal objects of his vituperations were the clergy, whose habits, at this period, were such as to afford ample scope to the pen of the satirist. He, however, with equal freedom exposed the abuses of the court, though at the time he was a state officer of high standing, and much influence. His principal poems are, *The Dreme*, *The Complaynt*, *The Complaynt of the King's Peacock*, *The Satire of the Three Estates*, *Kitteis' Confession*, *The History of Squire Meldrum*, and *The Monarchie.*

'The History of Squire Meldrum' is, perhaps, the most pleasing of all this author's works, and is considered the last British poem that in any degree partakes of the character of the metrical romance. This poem, together with the various other Satires and Burlesques of this author, is said to have contributed greatly to the Reformation in Scotland. 'The Monarchie' was the last of his poems. It was written just before his death, and from it we select the following curious passage:—

THE BUILDING OF THE TOWER OF BABEL, AND THE CONFUSION OF TONGUES.

Their great fortress then did they found,
And cast till they gat sure ground.
All fell to work both man and child
Some howkit clay, some burnt the tyld.
Nimron, that curious champion,
Deviser was of that dungeon.
Nathing they spared their labours,
Like busy bees upon the flowers,
Or emmets travelling into June;
Some under wrocht, and some aboon,
With strang ingenious masonry,
Upward their work did fortify;
The land about was fair and plain,
And it rase like ane heich montane.
Those fulish people did intend,
That till the heaven it should ascend:
Sae great ane strength was never seen
Into the warld with men's een.
The wallis of that waik they made,
Twa and fifty fathoms braid:
Ane fathom then as some men says,
Micht been twa fathom in our days;
Ane man was then of mair stature
Nor twa be now, of this be sure.

The translator of Orosius
Intil his chronocle writes thus;

That when the sun is at the hicht,
At noon, when it doth shine maist bricht,
The shadow of that hideous strength
Sax mile and mair it is of length:
Thus may ye judge into your thocht,
Gif Babylon be heich or nocht.

Then the great God omnipotent,
To whom all things been present,
He sceand the ambition,
And the prideful presumption,
How thir proud people did pretend,
Up through the heavens till ascend,
Sic languages on them he laid,
That nane wist what ane other said;
Where was but ane language afore,
God send them languages three-score;
Afore that time all spak Hebrew,
Then some began for to speak Grew,
Some Dutch, some language Saracen,
And some began to speak Latin.
The maister men gan to ga wild,
Cryand for trees, they brocht them tyld.
Some said, Bring mortar here at ance,
Then brocht they to them stocks and stanes;
And Nimrod, their great champion,
Ran ragand like ane wild lion,
Menacing them with words rude,
But never ane word they understood.
————for final conclusion,
Constrained were they for till depart
Ilk company in ane sundry airt.

Lyndsay also wrote a history of Scotland in three volumes, which, however, has never been published, but still remains in manuscript in the Advocates' Library, Edinburgh.

To the poets of the period of Scottish literature which we have had under consideration in the present lecture, we shall add the ballad of Sir Patrick Spens—a poem of such antiquity that its origin even, is doubtful. The incident upon which it is founded is as follows:—In 1280, a company of distinguished noblemen attended Margaret, daughter of Alexander the Third of Scotland, when she embarked for Norway to become the bride of Eric, king of that country. On the return of these noblemen from Norway their vessel was overtaken by a violent storm, and most of them perished.

SIR PATRICK SPENS.

The king sits in Dunfermline town,
Drinking the blude-red wine;
'O where will I get a skeely skipper[1]
To sail this new ship of mine?'

[1] Skillful mariner.

Oup and spake an eldern knight,
  Sat at the king's right knee:
'Sir Patrick Spens is the best sailor
  That ever sailed the sea.'

Our king has written a braid[1] letter,
  And sealed it with his hand,
And sent it to Sir Patrick Spens,
  Was walking on the strand.

'To Noroway, to Noroway,
  To Noroway o'er the faem;
The king's daughter of Noroway,
  'Tis thou maun bring her hame!'

The first word that Sir Patrick read,
  Sae loud loud laughed he;
The neist word that Sir Patrick read,
  The tear blindit his e'e.

'O wha is this has done this deed,
  And tauld the king o' me,
To send us out at this time of the year,
  To sail upon the sea?

'Be it wind, be it weet, be it hail, be it sleet,
  Our ship must sail the faem;
The king's daughter of Noroway,
  'Tis we must fetch her hame.'

They hoysed their sails on Monenday morn,
  Wi' a' the speed they may;
They hae landed in Noroway
  Upon a Wodensday.

They hadna been a week, a week
  In Noroway, but twae,
When that the lords o' Noroway
  Began aloud to say:

'Ye Scottishmen spend a' our king's gowd[2]
  And a' our queenis fee.'
'Ye lie, ye lie, ye liars loud!
  Fu' loud I hear ye lie!

'For I hae brought as much white monie
  As gane[3] my men and me—
And I hae brought a half-fou[4] o' gude red gowd
  Out owre the sea wi' me.

'Make ready, make ready, my merry men a'!
  Our gude ship sails the morn.'
'Now, ever alake! my master dear,
  I fear a deadly storm!

'I saw the new moon, late yestreen,
  Wi' the auld moon in her arm;

[1] Broad, large.
[2] Gold.
[3] Suffice.
[4] The eighth part of a peck.

And if we gang to sea, master,
  I fear we'll come to harm.'

They hadna sailed a league, a league,
  A league, but barely three,
When the lift[1] grew dark, and the wind blew loud,
  And gurly grew the sea.

The ankers brak, and the topmasts lap,[2]
  It was sic a deadly storm;
And the waves came o'er the broken ship
  Till a' her sides were torn.

'O where will I get a gude sailor
  To take my helm in hand,
Till I get up to the tall topmast,
  To see if I can spy land?'

'O here am I, a sailor gude,
  To take the helm in hand,
Till you go up to the tall topmast—
  But I fear you'll ne'er spy land.'

He hadna gane a step, a step,
  A step, but barely ane,
When a boult flew out of our goodly ship,
  And the salt sea it came in.

'Gae fetch a web o' the silken claith,
  Another o' the twine,
And wap them into our ship's side,
  And letna the sea come in.'

They fetched a web o' the silken claith,
  Another o' the twine,
And they wapped them roun' that gude ship's side,
  —But still the sea came in.

O laith[3] laith were our gude Scots lords
  To weet their cork-heeled shoon![4]
But lang or a' the play was played,
  They wat their hats aboon.

And mony was the feather-bed
  That floated on the faem;
And mony was the gude lord's son
  That never mair came hame.

The ladyes wrang their fingers white—
  The maidens tore their hair;
A' for the sake of their true loves—
  For them they 'll see na mair.

O lang lang may the ladyes sit,
  Wi' their fans into their hand,
Before they see Sir Patrick Spens
  Come sailing to the strand!

---

[1] Sky. [2] Spring. [3] Loath. [4] Shoes

And lang lang may the maidens sit,
  Wi' their gowd kairns in their hair,
A' waiting for their ain dear loves—
  For them they 'll see na mair.

O forty miles off Aberdeen
  'Tis fifty fathoms deep,
And there lies gude Sir Patrick Spens
  Wi' the Scots lords at his feet.

Lecture the Fourth.

JOHN THE CHAPLAIN—THOMAS OCCLEVE—JOHN LYDGATE—JOHN SKELTON—HENRY HOWARD, EARL OF SURREY—SIR THOMAS WYATT—THOMAS TUSSER—ANDREW BOURD—MISCELLANEOUS POEMS—PROSE WRITERS—SIR JOHN FORTESCUE—WILLIAM CAXTON.

IN our last lecture we fully considered the Scottish poets who flourished between the age of Edward the Third, and that of Elizabeth, and we shall now return to review those of England during the same period. We must here, however, at the outset remark, that though a few names of some degree of eminence will pass before us, yet we should look in vain for the same order of genius among them which was displayed by Dunbar, or even by James the First.

Of these poets the two first that present themselves are John the Chaplain, and Thomas Occleve. Of the former little is now known; and of the latter comparatively nothing, farther than that he was by profession a lawyer, and though a tolerably smooth versifier, yet nothing more. John Lydgate, the third of these writers, will require a little more attention.

LYDGATE was born in Suffolk, in 1380, the fourth year of the reign of Richard the Second. He was an Augustine monk of St. Edmondsberry, and though both a philosopher and a divine, his chief attention was devoted to the muses. Having travelled in France and Italy, and carefully studied the poetry of those countries, he returned to his monastery, and there established a school for the instruction of young men of the upper ranks, in the art of versification—a fact which proves that poetry had become a favorite study among the few who acquired any tincture of letters in that age. Lydgate died at Bury, in 1440, in the sixty-first year of his age.

The genius of this author was, perhaps, not above mediocrity; but by study and care he acquired such excellence in versification, as, in this particular, to excel, according to the judgment of some critics, even Chaucer himself. His poetical compositions range over a great variety of styles, embracing besides *The History of Thebes*, *The Fall of Princes*, and *The Destruction of*

Troy, which are his three principal performances, many *Odes*, *Eclogues*, and *Satires*. 'His muse,' says Warton, 'was of universal access; and he was not only the poet of the monastery, but of the world in general. If a disguising was contemplated by the company of goldsmiths, a mask before his majesty at Eltham, a May game for the sheriffs and aldermen of London, a mumming before the Lord Mayor, or a carol for the coronation, Lydgate was consulted, and gave the poetry.' In the words of the same writer, 'there is great softness and facility' in the following passage found in his Destruction of Troy:—

DESCRIPTION OF A SYLVAN RETREAT.

Till at the last, among the bowes glade,
Of adventure, I caught a pleasant shade;
Full smooth, and plain, and lusty for to seen,
And soft as velvet was the yonge green:
Where from my horse I did alight as fast,
And on the bow aloft his reine cast.
So faint and mate of weariness I was,
That I me laid adown upon the grass,
Upon a brinke, shortly for to tell,
Beside the river of a crystal well;
And the water, as I reherse can,
Like quicke silver in his streams y-ran.
Of which the gravel and the brighte stone,
As any gold, against the sun y-shone.

After Lydgate no poet appeared in England for more than a half century, whose name has been preserved from oblivion; for the reigns of Edward the Fourth, Richard the Third, and Henry the Seventh, extending from 1461 till 1509, were barren of every thing like true poetic genius. We descend, therefore, down the current of English literature without meeting with any thing to attract our attention until we reach the age of Henry the Eighth. The first name that occurs at this period is that of John Skelton.

SKELTON was born in Cumberland, but at what precise time is unknown. He was educated at the university of Oxford, and in 1489 was there invested with the laurel—a sort of poetical degree occasionally conferred upon the favorites of the muses. He took orders, and became rector of Dysse in Norfolk; but he was eventually suspended by his diocesan for writing loose and obscene verses, not only against obscure individuals, but even against Cardinal Wolsey, from whose resentment he took refuge in the sanctuary of Westminster, under the protection of abbot Islip. His death occurred on the twenty-first of June, 1529.

Skelton's poems consist chiefly of *Sonnets* and *Satires*, and his genius, according to Warton, was peculiarly suited to the low burlesque, though he occasionally assumed a more amiable and poetic manner, as in the following canzonet:—

TO MISTRESS MARGARET HUSSEY.

Merry Margaret,
As midsummer flower,
Gentle as falcon,
Or hawk of the tower;
With solace and gladness,
Much mirth and no madness,
All good and no badness;
So joyously,
So maidenly,
So womanly,
Her demeaning,
In every thing,
Far, far, passing,
That I can indite,
Or suffice to write
Of merry Margaret,
As midsummer flower,
Gentle as falcon,
Or hawk of the tower;
As patient and as still,
And as full of good will,
As fair Isiphil,
Coliander,
Sweet pomander,
Good Cassander;
Stedfast of thought,
Well made, well wrought
Far may be sought,
Ere you can find
So courteous, so kind,
As merry Margaret,
This midsummer flower,
Gentle as falcon,
Or hawk of the tower.

Henry Howard, Earl of Surrey, the English poet who follows Skelton in the order of time, was a genius of a very different character. He was the eldest son of the Duke of Norfolk, and was born in 1516. He was educated at Windsor, in company with a natural son of Henry the Eighth, the future Duke of Richmond, and in early life he became accomplished not only in the learning of the times, but also in all kinds of courtly and chivalrous exercises. Having completed his studies at home, he travelled into Italy, and was there a devoted student of the poets of that country—Dante, Petrarch, Boccaccio, and Ariosto—and formed his own poetical style upon theirs.

Surrey was also a valiant soldier as well as poet, and remarkably distinguished himself on many occasions, particularly in conducting an important expedition in 1542, for the destruction of the Scottish borderers. But he finally fell under the displeasure of his fickle monarch, who caused him to be apprehended and imprisoned in Windsor Castle, whence he was soon after removed to the Tower, and thence to the scaffold on Tower Hill, where he was beheaded on the nineteenth of January 1547, not yet having attained the thirty-first year of his age.

Surrey's attainments for the time at which he lived, were unusually great. He was entirely familiar with the Latin, the French, the Italian, and the Spanish languages, and also with all the gentlemanly accomplishments of the age. His poetry is distinguished for its flowing melody, correctness of style, and purity of expression: he has the honor also to have been the first writer of English narrative blank verse in the language.

The gentle and melancholy pathos of his manner is well exemplified in the following verses, which he wrote during his confinement in Windsor Castle, when about to yield his life a sacrifice to tyrannical caprice. They are so beautiful as to hold a permanent place among the finest poetical productions in the language. The noble poet is recounting the pleasure there enjoyed in former days:—

A PRISONER IN WINDSOR CASTLE.

So cruel prison how could betide, alas!
  As proud Windsor? where, in lust and joy,
With a king's son, my childish years did pass,
  In greater feast than Priam's son of Troy:

Where each sweet place returns a taste full sour!
  The large green courts where we were wont to hove,[1]
With eyes cast up into the Maiden Tower,
  And easy sighs such as folks draw in love.

The stately seats, the ladies bright of hue;
  The dances short, long tales of great delight,
With words and looks that tigers could but rue,
  Where each of us did plead the other's right.

The palm-play, where, despoiled for the game,
  With dazed eyes oft we by gleams of love,
Have missed the ball and got sight of our dame,
  To bait her eyes, which kept the leads above.

The gravel ground, with sleeves tied on the helm
  Of foaming horse,[2] with swords and friendly hearts;
With cheer, as though one should another whelm,
  Where we have fought, and chased oft with darts;

With silver drops the mead yet spread for ruth,
  In active games of nimbleness and strength,
Where we did strain, trained with swarms of youth,
  Our tender limbs that yet shot up in length:

The secret groves which oft we made resound,
  Of pleasant plaint, and of our ladies' praise,
Recording oft what grace each one had found,
  What hope of speed, what dread of long delays:

---

[1] Hover, loiter.

[2] A lover tied the sleeve of his mistress on the head of his horse.

The wild forest, the clothed holts with green,
  With reins availed[1] and swiftly breathed horse;
With cries of hounds and merry blasts between,
  Where we did chase the fearful hart of force.

The wide vales, eke, that harboured us each night,
  Wherewith, alas, reviveth in my breast,
The sweet accord such sleeps as yet delight,
  The pleasant dreams, the quiet bed of rest:

The secret thoughts imparted with such trust,
  The wanton talk, the divers change of play,
The friendship sworn, each promise kept so just;
  Wherewith we passed the wintei night away.

And with this thought the blood forsakes the face
  The tears berain my cheeks of deadly hue,
The which, as soon as sobbing sighs, alas,
  Upsupped have, thus I my plaint renew:

O place of bliss! renewer of my woes,
  Give me accounts, where is my noble fere;[2]
Whom in thy walls thou dost each night enclose;
  To other leef,[3] but unto me most dear:

Echo, alas! that doth my sorrow rue,
  Beturns thereto a hollow sound of plaint.
Thus I alone, where all my freedom grew,
  In prison pine with bondage and restraint,

And with remembrance of the greater grief
To banish the less, I find my chief relief.

To this sweet poem we add the following stanzas on

THE MEANS TO ATTAIN HAPPY LIFE.

Martial, the things that do attain
  The happy life, be there, I find,
The riches left, not got with pain;
  The fruitful ground, the quiet mind,

The equal friend; no grudge, no strife;
  No charge of rule, nor governance;
Without disease, the healthful life;
  The household of continuance;

The mean diet, no delicate fare;
  True wisdom joined with simpleness;
The night discharged of all care;
  Where wine the wit may not oppress.

The faithful wife, without debate;
  Such sleeps as may beguile the night;
Content with thine own estate,
  Ne wish for death, ne fear his might.

---

[1] Reins dropped. [2] Companion. [3] Agreeable.

SIR THOMAS WYATT, the contemporary and intimate friend of the Earl of Surrey, was born at Arlington Castle, in Kent, in 1503. His family was respectable but not distinguished; and as he early evinced more than ordinary talents, his education soon became a matter of parental solicitude. In 1518, he entered St. John's College, Cambridge, but eventually left that seat of learning to enjoy the superior advantages in classical studies that the university of Oxford at that time afforded. Wyatt was graduated at the latter institution in 1523, immediately after which he turned his attention to the careful study of modern languages; and before he had reached the twenty-fourth year of his age, he was critically familiar with the French, the Italian, and the Spanish. To these intellectual attainments he added all those personal accomplishments for which the Earl of Surrey was so much celebrated; and it was not surprising, therefore, that he should have become, almost immediately after he was presented at court, a recipient of royal confidence and favor.

Wyatt was knighted by Henry the Eighth, and for a number of years almost constantly employed by that monarch upon foreign embassies. He thus enjoyed the opportunity of commingling with the more refined courts and courtiers of the continent. In 1541, he was ordered by the king to re pair to Falmouth, there to meet the ambassador of Charles the Fifth of Spain, and conduct him to the English court. Anxious to execute this mission with the greatest possible celerity, he overheated himself on the way, and thus brought on a fever of which he soon after died, being in the thirty-ninth year of his age.

The traits of similarity in genius and character between Wyatt and the Earl of Surrey were so striking that a learned critic has, in contemplating them, indulged in the following strain:—'They were men whose minds may be said to have been cast in the same mould; for they differ only in those minuter shades of character which must always exist in human nature. In their love of virtue, and their instinctive hatred and contempt of vice; in their freedom from personal jealousy; in their thirst after knowledge and intellectual improvement; in nice observation of nature, promptitude to action, intrepidity, and fondness for romantic enterprise; in magnificence and liberality; in generous support of others, and high-spirited neglect of themselves; in constancy and friendship, and tender susceptibility of affections of a still warmer nature, and in every thing connected with sentiment and principle, they were one and the same; but when these qualities branch out into particulars, they will be found in some respects to differ. . . . . . In Wyatt's complaints, we hear a strain of manly grief which commands attention; and we listen to it with respect for the sake of him that suffers. Surrey's distress is painted in such natural terms, that we make it our own, and recognize in his sorrows, emotions which we are conscious of having felt ourselves.'*

The *Songs* and *Sonnets* of Wyatt, though somewhat conceited, are not

* Dr. Nott.

without refinement, and a very considerable share of poetic feeling; and he has the honor to be the first writer who attempted to turn the Psalms of David into English metre. His poems were originally published in 1565, along with those of the Earl of Surrey; and from this copy we select the following songs, and the stanza which follows them:—

THE LOVER'S LUTE CAN NOT BE BLAMED, THOUGH IT SING OF HIS LADY'S UNKINDNESS.

Blame not my Lute! for he must sound
  Of this or that as liketh me;
For lack of wit the Lute is bound
  To give such tunes as pleaseth me;
Though my songs be somewhat strange,
And speak such words as touch my change,
    Blame not my Lute!

My Lute, alas! doth not offend,
  Though that perforce he must agree
To sound such tunes as I intend
  To sing to them that heareth me;
Then though my songs be somewhat plain,
And toucheth some that use to feign,
    Blame not my Lute!

My Lute and strings may not deny,
  But as I strike they must obey;
Break not them then so wrongfully,
  But wreak thyself some other way;
And though the songs which I indite,
Do quit thy change with rightful spite,
    Blame not my Lute!

Spite asketh spite, and changing change,
  And falsed faith, must needs be known;
The faults so great, the case so strange;
  Of right it must abroad be blown:
Then since that by thine own desert
My songs do tell how true thou art,
    Blame not my Lute!

Blame but thyself that hath misdone,
  And well deserved to have blame;
Change thou thy way, so evil begone,
  And then my Lute shall sound that same;
But if till then my fingers play
By thy desert their wonted way,
    Blame not my Lute!

Farewell! unknown; for though thou break
  My strings in spite with great disdain,
Yet have I found out for thy sake,
  Strings for to string my Lute again:
And if perchance this silly rhyme,
Do make thee blush at any time,
    Blame not my Lute!

THE RE-CURED LOVER EXULTETH IN HIS FREEDOM, AND VOWETH TO REMAIN FREE UNTIL DEATH.

I am as I am, and so will I be;
But how that I am none knoweth truly.
Be it ill, be it well, be I bond, be I free,
I am as I am, and so will I be.

I lead my life indifferently;
I mean nothing but honesty;
And though folks judge full diversely,
I am as I am, and so will I die.

I do not rejoice, nor yet complain,
Both mirth and sadness I do refrain,
And use the means since folks will feign;
Yet I am as I am, be it pleasant or pain.

Divers do judge as they do trow,
Some of pleasure and some of woe,
Yet for all that nothing they know;
But I am as I am, wheresoever I go.

But since judgers do thus decay,
Let every man his judgment say;
I will take it in sport or play,
For I am as I am, whosoever say nay.

Who judges well, will God them send;
Who judges evil, God them amend;
To judge the best therefore intend,
For I am as I am, and so will I end.

Yet some there be that take delight,
To judge folk's thought for envy and spite;
But whether they judge me for wrong or rig]
I am as I am, and so do I write.

Praying you all, that this do read,
To trust it as you do your creed;
And not to think I change my weed,
For I am as I am, however I speed.

But how that is I leave to you;
Judge as you list, false or true,
Ye know no more than afore ye knew,
Yet I am as I am, whatever ensue.

And from this mind I will not flee,
But to you all that misjudge me,
I do protest as ye may see,
That I am as I am, and so will be.

THAT PLEASURE IS MIXED WITH EVERY PAIN

Venomous thorns that are so sharp and keen,
  Bear flowers, we see, full fresh and fair of hue,
Poison is also put in medicine,
  And unto man his health doth oft renew.

The fire that all things eke consumeth clean,
  May hurt and heal: then if that this be true,
I trust some time my harm may be my health,
Since every woe is joined with some wealth.

Thomas Tusser, another poet of the age of Henry the Eighth, though in genius much inferior to either the Earl of Surrey or Sir Thomas Wyatt, was of an ancient family, and was born in 1523, but at what place is unknown. He received a liberal education, and commenced life at court, under the patronage of Lord Paget; but not being adapted to a court life, he turned his attention to farming, and for a number of years pursued that course of life, successively in Sussex, Ipswich, Essex, Norwich, and other places. Not succeeding in that calling, he left it and followed other occupations, among which was that of a chorister, and it is said, a fiddler. As might be expected of one so inconstant, he did not prosper in the world, but died poor in London, in 1580, in the fifty-eighth year of his age.

Tusser's poem, entitled a *Hundreth Good Points of Husbandrie*, which was first published in 1557, contains a series of practical directions for farming, expressed in simple and inelegant, though not always, dull verse. It has, however, the honor of being the first regular didactic poem in the language. From this poem we select the two following extracts:—

HOUSEWIFELY PHYSIC.

Good huswife provides, ere a sickness do come,
Of sundry good things in her house to have some.
Good aqua composita, and vinegar tart,
Rose-water and treacle to comfort thine heart.
Cold herbs in her garden, for agues that burn,
That over-strong heat to good temper may turn.
White endive, and succory, with spinach enow;
All such with good pot herbs, should follow the plough.
Get water of fumitory, liver to cool,
And others the like, or else lie like a fool.
Conserves of barbary, quinces and such,
With sirops that easeth the sickly so much.
Ask Medicus' counsel, ere medicine ye take,
And honour that man for necessity's sake.
Though thousands hate physic, because of the cost,
Yet thousands it helpeth, that else should be lost.
Good broth, and good keeping, do much now and than
Good diet, with wisdom, best comforteth man.
In health, to be stirring shall profit thee best;
In sickness, hate trouble; seek quiet and rest.
Remember thy soul; let no fancy prevail;
Make ready to God-ward; let faith never quail:
The sooner thyself thou submittest to God,
The sooner he ceaseth to scourge with his rod.

MORAL REFLECTIONS ON THE WIND.

Though winds do rage as winds were wood,[1]
And cause spring-tides to raise great flood;
And lofty ships leave anchor in mud,
Bereaving many of life and of blood;
Yet, true it is, as cow chews cud,
And trees, at spring, doth yield forth bud,
Except wind stands as never it stood,
It is an ill wind turns none to good.

ANDREW BOURD, physician to Henry the Eighth, was contemporary with Tusser, and was the author of the following lines, which form an inscription under the picture of an Englishman, naked, with a roll of cloth in one hand and a pair of scissors in the other. The poem is chiefly valuable at present time as indicating the English spirit of that age.

CHARACTERISTIC OF AN ENGLISHMAN.

I am an Englishman, and naked I stand here,
Musing in my mind what garment I shall wear,
For now I will wear this, and now I will wear that,
Now I will wear I can not tell what:
All new fashions be pleasant to me,
I will have them whether I thrive or thee:
Now I am a fisher, all men on me look
What should I do but set cock on the hoop?
What do I care if all the world me fail,
I will have a garment reach to my tail.
Then I am a minion, for I wear the new guise,
The next year after I hope to be wise—
Not only in wearing my gorgeous array,
For I will go to learning a whole summer's day;
I will learn Latin, Hebrew, Greek and French,
And I will learn Dutch sitting on my bench.
I do fear no man, each man feareth me;
I overcome my adversaries by land and by sea:
I had no peer if to myself I were true;
Because I am not so diverse times do I rue:
Yet I lack nothing, I have all things at will,
If I were wise, and would hold myself still,
And meddle with no matters but to me pertaining,
But ever to be true to God and my king.
But I have such matters rolling in my pate,
That I will and do—I can not tell what.
No man shall let me, but I will have my mind,
And to father, mother, and friend, I'll be unkind.
I will follow mine own mind, and mine old trade;
Who shall let me? The devil's nails are unpared.
Yet above all things new fashions I love well,
And to wear them my thrift I will sell.
In all this world I shall have but a time:
Hold the cup, good fellow, here is thine and mine!

---

[1] Mad.

We shall conclude our remarks upon the English poets and poetry of the period extending from Chaucer to Elizabeth, by the introduction of a few miscellaneous poems, written, in all probability, during the reign of Henry the Eighth, and that of his son and successor Edward the Sixth. The first two of these poems are remarkable for being among the earliest verses in which the metaphysical refinements, so manifest in the subsequent period, are discerned. The first is a poet's praise of his lady, but of the writer we have no knowledge.

A PRAISE OF HIS (THE POET'S) LADY.

Give place, you ladies, and be gone.
  Boast not yourselves at all!
For here at hand approacheth one,
  Whose face will stain you all!

The virtue of her lively looks
  Excels the precious stone:
I wish to have none other books
  To read or look upon.

In each of her two crystal eyes
  Smileth a naked boy:
It would you all in heart suffice
  To see that lamp of joy.

I think nature hath lost the mold,
  Where she her shape did take;
Or else I doubt if nature could
  So fair a creature make.

She may be well compared
  Unto the phœnix kind,
Whose like was never seen nor heard,
  That any man can find.

In life she is Diana chaste,
  In troth Penelope,
In word and eke in deed steadfast:
  What will you more we say?

* * * * *

Her roseal colour comes and goes
  With such a comely grace,
More ruddier, too, than doth the rose,
  Within her lively face.

At Bacchus' feast none shall her meet,
  Nor at no wanton play;
Nor gazing in an open street,
  Nor gadding as a stray.

The modest mirth that she doth use
  Is mixed with shamefac'dness;
All vice she doth wholly refuse,
  And hateth idleness.

O Lord, it is a world to see
  How virtue can repair,
And deck in her such honesty
  Whom nature made so fair!

Truly she doth as far exceed
  Our women now-a-days,
As doth the gilly flower a weed,
  And more a thousand ways.

How might I do to get a graff
  Of this unspotted tree?
For all the rest are plain but chaff,
  Which seem good corn to be.

This gift alone I shall her give:
  When Death doth what he can,
Her honest fame shall ever live
  Within the mouth of man.

The second of these poems, *Amantium Iræ amoris redintegratio est*, was written by RICHARD EDWARDS, a court musician and poet, who was born in 1523, and died in 1566; but no farther information of him has been left on record.

AMANTIUM IRÆ AMORIS REDINTEGRATIO EST.

In going to my naked bed, as one that would have slept,
I heard a wife sing to her child, that long before had wept.
She sighed sore, and sang full sweet, to bring the babe to rest,
That would not cease, but cried still, in sucking at her breast.
She was full weary of her watch, and grieved with her child,
She rocked it, and rated it, until on her it smil'd;
Then did she say, 'Now have I found the proverb true to prove,
The falling out of faithful friends renewing is of love.'

Then took I paper, pen, and ink, this proverb for to write,
In register for to remain of such a worthy wight.
As she proceeded thus in song unto her little brat,
Much matter utter'd she of weight in place whereas she sat;
And proved plain, there was no beast, nor creature bearing life,
Could well be known to live in love without discord and strife:
Then kissed she her little babe, and sware by God above,
'The falling out of faithful friends renewing is of love.'

* * * * * * * * *

'I marvel much, pardie,' quoth she, 'for to behold the rout,
To see man, woman, boy, and beast, to toss the world about;
Some kneel, some crouch, some beck, some check, and some can smoothly smile
And some embrace others in arms, and there think many a wile.
Some stand aloof at cap and knee, some humble and some stout,
Yet are they never friends indeed until they once fall out.'
Thus ended she her song, and said, before she did remove,
'The falling out of faithful friends renewing is of love.'

The third of these poems is the far famed *Nut-Brown Maid*. With regard to the date and author of this poem, no certainty exists. Prior, who founded his 'Henry and Emma' upon it, fixes its date about 1400; but others, judging from its comparatively modern language, suppose it to have been composed subsequently to the time of Surrey. The poem opens with a declaration of the author that the faith of woman is stronger than is generally supposed; in proof of which he purposes to relate the trial to which the 'Nut-Brown Mayde' was exposed by her lover. The following stanzas form a dialogue between the pair:—

THE NUT-BROWN MAID.

HE.—It standeth so; a deed is do',
  Whereof great harm shall grow:
My destiny is for to die
  A shameful death I trow;
Or else to flee: the one must be,
  None other may I know,
But to withdraw as an outlaw,
  And take me to my bow,
Wherefore adieu, my own heart true!
  None other rede I can:
For I must to the green wood go,
  Alone, a banished man.

SHE.—O Lord what is this world's bliss,
  That changeth as the moon!
My summer's day in lusty May
  Is darked before the noon.
I hear you say, Farewell: Nay, nay,
  We depart not so soon.
Why say ye so? whither will ye go?
  Alas! what have ye done?
All my welfáre to sórrow and care
  Should change if ye were gone;
For in my mind, of all mankind
  I love but you alone.

HE.—I can believe, it shall you grieve,
  And somewhat you distrain:
But afterwards, your paines hard
  Within a day or twain
Shall soon aslake; and ye shall take
  Comfort to you again.
Why should ye ought, for to make thought?
  Your labor were in vain.
And thus I do, and pray to you,
  As heartily as I can;
For I must to the green wood go,
  Alone, a banished man.

SHE.—Now sith that ye have showed to me
  The secret of your mind,
I shall be plain to you again,
  Like as ye shall me find.
Sith it is so that ye will go,
  I will not live behind;

Shall never be said, the Nut-Brown Maid
  Was to her love unkind:
Make you ready', for so am I,
  Although it were anon;
For in my mind, of all mankind
  I love but you alone.

He.—I counsel you, remember how
  It is no maiden's law
Nothing to doubt, but to run out
  To wood with an outlaw;
For ye must there in your hand bear
  A bow, ready' to draw;
And as a thief, thus must you live,
  Ever in dread and awe.
Whereby to you great harm might grow:
  Yet had I lever than,
That I had to the green wood go,
  Alone, a banished man.

She.—I think not nay, but, as ye say,
  It is no maiden's lore:
But love may make me for your sake,
  As I have said before,
To come on foot, to hunt and shoot
  To get us meat in store;
For so that I your company
  May have, I ask no more:
From which to part it makes my heart
  As cold as any stone;
For, in my mind, of all mankind
  I love but you alone.

He.—Yet take good heed, for ever I dread
  That ye could not sustain
The thorny ways, the deep valley's,
  The snow, the frost, the rain,
The cold, the heat; for, dry or weet,
  We must lodge on the plain;
And us above, none other roof
  But a brake bush or twain:
Which soon should grieve you I believe,
  And ye would gladly than
That I had to the green wood go,
  Alone, a banished man.

She.—Sith I have here been partinèr
  With you of joy and bliss,
I must also part of your wo
  Endure, as reason is.
Yet I am sure of one pleasùre,
  And shortly, it is this,
That, where ye be, me seemeth, pardie,
  I could not fare amiss.
Without more speech, I you beseech
  That ye were soon agone,

For, to my mind, of all mankind
  I love but you alone.

He.—If ye go thither, ye must consider,
  When ye have list to dine,
There shall no meat be for your gete,
  Nor drink, beer, ale, nor wine,
Nor sheets clean, to lie between,
  Made of thread and twine;
None other house but leaves and boughs,
  To cover your head and mine.
Oh mine heart sweet, this evil diet,
  Should make you pale and wan;
Wherefore I will to the green wood go,
  Alone, a banished man.

She.—Among the wild deer, such an archér,
  As men say that ye be,
Ye may not fail of good vittail,
  Where is so great plentie.
And water clear of the rivér,
  Shall be full sweet to me,
With which in heal, I shall right weel
  Endure, as ye shall see;
And, ere we go, a bed or two
  I can provide anone;
For, in my mind, of all mankind
  I love but you alone.

He.—Lo yet before, ye must do more,
  If ye will go with me;
As cut your hair up by your ear,
  Your kirtle to the knee;
With bow in hand, for to withstand
  Your enemies, if need be;
And this same night, before daylight,
  To the wood-ward will I flee.
If that ye will all this fulfil,
  Do't shortly as ye can:
Else will I to the green wood go,
  Alone, a banished man.

She.—I shall, as now, do more for you,
  Than 'longeth to womanheed,
To short my hair, a bow to bear,
  To shoot in time of need.
Oh, my sweet mother, before all other
  For you I have most dread;
But now adieu! I must ensue
  Where fortune doth me lead.
All this make ye: Now let us flee;
  The day comes fast upon:
For, in my mind, of all mankind
  I love but you alone.

He.—Nay, nay, not so; ye shall not go
  And I shall tell you why;

Your appetite[1] is to be light
  Of love I weel espy:
For like as ye have said to me,
  In likewise, hardily,
Ye would answér whoever it were,
  In way of company.
It is said of old, soon hot, soon cold;
  And so is a woman,
Wherefore I to the wood will go,
  Alone, a banished man.

She.—If ye take heed, it is no need
  Such words to say by me;
For oft ye prayed and me assayed,
  Ere I loved you, pardie:
And though that I, of ancestry,
  A baron's daughter be,
Yet have you proved how I you loved,
  A squire of low degree;
And ever shall whatso befal;
  To die therefore anon;
For, in my mind, of all mankind
  I love but you alone.

He.—A baron's child to be beguiled,
  It were a cursed deed!
To be fellàw with an outlaw,
  Almighty God forbid!
It better were, the poor squièr
  Alone to forest yede,
Than I should say, another day,
  That, by my cursed deed,
We were betrayed: wherefore, good maid,
  The best rede that I can,
Is that I to the green wood go
  Alone, a banished man.

She.—Whatever befall, I never shall,
  Of this thing you upbraid;
But, if ye go, and leave me so,
  Then have ye me betrayed;
Remember weel, how that you deal;
  For if ye, as ye said,
Be so unkind to leave behind,
  Your love, the Nut-Brown Maid,
Trust me truly, that I shall die
  Soon after ye be gone;
For in my mind, of all mankind
  I love but you alone.

He.—If that ye went, ye should repent;
  For in the forest now
I have purveyed me of a maid,
  Whom I love more than you;

[1] Disposition.

Another fairèr than ever ye were,
  I dare it weel avow,
And of you both each should be wroth
  With other, as I trow:
It were mine ease to live in peace;
  So will I, if I can;
Wherefore I to the wood will go,
  Alone, a banished man.

SHE.—Though in the wood I understood
  Ye had a paramour,
All this may not remove my thought,
  But that I will be your.
And she shall find me soft and kind
  And courteous every hour;
Glad to fulfill all that she will
  Command me to my power.
For had ye, lo, an hundred mo,
  Of them I would be one;
For, in my mind, of all mankind
  I love but you alone.

HE.—Mine own dear love, I see thee prove,
  That ye be kind and true;
Of maid and wife, in all my life,
  The best that ever I knew.
Be merry and glad; no more be sad;
  The case is changed now;
For it were ruth, that, for your truth,
  Ye should have cause to rue.
Be not dismayed; whatever I said
  To you, when I began;
I will not to the green wood go,
  I am no banished man.

SHE.—These tidings be more glad to me,
  Than to be made a queen,
If I were sure they would endure:
  But it is often seen,
When men will break promise, they speak
  The wordes on the spleen.
Ye shape some wile me to beguile,
  And steel from me, I ween:
Than were the case worse than it was,
  And I more woe-begone:
For, in my mind, of all mankind
  I love but you alone.

HE.—Ye shall not need further to dread:
  I will not disparàge,
You (God defend!) sith ye descend
  Of so great a lineàge.
Now understand; to Westmoreland,
  Which is mine heritage,
I will you bring; and with a ring,
  By way of marriàge,

I will you take, and lady make
  As shortly as I can:
Thus have you won an earl's son,
  And not a banished man.

The most celebrated of these poems, and the last that we shall notice, is the ballad of *Chevy Chase.* The incident which induced this ballad occurred in the early part of the reign of Henry the Fourth, and was as follows:—Percy, Earl of Northumberland, resolved to hunt for three days in the Scottish border, without asking leave of Douglas, the Scottish Earl, upon whose lands he would thus trespass. This was an insult which the gallant Douglas immediately resented, and as he resolved to repel the intruders by force, the conflict, which the poet has so graphically described, was the consequence. The scene of the action was the Cheviot hills. Of this ballad, Sir Phillip Sydney, in his 'Defense of Poetry,' remarks, 'I never heard the old song of Percy and Douglas that I found not my heart more moved than with the sound of a trumpet.' The spelling of the original poem is now so nearly obsolete that we shall present it in a form in which it will be more readily understood:—

CHEVY-CHASE.

God prosper long our noble king,
  Our lives and safeties all;
A woful hunting once there did
  In Chevy-Chase befall;

To drive the deer with hound and horn,
  Earl Percy took his way;
The child may rue that is unborn,
  The hunting of that day.

The stout Earl of Northumberland,
  A vow to God did make,
His pleasure in the Scottish woods
  Three summer's days to take;

The chiefest harts in Chevy-Chase
  To kill and bear away.
These tidings to Earl Douglas came,
  In Scotland where he lay:

Who sent Earl Percy present word,
  He would prevent his sport.
The English Earl, not fearing that,
  Did to the woods resort

With fifteen hundred bow-men bold,
  All chosen men of might,
Who knew full well in time of need,
  To aim their shafts aright.

The gallant greyhounds swiftly ran,
  To chase the fallow-deer:
On Monday they began to hunt,
  Ere daylight did appear;

And long before high noon they had
  An hundred fat bucks slain:
Then having dined, the drovers went
  To rouse the deer again.

The bow-men muster'd on the hills,
  Well able to endure;
Their backsides all, with special care,
  That day were guarded sure.

The hounds ran swiftly through the woods,
  The nimble deer to take,
That with their cries the hills and dales
  An echo shrill did make.

Lord Percy to the quarry went,
  To view the slaughter'd deer,
Quoth he, Earl Douglas promised
  This day to meet me here.

But if I thought he would not come,
  No longer would I stay.
With that, a brave young gentleman
  Thus to the Earl did say:

Lo, yonder doth Earl Douglas come,
  His men in armor bright;
Full twenty hundred Scottish spears
  All marching in our sight;

All men of pleasant Tivydale,
  Fast by the river Tweed:
O cease your sports, Earl Percy said,
  And take your bows with speed:

And now with me, my countrymen,
  Your courage forth advance;
For there was never champion yet,
  In Scotland or in France,

That ever did on horseback come,
  But if my hap it were,
I durst encounter man for man,
  With him to break a spear.

Earl Douglas on his milk-white steed,
  Most like a baron bold,
Rode foremost of his company,
  Whose armor shone like gold.

Show me, said he, whose men you be
  That hunt so boldly here,
That, without my consent, do chase
  And kill my fallow-deer.

The first man that did answer make,
  Was noble Percy he;
Who said, We list not to declare,
  Nor show whose men we be:

Yet we will spend our dearest blood
  Thy chiefest harts to slay.
Then Douglas swore a solemn oath,
  And thus in rage did say,

Ere thus I will out-braved be,
  One of us two shall die:
I know thee well, an earl thou art,
  Lord Percy, so am I.

But trust me, Percy, pity it were,
  And great offense to kill
Any of these our guiltless men,
  For they have done no ill.

Let thou and I the battle try,
  And set our men aside.
Accurst be he, Earl Percy said,
  By whom this is denied.

Then stepp'd a gallant squire forth,
  Witherington was his name,
Who said, I would not have it told
  To Henry our king for shame,

That e'er my captain fought on foot,
  And I stood looking on;
You be two earls, said Witherington,
  And I a squire alone:

I'll do the best that do I may,
  While I have power to stand:
While I have power to wield my sword,
  I'll fight with heart and hand.

Our English archers bent their bows,
  Their hearts were good and true;
At the first flight of arrows sent,
  Full threescore Scots they slew.

* * * * * *

They closed full fast on every side,
  No slackness there was found;
And many a gallant gentleman
  Lay gasping on the ground.

O dear! it was a grief to see,
  And likewise for to hear,
The cries of men lying in their gore,
  And scatter'd here and there.

* * * * * *

This fight did last from break of day
  Till setting of the sun;
For when they rung the evening bell,
  The battle scarce was done.

With stout Earl Percy, there was slain
  Sir John of Egerton,

Sir Robert Ractliff, and Sir John,
  Sir James that bold baron:

And with Sir George and stout Sir James,
  Both knights of good account,
Good Sir Ralph Raby there was slain,
  Whose prowess did surmount.

For Witherington needs must I wail,
  As one in doleful dumps;
For when his legs were smitten off
  He fought upon his stumps.

* * * * * *

Of fifteen hundred Englishmen,
  Went home but fifty-three;
The rest were slain in Chevy-Chase,
  Under the greenwood tree.

Next day did many widows come,
  Their husbands to bewail;
They washed their wounds in brinish tears,
  But all would not prevail.

Their bodies, bathed in purple gore,
  They bare with them away:
They kiss'd them dead a thousand times,
  Ere they were clad in clay.

* * * * * *

God save our king and bless this land
  With plenty, joy, and peace;
And grant henceforth, that foul debate
  'Twixt noblemen may cease.

From these remarks upon the poetry of England between the age of Chaucer and that of Elizabeth, we proceed to notice the prose writers of the same period. These will be found both more numerous, and of more elevated merit than the former.

Sir John Fortescue, the first prose writer that appeared after Chaucer and Wickliffe, was born of an ancient family at Wear Gifford, in Devonshire about 1405. He was educated at Exeter College, Oxford, whence he removed to Lincoln's Inn, London, for the purpose of preparing for the law. His legal attainments soon became so great as to attract the attention of the court, and in 1430 he received the degree of sergeant-at-law. In 1441 he was made king's sergeant-at-law, and the next year appointed chief-justice of the king's bench at Westminster. These marks of royal confidence and favor were the result of Fortescue's integrity, wisdom, and firmness; but his attachment to the house of Lancaster proved the source of bitter persecutions; for in the first parliament of Edward the Fourth, he was attainted of high treason. Henry the Sixth had, meantime, escaped into Scotland, whither Fortescue immediately followed him, and was nominated by the exiled monarch, Chancellor of England.

From Scotland he embarked with queen Margaret and her son prince Edward, in 1463, for Holland, and remained for several years in exile in Lorraine. It was during his residence abroad that the chancellor composed most of his literary works, after which he returned to England, became reconciled to the reigning sovereign, and passed the remainder of his life in the quiet of retirement. He lived to reach nearly the ninetieth year of his age, and must therefore have died about 1495.

Besides several performances in the Latin language, chief-justice Fortescue wrote, *The difference between an Absolute and a Limited Monarchy, as it more particularly regards the English Constitution*, in English; in which he draws a striking, though, perhaps, exaggerated contrast between the condition of the French under an arbitrary monarch, and that of his own countrymen, who even at that time possessed very considerable privileges as subjects. The following extract from this work conveys at the same time, an idea of the literary style, and of the manner of thinking of that age.

ENGLISH COURAGE.

It is cowardice and lack of hearts and courage, that keepeth the Frenchmen from rising, and not poverty; which courage no Frenchman hath like to the Englishman. It hath been often seen in England that three or four thieves, for poverty, hath set upon seven or eight true men, and robbed them all. But it hath not been seen in France, that seven or eight thieves have been hardy to rob three or four true men. Wherefore it is right seld[1] that Frenchmen be hanged for robbery, for that they have no hearts to do so terrible an act. There be therefore mo men hanged in England, in a year, for robbery and manslaughter, than there be hanged in France for such cause of crime in seven years. There is no man hanged in Scotland in seven years together for robbery, and yet they be oftentimes hanged for larceny, and stealing of goods in the absence of the owner thereof; but their hearts serve them not to take a man's goods while he is present and will defend it; which manner of taking is called robbery. But the Englishman be of an other courage; for if he be poor, and see an other man having riches which may be taken from him by might, he wal not spare to do so, but if[2] that poor man be right true. Wherefore it is not poverty, but it is lack of heart and cowardice, that keepeth the Frenchmen from rising.

William Caxton, the English prose writer who follows Fortescue, and who is worthy to be held in immortal remembrance as the first who gave to England the means of diffusing knowledge through the medium of printing,[3] was born in the weald of Kent about 1410. Having been brought up a mercer, he was employed by the Mercer's Company of London as their agent in the Netherlands—a situation which he filled with great credit to himself for the space of twenty-three years. During this agency he was employed by Edward the Fourth to negotiate a treaty between that

[1] Seldom.

[2] But if—unless.

[3] The art of impressing characters upon paper with blocks of carved wood, was discovered in 1430, by Laurence Coster of Haarlem, in the Netherlands; and movable types were invented by John Guttenburgh of Mentz, in Germany, 1440; soon after which Shoeffer and Faust founded types of metal.

prince and the Duke of Burgundy, and was subsequently in the employment of Lady Margaret, the duke's wife.

Some years after he commenced his residence in the Netherlands, Caxton acquired a knowledge of the art of printing, and at the request of the duchess he translated *The Recuyell of the Histories of Troye*, from the French, and printed it at Cologne in 1471. This is the earliest typographical production in the English language, and is now very scarce, and therefore of very great value. Soon after this event he returned to England, and in 1476, established a printing press in Westminster Abbey, the first w issued from which was the *Game and Playe of Chesse*. From this peri he continued his typographical labors for about eighteen years, and die in 1492, in his eighty-third year. From the writings of this author we quote the following characteristic passage, found at the conclusion of his translation of the *Golden Legends*.

LEGEND OF ST. FRANCIS.

Francis, servant and friend of Almighty God, was born in the city of Assyse, and was made a merchant unto the 25th year of his age, and wasted his time by living vainly, whom our Lord corrected by the scourge of sickness, and suddenly changed him into an other man; so that he began to shine by the spirit of prophecy. For on a time, he, with other men of Peruse, was taken prisoner, and were put in a cruel prison, where all the other wailed and sorrowed, and he only was glad and enjoyed. And when they had repreved[1] him thereof, he answered 'Know ye,' said he, 'that I am joyful: for I shall be worshipped as a saint throughout all the world.' * * *

On a time as this holy man was in prayer, the devil called him thrice by his own name. And when the holy man had answered him, he said, none in this world is so great a sinner, but if he convert him, our Lord would pardon him; but who that sleeth himself with hard penance, shall never find mercy. And anon, this holy man knew by revelation the fallacy and deceit of the fiend, how he would have withdrawn him fro to do well. And when the devil saw that he might not prevail against him, he tempted him by grievous temptation of the flesh. And when this holy servant of God felt that, he despoiled[2] his cloaths, and beat himself right hard with an hard cord, saying, 'Thus, brother ass, it behoveth thee to remain and to be beaten.' And when the temptation departed not, he went out and plunged himself in the snow, all naked, and made seven great balls of snow, and purposed to have taken them into[3] his body, and said, 'This greatest is thy wife; and these four, two ben thy daughters and two thy sons; and the other twain, that one thy chambrere, and that other thy valet or yeman; haste and clothe them: for they all die for cold. And if thy business that thou hast about them, grieve ye sore, then serve our Lord perfectly.' And anon, the devil departed all confused; and St. Francis returned again unto his cell glorifying God.

* * * * * * * * * *

He was ennobled in his life by many miracles * * * and the very death, which is to all men horrible and hateful, he admonished them to praise it. And also he warned and admonished death to come to him, and said, 'Death, my sister, welcome be you.' And when he came at the last hour, he slept in our Lord; of whom a friar saw the soul, in manner of a star, like to the moon in quantity, and the sun in clearness.

---

[1] Reproved. [2] Took off. [3] Unto.

Lecture the Fifth.

ROBERT FABIAN AND EDWARD HALL—SIR THOMAS MORE—ALEXANDER BARCLAY —JOHN FISCHER—SIR THOMAS ELYOT—HUGH LATIMER—JOHN BALE.

TOWARD the close of the last lecture we commenced our remarks upon the prose writers of the period at present under consideration. This subject we shall now resume.

Of English historical prose writers, the earliest of whom we have any knowledge are Robert Fabian, and Edward Hall. They both were extremely simple in their manner of writing, and aimed in their compositions at no literary excellence, not even perspicuity of arrangement—their object being merely to narrate minutely, and as far as opportunity afforded, faithfully, the events in the history of their country, of which they were treating. These Chronicles, therefore, form masses of matter which a modern writer in search of materials alone, would now be likely to peruse. Yet it must be admitted, that to their minute and indiscriminate character, we are indebted for the preservation of many curious facts, and illustrations of manners, which otherwise would have been lost.

FABIAN flourished during the reign of Henry the Seventh. He was an alderman and afterward sheriff of London, and died in 1512, but at what age is uncertain. He wrote a general chronicle of English history under the title of *The Concordance of Stories.* His work is particularly minute with regard to what would probably appear the most important of all things to the worthy alderman—the succession of officers of all kinds in the city of London; and he also carefully repeats all the fabulous stories of early English history, first circulated by Geoffrey of Monmouth. In order to present an idea of the first English historical writer's style, we quote the following passage:—

THE DEPOSITION OF KING VORTIGERN.

* * * * * An heresy, called Arian's heresy, began then to spring up in Britain. For the which, two holy bishops, named Germanus and Lupus, as of Gaufryde is witnessed, came into Britain to reform the king, and all other that erred from the way of truth.

Of this holy man, Germanus, Vincent Historial saith, that upon an evening when the weather was passing cold, and the snow fell very fast, he axed lodging of the King of Britain, for him and his compeers, which was denied. Then he, after sitting under a bush in the field, the king's herdman passed by, and seeing this bishop with his company sitting in the weather, desired him to his house to take there such poor lodging as he had. Whereof the bishop being glad and fain, yode[1] unto the house of the said herdman, the which received him with glad cheer. And for him and his company, willed his wife to kill his only calf, and to dress it for his guests' supper; the which was also done. When the holy man had supped, he called to him his hostess, willing and desiring her, that she should diligently gather together all the bones of the dead calf; and them so gathered, to wrap together within the skin of the said calf. And then it lay in the stall before the rack near unto the dame. Which done according to the commandment of the holy man, shortly after the calf was restored to life; and forewith ate hay with the dam at the rack. At which marvel all the house was greatly astonished, and yielded thanking unto Almighty God, and to that holy bishop.

Upon the morrow, the holy bishop took with him the herdman, and yode unto the presence of the king, and axed of him in sharp wise, why that over-night he had denied to him lodging. Wherewith the king was so abashed, that he had no power to give unto the holy man answer. Then, St. Germain said to him: I charge thee, in the name of the Lord God, that thou and thine depart from this palace, and resign it and the rule of thy land to him that is more worthy this room than thou art. The which all things by power divine was observed and done; and the said herdman, by the holy bishop's authority, was set into the same dignity; of whom after descended all the kings of Britain.

HALL was a man of greatly superior attainments to Fabian, being an accomplished scholar, a lawyer, and a judge in the sheriff's court of London. He flourished throughout the whole of the reign of Henry the Eighth, and died at an advanced age, in 1547. He compiled a copious Chronicle of English history during the reigns of the houses of Lancaster and York, under the title of *The Union of the two Noble and Illustre Families of Lancastre and York, with all the actes done in both the tymes of the Princes both of the one lineage and the other.*

Hall is very minute in his narratives of the fashions of the times; and when his work is considered as the only compilation of English history at the command of the wits of Elizabeth's reign, and as furnishing the foundations of many scenes and even whole plays by the most illustrious of those wits, the 'Chronicles' have a value in our eyes beyond that which intrinsically belongs to them. In the following extract, the materials of a remarkable scene in Richard the Third are found; and it is worth our attention to notice, how well the prose narration reads by the side of the poetical one:—

SCENE IN THE COUNCIL-ROOM OF THE PROTECTOR GLOUCESTER.

The Lord Protector caused a council to be set at the Tower, on Friday the thirteenth day of June, where there was much communing for the honourable solemnity of the coronation, of the which the time appointed approached so near that the pageants were a making day and night at Westminster, and victual killed which afterwards was cast away.

[1] Went.

These lords thus sitting, communing of this matter, the Protector came in among them, about nine of the clock, saluting them courteously, excusing himself that he had been from them so long, saying merrily that he had been a sleeper that day. And after a little talking with him, he said to the Bishop of Ely, 'My Lord, you have very good strawberries in your garden at Holborn; I require you let us have a mess of them.' 'Gladly my Lord,' quoth he, 'I would I had some better thing, as ready to your pleasure as that;' and with that in all haste he sent his servant for a dish of strawberries. The Protector set the lords fast in communing, and thereupon prayed them to spare him a little; and so he departed, and came again between ten and eleven of the clock into the chamber, all changed, with a sour angry countenance, knitting the brows, frowning and fretting, and gnawing on his lips; and so set him down in his place. All the lords were dismayed, and sore marvelled of this manner and sudden change, and what thing should him ail. When he had sitten a while, thus he began: 'What were they worthy to have, that compass and imagine the destruction of me, being so near of blood to the king, and protector of this his royal realm?' At which question, all the lords sat sore astonished, musing much by whom the question should be meant, of which every man knew himself clear.

Then the Lord Hastings, as he that, for the familiarity that was between them, thought he might be boldest with him, answered and said, that they were worthy to be punished as heinous traitors, whatsoever they were; and all the other affirmed the same. 'That is,' quoth he, 'yonder sorceress, my brother's wife, and other with her;' meaning the queen. Many of the lords were sore abashed which favoured her; but the Lord Hastings was better content in his mind, that it was moved by her than by any other that he loved better; albeit his heart grudged that he was not afore made of counsel of this matter, as well as he was of the taking of her kindred, and of their putting to death, which were by his assent before devised to be beheaded at Pomfret, this self-same day; in the which he was not ware, that it was by other devised that he himself should the same day be beheaded at London. 'Then,' said the Protector, 'in what wise that sorceress and other of her counsel, as Shore's wife, with her affinity, have by their sorcery and witchcraft thus wasted my body!' and therewith plucked up his doublet sleeve to his elbow, on his left arm, where he showed a very withered arm, and small, as it was never other. And thereupon every man's mind misgave them, well perceiving that this matter was but a quarrel; for well they wist that the queen was both too wise to go about any such folly, and also, if she would, yet would she of all folk make Shore's wife least of her counsel, whom of all woman she most hated, as that concubine whom the king, her husband, most loved.

Also, there was no man there but knew that his arm was ever such, sith the day of his birth. Nevertheless, the Lord Hastings, which from the death of King Edward, kept Shore's wife, his heart somewhat grudged to have her whom he loved so highly accused, and that as he knew well untruly; therefore he answered and said, 'Certainly, my Lord, if they have so done, they be worthy of heinous punishment.' 'What!' quoth the Protector, 'thou servest me, I ween, with if and with and; I tell thee, they have done it, and that will I make good on thy body, traitor!' And therewith, as in a great anger, he clapped his fist on the board with a great rap, at which token given, one cried treason without the chamber, and therewith a door clapped, and in came rushing men in harness, as many as the chamber could hold. And anon the Protector said to the Lord Hastings, 'I arrest thee, traitor!' 'What! me! my Lord,' quoth he. 'Yea, the traitor,' quoth the Protector. And one let fly at the Lord Stanley, which shrunk at the stroke, and fell under the table, or else his head had been cleft to the teeth; for as shortly as he shrunk, yet ran the blood about his ears. Then was the Archbishop of York, and Doctor Morton, Bishop of Ely, and the Lord Stanley taken, and divers others which were bestowed in divers chambers, save the Lord Hastings, whom the Protector commanded to speed and shrive him apace. 'For, by Saint Poule,' quoth he, 'I will not dine till I see thy head off.' It booted him not to ask why, but heavily he took a priest at a venture, and made a short shrift, for a longer would not be suffered, the Protector made so much haste to his dinner, which might not go to it till this murder were done, for saving of his ungracious oath. So was he brought forth into the green, beside the chapel within the Tower, and his head laid down on a log of timber, that lay there for building of the chapel, and there tyrannously stricken off, and after his body and head were interred at Windsor, by his master, King Edward the Fourth; whose souls Jesu pardon. Amen.

After Fortescue, the first prose writer who mingled just and striking thought with his language, and was entitled to the appellation of a man of genius, was unquestionably Sir Thomas More, the celebrated chancellor of Henry the Eighth.

THOMAS MORE, was the son of Sir John More, and was born in London in 1480. His early education was conducted at St. Anthony's free school in London, after which he was placed, for instruction, in the family of cardinal Morton, archbishop of Canterbury—a method of education much practiced at that time in England, though such favors were generally extended to the sons of the nobility only. The cardinal was so greatly pleased with young More's ingenuous modesty, and with the vivacity and quickness of his wit, that he bestowed especial attention upon his studies, and was accustomed to remark to his friends, that 'More, whoever should live to see it would one day prove a marvellous man.'

In 1497, he entered Canterbury College, Oxford, soon after which he gave evidence of remarkable attainments for one so young in both the Latin and the Greek languages, by the production of some Epigrams and translations of very rare merit. After having passed two years at Oxford he removed thence to New Inn, London, in order to enter upon the study of the law. He soon discovered, however, that Lincoln's Inn would be more favorable to his purpose, and thither he accordingly removed, and there remained until he became a barrister.

At the age of twenty-one, More became a member of parliament, and two years after, greatly distinguished himself by opposing a subsidy demanded by Henry the Seventh, with such strength of argument, that the parliament actually refused to grant the king's request. As soon as the vote to this effect was taken, one of the king's privy-council hastened to his majesty and informed him that his design had been overthrown by a beardless boy. This so incensed the king that he devised a causeless quarrel against More's father, who was a judge of the king's bench, caused him to be conveyed to the Tower, and would not suffer him to be released until he had paid a fine imposed upon him of a hundred pounds.

This event so powerfully wrought upon the mind of the young barrister that he seriously designed an abode upon the continent; and with this view he made himself familiar with the French language, and also with such sciences as he might there find useful: but by the death of Henry the

Seventh, which occurred before these preparations were completed, his apprehensions were removed, and he accordingly, returned to his legal practice. In 1510, he was appointed judge of the sheriff's court in the city of London; made a justice of the peace; and became so eminent in the practice of the law, that scarcely a case of importance was tried at the bar, in which he was not concerned.

Before More entered directly into the service of Henry the Eighth, he was repeatedly engaged in connection with different embassies upon the continent, in all of which he evinced such learning, ability in the law, and dexterity in the management of business, that on his return from the last of these embassies, the king ordered cardinal Wolsey to engage him in the service of the court. With this view the cardinal offered him a pension; but this More refused, not thinking it equal to his deserts. With this spirited conduct on his part, the king was so well pleased that he insisted upon his accepting the office of Master of the Requests, within a month after which he was knighted, and appointed one of the king's privy-council.

In 1520, Sir Thomas was made treasurer of the Exchequer; and as his income was now such as to render his circumstances easy, he bought a house at Chelsea, and there settled with his family. With all his excellent endowments for public business, Sir Thomas was particularly formed for the enjoyment of the sweets of private life; and the king having once realized this engaging part of his new favorite's character, became impatiently eager for his society and conversation. With this view he was in the habit of sending for him into his private apartments, and there conversing familiarly with him on divinity, and various other parts of learning. There was, perhaps, another motive which induced this familiarity on the part of the king; for as he was at this time preparing his famous answer to Luther, he required the assistance of Sir Thomas to mould the work into proper shape.

In 1523, Sir Thomas More was chosen speaker of the House of Commons; and soon after evinced great intrepidity in frustrating a motion for an oppressive subsidy, promoted by Cardinal Wolsey. The cardinal afterward, in the gallery at Whitehall, severely reproached him for it, and said, 'Would to God, you had been at Rome, Mr. More, when I made you speaker.' To which Sir Thomas immediately replied, 'Your grace not offended, so would I too.' The cardinal now perceiving that he could not make More's course of conduct subservient to his own purposes, endeavored to have him sent abroad; but the king had other designs in view with regard to him, and he therefore accepted Sir Thomas's plea of delicate health, and allowed him to remain at home, with an occasional short embassy to France, and other neighboring countries.

When Cardinal Wolsey was disgraced, Henry intrusted the Great Seal to Sir Thomas, which was delivered to him on the 25th of October, 1530. This favor was the more signal as he was the first layman who had ever enjoyed it; but the evident object of the king was to engage Sir Thomas to favor his intended divorce from Catherine of Arragon. More was, however, a rigid Romanist, and he not only opposed the divorce, but when the king's supremacy in the church was declared by parliament, he refused to take the oath which it required, and was, therefore, condemned to be executed, and accordingly beheaded on Tower Hill, on the 5th of July, 1535, in the fifty-sixth year of his age. Thus ignominiously perished Sir Thomas More, confessedly the most illustrious personage of Henry the Eighth's reign.

The benignity and kindness of Sir Thomas More's character are strikingly evinced in the letter which he wrote to his ill-tempered wife after the accidental burning of some of his property during his absence upon the continent. It is at the same time a good specimen of his English prose. Most of his other English writings are tracts on the religious controversies of the day, besides which he wrote a history of *Richard the Third*, which, though an unfinished production, is regarded by Mr. Hallam as the first English prose work free from vulgarisms and pedantry.

The Utopia, written in Latin, is, however, Sir Thomas More's greatest literary performance. It is a pure romance, and was composed in 1516. The design of the author was to set forth his idea of those social arrangements by which the happiness and improvement of the people might be secured to the utmost extent of which human nature is susceptible. He imagines an island all the inhabitants of which are contented with the necessities of life; all are employed in useful labor; no one desires, in clothing, any other quality than durability; and since wants are few, and every member of the community engages in labor, there is no need for working more than six hours a day. Neither laziness nor avarice finds a place in this happy region; for the people have no inducement to be indolent when they have so little toil, or avaricious when they know that there is an abundance for all. This, however, is all incompatible with principles inherent in human nature: man requires the stimulus of self-interest to render him industrious and persevering; he loves not utility merely, but ornament also; he possesses a spirit of emulation which induces him to strive to outstrip his fellows, and a desire to accumulate property even for its own sake.

But with much that is chimerical, the 'Utopia' still contains many sound suggestions. Thus, instead of severe punishment for theft, the author would improve the morals and condition of the people, so as to take away the temptation to crimes; for he observes, 'If you suffer your people to be ill-educated, and their manners to be corrupted from their infancy, and then punish them for those crimes to which their early education disposed them, what else is to be concluded from this, than that you first make thieves and then punish them.' And again, 'It being a fundamental opinion among them, that a man can not make himself believe any thing he pleases; nor do they drive any to dissemble their thoughts by threatnings, so that men are not tempted to lie or disguise their feelings among them; which, being a sort of fraud, is abhorred by the Utopians. Every man may endeavor to convert others to his views by the force of amicable and modest argument, without bitterness against those of other opinions; but whoso adds reproach and violence to persuasion, is to be condemned to banishment or slavery.'

Such liberal views were extremely rare in the days of Sir Thomas More, and in later life were lamentably departed from by himself in practice; for in persecuting the Protestants, he displayed a degree of intolerance and severity which were strangely at variance, both with the opinions of his youth, and the general mildness of his disposition.

The descriptive parts of the work are beautiful beyond any thing that had hitherto appeared in the language; but as the style in which the whole performance is dressed in English is bishop Burnet's, and not Sir Thomas More's, we do not deem it necessary to make any quotation from it.

The following is the letter to his wife, to which we have already alluded:—

Mistress Alice, in my most hearty wise, I recommend me to you. And whereas I am informed by my son Heron of the loss of our barns and our neighbour's also, with all the corn that was therein; albeit (saving God's pleasure) it is a great pity of so much good corn lost; yet since it has liked him to send us such a chance, we must and are bounden not only to be content, but also to be glad of his visitation. He sent us all that we have lost; and since he hath by such a chance taken it away again, his pleasure be fulfilled! Let us never grudge thereat, but take it in good worth, and heartily thank him, as well for adversity as for prosperity. And peradventure we have more cause to thank him for our loss than for our winning, for his wisdom better seeth what is good for us than we do ourselves. Therefore, I pray you be of good cheer, and take all the household with you to church, and there thank God, both for that he has given us and that he has taken from us, and for that he has left us; which, if it please him, he can increase when he will, and if it please him to leave us yet less, at his pleasure be it!

I pray you to make some good onsearch what my poor neighbours have lost, and bid them take no thought therefore; for, if I should not leave myself a spoon, there shall no poor neighbour of mine bear no loss by my chance, happened in my house. I pray you be, with my children and your household, merry in God; and devise somewhat with your friends what way were best to take, for provision to be made for corn for our household, and for seed this year coming, if we think it good that we keep the ground still in our hands. And whether we think it good that we so shall do or not, yet I think it were not best suddenly thus to leave it all up, and to put away our folk from our farm, till we have somewhat advised us thereon. Howbeit, if we have more now than ye shall need, and which can get them other masters, ye may then discharge us of them. But I would not that any man were suddenly sent away, he wot not whither.

At my coming hither, I perceived none other but that I should tarry still with the king's grace. But now I shall, I think, because of this chance, get leave this next week to come home and see you, and then shall we farther devise together upon all things, what order shall be best to take.

And thus as heartily fare you well, with all our children, as ye can wish. At Woodstock, the third day of September, by the hand of Thomas More.

To this letter we shall add our author's account of Richard the Third, which was closely followed by Shakspeare in his tragedy of the same name.

CHARACTER OF RICHARD III.

Richard, the third son, of whom we now entreat, was in wit and courage egal[1] with either of them; in body and prowess, far under them both; little of stature, ill-featured of limbs, crook-backed, his left shoulder much higher than his right, hard-favoured of visage. He was malicious, wrathful, envious, and from afore his birth ever froward. It is for truth reported, that the duchess his mother had so much ado in her travail, that she could not be delivered of him uncut; and that he came into the world with the feet forward, as men be born outward; and (as the fame runneth) also not untoothed (whether men of hatred report above the truth, or else that nature changed her course in his beginning, which, in the course of his life, many things unnaturally committed.)

None evil captain was he in the war, as to which his disposition was more meetly than for peace. Sundry victories had he, and sometime overthrows, but never in default for his own person, either of hardiness or politic order. Free was he called of dispense, and somewhat above his power liberal. With large gifts he get him unsteadfast friendship, for which he was fain to pil and spoil in other places, and get him stedfast hatred. He was close and secret; a deep dissimuler, lowly of countenance, arrogant of heart; outwardly coumpinable where he inwardly hated, not letting to kiss whom he thought to kill; dispitious and cruel, not for evil will alway, but oftener for ambition, and either for the surety and increase of his estate. Friend and foe was indifferent, where his advantage grew; he spared no man's death, whose life withstood his purpose. He slew with his own hands king Henry VI., being prisoner in the Tower.

Contemporary with Sir Thomas More though greatly inferior to him in intellect, was Alexander Barclay, an English clergyman. He was born at Barclay in Somersetshire, and educated at Oriel College, Oxford. After having completed his studies at home, he travelled abroad, visiting Holland, Germany, France, and Italy; and on his return to England he was preferred, first to Baddow Magna, in Essex, and afterward to Allhollows, Lombard St., London. He died at a very advanced age at Croydon, but in what year is uncertain.

Besides a curious work in prose and verse, entitled *The Ship of Fooles*, in which is described a great variety of human absurdities, Barclay translated many Latin works, including Sallust's History of the Jugurthine War, which was among the earliest English versions of classical authors produced in England.

JOHN FISCHER, a fellow-martyr with Sir Thomas More, and somewhat his seniour in years, was born at Beverley in Yorkshire, in 1459. He lost his father when very young; but by the assiduous care of his mother, he was prepared for college in his native place, and educated at the university of Cambridge. In consequence of his extensive learning and exemplary virtues, he was selected, in 1495, by the Countess of Richmond, mother of king Henry the Seventh, as her chaplain and confessor; and such were his wisdom and piety, that she committed herself entirely to his government and

[1] Equal.

direction. In 1501, he took the degree of doctor of divinity, and was immediately after made vice-chancellor of the university of Cambridge. In 1504, he was elevated to the See of Rochester; and, notwithstanding, it was the poorest See in the kingdom, yet such was his attachment to it, that he could never be induced to change it for a richer.

In 1505, Fischer accepted the headship of Queen's College, Cambridge, and when Luther appeared as the advocate of religious liberty, he boldly stood forth as the champion of Rome. Though long favored by the king, he finally, in 1527, fell under his displeasure, for siding with queen Catherine in the affair of her divorce. When the question of the king's supremacy was agitated in 1531, he opposed it with great freedom and warmth, in consequence of which he was committed to the Tower, where he would doubtless have been permitted to linger out the remainder of his life, had not pope Paul the Third, pleased with his devotion to the Romish church, created him a cardinal. This so incensed the king that he caused him to be condemned for high treason, and he was, accordingly, beheaded on the 22d of June, 1535, in the seventy-eighth year of his age.

As Fischer was the literary opponent of Erasmus, the opinion of that illustrious scholar with regard to his merits, should carry great weight. He represents him as 'a man of great and extensive powers of mind, and for integrity, sweetness of temper, and greatness of soul, far superior to all the men of his age.' The English writings of Fischer consist of sermons, and a few small tracts on religious subjects. From a funeral sermon occasioned by the death of the Countess of Richmond, and preached in 1509, we extract the following remarkable portraiture of that pious lady's daily devotions:—

In prayer, every day at her uprising, which commonly was not long after five of the clock, she began certain devotions, and so after them, with one of her gentlewomen, the matins of our lady, which kept her to[1] —— then she came into her closet, where then with her chaplain, she said also matins of the day, and after that daily heard four or five masses upon her knees; so continuing in her prayers and devotions unto the hour of dinner, which of the eating day, was ten of the clock, and upon the fasting day, eleven. After dinner full truly she would go her stations to three altars daily; daily her dirges and commendations she would say, and her even songs before supper, both of the day and of our lady, beside many other prayers and psalters of David throughout the year; and at night before she went to bed, she failed not to resort unto her chapel, and there a large quarter of an hour to occupy her devotions. No marvel, though all this long time her kneeling was to her painful, and so painful that many times it caused in her back pain and desease. And yet, nevertheless, daily when she was in health, she failed not to say the crown of our lady, which after the manner of Rome, containeth sixty and three aves, and at every ave to make a kneeling. As for meditation, she had divers books in French, wherewith she would occupy herself when she was weary of prayer. Wherefore divers she did translate out of the French into English. Her marvellous weeping they can bear witness of, which here before have heard her confession, which be divers and many, and at many seasons in the year, lightly every third day. Can also record the same

[1] There is an omission here.

tho that were present at any time when she was houshilde,[1] which was full nigh a dozen times every year, what floods of tears there issued forth of her eyes!

THOMAS ELYOT, a gentleman of eminent learning, and a distinguished physician of the reign of Henry the Eighth, was descended from an ancient family in the county of Suffolk, and was the son of Sir Richard Elyot; but the period of his birth has not been preserved. He was educated at St. Mary's Hall, Oxford, and was particularly distinguished for his attainments in philosophy and logic. After having passed some years at the university, and having also acquired a thorough knowledge of his profession, he travelled upon the continent; and upon his return to England he was introduced at court. His unusual genius and extensive learning recommending him to the favor of Henry the Eighth, who, with all his faults, was a great patron of men of letters, his majesty conferred upon him the honor of knighthood, and employed him in several important embassies, one of which was to Rome in 1532, relating to the king's divorce from queen Catherine; and another, four years after, to the emperor Charles the Fifth of Spain. He died on the 25th of March, 1546, and was buried in the church of Carlton in Cambridgeshire, where a magnificent monument was soon after erected to his memory.

Mr. Wood remarks that 'Sir Thomas Elyot was an excellent grammarian, poet, rhetorician, philosopher, physician, and historian; and distinguished as much for his candor, and the innocence and integrity of his life, as for his accomplishments. He was admired and beloved by all the men of learning who were his contemporaries; and his memory is celebrated by them in their respective works, particularly by Leland.'

Of the numerous productions of Elyot, the most popular are, *The Castle of Health*, and *The Governor*. The former is a professional work, and contains many sound precepts with regard to diet and regimen; and the latter is devoted chiefly to the subject of education. He recommends that children be taught to speak Latin from their infancy; and he deprecates 'cruel and yrous[2] schoolmasters, by whom the wits of children be dulled, whereof we need no better author to witness than daily experience.' Mr. Hallam observes, in reference to this passage, that, 'all historians concur to this savage ill-treatment of boys in the schools of this period. The fierceness of the Tudor government, the religious intolerance, the polemical brutality, the rigorous justice, when justice it was, of our laws, seemed to have engendered a hardness of character, which displayed itself in severity of discipline, when it did not even reach the point of arbitrary or malignant cruelty.'

The following brief passage from 'The Castle of Health,' gives a very fair idea of Elyot's style, and at the same time of the habits recommended by the medical men of that period:—

* * * * * The muscles are best exercised with holding of the breath in a long time, so that he which doth exercise hath well digested his meat and is not troubled with much wind in his body. Finally, loud reading, counterfeit

[1] Received the sacrament of the Lord's Supper.

[2] Irascible.

battle, tennis or throwing the ball, running, walking, adde(d) to shooting, which, in my opinion, exceeds all the other, do exercise the body commodiously. Alway remember that the end of violent exercise is difficulty in fetching of the breath; of moderate exercise, alteration of breath only, or the beginning of sweat. Moreover, in winter, running and wrestling is convenient; in summer, wrestling a little, but not running; in very cold weather, much walking; in hot weather rest is more expedient. They which seem to have moist bodies, and live in idleness, they have need of violent exercise. They which are lean and choleric must walk softly, and exercise themselves very temperately. The plummets, called of Galen, alteres, which are now much used with great men, being of equal weight and according to the strength of him that exerciseth, are very good to be used.

At the period at present under consideration bishop Latimer distinguished himself as a zealous Reformer, not less than Sir Thomas More, and bishop Fischer did as Romanists.

Hugh Latimer was born at Thirkesson, Leicestershire, in 1470. His father rented a small farm, and though he had a family of seven children, yet by industry and frugality he succeeded in bringing them all up at home, and finally establishing them respectably in life. Hugh, his only son, was early sent to the grammar-school of his native place, and the facility with which he acquired knowledge was such, that his father at once resolved to educate him for the church. With this view, as soon as suitable preparations had been made, he sent him to the university of Cambridge, where he greatly distinguished himself in scholastic learning; and having taken the degree of master of arts, he entered into priest's orders as a devoted advocate of Popery. He remained attached to the Romish church, however, but a few years; for forming an acquaintance with Thomas Bilney, a celebrated defender of the doctrines of the Reformation, he became convinced of his error, and thenceforth boldly maintained both in private and in the pulpit, the views of the Protestant party. His preaching at Cambridge gave great offense to the Romish clergy, at whose instigation cardinal Wolsey instituted a court of bishops and deacons to execute the laws against heretics. Before this court Bilney and Latimer were summoned, when the recantation of the former, who was regarded as the principal offender, caused both to be liberated. Bilney afterward disclaimed his abjuration, and was burnt. This, however, did not abate the boldness of Latimer, who not only continued to preach openly in favor of Protestantism, but even wrote to Henry the Eighth, remonstrating with that arbitrary sovereign against the prohibition of the use of the Bible in English. This boldness, although it failed to produce the desired result, gave no offense to the king, who soon after presented Latimer to a living in Wiltshire, and in 1535, appointed him bishop of Worcester. The fall of Anne Boleyn was followed by the passing of the six articles establishing the doctrines of Popery, in consequence of which Latimer resigned his bishopric.

During the latter part of Henry's reign the bishop suffered imprisonment; but being liberated after the accession of Edward the Sixth, he became popular at court as a preacher, but could never be prevailed upon to resume his Episcopal functions. In Mary's reign, when measures were taken for the restoration of Popery, Latimer was summoned before the council, and although allowed an opportunity to escape, he readily obeyed the citation, exclaiming as he passed through Smithfield, 'This place has long groaned for me.' After a tedious imprisonment, he still persisted in refusing to subscribe to certain articles which were submitted to him; and he and Ridley, bishop of London, were led to the stake together at Oxford, and committed to the flames on the 16th of October, 1555. On their way to their execution Latimer exclaimed to his fellow-martyr, 'Be of good comfort Doctor Ridley, and play the man: we shall this day light such a candle, by God's grace, in England, as I trust shall never be put out.' Thus died bishop Latimer, one of the leaders of that glorious army of martyrs who successfully introduced the reformation into England.

Latimer's sermons, his only literary preformances, are remarkable for a familiarity and drollery of style, which, though it would now be considered very singular in the pulpit, was highly popular in his own time, and produced a wonderful impression upon his hearers. He was also chiefly instrumental in effecting a great improvement in the quality of clerical discourses, by substituting topics connected with moral duties for those incredible and often ridiculous legendary tales of saints and martyrs, which was at that time the common subject-matter of sermons.

The following extracts from his discourses will afford a pretty correct idea of his style, and peculiar manner of preaching:—

HASTY JUDGMENT.

Here I have occasion to tell you a story which happened at Cambridge. Master Bilney, or rather Saint Bilney, that suffered death for God's word's sake, the same Bilney was the instrument whereby God called me to knowledge, for I may thank him, next to God, for that knowledge that I have in the word of God. For I was as obstinate a papist as any was in England, insomuch that, when I should be made Bachelor of Divinity, my whole oration went against Philip Melancthon and against his opinions. Bilney heard me at that time, and perceived that I was zealous without knowledge; he came to me afterward in my study, and desired me for God's sake to hear his confession; I did so; and, to say the very truth, by his confession I learned more than before in many years; so from that time forward I began to smell the word of God, and forsook the school-doctors and such fooleries.

Now after I had been acquainted with him, I went with him to visit the prisoners in the tower at Cambridge, for he was ever visiting prisoners and sick folk. So we went together, and exhorted them as well as we were able to do; minding them to patience, and to acknowledge their faults. Among other prisoners, there was a woman which was accused that she had killed her child, which act she plainly and steadfastly denied, and could not be brought to confess the act; which denying gave us occasion to search for the matter, and so we did; and at length we found that her husband loved her not, and therefore he sought means to make her out of the way. The matter was thus:—A child of hers had been sick by the space of a year, and so decayed, as it were, in a consumption. At length it died in harvest-time; she went to her neighbours and other friends to desire their help to prepare the child for burial; but there was nobody at home, every man was in the field. The woman, in a heaviness and trouble of spirit, went, and being herself alone, prepared the child for burial. Her husband coming home, not having great love toward her, accused her of the murder, and so she was taken and brought to Cambridge. But as far forth as I could learn, through earnest inquisition, I thought in my conscience the woman was not guilty, all the circumstances well considered.

Immediately after this I was called to preach before the king, which was my first sermon that I made before his majesty, and it was done at Windsor; where his majesty, after the sermon was done, did most familiarly talk with me in a gallery. Now, when I saw my time, I kneeled down before his majesty, opening the whole matter, and afterward most humbly desired his majesty to pardon that woman. For I thought in my conscience she was not guilty, or else I would not for all the world sue for a murderer. The king most graciously heard my humble request, insomuch that I had a pardon ready for her at my returning homeward. In the mean season, that woman was delivered of a child in the town of Cambridge, whose god-father I was, and Mistress Cheek was god-mother. But all that time I hid my pardon, and told her nothing of it, only exhorting her to confess the truth. At length the time came when she looked to suffer; I came as I was wont to do, to instruct her; she made great moan to me. So we travailed with this woman till we brought her to a good opinion; and at length showed her the king's pardon, and let her go.

This tale I told you by this occasion, that though some women be very unnatural, and forget their children, yet when we hear any body so report, we should not be too hasty in believing the tale, but rather suspend our judgments till we know the truth.

THE SHEPHERDS OF BETHLEHEM.

I pray you to whom was the nativity of Christ first opened? To the bishops or great lords which were at this time at Bethlehem? Or to those jolly damsels with their fardingales, with their round-abouts, or with their bracelets? No, no, they had too many lets to trim and dress themselves, so that they could have no time to hear of the nativity of Christ; their minds were so occupied otherwise, that they were not allowed to hear of him. But his nativity was revealed first by the Shepherds, and it was revealed unto them in the night-time, when every body was at rest; then they heard this joyful tidings of the Saviour of the world; for these shepherds were keeping their sheep in the night season from the wolf and other beasts, and from the fox; for the sheep in that country do lamb two times in a year, and therefore it was needful for the sheep to have a shepherd to keep them. And here note the diligence of these shepherds; for whether the sheep were their own, or whether they were servants, I can not tell, for it is not expressed in the book; but it is most like they were servants, and their masters had put them in trust to keep their sheep. Now, if these shepherds had been deceitful fellows, that when their masters had put them in trust to keep their sheep, they had been drinking in the ale-house all night, as some of our servants do now-a-days, surely the angel had not appeared unto them to have told them this great joy and good tidings. And here all servants may learn by these shepherds, to serve truly and diligently unto their masters; in what business soever they are set to do, let them be painful and diligent like as Jacob was unto his master Laban.

Now these shepherds, I say, they watch the whole night, they attend upon their vocation, they do according to their calling, they keep their sheep, they run not hither and thither spending the time in vain, and neglecting their office and calling No, they did not so. Here by these shepherds men may learn to attend upon their offices and callings: I would wish that clergymen, the curates, parsons, and vicars, the bishops and all other spiritual persons, would learn this lesson by these poor shepherds; which is this, to abide by their flocks, and by their sheep, to tarry among them, to be careful over them, not to run hither and thither after their own pleasure, but to tarry by their benefices and feed their sheep with the food of God's word, and to keep hospitality, and so to feed them both soul and body. For I tell you, these poor unlearned shepherds shall condemn many a stout and great learned clerk; for these shepherds had but the care and charge over brute beasts, and yet were diligent to keep them, and to feed them, and the other have the cure over God's lambs which he bought with the death of his son, and yet they are so careless, so negligent, so slothful over them; yea, and the most part intendeth not to feed the sheep, but they long to be fed of the sheep; they seek only their own pastimes, they care for no more. But, what said Christ to Peter? What said he? Petre, amas me? (Peter, lovest thou me?) Peter made answer, yes. Then feed my sheep. And so the third time he commanded Peter to feed his sheep. But our clergymen do declare plainly that they love not Christ, because they feed not his flock. If they had earnest love to Christ, no doubt they would show their love, they would feed his sheep. * * *

'And the shepherds returned lauding and praising God, for all the things that they had heard and seen,' &c. They were not made religious men, but returned again to their business and to their occupation. Here we learn every man to follow his occupation and his vocation, and not to leave the same, except God call him from it to another, for God would have every man to live in that order that he hath ordained for him. And no doubt the man that plieth his occupation truly, without any fraud or deceit, the same is acceptable to God, and he shall have everlasting life.

We shall close our present remarks with a brief sketch of Bale, the celebrated Bishop of Ossory, in Ireland.

JOHN BALE was born at Cove, Suffolk, in 1495. His parents being in narrow circumstances, he was sent, when only twelve years of age to the monastery of *Camelites* in Norwich, and moved, a few years after, to Jesus College, Cambridge. His whole education, both in school and at college, was strictly in accordance with the doctrines and practices of the Romish church, but before he entered into orders he became a devoted Protestant. He informs us in reference to this change, 'that he was involved in the utmost ignorance and darkness of mind, both at Norwich and Cambridge, till the word of God shining forth, the churches began to return to the true fountains of divinity. That the instrument of his conversion was not a priest or a monk, but the most noble Earl of Wentworth.' His conversion, however, exposed him to the severest persecutions from the Romish clergy, and he would doubtless have felt the full force of their resentment had he not been protected by Lord Cromwell, one of Henry the Eighth's principal favorites. But after the death of that nobleman, Bale was obliged to take refuge in Holland, where he remained for six years. When Edward the Sixth ascended the throne, he was recalled by that youthful monarch to England, and on the 15th of August, 1552, nominated to the See of Ossory in Ireland. Upon his arrival in that country, he immediately began to introduce such reformations in his diocess as would have a tendency to correct the extensive abuses which there prevailed, particularly the vicious and irregular lives of the priests; but all his schemes were frustrated by the premature death of Edward, and the accession of Mary to the throne. The priests of Ossory now resolved to retaliate upon their bishop; and while they were endeavoring to compass his death, he fled once more to Holland, and thence passed to Basil in Switzerland, where he remained until Mary's death. In the beginning of Elizabeth's reign, he returned from exile, but instead of resuming the duties of bishop of Ossory, he became prebend of Canterbury, and in this office remained until his death, which occurred in the month of November, 1563, and in the sixty-eighth year of his age.

Bale was the author of many severe and intemperate tracts against popery; but his most celebrated production is an Account, in Latin, of Lives of Eminent Writers of Great Britain, extending from Japhet, one (the sons of Noah, to the year 1557. He left, also, many curious metrica productions in the English language, including several dramatic pieces on sacred subjects, which to a modern taste appear utterly burlesque. Among these are plays on *John the Baptist's preaching*; on *The childhood, temptation, passion, and resurrection of Christ;* on *The Lord's Supper*, *The washing of the disciples' feet*, and on *God's promises*—the performance of all of which formed a part of the exercises of the Sabbath, at Kilkenny, during Bale's residence in Ireland. In 1544, he published a *Brefe Chronycle concernynge the Examinacyon and Death of Sir John Oldecastell the Lorde Cobham*, from which we extract the account of Cobham's death. Cobham was executed in 1417, in the reign of Henry the Fifth, for supporting the doctrines of Wickliffe, and was the first martyr among the English nobility.

DEATH OF LORD COBHAM.

Upon the day appointed, he was brought out of the Tower with his arms bound behind him, having a very cheerful countenance. Then was he laid upon a hurdle, as though he had been a most heinous traitor to the crown, and so drawn forth into Saint Giles' Field, where as they had set up a new pair of gallows. As he was coming to the place of execution, and was taken from the hurdle, he fell down devoutly upon his knees, desiring Almighty God to forgive his enemies. Than stood he up, and beheld the multitude, exhorting them in most godly manner to follow the laws of God written in the Scriptures, and in any wise to beware of such teachers as they see contrary to Christ in their conversation and living, with many other special counsels. Then he was hanged up there by the middle in chains of iron, and so consumed alive in the fire, praising the name of God, so long as his life lasted. In the end he commended his soul into the hand of God, and so departed hence most Christenly, his body resolved into ashes.

Lecture the Sixth.

THE STATE OF THE POPULAR MIND—WILLIAM TYNDALE—MILES COVERDALE—JOHN FOX—JOHN LELAND—GEORGE CAVENDISH—LORD BERNERS—JOHN BELLENDEN—SIR JOHN CHEKE—THOMAS WILSON—ROGER ASCHAM.

ONE of the most striking features of the popular mind of England during the reign of Henry the Eighth, was a disposition to throw off the oppressive yoke of the Romish Church; and the measures which were taken to effect this great object, were wonderfully facilitated by the insufferable pride and pomp of the prelates of that church, and the shameful debaucheries of the monks. The latter had become so notorious that even the advocates themselves of popery did not attempt to deny it; and, accordingly, when it was pressed upon the consciousness of Sir Thomas More, his only reply was, 'Our mater is not of the lyuynge but of the doctryne.' This, it was early perceived, could be done so effectually in no other way as by affording to the people the means of reading the Scriptures in their vernacular language. To the attainment of this great end, the life of Tyndale was therefore devoted.

WILLIAM TYNDALE, the son of John Tyndale, of baronial dignity, was born at Hunt's Court in Gloucestershire, in 1477. From childhood he was destined for the church, and at a very early age he, accordingly, became a diligent student in the university at Oxford. He continued at Oxford till his proficiency in the Greek and Latin languages enabled him to read the New Testament to his fellow-students in Magdalen Hall, and also to those of Magdalen College. In this manner he laid the foundation of that skill in the learned languages so essential to the successful accomplishment of the great enterprise upon which he was soon to enter. Having taken his degrees at Oxford, Tyndale, for some reason not now known, entered the university of Cambridge, where he also took a degree, immediately after which he was ordained, and on the eleventh of March, 1502, was set apart as priest to the nunnery of Lambley in the diocess of Carlisle. He took the vows and became a friar in the monastery of Greenwich, in 1508. For some years previous to taking the vows, he had not only read the Scriptures to his fellow-students, but by presenting, in an English dress, various portions of the New Testament, evinced his early zeal for the noble enterprise which has perpetuated his name.

How long Tyndale remained with the Greenwich community is uncertain; but having returned to his native county, he exchanged the life of a friar for that of tutor and chaplain in the family of Sir John Welch, a knight of Gloucestershire, whose liberal table was certain to procure him the frequent visits of the neighboring prelates and clergy. Luther, at this time, having become, from his bold defiance of the Pope, the all-absorbing topic, the chaplain was often betrayed into disputes with his patron's guests on the new heresy. When mortified at the ignorance of his authorized guides, he would warmly urge upon them the study of the New Testament. This led them, in Fuller's witty phrase, 'to prefer resigning Squire Welch's good cheer, rather than to have the sour sauce of Master Tyndale's company.' At this display of Tyndale's independence and conscientious integrity, Sir John Welch's lady expressed strong disapprobation; but Tyndale took no other notice of her displeasure, than to translate and to dedicate to herself and Sir John 'Erasmus Enchiridion,' the attentive reading of which resulted in the happy conversion of both. He was now firmly seated anew in their regard; but the hostility of the beneficed clergy had been thoroughly aroused, and was not quieted until he was cited to appear before the ordinary. 'With a deep sense of his danger, it was his earnest prayer on the way, that God would strengthen him to contend firmly, at all hazards, for the truth of his word. His persecutors had assembled strong; but whether from the influence of his protecting knight, or the secret providence of God, their courage failed, and he escaped without accusation. The ordinary, however, 'rated him like a dog.'[1]

Tyndale now found it necessary, for better security, to leave the service of Sir John Welch, and he, therefore, made application to Tonstall, bishop of London, to become one of his chaplains; but while the fate of his application was pending, he happened to fall in company with a popish divine, with whom he argued the necessity of a vernacular translation of the Bible so conclusively, that the priest, unable to answer him, exclaimed, 'We had better be without God's law than the Pope's.' This audacity so fired the spirit of Tyndale that he indignantly replied, 'I defy the Pope and all his laws; and if God give me life, ere many years the plow-boys shall know more of the Scriptures than you do'—a pledge which he afterward amply redeemed.

Having failed in his application for a chaplaincy under the protection of the bishop of London, Tyndale found an asylum in the house of Humphrey Munmouth, a wealthy alderman of London, with whom he continued to reside for about six months. The design of translating the New Testament into the English language, had now become the settled purpose of his life; and finding that his native country would no longer afford him even a

[1] Offor.

temporary retreat in which to effect this purpose, he left England in 1523, and for conscience' sake became a voluntary exile from his native land for the remainder of his life. Having arrived at Hamburgh in Germany, he immediately passed thence into Saxony, and after a conference with Luther, who had just then published the New Testament in the German language, he at once completed and published at Wyttemburg in 1526, the first translation of the New Testament ever made from the original Greek into the English language. The sensation produced in England by this publication was intense; and notwithstanding every effort that the strength of the government could put forth, or the rage of the clergy invent to suppress it, still the word of God in the vernacular tongue, 'grew and prevailed.'

From this period Tyndale became the object of such deep hatred by the Romish clergy, that they hunted him from place to place without intermission, until 1530, when he found, for a few years, comparative repose as chaplain to a company of English merchants at Antwerp, in Holland. During his sojourn in this city, he literally went about doing good.' 'He was,' says Mr. Offor, 'the almoner of his more wealthy countrymen. Saturday and Sunday were his days of relaxation from severe study: on the former, he visited the sick and dying foreigners, and on Sunday, both before and after divine service, he visited and relieved his fellow-exiles. Persecution for conscience' sake, swept like a pestilence over his native land; and carried along with it, the worthiest of her sons. Many fled to Antwerp as their asylum in the greatest distress; and found from Tyndale's generous sympathy, both refreshment to the spirit, and assistance in purse; he, in his charities, appearing like an angel of mercy; in preaching, like an apostle.'

At length, however, in 1534, he was treacherously apprehended through the agency of one Philips, an emissary of the English king, and immediately conveyed to a prison at Vilvoord, a small village situated between Brussels and Malines. During the greater part of his imprisonment, which lasted two years, he was treated by his jailor with great kindness; and he, therefore, improved the lenity thus extended to him by redeeming the pledge long before given to the priest of Gloucestershire that 'the plow-boys should have the New Testament to read.' With this view he caused to be printed in 1535, an edition of his version, in a provincial orthography, probably that of his native county, peculiarly adapted to agricultural laborers. The formalities of a trial were at length gone through with, and he was condemned, by virtue of a decree made at Augsburgh, against what was called heresy. In September 1536, he suffered the dreadful sentence of death by strangulation, immediately after which his body was bound to a stake and burned; and in his dying moments he uttered the fervent ejaculation, 'Lord, open the king of England's eyes.'

Besides the New Testament from the Greek, Tyndale translated the Pentateuch and other portions of the Old Testament from the Hebrew. He also wrote many tracts of a controversial character, in vindication of his conduct in endeavoring to give the Scriptures to the laity; the principal of which are *The Wicked Mammon*, *The Practice of Prelates*, *The Revelation of Anti-Christ*, *The Sum of Scripture*, *The Book of Beggars*, and *The Obedience of a Christian Man*. In the latter of these works, which is considered the most valuable of his original compositions, he maintains, at some length, the necessity of a free circulation of the Scriptures in the vernacular language of every country; and after his Christian salutation, proceeds: 'Let it not make thee dispayre, neither yet discorage thee (oh reader) that it is forbidden thee in payne of lyfe and goodes, or that it is made breakynge of the kynges peace, or treason vnto his highnes to reade ye worde of thy soules health. But much rather be bold in the Lorde, and comfort thy soule. For as much as thou art sure and haste an euydent token thorow suche persecutyon, that it is the true worde of God, which worde euer hated of the worlde.' But the literary performance of Tyndale which should embalm his name in the heart of every Christian reader of the English language, is his translation of the New Testament. From this great work we extract the Lord's Prayer in the original spelling, and the third chapter of St. Matthew's Gospel, in the spelling of Offor's edition published in 1836.

THE LORD'S PRAYER.

Oure Father which arte in heven, halowed be thy name. Let thy kingdom come. Thy wyll be fulfilled as well in erth, as hit ys in heven. Geve vs this daye oure dayly breade. And forgeve vs oure treaspases, even as we forgeve them which treaspas vs Leede vs not into temptacion, but delyvre vs from yvell. Amen.

THE THIRD CHAPTER OF ST. MATTHEW'S GOSPEL.

In those dayes Jhon the baptiser cam and preached in the wildernes off iury saynge: Repente the kingdome of heven is at honde. This is he of whom it is spoken be the prophet Esay, which sayeth: The voyce off a cryer in wyldernes prepare the lordes way, and make hys pathes strayght.

This Jhon had his garment off camels heer, and a gerdell off a skynne about his loynes. Hys meate was locustes and wyld hony. Then went out to hym Jerusalem, and all Jury, and all the region rounde aboute Jordan, and were baptised of hym in Jordon, knoledging their synnes.

When he sawe many of the pharises and off the saduces come to his baptism, he sayde vnto them: O generacion of vipers, who hath taught you to fle from the vengeaunce to come? brynge forthe therefore the frutes belongynge to repentaunce. And se that ye ons thinke not to saye in yourselves, we have Abraham to oure father. For I say vnto you, that God is able off these stones, to rayse up chyldren vnto Abraham. Even nowe is the ax put vnto the rote of the trees: soo that every tree which bringeth not fforthe goode frute, shal be hewne downe, and cast into the fyre.

I Baptise you in water in token of repentaunce, but he that cometh after me, is myghtier than I: whose shues I am not worthy to beare, he shal baptise you with the holy gost, and with fyre, which hath also his fan in his hond, and will pourge his floore, and gadre the wheet into his garner, and will burne the chaffe with everlastynge fyre.

Then cam Jesus from Galile into Jordon, to Jhon, ffor to be baptised off hym. But Jhon fforbade him,sayinge: I ought to be baptised off the: and commest thou to me? Jesus answered and sayde to hym: Lett hyt be so nowe. For thus hyt becommeth vs to fulfyll all rightewesnes. Then he suffred hym. And Jesus as sone as he was baptised, came strayght out of the water: And lo heven was open vnto hym: and he saw the spirite of God descend lyke a dove, and lyght vpon hym. And lo there came a voice from heven sayng: thys ys my deare sonne in whom is my delyte.

In translating the Pentateuch, Tyndale was assisted by Miles Coverdale, who, in 1535, while Tyndale was in prison at Velvoord, published the first English translation of the whole Scriptures, with this title:—*Biblia, the Bible; That is, the Holy Scriptures of the Olde and New Testament, faithfully translated out of the Doutche and Latyn into English.*

Coverdale was born in Yorkshire, in 1487, and educated at the university of Cambridge. He early became a Protestant, in consequence of which he left England for the continent. In 1551, he was made bishop of Exeter, but on the accession of Mary he again retired to the continent, where he remained until Elizabeth ascended the throne. He then returned to England, and lived in retirement until his death, which occurred in 1568, in his sixty-eighth year.

The translations of Tyndale and Coverdale were soon followed by others, so that the desire of the people for Scriptural knowledge was amply gratified. The dissemination of so many copies of the sacred volume, where neither the Bible nor any considerable number of other books had previously been in use, produced very remarkable effects. The people being now allowed to read the Scriptures for themselves, and to form their own judgment with regard to their meaning, perused them with such avidity, that their minds thence received that impulse for reading which is generally allowed to have been one of the causes of the flourishing literary era which so soon followed.

John Fox, another of the theologians of this period, whose adoption of the principles of the Reformation brought them into difficulty, was born at Boston in Lincolnshire, in 1517. He was of respectable though not distinguished parentage, and having lost his father in infancy, his mother, by a second marriage, placed him under the care of a step-father; by whom, however, his early education was so carefully attended to, that he entered the university of Oxford at the age of sixteen. He took the degree of bachelor of arts in 1538, and for ability and learning was so distinguished that he was immediately after chosen fellow of the Magdalen College, and received thence his master's degree, in 1543.

Fox early discovered a genius for poetry, and while at the university, and before he had commenced the study of divinity, he wrote, in the Latin language, several comedies, the subjects of all of which were taken from Scripture. One of the comedies, *De Christo Triumphante*, was translated into English during the reign of Elizabeth by Richard Day, and has since been repeatedly bpulished under the title of *Christ Jesus Triumphant, wherein is described the glorious triumph and conquest of Christ over sin, death, and the law.*

After a few years passed in this manner, Fox abandoned poetry altogether, and turned his exclusive attention to the study of divinity. He was still at Oxford; and so closely did he now apply himself to his studies, particularly to the investigation of those controverted points which were then engaging so much of the public attention, that he entirely withdrew from society, and often sat up during the greater part of the night. Becoming, after the most painful investigation, convinced of the errors of Popery, he avowed his conversion when examined on a charge of heresy in 1543, and was in consequence expelled from his college. After this event, being deserted by his friends, he passed some time in extreme poverty, but was at length employed by a gentleman of Warwickshire as tutor to his family. He must have remained in this situation, however, but a very short time; for toward the close of the reign of Henry the Eighth he went to London, where he again became so reduced in circumstances that he would have perished through absolute want, had not relief been afforded him by some unknown person, who was deeply affected by his wretched appearance as he was sitting in St. Paul's Cathedral.

The unknown stranger who so unexpectedly relieved Fox's wants, bade him, at the same time, not to give way to despondency, as a happy change was about to occur in his fortunes. The truth of this seasonable encouragement was almost immediately realized; for within a very few days, the Duchess of Richmond invited him to take up his residence in her family at Ryegate, in Surrey, as tutor to the children of her nephew, the Earl of Surrey. In this peaceful retreat, he remained until the persecutions of Mary's reign compelled him to flee for safety to the continent. Proceeding through Antwerp and Strasburg to Basle, in Germany, he there, for some years, supported himself by correcting the press for Oporimus, a celebrated printer; but upon the accession of queen Elizabeth to the throne he returned to England, and was kindly received and provided for by the Duke of Norfolk, who had been his pupil at Ryegate. Through other powerful friends, such as Sir Francis Drake, Sir Francis Walsingham, Bishop Grindal, and Bishop Pinkington, he might now have obtained considerable preferment; but entertaining conscientious scruples as to the articles to which it would be necessary for him to subscribe, and disapproving of some of the ceremonies of the church, he declined all offers made to him except that of a prebend in the church of Salisbury, which he accepted with great reluctance. He died on the eighteenth of April, 1587, in the seventieth year of his age, much respected for the piety, modesty, humanity, and conscientiousness of his character, as well as for his extensive acquirements in ecclesiastical antiquities, and other branches of learning.

Fox was the author of a number of Latin treatises, chiefly on theological subjects; but the work on which his fame rests is his history of the *Acts and Monuments of the Church*, popularly denominated *Fox's Book of Martyrs*. This celebrated production, on which the author labored for eleven years, was published in 1563, and was received with great favor by the

Protestants; but, of course, occasioned much exasperation among the opposite party, who did every thing in their power to undermine its credit. That the author has frequently erred, and, like other controversial writers of the time, sometimes lost his temper and sullied his pages with coarse language, can not be denied; but that mistakes were willfully or malignantly committed by him, no one has ever been able to prove. With regard to what he derived from written documents, Bishop Burnet, in the preface to his 'History of the Reformation,' bears strong testimony in his favor, by declaring that, 'having compared the Acts and Monuments with the records, he had never been able to discover any error or prevarication in them, but the utmost fidelity and exactness.'

Few writers of the period that we are at present considering, afford more ample scope for extracts than Fox; but our limits will permit us to introduce only the following:—

THE INVENTION OF PRINTING.

What man soever was the instrument (whereby this invention was made), without all doubt God himself was the ordainer and disposer thereof, no otherwise than he was of the gift of tongues, and that for a similar purpose. And well may this gift of printing be resembled to the gift of tongues: for like as God then spake with many tongues, and yet all that would not turn the Jews; so now, when the Holy Ghost speaketh to the adversaries in innumerable sorts of books, yet they will not be converted, nor turn to the gospel.

Now to consider to what end and purpose the Lord hath given this gift of printing to the earth, and to what great utility and necessity it serveth, it is not hard to judge, who so wisely perpendeth both the time of the sending, and the sequel which thereof ensueth.

And first, touching the time of this faculty given to the use of man, this is to be marked: that when as the bishop of Rome with all and full the consent of the cardinals, patriarchs, archbishops, bishops, abbots, priors, lawyers, doctors, provoses, deans, archdeacons, assembled together in the Council of Constance, had condemned poor John Huss and Hierome of Prague, to death for heresy, notwithstanding they were no heretics; and after they had subdued the Bohemians, and all the whole world, under the supreme authority of the Romish see; and had made all Christian people obedienciaries and vassals unto the same, having (as one would say) all the world at their will, so that the matter now was past not only the power of all men, but the hope also of any man to be recovered: in this very time so dangerous and desperate, when man's power could do no more, there the blessed wisdom and omnipotent power of the Lord began to work for his church, not with sword and target to subdue his exalted adversary, but with printing, writing, and reading to convince darkness by light, error by truth, ignorance by learning. So that by this means of printing, the secret operation of God hath heaped upon that proud kingdom a double confusion. For whereas the bishop of Rome had burned John Huss before, and Hierome of Prague, who neither denied his transubstantiation, nor his supremacy, nor yet his popish mass, but said mass, and heard mass themselves; neither spake against his purgatory, nor any other great matter of his popish doctrine, but only exclaimed against his excessive and pompous pride, his unchristian or rather antichristian abomination of life: thus while he could not abide his wickedness only of life to be touched, but made it heresy, or at least matter of death, whatsoever was spoken against his detestable conversation and manners, God of his secret judgment, seeing time to help his church, hath found a way by this faculty of printing, not only to confound his life and conversation, which before he could not abide to be touched, but also to cast down the foundation of his standing, that is, to examine, confute, and detect his doctrine, laws, and institutions most detestable, in such sort, that though his life were never so pure, yet his doctrine standing as it doth, no man is so blind but may see, that either the pope is anti-christ, or also that anti-christ is near cousin to the pope: and all this doth, and will hereafter more and more, appear by printing.

The reason whereof is this: for that hereby tongues are known, knowledge groweth, judgment encreaseth, books are dispersed, the scripture is seen, the doctors be read, stories be opened, times compared, truth discerned, falsehood detected, and with finger pointed, and all (as I said) through the benefit of printing. Wherefore I suppose, that either the pope must abolish printing, or he must seek a new world to reign over: for else, as the world standeth, printing doubtless will abolish him. But the pope, and all his college of cardinals, must this understand, that through the light of printing, the world beginneth now to have eyes to see, and heads to judge. He can not walk so invisible in a net, but he will be spied. And although, through might, he stopped the mouth of John Huss before, and of Hierome, that they might not preach, thinking to make his kingdom sure; yet, instead of John Huss and other, God hath opened the press to preach, whose voice the pope is never able to stop with all the puissance of his triple crown. By this printing, as by the gift of tongues, and as by the singular organ of the Holy Ghost, the doctrine of the gospel soundeth to all nations and countries under heaven: and what God revealeth to one man, is dispersed to many; and what is known in one nation, is opened to all.

JOHN LELAND, another ornament of this period, was born in the city of London about 1495. He lost both his parents in his infancy, but was immediately adopted by Mr. Thomas Myles, who not only supported him at school, but also, through admiration of his genius, sent him to Christ's College, Cambridge, whence, however, he soon after removed to All-Souls-College, Oxford. At Oxford, Leland devoted himself for several years with very great assiduity to his studies, particularly to the Greek language and literature. Having left Oxford he went to Paris, and there continued to reside for some years, enjoying the friendship and even intimacy of most of the learned men of that city.

In addition to a very profound knowledge of the Latin and Greek languages, Leland became, while abroad, familiar with the French, the Italian, and the Spanish; and what was still more unusual at that time, he gave, after his return to England, much attention to the Welsh and Saxon. Henry the Eighth, through admiration for his learning, appointed him one of his chaplains, and made him his librarian; and as he had a strong inclination for researches into the antiquities of his native country, the king gave him a commission to inspect records, wherever placed; and armed with this authority, he proceeded upon a tour of the whole kingdom, at once to visit the remains of ancient buildings, tumuli, and other objects surviving from an early age, and to make researches into the libraries of colleges, abbeys, and cathedrals. In the course of six years thus employed, he collected an immense mass of materials, some of which he deposited in the king's library, in consequence of which Henry named him his antiquarian.

The works which Leland subsequently composed with reference to his favorite pursuits, convey a very flattering impression of his diligence, and of the value of his labors; but they present little attraction except to readers of a peculiar taste. Some of his writings are in Latin; but the *Itinerary*—an account of his travels, and of the ancient remains which he visited, together with a catalogue of English writers—is in English. Leland was, for the last two years of his life, insane—a disease superinduced, in all probability, by too severe study. He died in London, in 1552.

George Cavendish, gentleman usher to cardinal Wolsey, and afterwards to Henry the Eighth, belongs to the writers of this period, but the time of his birth has not been preserved. To Wolsey he was strongly attached, and after that prelate's fall, he continued to serve him faithfully until his death.

Cavendish himself died in 1557, leaving in manuscript the *Life of Cardinal Wolsey*, in which, while he admits the arrogant disposition of the cardinal, he highly extols his general character. *The Metrical Visions* of Cavendish treat of the fortunes and fall of some of the most eminent persons of his time. Respecting the life of Wolsey a recent editor observes:—'There is a sincere and impartial adherence to truth, a reality, in Cavendish's narrative, which bespeaks the confidence of his reader, and very much increases his pleasure. It is a work without pretensions, but full of natural eloquence, devoid of the formality of a set rhetorical composition, unspoiled by the affectation of that classical manner in which all biography and history of old time was prescribed to be written, and which often divests such records of the attraction to be found in the conversational style of Cavendish. Shakspeare has literally followed him in several passages of his king Henry VIII., merely putting his language into verse. Add to this the historical importance of the work, as the only sure and authentic source of information upon many of the most interesting events of that reign; and from which all historians have largely drawn, (through the secondary medium of Holinshed and Stow, who adopted Cavendish's narrative,) and its intrinsic value need not be more fully expressed.'

From this work we extract the following curious account of the familiar visits of Henry the Eighth to the house of cardinal Wolsey:—

And when it pleased the king's majesty, for his recreation, to repair unto the Cardinal's house, as he did divers times in the year, at which time there wanted no preparations, or goodly furniture, with viands of the finest sort that might be provided for money or friendship; such pleasures were then devised for the king's comfort and consolation, as might be invented, or by man's wit imagined. The banquets were set forth with masks and mummeries, in so gorgeous a sort and costly manner, that it was a heaven to behold. There wanted no dames or damsels, meet or apt to dance with the maskers, or to garnish the place for the time with other goodly disports. Then was there all kinds of music and harmony set forth, with excellent voices both of men and children. I have seen the king come suddenly in thither in a mask, with a dozen of other maskers, all in garments like shepherds, made of fine cloth of gold, and fine crimson satin paned, and caps of the same, with visors of good proportion of visnomy; their hairs, and beards, either of fine gold wire, or else of silver, and some being of black silk; having sixteen torch bearers, besides their drums, and other persons attending upon them, with visors, and clothed all in satin, of the same colours And at his coming, and before he came into the hall, ye shall understand that he came by water to the watergate, without any noise, where, against his coming, were laid charged many chambers,[1] and at his landing they were all shot off, which made such a rumble in the air, that it was like thunder. It made all the noblemen, ladies, and gentlewomen, to muse what it should mean coming so suddenly, they sitting quietly at a solemn banquet. * * * * Then, immediately after this great shot of guns, the cardinal desired the lord chamberlain and comptroller to look what this sudden shot should mean, as though he knew nothing of the matter. They thereupon, looking out of the windows into Thames, returned again and showed him, that it seemed to them there should be some noblemen and strangers arrived at his bridge, as ambassadors from some foreign prince. * * * * Then quoth the cardinal to my lord chamberlain, 'I pray you,' quoth he, 'show them that it seemeth me that there should be among them some noblemen, whom I suppose to be much more worthy of honour to sit and occupy this room and place than I; to whom I would most gladly, if I knew him, surrender my place according to my duty.' Then spake my lord chamberlain unto them in French, declaring my lord cardinal's mind; and they rounding[2] him again in the ear, my lord chamberlain said to my lord cardinal, 'Sir, they confess,' quoth he, 'that among them is such a noble personage, whom, if your Grace can appoint him from the other, he is contented to disclose himself, and to accept your place most worthily.' With that the cardinal, taking a good advisement among them, at the last, quoth he, 'Me seemeth the gentleman with the black beard should be even he.' And with that he arose out of his chair, and offered the same to the gentleman in the black beard, with his cap in his hand. The person to whom he offered then his chair, was Sir Edward Neville, a comely knight of a goodly personage, that much more resembled the king's person in that mask than any other. The king, hearing and perceiving the cardinal so deceived in his estimation and choice, could not forbear laughing; but plucked down his visor, and Master Neville's also, and dashed out with such a pleasant countenance and cheer, that all noble estates[3] there assembled, seeing the king to be there amongst them, rejoiced very much. The cardinal eftsoons[4] desired his highness to take the place of estate, to whom the king answered, that he would go first and shift his apparel; and so departed and went straight into my lord's bedchamber, where there was a great fire made and prepared for him, and there new apparelled him with rich and princely garments. And in the time of the king's absence, the dishes of the banquet were clean taken up, and the table spread again with new and sweet perfumed cloths; every man sitting still until the king and his maskers came in among them again, every man being newly apparelled. Then the king took his seat under the cloth of estate, commanding no man to remove, but sit still, as they did before. Then in came a new banquet before the king's majesty, and to all the rest through the tables, wherein, I suppose, were served two hundred dishes, or above, of wondrous costly meats and devices, subtilly devised. Thus passed they forth the whole night with banquetting, dancing, and other triumphant devices, to the great comfort of the king, and pleasant regard of the nobility there assembled.

LORD BERNERS, another popular writer of the age of Henry the Eighth, and a very great favorite of that monarch, being first made by him chancellor of the Exchequer, and afterward governor of Calais, is known chiefly as the author of a translation of the French chronicles of Froissart. His versions of that fascinating narrative of cotemporary events in England, France,

[1] Short guns, or cannon, without carriages, chiefly used for festive occasions.
[2] Whispering. [3] Persons of rank. [4] Immediately.

Flanders, Scotland, and other countries, was executed by the king's command, and was published in 1523. Froissart, the original author, resided in England as secretary to the queen of Edward the Third, from 1361, till 1366, and again visited that country in 1395. The translation is an excellent sample of the English language of that period, being remarkable for the purity and nervousness of its style. Besides the translation from Froissart, Lord Berners wrote *The History of the Most Noble and Valiant Knight, Arthur of Little Britain*, and *The Duties of the Inhabitants of Calais*. From his translation of Froissart, we extract the following passage :—

THE BATTLE OF CRESSY.

When the French king saw the Englishmen, his blood changed, and (he) said to his marshalls, 'Make the Genoese go on before, and begin the battle in the name of God and St. Denis.' There were of the Genoese cross-bows about a fifteen thousand, but they were so weary of going a-foot that day, a six leagues, armed with their cross-bows, that they said to their constables, 'We be not well ordered to fight this day, for we be not in the case to do any great deed of arms; we have more need of rest.' These words came to the Earl of Alençon, who said, 'A man is well at ease to be charged with such a sort of rascals, to be faint and fail now at most need.' Also, the same season, there fell a great rain and an eclipse, with a terrible thunder; and before the rain, there came flying over the battles a great number of crows for fear of the tempest coming. Then anon the air began to wax clear, and the sun to shine fair and bright, the which was right in the Frenchmen's eyen, and on the Englishmen's back. When the Genoese were assembled together, and began to approach, they made a great leap and cry, to abash the Englishmen; but they stood still, and stirred not for all that. Then the Genoese again the second time made another leap and a fell cry, and stepped forward a little; and the Englishmen removed not one foot. Thirdly again, they leaped and cried, and went forth till they came within shot; then they shot fiercely with their cross-bows. Then the English archers stepped forth one pace, and let fly their arrows so wholly and thick that it seemed snow. When the Genoese felt the arrows piercing through heads and arms and breasts, many of them cast down their cross-bows, and did cut their strings, and returned discomfited. When the French king saw them flee away, he said, 'Slay these rascals, for they shall let and trouble us without reason.' Then ye should have seen the men-at-arms dash in among them, and killed a great number of them, and ever still the Englishmen shot whereas they saw the thickest press; the sharp arrows ran into the men-at-arms and into their horses; and many fell horse and men among the Genoese; and when they were down, they could not relieve again; the press was so thick that one overthrew another. And also, among the Englishmen, there were certain rascals that went on foot with great knives, and they went in among the men-at-arms, and murdered many as they lay on the ground, both earls, barons, knights, and squires, whereof the King of England was after displeased, for he had rather they had been taken prisoners.

Contemporary with Lord Berners was JOHN BELLENDEN, archdeacon of Moray, a favorite of James the Fifth of Scotland, and one of the lords of session in the reign of queen Mary. Besides writing a topography of Scotland, epistles to James the Fifth, and some poems, Bellenden translated, by order of the king, Hector Boece's *History of Scotland*, and also the first five books of Livy. The translation of Boece was published in 1536, and constitutes the earliest existing specimen of Scottish literary prose. It is, however, rather a free translation, and additions to the original are sometimes made by the translator. Another translation of Boece's History was published some years after in England by Holinshed, an English chronicler in the reign of Elizabeth, and was the source whence Shakspeare derived the historical materials of his tragedy of Macbeth. As the language of Bellenden's translation is now nearly obsolete, and as Holinshed's is easily accessible, we do not consider it necessary to introduce any extract from the former work.

Among the distinguished men of this age SIR JOHN CHEKE holds a very conspicuous place. He was descended from an ancient family in the Isle of Wight, and was born at Cambridge on the sixteenth of June 1514. At the age of seventeen he entered St. John's College, Cambridge, and such was his proficiency in the Greek language and literature that immediately after he had taken his degrees he was chosen Greek lecturer of the university. In 1540, when Henry the Eighth founded the Greek professorship at Cambridge, Cheke was chosen the first professor, and at the same time made university orator. In 1544, he was appointed tutor to prince Edward, and upon the accession of that prince to the crown, he obtained an annuity of one hundred marks, and by virtue of the king's mandamus, was elevated provost of King's College. In 1550, he was raised to the position of chief gentleman of the king's privy chamber, and in the following year his majesty conferred upon him the honor of knighthood. With a celerity almost unparalleled he passed from gentleman of the king's privy chamber, to the office of chancellor of the exchequer, and thence to the clerkship of the council, immediately after which he became one of the secretaries of state, and privy-counsellor.

At the period of King Edward's death, Sir John Cheke's cup of prosperity was full, but having acted as secretary to Lady Jane Grey, and her council, he was, on the accession of Mary, committed to the Tower. In 1554, however, he obtained his liberty, and soon after left England for the continent. He travelled through France and Italy, but on his arrival at Strasburgh, in Germany, he was reduced to the necessity of teaching Greek for a subsistence. In 1556, he was insidiously drawn to Brussels, and by order of King Philip, Mary's consort, apprehended, sent to England, and again committed to the Tower. The dreadful alternative was now presented to him by Cardinal Pole, 'either to comply or burn;' and in a moment of weakness he renounced Protestantism, and was received into the bosom of the Romish church. The grief, remorse, and shame, however, which immediately followed, hastened his end, and he, accordingly, died soon after, on the thirteenth of September, 1557, in his forty-fourth year.

Sir John Cheke was chiefly distinguished for the exertions he made to introduce the study of the Greek language and literature into England. Having dictated to his pupils an improved method for pronouncing Greek words, he was violently assailed by Bishop Gardiner, then Chancellor of

Cambridge university; but notwithstanding the fulminations of that severe prelate, the system of Cheke prevailed, and prevails even to the present day. At his death he left several works in manuscript, among which was a *Translation of the Gospel by St. Matthew*, the design of which was to exemplify a plan that he had conceived of reforming the English language by eradicating all words except those derived from Saxon roots.

Cheke's only original work in English is a pamphlet under the title of *The Hurt of Sedition, how grievous it is to a Commonwealth*, the design of the writer being to admonish the people who had risen under Ket the tanner. From this pamphlet we select the following specimen :—

REMONSTRANCE WITH LEVELLERS.

Ye pretend to a commonwealth. How amend ye it by killing of gentlemen, by spoiling of gentlemen, by imprisoning of gentlemen? A marvellous tanned[1] commonwealth. Why should ye hate them for their riches, or for their rule? Rule, they never took so much in hand as ye do now. They never resisted the king, never withstood his council, be faithful at this day, when ye be faithless, not only to the king, whose subjects ye be, but also to your lords, whose tenants ye be. Is this your true duty—in some of homage, in most of fealty, in all of allegiance—to leave your duties, go back from your promises, fall from your faith, and contrary to law and truth, to make unlawful assemblies, ungodly companies, wicked and detestable camps, to disobey your betters, and to obey your tanners, to change your obedience from a king to a Ket, to submit yourselves to traitors, and break your faith to your true king and lords? * * *

If riches offend you, because ye would have the like, then think that to be no commonwealth, but envy to the commonwealth. Envy it is to appair[2] another man's estate, without the amendment of your own; and to have no gentlemen, because ye be none yourselves, is to bring down an estate, and to mend none. Would ye have all alike rich? That is the overthrow of all labour, and utter decay of work in this realm. For, who will labour more, if, when he hath gotten more the idle shall by lust, without right, take what him list from him, under pretence of equality with him? This is the bringing in of idleness, which destroyeth the commonwealth, and not the amendment of labour, which maintaineth the commonwealth. If there should be such equality, then ye take all hope away from yours, to come to any better estate than you now leave them. And as many mean men's children come honestly up, and are great succour to all their stock, so should none be hereafter holpen by you. But because you seek equality, whereby all cannot be rich, ye would that be like, whereby every man should be poor. And think, beside, that riches and inheritance be God's providence, and given to whom of his wisdom he thinketh good.

Of the period at present under consideration, we have still to notice Thomas Wilson and Roger Ascham.

Of the time of Wilson's birth, of his birth-place, of his family, and of his early education, we are entirely ignorant. That his scholarship must have been respectable is evident; for he not only became a fellow of King's College, Cambridge, but soon after rose to the Deanery of Durham, and to various state employments under Elizabeth. He died in 1581, well advanced in years.

[1] Alluding to the profession of the ringleader.

[2] Impair.

Wilson, according to Burnet, may be regarded as the earliest writer on the English language. He published, in 1553, a *System of Rhetoric and Logic*, in which the principles of eloquence and composition are laid down with considerable ability. He strenuously advocates, in this treatise, simplicity of language, and condemns those writers who disturb the natural arrangement of their words, and reject familiar and appropriate phrases for the sake of others more refined and curious. The effect which the publication of this work produced was very remarkable; for his doctrines were considered by the Church so great and dangerous an innovation, that, upon a visit to Rome, he was cast into prison as a heretic. Among other false styles censured by Wilson, is that of alliteration, in illustration of which he gives the following caricatured example:—'Pitiful poverty prayeth for a penny, but puffed presumption passeth not a point, pampering his paunch with pestilent pleasure, procuring his passport to post it to hell-pit, there to be punished with pains perpetual.' The following passages from his *Art of Rhetoric* contain much good sense:—

SIMPLICITY OF STYLE RECOMMENDED.

Among other lessons, this should first be learned, that we never affect any strange inkhorn terms, but to speak as is commonly received; neither seeking to be over fine, nor yet living over careless; using our speech as most men do, and ordering our wits as the fewest have doen. Some seek so far for outlandish English, that they forget altogether their mother's language. And I dare swear this, if some of their mothers were alive, they were not able to tell what they say, and yet these fine English clerks will say they speak in their mother tongue, if a man should charge them with counterfeiting the king's English. Some far journied gentlemen, at their return home, like as they love to go in foreign apparel, so they will ponder their talk with over-sea language. He that cometh lately out of France will talk French English, and never blush at the matter. Another chops in with English Italianated, and applieth the Italian phrase to one English, speaking; the which is, as if an oration that professeth to utter his mind in plain Latin would needs speak poetry, and far-fetched colours of strange antiquity. The lawyer will store his stomach with the prating of pedlars. The auditor in making his account and reckoning, cometh in with *sise sould, et cater denere*, for 6*s*. and 4*d*. The fine courtier will talk nothing but Chaucer. The mystical wise men, and poetical clerks, will speak nothing but quaint proverbs and blind allegories; delighting much in their own darkness, especially when none can tell what they do say. The unlearned or foolish fantastical, that smells but of learning (such fellows as have seen learned men in their days), will so Latin their tongues, that the simple cannot but wonder at their talk, and think surely they speak by some revelation. I know them, that think rhetoric to stand wholly upon dark words; and he that can catch an inkhorn term by the tail, him they count to be a fine Englishman and a good rhetorician.

MORAL AIM OF POETRY.

The saying of poets, and all their fables, are not to be forgotten. For by them we may talk at large, and win men by persuasion, if we declare beforehand, that these tales were not feigned of such wise men without cause, neither yet continued until this time and kept in memory, without good consideration; and thereupon declare the true meaning of all such writing. For undoubtedly, there is no one tale among all the poets, but under the same is comprehended something that pertaineth either to the amendment of manners, to the knowledge of truth, to the setting forth nature's work, or else to the understanding of some notable thing doen. For what other is the painful travail of Ulysses, described so largely by Homer, but a lively picture of man's misery in this life? And as Plutarch saith, and likewise Basilius Magnus, in the Iliads are described strength and valiantness of body: in Odessea is set forth a lively pattern of the mind. The poets are wise men, and wished in heart the redress of things; the which when for fear they durst not openly rebuke, they did in colours paint them out, and told men by shadows what they should do in good sothe: or else, because the wicked were unworthy to hear the truth, they spake so that none might understand but those unto whom they please to utter their m.-ing, and knew them to be of honest conversation.

Roger Ascham was a still more distinguished and instructive writer thar Thomas Wilson. Ascham was born at Kirkby-Wiske, in Yorkshire, in 1515. As his parents were poor, and as he early discovered more than an ordinary share of genius, he was taken into the family of Sir Anthony Wingfield, and there educated in company with that noble knight's two sons. As young Ascham evinced great taste for the learned languages, Sir Anthony sent him, in 1530, to St. John's College, Cambridge, where his assiduity and application eventually secured for him the intimate friendship of all the celebrated scholars of that college. He took the degree of bachelor of arts at the early age of eighteen, and such was then his scholarship that within a month after, he was elected one of the fellows of his college. These honors incited him to a still greater and more vigorous prosecution of his studies; and in the Greek language his attainments soon became such that he read it publicly, in his college, with universal applause. In the twenty-first year of his age he was made master of arts, and soon after appointed, by the university, teacher of Greek, with a liberal salary. In order to relax his mind after so severe a course of study, he now composed *Toxophilus, or a Treatise on Archery*, which he dedicated to the king. His majesty being pleased with the performance, settled a pension upon the author, and employed him to teach the young prince Edward, and the princess Elizabeth writing—an art in which he particularly excelled.

In 1548, Ascham became the instructor of Elizabeth in the learned languages, and filled that situation for two years, at the expiration of which he returned to Cambridge and resumed his position of public orator, with a pension from the young king Edward. In 1550 he was appointed to attend Sir Richard Morysine in his embassy to the Emperor Charles the Fifth; and while in Germany, where he remained three years, he wrote his Discourse on the affairs of that country, which introduced him to all the men of letters of the German court. From Germany he was recalled to become Latin secretary to king Edward—a post which he held under queen Mary also, and to which he passed on the accession of Elizabeth. A discussion between several of the eminent members of Elizabeth's court, on the different modes of education then practiced, gave rise to his treatise on that subject—a work still held in high esteem among the best judges of the art of instruction. Ascham died on the fourth of January, 1568, in the fifty-fourth year of his age, universally lamented; especially by queen Elizabeth, who did his memory the honor to remark that 'she would rather have given ten thousand pounds than to have lost him.'

Ascham was the earliest writer on education in the English language, and his writings themselves not only furnish an improved example of style, but abound also in sound sense and excellent instructions. *The Schoolmaster*, which was published by his widow after his death, contains, besides the correct views of education already alluded to, what Dr. Johnson acknowledged to be 'perhaps the best advice that was ever given for the study of languages.' From this deeply interesting work we extract the two following passages, to which we shall add *The Qualifications of a Historian*, from the *Discourse on the Affairs of Germany*.

THE CHOICE OF A TUTOR.

It is pity that commonly more care is had, and that among very wise men, to find out rather a cunning man for their horse, than a cunning man for their children. To the one they will gladly give a stipend of 200 crowns by the year, and loth to offer the other 200 shillings. God, that setteth in heaven, laugheth their choice to scorn, and rewardeth their liberality as it should; for he suffereth them to have tame and well-ordered horse, but wild and unfortunate children.

One example, whether love or fear doth work more in a child for virtue and learning, I will gladly report; which may be heard with some pleasure, and followed with more profit. Before I went into Germany, I came to Broadgate, in Leicestershire, to take my leave of that noble Lady Jane Grey, to whom I was exceedingly much beholden. Her parents, the duke and the duchess, with all the household, gentlemen and gentlewomen, were hunting in the park. I found her in her chamber reading Phoëdon Platonis in Greek, and that with as much delight, as some gentlemen would read a merry tale in Bocace. After salutation and duty done with some other talk, I asked her, why she would lose such pastime in the park? Smiling, she answered me, 'I wiss, all their sport in the park is but a shadow to that pleasure that I find in Plato. Alas! good folk, they never felt what true pleasure meant.' 'And how came you, madam,' quoth I, 'to this deep knowledge of pleasure? And what did chiefly allure you unto it, seeing not many women, but very few men, have attained thereunto?' 'I will tell you,' quoth she, 'and tell you a truth which, perchance, ye will marvel at. One of the greatest benefits that ever God gave me, is that he sent me so sharp and severe parents, and so gentle a schoolmaster. For when I am in presence either of father or mother, whether I speak, keep silence, sit, stand, or go, eat, drink, be merry or sad, be sewing, playing, dancing, or doing any thing else, I must do it, as it were, in such weight, measure, and number, even so perfectly as God made the world, or else I am so sharply taunted, so cruelly threatened, yea, presently, sometimes with pinches, nips, and bobs, and other ways, which I will not name for the honour I bear them, so without measure misordered, that I think myself in hell, till time come that I must go to Mr. Elmer; who teacheth me so gently, so pleasantly, with such fair allurements to learning, that I think all the time nothing, while I am with him. And when I am called from him, I fall on weeping, because, whatever I do else, but learning, is full of grief, trouble, fear, and whole misliking unto me. And thus my book has been so much my pleasure, and bringeth daily to me more pleasure and more, that, in respect of it, all other pleasures, in very deed, be but trifles and troubles unto me.'

THE NECESSITY OF LEARNING MORE THAN ONE LANGUAGE.

I have been a looker on in the cockpit of learning these many years; and one cock only have I known, which, with one wing, even at this day, doth pass all other, in mine opinion, that ever I saw in England though they had two wings. Yet nevertheless, to fly well with one wing, to run fast with one leg, are masteries, much to be marvelled at than sure examples, safely to be followed. A bishop that now liveth, a good man, whose judgment in religion I better like, than his opinion in perfectness in other learning, said once unto me; 'We have no need now of the Greek tongue, when all things be translated into Latin.' But the good man understood not, that even the best translation, is for mere necessity but an evil imped wing to fly withal, or a heavy stump leg of wood to go withal. Such, the higher they fly, the sooner they falter and fail: the faster they run the ofter they stumble and sorer the fall. Such as will needs so fly, may fly at a pye, and catch a daw: and such runners, as commonly they, shove and shoulder, to stand foremost, yet in the end they come behind others, and deserve but the hopshakles, if the masters of the game be right iudgers.

QUALIFICATIONS OF A HISTORIAN.

When you and I read Livy together (if you do remember), after some reasoning we concluded both what was in our opinion to be looked for at his hand, that would well and advisedly write an history. First point was, to write nothing false; next, to be bold to say any truth: whereby is avoided two great faults—flattery and hatred. For which two points, Cæsar is read to his great praise; and Jovius the Italian to his just reproach. Then to mark diligently the causes, counsels, acts, and issues, in all great attempts: and in causes, what is just or unjust; in counsels, what is purposed wisely or rashly; in acts, what is done courageously or faintly; and of every issue, to note some general lesson of wisdom and weariness for like matters in time to come, wherein Polybius in Greek, and Philip Comines in French, have done the duties of wise and worthy writers. Diligence also must be used in keeping truly the order of time, and describing lively both the site of places and nature of persons, not only for the outward shape of the body, but also for the inward disposition of the mind, as Thucydides doth in many places very trimly; and Homer everywhere, and that always most excellently; which observation is chiefly to be marked in him. And our Chaucer doth the same, very praiseworthy: mark him well, and confer him with any other that writeth in our time in their proudest tongue, whosoever list. The style must be always plain and open; yet sometime higher and lower, as matters do rise and fall. For if proper and natural words, in well-joined sentences, do lively express the matter, be it troublesome, quiet, angry, or pleasant, a man shall think not to be reading, but present in doing of the same. And herein Livy of all other in any tongue, by mine opinion, carrieth away the praise.

After the publication of Ascham's work, it became more usual for learned men to compose in English, especially when they aimed to influence public opinion; English literature fi ɔm that period therefore, assumes a new aspect.

Lecture the Seventh.

THE AGE OF ELIZABETH—JOHN HARRINGTON—THOMAS SACKVILLE—SIR PHILIP SIDNEY—SIR WALTER RALEIGH—NICHOLAS BRETON—HENRY CONSTABLE—JOSHUA SYLVESTER—RICHARD BARNFIELD—EDMUND SPENSER.

WE have thus brought the history of English literature down to the period at which its infancy may be said to cease, and its manhood to commence. In the early part of the sixteenth century, it was sensibly effected by a variety of influences, which, for one or two ages before, had operated powerfully in extending the intellect of all the different nations of Europe. The study of classical literature, the invention of the art of printing, and the freedom of religious discussion, had everywhere given activity and strength to the minds of men. The immediate effect of these circumstances upon English literature, were, the enriching of the language by a great variety of words from the classic tongues, the establishing of better models of thought and style, and the allowing of greater freedom to the fancy and powers of observation in the exercise of literary efforts. Not only the Greek and Roman writers, but those also of modern Italy and France, where letters had experienced an earlier revival, were now freely translated into English, and being, through the press, extensively diffused, served to excite a taste for elegant reading in the lower order of society, where the genial influence of literature had never before been felt. The dissemination of the Scriptures in the vernacular tongue, while it greatly affected the language and ideas of the people, was also of no small advantage in giving a new direction to the thoughts of literary men, to whom these antique Oriental compositions presented numberless incidents, images, and sentiments, unknown before, and of the richest and most interesting kind.

Among other circumstances favorable to the literature of this period, must be named the encouragement given to it by queen Elizabeth, who was, herself, a very accomplished scholar, addicted to poetical composition, and had the art of filling her court with men qualified to shine in almost any department of intellectual exertion. Her successors, James and Charles, resembled her in some of these respects, and during their reigns, the impulse which she had given to literature was rather increased than retarded. There was, indeed, something in the policy, as well as in the personal character of all these sovereigns, which proved favorable to literature. The study of the *Belles Lettres* was, in some measure, identified with the courtly and arbitrary principles of the time; not, perhaps, so much from any enlightened spirit in those who supported such principles, as from a desire to oppose the *Puritans*, and other malcontents, whose religious doctrines taught them to despise some departments of elegant literature, and utterly to condemn others. The drama, for instance, doubtless owed the encouragement which it received under Elizabeth and her successors, chiefly, if not entirely, to a spirit of hostility to the 'Puritans,' who justly repudiated it for its immorality. We must, at the same time, allow much to the influence which such a court as that of England during these three reigns, was calculated to have upon men of literary tendencies. Almost all the poets, and many of the prose writers, were either courtiers themselves, or were under the immediate protection of courtiers, and were constantly experiencing the smiles, and occasionally the solid benefactions of royalty. Whatever was refined, or gay, or sentimental, at that time in England, came with its full influence upon literature.

The works brought forth under such circumstances have been very aptly compared, by a recent writer in the Edinburgh Review, to the productions of a soil for the first time broken up, 'where all indigenous plants spring up at once with a rank and irrepressible fertility, and display whatever is peculiar and excellent in their nature on a scale the most conspicuous and magnificent.' The ability to write having been, as it were, suddenly created, the whole world of character, imagery, and sentiment, as well as of information and philosophy, lay ready for the use of those who possessed the gift, and was appropriated accordingly. As might be expected, where there was less rule of art than opulence of materials, the productions of these writers are often deficient in taste, and contain much that is totally irrelevant to their purpose. To pursue the simile just quoted, the crops are not so clean as if they had been reared under systematic cultivation. On this account, the refined taste of the eighteenth century condemned most of the productions of the sixteenth and seventeenth to oblivion, and it is only lately that they have once more obtained their deserved reputation.

After every proper deduction has been made, enough remains to fix the era as 'by far the mightiest in the history of English literature, or indeed of human intellect and capacity.'[1] There never was any thing elsewhere like the sixty or seventy years that elapsed from the middle of Elizabeth's reign to the period of the Restoration. In point of real force and originality of genius, neither the age of Pericles, nor that of Augustus, nor the age of Leo the Tenth, nor that of Louis the Fourteenth, can at all compare with it. In that short period, we find the names of most of the great men that England has ever produced—the names of Shakspeare, and Spen-

[1] Henry Neale.

ser, and Bacon, and Sidney, and Hooker, and Taylor, and Barrow, and Raleigh, and Napier, and a host of others—men, all of them not merely of great talents and accomplishments, but of vast compass and reach of understanding, and of minds truly creative and original; not perfecting art by the delicacy of their taste, or digesting knowledge by the justness of their reasonings, but making vast and substantial additions to the materials upon which taste and reason must, hereafter be employed, and enlarging, to an incredible and unparalleled extent, both the stores and the resources of the human faculties. This important period of English literature commences about 1575, and closes with the death of Charles the First, in 1649; and in our examination of the authors which it produced, we shall first notice the miscellaneous poets, then the dramatic, and afterward the writers in prose. Queen Elizabeth herself first demands our attention.

Elizabeth was the daughter of Henry the Eighth and of Anne Boleyn, his second wife. She was born the seventeenth of September, 1533, and was committed by her mother, just before that unfortunate princess was executed, to the care of Doctor Parker, a strenuous friend of the Reformation, and subsequently archbishop of Canterbury. Doctor Parker having the exclusive supervision of Elizabeth's education for a number of years, was careful to have her instructed in the principles of the Protestant faith, and by this means he thoroughly prepared her for the important and decisive stand which she took in favor of Protestantism, as soon as she became queen. At the time of her father's death, she had just attained the fourteenth year of her age, and her letters at that early period of life, both in English and Italian, were the subject of universal admiration. During the entire reign of Edward the Sixth, and the early part of the reign of Mary, she devoted her exclusive attention to study; and such was the wonderful facility with which she acquired knowledge, that before she reached her seventeenth year she had become familiarly acquainted with the Latin, the Greek, the French, and the Italian languages, and was not unacquainted with other European tongues. Nor did she confine herself merely to the knowledge of languages, but cultivated philosophy, rhetoric, history, divinity, music and poetry also, and, indeed, every thing that would have a tendency to improve and adorn her mind. Her studies were, however, for a short time interrupted; for being suspected by Mary of favoring the pretensions of Lady Jane Grey to the crown, she was apprehended on the eleventh of March, 1554, and committed to the Tower. After a tedious confinement, she was eventually, through the direct agency of king Philip, Mary's consort, released; and the rest of her time was passed in the retirement of a private personage until the death of Mary, when she succeeded to an undisputed crown, on the sixteenth of November, 1558. Her reign was one of unparalleled brilliancy, and terminated on the twenty-fourth of March, 1603, in the seventieth year of her age.

The poetry of Elizabeth, though not of a high order of merit, is such as to entitle it to a passing notice. It consists chiefly of brief and unpremeditated effusions, of which the following stanzas afford a fair sample:—

VERSES ON HER OWN FEELINGS.

I grieve, and dare not show my discontent,
I love, and yet am forced to seem to hate;
I do, yet dare not say I ever meant,
I seem stark mute, but inwardly do prate:
    I am, and not, I freeze, and yet am burn'd,
    Since from myself my other self I turn'd.

My care is like my shadow in the sun,
Follows me flying, flies when I pursue it;
Stands and lies by me, does what I have done,
This too familiar care does make me rue it.
    No means I find to rid him from my breast,
    Till by the end of things it be suppressed.

Some gentler passions slide into my mind,
For I am soft and made of melting snow;
Or be more cruel, Love, and so be kind,
Let me or float or sink, be high or low,
    Or let me live with some more sweet content,
    Or die, and so forget what love e'er meant.

JOHN HARRINGTON, the first English poet after queen Elizabeth, was born in 1534, but at what place is unknown. Few incidents of the history of his life have been preserved, farther than that he was imprisoned in the Tower by queen Mary for holding correspondence with Elizabeth, and that the latter, on her accession to the throne, rewarded him with many favors. He died in 1582, in his forty-ninth year. The following brief specimen of Harrington's poetry sufficiently shows that he must have been a man of taste and refined feelings:—

SONNET ON ISABELLA MARKHAM.

Whence comes my love? Oh heart, disclose;
It was from cheeks that shamed the rose,
From lips that spoil the ruby's praise,
From eyes that mock the diamond's blaze:
Whence comes my woe, as freely own;
Ah me! 'twas from a heart like stone.

The blushing cheek speaks modest mind,
The lips befitting words most kind,
The eye does tempt to love's desire,
And seems to say 'tis Cupid's fire;
Yet all so fair but speak my moan,
Sith nought doth say the heart of stone.

Why thus, my love, so kind bespeak
Sweet eye, sweet lip, sweet blushing cheek—
Yet not a heart to save my pain;
Oh Venus, take thy gifts again!
Make not so fair to cause our moan,
Or make a heart that's like our own.

Among the English miscellaneous poets of the age of Elizabeth, who preceded Spenser, Sackville unquestionably holds the first rank.

THOMAS SACKVILLE was of a very ancient family, and was born at Buckhurst, Sussex, in 1536. Having prepared for college at Eton school, he entered the university of Oxford, but sometime after removed to Cambridge, where he remained until he took the degree of master of arts. From Cambridge he passed to the Inner Temple, London, and proceeded so far in the study of the law as to be called to the bar; not, however, with the view of practicing the legal profession, but merely to prepare himself the more effectually to serve his country in parliament, into which he entered toward the close of the reign of Mary.

Sackville had acquired, while at the university, the reputation of a good poet; and in 1557, he formed the design of writing a series of poems under the title of *The Mirror for Magistrates*, the object of which was to exhibit the career of eminently bad men who had come to an unhappy end. Of this poem he executed little more than the *Induction*, or introduction, which was immediately published, and received with unbounded applause. In 1561, he aided Thomas Norton in the composition of *Gorboduc*, the first regular tragedy produced in the English language. This performance we shall, however, have occasion more particularly to notice under the department of dramatic literature.

Having, in this way, succeeded in establishing the reputation of being the best poet of the age, Sackville suddenly abandoned the muses, made the tour of France and Italy, and on his return to England assumed the character of a statesman. He soon became a great favorite with queen Elizabeth, to whom he was distantly related, and by whom he was raised to the peerage under the title of Lord Buckhurst. In 1591, he was, by the queen's special interposition, made chancellor of Oxford, and in 1598, on the death of Lord Burleigh, he succeeded to the treasury, and thus became the queen's recognized prime minister. After the death of Elizabeth he retained the office of lord high treasurer under king James, and was created, by that monarch, on the thirteenth of March, 1604, earl of Dorset. In the height of his power and influence, Sackville was still unremitting in his attention to business, and at his death, which occurred on the nineteenth of April, 1608, he left a universal regret for his departure.

In 'The Mirror for Magistrates,' Sackville, like Dante, and several other poets, lays the scene of his poem in the infernal regions, whither he is conducted under the guide of an allegorical personage named *Sorrow*. It was his object to make all the great persons of English history, from the Conquest downwards, pass here in review, and each tell his own story as a warning to existing statesmen; but other duties compelled the poet, after he had written the 'Induction,' and a legend on the life of the Duke of Buckingham, to leave the completion of the work to the inferior hands of Baldwyne and Ferrers. The part of this poem executed by Sackville frequently exhibits a strength of description, and a power of drawing allogorical characters, scarcely inferior to Spenser. From this poem we extract the following descriptions of its various allegorical characters :—

ALLEGORICAL PERSONAGES IN THE INFERNAL REGIONS.

And first, within the porch and jaws of hell,
  Sat deep Remorse of Conscience, all bespent
With tears; and to herself oft would she tell
  Her wretchedness, and, cursing, never stent
  To sob and sigh, but ever thus lament
With thoughtful care; as she that, all in vain,
Would wear and waste continually in pain.

Her eyes unsteadfast rolling here and there,
  Whirl'd on each place, as place that vengeance brought,
So was her mind continually in fear,
  Tost and tormented with the tedious thought
  Of those detested crimes which she had wrought;
With dreadful cheer, and looks thrown to the sky,
Wishing for death, and yet she could not die.

Next, saw we Dread, all trembling how he shook,
  With foot uncertain, proffer'd here and there;
Benumb'd with speech, and with a ghastly look,
  Searched every place, all pale and dead for fear,
  His cap borne up with staring of his hair;
'Stoin'd and amazed at his own shade for dread,
And fearing greater dangers than was need.

And, next, within the entry of this lake,
  Sat fell Revenge, gnashing her teeth for ire;
Devising means how she may vengeance take;
  Never in rest, till she have her desire;
  But frets within so far forth with the fire
Of wreaking flames, that now determines she
To die by death, or 'veng'd by death to be.

When fell Revenge, with bloody foul pretense,
  Had show'd herself, as next in order set,
With trembling limbs we softly parted thence,
  Till in our eyes another sight we met;
  When fro my heart a sigh forthwith I fet,
Rueing, alas, upon the woful plight
Of Misery, that next appear'd in sight:

His face was lean, and some-deal pin'd away,
  And eke his hands consumed to the bone;
But, what his body was, I can not say,
  For, on his carcass raiment had he none,
  Save clouts and patches pieced one by one;
With staff in hand, and scrip on shoulders cast,
His chief defense against the winter's blast:

His food, for most, was wild fruits of the tree,
  Unless sometime some crumbs fell to his share,

Which in his wallet long, Got wot, kept he,
  As on the*which full daintily would he fare;
  His drink, the running stream; his cup, the bare
Of his palm closed; his bed, the hard cold ground:
To this poor life was Misery y-bound.

Whose wretched state when we had well beheld,
  With tender ruth on him, and on his fears,
In thoughtful cares forth then our pace we held;
  And, by and by, another shape appears
  Of greedy Care, still brushing up the briers;
His knuckles knob'd, his flesh deep dinted in
With tawed hands, and hard y-tanned skin:

The morrow gray no sooner had begun
  To spread his light e'en peeping in our eyes,
But he is up, and to his work y-run;
  But let the night's black misty mantles rise,
  And with foul dark never so much disguise
The fair bright day, yet ceaseth he no while,
But hath his candles to prolong his toil.

By him lay heavy Sleep, the cousin of Death,
  Flat on the ground, and still as any stone,
A very corpse, save yielding forth a breath,
  Small keep took he, whom fortune frowned on,
  Or whom she lifted up into the throne
Of high renown; but as a living death,
So dead alive, of life he drew the breath:

* * * * * *

And next in order sad, Old Age we found:
  His beard all hoar, his eyes hollow and blind;
With drooping cheer still poring on the ground,
  As on the place where nature him assign'd
  To rest, when that the sisters had untwined
His vital thread, and ended with their knife
The fleeting course of fast declining life.

There heard we him with broke and hollow plaint
  Rue with himself his end approaching fast,
And all for nought, his wretched mind torment
  With sweet remembrance of his pleasures past.
  And fresh delights of lusty youth forewaste;
Recounting which, how would he sob and shriek,
And to be young again of Jove beseek!

* * * * * *

Crook-back'd he was, tooth-shaken, and blear-eyed;
  Went on three feet, and sometime crept on four;
With old lame bones, that rattled by his side;
  His scalp all piled, and he with eld forelore,
  His wither'd fist still knocking at death's door;
Fumbling, and drivelling, as he draws his breath;
For brief, the shape and messenger of Death.

And fast by him pale Malady was placed:
  Sore sick in bed, her colour all foregone;

Bereft of stomach, savor, and of taste.
  Ne could she brook no meat but broths alone;
  Her breath corrupt; her keepers every one
Abhorring her; her sickness past recure,
Detesting physic, and all physic's cure.

But oh, the doleful sight that then we see!
  We turn'd our look, and on the other side
A grisly shape of Famine mought we see:
  With greedy looks, and gasping mouth, that cried
  And roar'd for meat, as she should there have died;
Her body thin and bare as any bone,
Whereto was left nought but the case alone.

And that, alas, was gnawen every where,
  All full of holes; that I me nought refrain
From tears, to see how she her arms could tear,
  And with her teeth gnash on the bones in vain,
  When, all for nought, she fain would so sustain
Her starven corpse, that rather seem'd a shade
Than any substance of a creature made:

Great was her force whom stone wall could not stay:
  Her tearing nails snatching at all she saw;
With gaping jaws, that by no means ymay
  Be satisfied from hunger of her maw,
  But eats herself as she that hath no law;
Gnawing, alas, her carcass all in vain,
Where you may count each sinew, bone, and vein.

* * * * * * *

Lastly, stood War, in glittering arms yclad,
  With visage grim, stern look, and blackly hued:
In his right hand a naked sword he had,
  That to the hilts was all with blood imbued;
  And in his left (that kings and kingdoms rued)
Famine and fire he held, and therewithal
He razed towns and threw down towers and all:

Cities he sack'd, and realms that (whilom flower'd
  In honour, glory, and rule, above the rest)
He overwhelm'd, and all their fame devour'd,
  Consum'd, destroy'd, wasted, and never ceas'd,
  Till he their wealth, their name, and all oppress'd:
His face forehew'd with wounds; and by his side
There hung his targe, with gashes deep and wide.

Sir Philip Sidney and Sir Walter Raleigh deserve a passing notice among the early poets of Elizabeth's reign, though it is chiefly for their compositions in prose that their memories are cherished. The former has left us a few *Sonnets*, delicate in sentiment, and sweet and flowing in expression, of which the following are specimens:—

Because I oft in dark abstracted guise
Seem most alone in greatest company,
With dearth of words, or answers quite awry
To them that would make speech of speech arise,
They deem, and of their doom the rumour flies,

That poison foul of bubbling Pride doth lie
So in my swelling breast, that only I
Fawn on myself, and others do despise.
Yet Pride, I think, doth not my soul possess,
Which looks too oft in his unflattering glass;
But one worst fault Ambition I confess,
That makes me oft my best friends overpass,
Unseen, unheard, while thought to highest place
Bends all his powers, even unto Stella's grace.

Come, Sleep, O Sleep, the certain knot of peace,
The baiting place of wit, the balm of woe,
The poor man's wealth, the prisoner's release,
The indifferent judge between the high and low
With shield of proof shield me from out the prease[1]
Of those fierce darts, Despair at me doth throw;
O make in me those civil wars to cease:
I will good tribute pay, if thou do so.
Take thou of me smooth pillows, sweetest bed;
A chamber, deaf to noise, and blind to light;
A rosy garland, and a weary head.
And if these things as being thine by right,
Move not thy heavy grace, thou shalt in me
Livelier than elsewhere, Stella's image see.

O happy Thames, that didst my Stella bear!
I saw thee with full many a smiling line
Upon thy cheerful face joy's livery wear,
While those fair planets on thy streams did shine.
The boat for joy could not to dance forbear;
While wanton winds, with beauties so divine
Ravish'd, staid not, till in her golden hair
They did themselves (O sweetest prison) twine:
And fain those Œols' youths there would their stay
Have made; but, forced by nature still to fly,
First did with puffing kiss those locks display.
She, so dishevell'd, blush'd. From window I,
With sight thereof, cried out, 'O fair disgrace;
Let Honour's self to thee grant highest place.'

Sir Walter Raleigh wrote comparatively little poetry, but that which we have is sufficient to satisfy us that had he courted the poetic muse exclusively, he would have attained to a very high degree of celebrity. The following extracts from a poem under the title of *The Country's Recreations* breathe a melancholy tenderness that poetic feeling alone could inspire:—

Heart-tearing cares and quiv'ring fears,
Anxious sighs, untimely tears,
  Fly, fly to courts,
  Fly to fond worldling's sports;
Where strained sardonic smiles are glozing still,
And grief is forced to laugh against her will;

[1] Press, throng.

Where mirth's but mummery,
And sorrows only real be.

Fly from our country pastimes, fly,
Sad troop of human misery!
Come, serene looks,
Clear as the crystal brooks,
Or the pure azur'd heaven that smiles to see
The rich attendance of our poverty.
Peace and a secure mind,
Which all men seek, we only find.

Abused mortals, did you know
Where joy, heart's ease, and comforts grow,
You'd scorn proud towers,
And seek them in those bowers
Where winds perhaps our woods may sometimes shake,
But blustering care could never tempest make,
Nor murmurs e'er come nigh us,
Saving of fountains that glide by us.

* * * * * *

Blest silent groves! O may ye be
Forever mirth's best nursery!
May pure contents
Forever pitch their tents
Upon these downs, these meads, these rocks, these mountains,
And peace still slumber by these purling fountains,
Which we may every year
Find when we come a-fishing here.

To the preceding extract from 'The Country's Recreations' we shall add Sir Walter Raleigh's response to *The Passionate Shepherd* of Christopher Marlow. The author of the latter poem will occupy so conspicuous a place in our remarks upon the dramatic writers of the age at present under consideration, that no farther notice of him is here required. The poem itself, and the response to it both, richly deserve the great popularity which they have, for more than two and a half centuries, enjoyed:—

THE PASSIONATE SHEPHERD TO HIS LOVE.—MARLOW.

Come live with me, and be my love,
And we will all the pleasures prove
That valleys, groves, and hills and fields,
Woods or steepy mountains yields.

And we will sit upon the rocks,
Seeing the shepherds feed their flocks,
By shallow rivers, to whose falls
Melodious birds sing madrigals.

And I will make thee beds of roses,
And a thousand fragrant posies;
A cap of flowers and a kirtle
Embroider'd all with leaves of myrtle:

A gown made of the finest wool,
Which from our pretty lambs we pull;
Fair lined slippers for the cold,
With buckles of the purest gold:

A belt of straw and ivy buds
With coral clasps and amber studs!
And if these pleasures may thee move,
Come live with me and be my love.

The shepherd swains shall dance and sing,
For thy delight each May-morning;
If these delights thy mind may move,
Then live with me and be my love.

THE NYMPH'S REPLY TO THE PASSIONATE SHEPHERD.—Raleigh

If all the world and love were young,
And truth in every shepherd's tongue,
These pretty pleasures might one move
To live with thee and be thy love.

Time drives the flocks from field to fold,
When rivers rage and rocks grow cold;
And Philomel becometh dumb,
The rest complain of cares to come.

The flowers do fade, and wanton fields
To wayward winter reckoning yields;
A honey tongue—a heart of gall,
Is fancy's spring, but sorrow's fall.

Thy gowns, thy shoes, thy beds of roses,
Thy cap, thy kirtle, and thy posies,
Soon break, soon wither, soon forgotten.
In folly ripe, in reason rotten.

Thy belt of straw and ivy buds,
Thy coral clasps and amber studs;
All these in me no means can move
To come to thee and be thy love.

But could youth last, and love still breed,
Had joys no date, nor age no need,
Then these delights my mind might move
To live with thee and be thy love.

Sidney, Raleigh, and Marlow, had for their contemporaries Breton, Constable, Sylvester, and Barnfield, all of whom justly rank among the second rate miscellaneous poets of this period, though the number of their poems was generally limited.

Nicholas Breton was born in 1555, but at what place we have not been able to ascertain. Indeed, of his entire history no particulars have been preserved farther than that he first acquired very considerable popularity as a writer of pastorals, and then published a volume of poems under the title of *The Works of a Young Wit.* Breton died in 1624, in his seventieth year. The following stanzas from this author well deserve preservation:

FAREWELL TO TOWN.

* * * * * *

Thou gallant court, to thee farewell!
For froward fortune me denies
Now longer near to thee to dwell.
I must go live, I wot not where,
Nor how to live when I come there.

And next, adieu you gallant dames,
The chief of noble youth's delight.
Untoward Fortune now so frames,
That I am banish'd from your sight.
And, in your stead, against my will,
I must go live with country Jill.

Now next, my gallant youths, farewell;
My lads that oft have cheered my heart!
My grief of mind no tongue can tell,
To think that I must from you part.
I now must leave you all, alas,
And live with some old lobcock ass!

And now farewell thou gallant lute,
With instruments of music's sounds!
Recorder, citern, harp, and flute,
And heavenly descants on sweet grounds.
I now must leave you all, indeed,
And make some music on a reed!

And now, you stately stamping steeds,
And gallant geldings fair, adieu.
My heavy heart for sorrow bleeds,
To think that I must part with you:
And on a strawen pannel sit,
And ride some country carting tit!

And now farewell both spear and shield,
Caliver, pistol, arquebuss,
See, see, what sighs my heart doth yield
To think that I must leave you thus;
And lay aside my rapier blade,
And take in hand a ditching spade!

And you farewell, all gallant games,
Primero and *Imperial*,
Wherewith I us'd with courtly dames
To pass away the time withal:
I now must learn some country plays
For ale and cakes on holydays.

And now farewell each dainty dish,
With sundry sorts of sugar'd wine!
Farewell I say, fine flesh and fish,
To please this dainty mouth of mine!

I now, alas, must leave all these,
And make good cheer with bread and cheese!

And now, all orders due, farewell!
  My table laid when it was noon;
My heavy heart it irks to tell
  My dainty dinners are all done;
With leeks and onions, whig and whey,
I must content me as I may.

And farewell all gay garments now,
  With jewels rich of rare device!
Like Robin Hood, I wot not how,
  I must go range in woodman's wise;
Clad in a coat of green or gray,
And glad to get it if I may.

What shall I say, but bid adieu
  To every dream of sweet delight,
In place where pleasure never grew
  In dungeon deep of foul despite.
I must, ah me! wretch as I may,
Go sing the song of welaway!

Of Henry Constable less even is known than of Breton. He was a very popular writer of sonnets, though his sentiments are usually strained and conceited. But in the midst of his affectations and conceits, many happy thoughts and much beautiful imagery may be found. The following sonnet from his *Diana* contains much epigrammatic power :—

To live in hell, and heaven to behold,
To welcome life, and die a living death,
To sweat with heat, and yet be freezing cold,
To grasp at stars, and lie the earth beneath,
To tread a maze that never shall have end,
To burn in sighs, and starve in daily tears,
To climb a hill, and never to descend,
Giants to kill, and quake at childish fears,
To pine for food, and watch the Hesperian tree,
To thirst for drink, and nectar still to draw,
To live accurs'd, whom men hold blest to be,
And weep those wrongs, which never creature saw;
If this be love, if love in these be founded,
My heart is love, for these in it are grounded.

Joshua Sylvester was born in 1563. He was bred to ordinary mercantile pursuits, but the delicacy of his wit eventually brought him into notice, and he was patronized both by Elizabeth and James. For some cause, not now known, he was obliged to leave England, and he soon after died in Holland, on the twenty-eighth of September, 1618. Sylvester was the author of the following impressive poem, long attributed to Sir Walter Raleigh :—

THE SOUL'S ERRAND.

Go, soul, the body's guest,
  Upon a thankless errand!
Fear not to touch the best,
  The truth shall be thy warrant;
    Go, since I needs must die,
    And give the world the lie.

Go, tell the court it glows,
  And shines like rotten wood;
Go, tell the church it shows
  What's good, and doth no good:
    If church and court reply,
    Then give them both the lie.

Tell potentates, they live
  Acting by others' actions,
Not loved unless they give,
  Not strong but by their factions.
    If potentates reply,
    Give potentates the lie.

Tell men of high condition
  That rule affairs of state,
Their purpose is ambition,
  Their practice only hate.
    And if they once reply,
    Then give them all the lie.

Tell them that brave the most,
  They beg for more by spending,
Who in their greatest cost,
  Seek nothing but commending.
    And if they make reply,
    Then give them all the lie.

Tell zeal it lacks devotion,
  Tell love it is but lust,
Tell time it is but motion,
  Tell flesh it is but dust;
    And wish them not reply,
    For thou must give the lie.

Tell age it daily wasteth,
  Tell honour how it alters,
Tell beauty how she blasteth,
  Tell favour how she falters.
    And as they shall reply,
    Give every one the lie.

Tell wit how much it wrangles,
  In tickle points of niceness:
Tell wisdom she entangles
  Herself in over-wiseness.
    And when they do reply,
    Straight give them both the lie.

Tell physic of her boldness,
Tell skill it is pretension,
Tell charity of coldness,
Tell law it is contention.
And as they do reply,
So give them still the lie.

Tell fortune of the blindness,
Tell nature of decay,
Tell friendship of unkindness
Tell justice of delay.
And if they will reply,
Then give them all the lie.

Tell arts they have no soundness,
But vary by esteeming,
Tell schools they want profoundness
And stand too much on seeming,
If arts and schools reply,
Give arts and schools the lie.

Tell faith it's fled the city,
Tell how the country erreth,
Tell, manhood shakes off pity,
Tell, virtue least preferreth.
And if they do reply,
Spare not to give the lie.

So then thou hast, as I
Commanded thee, done babbling:
Although to give the lie
Deserves no less than stabbing;
Yet stab at thee who will
No stab the soul can kill.

RICHARD BARNFIELD was the author of a volume of poems of very unequal merit, published between 1594 and 1598. Among these poems, however, is found the following *Address to the Nightingale*, which is of so rare excellence, that it was, for a long time, ascribed to Shakspeare.

ADDRESS TO THE NIGHTINGALE.

As it fell upon a day,
In the merry month of May,
Sitting in a pleasant shade
Which a grove of myrtles made;
Beasts did leap and birds did sing,
Trees did grow, and plants did spring;
Every thing did banish moan,
Save the Nightingale alone.
She, poor bird, as all forlorn,
Lean'd her breast up-till a thorn;
And there sung the dolefull'st ditty,
That to hear it was great pity.
Fie, fie, fie, now would she cry;
Teru, teru, by and by;

That, to hear her so complain,
Scarce I could from tears refrain;
For her griefs so lively shown,
Made me think upon mine own.
Ah! (thought I,) thou mourn'st in vain;
None takes pity in thy pain:
Senseless trees they can not hear thee,
Ruthless bears they will not cheer thee:
King Pandion he is dead;
All thy friends are lapp'd in lead;
All thy fellow-birds do sing,
Careless of thy sorrowing!
While as fickle Fortune smil'd,
Thou and I were both beguil'd.
Every one that flatters thee
Is no friend in misery.
Words are easy, like the wind;
Faithful friends are hard to find.
Every man will be thy friend
While thou hast wherewith to spend:
But, if store of crowns be scant.
No man will supply thy want.
If that one be prodigal,
Bountiful they will him call;
And with such like flattering,
'Pity but he were a king.'
If he be addict to vice,
Quickly him they will entice;
But if fortune once do frown,
Then farewell his great renown:
They that fawn'd on him before
Use his company no more.
He that is thy friend indeed,
He will help thee in thy need;
If thou sorrow, he will weep,
If thou wake he can not sleep:
Thus of every grief in heart
He with thee doth bear a part.
These are certain signs to know,
Faithful friend from flattering foe.

It must be remembered, that this was the age when collections of fugitive and miscellaneous poems first became common in England. Several volumes of this kind, published in the reign of Elizabeth, contain poems of high merit without any author's name attached to them; and, therefore, it is not remarkable that the last two poems introduced, should have been so long attributed to Raleigh and Shakspeare.

The miscellaneous poets of the reign of Elizabeth thus far noticed, bring us down to Spenser, whose genius is one of the peculiar glories of that romantic age.

Edmund Spenser was of an ancient though poor family, and was born in the city of London, in 1553. From the circumstances of his parents it is difficult to conjecture how he obtained his preparation for admission into the university; but it is certain that in May, 1569, he entered Pembroke College, Cambridge, as a charity student, and there continued until 1576, when he took his master's degree. His design evidently was to remain permanently attached to the university, and with this view, immediately after he was graduated, he made every effort that his limited resources would permit, to obtain a fellowship. But having neither friends nor influential patrons to make interest for him, he was disappointed in this important object, in consequence of which he accepted an invitation from some distant relatives in the north of England, to take up his residence with them until his future prospects should, in some degree, become determined.

While residing in the North, Spenser formed an attachment for a young lady whom he designates as *Rosalind*, and whose attractive beauty and graces first inspired his muse. To win her favor he composed his *Shepherd's Calender*, a pastoral poem, in twelve eclogues, one for each month, but without strict *keeping* as to natural description and rustic character, and deformed by a number of obsolete uncouth phrases; yet containing traces of a superior original genius. The fable of the *Oak and Brier* is finely told; and in verses like the following we see the germ of that tuneful harmony and pensive reflection in which the author afterward so remarkably excelled:—

> You naked buds, whose shady leaves are lost,
> Wherein the birds were wont to build their bower,
> And now are clothed with moss and hoary frost,
> Instead of blossoms wherewith your buds did flower:
> I see your tears that from your boughs do rain,
> Whose drops in dreary icicles remain.
>
> All so my lustful life is dry and sere,
> My timely buds with wailing all are wasted;
> The blossom which my branch of youth did bear,
> With breathed sighs is blown away and blasted,
> And from mine eyes the drizzling tears descend,
> As on your boughs the icicles depend.

The fair Rosalind, however, preferred a less poetical rival, and Spenser soon after left the country and repaired to London, there to seek his fortune in the midst of the more busy scenes of life. To this step he was induced by Gabriel Harvey, a fellow-student at Cambridge, and by whom he was introduced to Sir Philip Sidney, 'one of the very diamonds of her majesty's court.' Sir Philip being himself a man of wit and polite accomplishments, immediately became sensible of Spenser's merit, and so long as that nobleman remained at court, the poet never wanted a judicious friend, nor a generous patron. In gratitude for Sidney's kindness, Spenser now revised and published the 'Shepherd's Calender,' with an appropriate dedication to him.

The 'Shepherd's Calender' appeared in 1579, and such was its popularity that even royalty itself smiled upon its author, and Spenser was raised to the *Laureate.* This, however, he soon found to be but an empty honor, and he was accordingly left, for some years, to pine over his penury and neglect, though in constant attendance at court. While thus circumstanced he composed and published *Mother Hubbard's Tale*, which appeared in 1581, and which contains the following picture of the aggravations attending the life of disappointment and mortification which he then led:—

Full little knowest thou that hast not tried,
What hell it is in suing long to bide;
To lose good days that might be better spent;
To waste long nights in pensive discontent;
To speed to-day, to be put back to-morrow;
To feed on hope, to pine with fear and sorrow;
To have thy prince's grace, yet want her peers';
To have thy asking, yet wait many years;
To fret thy soul with crosses and with cares;
To eat thy heart through comfortless despairs;
To fawn, to crouch, to wait, to ride, to run,
To spend, to give, to wait, to be undone!

Spenser was, however, during this period, occasionally employed on inferior state missions, and thus his immediate necessities were supplied; but at length he received an important and lucrative appointment. Lord Grey of Wilton was sent to Ireland as lord-deputy, and Spenser accompanied him in the capacity of secretary. They remained in that country two years, when the deputy was recalled, and the poet also returned to England. In June, 1586, Spenser obtained, from the crown, three thousand and twenty-eight acres in the county of Cork, out of the forfeited lands of the Earl of Desmond. One of the conditions of the grant was, that the poet should reside upon his estate, and he accordingly repaired to Ireland, and took up his abode in Kilcolman Castle, near Doneraile, which had been one of the ancient strongholds of the Earl of Desmond. Spenser's castle stood in the midst of a large plain, by the side of a lake; the river Mulla ran through his grounds, and a chain of mountains at a distance seemed to bulwark in the romantic retreat. To this castle he introduced, soon after it was repaired, the 'Elizabeth' of his sonnets, as its future mistress, and welcomed her with that noble strain of pure and fervent passion, which he has styled the *Epithalamium*, and which forms the most magnificent 'spousal verse' in the language. The following passages from this gem of poetry, show that the poem itself needs no farther comment:—

Wake now, my love, awake; for it is time;
The rosy morn long since left Tithon's bed,
All ready to her silver coach to climb;
And Phœbus 'gins to show his glorious head.
Hark! now the cheerful birds do chant their lays,
And carol of Love's praise.
The merry lark her matins sings aloft;
The thrush replies; the marvis descant plays;
The ouzel shrills; the ruddock warbles soft;

So goodly all agree, with sweet consent,
To this day's merriment.
Ah! my dear love, why do you sleep thus long,
When meeter were that you should now awake,
T' await the coming of your joyous make,
And hearken to the birds' love-learned song,
The dewy leaves among!
For they of joy and pleasance to you sing,
That all the woods them answer and their echo ring.

My love is now awake out of her dream,
And her fair eyes, like stars that dimmed were
With darksome cloud, now show their goodly beams
More bright than Hesperus his head doth rear.
Come now, ye damsels, daughters of delight,
Help quickly her to dight;
But first come, ye fair Hours, which were begot,
In Jove's sweet paradise, of Day and Night;
Which do the seasons of the year allot,
And all, that ever in this world is fair,
Do make and still repair;
And ye three handmaids of the Cyprian Queen,
The which do still adorn her beauties' pride,
Help to adorn my beautifullest bride:
And, as ye her array, still throw between
Some graces to be seen;
And as ye use to Venus, to her sing,
The whiles the woods shall answer, and your echo ring.

* * * * * * * *

Open the temple gates unto my love,
Open them wide that she may enter in,
And all the posts adorn as doth behove,
And all the pillars deck with garlands trim,
For to receive this saint with honour due,
That cometh in to you
With trembling steps, and humble reverence,
She cometh in, before the Almighty's view:
Of her, ye virgins, learn obedience,
When so ye come into those holy places,
To humble your proud faces:
Bring her up to the high altar, that she may,
The sacred ceremonies there partake,
The which do endless matrimony make;
And let the roaring organs loudly play
The praises of the Lord in lively notes;
The whiles, with hollow throats,
The choristers the joyous anthem sing,
That all the woods may answer, and their echo ring.

Behold, while she before the altar stands,
Hearing the holy priest that to her speaks,
And blesseth her with his two happy hands,
How the red roses flush up in her cheeks,
And the pure snow, with goodly vermeil stain,
Like crimson dyed in grain;

That even the angels, which continually
About the sacred altar do remain,
Forget their service and about her fly,
Oft peeping on her face, that seems more fair,
The more they on it stare.
But her sad eyes, still fastened on the ground,
Are governed with goodly modesty,
That suffers not a look to glance awry,
Which may let in a little thought unsound.
Why blush you, love, to give to me your hand,
The pledge of all our band?
Sing, ye sweet angels, alleluya sing
That all the woods may answer, and your echo ring.

Kilcolman Castle is now a ruin, but the spot must ever remain dear to every lover of genius. It was there that Spenser wrote the *Faery Queen*, and there also he received the visit of Sir Walter Raleigh, in 1589, when, in the figurative language of the poet himself, the two illustrious friends, while reading the manuscript of that poem, sat

Amongst the coolly shade,
Of the green alders, by the Mulla's shore.

We may easily conceive the transports of delight with which Raleigh listened to those strains of chivalry and gorgeous description, which revealed to him a land still brighter than any that he had seen in his distant wanderings, or could have been present even to his own romantic imagination. When Raleigh left Kilcolman Castle to return to England, he persuaded Spenser to accompany him thither, that the poem might be published without unnecessary delay. The first, the second, and the third books of the 'Faery Queen,' accordingly, appeared in January, 1590, and was dedicated to the Queen in that strain of adulation which was the fashion of the age. Elizabeth was so much pleased with the work, that she settled upon the author an annual pension of fifty pounds, and Spenser returned to Ireland to complete his great design. The original plan of the Faery Queen embraced twelve books, and in 1596, Spenser having completed the fourth, the fifth, and the sixth, again visited London for the purpose of superintending their publication. The remaining six books, it is not probable, were ever written, though the story was long rife that they were committed, by the author, to the care of a servant to convey them to his publishers in London, and were, through carelessness, lost on the way.

At the time of the publication of the second part of the 'Faery Queen,' Spenser had resided in Ireland ten years, and during the whole of that period the Irish people had been very restive under English oppression. Rebellion after rebellion succeeding each other, the spirit of revolt finally reached Munster. The insurgents attacked Kilcolman, and having first robbed and plundered the castle, then set fire to it. Spenser and his wife escaped; but either in the confusion incident to such a calamity, or from inability to render assistance, an infant child of the poet was left behind, and perished in the flames. The poet himself, impoverished and broken-hearted, reached London, and died three months after, on the sixteenth of January, 1599, in the forty-seventh year of his age. He was buried in Westminster Abbey, near the tomb of Chaucer, and thirty years after his death, a monument was erected over his remains, by the Countess of Dorset.

The genius of Spenser was such as to place him in the very first class of English poets. In his great performance, the 'Faery Queen,' his creations are infinite, and in free and sonorous versification, he has rarely been surpassed. His lofty rhyme has a swell and cadence, and a continuous sweetness in it, that we in vain look for in any other poet. In luxuriant description also, and in richness of fancy and invention, he has scarcely ever been equalled. With all these great excellencies, however, Spenser is not without his faults, though these may be said to have arisen out of the very fullness of his riches. His inexhaustible power of circumstantial description, betrayed him into a minuteness which sometimes, in the delineation of his personified passions, becomes repulsive, and in the painting of natural objects, led him to group together trees and plants, and assemble sounds and instruments which were never seen or heard in unison out of *Faery Land*. His command of musical language also induced him to protract his narrative to so great a length, that the attention becomes exhausted even with its very melody. Had he, therefore, lived to finish his great poem it is doubtful whether he would not have diminished the number of his readers. His own fancy had evidently begun to give away; for the last three books have not the same unity of design, or plenitude of imagination, which fills the earlier cantos with so many interesting, lofty, and ethereal conceptions, and steeps them in such a flood of ideal and poetical beauty. But notwithstanding the lengthened allegory may sometimes fatigue us, yet the general impression remains: we can never think of the 'Faery Queen' without recalling its wondrous scenes of enchantment and beauty, and feeling ourselves lulled, as it were, by the recollected music of the poet's verse, and the endless flow and profusion of his fancy. It remains only for us to select from this poem a few passages illustrative of these remarks, and with this view we present the following:—

UNA AND THE RED-CROSS KNIGHT.

A gentle knight was pricking on the plain,
Y-clad in mighty arms and silver shield,
Wherein old dints of deep wounds did remain,
The cruel marks of many a bloody field;
Yet arms till that time did he never wield:
His angry steed did chide his foaming bit,
As much disdaining to the curb to yield:
Full jolly knight he seem'd, and fair did sit,
As one for knightly jousts and fierce encounters fit.

And on his breast a bloody cross he bore,
The dear remembrance of his dying Lord.

For whose sweet sake that glorious badge he wore,
And dead (as living) ever him adored:
Upon his shield the like was also scored,
For sovereign hope, which in his help he had:
Right faithful true he was in deed and word;
But of his cheer did seem too solemn sad:
Yet nothing did he dread, but ever was ydrad.

Upon a great adventure he was bound,
That greatest Gloriana to him gave,
(That greatest glorious queen of fairy lond,)
To win him worship, and her grace to have,
Which of all earthly things he most did crave;
And ever as he rode his heart did yearn
To prove his puissance in battle brave
Upon his foe, and his new force to learn;
Upon his foe, a dragon horrible and stern.

A lovely lady rode him fair beside,
Upon a lowly ass more white than snow;
Yet she much whiter, but the same did hide
Under a veil that wimpled was full low,
And over all a black stole she did throw,
As one that inly mourn'd: so was she sad,
And heavy sat upon her palfrey slow;
Seemed in heart some hidden care she had,
And by her in a line a milk-white lamb she led.

So pure and innocent, as that same lamb,
She was in life and every virtuous lore,
And by descent from royal lineage came
Of ancient kings and queens, that had of yore
Their sceptres stretcht from east to western shore,
And all the world in their subjection held;
Till that infernal fiend with foul uproar
Forewasted all their land, and them expell'd:
Whom to avenge, she had this knight from far compell'd.

Behind her far away a dwarf did lag,
That lazy seem'd in being ever last,
Or wearied with bearing of her bag
Of needments at his back. Thus as they past
The day with clouds was sudden overcast,
And angry Jove an hideous storm of rain
Did pour into his leman's lap so fast,
That every wight to shroud it did constrain,
And this fair couple eke to shroud themselves were fain.

Enforced to seek some covert nigh at hand,
A shady grove not far away they spied,
That promised aid the tempest to withstand;
Whose lofty trees, yclad with summer's pride,
Did spread so broad, that heaven's light did hide,
Nor pierceable with power of any star:
And all within were paths and alleys wide,
With footing worn, and leading inward far:
Fair harbour, that them seems; so in they entered are.

And forth they pass, with pleasure forward led,
Joying to hear the bird's sweet harmony,
Which therein shrouded from the tempest dread,
Seem'd in their song to scorn the cruel sky.
Much can they praise the trees so straight and high,
The sailing Pine, the Cedar proud and tall,
The vine-prop Elm, the Poplar never dry,
The builder Oak, sole king of forests all,
The Aspen good for staves, the Cypress funeral.

The Laurel, meed of mighty conquerors
And poets sage, the Fir that weepeth still,
The Willow, worn of forlorn paramours,
The Yew obedient to the bender's will,
The Birch for shafts, the Sallow for the mill,
The Myrrh sweet bleeding in the bitter wound,
The warlike Beech, the Ash for nothing ill,
The fruitful Olive, and the Plantain round,
The carver Holme, the Maple seldom inward sound;

Led with delight, they thus beguile the way,
Until the blustering storm is overblown,
When, weening to return, whence they did stray,
They can not find that path which first was shown,
But wander to and fro in ways unknown,
Furthest from end then, when they nearest ween,
That makes them doubt their wits be not their own:
So many paths, so many turnings seem,
That which of them to take, in divers doubt they been.

ADVENTURE OF UNA WITH THE LION.

Yet she, most faithful lady, all this while
Forsaken, woful, solitary maid,
Far from all people's prease, as in exile,
In wilderness and wasteful deserts strayed,
To seek her knight; who subtilly betrayed
Through that late vision which th' enchanter wrought,
Had her abandoned; she of naught afraid
Through woods and wasteness wide him daily sought;
Yet wished tidings none of him unto her brought.

One day nigh weary of the irksome way,
From her unhasty beast she did alight;
And on the grass her dainty limbs did lay,
In secret shadow, far from all men's sight;
From her fair head her fillet she undight,
And laid her stole aside; her angel's face
As the great eye of Heaven, shined bright
And made a sunshine in the shady place;
Did never mortal eye behold such heavenly grace.

It fortuned, out of the thicket wood
A ramping lion rushed suddenly,
Hunting full greedy after savage blood:
Soon as the royal virgin he did spy,

With gaping mouth at her ran greedily,
To have at once devour'd her tender corse:
But to the prey when as he drew more nigh,
His bloody rage assuaged with remorse,
And with the sight amazed forgat his furious force.

Instead thereof he kiss'd her weary feet,
And lick'd her lily hands with fawning tongue;
As he her wronged innocence did weet.
O how can beauty master the most strong,
And simple truth subdue avenging wrong!
Whose yielded pride and proud submission,
Still dreading death, when she had mark'd long,
Her heart 'gan melt in great compassion,
And drizzling tears did shed for pure affection.

The lion, lord of every beast in field,'
Quoth she, 'his princely puissance doth abate,
And mighty proud to humble weak does yield,
Forgetful of the hungry rage, which late
Him prick'd, in pity of my sad estate:
But he, my lion, and my noble lord
How does he find in cruel heart to hate
Her that him loved, and ever most adored,
As the God of my life! why hath he me abhorred?'

Redounding tears did choke th' end of her plaint,
Which softly echoed from the neighbour wood;
And, sad to see her sorrowful constraint,
The kingly beast upon her gazing stood:
With pity calm'd down fell his angry mood.
At last, in close heart shutting up her pain,
Arose the virgin born of heav'nly brood,
And to her snowy palfry got again,
To seek her strayed champion if she might attain.

The lion would not leave her desolate,
But with her went along, as a strong guard
Of her chaste person, and a faithful mate
Of her sad troubles and misfortunes hard:
Still when she slept, he keep both watch and ward;
And when she waked, he waited diligent,
With humble service to her will prepared;
From her fair eyes he took commandèment,
And ever by her looks conceived her intent.

THE BOWER OF BLISS.

There the most dainty paradise on ground
Itself doth offer to his sober eye,
In which all pleasures plenteously abound.
And none does other's happiness envy;
The painted flowers, the trees upshooting high,
The dales for shade, the hills for breathing space,
The trembling groves, the crystal running by;
And that which all fair works doth most aggrace
The art, which all that wrought, appeared in no plac

One would have thought (so cunningly the rude
And scorned parts were mingled with the fine)
That nature had for wantonness ensued
Art, and that art at nature did repine;
So striving each th' other to undermine,
Each did the other's work more beautify;
So differing both in wills, agreed in fine:
So all agreed through sweet diversity,
This garden to adorn with all variety.

And in the midst of all a fountain stood
Of richest substance that on earth might be
So pure and shiny, that the silver flood
Through every channel running one might see;
Most goodly it with curious imagery
Was overwrought, and shapes of naked boys,
Of which some seem'd with lively jollity
To fly about, playing their wanton toys,
While others did embaye themselves in liquid joys.

And over all, of purest gold was spread
A trail of ivy in his native hue:
For the rich metal was so coloured,
That wight, who did not well advis'd it view,
Would surely deem it to be ivy true:
Low his lascivious arms adown did creep,
That themselves dipping in the silver dew,
Their fleecy flowers they fearfully did steep,
Which drops of crystal seem'd for wantonness to weep.

Infinite streams continually did well
Out of this fountain, sweet and fair to see,
The which into an ample laver fell,
And shortly grew to be so great quantity,
That like a little lake it seem'd to be;
Whose depths exceeded not three cubits height,
That through the waves one might the bottom see,
All pav'd beneath with jasper shining bright,
That seem'd the fountain in that sea that did sail upright.

And all the margin round about was set
With shady laurel trees, thence to defend
The sunny beams, which in the billows beat,
And those which therein bathed might offend.

* * * * * * *

Eftsoons they heard a most melodious sound,
Of all that might delight a dainty ear,
Such as at once might not on living ground,
Save in this paradise, be heard elsewhere:
Right hard it was for wight which did it hear,
To read what manner music that might be:
For all that pleasing is to living ear,
Was there consorted in one harmony:
Birds, voices, instruments, winds, waters, all agree.

The joyous birds, shrouded in cheerful shade,
Their notes unto the voice attemper'd sweet;

Th' angelical soft trembling voices made
To th' instruments divine respondence meet
The silver sounding instruments did meet,
With the base murmur of the water's fall;
The water's fall with difference discreet,
Now soft, now loud, unto the wind did call:
The gentle warbling wind low answered to all.

The while, some one did chant this lovely lay;
Ah see, whoso fair thing thou dost fain to see,
In springing flower the image of thy day;
Ah see the virgin rose, how sweetly she
Doth first peep forth with bashful modesty,
That fairer seems, the less ye see her may;
Lo, see soon after, how more bold and free
Her bared bosom she doth broad display;
Lo, see soon after, how she fades and falls away

So presseth, in the passing of a day,
Of mortal life, the leaf, the bud, the flower,
No more doth flourish after first decay,
That erst was sought to deck both bed and bower
Of many a lady, and many a paramour;
Gather, therefore, the rose, while yet is prime,
For soon comes age, that will her pride deflower:
Gather the rose of love, while yet is time,
While loving thou mayst loved be with equal crime.'

To the preceding extracts from the 'Fairy Queen,' which we have given in a modernized spelling, we shall add the following highly poetical description, in the poet's own orthography.

DESCRIPTION OF BELPHŒBE.

In her faire eyes two living lamps did flame,
Kindled above at th' heavenly Maker's light,
And darted fyrie beames out of the same,
So passing persant, and so wondrous bright,
That quite bereav'd the rash beholder's sight:
In them the blinded God his lustfull fyre
To kindle oft assayd, but had no might;
For, with dredd majestie and awfull yre,
She broke his wanton darts, and quenched base desyre.

Her yvorie forhead, full of bountie brave
Like a broad table did itselfe dispred,
For Love his loftie triumphes to engrave,
And write the battailes of his great godhed:
All good and honour might therein be red;
For there their dwelling was. And, when she spake,
Sweete wordes, like dropping honey, she did shed;
And 'twixt the perles and rubins softly brake
A silver sound, that heavenly musicke seem'd to make.

Upon her eyelids many Graces sate,
Under the shadow of her even browes,

Working belgardes and amorous retrate;
And everie one her with a grace endowes,
And everie one with meekenesse to her bowes:
So glorious mirrhour of celestiall grace,
And soveraine moniment of mortall vowes,
How shall frayle pen descrive her heavenly face,
For feare, through want of skill, her beauty to disgrace!

So faire, and thousand thousand times more faire,
She seem'd, when she presented was to sight;
And was y-clad, for heat of scorching aire,
All in a silken Camus lily white,
Purfled upon with many a folded plight,
Which all above besprinkled was throughout
With golden aygulets.

* * * * * * *

And in her hand a sharpe bore-speare she held,
And at her backe a bow, and quiver gay
Stuft with steel-headed dartes, wherewith she queld
The salvage beastes in her victorious play,
Knit with a golden bauldricke which forelay
Athwart her snowy brest, and did divide
Her daintie paps; which, like young fruit in May,
Now little gan to swell, and being tide
Through her thin weed their places only signifide.

Her yellow lockes, crisped like golden wyre,
About her shoulders weren loosely shed,
And, when the winde emongst them did inspyre,
They waved like a penon wyde despred,
And low behinde her backe were scattered:
And, whether art it were or heedlesse hap,
As through the flouring forrest rash she fled,
In her rude heares sweet flowres themselves did lap,
And flourishing fresh leaves and blossomes did enwrap.

Besides the important productions that we have noticed, Spenser was the author of some beautiful minor poems, the principal of which are *The Tears of the Muses*, *Daphnaida*, *Amoretti*, and the *Elegy of Astrophel*, the last of which was occasioned by the death of his lamented friend and early patron, Sir Philip Sidney.

Lecture the Eighth.

ROBERT SOUTHWELL—SAMUEL DANIEL—MICHAEL DRAYTON—EDWARD FAIRFAX —JOHN HARRINGTON—HENRY WOTTON—JOHN DAVIES—JOHN DONNE—ROBERT CORBET.

THE bitter and acrimonious spirit of religious intolerance and oppression which pervaded the entire administration of the House of Tudor, unfortunately did not cease, even after Protestantism had gained a fixed and permanent ascendency under Elizabeth. The mild and amiable Southwell suffered as unjustly for conscience' sake, in her reign, as either Latimer or Tyndale had in that of her rigorous father, Henry the Eighth.

ROBERT SOUTHWELL was of Roman Catholic parentage, and was born at St. Farths, in 1560. His parents being anxious to have him carefully educated, sent him, when very young, to the English College at Douay, in Flanders, where he advanced in his studies with unusual rapidity, and at the early age of sixteen he left Douay for Rome, and immediately entered the society of Jesuits. In 1584, having completed his studies, and taken priest's orders, he returned to England as a missionary of the society to which he belonged, and during eight successive years administered, unostentatiously, but zealously, to the scattered adherents of his creed, without, as far as has ever been ascertained, doing any thing to disturb the peace of society, or the faith of the established church. In 1592, he was apprehended in a gentleman's house at Uxenden in Middlesex, and committed to a dungeon in the Tower, so filthy, that when he was brought out for examination, his clothes, even, were noisomely offensive. When his father, who was a man of good family, beheld his situation, he presented a petition to the queen, requesting that, 'if his son had committed any thing for which, by the laws, he deserved death, he might suffer death; if not, as he was a gentleman, he hoped her majesty would be pleased to order him to be treated as a gentleman.' Southwell was afterward somewhat better lodged, but an imprisonment of three years, with ten inflictions of the rack, at length wore out his patience, and he entreated to be brought to trial. Being found guilty of heresy, on his own confession that he was a Romish priest, he was condemned to death, and executed at Tyburn accordingly, in 1595, in the thirty-sixth year of his age. Throughout all the scenes of suffering to which he was exposed, Southwell conducted himself with a mildness and fortitude which nothing but a well-regulated mind and a satisfied conscience could have induced.

The life of Southwell, though short, was full of sorrow; and the prevailing tone of his poetry is, therefore, that of religious resignation under grief. His two principal poems, *St. Peter's Complaint*, and *Mary Magdalene's Farewell Tears*, were, like many other works of which the world has had reason to be proud, written in prison; and it is remarkable that, though composed while suffering under the most unfeeling persecution, no trace of anger against any human being or any human institution, occurs throughout either work. The general tone and quality of the author's writings may be gathered from the following pieces:—

THE IMAGE OF DEATH.

Before my face the picture hangs,
  That daily should put me in mind
Of those cold names and bitter pangs
  That shortly I am like to find;
But yet, alas! full little I
Do think hereon, that I must die.

I often look upon a face
  Most ugly, grisly, bare and thin;
I often view the hollow place
  Where eyes and nose had sometime been;
I see the bones across that lie,
Yet little think that I must die.

I read the label underneath,
  That telleth me whereto I must;
I see the sentence, too, that saith,
  'Remember, man, thou art but dust.'
But yet, alas! how seldom I
Do think, indeed, that I must die!

Continually at my bed's head
  A hearse doth hang, which doth me tell
That I ere morning may be dead,
  Though now I feel myself full well;
But yet, alas! for all this, I
Have little mind that I must die.

The gown which I am used to wear,
  The knife wherewith I cut my meat;
And eke that old and ancient chair,
  Which is my only usual seat;
All these do tell me I must die,
And yet my life amend not I.

My ancestors are turn'd to clay,
  And many of my mates are gone;

My youngers daily drop away,
  And can I think to 'scape alone?
No, no; I know that I must die,
And yet my life amend not I.

* * * * *

If none can 'scape Death's dreadful dart;
  If rich and poor his beck obey;
If strong, if wise, if all do smart,
  Then I to 'scape shall have no way:
Then grant me grace, O God! that I
My life may mend, since I must die.

SCORN NOT THE LEAST.

Where words are weak, and foes encount'ring strong,
  Where mightier to assault than to defend,
The feebler part puts up enforced wrong,
  And silent sees, that speech could not amend;
Yet higher powers must think, though they repine,
When sun is set, the little stars will shine.

While pike doth range, the silly tench doth fly
  And crouch in privy creeks with smaller fish;
Yet pikes are caught when little fish go by,
  These fleet afloat, while those do fill the dish;
There is a time even for the worms to creep,
And suck the dew while all their foes do sleep.

The merlin can not ever soar on high,
  Nor greedy greyhound still pursue the chase;
The tender lark will find a time to fly,
  And fearful hare to run a quiet race.
He that high growth on cedars did bestow,
Gave also lowly mushrooms leave to grow.

In Haman's pomp poor Mardocheus wept,
  Yet God did turn his fate upon his foe.
The Lazar pin'd, while Dives' feast was kept,
  Yet he to heaven—to Hell did Dives go.
We trample grass, and prize the flowers of May;
Yet grass is green, when flowers do fade away.

DANIEL, the writer next to be noticed among the miscellaneous poets of England, divided his attention so equally between different departments of literature, that it is difficult to determine with which to assign him his place. As his minor poems, however, more particularly marked the peculiar character of his genius than any other of his performances, we have concluded to notice him in the present connection.

Samuel Daniel was the son of a music-master, and was born near Taunton, in Somersetshire, in 1562. In 1579, he was admitted a commoner in Magdalene College, Oxford, where he continued three years, and being aided in his studies, during the whole of that period, by an excellent tutor, he made very considerable progress in academical learning; but his genius and taste inclining him more to poetry and history than to severer studies, he left the university without his degree, and immediately repaired to London, to mingle with the wits of the metropolis. His first literary performance after he arrived in London, was the translation of a tract of Paul Jovius, containing *A Discourse of rare Inventions, both Military and Civil*, the reception of which was very flattering. On the death of Spenser, he succeeded to the vacant laureate, but was soon after displaced by Ben Jonson.

On the accession of James the First to the crown of England, Daniel became one of the grooms of the privy chamber, and was patronized by the king's consort, Queen Anne, who took much pleasure in his conversation The royal favor thus extended to him, together with his own personal qualifications, readily introduced him to the acquaintance and friendship of many of his ingenious and learned contemporaries; and occupying a house in the suburbs of London, he was accustomed there to receive and entertain his literary associates with much taste and elegance. After spending some years in this manner, Daniel became tutor to Lady Anne Clifford, and having closed the duties which this interesting and important relation imposed upon him, he retired into the country, where he passed the remainde of his days in devotion to poetry and to religious contemplation, and where he died in the month of October, 1619, in the fifty-eighth year of his age. He was buried in the church at Beckington, and a splendid monument was erected over his grave by Lady Anne Clifford, afterward Countess of Pembroke, in testimony of her gratitude to his memory, for the assiduous care and attention which he had bestowed upon her education.

The works of Daniel are numerous, and consist of dramas, histories, and miscellaneous poems. Of his dramas, *Hymen's Triumphs*, *The Vision*, *The Tragedy of Cleopatra*, and *The Tragedy of Philotus*, are the chief. His principal historical work treated of that period of English history which extended from the Conquest, in 1066, to the close of the reign of Edward the Third, in 1377. Of this historical performance, the following remark is made in the preface to Kennet's *Complete History of England*. 'The author had a place at court, in the reign of King James the First, and seems to have taken all the refinement a court could give him. It is said, he had a good vein in poetry; and it is certain, he has shown great judgment in keeping it, as he did, from infecting his prose, and destroying that simplicity which is the principal beauty in the style of an historian. His narrative is smooth and clear, and carries everywhere an air of good sense and just eloquence, and his English is much more modern than Milton's, though he lived before him.'

It is, however, chiefly through his minor pieces and sonnets that Daniel preserves his literary reputation; and from these therefore we shall take our extracts. *His Epistle to the Countess of Cumberland*, from which the following passage is selected, is a fine effusion of meditative thought:—

TO THE COUNTESS OF CUMBERLAND.

He that of such a height hath built his mind,
And reared the dwelling of his thoughts so strong,
As neither hope nor fear can shake the frame
Of his resolved powers; nor all the wind
Of vanity or malice pierce to wrong
His settled peace, or to disturb the same:
What a fair seat hath he, from whence he may
The boundless wastes and wilds of man survey.

And with how free an eye doth he look down
Upon these lower regions of turmoil,
Where all the storms of passions mainly beat
On flesh and blood! where honour, power, renown,
Are only gay afflictions, golden toil;
Where greatness stands upon as feeble feet
As frailty doth; and only great doth seem
To little minds who did it so esteem.

He looks upon the mightiest monarch's wars,
But only as on stately robberies;
Where evermore the fortune that prevails
Must be the right: the ill-succeeding mars
The fairest and the best-fac'd enterprise.
Great pirate Pompey lesser pirates quails:
Justice he sees, as if reduced, still
Conspires with power, whose cause must not be ill.

* * * * * * * *

He sees the face of right t' appear as manifold
As are the passions of uncertain man;
Who puts it in all colours, all attires,
To serve his ends, and makes his courses hold.
He sees that, let deceit work what it can,
Plot and contrive base ways to high desires;
That the all-guiding Providence doth yet
All disappoint and mocks this smoke of wit.

To this passage we shall add the following very beautiful *Sonnet* on Sleep—a most fruitful subject with the sonnet writers of that period.

Care-charmer Sleep, son of the sable Night,
Brother to Death, in silent darkness born,
Relieve my anguish, and restore the light,
With dark forgetting of my care, return,
And let the day be time enough to mourn
The shipwreck of my ill-advised youth;
Let waking eyes suffice to wail their scorn,
Without the torments of the night's untruth.
Cease, dreams, the images of day-desires,
To model forth the passions of to-morrow;
Never let the rising sun prove you liars,
To add more grief, to aggravate my sorrow.
Still let me sleep embracing clouds in vain,
And never wake to feel the day's disdain

Michael Drayton, a poet of very different genius from Daniel, was born at Harshall in the parish of Atherston, Warwickshire, in 1563. His family, though poor, was very ancient, and originally belonged to the town of Drayton in Leicestershire, the place whence his ancestors derived their name. His genius so early developed itself that when only ten years of age, he became page to some person of quality—a situation which was not, in that age, thought too humble for the sons of gentlemen. He entered the university of Oxford, but for some reason did not remain there long enough to take a degree. Immediately after he left the university, he entered into the service of the Countess of Bedford, with whom he remained for a number of years, and by whom he was very highly esteemed.

In 1593, Drayton appeared before the public as an author, in the publication of a collection of his pastorals; and in the course of the few following years he gave to the world his more elaborate poems, *The Baron's Wars*, and *England's Heroical Epistles.* In the latter productions we see the first symptoms of that taste for poetized history, as it may be called, which marked the age—which is first seen in Sackville's design of 'The Mirror for Magistrates,' and was now developing itself strongly in the historical plays of Marlow, Shakspeare, and others.

On the accession of James the First in 1603, Drayton acted as squire to Sir Walter Aston, in the ceremony of his installation as a Knight of the Bath. The poet now expected some patronage from the new sovereign, but being disappointed, he again courted the muses, and in 1612, published the first part of his most elaborate work, the *Polyolbion*, the second part of which appeared in 1622. This great performance forms a poetical description of England in thirty books, and is, both in its subject, and in the manner of its execution, entirely unlike any other work in English poetry. It is full of topographical and antiquarian details, with innumerable allusions to remarkable events and persons, as connected with various localities; yet such is the poetical genius of the author, so happily does he idealize almost every thing upon which he touches, and so lively is the flow of his verse, that we do not readily tire in perusing this vast map of intelligence. The information which the 'Polyolbion' imparts, is in general so accurate that it is frequently quoted as authority.

In 1627 Drayton published a volume containing *The Battle of Agincourt*, *The Court of Faerie*, and other poems; and three years after appeared his last volume, entitled *The Muse's Elysium*, from which it appears that he had found a final shelter in the family of the Earl of Dorset. On his death, which occurred in 1631, he was buried in Westminster Abbey, where a monument, containing an inscription in letters of gold, was raised to his memory by the wife of that nobleman, the celebrated Lady Anne Clifford, Countess of Pembroke.

Drayton, throughout the whole of his writings, voluminous as they are, shows the fancy and feeling of the true poet. 'He possessed a very considerable fertility of mind, which enabled him to distinguish himself in almost every species of poetry, from a trifling sonnet to a long topographical poem. If he anywhere sinks below himself, it is in his attempts at satire. In a most pedantic era, he was unaffected, and seldom exhibits his learning at the expense of his judgment.'[1] Our limited space will allow us room for two brief extracts only from the writings of this truly interesting poet; and both those we shall select from the 'Polyolbion.' The first is a description of *Morning in Warwickshire*, and the other, a description of the *River Trent*.

MORNING IN WARWICKSHIRE.

When Phœbus lifts his head out of the winter's wave,
No sooner doth the earth her flowery bosom brave,
At such a time as the year brings on the pleasant spring,
But hunts up to the morn the feath'red sylvans sing:
And in the lower grove, as on the rising knole,
Upon the highest spray of every mounting pole,
Those quiristers are perch't, with many a speckled breast,
Then from her burnisht gate the goodly glitt'ring east
Gilds every lofty top, which late the humorous night
Bespangled had with pearl, to please the morning's sight;
On which the mirthful quires, with their clear open throats,
Unto the joyful morn so strain their warbling notes,
That hills and valleys ring, and even the echoing air
Seems all composed of sounds, about them everywhere.
The throstle, with shrill sharps; as purposely he sang
T' awake the listless sun; or chiding, that so long
He was in coming forth, that should the thickets thrill;
The ouzel near at hand, that hath a golden bill,
As nature him had markt of purpose, t' let us see
That from all other birds his tunes should different be:
For with their vocal sounds they sang to pleasant May;
Upon his dulcet pipe the merle[2] doth only play.
When in the lower brake, the nightingale hard by,
In such lamenting strains the joyful hours doth ply,
As though the other birds she to her tunes would draw;
And, but that nature (by her all-constraining law)
Each bird to her own kind this season doth invite,
They else, alone to hear that charmer of the night,
(The more to use their ears,) their voices sure would spare,
That moduleth her tunes so admirably rare,
As man to set in parts at first had learn'd of her.
  To Philomel the next, the linnet we prefer;
And by that warbling bird, the wood-lark place we then,
The red-sparrow, the nope, the red-breast and the wren.
The yellow-pate; which though she hurt the blooming tree,
Yet scarce hath any bird a finer pipe than she.
And of these chanting fowls, the goldfinch not behind,
That hath so many sorts descending from her kind.
The tydy for her notes as delicate as they,
The laughing hecco, then the counterfeiting jay.
The softer with the shrill (some hid among the leaves,
Some in the taller trees, some in the lower greaves)

---

[1] Headley.

[2] Of all birds only the blackbird whistleth.

Thus sing away the morn, until the mounting sun,
Through thick exhaled fogs his golden head hath run,
And through the twisted tops of our close covert creeps
To kiss the gentle shade, this while that sweetly sleeps.

THE RIVER TRENT.

But, Muse, return at last, attend the princely Trent,
Who straining on in state, the north's imperious flood,
The third of England call'd, with many a dainty wood,
Being crown'd to Burton comes, to Needwood where she shows
Herself in all her pomp; and as from thence she flows,
She takes into her train rich Dove, and Darwin clear,
Darwin, whose font and fall are both in Derbyshire;
And of those thirty floods, that wait the Trent upon,
Doth stand without compare the very paragon.
Thus wand'ring at her will, as uncontroll'd she ranges,
Her often varying form, as variously and changes;
First Erwash, and then Lyne, sweet Sherwood sends her in;
Then looking wide, as one that newly wak'd had been,
Saluted from the north, with Nottingham's proud height,
So strongly is surpris'd, and taken with the sight,
That she from running wild, but hardly can refrain,
To view in how great state, as she along doth strain,
That brave exalted seat beholdeth her in pride,
As how the large-spread meads upon the other side,
All flourishing in flowers, and rich embroideries dress'd,
In which she sees herself above her neighbours bless'd.
As wrapp'd with the delights, that her this prospect brings
In her peculiar praise, lo thus the river sings:
'What should I care at all, from what my name I take,
That thirty doth import, that thirty rivers make;
My greatness what it is, or thirty abbeys great,
That on my fruitful banks, times formerly did seat;
Or thirty kinds of fish that in my streams do live,
To me this name of Trent, did from that number give?
What reck I? let great Thames, since by his fortune he
Is sovereign of us all that here in Britain be;
From Isis and old Fame his pedigree derive;
And for the second place, proud Severn that doth strive,
Fetch her descent from Wales, from that proud mountain sprung,
Plinillimon, whose praise is frequent them among,
As of that princely maid, whose name she boasts to bear,
Bright Sabine, whom she holds as her undoubted heir,
Let these imperious floods draw down their long descent,
From these so famous stocks, and only say of Trent,
That Moreland's barren earth me first to light did bring,
Which though she be but brown, my clear complexion'd spring
Gain'd with the nymphs such grace, that when I first did rise,
The Naiads on my brim danc'd wanton hydagies,
And on her spacious breast (with heaths that doth abound)
Encircled my fair fount with many a lusty round:
And of the British floods, though but the third I be,
Yet Thames and Severn both in this come short of me,

For that I am the mere of England, that divides
The north part from the south, on my so either sides,
That reckoning how these tracts in compass be extent,
Men bound them on the north, or on the south of Trent;
Their banks are barren sands, if but compar'd with mine,
Through my perspicuous breast, the pearly pebbles shine:
I throw my crystal arms along the flow'ry valleys,
Which lying sleek and smooth as any garden alleys,
Do give me leave to play, whilst they do court my stream,
And crown my winding banks with many an anadem;
My silver-scaled scrolls about my streams do sweep
Now in the shallow fords, now in the falling deep:
So that of every kind, the new spawn'd numerous fry
Seem in me as the sands that on my shore do lie.

Edward Fairfax, the celebrated translator of Tasso's *Jerusalem Delivered*, lived at the period before us, though of the history of his life we have very little knowledge. He was the natural son of Sir Thomas Fairfax, but neither the date of his birth, nor that of his death, has been preserved. That he flourished during the age of Elizabeth is entirely evident, for his great literary performance is dedicated to that princess; and it also appears that he was living in 1631; but nothing farther of him is certainly known, only that he spent his life at Fuystone, in the forest of Knaresborough, in the enjoyment of many blessings which rarely fall to the poetical race —competence, ease, rural scenes, and in ample command of the means of study.

The poetical beauty and freedom of Fairfax's version of Tasso has been the theme of almost universal praise. Dryden ranked him with Spenser as a master of the English language, and Waller declared that he derived from him the harmony of his numbers. Collins too has finely alluded to his poetical and imaginative genius in the following lines:—

Prevailing poet, whose undoubting mind
Believed the magic wonders which he sung.

Besides the translation of the 'Jerusalem Delivered, Fairfax' wrote some minor poems, and also a work on *Demonology*, in the preface to which he remarks that 'in religion I am neither a fanatic Puritan, nor superstitious Papist; but so settled in conscience, that I have the sure ground of God's word to warrant all I believe, and the commendable ordinances of our English church to approve all I practice: in which course I live a faithful Christian, and an obedient subject, and so teach my family.'

As Fairfax's original poems are comparatively little known, we shall pass them over, and take the following passage from the eighteenth book of the 'Jerusalem,' commencing with the twelfth stanza:—

RINALDI AT MOUNT OLIVET AND THE ENCHANTED WOOD.

XII.

It was the time, when 'gainst the breaking day,
Rebellious night yet strove, and still repined,
For in the east appear'd the morning gray,
And yet some lamps in Jove's high palace shined,

When to Mount Olivet he took his way,
And saw, as round about his eyes he twined,
Night's shadows hence, from thence the morning's shine,
This bright, that dark; that earthly, this divine.

XIII.

Thus to himself he thought: how many bright
And 'splendent lamps shine in heaven's temple high!
Day hath his golden sun, her moon the night,
Her fix'd and wand'ring stars the azure sky;
So framed all by their Creator's might,
That still they live and shine, and ne'er will die,
Till in a moment, with the last day's brand
They burn, and with them burn sea, air, and land.

XIV.

Thus as he mused, to the top he went,
And there kneel'd down with reverence and fear;
His eyes upon heaven's eastern face he bent;
His thoughts above all heavens uplifted were—
The sins and errors which I now repent,
Of my unbridled youth, O Father dear,
Remember not, but let thy mercy fall
And purge my faults and my offenses all.

XV.

Thus prayed he; with purple wings up-flew,
In golden weed, the morning's lusty queen,
Begilding with the radiant beams she threw,
His helm, the harness, and the mountain green:
Upon his breast and forehead gently blew
The air, that balm and nardus breath'd unseen;
And o'er his head, let down from clearest skies,
A cloud of pure and precious dew there flies.

XVI.

The heavenly dew was on his garments spread,
To which compar'd, his clothes pale ashes seem,
And sprinkled so that all that paleness fled,
And thence of purest white bright rays outstream:
So cheered are the flowers, late withered,
With the sweet comfort of the morning beams;
And so return'd to youth, a serpent old
Adorns herself in new and native gold.

XVII.

The lovely whiteness of his changed weed
The prince perceived well and long admired;
Toward the forest march'd he on with speed,
Resolv'd, as such adventures great required:
Thither he came, whence, shrinking back for dread
Of that strange desert's sight, the first retired;
But not to him fearful or loathsome made
That forest was, but sweet with pleasant shade.

XVIII.

Forward he pass'd, and in the grove before,
He heard a sound, that strange, sweet, pleasing was;
There roll'd a crystal brook with gentle roar,

There sigh'd the winds, as through the leaves they pass;
There sang the swan, and singing died, alas!
There lute, harp, cittern, human voice he heard,
And all these sounds one sound right well declared.

XIX.

A dreadful thunder-clap at last he heard,
The aged trees and plants well nigh, that rent,
Yet heard the nymphs and syrens afterward,
Birds, winds, and waters sing with sweet consent;
Whereat amazed, he stay'd and well prepar'd
For his defense, heedful and slow forth-went,
Nor in his way his passage aught withstood,
Except a quiet, still, transparent flood.

XX.

On the green banks, which that fair stream inbound,
Flowers and odours sweetly smil'd and smell'd,
Which reaching out his stretched arms around,
All the large desert in his bosom held,
And through the grove one channel passage found;
This in the wood, that in the forest dwell'd:
Trees clad the streams, streams green those trees aye made,
And so exchang'd their moisture and their shade.

Sir John Harrington, the first translator of Ariosto's *Orlando Furioso* into English, though a writer of greatly inferior genius to Fairfax, deserves to be noticed in connection with him. He was the son of that John Harrington who was imprisoned in the Tower by Mary, and was born at Kelston, near Bath, in 1561. He prepared for college at Eton Grammar School, and thence removed to the university of Cambridge, where he remained until he had taken his master's degree. Harrington was knighted by James the First, and after having passed a number of years as a successful courtier, he died in 1612, in his fifty-second year.

The translation of the 'Orlando Furioso' was an early performance, having been published before the author was thirty years of age. As a version of the original, the work is literally correct, but as a poetical performance, it is cold and prosaic. Besides the translation of the 'Orlando Furioso,' Harrington published a volume of *Epigrams*, many of which, such as the following, exhibit much talent for that department of writing:—

OF A PRECISE TAILOR.

A tailor, thought a man of upright dealing—
True, but for lying—honest but for stealing,
Did fall one day extremely sick by chance,
And on the sudden was in wondrous trance;
The fiends of hell mustering in fearful manner,
Of sundry colour'd silks displayed a banner
Which he had stolen, and wish'd, as they did tell,
That he might find it all one day in hell,
The man, affrighted with this apparition,
Upon recovery grew a great precisian:
He bought a bible of the best translation,
And in his life he show'd great reformation;

He walked mannerly, he talked meekly,
He heard three lectures and two sermons weekly;
He vow'd to shun all company unruly,
And in his speech he used no oath but truly;
And zealously to keep the Sabbath's rest,
His meat for that day on the eve was drest;
And lest the custom which he had to steal,
Might cause him sometimes to forget his zeal,
He gives his journeyman a special charge,
That if the stuff, allowance being large
He found his fingers were to filch inclined,
Bid him to have the banner in his mind.
This done (I scant can tell the rest for laughter)
A captain of a ship came three days after,
And brought three yards of velvet and three quarters,
To make Venetians down below the garters.
He, that precisely knew what was enough,
Soon slipt aside three quarters of the stuff;
His man, espying it, said in derision,
Master, remember how you saw the vision!
Peace, knave! quoth he, I did not see one rag
Of such a color'd silk in all the flag.

SIR HENRY WOTTON, the miscellaneous poet who follows Fairfax and Harrington, was born at Bocton Hall, in Kent, on the thirtieth of March, 1568. His early education was conducted by private tutors at home, after which he was sent to Winchester school, whence he passed, in 1584, to New College, Oxford. He did not, however, long remain there, but soon entered Queen's College, where he became well versed in logic and rhetoric; and being also distinguished for various other learning, and for his wit, he was selected to write a tragedy for the private use of his college. The name of the tragedy was *Tancredo*, and Walton, Sir Henry's biographer, remarks that 'it was interwoven with sentences, and for the method and exact personating those humors, passions, and dispositions, which he proposed to represent, so performed, that the gravest of the society declared, he had in a slight employment, given an early and solid testimony of his future abilities.'

Wotton having, in the twentieth year of his age, taken his master's degree, left the university, and after travelling a number of years on the continent, returned to England, and attached himself to the service of the Earl of Essex, the chief favorite of Queen Elizabeth. Having afterward gained the friendship of king James, by communicating the secret of a conspiracy formed against him, while yet only king of Scotland, he was employed by that monarch, when he ascended the English throne, as ambassador to Venice. A versatile and lively disposition qualified Sir Henry, in an eminent degree, for this situation, of the duties of which we have his own idea in the well-known punning expression, in which he defines an ambassador to be 'an honest gentleman, sent to lie abroad for the good of his country.' Late in life Wotton took orders to qualify himself to be provost of Eton, and in that situation he died, in 1639, in the seventy-second year of his age. The poems of this author are generally brief unstudied effusions, of very consid erable merit, and from them we select the following:—

A FAREWELL TO THE VANITIES OF THE WORLD.

Farewell, ye gilded follies, pleasing troubles;
Farewell, ye honour'd rags, ye glorious bubbles!
Fame 's but a hollow echo; gold, pure clay;
Honour, the darling but of one short day;
Beauty, th' eye's idol, but a damask'd skin;
State, but a golden prison to live in,
And torture free-born minds; embroider'd trains
Merely but pageants for proud swelling veins;
And blood allied to greatness, is alone
Inherited, not purchased, nor our own:
Fame, honour, beauty, state, train, blood, and birth,
Are but the fading blossoms of the earth.
* * * * * *
Welcome pure thoughts, welcome ye silent groves,
These guests, these courts, my soul most dearly loves:
Now the wing'd people of the sky shall sing
My cheerful anthems to the gladsome spring:
A prayer-book now shall be my looking-glass,
In which I will adorn sweet Virtue's face.
Here dwell no hateful looks, no palace cares,
No broken vows dwell here, nor pale-faced fears:
Then here I'll sigh, and sigh my hot love's folly,
And learn t' affect an holy melancholy;
And if Contentment be a stranger then,
I'll ne'er look for it, but in heaven again.

THE CHARACTER OF A HAPPY LIFE.

How happy is he born and taught,
That serveth not another's will;
Whose armour is his honest thought,
And simple truth his utmost skill.

Whose passions not his masters are,
Whose soul is still prepared for death,
Untied unto the worldly care
Of public fame or private breath;

Who envies none that chance doth raise,
Or vice; who never understood
How deepest wounds are given by praise;
Nor rules of state, but rules of good:

Who hath his life from rumours freed,
Whose conscience is his strong retreat;
Whose state can neither flatterers feed,
Nor ruin make oppressors great.

Who God doth late and early pray,
More of his grace than gifts to lend;
And entertains the harmless day
With a religious book or friend;

This man is freed from servile bands
Of hope to rise, or fear to fall;
Lord of himself, though not of lands;
And having nothing yet hath all.

SIR JOHN DAVIES, the poet to whom our attention is next directed, was of low origin, being the son of a tanner. He was born at Chisgrove in Wiltshire in 1570, and after careful preparation, became, in 1585, a commoner of Queen's College, Oxford. He remained at the university until he had taken his bachelor's degree, immediately after which he repaired to London, and entered the Middle Temple, where he applied himself so closely to the study of the common law, that he was soon called to the bar. An unfortunate quarrel, however, the cause of which is not known, with a gentleman of the society to which he belonged, resulted in his expulsion thence, and he returned to Oxford and continued the prosecution of his studies there; but being eventually reinstated in the Temple, he returned thither and practiced, for some time, as a counsellor; and in 1601, he became a member of parliament. Upon the death of Queen Elizabeth, he accompanied lord Hunsdon into Scotland to congratulate king James upon his accession to the crown of England; and being introduced into his majesty's presence, he was particularly noticed by him; and when the king was informed by lord Hunsdon that Davies was the author of *Nosce tiepsum*, his majesty graciously embraced him, and assured him of his favor. The 'Nosce tiepsum,' a poem on the origin, nature, and immortality of the soul, was published in 1599, and dedicated to queen Elizabeth, by whom it was very favorably received.

Davies, soon after the accession of James, published a small volume of poems containing *Hymns of Astrea*, in acrostic verse; *Orchestra*, or a poem expressing the antiquity and excellency of dancing, and other pieces, which not only placed him in a high rank among his contemporary poets, but so far increased the favor of the king toward him, that he appointed him, first, his solicitor, and then his attorney-general, in Ireland; where, in 1606, he became one of his majesty's sergeants at law; and was afterward speaker in the House of Commons in that kingdom. In 1607, Davies received the honor of knighthood from the king at Whitehall; and in 1612, he quitted the post of attorney-general in Ireland, and was made one of the king's English sergeants at law; and, soon after he settled in England, one of the judges of assize on the circuit. In 1626, he was appointed by Charles the First, lord chief-justice of the King's Bench; but, before his installation, he died suddenly of apoplexy in the fifty-seventh year of his age.

Sir John Davies was a man of bold spirit, sharp and ready wit, and of most thorough and extensive learning; and among the minor poets of this period, he holds a very high rank. His philosophical poem, *On the Soul of Man, and the Immortality thereof*, is one of the earliest poems of that kind in the language. The author shows that he was a profound thinker, and close reasoner. 'In the happier parts of his poem,' says Campbell, 'we come to logical truths so well illustrated by ingenious similes, that we know not whether to call the thoughts more poetical or philosophically just. The judgment and the fancy are reconciled, and the imagery of the poem seems to start more vividly from the surrounding shades of abstraction.' From this poem, the versification of which was afterward copied by Davenant and Dryden, we extract the following passage:—

THE DIGNITY OF MAN.

Oh! what is man, great Maker of mankind!
  That thou to him so great respect dost bear;
That thou adorn'st him with so bright a mind,
  Mak'st him a king, and even an angel's peer?

Oh! what a lively life, what heav'nly pow'r,
  What spreading virtue, what a sparkling fire,
How great, how plentiful, how rich a dow'r
  Dost thou within this dying flesh inspire!

Thou leav'st thy print in other works of thine,
  But thy whole image thou in man has writ;
There can not be a creature more divine,
  Except, like thee, it should be infinite.

But it exceeds man's thought, to think how high
  God hath rais'd man, since God a man became;
The angels do admire this mystery,
  And are astonish'd when they view the same:

Nor hath he given these blessings for a day,
  Nor made them on the body's life depend;
The soul, though made in time, survives for aye;
  And though it hath beginning, sees no end.

In another production, the 'Orchestra, or Poem of Dancing, in a Dialogue between Penelope and one of her Wooers,' Davies is much more fanciful than in the previous poem. He there represents Penelope as declining to dance with Antinous, and the latter as proceeding to lecture her upon the antiquity of that elegant exercise, the merit of which he describes in verses partaking peculiarly of the flexibility and grace of the subject. Of this performance, the following is one of the most imaginative passages:—

THE DANCING OF THE AIR.

And now behold your tender nurse, the air,
  And common neighbour, that aye runs around,
How many pictures and impressions fair
  Within her empty regions are there found,
  Which to your senses dancing do propound;
For what are breath, speech, echoes, music, winds,
But dancings of the air in sundry kinds.

For when you breathe, the air in order moves,
  Now in, now out, in time and measure true,
And when you speak, so well she dancing loves,
  That doubling oft, and oft redoubling new,
  With thousand forms she doth herself endue:

For all the words that from your lips repair,
Are naught but tricks and turnings of the air.

Hence is her prattling daughter, Echo, born,
  That dances to all voices she can hear:
There is no sound so harsh that she doth scorn,
  Nor any time wherein she will forbear
  The airy pavement with her feet to wear:
And yet her hearing sense is nothing quick,
For after time she endeth ev'ry trick.

And thou, sweet Music, dancing's only life,
  The ear's sole happiness, the air's best speech,
Loadstone of fellowship, charming rod of strife,
  The soft mind's paradise, the sick mind's leech,
  With thine own tongue thou trees and stones can teach,
That when the air doth dance her finest measure,
Then art thou born, the gods, and men's sweet pleasure.

Lastly where keep the Winds, their revelry,
  Their violent turnings, and wild whirling hays,
But in the air's translucent gallery?
  Where she herself is turn'd a hundred ways,
  While with those maskers wantonly she plays:
Yet in this misrule, they shall rule embrace,
As two at once encumber not the place.

Davies wrote a number of pieces in prose also; and the first Reports of Law Cases, published in Ireland, proceeded from his able and accomplished pen. The preface to the volume containing these Reports is considered the best that was ever prefixed to a law-book.

JOHN DONNE, the poet whom we are next to notice, was of respectable parentage, and was born in London, 1573. His mother was descended from the family of Sir Thomas More, and his parents being both rigidly attached to the Romish religion, had their son's education attended to at home until he reached the eleventh year of his age, when he was sent to the university of Oxford; where, such was the precociousness of intellect that he evinced, that one of his tutors, through admiration of his early genius, remarked, that 'he was rather born wise than made so by study.' His acquirements in learning at the university realized all that his early mental developments had promised; so that at the expiration of three years he was prepared for the bachelor's degree—an honor which he was compelled to forego, as the religious sentiments of his parents would not allow him to take the oath of allegiance which the occasion required. Having passed three years at Oxford he entered the university of Cambridge, where he also remained for the same length of time; but as the difficulties in the way of obtaining university honors prevailed there also, which had existed at Oxford, he now relinquished collegiate studies, repaired to London, and entered Lincoln's Inn as a student of law. He had, however, no predilection for the legal profession; and as his father, who had been a merchant, died before he was admitted into Lincoln's Inn society, and left him a fortune of three thousand pounds, he at once relinquished the law, and resolved to pass some years upon the continent. Before he should leave England, however, he determined thoroughly to investigate the relative claims the Romish faith, in which he had been brought up, and the Protestant, had upon his belief. Of this investigation he himself gives the following account:—'I had a longer work to do in this inquiry than many other men: for I was first to blot out certain impressions of the Roman religion, and to wrestle against the examples, and against the reasons by which some hold was taken, and some anticipations early laid upon my conscience, both by persons who by nature had a power and superiority over my will, and others, who, by their learning and good life, seemed to me justly to claim an interest for the guiding and rectifying of mine understanding in these matters.' The result of this inquiry was a thorough conversion to Protestantism; of which he remarks, 'I was not transported by any sudden and violent determination, till I had, to the measure of my poor wit and judgment, surveyed and digested the whole body of divinity, controverted between ours and the Romish church. In which such an disquisition that God, which awakened me then, and hath never forsaken me in that industry, as he is the author of that purpose, so he is a witness of this protestation, that I proceeded therein with humility and diffidence in myself, and by that, which by his grace, I took to be the ordinary means, frequent prayer and equal actions.'

Having thus settled the momentous question of his religious faith, Donne, in 1596, accompanied the Earl of Essex into Spain, and after spending about a year in that country and acquiring a knowledge of the Spanish language, he visited Italy, intending to embark thence for Palestine, to view Jerusalem and the sepulchre of our Saviour. He was, however, disappointed in the company with whom he had arranged to make the journey, and he therefore returned to England, after having remained in Italy a sufficient length of time to become familiar with the language of that country.

Soon after his return to England, Donne was appointed by Sir Thomas Egerton, lord-keeper of the great seal, his chief secretary; but he had filled this important place only a few years before he clandestinely married Anne, the daughter of Sir George More, and niece of the lord-keeper. Sir George was so incensed at this conduct on the part of Donne, as to insist that Sir Thomas Egerton should dismiss him from his service. Sir Thomas complied with his friend and relative's request, but in parting with his secretary he remarked that 'Mr. Donne was fitter to serve a king than a subject.' A long altercation, and even a law-suit followed between Donne and his father-in-law, during the whole of which the former resided with his relative, Sir Francis Wolley, who eventually succeeded in reconciling the parties, and obtaining from Sir George eight hundred pounds as his daughter's marriage portion. Sir Francis Wolley dying soon after, Donne sought a home and employment with Sir Robert Drury, through whose influence he obtained in 1610 the degree of master of arts from the university of Oxford.

In 1612, Sir Robert Drury was sent ambassador to the court of France, and thither Donne accompanied him as his secretary. Meantime, many of the nobility were urgent with the king to confer some secular employment upon him worthy of his singular merits; but James who was familiar with his talents and attainments, desired him to enter the church, and would hear of no other arrangement. About this important step Donne for some time hesitated; but at length he consented to comply with the king's request, and was, accordingly, ordained by Doctor King, bishop of London, and soon after appointed by his royal patron, dean of St. Paul's with the degree of doctor of divinity conferred upon him, at the king's request, by the university of Cambridge. In this position Donne passed the remainder of his life, honored and respected even by nobility itself, until his death, which occurred on the thirty-first of March, 1631. He was buried in the cathedral church of St. Paul's, where a suitable monument was soon after erected to his memory.

The poetical works of Donne consist of satires, elegies, religious poems, complimentary verses, and epigrams. His reputation as a poet, was, in his own day, very great; and though during the latter part of the seventeenth and the whole of the eighteenth century it was comparatively low, it has lately revived again. It is now generally acknowledged that amid much rubbish, there is much real poetry, and that of a high order, in his writings. He is usually considered as the first of a series of poets of the seventeenth century, who, under the name of *Metaphysical Poets*, fill a conspicuous place in English literary history. The directness of thought, the naturalness of description, the rich abundance of genuine poetical feeling and imagery, which distinguished the poets of Elizabeth's reign, now began to give way to cold and forced conceits, mere vain workings of the intellect, a kind of poetry as unlike the former as punning is unlike genuine wit. This quality, it should be remarked, however, did not characterize the whole of the poetry of Donne and his followers. These writers are often direct, natural, and truly poetical. Donne is usually considered the first writer of that kind of satire which Pope afterward carried to perfection. From this poet's various poems we select the following curious specimen:—

THE WILL.

Before I sigh my last gasp, let me breathe,
Great Love, some legacies: I here bequeath
Mine eyes to Argus, if mine eyes can see;
If they be blind, then, Love, I give them thee;
My tongue to Fame; to ambassadors mine ears;
    To women, or the sea, my tears;
Thou, Love, hast taught me here to fall,
By making me serve her who had twenty more,
That I should give to none but such as had too much before.

My constancy I to the planets give;
My truth to them who at the court do live;

Mine ingenuity and openness
To Jesuits; to buffoons my pensiveness;
My silence to any who abroad have been;
    My money to a Capuchin.
Thou, Love, taught'st me, by appointing me
To love there, where no love received can be,
Only to give to such as have no good capacity.

My faith I give to Roman Catholics;
All my good works unto the schismatics
Of Amsterdam; my best civility
And courtship to an university;
My modesty I give to soldiers bare;
    My patience let gamesters share;
Thou, Love, taught'st me, by making me
Love her that holds my love disparity,
Only to give to those that count my gifts indignity.

I give my reputation to those
Which were my friends; mine industry to foes;
To schoolmen I bequeath my doubtfulness;
My sickness to physicians, or excess;
To Nature all that I in rhyme have writ!
    And to my company, my wit:
Thou, Love, by making me adore
He who begot this love in me before,
Taught'st me to make as though I gave, when I do but restore.

To him for whom the passing bell next tolls
I give my physic books; my written rolls
Of moral counsels I to Bedlam give;
My brazen medals, unto them which live
In want of bread; to them which pass among
    All foreigners, my English tongue:
Thou, Love, by making me love one
Who thinks her friendship a fit portion
For younger lovers, dost my gifts thus disproportion.

Therefore I'll give no more, but I'll undo
The world by dying, because love dies too.
Then all your beauties will be no more worth
Than gold in mines, where none doth draw it forth,
And all your graces no more use shall have
    Than a sun-dial in a grave.
Thou Love, taught'st me, by making me
Love her who doth neglect both me and thee,
To invent and practice this one way to annihilate all three.

Doctor DONNE's poems, it must be remembered, were written chiefly in early life. After he took orders he indulged very little in the poetic vein, though his fancy, as will appear from the following extract from his sermons, was still very fruitful :—

GOD SHOULD BE WORSHIPED EVERYWHERE.

It is true, God may be devoutly worshiped anywhere; in all places of his dominion, my soul shall praise the Lord, says David. It is not only a concurring of men, a meeting of so many bodies that makes a church; if thy soul and body be met together, an humble preparation of the mind, and a reverent disposition of the body; if thy knees be bent to the earth, thy hands and eyes lifted up to heaven; if thy tongue pray and praise, and thine ears hearken to his answer; if all thy senses, and powers, and faculties, with one unanime purpose to worship thy God, thou art, to this intendment, a church, thou art a congregation; here are two or three met together in his name, and he is in the midst of them though thou be alone in thy chamber. The church of God should be built upon a rock, and yet Job had his church upon a dunghill; the church is to be placed upon the top of a hill, and yet the prophet Jeremy had his church in a miry dungeon; constancy and settledness belong to the church, and yet Jonah had his church in the whale's belly; the lion that roars and seeks whom he may devour, is an enemy to this church, and yet Daniel had his church in the lion's den; the waters of rest in the Psalms were a figure of the church, and yet the three children had their church in the fiery furnace; liberty and life appertain to the church, and yet Peter and Paul had their church in prison, and the thief had his church upon the cross. Every particular man is himself a temple of the Holy Ghost; yea, destroy his body by death and corruption in the grave, and yet here shall be a renewing, a re-edifying of all those temples, in the general resurrection; when we shall rise again, not only as so many Christians, but as so many Christian churches, to glorify the apostle and high-priest of our profession, Christ Jesus, in that eternal Sabbath. Every person, every place is fit to glorify God in.

We shall close our present remarks with a brief notice of the poet Corbet, Bishop of Oxford, and afterward of Norwich.

RICHARD CORBET was the son of a gardener, and was born at Ervill in Surrey, in 1582. He pursued his early studies at Westminster school, and thence passed, in 1598, to Christ-church College, Oxford, where he remained till he obtained his master's degree, immediately after which he took orders and soon became an eminent preacher. His wit and eloquence recommended him to the favor of James the First, by whom he was appointed one of his chaplains in ordinary, and in 1628, made dean of Christ-church. In 1629, Charles the First raised him to the see of Oxford, and in 1632, transferred him to that of Norwich. Corbet died on the twenty-eighth of July, 1638, and was buried in the Cathedral church at Norwich, where a free-stone monument was erected to his memory.

Bishop Corbet's poems are comparatively few in number, and those best known are a *Journey into France*, the *Farewell to the Fairies*, and *Lines to his son Vincent Corbet;* the second and third of which follow:—

FAREWELL TO THE FAIRIES.

Farewell rewards and fairies,
  Good housewives now may say,
For now foul sluts in dairies
  Do fare as well as they.
And, though they sweep their hearth no less
  Than maids were wont to do,
Yet who of late, for cleanliness,
  Finds sixpence in her shoe?

Lament, lament old Abbeys,
  The fairies' lost command;

They did but change priests' babies,
  But some have changed your land;
And all your children spring from thence
  Are now grown Puritans;
Who live as changelings ever since,
  For love of your domains.

At morning and at evening both,
  You merry were and glad,
So little care of sleep or sloth
  These pretty ladies had;
When Tom came home from labour,
  Or Cis to milking rose,
Then merrily went their labour,
  And nimbly went their toes.

Witness those rings and roundelays
  Of theirs which yet remain,
Were footed in queen Mary's days
  On many a grassy plain;
But since of late Elizabeth,
  And later, James came in,
They never danc'd on any heath
  As when the time hath been.

By which we note the fairies
  Were of the old profession,
Their songs were Ave-Maries,
  Their dances were procession
But now, alas! they are all dead,
  Or gone beyond the seas;
Or farther for religion fled,
  Or else they take their ease.

A tell-tale in their company
  They never could endure,
And whoso kept not secretly
  Their mirth, was punish'd sure:
It was a just and Christian deed,
  To pinch such black and blue:
O how the commonwealth doth need
  Such justices as you!

TO HIS SON.

What I shall leave thee none can tell,
But all shall say I wish thee well;
I wish thee, Vin, before all wealth,
Both bodily and ghostly health;
Nor too much wealth, nor wit come to thee,
So much of either may undo thee.
I wish thee learning not for show,
Enough for to instruct and know;
Not such as gentlemen require
To prate at table or at fire.
I wish thee all thy mother's graces,
Thy father's fortunes and his places.

I wish thee friends, and one at court
Not to build on, but to support;
To keep thee not in doing many
Oppressions, but from suffering any.
I wish thee peace in all thy ways,
Nor lazy nor contentious days;
And when thy soul and body part,
As innocent as now thou art.

Lecture the Ninth.

SIR JOHN BEAUMONT—PHINEAS FLETCHER—GILES FLETCHER—THOMAS CAREW—GEORGE WITHER—WILLIAM BROWNE—HENRY KING—FRANCIS QUARLES—GEORGE HERBERT—ROBERT HERRICK—JOSEPH HALL.

THE remaining English miscellaneous poets connected with the period which we are at present considering, though numerous, will not generally require notices so extended as those who have already passed in review before us. Of these poets, those who in the order of time first present themselves are, Beaumont, the Fletchers, Carew, Wither, Browne, King, and Quarles.

JOHN BEAUMONT was the son of Sir Francis Beaumont, and elder brother of the celebrated dramatic poet, Francis Beaumont. He was born at Grace-Dieu, in Leicestershire, in 1582, and admitted gentleman commoner of Broadgate Hall, Oxford, in 1596. After having passed three years at the university, he removed to one of the Inns of Court, London, but he soon relinquished the study of the law, and retired to the family estate in Leicestershire. In 1626, he was knighted by Charles the First, and died two years after, in the forty-seventh year of his age.

Sir John Beaumont wrote a number of pieces, the principal of which are *Bosworth Field*, and *Lines to the Memory of Ferdinando Pulton*. These poems are both in heroic verse—a measure which Beaumont wrote with great ease and correctness. 'Bosworth Field' is generally cold and unimpassioned, though there are in it occasional spirited passages; but the 'Lines to the Memory of Pulton' contain many passages of rare excellence, such as the following:—

Why should vain sorrow follow him with tears,
Who shakes off burdens of declining years?
Whose thread exceeds the usual bounds of life,
And feels no stroke of any fatal knife?
The destinies enjoin their wheels to run,
Until the length of his whole course be spun.
No envious clouds obscure his struggling light,
Which sets contented at the point of night:

Yet this large time no greater profit brings,
Than every little moment whence it springs;
Unless employ'd in works deserving praise,
Must wear out many years and live few days.
Time flows from instants, and of these each one
Should be esteem'd as if it were alone
The shortest space, which we so lightly prize
When it is coming, and before our eyes:
Let it but slide into the eternal main,
No realms, no worlds, can purchase it again:
Remembrance only makes the footsteps last,
When winged time, which fixed the prints, is past.

To the above extract we feel constrained to add the following fine epitaph upon Sir John's son, Gervase Beaumont :—

Can I, who have for others oft compiled
The songs of death, forget my sweetest child,
Which like a flow'r crush'd with a blast, is dead,
And ere full time hangs down his smiling head,
Expecting with clear hope to live anew,
Among the angels fed with heavenly dew?
We have this sign of joy, that many days,
While on the earth his struggling spirit stays,
The name of Jesus in his mouth contains
His only food, his sleep, his ease from pains.
O may that sound be rooted in my mind,
Of which in him such strong effect I find!
Dear Lord, receive my son, whose winning love
To me was like a friendship, far above
The course of nature, or his tender age;
Whose looks could all my better griefs assuage:
Let his pure soul—ordain'd seven years to be
In that frail body, which was part of me—
Remain my pledge in heaven, as sent to show
How to this port at every step I go.

PHINEAS and GILES FLETCHER were brothers, and were sons of the celebrated Doctor Giles Fletcher, who stood so high in the favor of Queen Elizabeth that she employed him on various important foreign embassies. Both these brothers were clergymen, and their lives, therefore, afford little variety of incident.

PHINEAS FLETCHER was born in 1584; and after passing through preparatory studies at Eton, he entered the university of Cambridge, whence being graduated, he took orders, and soon after settled at Kilgay, in Norfolk, where he passed his life in the quiet of the country. He died in 1650, in his sixty-seventh year.

The principal poems of Phineas Fletcher are, the *Purple Island*, or the *Isle of Man*, and *Piscatory Eclogues*. The name of the former poems suggests images of poetical and romantic beauty, such as we may suppose an admirer and follower of Spenser to have drawn; but a perusal of the work soon dispels this illusion. The 'Purple Island' of Fletcher is no 'sunny spot amid the melancholy main,' but is an elaborate and anatomical description of the body and soul of man. Its value, therefore, must not rest upon the plot, but upon isolated passages and poetical descriptions. Some of his stanzas have all the easy flow and mellifluous sweetness of the 'Faery Queen;' and clearly show a luxuriance of fancy, which had it been disciplined by taste and judgment, must have rivalled the softer scenes of Spenser. To justify this remark we take the following passage:—

DESCRIPTION OF PARTHENIA, OR CHASTITY.

With her, her sister went, a warlike maid,
Parthenia, all in steel and gilded arms;
In needle's stead, a mighty spear she sway'd,
With which in bloody fields and fierce alarms,
The boldest champion she down would bear,
And like a thunder-bolt wide passage tear,
Flinging all to the earth with her enchanted spear.

Her goodly armour seem'd a garden green,
Where thousand spotless lilies freshly blew;
And on her shield the lone bird might be seen,
Th' Arabian bird, shining in colours new;
Itself unto itself was only mate:
Ever the same, but new in newer date:
And underneath was writ, 'Such is chaste single state.'

Thus hid in arms she seem'd a goodly knight,
And fit for any warlike exercise:
But when she list lay down her armour bright,
And back resume her peaceful maiden's guise;
The fairest maid she was, that ever yet
Prison'd her locks within a golden net,
Or let them waving hang, with roses fair beset.

Choice nymph! the crown of chaste Diana's train,
Thou beauty's lily, set in heavenly earth;
Thy fairs unpattern'd, all perfection stain;
Sure Heaven with curious pencil at thy birth
In thy rare face her own full picture drew:
It is a strong verse here to write, but true,
Hyperboles in others are but half thy due.

Upon her forehead Love his trophies fits,
A thousand spoils in silver arch displaying:
And in the midst himself full proudly sits,
Himself in awful majesty arraying:
Upon her brows lies his bent ebon bow,
And ready shafts; deadly those weapons show;
Yet sweet the death appear'd, lovely that deadly blow.

* * * * * * * *

A bed of lilies flow'r upon her cheek,
And in the midst was set a circling rose;
Whose sweet aspect would force Narcissus seek
New liveries, and fresher colours choose

To deck his beauteous head in snowy 'tire;
But all in vain: for who can hope t' aspire
To such a fair, which none attain, but all admire?

Her ruby lips lock up from gazing sight
A troop of pearls, which march in goodly row;
But when she deigns these precious bones undight,
Soon heavenly notes from those divisions flow,
And with rare music charm the ravish'd ears,
Daunting bold thoughts, but cheering modest fears:
The spheres so only sing, so only charm the spheres.

Yet all these stars which deck this beauteous sky
By force of th' inward sun both shine and move;
Thron'd in her heart sits love's high majesty;
In highest majesty the highest love,
As when a taper shines in glassy frame,
The sparkling crystal burns in glittering flame,
So does that brightest love brighten this lovely dame.

GILES FLETCHER was younger than his brother, but neither the date of his birth, nor the period of his death has been preserved. His only important poetical production is a sacred poem entitled *Christ's Victory and Triumph.* There is a massive grandeur and earnestness about this performance, which strike the imagination with great force. The materials of the poem are more harmoniously linked together than those of the 'Purple Island.' Hallam remarks that, 'both of these brothers are deserving of much praise: they were endowed with minds eminently poetical, and not inferior in imagination to any of their contemporaries. But an injudicious taste, and an excessive fondness for a style which the public was fast abandoning, that of allegorical personification, prevented their powers from being effectively displayed.' Campbell also observes that, 'they were both the disciples of Spenser, and with his diction gently modernized, retained much of his melody and luxuriant expression. Giles, inferior as he is to Spenser and Milton, might be figured in his happiest moments, as a link of connection in our poetry between these congenial spirits, for he reminds us of both, and evidently gave hints to the latter in a poem on the same subject with Paradise Regained.'

We shall close our notice of these brother poets with the following passage from 'Christ's Victory and Triumph:'—

THE RAINBOW.

High in the airy element there hung
Another cloudy sea, that did disdain,
As though his purer waves from heaven sprung,
To crawl on earth, as doth the sluggish main:
But it the earth would water with his rain,
That ebb'd and flow'd as wind and season would;
And oft the sun would cleave the limber mould
To alabaster rocks, that in the liquid roll'd.

Beneath those sunny banks a darker cloud,
Dropping with thicker dew, did melt apace,
And bent itself into a hollow shroud,
On which, if Mercy did but cast her face,
A thousand colours did the bow enchase,
That wonder was to see the silk distain'd
With the resplendence from her beauty gain'd,
And Iris paint her locks with beams so lively feign'd.

About her head a cypress heaven she wore,
Spread like a vail, upheld with silver wire,
In which the stars so burnt in golden ore,
As seem'd the azure web was all on fire:
But hastily, to quench their sparkling ire,
A flood of milk came rolling up the shore,
That on his curded wave swift Argus wore
And the immortal swan, that did her life deplore.

Yet strange it was so many stars to see,
Without a sun to give their tapers light;
Yet strange it was not that it so should be;
For, where the sun centers himself by right,
Her face and locks did flame, that at the sight
The heavenly vail, that else should nimbly move,
Forgot his flight, and all incensed, with love,
With wonder and amazement, did her beauty prove.

Over her hung a canopy of state,
Not of rich tissue nor of spangled gold,
But of a substance, though not animate,
Yet of a heavenly and spiritual mould,
That only eyes of spirits might behold:
Such light as from main rocks of diamond,
Shooting their sparks at Phœbus, would rebound,
And little angels, holding hands, danced all around.

Thomas Carew was of an ancient family, and was born in Gloucestershire, in 1589. He was educated at Corpus Christi College, Oxford, after which he travelled, for some time, upon the continent, and on his return to England, entered into the service of Charles the First, by whom he was made gentleman of the privy chamber, and was personally very highly esteemed. From this period his life was that of a courtier—witty, affable, and accomplished—without reflection; and in a strain of loose revelry which, according to Lord Clarenden, 'he deeply repented in his latter days.' He died in 1639, not having quite attained the fiftieth year of his age.

Carew was the precursor and representative of a numerous class of poets—courtiers of a gay and gallant school, who, to personal accomplishments, rank, and education, united a taste and talent for the conventional poetry then most popular and most cultivated. Their visions of fame were, in general, bounded by the circle of the court and of the nobility. To live in future generations, or to sound the depth of the human heart, seems not to have entered into their contemplations. A 'rosy cheek or coral lip' formed their ordinary themes. The court applauded; the lady was flattered or appeased by the compliment; and the poet was praised for his wit and gallantry; while the heart had nothing to do with the poetical homage thus tendered and accepted.

Carew was capable, however, of ascending far beyond this heartless frivolity; and in his productions, therefore, we see only glimpes of a genius which might have been ripened into permanent and beneficial excellence. His short amatory pieces and songs were exceedingly popular in his day, and are now his only poems that are read. A few of these are here introduced, together with his lines on the *Approach of Spring*—a production which indicates that the passionate and imaginative view of the Elizabethan period had not wholly passed away, but that the 'genial and warm tints' of the elder muse still occasionally colored the landscape.

SONG.

Ask me no more where Jove bestows,
When June is past, the fading rose;
For in your beauties, orient deep,
These flowers, as in their causes, sleep.

Ask me no more whither do stray
The golden atoms of the day;
For in pure love heaven did prepare
Those powders to enrich your hair.

Ask me no more whither doth haste
The nightingale when May is past;
For in your sweet dividing throat
She winters, and keeps warm her note.

Ask me no more if east or west
The Phœnix builds her spicy nest;
For unto you at last she flies,
And in your fragant bosom dies.

THE COMPLIMENT.

I do not love thee for that fair
Rich fan of thy most curious hair;
Though the wires thereof be drawn
Finer than the threads of lawn,
And are softer than the leaves
On which the subtile spider weaves.

I do not love thee for those flowers
Growing on thy cheeks (love's bowers);
Though such cunning them hath spread,
None can paint them white and red:
Love's golden arrows thence are shot,
Yet for them I love thee not.

I do not love thee for those soft
Red coral lips I've kiss'd so oft;
Nor teeth of pearl, the double guard
To speech, whence music still is heard;

Though from those lips a kiss being taken,
Might tyrants melt, and death awaken.

I do not love thee, oh! my fairest,
For that richest, for that rarest
Silver pillar, which stands under
Thy sound head, that globe of wonder;
Tho' that neck be whiter far
Than towers of polish'd ivory are.

DISDAIN RETURNED.

He that loves a rosy cheek,
Or a coral lip admires,
Or from star-like eyes doth seek
Fuel to maintain his fires;
As old Time makes these decay,
So his flames must waste away.

But a smooth and steadfast mind,
Gentle thoughts and calm desires;
Hearts with equal love combined,
Kindle never-dying fires.
Where these are not, I despise
Lovely cheeks, or lips, or eyes!

No tears, Celia, now shall win
My resolv'd heart to return;
I have search'd thy soul within,
And find nought but pride and scorn;
I have learn'd thy arts, and now
Can disdain as much as thou.
Some power, in my revenge, convey
That love to her I cast away.

APPROACH OF SPRING.

Now that the winter's gone, the earth hath lost
Her snow-white robes, and now no more the frost
Candies the grass, or calls an icy cream
Upon the silver lake, or crystal stream;
But the warm sun thaws the benumb'd earth,
And makes it tender; gives a sacred birth
To the dead swallow; wakes in hollow tree
The drowsy cuckoo, and the humble bee;
Now do a choir of chirping minstrels bring
In triumph to the world the youthful spring.
The valleys, hills, and woods, in rich array
Welcome the coming of the long'd for May.
Now all things smile.

George Wither was born in Hampshire on the eleventh of June, 1588, and was educated at Magdalen College, Oxford. In the twenty-fifth year of his age he published a satire entitled *Abuses Stript and Whipt*, for which he was thrown into Marshalsea; but so far from allowing his imprisonment to depress his spirits, he there composed his fine poem, *The*

Shepherds' Hunting. When the abuses satirized by the poet had accumulated and brought on the civil war, Wither embraced the popular side, and sold his patrimonial estate to raise a troop of horse for the Parliament. He rose to the rank of a major, and in 1642, was made governor of Farnham Castle. During the struggle that immediately followed, Wither was made prisoner by the royalists, and stood in danger of capital punishment, but was saved by the interference of his brother poet, Denham. Nothing daunted by the perilous contentions of the times, he again joined the parliamentary army, became one of Cromwell's major-generals, and was appointed by that dauntless leader to keep watch over the royalists of Surrey. From the sequestrated estates of these gentlemen, Wither obtained a considerable fortune, but the *Restoration* came, and he was stript of all his possessions. Against this he remonstrated loudly and angrily; his remonstrances were voted libels, and the unfortunate poet was again thrown into prison. In 1663 he was released from prison under bond of good behaviour, and died in London on the second of May, 1665.

Wither's poetic fame is derived chiefly from those early productions which were composed while he was incarcerated in prison. His mind was extremely active, and though his body was confined within stone walls and iron bars, his fancy was among the hills and plains, with shepherds hunting; or loitering with Poesy, by rustling boughs or murmuring springs. There is hence a freshness and natural vivacity in his poetry, that render his early works a 'perpetual feast.' It is certainly not a feast 'where no crude surfeit reigns,' for he is often harsh, obscure, and affected; but he has an endless diversity of style and subject, and true poetical feeling and expression.

Wither, for more than a century and a half, shared the fate so common to poets of his own age and class, of being comparatively forgotten; but his reputation has recently been revived by Ellis, who, in his *Specimens of Early English Poets*, first pointed out 'that playful fancy, pure taste, and artless delicacy of sentiment, which distinguish the poetry of his early youth.' His 'Address to Poetry' in the 'Shepherds' Hunting' is worthy of the theme, and superior to most of the effusions of that period. The pleasure with which he recounts the various charms and the 'divine skill' of his muse, that had derived nourishment and delight from 'the meanest objects' of external nature—a daisy, a bush, or a tree; and which, when these picturesque and beloved scenes of the country were denied him, could gladden even the vaults and shades of a prison, is one of the richest offerings that has yet been made to the pure and hallowed shrine of poesy. The superiority of intellectual pursuits over the gratifications of sense, and al the malice of fortune, has never been more touchingly or finely illustrated The poem itself follows:—

THE COMPANIONSHIP OF THE MUSE.

See'st thou not, in clearest days,
Oft thick fogs cloud heaven's rays;

And the vapours that do breathe
From the earth's grass womb beneath,
Seem they not with their black steams
To pollute the sun's bright beams,
And yet vanish into air,
Leaving it, unblemish'd fair?
So my Willy, shall it be
With Detraction's breath and thee:
It shall never rise so high,
As to stain thy poesy.
As that sun doth oft exhale
Vapours from each rotten vale;
Poesy so sometime drains
Gross conceits from muddy brains;
Mists of envy, fogs of spite,
'Twixt men's judgments and her light:
But so much her power may do,
That she can dissolve them too.
If thy verse do bravely tower,
As she makes wing she gets power;
Yet the higher she doth soar,
She's affronted still the more:
Till she to the high'st hath past,
Then she rests with fame at last:
Let nought therefore thee affright,
But make forward in thy flight;
For, if I could match thy rhyme,
To the very stars I'd climb;
There begin again, and fly
Till I reach'd eternity.
But, alas! my muse is slow;
For thy page she flags too low:
Yea, the more's her hapless fate,
Her short wings were clipt of late:
And poor I, her fortune ruing,
Am myself put up a mewing:
But if I my cage can rid,
I'll fly where I never did:
And though for her sake I'm crost,
Though my best hopes I have lost,
And knew she would make my trouble
Ten times more than ten times double:
I should love and keep her too,
Spite of all the world could do.
For, though banish'd from my flocks,
And confin'd within these rocks,
Here I waste away the light,
And consume the sullen night,
She doth for my comfort stay,
And keeps many cares away.
Though I miss the flowery fields,
With those sweets the springtide yields,
Though I may not see those groves,
Where the shepherds chant their loves,

And the lasses more excel
Than the sweet-voiced Philomel.
Though of all those pleasures past,
Nothing now remains at last,
But Remembrance, poor relief,
That more makes than mends my grief
She's my mind's companion still,
Maugre Envy's evil will.
(Whence she would be driven, too,
Were 't in mortal's power to do.)
She doth tell me where to borrow
Comfort in the midst of sorrow:
Makes the desolatest place
To her presence be a grace;
And the blackest discontents
Be her fairest ornaments.
In my former days of bliss,
Her divine skill taught me this,
That from every thing I saw,
I could some invention draw;
And raise pleasure to her height,
Through the meanest objects' sight,
By the murmur of a spring,
Or the least boughs' rustleïng.
By a daisy whose leaves spread,
Shut when Titan goes to bed;
Or a shady bush or tree
She could more infuse in me;
Than all Nature's beauties can
In some other wiser man.
By her help I also now
Make this churlish place allow
Some things that may sweeten gladness,
In the very gall of sadness,
The dull loneness, the black shade,
That these hanging vaults have made;
The strange music of the waves,
Beating on these hollow caves;
This black den which rocks emboss,
Overgrown with eldest moss:
The rude portals that give light
More to terror than delight:
This my chamber of neglect,
Wall'd about with disrespect.
From all these, and this dull air,
A fit object for despair,
She hath taught me by her might
To draw comfort and delight.
Therefore, thou best earthly bliss,
I will cherish thee for this.
Poesy, thou sweet'st content
That e'er heaven to mortals lent:
Though they as a trifle leave thee,
Whose dull thoughts can not conceive thee,

Though thou be to them a scorn,
That to nought but earth are born,
Let my life no longer be
Than I am in love with thee:
Though our wise ones call thee madness,
Let me never taste of gladness,
If I love not thy madd'st fits
Above all their greatest wits.
And though some too seeming holy,
Do account thy raptures folly,
Thou dost teach me to contemn
What makes knaves and fools of them.

The poem on Christmas is another fine and graphic sketch, and affords a lively picture of the manners of the times. We have not, however, space to introduce it, and shall, therefore, close our remarks upon this writer with the following witty sonnet:—

A STOLEN KISS.

Now gentle sleep has closed up those eyes
Which, waking, kept my boldest thoughts in awe;
And free access unto that sweet lip lies,
From whence I long the rosy breath to draw.
Methinks no wrong it were, if I should steal
From those two melting rubies, one poor kiss;
None sees the theft that would the theft reveal,
Nor rob I her of ought what she can miss:
Nay should I twenty kisses take away,
There would be little sign I would do so;
Why then should I this robbery delay?
Oh! she may wake, and therewith angry grow!
Well, if she do, I'll back restore that one,
And twenty hundred thousand more for loan.

William Browne was a pastoral and descriptive poet, and adopted Spenser as his model. He was born at Tavistock, in Devonshire, in 1590, but where, and under what circumstances he received his education, is unknown. He was for a short time connected with the Inner Temple as a student of law, but seems never to have followed the legal profession. For a number of years he held the place of tutor to the Earl of Carnarvon, and after the death of that nobleman, who was killed at the battle of Newbury, in 1643, Browne received the patronage, and lived in the family of the Earl of Pembroke. In this situation he realized a competency, and purchased an estate, upon which he died, in 1645.

Browne's works consist of *Britannia's Pastorals*, *The Shepherd's Pipe*, and a masque called *The Inner Temple Masque*. As all these poems were produced before the writer was thirty years of age, and 'Britannia's Pastorals,' which are by far the best, when he was little more than twenty, we should not be surprised that they contain marks of juvenility, and frequent traces of resemblance to the performances of previous poets, especially Spenser, whom he warmly admired. 'Britannia's Pastorals' are written in the heroic couplet, and contain much beautiful descriptive poetry. The author had great facility of expression, and an intimate acquaintance with the phenomena of inanimate nature, and the characteristic features of the English landscape. His own beautiful Devonshire seems to have inspired his strains. The following lines contain an assemblage of the same images that are found in the morning picture of Milton's 'L'Allegro':—

By this had chanticleer, the village cock,
Bidden the goodwife for her maids to knock;
And the swart ploughman for his breakfast stayed,
That he might till those lands where fallow laid;
The hills and valleys here and there resound
With the re-echoes of the deep-mouth'd hound;
Each shepherd's daughter with her cleanly pail
Was come a-field to milk the morning meal;
And ere the sun had climb'd the eastern hills,
To gild the muttering bourns and pretty rills,
Before the labouring bee had left the hive,
And nimble fishes, which in rivers dive,
Began to leap and catch the drowned fly,
I rose from rest, not infelicity.

In one of Browne's pastorals he celebrates the death of a friend, and Milton is supposed to have copied his plan in Lycidas. There is also a faint similarity in some of the sentiments and images. Browne has the following very fine illustration of a rose:—

Look, as a sweet rose fairly budding forth
  Betrays her beauty to th' enamour'd morn,
Until some keen blast from the envious north
  Kills the sweet bud that was but newly born;
    Or else her rarest smells, delighting,
      Make herself betray
    Some white and curious hand, inviting
      To pluck her thence away.

The following beautiful sketches are from the 'Britannia's Pastorals:'—

EVENING.

As in an evening, when the gentle air
Breathes to the sullen night a soft repair,
I oft have sat on Thames' sweet bank, to hear
My friend with his sweet touch to charm mine ear:
When he hath play'd (as well he can) some strain,
That likes me, straight I ask the same again,
And he, as gladly granting, strikes it o'er
With some sweet relish was forgot before:
I would have been content if he would play,
In that one strain, to pass the night away;
But, fearing much to do his patience wrong,
Unwillingly have ask'd some other song:

So, in this diff'ring key, though I could well
A many hours, but as few minutes tell,
Yet, lest mine own delight might injure you,
(Though loath so soon) I take my song anew.

NIGHT.

The sable mantle of the silent night
Shut from the world the ever-joysome light,
Care fled away, and softest slumbers please
To leave the court for lowly cottages.
Wild beasts forsook their dens on woody hills,
And sleightful otters left the purling rills;
Rooks to their nests in high woods now were flung
And with their spread wings shield their naked young.
When thieves from thickets to the cross-ways stir,
And terror frights the lonely passenger;
When nought was heard but now and then the howl
Of some vile cur, or whooping of the owl.

Henry King, better known as a divine than as a poet, was the son of Doctor John King, chaplain to Queen Elizabeth, and afterwards bishop of London. He was born at Wornall, in January 1591, and after preparing for the university at Westminster school, was elected student of Christ's Church College, Oxford. Having taken his degrees, and entered into orders, he became chaplain to James the First, soon after which he was made archdeacon of Colchester. In 1625, he received the degree of doctor of divinity, and became chaplain to Charles the First; and though strongly suspected of inclining to the Puritanical party, he remained in that relation to the king for many years. In 1641, doctor King, as a conciliatory step toward the Puritans, was raised to the see of Chichester; but no sooner had the civil war broken out, and the dissolution of Episcopacy taken place, than he was treated by the very party whom he had been elevated to conciliate, with the utmost severity. At the Restoration, however, he was restored to his bishopric, and Wood informs us that, 'he was esteemed by his diocese and neighborhood, the epitome of all honors, virtues, and generous nobleness, and a person never to be forgotten by his tenants and the poor. He died on the first of October 1669, in his seventy-ninth year.

Bishop King was emphatically a religious poet, and besides composing many sacred songs, elegies, and sonnets, in all of which his language and imagery are chaste and refined, he turned the Psalms of David also into metre. His poems afford little variety, however, as literary performances, and the following specimen will, therefore, be sufficient to exhibit his style and manner:—

A DIRGE.

What is the existence of man's life,
But open war or slumber'd strife;
Where sickness to his sense presents
The combat of the elements;
And never feels a perfect peace
Till Death's cold hand signs his release.

It is a storm—where the hot blood
Outvies in rage the boiling flood;
And each loose passion of the mind
Is like a furious gust of wind,
Which beats his bark with many a wave,
Till he casts anchor in the grave.

It is a flower—which buds, and grows,
And withers as the leaves disclose;
Whose spring and fall faint seasons keep,
Like fits of waking before sleep;
Then shrinks into that fatal mould
Where its first being was enroll'd.

It is a dream—whose seeming truth
Is moraliz'd in age and youth;
Where all the comforts he can share,
As wandering as his fancies are:
Till in a mist of dark decay,
The dreamer vanish quite away.

It is a dial—which points out
The sunset, as it moves about;
And shadows out in lines of night
The subtle stages of Time's flight;
Till all-obscuring earth hath laid
His body in perpetual shade.

It is a weary interlude—
Which doth short joys, long woes, include;
The world the stage, the prologue tears,
The acts vain hopes and varied fears;
The scene shuts up with loss of breath,
And leaves no epilogue but death.

FRANCIS QUARLES was born at Stewards, in Essex, in 1592. His father was clerk of the green-cloth, and purveyor to Queen Elizabeth, and as the son was early designed for a court life, he was educated with reference to that object. He entered Christ's College, Cambridge, but seems to have left the university without a degree, soon after which he became a member of Lincoln's Inn, London. He was afterward cup-bearer to Eliza beth, daughter of James the First, Electress Palatine and Queen of Bo hemia; but upon the ruin of the elector's affairs, he quitted the queen's service, and went to Ireland, where he became secretary to Archbishop Usher. In this situation he remained until the breaking out of the Irish rebellion of 1641, when, after having suffered very severe pecuniary losses, he was obliged to fly for safety into England. In England, however, he did not realize the repose he had anticipated, for one of his productions, the *Royal Convert*, having given offense to the prevailing party, they stripped him of what remained of his possessions, and even seized his books and some valuable manuscripts, which he had prepared for the press. This last blow was more than his mental strength was sufficient to bear, and he died of a broken heart, in September, 1644.

The writings of Quarles are more like those of a divine, or contemplative recluse, than of a busy man of the world, who held various public situations, and died at the age of fifty-two. His principal poems are *Job Militant*, *Sion's Elegies*, *The History of Queen Esther*, *The Morning Muse*, *The Feast of Worms*, and *The Divine Emblems*. The latter was published the year after the writer's death, and was so popular, that Phillips, Milton's nephew, styles Quarles the 'darling of our plebeian judgments.' The eulogium, to some extent, is still appropriate, for the 'Divine Emblems,' with their quaint and grotesque illustrations, may be found, even at the present day, in the cottages of many of the English peasantry.

Quarles' style is that of his age—studded with conceits, often extravagant in conception, and presenting frequently the most ridiculous combinations. There is strength, however, amidst his contortions, and true wit intermingled with the false. His epigrammatic point, uniting wit and devotion, has been considered the precursor of Young's 'Night Thoughts.' The following pieces sufficiently exhibit all the peculiarities of this author's manner, to which we have alluded:—

THE SHORTNESS OF LIFE.

And what's a life?—a weary pilgrimage,
Whose glory in one day doth fill the stage
With childhood, manhood, and decrepit age.

And what's a life?—the flourishing array
Of the proud summer-meadow, which to-day
Wears her green plush, and is to-morrow hay.

Read on this dial, how the shades devour
My short-lived winter's day! hour eats up hour;
Alas! the total's but from eight to four.

Behold these lilies, which thy hands have made,
Fair copies of my life, and open laid
To view, how soon they droop, how soon they fade!

Shade not that dial, night will blind too soon;
My non-aged day already points to noon;
How simple is my suit!—how small my boon!

Nor do I beg this slender inch to wile
My time away, or falsely to beguile
My thoughts with joy: here's nothing worth a smile.

THE VANITY OF THE WORLD.

False world, thou ly'st: thou canst not lend
The least delight:
Thy favours can not gain a friend,
They are so slight:
Thy morning pleasures make an end
To please at night:
Poor are the wants that thou supply'st,
And yet thou vaunt'st, and yet thou vy'st
With heaven; fond earth, thou boasts; false world, thou ly'st.

Thy babbling tongue tells golden tales
Of endless treasure;
Thy bounty offers easy sales
Of lasting pleasure;
Thou ask'st the conscience what she ails,
And swear'st to ease her:
There's none can want where thou supply'st:
There's none can give where thou deny'st.
Alas! fond world, thou boasts; false world, thou ly'st.

What well-advised ear regards
What earth can say?
Thy words are gold, but thy rewards
Are painted clay:
Thy cunning can but pack the cards,
Thou can'st not play:
Thy game at weakest, still thou vy'st;
If seen, and then revy'd, deny'st;
Thou art not what thou seem'st; false world, thou ly'st.

Thy tinsel bosom seems a mint
Of new-coin'd treasure;
A paradise, that has no stint,
No change, no measure;
A painted cask, but nothing in't,
Nor wealth, nor pleasure:
Vain earth! that falsely thus comply'st
With man; vain man! that thou rely'st
On earth; vain man, thou dot'st; vain earth, thou ly'st.

What mean dull souls, in this high measure
To haberdash
In earth's base wares, whose greatest treasure
Is dross and trash?
The height of whose enchanting pleasure
Is but a flash?
Are these the goods that thou supply'st
Us mortals with? are these the high'st?
Can these bring cordial peace? false world, thou ly'st.

DELIGHT IN GOD ALONE.

I love, (and have some cause to love,) the earth
She is my Maker's creature; therefore good:
She is my mother, for she gave me birth;
She is my tender nurse—she gives me food;
But what's a creature, Lord, compared with thee?
Or what's my mother, or my nurse to me?

I love the air: her dainty sweets refresh
My drooping soul, and to new sweets invite me;
Her shrill-mouth'd quire sustains me with their flesh,
And with their polyphonian notes delight me:
But what's the air, or all the sweets that she
Can bless my soul withal, compared to thee?

I love the sea: she is my fellow-creature,
My careful purveyor; she provides me store:

She walls me round; she makes my diet greater;
She wafts my treasure from a foreign shore:
  But, Lord of oceans, when compared with thee.
  What is the ocean, or her wealth to me?

To heaven's high city I direct my journey,
Where spangled suburbs entertain mine eye;
Mine eye, by contemplation's great attorney,
Transcends the crystal pavement of the sky:
  But what is heaven, great God, compared to thee?
  Without thy presence heaven's no heaven to me.

Without thy presence earth gives no reflection;
Without thy presence sea affords no treasure;
Without thy presence air 's a rank infection;
Without thy presence heaven itself no pleasure:
  If not possess'd, if not enjoy'd in thee,
  What's earth, or sea, or air, or heaven to me?

The highest honours that the world can boast,
Are subjects far too low for my desire;
The brightest beams of glory are (at most)
But dying sparkles of thy living fire:
  The loudest flames that earth can kindle, be
  But mighty glow-worms if compared to thee.

Without thy presence wealth is bag of cares;
Wisdom but folly; joy disquiet—sadness:
Friendship is treason, and delights are snares;
Pleasures but pain, and mirth but pleasing madness;
  Without thee, Lord, things be not what they be,
  Nor have they being, when compared with thee.

In having all things, and not thee, what have I?
Not having thee, what have my labours got?
Let me enjoy but thee, what farther care I?
And having thee alone, what have I not?
  I wish nor sea nor land; nor would I be
  Possess'd of heaven, heaven unpossess'd of thee.

Herbert and Herrick, with a passing glance at Hall, will close the list of poets to be embraced within the present lecture.

George Herbert was of the ancient and honorable family of Pembroke, and was born at Montgomery Castle, Wales, on the third of April, 1593. His early studies were pursued at Westminster school, where he was eminently distinguished for both genius and application. In 1608, he was elected as King's scholar to Trinity College, Cambridge, and having there taken both his degrees, he soon after obtained a fellowship, and, in 1619, became orator of the university. Herbert was the intimate friend of Sir Henry Wotton, and Doctor Donne; and Lord Bacon is said to have entertained so high regard for his learning and judgment, that he usually submitted his works to him before their publication. The poet was also in favor with King James, who gave him a sinecure office worth one hundred and twenty pounds a year, which Queen Elizabeth had formerly given to Sir Philip Sidney. 'With this,' says Izaak Walton, 'and his annuity, and the advantages of his college and of his oratorship, he enjoyed his genteel humor for clothes and court-like company, and seldom looked toward Cambridge unless the King was there, but then he never failed.'

The death of the king and of two powerful friends, the Duke of Richmond and the Marquis of Hamilton, destroyed Herbert's court hopes, and he, therefore, entered into sacred orders. He was first prebend of Layton Ecclesia, and afterward rector of Bemerton, in Wiltshire. 'The third day after he was made rector of Bemerton,' says Walton, 'and had changed his sword and silk clothes into a canonical habit, he returned so habited with his friend Mr. Woodnot to Bainton; and immediately after he had seen and saluted his wife, he said to her, 'You are now a minister's wife, and must now so far forget your father's house as not to claim a precedence of any of your parishioners; for you are to know that a priest's wife can challenge no precedence or place but that which she purchases by her obliging humility; and I am sure places so purchased do best become them. And let me tell you, I am so good a herald as to assure you that this is truth.' 'And she was so meek a wife as to assure him it was no vexing news to her, and that he should see her observe it with a cheerful willingness.' Herbert remained at Bemerton till the close of his life, and to the last discharged his clerical duties with saint-like zeal and purity; but his strength was not equal to his self-imposed tasks, and he died at the early age of thirty-nine.

The principal production of Herbert is *The Temple, or Sacred Poems, and Private Ejaculations.* The lines on *Virtue* are the best in the collection; but even in them we find what mars all the poetry of this writer, ridiculous conceits and coarse unpleasant similes. The most sacred subject could not repress his love of fantastic imagery, or keep him for any number of consecutive verses in a serious and natural strain. It may be safely said, therefore, that his poetry alone would not have preserved his name, and that he is indebted for the reputation he enjoys to his excellent and amiable character, to his prose work, the *Country Parson*, and to the warm and fervent piety which gave a charm to his life, and breathes through all his writings. The following are the lines on 'Virtue' already alluded to, to which we shall add a much more elaborate poem on Sunday.

VIRTUE.

Sweet day! so cool, so calm, so bright,
The bridal of the earth and sky;
The dews shall weep thy fall to-night,
For thou must die.

Sweet rose! whose hue, angry and brave,
Bids the rash gazer wipe his eye;
Thy root is ever in its grave;
And thou must die.

Sweet spring! full of sweet days and roses
A box where sweets compacted lie;
Thy music shows ye have your closes;
And all must die.

Only a sweet and virtuous soul,
Like season'd timber never gives;
But, though the whole world turn to coal,
Then chiefly lives.

SUNDAY.

O day most calm, most bright,
The fruit of this the next world's bud,
The indorsement of supreme delight,
Writ by a friend, and with his blood;
The couch of time, care's balm and bay:
The week were dark, but for thy light;
Thy torch doth show the way.

The other days and thou
Make up one man; whose face thou art,
Knocking at heaven with thy brow;
The worky days are the back-part;
The burden of the week lies there,
Making the whole to stoop and bow,
Till thy release appear.

Man had straight-forward gone
To endless death: but thou dost pull
And turn us round, to look on one,
Whom, if we were not very dull,
We could not choose, but look on still;
Since there is no place so alone,
The which he doth not fill.

Sundays the pillars are,
On which heaven's palace arched lies;
The other days fill up the spare
And hollow room with vanities.
They are the fruitful beds and borders
In God's rich garden: that is bare,
Which parts their ranks and orders.

The Sundays of man's life,
Threaded together on Time's string,
Make bracelets to adorn the wife
Of the eternal glorious King.
On Sunday heaven's gate stands ope;
Blessings are plentiful and rife—
More plentiful than hope.

This day my Saviour rose,
And did inclose this light for his;
That, as each beast his manger knows,
Man might not of his fodder miss.
Christ hath took in this piece of ground,
And made a garden there for those
Who want herbs for their wound.

The rest of our creation
Our great Redeemer did remove
With the same shake, which at his passion
Did the earth and all things with it move.
As Samson bore the doors away,
Christ's hands, though nail'd, wrought our salvation,
And did unhinge that day.

The brightness of that day
We sullied by our foul offence:
Wherefore that robe we cast away,
Having a new at his expense,
Whose drops of blood paid the full price,
That was required to make us gay,
And fit for paradise.

Thou art a day of mirth:
And where the week-days trail on ground,
Thy flight is higher, as thy birth;
O let me take thee at the bound,
Leaping with thee from seven to seven,
Till that we both being toss'd from earth,
Fly hand in hand to heaven.

Robert Herrick, one of the most exquisite of the early English lyrical poets, was born in Cheapside, London, in 1591. He was educated at the university of Cambridge, and having taken orders, was presented, by Charles the First, in 1629, to the vicarage of Dean Prior, in Devonshire. After residing about twenty years in this rural parish, Herrick was ejected from his living by the storms of the civil war; but whatever regret the poet may have felt on being turned adrift upon the world, he could have experienced little pain on parting with his parishioners, whom he describes as a 'wild amphibious race, almost as rude as savages, and churlish as the seas.' Herrick, at the same time, gives us a glimpse of his own character:—

Born I was to meet with age,
And to walk life's pilgrimage:
Much, I know, of time is spent;
Tell I can't what's resident.
Howsoever, cares adieu!
I'll have nought to say to you;
But I'll spend my coming hours
Drinking wine and crown'd with flowers.

So light and genial a temperament would enable the poet to ride out the storm in comparative composure.

Herrick published his *Noble Numbers, or Pious Pieces*, in 1647, which must have been about the time that he lost his vicarage. In the following year appeared *The Hesperides, or the Works, both Humane and Divine, of Robert Herrick, Esquire.* The clerical prefix to his name seems now to have been abandoned by the poet, and there are certainly many pieces in his second volume which would not become one ministering at the altar, or belonging to the sacred profession. He now took up his residence in Westminster, associated with the jovial spirits of the age, and was supported or assisted by the wealthy royalists.

After the Restoration Herrick was restored to the Devonshire vicarage. How he was received by the 'rude savages' of Dean Prior, or how he felt on quitting the gayeties of the metropolis to resume his clerical duties and seclusion, is not recorded. He was at this time about seventy years of age, and was probably tired of wine and tavern jollities. He had an unquestionable taste for the pleasures of a country life, if we may judge from his works, and the fondness with which he dwells on old English festivals and rural scenes. Though his rhymes were sometimes wild, he says his life was chaste, and he repented of his errors :—

For these my unbaptized rhymes,
Writ in my wild unhallowed times,
For every sentence, clause, and word,
That's not inlaid with thee, O Lord!
Forgive me, God, and blot each line
Out of my book that is not thine;
But if, 'mongst all thou findest one
Worthy thy benediction,
That one of all the rest shall be
The glory of my work and me.

The poet would have better evinced the sincerity and depths of his contrition by blotting out the unbaptized rhymes himself; but the vanity of the author probably triumphed over the penitence of the Christian. Gayety was Herrick's natural element. His muse was a goddess fair and free, that did not move happily in serious numbers. The time of the poet's death has not been ascertained, but he must have lived to reach a ripe old age.

The poetical works of Herrick lay neglected for many years after his death, but they have recently become popular, especially his shorter Lyrics, some of which have, within a few years, been set to music, and are now sung and quoted by all lovers of song. His verses, *Cherry Ripe*, and *Gather the Rose-buds while ye may*, possess a delicious mixture of playful fancy and natural feeling. Those *To Blossoms*, *To Daffodils*, and *To Primroses*, have a tinge of pathos that at once wins its way to the heart. They abound, like all Herrick's poems, in lively imagery and conceits; but the pensive moral feeling predominates, and we feel that the poet's smiles might as well be tears. Shakspeare and Jonson had scattered such delicate fancies among their plays and masques, that Herrick was not without models of the highest excellence in this species of composition. There is, however, in his songs and anacreontics, an unforced gayety and natural tenderness, which show that he wrote chiefly from the impulses of his own cheerful and happy nature. The select beauty and picturesqueness of Herrick's language, when he is in his happiest vein, is worthy of his fine conceptions; and his versification is harmony itself. His verses bound and flow like some exquisite lively melody, that echoes nature, by wood and dell, and presents new beauties at every turn and winding. The strain is short, and sometimes fantastic, but the notes long linger in the mind, and take their place forever in the memory. One or two words, such as 'gather the rose-buds,' call up a summer landscape, with youth, beauty, flowers, and music. This is, and ever must be, true poetry.

We shall introduce Herrick's minor poems in the order in which they are enumerated above; and shall follow them by two that are more extended, the latter of which is one of the finest of his serious poetical performances.

CHERRY RIPE.

Cherry ripe, ripe, ripe, I cry,
Full and fair ones—come and buy;
If so be you ask me where
They do grow?—I answer, There,
Where my Julia's lips do smile—
There's the land, or cherry-isle;
Whose plantations fully show
All the year where cherries grow.

GATHER THE ROSE-BUDS.

Gather the rose-buds while ye may,
  Old Time is still a-flying,
And this same flower that smiles to-day,
  To-morrow will be dying.

The glorious lamp of heaven, the Sun,
  The higher he's a getting,
The sooner will his race be run,
  And nearer he's to setting.

That age is best which is the first,
  When youth and blood are warmer;
But being spent, the worse, and worst
  Time shall succeed the former.

Then be not coy, but use your time,
  And while ye may, go marry;
For, having lost but once your prime,
  You may forever tarry.

TO BLOSSOMS.

Fair pledges of a fruitful tree,
    Why do ye fall so fast?
    Your date is not so past,
But you may stay yet here a while,
    To blush and gently smile,
        And go at last.

What! were ye born to be
    An hour or half's delight,
    And so to bid good-night?
'Tis pity nature brought ye forth
    Merely to show your worth,
        And lose you quite.

But you are lovely leaves, where we
May read how soon things have
Their end, though ne'er so brave:
And after they have shown their pride,
Like you a while they glide
Into the grave.

TO DAFFODILS.

Fair daffodils, we weep to see
You haste away so soon;
As yet the early-rising sun
Has not attain'd his noon:
Stay, stay,
Until the hast'ning day
Has run
But to the even-song;
And having pray'd together, we
Will go with you along!
We have short time to stay as you;
We have as short a spring;
As quick a growth to meet decay
As you or any thing:
We die
As your hours do; and dry
Away
Like to the summer's rain,
Or as the pearls of morning dew
Ne'er to be found again.

TO PRIMROSES, FILLED WITH MORNING DEW.

Why do ye weep, sweet babes? Can tears
Speak grief in you,
Who were but born
Just as modest morn
Teem'd her refreshing dew?
Alas! you have not known that shower
That mars a flower,
Nor felt the unkind
Breath of a blasting wind;
Nor are ye worn with years,
Or warped as we,
Who think it strange to see
Such pretty flowers, like to orphans young,
Speaking by tears before ye have a tongue.

Speak whimp'ring younglings, and make known
The reason why
Ye droop and weep;
Is it for want of sleep,
Or childish lullaby?
Or that ye have not seen as yet
The violet?
Or brought a kiss
From that sweet heart to this?

No, no; this sorrow shown
By your tears shed,
Would have this lecture read—
'That things' of greatest, so of meanest worth,
Conceived with grief are, and with tears brought forth

TO CORINNA, TO GO A MAYING.

Get up, get up, for shame, the blooming morn
Upon her wings presents the god unshorn.
See how Aurora throws her fair
Fresh-quilted colours through the air;
Get up, sweet slug-a-bed, and see
The dew bespangled herb and tree.
Each flower has wept, and bow'd toward the east,
Above an hour since, yet you are not drest,
Nay, not so much as out of bed;
When all the birds have matins said,
And sung their thankful hymns: 'tis sin,
Nay, profanation, to keep in,
When as a thousand virgins on this day,
Spring sooner than the lark to fetch in May.

Rise, and put on your foliage, and be seen
To come forth, like the spring time, fresh and green,
And sweet as Flora. Take no care
For jewels for your gown or hair;
Fear not, the leaves will strew
Gems in abundance upon you;
Besides, the childhood of the day has kept,
Against you come, some orient pearls unwept.
Come and receive them while the light
Hangs on the dew-locks of the night:
And Titan on the eastern hill
Retires himself, or else stands still
Till you come forth. Wash, dress, be brief in praying;
Few beads are best, when once we go a Maying.

Come, my Corinna, come; and, coming, mark
How each field turns a street,[1] each street a park
Made green, and trimm'd with trees; see how
Devotion gives each house a bough,
Or branch; each porch, each door, ere this,
An ark, a tabernacle is,
Made up of white thorn neatly interwove;
As if here were those cooler shades of love.
Can such delights be in the street,
And open fields, and we not see't?
Come, we'll abroad, and let's obey
The proclamation made for May:
And sin no more, as we have done, by staying,
But, my Corinna, come, let's go a Maying.

[1] Herrick here alludes to the multitudes which were to be seen roaming in the fields on May morning; he afterward refers to the appearance of the towns and villages bedecked with evergreens.

There's not a budding boy or girl, this day,
But is got up, and gone to bring in May.
  A deal of youth, ere this, is come
  Back, and with white thorn laden home.
  Some have dispatch'd their cakes and cream
  Before that we have left to dream;
And some have wept, and woo'd, and plight'd troth,
And chose their priest, ere we can cast off sloth:
  Many a green gown has been given;
  Many a kiss, both odd and even;
  Many a glance, too, has been sent
  From out the eye, love's firmament;
Many a jest told of the key's betraying
This night, and locks pick'd; yet w' are not a Maying.

Come, let us go, while we are in our prime,
And take the harmless folly of the time.
  We shall grow old apace, and die
  Before we know our liberty.
  Our life is short, and our days run
  As fast away as does the sun;
And as a vapour, or a drop of rain
Once lost, can ne'er be found again;
  So when or you or I are made
  A fable, song, or fleeting shade;
  All love, all liking, all delight
  Lies drown'd with us in endless night.
Then, while time serves, and we are but decaying,
Come, my Corinna, come, let's go a Maying.

A THANKSGIVING FOR HIS HOUSE.

Lord, Thou hast given me a cell,
    Wherein to dwell;
A little house, whose humble roof
    Is weatherproof;
Under the spars of which I lie
    Both soft and dry.
Where Thou, my chamber for to ward
    Hast set a guard
Of harmless thoughts, to watch and keep
    Me while I sleep.
Low is my porch, as is my fate,
    Both void of state;
And yet the threshold of my door
    Is worn by the poor,
Who hither come, and freely get
    Good words or meat.
Like as my parlour, so my hall,
    And kitchen small;
A little buttery, and therein
    A little bin,
Which keeps my little loaf of bread
    Unchipt, unflead.
Some brittle sticks of thorn or brier
    Make me a fire,

Close by whose living coal I sit,
And glow like it.
Lord, I confess, too, when I dine,
The pulse is Thine,
And all those other bits that be
There placed by Thee.
The worts, the parslain, and the mess
Of water cress,
Which of Thy kindness Thou hast sent:
And my content
Makes those, and my beloved beet,
To be more sweet.
'Tis thou that crown'st my glittering hearth
With guiltless mirth;
And giv'st me wassail bowls to drink,
Spiced to the brink.
Lord, 'tis thy plenty-dropping hand
That sows my land:
All this, and better, dost Thou send
Me for this end:
That I should render for my part
A thankful heart,
Which, fir'd with incense, I resign
As wholly thine:
But the acceptance—that must be,
O Lord, by Thee.

JOSEPH HALL, Bishop of Norwich, though much more distinguished as a prose writer than as a poet, is yet allowed to be the first English author who wrote satirical verse with any degree of elegance. His satires refer to general objects, and present some just pictures of the more remarkable anomalies in human character: they are also written in a style of greater polish and volubility than most of the compositions of that age. Of these satires we present the following as a specimen:—

THE DOMESTIC TUTOR.

A gentle squire would gladly entertain
Into his house some trencher-chapelain:
Some willing man that might instruct his sons,
And that would stand to good conditions.
First, that he lie upon the truckle-bed,
While his young master lieth o'er his head.
Second, that he do, on no default,
Ever presume to sit above the salt.
Third, that he never change his trencher twice.
Fourth, that he use all common courtesies;
Sit bare at meals, and one half rise and wait.
Last, that he never his young master beat,
But he must ask his mother to define,
How many jerks he would his breech should line.
All these observed, he could contented be,
To give five marks and winter livery.

Lecture the Tenth.

JOHN CHALKHILL—WILLIAM HABINGTON—THOMAS RANDOLPH—SIR WILLIAM DAVENANT—SIR RICHARD FANSHAWE—SIR JOHN SUCKLING—WILLIAM CARTWRIGHT—JOHN CLEVELAND—RICHARD LOVELACE—RICHARD CRASHAW.

WE have long lingered with the English miscellaneous poets of the age of Elizabeth, James, and Charles the First, and yet our task is not done; for there still remain to be noticed and illustrated, Chalkhill, Habington, Randolph, Davenant, Fanshawe, Suckling, and a number of others of equal eminence.

JOHN CHALKHILL was born about the year 1600, but of his life comparatively little is known. Izaak Walton, who published, in 1683, a pastoral romance entitled *Thealma and Clearchus* by Chalkhill, remarks, 'that the author was, in his time, a man generally known, and as well beloved; for he was humble and obliging in his behaviour; a gentleman, a scholar, very innocent and prudent; and, indeed, his whole life was useful, quiet, and virtuous.' Chalkhill died in 1679, and was buried in Winchester Cathedral, upon the walls of which, his tombstone of black marble is still to be seen.

The scene of 'Thealma and Clearchus' is laid in Arcadia, and the author, like the ancient poets, describes the golden age and all its charms, which were succeeded by an iron age, in the introduction of ambition, avarice, and tyranny. The plot is complicated and obscure, and the characters are deficient in individuality; the poem must, therefore, be read, like the Faery Queen, for its romantic description and its occasional felicity of language. The versification is that of the heroic couplet, varied, like Milton's Lycidas, by breaks and pauses in the middle of the line. The following brief extracts will sufficiently illustrate these remarks:—

THE PRIESTESS OF DIANA.

Within a little silent grove hard by,
Upon a small ascent he might espy
A stately chapel, richly gilt without,
Beset with shady sycamores about:

And ever and anon he might well hear
A sound of music steal in at his ear
As the wind gave it being:—so sweet an air
Would strike a syren mute.

* * * * * *

A hundred virgins he might there espy
Prostrate before a marble deity,
Which, by its portraiture, appear'd to be
The image of Diana:—on their knee
They tender'd their devotions: with sweet airs,
Off'ring the incense of their praise and prayers.
Across their snowy silken robes, they wore
An azure scarf, with stars embroider'd o'er.
Their hair in curious tresses was knit up,
Crown'd with a silver crescent on the top,
A silver bow their left hand held; their right,
For their defence, held a sharp-headed flight,
Drawn from their 'broider'd quiver, neatly tied
In silken cords, and fasten'd to their side.
Under their vestments, something short before,
White buskins, lac'd with ribanding, they wore.
It was a catching sight for a young eye,
That love had fir'd before:—he might espy
One, whom the rest had sphere-like circled round,
Whose head was with a golden chaplet crown'd.
He could not see her face, only his ear
Was blest with the sweet words that came from her.

THE VOTARESS OF DIANA.

——— Clarinda came at last,
With all her train, who, as along she pass'd
Thorough the inward court, did make a lane,
Opening their ranks, and closing them again,
As she went forward, with obsequious gesture,
Doing their reverence. Her upward vesture
Was of blue silk, glistering with stars of gold,
Girt to her waist by serpents, that enfold
And wrap themselves together, so well wrought
And fashion'd to the life, one would have thought
They had been real. Underneath she wore
A coat of silver tinsel, short before,
And fring'd about with gold: white buskins hide
The naked of her leg; they were loose tied
With azure ribands, on whose knots were seen
Most costly gems, fit only for a queen.
Her hair bound up like to a coronet,
With diamonds, rubies, and rich sapphires set;
And on the top a silver crescent plac'd,
And all the lustre by such beauty grac'd,
As her reflection made them seem more fair;
One would have thought Diana's self were there
For in her hand a silver bow she held,
And at her back there hung a quiver fill'd
With turtle-feather'd arrows.

William Habington was descended from an ancient family, and born at Hendlip, Worcestershire, in 1605. He received his education at St. Omers and Paris, and when he had completed his studies was earnestly solicited to enter into the society of Jesuits; but as their habits of life suited neither his taste nor his genius, he left them and returned to England. Soon after his return to his native country, Habington married Lucia, daughter of the first Lord Powis, and from that time until his death, which occurred on the thirtieth of November, 1654, his life presents few incidents worthy of particular notice.

Habington had all the vices of the metaphysical school, excepting its occasional licentiousness. He tells us, in the preface to his works, that 'if the innocency of a chaste muse shall be more acceptable, and weigh heavier in the balance of esteem, than a fame begot in adultery of study, I doubt I shall leave fame no hope of competition.' And of a pure attachment he beautifully remarks, that, 'when love builds upon the rock of Chastity, it may safely contemn the battery of the waves and threatenings of the wind; since time, that makes a mockery of the firmest structures, shall itself be ruinated before that be demolished.'

Twenty years before his death, when he had scarcely attained the thirtieth year of his age, Habington published his poems under the title of *The Mistress*, *The Wife*, and *The Holy Man*. These titles included each several copies of verses, and the same design was afterward adopted by Cowley. The life of the poet seems to have glided quietly away, cheered by the society and affection of his Lucia. He had no stormy passions to agitate him, and no unruly imagination to control or subdue. His poetry is of the same unruffled description—placid, tender, and often elegant—but studded with conceits to show his wit and fancy. The following description of Lucia under the feigned name of Castara, is full of beauty:—

DESCRIPTION OF CASTARA.

Like the violet which, alone,
Prospers in some happy shade,
My Castara lives unknown,
To no looser eye betray'd,
    For she's to herself untrue
    Who delights i' th' public view.

Such is her beauty as no arts
Have enrich'd with borrow'd grace;
Her high birth no pride imparts
For she blushes in her place.
    Folly boasts a glorious blood,
    She is noblest being good.

Cautious, she knew never yet
What a wanton courtship meant;
Nor speaks loud to boast her wit:
In her silence eloquent:
    Of herself survey she takes,
    But 'tween men no difference makes.

She obeys with speedy will
Her grave parents' wise commands;
And so innocent, that ill
She nor acts, nor understands:
  Women's feet run still astray,
  If once to ill they know the way.

She sails by that rock the court,
Where oft honour splits her mast;
And retir'dness thinks the port,
Where her fame may anchor cast;
  Virtue safely cannot sit,
  Where vice is enthron'd for wit.

She holds that day's pleasure best,
Where sin waits not on delight;
Without masque, or ball, or feast,
Sweetly spends a winter's night:
  O'er that darkness whence is thrust
  Prayer and sleep, oft governs lust.

She her throne makes reason climb,
While wild passions captive lie:
And, each article of time
Her pure thoughts to heaven fly:
  All her vows religious be,
  And her love she vows to me.

Thomas Randolph was the son of the steward of Lord Zouch, and was born at Newnham in Northamptonshire, on the fifteenth of June 1605. He prepared for the university at Westminister school, and in 1623, was elected, as King's scholar, to Trinity College, Cambridge, where he remained until he had taken his master's degree, soon after which he was chosen to a fellowship.

Randolph's genius was so remarkably precocious that he acquired poetic celebrity even before he entered the university; having, when he had scarcely passed the tenth year of his age, written a *History of the Incarnation of our Saviour*, in verse. Such early evidences of genius being sustained as he advanced into manhood, Ben Jonson, through affectionate admiration, adopted him as one of his sons. But poet-like, Randolph evinced a thorough contempt of wealth, and a corresponding love of pleasure; and by these means he was drawn into excesses which so rapidly shortened his life, that he died in March 1634, not yet having attained the thirtieth year of his age.

Randolph was the author of five dramatic pieces, besides a volume of miscellaneous poems. Of his dramas, the *Muse's Looking-Glass* is a greatly superior production to the rest, and was for a long time, extremely popular; but his reputation rests chiefly upon his miscellaneous poems. Of these, the following address to a *Lady admiring herself in a Looking-Glass*, though somewhat fantastic, is both witty and elegant:—

Fair lady, when you see the grace
Of beauty, in your looking-glass;
A stately forehead, smooth and high,
And full of princely majesty;
A sparkling eye no gem so fair,
Whose lustre dims the Cyprian star;
A glorious cheek, divinely sweet,
Wherein both roses kindly meet;
A cherry lip that would entice
Even gods to kiss at any price;
You think no beauty is so rare
That with your shadow might compare;
That your reflection is alone
The thing that men most dote upon.
Madam, alas, your glass doth lie
And you are much deceived; for I
A beauty know of richer grace,
(Sweet, be not angry) 'tis your face.
Hence, then, O learn more mild to be,
And leave to lay your blame on me:
If me your real substance move,
When you so much your shadow love,
Wise nature would not let your eye
Look on her own bright majesty;
Which, had you once but gazed upon,
You could except yourself, love none:
What then you can not love, let me,
That face I can, you can not see.
Now you have what to love, you'll say,
What then is left for me, I pray?
My face, sweet heart, if it please thee;
That which you can, I can not see:
So either love shall gain his due,
Yours, sweet, in me, and mine in you.

WILLIAM DAVENANT was the son of a vintner, and was born at Oxford, where his father kept the 'Crown Tavern,' in 1605. The 'Crown' being a very popular stopping place, Shakspeare was in the habit of putting up there in his frequent journeyings from London to Stratford, and young Davenant, conceiving the strongest admiration for the great poet, poured forth his youthful feelings in an ode commencing with the following stanza:—

Beware, delighted poets, when you sing,
To welcome nature in the early spring,
  Your numerous feet not tread
The banks of Avon, for each flower
(As it ne'er knew a sun or shower)
  Hangs there the pensive head.

At this time Davenant was only ten years of age, and the evidence of unusual genius thus early given, induced his friends to enter him into the grammar-school of his native place, whence, after suitable preparation, he passed to Lincoln College, Oxford. He discovered, however, little taste for collegiate learning, and, therefore, soon left the university and entered into the service as page, first of Frances, Duchess of Richmond, and afterward of Lord Brooke, who being himself a poet, was much delighted with him.

In similar employments Davenant passed his life until 1628, when he turned his attention to the drama, and began to write for the stage; and in 1638, on the death of Ben Jonson, he was appointed poet-laureate. He was, soon after this period, drawn into the commotions and intrigues of the civil war, and being, with others, suspected by the parliamentary party of a design to bring their army into the interests of the king, he was apprehended and sent to the Tower. After a few months' imprisonment he obtained his release and retired into France; but he did not long remain abroad; and on his return to England so distinguished himself in the cause of the royalists, that in 1643 he received from the king the honor of knighthood.

On the decline of the king's affairs Davenant returned to France, and soon after engaged to sail for Virginia as a colonial projector; but the vessel in which he set sail was captured off the coast of France by one of the parliametary ships of war, and he was lodged in prison at Cowes, in the Isle of Wight. In 1650, he was removed to the Tower, preparatory to trial by the High Commission Court. His life was now considered in imminent peril; but through the influence of Milton, who was at the time all-powerful with the dominant party, it was spared, and after two years' imprisonment he obtained his liberty. It is said that Davenant did not forget the favor thus received at Milton's hands, but when, after the Restoration, the royalists were again in the ascendant, he interposed in turn his kind offices for Milton's safety, and that it was through his influence chiefly that the great poet was spared. Such instances of reciprocal admiration for genius afford a sweet relief to the general asperities of political contentions. After the Restoration, Davenant again basked in royal favor, and uninterrupted prosperity attended him until his death, which occurred on the seventh of April, 1668, in his sixty-third year.

Sir William Davenant is indebted chiefly for his fame to his heroic poem, *Gondibert*. This production, though regarded by his friends and admirers as a great and durable monument of genius, is now almost entirely forgotten. The plot is romantic, but defective in interest; and its extreme length, together with the long four-line stanza of alternate rhymes in which it is written, render the whole poem languid and tedious. Critics have been strangely at variance with each other with regard to its merits; and as to general readers the poem is almost entirely unknown, we shall introduce the following passage as a specimen of the work:—

DESCRIPTION OF BIRTHA.

To Astragon, heaven for succession gave
  One only pledge, and Birtha was her name,

Whose mother slept where flowers grew on her grave,
  And she succeeded her in face and fame.

Her beauty princes durst not hope to use,
  Unless like poets, for their morning theme;
And her mind's beauty they would rather choose,
  Which did the light on beauty's lanthorn seem.

She ne'er saw courts, yet courts could have undone
  With untaught looks, and an unpracticed heart;
Her nets, the most prepar'd could never shun,
  For nature spread them in the scorn of art.

She never had in busy cities been,
  Ne'er warm'd with hopes, nor ere allay'd with fears;
Not seeing punishment, could guess no sin,
  And sin not seeing, ne'er had use of tears.

But here her father's precepts gave her skill,
  Which with incessant business fill'd the hours;
In spring she gather'd blossoms for the still;
  In autumn, berries; and in summer, flowers.

And as kind nature, with calm diligence,
  Her own free virtue silently employs,
Whilst she unheard, does ripening growth dispense,
  So were her virtues busy without noise.

Whilst her great mistress, Nature, thus she tends,
  The busy household waits no less on her;
By secret law, each to her beauty bends,
  Though all her lowly mind to that prefer.

Gracious and free she breaks upon them all
  With morning looks; and they, when she does rise,
Devoutly at her dawn in homage fall
  And droop like flowers when evening shuts her eyes.

* * * * * * * *

Beneath a myrtle covert she does spend,
  In maid's weak wishes, her whole stock of thought;
Fond maids! who love with mind's fine stuff would mend
  Which nature purposely of bodies wrought.

She fashions him she loved of angels' kind;
  Such as in holy story were employ'd
To the first fathers from the Eternal Mind,
  And in short vision only are enjoy'd.

As eagles, then, when nearest heaven they fly,
  Of wild impossibles soon weary grow;
Feeling their bodies find no rest so high,
  And therefore perch on earthly things below;

So now she yields; him she an angel deem'd
  Shall be a man, the name which virgins fear;
Yet the most harmless to a maid he seem'd,
  That ever yet that fatal name did bear.

Soon her opinion of his hurtless heart,
  Affection turns to faith; and then love's fire

To heaven, though bashfully, she does impart,
  And to her mother in the heavenly quire.

'If I do love,' said she, 'that love, O Heaven!
  Your own disciple, Nature, bred in me;
Why should I hide the passion you have given,
  Or blush to show effects which you decree?

'And you, my alter'd mother, grown above
  Great Nature, which you read and reverenc'd here,
Chide not such kindness as you once call'd love,
  When you as mortal as my father were.'

This said, her soul into her breast retires;
  With love's vain diligence of heart she dreams
Herself into possession of desires,
  And trusts unanchor'd hopes in fleeting streams.

She thinks of Eden-life; and no rough wind
  In that pacific sea shall wrinkles make;
That still her lowliness shall keep him kind,
  Her ears keep him asleep, her voice awake.

She thinks, if ever anger in him sway,
  (The youthful warrior's most excus'd disease,)
Such chance her tears shall calm, as showers allay
  The accidental rage of winds and seas.

To this extract from 'Gondibert' we add, from Sir William Davenant's minor poems, the following very beautiful verses:—

SONG.

The lark now leaves his watery nest,
  And climbing shakes his dewy wings;
He takes his window from the east,
  And to implore your light, he sings,
Awake, awake, the morn will never rise,
Till she can dress her beauty at your eyes.

The merchant bows unto the seaman's star,
  The ploughman from the sun his season takes;
But still the lover wonders what they are,
  Who look for day before his mistress wakes:
Awake, awake, break through your veils of lawn!
Then draw your curtains and begin the dawn.

Richard Fanshawe was descended from an ancient family in Derbyshire, and was born at Ware Park, Hertfordshire, in 1607. He received the rudiments of his education from Thomas Farnaby, the most famous teacher of the age, and from under his care he passed to the university of Cambridge, where he remained until he had completed his studies. From the university Fanshawe went to the Continent, and by the means of intercourse with foreign nations for some years, he became highly accomplished both in mind and manners. His learning and ability so early distinguished him, that, in 1635, when he was but twenty-eight years of age, he was sent by Charles the First as minister to the court of Spain, and at that court remained until 1641, when the precarious state of affairs at home requiring his presence, he was recalled; and through all the disastrous events which immediately followed, adhered unfalteringly to the royal cause. In 1644, attending the court at Oxford, Fanshawe had the degree of doctor of the civil law conferred upon him, and being immediately after made secretary to Charles, Prince of Wales, he attended the prince in that capacity, first into the western part of England, and then to the Scilly Isles, and to Jersey.

In 1650, soon after the death of Charles the First, Fanshawe was created a baronet by Charles the Second, and sent as envoy extraordinary to the court of Spain; but was soon recalled thence to Scotland, where he, for some time, exercised the duties of Secretary of State. The struggle in Scotland proved unfavorable to the interests of Charles, and Fanshawe, being taken prisoner by the parliamentary forces, was, for a long time, kept in close confinement in London. He was at length, however, set at liberty, and in 1659, repaired to the king at Breda, and was knighted by him in the April following. Soon after the Restoration, Sir Richard Fanshawe was sent as ambassador to Philip the Fourth of Spain, and in that capacity served his country with signal ability until his death, which occurred at Madrid on the sixteenth of June, 1666, and in the sixtieth year of his age.

Though Fanshawe's life may be truly said to have been a life of business, yet in the midst of his various occupations, he still found time to devote much attention to literary pursuits. He was an elegant and accomplished scholar, and produced very acceptable translations of the *Lusiad of Camoens* from the Portuguese, and of the *Pastor Fido* of Guarini from the Italian; with the latter of which he published some miscellaneous poems, from which the following are selected :—

A ROSE.

Thou blushing rose, within whose virgin leaves
  The wanton wind to sport himself presumes,
Whilst from their rifled wardrobe he receives
  For his wings purple, for his breath perfumes!

Blown in the morning, thou shalt fade ere noon:
  What boots a life which in such haste forsakes thee?
Thou 'rt wondrous frolic being to die so soon:
  And passing proud a little colour makes thee.

If thee thy brittle beauty so deceives,
  Know, then, the thing that swells thee is thy bane;
For the same beauty doth in bloody leaves
  The sentence of thy early death contain.

Some clown's coarse lungs will poison thy sweet flower,
  If by the careless plough thou shalt be torn:
And many Herods lie in wait each hour
  To murder thee as soon as thou art born;
Nay, force thy bud to blow; their tyrant breath
Anticipating life, to hasten death.

THE SAINT'S ENCOURAGEMENT.—A Song.

Fight on, brave soldiers, for the cause;
  Fear not the cavaliers;
Their threat'nings are as senseless, as
  Our jealousies and fears.
'Tis you must perfect this great work,
  And all malignants slay,
You must bring back the King again
  The clean contrary way.

'Tis for Religion that you fight
  And for the kingdom's good,
By robbing churches, plundering men,
  And shedding guiltless blood.
Down with the orthodoxal train,
  All loyal subjects slay;
When these are gone, we shall be blest,
  The clean contrary way.

When Charles we've bankrupt made like us,
  Of crown and power bereft him,
And all his loyal subjects slain,
  And none but rebels left him.
When we've beggar'd all the land,
  And sent our trunks away,
We'll make him then a glorious prince,
  The clean contrary way.

'Tis to preserve his majesty,
  That we against him fight,
Nor are we ever beaten back,
  Because our cause is right:
If any make a scruple on't,
  Our declarations say,
Who fight for us, fight for the king
  The clean contrary way.

At Keynton, Branford, Plymouth, York,
  And divers places more,
What victories we saints obtain'd
  The like ne'er seen before!
How often we Prince Rupert kill'd,
  And bravely won the day;
The wicked cavaliers did run
  The clean contrary way.

The true religion we maintain,
  The kingdom's peace and plenty;
The privilege of parliament
  Not known to one of twenty;
The ancient fundamental laws;
  And teach men to obey
Their lawful sovereign; and all these
  The clean contrary way.

We subjects' liberties preserve,
  By prisonments and plunder,
And do enrich ourselves and state
  By keeping the wicked under.
We must preserve mechanics now,
  To lecturize and pray;
By them the gospel is advanced
  The clean contrary way.

And though the king be much misled
  By that malignant crew!
He'll find us honest, and at last
  Give all of us our due.
For we do wisely plot, and plot,
  Rebellion to destroy,
He sees we stand for peace and truth,
  The clean contrary way.

The public works shall save our souls,
  And good out-works together;
And ships shall save our lives, that stay
  Only for wind and weather.
But when our faith and works fall down,
  And all our hopes decay,
Our acts will bear us up to heaven,
  The clean contrary way.

Sir John Suckling, whom we next notice, possessed such a natural liveliness of fancy, and exuberance of animal spirits, that he often broke through the artificial restraints imposed upon him by the literary taste of the age, but he never rose into the poetry of passion and imagination. He is a delightful writer of what are called 'occasional poems.' His polished wit, playful fancy, and knowledge of life and society enabled him to give interest to trifles, and to clothe familiar thoughts in the garb of poetry.

Suckling was born at Witham, in Essex, in 1608. He was of a very eminent family, his father Sir John Suckling being Secretary of State to James the First, and afterward Comptroller of the household of that monarch's successor, Charles. The poet was distinguished almost from his infancy, being able to speak Latin at five years of age, and to write it with accuracy at nine. When sixteen years old he entered into public life as a soldier under the celebrated Gustavus Adolphus, with whom he served out an entire campaign. On his return to England he entered warmly into the cause of Charles the First, and raised a troop of horse in his support. He also intrigued with his brother cavaliers to rescue the Earl of Stratford, and was impeached by the House of Commons. To evade a trial he fled to France, but a fatal accident befell him on the way. His servant having robbed him at an inn, Suckling learning the circumstances, drew on his boots hurriedly to pursue him; but a rusty nail, or the blade of a knife, had been concealed in one of them, which, wounding him, produced mortification, of which he soon after died, in 1641, and in his thirty-fourth year.

The works of Suckling consist of miscellaneous poems, five plays, and some letters. His poems are all short, and the best of them are dedicated to love and gallantry. With the freedom of a cavalier he has greater purity of expression than most of his contemporaries. His sentiments are sometimes voluptuous, but rarely coarse; and there is so much elasticity and vivacity in his verses, that he never becomes tedious. His *Ballad upon a Wedding* is inimitable for witty levity and choice beauty of expression. It contains touches of graphic description and liveliness equal to the pictures of Chaucer. The following well-known stanza has, perhaps, never been excelled:—

Her feet beneath her petticoat,
Like little mice, stole in and out,
As if they fear'd the light;
But oh! she dances such a way!
No sun upon an Easter-day
Is half so fine a sight.

This 'Ballad,' and the fine lines on *Detraction* which follow it, are the only poems that our space will allow us to introduce from this spirited writer.

A BALLAD UPON A WEDDING.

I tell thee, Dick, where I have been,
Where I the rarest things have seen;
Oh, things without compare!
Such sights again can not be found
In any place on English ground,
Be it at wake or fair.

At Charing Cross, hard by the way
Where we (thou knowest) do sell our hay,
There is a house with stairs;
And there did I see coming down
Such folk as are not in our town,
Vorty at least, in pairs.

Amongst the rest, one pest'lent fine,
(His beard no bigger, though, than thine)
Walk'd on before the rest:
Our landlord looks like nothing to him:
The king, God bless him, 'twould undo him,
Should he go still so drest.

* * * * * *

But wot you what? the youth was going
To make an end of all his wooing;
The parson for him staid:
Yet by his leave, for all his haste,
He did not so much wish all past
Perchance, as did the maid.

The maid, and thereby hangs a tale,
For such a maid, no Whitsun-ale[1]
Could ever yet produce:

[1] Whitsun-ales were festive assemblies of the people of whole parishes at Whitsunday.

No grape that's kindly ripe could be
So round, so plump, so soft as she,
    Nor half so full of juice.

Her finger was so small, the ring
Would not stay on which they did bring;
    It was too wide a peck:
And to say truth (for out it must),
It look'd like the great collar, (just)
    About our young colt's neck.

Her feet beneath her petticoat,
Like little mice stole in and out,
    As if they fear'd the light;
But oh! she dances such a way!
No sun upon an Easter-day
    Is half so fine a sight.

* * * * * *

Her cheeks so rare a white was on,
No daisy makes comparison;
    Who sees them is undone;
For streaks of red were mingled there,
Such as are on a Cath'rine pair,
    The side that's next the sun.

Her lips were red; and one was thin,
Compar'd to that was next her chin,
    Some bee had stung it newly;
But Dick, her eyes so guard her face,
I durst no more upon them gaze,
    Than on the sun in July.

Her mouth so small, when she does speak,
Thou'dst swear her teeth her words did break,
    That they might passage get:
But she so handled still the matter
They came as good as ours, or better,
    And are not spent a whit.

* * * * * *

Passion, oh me! how I run on!
There's that that would be thought upon,
    I trow, besides the bride:
The bus'ness of the kitchen's great,
For it is fit that men should eat
    Nor was it there denied.

Just in the nick, the cook knock'd thrice,
And all the waiters in a trice
    His summons did obey;
Each serving-man, with dish in hand
March'd boldly up, like our train'd band,
    Presented, and away.

When all the meat was on the table,
What man of knife, or teeth, was able
    To stay to be entreated?

And this the very reason was,
Before the parson could say grace,
The company was seated.

Now hats fly off, and youths carouse;
Healths first go round, and then the house,
The bride's came thick and thick;
And, when 'twas nam'd another's health,
Perhaps he made it her's by stealth,
And who could help it, Dick?

O' th' sudden up they rise and dance;
Then sit again, and sigh, and glance;
Then dance again, and kiss.
Thus sev'ral ways the time did pass,
Till every woman wish'd her place,
And every man wish'd his.

By this time all were stol'n aside
To counsel and undress the bride;
But that he must not know:
But yet 'twas thought he guess'd her mind.
And did not mean to stay behind
Above an hour or so.

* * * * * *

DETRACTION EXECRATED.

Thou vermin slander, bred in abject minds,
Of thoughts impure, by vile tongues animate,
Canker of conversation! could'st thou find
Nought but our love whereon to show thy hate?
Thou never wert, when we two were alone;
What canst thou witness then? thou, base dull aid,
Wast useless in our conversation,
Where each meant more than could by both be said.
Whence hadst thou thy intelligence—from earth?
That part of us ne'er knew that we did love:
Or, from the air? our gentle sighs had birth
From such sweet raptures as to joy did move;
Our thoughts as pure as the chaste morning's breath,
When from the night's cold arms it creeps away,
Were clothed in words, and maiden's blush, that hath
More purity, more innocence than they.
Nor from the water could'st thou have this tale;
No briny tears has furrowed her smooth cheek;
And I was pleas'd: I pray what should he ail,
That had her love; for what else could he seek?
We shorten'd days to moments by love's art,
Whilst our two souls in amorous ecstasy
Perceiv'd no passing time, as if a part
Our love had been of still eternity.
Much less could'st have it from the purer fire;
Our heat exhales no vapour from coarse sense,
Such as are hopes, or fears, or fond desire:
Our mutual love itself did recompense.

Thou hast no correspondence had in heaven,
And th' elemental world, thou see'st is free.
Whence hadst thou, then, this talking monster? even
From hell, a harbour fit for it and thee.
Curst be th' officious tongue that did address
Thee to her ears, to ruin my content:
May it one minute taste such happiness,
Deserving lost, unpitied it lament!
I must forbear her sight, and so repay
In grief, those hours' joy short'ned to a dream;
Each minute I will lengthen to a day,
And in one year outlive Methusalem.

Cartwright, Cleveland, Lovelace and Crashaw close the long list of English miscellaneous poets who have occupied our attention during the last four lectures.

William Cartwright, one of Ben Jonson's sons of the muses, was born at Cirencester, Gloucestershire, in 1611. He received his early education at the free school of his native place, whence he removed to Westminster school, and in 1628 entered Christ College, Oxford. Having remained at Oxford until he had taken his master's degree, he entered into orders, and soon became a very popular preacher in the university. In 1643 he was chosen junior proctor of the university and reader in metaphysics; and was at that time in the habit of studying sixteen hours a day. Toward the close of the same year he unfortunately caught a malignant fever then prevalent at Oxford, and died on the twenty-third of December, 1643, in his thirty-third year. The king, who was at that time at Oxford, went into mourning for Cartwright's death; and when his works were published in 1651, no less than fifty copies of encomiastic verses were prefixed to them by the wits and scholars of that period.

It is difficult to conceive, from the perusal of Cartwright's poems, why he should have obtained such extensive applause and reputation. His pieces are generally short, occasional productions, addressed to ladies and noblemen, or to his brother poets, Fletcher and Jonson; or slight amatory effusions, not distinguished either for elegance or fancy. Admiration of his genius, his youthful virtues, his learning, and his devoted loyalty to the king, seemed to have mainly contributed to his popularity; and his premature death doubtless renewed and deepened the impression of his worth and talents. Cartwright must have cultivated poetry in his youth; for he was only twenty-six years old when Ben Jonson died, and previous to that period the veteran poet paid him the compliment to remark, 'My son Cartwright writes all like a man.' The following effusions are both witty and pretty, but possess no higher merit:—

THE DREAM.

I dream'd I saw myself lie dead,
  And that my bed my coffin grew,

Silence and sleep this strange sight bred,
But, wak'd, I found I liv'd anew.
Looking next morn on your bright face,
Mine eyes bequeath'd mine heart fresh pain;
A dart rush'd in with every grace,
And so I kill'd myself again:
O eyes, what shall distressed lovers do,
If open you can kill, if shut you view!

TO CUPID.

Thou, who didst never see the light,
Nor know'st the pleasure of the sight,
But always blinded, canst not say,
Now it is night, or now 'tis day;
So captivate her sense, so blind her eye,
That still she love me, yet she ne'er know why.

Thou who dost wound us with such art,
We see no blood drop from the heart,
And, subt'ly cruel, leav'st no sign
To tell the blow or hand was thine;
O gently, gently wound my fair, that she
May thence believe the wound did come from thee!

TO A LADY VAILED.

So love appear'd, when, breaking out his way
From the dark chaos, he first shed the day;
Newly awak'd out of the bud, so shows
The half seen, half hid glory of the rose,
As you do through your vails; and I may swear,
Viewing you so, that beauty doth bide there.
So Truth lay under fables, that the eye
Might reverence the mystery, not descry;
Light being so proportion'd, that no more
Was seen, but what might cause men to adore:
Thus is your dress so order'd, so contrived,
As 'tis but only poetry revived.
Such doubtful light had sacred groves, where rods
And twigs at last did shoot up into gods;
Where, then, a shade darkeneth the beauteous face,
May I not pay a reverence to the place?
So, under water, glimmering stars appear,
As those (but nearer stars) your eyes do here;
So deities darkened sit, that we may find
A better way to see them in our mind.
No bold Ixion, then, be here allow'd,
Where Juno dares herself be in the cloud.
Methinks the first age comes again, and we
See a retrieval of simplicity.
Thus looks the country virgin, whose brown hue
Hoods her, and makes her show even veil'd as you.
Blest mean, that checks our hope, and spurs our fear
Whiles all doth not lie hid, nor all appear:

O fear ye no assaults from bolder men;
When they assail, be this your armour then.
A silken helmet may defend those parts,
Where softer kisses are the only darts!

John Cleveland was born at Henkley, Leicestershire, in 1613. His father being rector of the parish, and also a man of sound learning, the future poet's early studies were carefully attended to at home, supervised by an able teacher connected with the grammar-school of the place. When well prepared, he was sent to Christ's College, Cambridge, where he soon became distinguished for both talents and learning. As an orator especially, he was unrivalled; and such was his general popularity, that as soon as he had taken his degrees he was elected to a fellowship in St. John's College. Cleveland continued at the university about nine years, the delight and ornament of the college to which he belonged, and during that time he became as eminent as a poet as he was as an orator. Upon the breaking out of the civil war, he espoused the royal cause with all the ardor of his nature, in consequence of which, as soon as the reins of power passed into the hands of the parliamentary party, he was ejected from his fellowship, and turned upon the world. He now repaired to Oxford, the head-quarters of the king, and there employed his talents in the composition of those severe and biting satires which rendered him, at the time, the delight of his party, and the terror of their foes.

From Oxford, Cleveland, on invitation of Sir Richard Willis, governor of Newark, removed to that city, and there was immediately elevated to the office of Judge-advocate—a situation which he continued to fill till Newark was, by the king's order, surrendered to the parliament. In 1655, he was seized at Norwich and cast into prison, being 'a person of great ability, and so able to do the greater disservice.' He remained in prison for some time, enduring all the wretchedness that poverty and destitution could inflict; but at length becoming exhausted from his sufferings, he petitioned Cromwell for his release in terms so pathetic and moving, that the heart of the Protector was melted, and he set him at liberty. Cleveland now repaired to London to resume his literary pursuits, but he died soon after, on the fourteenth of April, 1658, and was buried in the church of St. Michael in that city.

Besides his strong and caustic satires, which were the chief source of his popularity while living, and which Butler afterward partially imitated in his 'Hudibras,' Cleveland wrote some love verses containing morsels of genuine poetry, amid a mass of affected metaphors and fancies. He carried gal lantry to an extent bordering on the ridiculous, making all nature—sun and shade—do homage to his mistress. To illustrate this remark we need only present the following lines:—

ON PHILLIS, WALKING BEFORE SUNRISE.

The sluggish morn as yet undress'd,
My Phillis brake from out her rest,
As if she 'd made a match to run
With Venus, usher to the sun.
The trees, (like yeomen of her guard
Serving more for pomp than ward,
Rank'd on each side with loyal duty,)
Wave branches to inclose her beauty.
The plants, whose luxury was lopp'd,
Or age with crutches underpropp'd,
Whose wooden carcasses are grown
To be but coffins of their own,
Revive, and at her general dole,
Each receives his ancient soul.
The winged choiristers began
To chirp their matins; and the fan
Of whistling winds, like organs play'd
Unto their voluntaries, made
The waken'd earth in odours rise
To be her morning sacrifice;
The flowers, call'd out of their beds,
Start and raise up their drowsy heads;
And he that for their colour seeks,
May find it vaulting in her cheeks,
Where roses mix; no civil war
Between her York and Lancaster.
The marigold, whose courtier's face
Echoes the sun, and doth unlace
Her at his rise, at his full stop,
Packs and shuts up his gaudy shop,
Mistakes her cue, and doth display;
Thus Phillis antedates the day.
These miracles had cramp'd the sun,
Who, thinking that his kingdom's won,
Powders with light his frizzled locks,
To see what saint his lustre mocks.
The trembling leaves through which he play'd,
Dappling the walk with light and shade,
(Like lattice windows) give the spy
Room but to peep with half an eye,
Lest her full orb his sight should dim,
And bid us all good night in him:
Till she would spend a gentle ray,
To force us a new-fashion'd day.
But what new-fashion'd palsy 's this,
Which makes the boughs divest their bliss?
And that they might her footsteps straw,
Drop their leaves with shivering awe;
Phillis perceives, and (lest her stay
Should wed October into May,
And as her beauty caus'd a spring,
Devotion might an autumn bring)

Withdrew her beams, yet made no night,
But left the sun her curate light.

Richard Lovelace was the son of Sir William Lovelace, and was born at Woolridge, Kent, in 1618. He was educated at Oxford, and Wood describes him, at the age of sixteen, 'as the most amiable and beautiful person that eye ever beheld; a person also of innate modesty, virtue, and courtly deportment, which made him then, but especially after, when he retired to the great city, much admired and adored by the female sex.' Soon after Lovelace had completed his studies he was introduced at court, and being thus personally distinguished, and a royalist in principle, he was chosen by the county of Kent to deliver a petition to the House of Commons, praying that the king might be restored to his rights, and the government settled. The 'Long Parliament' was then in the ascendant, and Lovelace was thrown into prison for his temerity. He was eventually liberated on heavy bail, and soon after spent the balance of his fortune in fruitless efforts to succour the royal cause.

Lovelace afterward obtained the command of a regiment in the French army, but being wounded at Dunkirk, he relinquished his command, and in 1648 returned to England. He had, however, scarcely reached his native shore before he was apprehended and again cast into prison; and seeing no prospect of a second retrieve, he beguiled the time of his imprisonment by collecting and arranging his poems for publication. They appeared in 1649, under the title of *Lucastra: Odes, Sonnets, and Songs.* The general title was bestowed upon them on account of the 'lady of his love,' Lucy Sackeverell, whom he usually called *Lux Castra.* This attachment proved, in the event, unfortunate; for the lady, hearing that Lovelace died of his wounds at Dunkirk, married another man. From this time the course of the poet was downward. The dominant party did, indeed, release his person, when the death of the king had left them the less to fear from their opponents; but Lovelace was now penniless, and the reputation of a broken cavalier was no passport to better circumstances. Oppressed with want and melancholy, he gradually sunk into a consumption, and finally died in a miserable alley near Shore Lane, London, in 1658,—a death presenting a striking contrast to the gay and splendid scenes of his youth.

The poetry of Lovelace, like his life, was very unequal. There is a spirit and nobleness in some of his verses and sentiments, that charms the reader as much as his gallant bearing and fine person captivated the fair. His genius was exalted, but his taste was perverted by the affected wit and ridiculous gallantry of the day. That he knew, however, how to appreciate true taste and nature, may be seen from the following lines on Lely's portrait of Charles the First:—

See what an humble bravery doth shine,
And grief triumphant breaking through each line,
How it commands the face! So sweet a scorn
Never did happy misery adorn!

So sacred a contempt that others show
To this (o'. the height of all the wheel) below;
That mightiest monarchs by this shaded book
May copy out their proudest, richest look.

Lovelace's lighter poems bear a strong resemblance to those of Herrick, though they are less buoyant in spirit, and less natural in imagery and fancy. From these poems we select the following addresses, both of which are certainly very beautiful :—

TO LUCASTA, ON GOING TO THE WARS.

Tell me not, sweet, I am unkind,
  That from the nunnery
Of thy chaste breast and quiet mind,
  To war and arms I fly.

True, a new mistress now I chase,
  The first foe in the field;
And with a stronger faith embrace
  A sword, a horse, a shield.

Yet this inconstancy is such,
  As you, too, shall adore;
I could not love thee, dear, so much,
  Lov'd I not honour more.

TO ALTHEA, FROM PRISON.

When love with unconfined wings
  Hovers within my gates,
And my divine Althea brings
  To whisper at my grates;
When I lie tangled in her hair,
  And fetter'd with her eye,
The birds that wanton in the air,
  Know no such liberty.

When flowing cups run swiftly round
  With no allaying Thames,
Our careless heads with roses crown'd,
  Our hearts with loyal flames;
When thirsty grief in wine we steep,
  When healths and draughts go free,
Fishes that tipple in the deep,
  Know no such liberty.

When linnet-like, confined, I
  With shriller note shall sing
The mercy, sweetness, majesty,
  And glories of my king;
When I shall voice aloud how good
  He is, how great should be,
Th' enlarged winds that curl the flood,
  Know no such liberty.

Stone walls do not a prison make,
  Nor iron bars a cage;

Minds, innocent and quiet, take
  That for an hermitage:
If I have freedom in my love,
  And in my soul am free;
Angels alone, that soar above,
  Enjoy such liberty.

Richard Crashaw was the son of William Crashaw, an eminent preacher at the Temple Church, London; but the time of his birth is unknown. He received the early part of his education at the 'Charter House' near London, and thence passed to Pembroke Hall, Cambridge, whence, after a brief period, he entered Peter House College, of which he was soon after chosen a fellow. When the parliamentary party gained the ascendency in the university, he was, with many others, ejected from his fellowship; and being of an enthusiastic disposition he lived for several years in St. Mary's Church, near Peter House, engaged, chiefly, in religious offices and writing devotional poetry; and 'like a primitive saint, offering more prayers by night, than others usually offer in the day.' Foreseeing, as he supposed, that the church of England would be subverted, Crashaw removed to France and became a proselyte to the Roman Catholic faith; and soon after, through the friendship of Cowley, he obtained the notice of queen Henrietta Maria, who was at that time in Paris, and who recommended him to the dignitaries of the church in Italy. He there became secretary to one of the cardinals, and a canon of the church of Loretto. In this situation he died about 1650, and when intelligence of the event reached England, Cowley honored his memory with—

The meed of a melodious tear.

Crashaw was a very accomplished scholar, and his translations from the Latin and the Italian languages possess great freedom, force, and beauty. He translated part of the *Sospetto d'Herode* from the Italian of Merino; and passages from his version are not unworthy of even Milton. He thus describes the abode of Satan:—

Below the bottom of the great abyss,
There, where one centre reconciles all things,
The world's profound heart pants; there placed is
Mischief's old master; close about him clings
A curl'd knot of embracing snakes, that kiss
His corresponding cheeks: these loathsome strings
Hold the perverse prince in eternal ties
Fast bound, since first he forfeited the skies.

* * * * * *

Fain would he have forgot what fatal strings
Eternally bind each rebellious limb;
He shook himself and spread his spacious wings,
Which, like two bosom'd sails, embrace the dim
Air with a dismal shade, but all in vain;
Of sturdy adamant is his strong chain.

While thus Heaven's highest counsels, by the low
Footsteps of their effects, he trac'd too well,
He toss'd his troubled eyes—embers that glow
Now with new rage, and wax too hot for hell;
With his foul claws he fenc'd his furrow'd brow,
And gave a ghastly shriek, whose horrid yell
Ran trembling through the hollow vault of night.

The felicity and copiousness of Crashaw's language are, perhaps, better seen from his translations than from his original poems; and did our space permit, we should, therefore, be happy to introduce, entire, his version of *Music's Duel*, from the Latin of Strada: it is seldom that, in our poetical pilgrimage, so sweet and luxurious a strain of pure description and sentiment greets us as it contains.

While residing at Cambridge, Crashaw published a volume of Latin poems and epigrams, in one of which occurs the well-known conceit relative to the sacred miracle of water being turned into wine—

The conscious water saw its God and blush'd.

In 1646, his English poems appeared under the title of *Steps to the Temple*, *The Delights of the Muses*, and *Carmen Deo Nostro*. The greater part of the volume consists of religious poetry, much of which, though deficient, occasionally, in taste and judgment, indicates genius of a very high order. No poet of his day is so rich in 'barbaric pearl and gold,' the genuine ore of poetry, as he. It is, therefore, deeply to be regretted that his life had not been longer, more calm and fortunate—realizing his own exquisite lines—

A happy soul that all the way
To heaven, hath a summer's day.

Of the two beautiful similes which the following lines contain, the first reminds us of a passage in Jeremy Taylor's *Holy Dying*, and the other, of one of Shakspeare's best sonnets:—

I've seen, indeed, the hopeful bud
Of a ruddy rose, that stood,
Blushing to behold the ray
Of the new-saluted day;
His tender top not fully spread;
The sweet dash of a shower new shed,
Invited him no more to hide
Within himself the purple pride
Of his forward flower, when lo,
While he sweetly 'gan to show
His swelling glories, Auster spied him;
Cruel Auster thither hied him,
And with the rush of one rude blast
Sham'd not spitefully to waste
All his leaves so fresh and sweet,
And lay them trembling at his feet.

I've seen the morning's lovely ray
Hover o'er the new-born day,
With rosy wings, so richly bright,
As if he scorn'd to think of night,
When a ruddy storm, whose scowl
Made Heaven's radiant face look foul,
Call'd for an untimely night
To blot the newly-blossom'd light.

The following Hymn will form an appropriate close for our brief sketch of this deeply interesting poet :—

HYMN TO THE NAME OF JESUS.

I sing the Name which none can say,
But touch'd with an interior ray ;
The name of our new peace; our good;
Our bliss, and supernatural blood;
The name of all our lives and loves:
Hearken and help, ye holy doves!
The high-born brood of day; you bright
Candidates of blissful light,
The heirs elect of love; whose names belong
Unto the everlasting life of song;
All ye wise souls, who in the wealthy breast
Of this unbounded Name build your warm nest.
Awake, my glory! soul (if such thou be,
And that fair word at all refer to thee),
    Awake and sing,
    And be all wing!
Bring hither thy whole self; and let me see
What of thy parent heaven yet speaks in thee.
    O thou art poor
    Of noble powers, I see,
And full of nothing else but empty me;
Narrow and low, and infinitely less
Than this great morning's mighty business.
    One little world or two,
    Alas! will never do;
    We must have store;
Go, soul, out of thyself, and seek for more;
    Go and request
Great Nature for the key of her huge chest,
Of heav'ns the self-involving set of spheres,
Which dull mortality more feels than hears;
    Then rouse the nest
Of nimble art, and traverse round
The airy shop of soul-appeasing sound:
And beat a summons in the same
    All-sovereign name,
To warn each several kind
And shape of sweetness—be they such
    As sigh with supple wind
    Or answer artful touch—

That they convene and come away
To wait at the love-crowned doors of that illustrious day.
* * * * * * * *
Come, lovely name! life of our hope!
Lo we hold out our hearts wide ope!
Unlock thy cabinet of day,
Dearest sweet, and come away.
Lo, how the thirsty lands
Gasp for thy golden show'rs, with long-stretch'd hands!
Lo how the labouring earth,
That hopes to be
All heaven by thee
Leaps at thy birth!
The attending world, to wait thy rise,
First turn'd to eyes;
And then, not knowing what to do,
Turn'd them to tears, and spent them too.
Come, royal name! and pay the expense
Of all this precious patience:
Oh, come away
And kill the death of this delay.
Oh see, so many worlds of barren years
Melted and measur'd out in seas of tears!
Oh, see the weary lids of wakeful hope
(Love's eastern windows) all wide ope
With curtains drawn,
To catch the daybreak of thy dawn!
Oh, dawn at last, long look'd for day!
Take thine own wings and come away.
Lo, where aloft it comes! It comes, among
The conduct of adoring spirits, that throng
Like diligent bees, and swarms about it.
Oh, they are wise,
And know what sweets are suck'd from out it.
It is the hive
By which they thrive,
Where all their hoard of honey lies.
Lo, where it comes, upon the snowy dove's
Soft back, and brings a bosom big with loves,
Welcome to our dark world, thou womb of day!
Unfold thy fair conceptions; and display
The birth of our bright joys.
Oh, thou compacted
Body of blessings! spirits of souls extracted!
Oh, dissipate thy spicy powers,
Cloud of condensed sweets! and break upon us
In balmy showers!
Oh, fill our senses, and take from us
All force of so profane a fallacy,
To think aught sweet but that which smells of thee.
Fair flow'ry name! in none but thee,
And thy nectareal fragrancy,
Hourly there meets
An universal synod of all sweets;

By whom it is defined thus—
    That no perfume
    Forever shall presume
To pass for odoriferous
But such alone whose sacred pedigree
Can prove itself some kin, sweet name, to thee.
Sweet name! in thy each syllable
A thousand blest Arabias dwell;
A thousand hills of frankincense;
Mountains of myrrh and beds of spices,
And ten thousand paradises,
The soul that tastes thee takes from thence.
How many unknown worlds there are
Of comforts, which thou hast in keeping!
How many thousand mercies there
In pity's soft lap lie a sleeping!
Happy he who has the art
    To awake them,
    And to take them
Home, and lodge them in his heart.
Oh, that it were as it was wont to be,
When thy old friends, on fire all full of thee,
Fought against frowns with smiles; gave glorious chase
To persecutions; and against the face
Of death and fiercest dangers, durst with brave
And sober pace march on to meet a grave.
On their bold breasts about the world they bore thee,
And to the teeth of hell stood up to teach thee;
In centre of their inmost souls they wore thee,
Where racks and torments striv'd in vain to reach thee.
    Little alas! thought they
Who tore the fair breasts of thy friends,
    Their fury but made way
For thee, and serv'd them in thy glorious ends.
What did their weapons, but with wider pores
Enlarge thy flaming-breasted lovers,
    More freely to transpire
    That impatient fire
The heart that hides thee hardly covers?
What did their weapons. but set wide the doors
For thee? fair purple doors, of love's devising;
The ruby windows which enrich'd the east
Of thy so oft-repeated rising
Each wound of theirs was thy new morning,
And re-enthron'd thee in thy rosy nest,
With blush of thine own blood thy day adoring:
It was the wit of love o'erflow'd the bounds
Of wrath, and made the way through all these wounds.
Welcome, dear all-adored name!
    For sure there is no knee
    That knows not thee;
Or if there be such sons of shame,
    Alas! what will they do,
When stubborn rocks shall bow,

And hills hang down their heav'n-saluting heads
        To seek for humble beds
Of dust, where, in the bashful shades of night,
Next to their own low nothing they may lie,
And couch before the dazzling light of thy dread majesty.
They that by love's mild dictate now
        Will not adore thee,
Shall then, with just confusion, bow
        And break before thee.

Lecture the Eleventh.

ALEXANDER SCOT—SIR RICHARD MAITLAND—ALEXANDER MONTGOMERY—ALEXANDER HUME—GEORGE BUCHANAN—JAMES THE SIXTH—SIR ROBERT AYTON—EARL OF ANCRUM—EARL OF STIRLING—WILLIAM DRUMMOND—DOCTOR ARTHUR JOHNSTON—SIR ROGER L'ESTRANGE.

HAVING, in the last lecture, closed our remarks upon the English miscellaneous poets who graced the age of Elizabeth and her immediate successors, we now pass to notice briefly their contemporaneous bards in Scotland, where the muses were not wholly neglected. There was, however, so little intercourse between the two nations at this time, that the works of the English poets seem to have been comparatively unknown in the north, and to have had no Scottish imitators. The country was then in a rude and barbarous state, tyrannized over by the nobles, and torn by internal feuds and dissensions. In England, the Reformation had proceeded from the throne, and was accomplished without violence or disorder; but in Scotland it uprooted the whole form of society, and was marked by fierce contentions and lawless turbulence. The absorbing influence of this ecclesiastical struggle was altogether unfavorable to the cultivation of poetry. It shed a gloomy spirit over the nation, and almost proscribed the study of romantic literature. The drama, which in England was the nurse of so many fine thoughts, so much stirring passion, and beautiful imagery, was shunned as a leprosy, fatal to both religion and morality. The very songs in Scotland partook of this religious character; and so widely was the polemical spirit diffused, that ALEXANDER SCOT, the earliest poet of this period, in his *New Year Gift to the Queen*, in 1562, says—

> That trimmer lads and little lasses, lo,
> Will argue baith with bishop, priest, and friar.

The history of Scot's life is so little known, that neither the date of his birth, nor the period of his death, has been preserved. He wrote several short satires, and some other miscellaneous poems, the prevailing amatory character of which has caused him to be called the Scottish Anacreon, though there are many points wanting to complete his resemblance to the Teian bard. As a specimen of his talents, we present the following piece:—

TO HIS HEART.

Hence, heart, with her that must depart,
And hald thee with thy soverain,
For I had lever[1] want ane heart,
Nor have the heart that does me pain;
Therefore go with thy luve remain,
And let me live thus unmolest;
See that thou come not back again,
But bide with her thou luvis best.

Sen she that I have servit lang,
Is to depart so suddenly,
Address thee now, for thou sall gang
And beir thy lady company.
Fra she be gone, heartless am I;
For why? thou art with her possest.
Therefore, my heart! go hence in hy,
And bide with her thou luvis best.

Though this belappit body here
Be bound to servitude and thrall,
My faithful heart is free inteir,
And mind to serve my lady at all.
Wald God that I were perigall[2]
Under that redolent rose to rest!
Yet at the least, my heart, thou sall
Abide with her thou luvis best.

Sen in your garth[3] the lily whyte
May not remain amang the lave,
Adieu the flower of haill delyte;
Adieu the succour that may me save;
Adieu the fragrant balme suaif,[4]
And lamp of ladies lustiest!
My faithful heart she sall it have,
To bide with her it luvis best.

Deplore, ye ladies clear of hue,
Her absence, sen she must depart,
And specially ye luvers true,
That wounded be with luvis dart,
For ye sall want you of ane heart
As weil as I, therefore at last
Do go with mine, with mind inwart,
And bide with her thou luvis best.

Contemporary with Scot, lived Maitland, Montgomery, Hume, and Buchanan, the last of whom distinguished himself equally in both prose and verse, but is particularly celebrated for the purity and classic elegance of his Latin poems.

SIR RICHARD MAITLAND was born at Lethington, in 1496. He passed

[1] Rather.
[2] Competent; had it in my power
[3] Garden.
[4] Embrace.

an active life as a judge and statesman, and during his latter years he relieved the duties of his official station by composing some moral and conversational pieces, and by collecting into the well-known manuscript that bears his name, the best productions of his contemporaries. Maitland's familiar style reminds us of that of Lyndsay. His death occurred in 1586, when he was in his ninety-first year. The following satire will well reward the labor of a careful perusal :—

SATIRE ON THE TOWN LADIES.

Some wifis of the borrowstoun
Sae wonder vain are, and wantoun,
In warld they wait not[1] what to weir:
On claithis they ware[2] mony a crown;
And all for newfangleness of geir.[3]

And of fine silk their furrit clokis,
With hingan sleeves, like geil pokis;
Nae preaching will gar them forbeir
To weir all thing that sin provokis;
And all for newfangleness of geir.

Their wilicoats maun weel be hewit,
Broudred richt braid, with pasments sewit.
I trow wha wald the matter speir,
That their gudemen had cause to rue it,
That evir their wifis wore sic geir.

Their woven hose of silk are shawin,
Barrit aboon with taisels drawin;
With gartens of ane new maneir
To gar their courtliness be knawin;
And all for newfangleness of geir.

Sometime they will beir up their gown
To shaw their wilicoat hingan down;
And sometime baith they will upbeir,
To shaw their hose of black or brown;
And all for newfangleness of geir.

Their collars, carcats, and hause beidis![4]
With velvet hat heigh on their heidis,
Cordit with gold like ane younkeir.
Braidit about with golden threidis;
And all for newfangleness of geir.

Their shoon of velvet, and their muilis!
In kirk they are not content of stuilis,
The sermon when they sit to heir,
But carries cusheons like vain fulis;
And all for newfangleness of geir.

And some will spend mair, I hear say,
In spice and drugis in ane day,

[1] Wot, or know not
[2] Spend.
[3] Attire.
[4] Beads for tne throat.

Nor wald their mothers in ane yeir.
Whilk will gar mony pack decay,
When they sae vainly waste their geir.

Leave, burgess men, or all be lost,
On your wifis to mak sic cost,
Whilk may gar all your bairnis bleir,[1]
She that may not want wine and roast,
Is able for to waste some geir.

Between them, and nobles of blude,
Nae difference but ane velvet hude!
Their cumrock curchies are as deir,
Their other claithis are as gude,
And they as costly in other geir.

Of burgess wifis though I speak plain,
Some landwart ladies are as vain,
And by their claithing may appeir,
Wearing gayer nor them may gain,
On ower vain claithis wasting geir.

ALEXANDER MONTGOMERY, of whose history little has been preserved, was known as a poet of reputation as early as 1568, but his principal work, *The Cherry and the Slae*, was not published until 1597. 'The Cherry and the Slae' is an allegorical poem, representing virtue and vice. The allegory is defective, but some of Montgomery's descriptions are lively and vigorous, and the style of verse adopted in this poem was afterward followed by Burns. Divested of some of the antique spelling, parts of the poem seem as modern, and are as smoothly versified as the Scottish poetry of a century and a half later. To illustrate this remark we need only take the following sample:—

The cushat crouds, the corbie cries,
The cuckoo couks, the prattling pyes
  To geck there they begin;
The jargon of the jangling jays,
The craiking caws and keckling kays,
  They deave't me with their din.
The painted pawn with Argus eyes
  Can on his May-cock call;
The turtle wails on wither'd trees,
  And Echo answers all,
    Repeating, with greeting,
    How fair Narcissus fell,
    By lying and spying
    His shadow in the well.

I saw the hurcheon and the hare
In hidlings hirpling here and there,
  To make their morning mange.
The con, the cuning, and the cat,
Whose dainty downs with dew were wat,
  With stiff mustachios strange.

[1] Crv till their eyes become red.

The hart, the hind, the dae, the rae,
  The foumart and false fox;
The bearded buck clamb up the brae
  With birsy bairs and brocks;
    Some feeding, some dreading
    The hunter's subtle snares,
    With skipping and tripping,
    They play'd them all in pairs.

The air was sober, saft, and sweet,
Nae misty vapours, wind, nor weet,
  But quiet, calm, and clear,
To foster Flora's fragrant flowers,
Whereon Apollo's paramours
  Had trinkled mony a tear;
The which like silver shakers shined,
  Embroidering Beauty's bed,
Wherewith their heavy heads declined
  In May's colours clad.
    Some knoping, some dropping
    Of balmy liquor sweet,
    Excelling and swelling
    Through Phœbus' wholesome heat.

Alexander Hume, of the Humes of Polwarth, was brought up to the legal profession, but abandoning the law, he became a clergyman of the stern Puritan faith. He was the minister of Logie, where he died in 1609, but at what age is uncertain, so that the period of his birth can not be ascertained.

Hume published,in 1599, a volume of *Hymns or Sacred Songs*, the most finished of which is the description of a summer's day, which he calls the *Day Estival*. The various objects of external nature, characteristic of a Scottish landscape, are painted with truth and clearness, and a calm devotional feeling is spread over the whole poem. It opens as follows :—

O perfect light, which shed away
  The darkness from the light,
And set a ruler o'er the day,
  Another o'er the night.

Thy glory when the day forth flies,
  More vively does appear,
Nor at mid-day unto our eyes
  The shining sun is clear.

The shadow of the earth anon
  Removes and drawis by,
Syne in the east, when it is gone,
  Appears a clearer sky.

Whilk soon perceive the little larks,
  The lapwing and the snipe;
And tune their song like Nature's clerks,
  O'er meadow, muir, and stripe.

The summer day of the poet is one of unclouded splendor.

The time so tranquil is and clear,
  That nowhere shall ye find,
Save on a high and barren hill,
  An air of passing wind.

All trees and simples, great and small,
  That balmy leaf do bear,
Than they were painted on a wall,
  No more they move or steir.

The rivers fresh, the caller streams
  O'er rocks can swiftly rin,
The water clear like crystal beams,
  And makes a pleasant din.

The condition of the Scottish laborer must have been, at that time, more comfortable than it is at present, and the climate warmer; for Hume describes those working in the fields as stopping at mid-day, 'noon meat and sleep to take,' and refreshing themselves with 'caller wine' in a cave, and 'sallads steep'd in oil.' At length 'the gloaming comes, the day is spent,' and the poet concludes in the following strain of pious gratitude and delight:—

What pleasure, then, to walk and see
  End-lang a river clear
The perfect form of every tree
  Within the deep appear.

The salmon out of cruives and creels,
  Uphailed into scouts,
The bells and circles on the weills
  Through leaping of the trouts.

O sure it were a seemly thing,
  While all is still and calm,
The praise of God to play and sing,
  With trumpet and with shalm.

Through all the land great is the gild
  Of rustic folks that cry;
Of bleating sheep fra they be kill'd
  Of calves and rowting kye.

All labourers draw hame at even,
  And can to others say,
Thanks to the gracious God of heaven,
  Whilk sent this summer day.

George Buchanan, who by early and intense study acquired all the freedom and fluency of a native in the Latin tongue, and who has been called the Scottish Virgil, was born in Dumbartonshire, in the month of February 1506. His parents were poor, and he had also in his childhood, the misfortune to lose his father, so that his early training devolved entirely upon a widowed mother who had, besides him, a number of other children.

By great care and prudent management she succeeded in obtaining for him the rudiments of an education, and his maternal uncle, perceiving in him the promise of future eminence, sent him to the university of Paris. After having remained two years in Paris, Buchanan returned to Scotland and finished his studies at the university of St. Andrews, of one of the colleges of which he afterward became master. He was now invited by King James the Fifth to become tutor to the Earl of Murray, and having previously adopted the sentiments of Luther, he, while employed in his new vocation, wrote a satirical poem upon the monks, which gave such offence to the clergy generally, that he was obliged to take refuge on the continent, from which he did not return to Scotland till 1560. It was during his long residence abroad that Buchanan acquired that familiarity with the Latin tongue, which rendered him so skillful a writer of Latin poetry; for as, during a period of more than twenty years, much of which he spent in teaching, either in France or in Portugal, he made that language the common medium of communication with his scholars, it became to him more familiar even, than his mother tongue.

Though he had embraced the Protestant faith, yet Buchanan's reception at the court of Mary, when he returned to Scotland, was not only favorable but even flattering. He assisted her in her studies, was employed to regulate the universities, and became principal of St. Leonard's College in the university of St. Andrews. He joined, however, the Earl of Murray's party against the queen, and was appointed tutor to James the Sixth, whose pedantry was probably, in some degree, the result of his instructions.

In 1571, Buchanan violently attacked the conduct and character of the queen, in a Latin work entitled *Detectio Mariæ Reginæ*. After the assassination of his patron, Regent Murray, he still continued to enjoy the favor of the dominant party, whose opinions that the people are entitled to judge of the conduct of their governors, and control it, he maintained with great spirit and ability in a treatise, *De Jure Regni*, published in 1579. Having by this work offended his royal pupil, he passed, in retirement, the last few years of his life, during which he composed in Latin, his well-known *History of Scotland*, which was published in 1582, under the title of *Rerum Scoticarum Historia*. He died during the same year in such abject poverty as not to leave the means of defraying the ordinary expenses of his funeral.

As a Latin historical writer, Buchanan's style, it is conceded, unites the excellencies of both Livy and Tacitus. Like the former, however, he is sometimes too declamatory, and largely embellishes his narrative with fables. 'If his accuracy and impartiality,' says Dr. Robertson, 'had been in any degree equal to the elegance of his taste, and to the purity and vigor of his style, his history might be placed on a level with the most admired compositions of the ancients. But, instead of rejecting the improbable tales of chronicle writers, he was at the utmost pains to adorn them; and has clothed, with all the beauties and graces of fiction, those legends which formerly had only its wildness and extravagance.'

Buchanan's poetical performances are numerous ; but the most important is a Latin paraphrase of the Psalms of David. This great work was commenced in a monastery in Portugal, about 1550, continued afterward in France, and completed in Scotland after Mary had assumed the duties of sovereignty. He also wrote, about the same time, the most finished and beautiful of his productions, the *Epithalamium*—a poem occasioned by Mary's first marriage. Of Buchanan's minor poems, his *Ode on the First of May* is absolutely inimitable. This season of the year usually excites emotions of 'vernal joy ;' but in this ode, the circumstances which the poet has selected, are of a kind that appear inexpressibly grand. We shall, therefore, venture here to present a translation of the work, adhering as closely to the original as the difference between the languages will permit :—

THE FIRST OF MAY.

Hail to thee, delicious day,
Fair and sacred first of May!
Sacred unto wine and mirth,
Where the game and feast have birth—
Sacred to the gentle dance
Where the Graces' dark eyes glance.
Hail! delight and shining grace!
Ever following the pace
Of the aye revolving year,
Time's unwearied traveller!
When spring's life-inspiring rays
Lit the world in other days,
Those delicious days of old
In the blessed age of gold,
Such unceasing mildness charm'd
Fields which soft Favonius warm'd:
Earth's unsown fertility
Gave forth fruits spontaneously.
Such a warmth of æther smiles
Ever on the blessed Isles,
And the fields where sad decay
And old age held never sway!
Such a gentle murmur blows
Through the silent grove where flows
Lethe's quiet water on,
Fraught with sweet oblivion!
When God sends his judgment fires,
Purging earth till sin expires,
Perchance an air like this will cherish!
Ethereal souls that can not perish.
Hail! glory of the fleeting age—
Praiseworthy in man's pilgrimage—
Image of earth's early bloom,
And type of life beyond the tomb.

To the above translation from the Latin of Buchanan, we add the following version of another ode by the late accomplished Robert Hogg.

ON NEÆRA.

My wreck of mind, and all my woes,
And all my ills, that day arose,
When on the fair Neæra's eyes,
  Like stars that shine,
At first, with hapless fond surprise,
  I gazed with mine.

When my glance met her searching glance,
  A shivering o'er my body burst,
As light leaves in the green woods dance
  When western breezes stir them first;
My heart forth from my breast to go,
  And mine with hers already wanting,
Now beat, now trembled, to and fro,
  With eager fondness leaping, panting.

Just as a boy, whose nourice woos him,
Folding his young limbs in her bosom,
Heeds not caresses from another
But turns his eyes still to his mother,
When she may once regard him watches,
And forth his little fond arms stretches.
Just as a bird within the nest
  That can not fly, yet constant trying,
Its weak wings on its tender breast
  Beats with the vain desire of flying.

Thou, wary mind, thyself preparing
To live at peace, from all ensnaring,
That thou might'st never mischief catch,
Plac'd'st you, unhappy eyes, to watch
With vigilance that knew no rest,
Beside the gateways of the breast.

But you, induc'd by dalliance deep,
Or guile, or overcome by sleep;
Or else have of your own accord
Consented to betray your lord;
Both heart and soul then fled and left
Me spiritless, of mind bereft.

Then cease to weep; use is there none
To think by weeping to atone;
Since heart and spirit from me fled,
You move not by the tears you shed;
But go to her, entreat, obtain;
If you do not entreat, and gain,
Then will I ever make you gaze
Upon her, till in dark amaze
You sightless in your sockets roll,
Extinguish'd by her eyes' bright blaze,
As I have been depriv'd of heart and soul.

In 1584, two years after Buchanan's death, James the Sixth himself ventured into the magic circle of poetry, and published a volume entitled *Es-*

says of a Prentice in the Divine art of Poesie. The young king's verses, considering that he was not yet eighteen years of age, are certainly very creditable to him; and we shall therefore quote, in the original spelling, the following poem from the volume alluded to:—

ANE SCHORT POEME OF TYME.

As I was pausing in a morning aire,
  And could not sleip nor nawyis take me rest,
Furth for to walk, the morning was so faire,
  Athort the fields, it seemed to me the best.
  The East was cleare, whereby belyve I gest
That fyrier Titan cumming was in sight,
Obscuring chaste Diana by his light.

Who by his rising in the azure skyes,
  Did dewlie helse all thame on earth do dwell.
The balmie dew through birning drouth he dryis,
  Which made the soile to savour sweit and smell,
  By dew that on the night before downe fell,
Which then was soukit up by the Delphienus heit
Up in the aire: it was so light and weit.

Whose hie ascending in his purpour chere
  Provokit all from Morpheus to flee:
As beasts to feid, and birds to sing with beir,
  Men to their labour, bissie as the bee:
  Yet idle men devysing did I see,
How for to drive the tyme that did them irk,
By sindrie pastymes, quhile that it grew mirk.

Then woundred I to see them seik a wyle,
  So willingly the precious tyme to tine:
And how they did themselfis so farr begyle,
  To fushe of tyme, which of itself is fyne.
  Fra tyme be past to call it backwart syne
Is bot in vaine: therefore men sould be warr,
To sleuth the tyme that flees fra them so farr.

For what hath man bot tyme into this lyfe,
  Which gives him dayis his God aright to know?
Wherefore then sould we be at sic a stryfe,
  So spedelie our selfis for to withdraw
  Evin from the tyme, which is on nowayes slaw
To flie from us, suppose we fled it noght?
More wyse we were, if we the tyme had soght.

But sen that tyme is sic a precious thing,
  I wald we sould bestow it into that
Which were most pleasour to our heavenly King.
  Flee ydilteth, which is the greatest lat;
  Bot, sen that death to all is destinat,
Let us employ that tyme that God hath send us,
In doing weill, that good men may commend us.

Ayton, the Earl of Ancrum, the Earl of Stirling, Drummond, and Doctor Arthur Johnston, close the brief list of Scottish poets whom this important period in English literature produced.

ROBERT AYTON was born in Fifeshire in 1570. He was well educated, a devoted courtier, and enjoyed the advantages of foreign travel and intercourse with the poets of other nations, particularly with those of England. After king James succeeded to the English crown, he invited Ayton to that court, appointed him one of the gentlemen of the bed-chamber, and private secretary to the queen, besides conferring upon him the honor of knighthood. In England, Ayton, unlike the majority of his countrymen, was very popular; and even Ben Jonson was so proud of his friendship and affection that he boasted of it to Drummond. His death occurred in 1638, but under what circumstances is unknown.

Sir Robert Ayton was the author of only a comparatively limited number of poems, but the few that we have are written in very pure English, and evince a smoothness of style and delicacy of fancy that have rarely been surpassed. To illustrate this remark the following stanzas will be sufficient:—

WOMAN'S INCONSTANCY.

I lov'd thee once, I'll love no more,
  Thine be the grief as is the blame;
Thou art not what thou wast before,
  What reason I should be the same?
    He that can love unlov'd again,
    Hath better store of love than brain:
  God send me love my debts to pay,
  While unthrifts fool their love away.

Nothing could have my love o'erthrown,
  If thou hadst still continued mine;
Yea, if thou hadst remain'd thy own,
  I might perchance have yet been thine.
    But thou thy freedom did recall,
    That if thou might elsewhere inthrall;
  And then how could I but disdain
  A captive's captive to remain?

When new desires had conquer'd thee,
  And chang'd the object of thy will,
It had been lethargy in me,
  Not constancy to love thee still.
    Yea, it had been a sin to go
    And prostitute affection so,
  Since we are taught no prayers to say.
  To such as must to others pray.

Yet do thou glory in thy choice,
  Thy choice of his good fortune boast;
I'll neither grieve nor yet rejoice,
  To see him gain what I have lost;

The height of my disdain shall be,
To laugh at him, to blush for thee;
To love thee still, but go no more
A begging to a beggar's door.

The EARL OF ANCRUM was a younger son of Sir Andrew Ker of Ferneihurst, and was born in 1578. He early became a very great favorite with king James, and was held in equal esteem by that monarch's son and successor Charles the First. He was possessed of a competent fortune, and his life seems to have passed calmly and smoothly along until an advanced age. His death occurred in 1654.

The Earl's poems are generally brief fugitive pieces, and the following sonnet, which he addressed to Drummond the poet in 1624, shows how greatly the union of crowns under James had contributed toward the cultivation of the English style and language in Scotland :—

IN PRAISE OF A SOLITARY LIFE.

Sweet solitary life! lovely, dumb joy,
  That need'st no warnings how to grow more wise,
By other men's mishaps, nor the annoy
  Which from sore wrongs done to one's self doth rise.
The morning's second mansion, truth's first friend,
  Never acquainted with the world's vain broils,
When the whole day to our own use we spend,
  And our dear time no fierce ambition spoils.
Most happy state, that never tak'st revenge
  For injuries received, nor dost fear
The court's great earthquake, the griev'd truth of change,
  Nor none of falsehood's savoury lies dost hear;
Nor knows hope's sweet disease that charms our sense,
  Nor its sad cure—dear-bought experience.

WILLIAM ALEXANDER, afterward Earl of Stirling, was born at Menstrie, in 1580. Having received a liberal education, he travelled abroad with the Duke of Argyle, either as his tutor or his companion; and upon his return to Scotland he selected, as his residence, a rural retreat, where he passed some time in study, and in the composition of the *Aurora*, his first important poem. On leaving his rural abode, Alexander repaired to Edinburgh, with the design of devoting himself exclusively to poetical pursuits. Here he composed his four tragedies, *Darius*, *Crœsus*, *Alexander*, and *Julius Cæsar*, which were published in London, in 1607, with a dedication to the King. In 1613, Alexander published a sacred poem in twelve books on the *Day of Judgment;* and during the same year he was appointed one of the gentlemen ushers to Prince Charles, and knighted.

Relinquishing, soon after these events occurred, the character of the poet, and assuming that of the statesman, Sir William was appointed by Charles the First, in 1626, secretary of state for Scotland; and with such faithfulness and fidelity did he discharge the duties of this important office, that in

1633, the king created him, by letters patent, Earl of Stirling. He continued to fill the important office which he had so long held, for seven years after this last honor was conferred upon him, and died in his own castle, on the twelfth of February, 1640, in his sixty-first year.

The Earl of Stirling published in 1637, a complete edition of his works under the title of *Recreations with the Muses*, embracing, in addition to the productions already mentioned, a heroic poem entitled *Jonathan*, and an address to Prince Henry. 'Julius Cæsar,' one of the Earl's tragedies, contains several passages resembling parts of Shakspeare's tragedy of the same name; but it can not be ascertained which was first published. The genius of Shakspeare did not disdain to gather hints and expressions from comparatively obscure authors—the lesser lights of the age—and a famous passage in the 'Tempest' is supposed to have been also derived from the Earl of Stirling. In the play of *Darius*, occurs the following reflection:—

Let greatness of her glassy sceptres vaunt,
Not sceptres, no, but reeds, soon bruised, soon broken:
And let this worldly pomp our wits enchant,
All fades, and scarcely leaves behind a token.

The lines of Shakspeare will, of course, instantly suggest themselves—

And like this insubstantial pageant, faded,
Leave not a wreck behind.

None of the productions of the Earl of Stirling, touch the heart or entrance the imagination. He has nothing of the humble, but genuine inspiration of Alexander Hume; yet he was a calm aad elegant poet, with considerable fancy, and an ear for refined metrical harmony. The following is one of his best sonnets:—

TO AURORA.

I swear, Aurora, by thy starry eyes,
And by those golden locks, whose lock none slips,
And by the coral of thy rosy lips,
And by the naked snows which beauty dyes;
I swear by all the jewels of thy mind,
Whose like yet never worldly treasure bought,
Thy solid judgment, and thy generous thought,
Which in this darken'd age have clearly shin'd;
I swear by those, and by my spotless love,
And by my secret, yet most fervent fires,
That I have never nurst but chaste desires,
And such as modesty might well approve.
Then, since I love those virtuous parts in thee,
Should'st thou not love this virtuous mind in me?

William Drummond, a contemporary of the Earl of Stirling, and a poet of greatly superior genius, was born at Hawthornden, on the thirteenth of November, 1585. His father, Sir John Drummond, was gentleman usher to James the Sixth, and the future poet received his education, first at the university of Edinburgh, and afterward in France. In 1606 he commenced the study of the civil law, with the intention of following the legal profession; but in 1611, on the death of his father, he succeeded to an independent estate, and immediately took up his residence at Hawthornden. 'If beautiful and romantic scenery,' remarks a writer of that period, 'could create or nurse the genius of a poet, Drummond was peculiarly blessed with the means of inspiration. In all Scotland, there is no spot more finely varied—more rich, graceful, or luxuriant—than the cliffs, caves, and wooded banks of the river Esk, and the classic shades of Hawthornden. In the immediate neighbourhood is Roslin Castle, one of the most interesting of Gothic ruins; and the whole course of the stream and the narrow glen is like the groundwork of some fairy dream.'

Drummond had been in the habit of relieving the oppressive weight of his legal studies in France by occasionally courting the muse; but it was not until after he was established at Hawthornden that he assumed a distinct position as an author. His first publication was a volume of miscellaneous poems; to which soon after succeeded a moral treatise in prose, entitled, the *Cypress Grove*, and another poetical work termed the *Flowers of Zion.* The death, which occurred about this time, of the young lady to whom he was betrothed, affected him so deeply that he sought relief in change of scene and the excitement of foreign travel. He first visited Paris, and thence passed to Rome, spending, between those two cities, and the intermediate countries, Germany and Switzerland, nearly eight years. He embraced the opportunity also, thus afforded, of making a large collection of the choicest works to be obtained in the Greek, the Latin, the French, and the Italian languages; and enriched with the literary lore of both the ancient and the modern world, he returned to Scotland, and resumed his abode at Hawthornden. On his way thither, he met, by accident, a young lady named Logan, who bore so strong a resemblance to the former object of his affections, that he solicited and obtained her hand in marriage. From this period Drummond passed many years in his delightful retreat at Hawthornden, relieving the sameness of a retired abode by occasional visits to his brother bards of England, and receiving visits in return from Ben Jonson, Drayton, and others, at his hospitable home.

Drummond inherited from his father, the deepest reverence for royalty, and the trial and execution of Charles the First, is said to have so deeply affected him as to hasten his own death, which occurred in the latter part of the same year 1649, and in the sixty-fifth year of his age.

The poetry of Drummond has singular sweetness and harmony of versification. His *Tears on the Death of Mocliades*, or Prince Henry, was written in 1612; his *Wandering Muses*, or *The River of Forth Feasting*, a congratulatory poem to King James The First on his revisiting Scotland, appeared in 1617, and placed him among the greatest poets of the age. His sonnets are of a still higher cast, have fewer conceits, and more natural feeling, elevation of sentiment, and grace of expression. The general purity of his language, the harmony of his verse, and the play of fancy in all his principal productions, are his distinguishing characteristics. With more energy and force of mind he would have been a greater favorite both with his contemporaries and with posterity. We shall close our notice of this eminent Scottish poet with a few of his *Sonnets*, and an extract from the *River of Forth Feasting.*

EPITATH ON PRINCE HENRY.

Stay, passenger, see where inclosed lies
The paragon of Princes, fairest frame
Time, nature, place, could show to mortal eyes,
In worth, wit, virtue, miracle of fame:
At least that part the earth of him could claim
This marble holds (hard like the Destinies):
For as to his brave spirit, and glorious name,
The one the world, the other fills the skies.
Th' immortal amaranthus, princely rose,
Sad violet, and that sweet flower that bears
In sanguine spots the tenor of our woes,[1]
Spread on this stone, and wash it with your tears;
Then go and tell from Gades unto Ind
You saw where Earth's perfections were confin'd.

TO HIS LUTE.

My lute, be as thou wert when thou didst grow
With thy green mother in some shady grove,
When immelodious winds but made thee move,
And birds their ramage[2] did on thee bestow.
Since that dear voice which did thy sounds approve,
Which wont in such harmonious strains to flow,
Is reft from earth to tune the spheres above,
What art thou but a harbinger of woe?
Thy pleasing notes be pleasing notes no more,
But orphan wailings to the fainting ear,
Each stroke a sigh, each sound draws forth a tear;
For which be silent as in woods before:
Or if that any hand to touch thee deign,
Like widow'd turtle still her loss complain.

THE PRAISE OF A SOLITARY LIFE.

Thrice happy he who by some shady grove,
Far from the clamorous world, doth live his own.
Thou solitary, who is not alone,
But doth converse with that eternal love.
O how more sweet is bird's harmonious moan,
Or the hoarse sobbings of the widow'd dove,

---

[1] Milton has copied this image in his Lycidas:—

'Inwrought with figures dim, and on the edge
Like to that sanguine flower, inscribed with woe.'

[2] Warbling: from ramage, French.

Than those smooth whisperings near a prince's throne,
Which good make doubtful, do the evil approve!
O how more sweet is Zephyr's wholesome breath,
And sighs embalm'd which new-born flowers unfold,
Than that applause vain honour doth bequeath!
How sweet are streams to poison drank in gold!
The world is full of horror, troubles, slights:
Woods' harmless shades have only true delights.

TO A NIGHTINGALE.

Sweet bird! that sing'st away the early hours
Of winters past, or coming, void of care.
Well pleased with delights which present are,
Fair seasons, budding sprays, sweet-smelling flowers:
To rocks, to springs, to rills, from leafy bowers,
Thou thy Creator's goodness dost declare,
And what dear gifts on thee he did not spare,
A stain to human sense in sin that low'rs.
What soul can be so sick which by thy songs
(Attir'd in sweetness) sweetly is not driven
Quite to forget earth's turmoils, spites, and wrongs,
And lift a reverend eye and thought to heaven?
Sweet artless songster! thou my mind dost raise
To airs of spheres—yes, and to angels' lays.

THE RIVER OF FORTH FEASTING.

What blustering noise now interrupts my sleeps?
What echoing shouts thus cleave my crystal deeps?
And seems to call me from my watery court?
What melody, what sounds of joy and sport,
Are convey'd hither from each night-born spring?
With what loud murmurs do the mountains ring,
Which in unusual pomp on tiptoes stand,
And, full of wonder, overlook the land?
Whence come these glittering throngs, these meteors bright,
This golden people glancing in my sight?
Whence doth this praise, applause, and love arise;
What load-star draweth us all eyes?
Am I awake, or have some dreams conspir'd
To mock my sense with what I most desir'd?
View I that living face, see I those looks,
Which with delight were wont t' amaze my brooks?
Do I behold that worth, that man divine,
This age's glory, by these banks of mine?
Then find I true what long I wish'd in vain;
My much-beloved prince is come again.
So unto them whose zenith is the pole,
When six black months are past, the sun does roll:
So after tempest to sea-tossed wights,
Fair Helen's brothers show their cheering lights:
So comes Arabia's wonder from her woods,
And far, far off is seen by Memphis' floods;

The feather'd sylvans, cloud-like by her fly,
And with triumphing plaudits beat the sky;
Nile marvels, Serap's priests entranced rave,
And in Mygdonian stone her shape engrave;
In lasting cedars they do mark the time
In which Apollo's bird came to their clime.
  Let mother earth now deck'd with flowers be seen,
And sweet-breath'd zephyrs curl the meadows green:
Let heaven weep rubies in a crimson shower,
Such as on India's shores they use to pour:
Or with that golden storm the fields adorn
Which Jove rain'd when his blue-eyed maid was born.
May never hours the web of day outweave;
May never night rise from her sable cave!
Swell proud my billows, faint not to declare
Your joys as ample as their causes are:
For murmurs hoarse sound like Arion's harp,
Now delicately flat, now sweetly sharp;
And you, my nymphs, rise from your moist repair,
Strew all your springs and grots with lilies fair.
Some swiftest footed, get them hence, and pray
Our floods and lakes may keep this holyday;
Whate'er beneath Albania's hills do run,
Which see the rising or the setting sun,
Which drink stern Grampus' mists, or Ochil's snows:
Stone-rolling Tay, Tyne, tortoise-like, that flows;
The pearly Don, the Dees, the fertile Spray,
Wild Severn, which doth see our longest day;
Ness, smoking sulphur, Leve, with mountains crown'd,
Strange Lomond for his floating isles renown'd,
The Irish Rian, Ken, the silver Ayr,
The snaky Doon, the Orr with rushy hair,
The crystal-streaming Nith, loud-bellowing Clyde,
Tweed which no more our kingdoms shall divide;
Rank-swelling Annan, Lid with curl'd streams,
The Esks, the Solway where they lose their names;
To every one proclaim our joys and feasts,
Our triumphs; bid all come and be our guests;
And as they meet in Neptune's azure hall,
Bid them bid sea-gods keep this festival;
This day shall by our currents be renown'd:
Our hills about shall still this day resound:
Nay, that our love more to this day appear,
Let us with it henceforth begin our year.
To virgins flowers, to sun-burnt earth the rain,
To mariners fair winds amidst the main;
Cool shades to pilgrims, which hot glances burn,
Are not so pleasing as thy blest return,
That day, dear Prince.

Arthur Johnston, the last of the poets of this period, was so celebrated as a writer of Latin verse, that he received the name of the Scottish Ovid, and even contested the supremacy in Latinity with Buchanan himself. He was born at Caskieben, near Aberdeen, in 1587; and having first pursued collegiate studies in the university of Aberdeen, he afterward went to Rome, and thence to Padua, where he studied medicine, and took his doctor's degree in 1610. Being at this time only in the twenty-fourth year of his age, he resolved to acquire, before he entered upon his profession, those accomplishments which he well knew nothing but foreign travel could impart. With this view he made the tour of Italy, Germany, Denmark, Holland, and England, and finally settled in Paris, where he continued to practice his profession with uninterrupted success for nearly twenty years.

In 1632, Doctor Johnston returned to Scotland, and being introduced to Archbishop Laud, who was at that time in the north with Charles the First, he became, through the influence of that prelate, physician to the king. In this important relation to his majesty, he remained until 1641, when, being on a visit to a married daughter residing at Oxford, he was there seized with a serious illness of which he soon after died, in the fifty-fifth year of his age.

Doctor Johnston was an extensive writer of Latin verse, and produced in that language a number of elegies, epigrams, a paraphrase of the Song of Solomon, a collection of short poems entitled *Musæ Aulicæ*, and a complete ***Version of the Psalms of David***, the last of which is his great performance. He also edited and contributed largely to the *Deliciæ Poetarum Scotorum*—a collection of congratulatory poems by various authors, which reflected great honor on the taste and scholarship of Scotland at that time. The celebrity of Dr. Johnston's name throughout the learned world, requires this brief notice of his life; but we shall neither make any extracts, nor attempt any translations from his poems.

The following beautiful verses will afford an appropriate close to our present remarks. They are supposed to have been written by SIR ROGER L'ESTRANGE, while he was confined in prison on account of his adherence to his unfortunate monarch, Charles the First.

LOYALTY CONFINED.

Beat on, proud billows; Boreas, blow;
  Swell, curl'd waves, high as Jove's roof;
Your incivility doth show
  That innocence is tempest-proof;
Though surely Nereus frown, my thoughts are calm;
Then strike affliction, for thy wounds are balm.

That which the world miscalls a jail,
  A private closet is to me:
While a good conscience is my bail,
  And innocence my liberty:
Locks, bars, and solitude, together met,
Make me no prisoner, but an anchoret.

I, while I wish'd to be retired,
  Into this private room was turn'd;

As if their wisdoms had conspir'd
The salamander should be burn'd;
Or like those sophists, that would drown a fish,
I am constrain'd to suffer what I wish.

The cynic loves his poverty,
The pelican her wilderness,
And 'tis the Indian's pride to be
Naked on frozen Caucasus:
Contentment can not smart, stoics we see
Make torments easy to their apathy.

These manacles upon my arm,
I, as my mistress' favours, wear;
And for to keep my ankles warm,
I have some iron shackles there:
These walls are but my garrison; this cell,
Which men call jail, doth prove my citadel.

I'm in the cabinet lock'd up,
Like some high-prized margarite;
Or like the great Mogul or Pope,
Am cloister'd up from public sight.
Retiredness is a piece of majesty,
And thus, proud sultan, I'm as great as thee.

Here sin for want of food must starve,
Where tempting objects are not seen;
And these strong walls do only serve
To keep vice out, and keep me in:
Malice of late 's grown charitable sure;
I'm not committed, but am kept secure.

So he that struck at Jason's life,
Thinking t' have made his purpose sure,
By a malicious friendly knife
Did only wound him to a cure:
Malice, I see, wants wit; for what is meant
Mischief, ofttimes proves favour by th' event.

When once my prince affliction hath,
Prosperity doth treason seem;
And to make smooth so rough a path,
I can learn patience from him:
Now not to suffer shows no loyal heart—
When kings want ease, subjects must bear a part.

What though I can not see my king,
Neither in person, or in coin;
Yet contemplation is a thing
That renders what I have not, mine:
My king from me what adamant can part,
Whom I do wear engraven on my heart.

Have you not seen the nightingale
A prisoner-like, coop'd in a cage,
How doth she chant her wonted tale,
In that her narrow hermitage!

Even then her charming melody doth prove
That all her bars are trees, her cage a grove.
  I am that bird whom they combine
    Thus to deprive of liberty;
  But though they do my corpse confine,
    Yet, maugre hate, my soul is free:
And, though immur'd, yet can I chirp and sing
Disgrace to rebels, glory to my king.

  My soul is free as ambient air,
    Although my baser part 's immur'd;
  Whilst loyal thoughts do still repair
    T' accompany my solitude;
Although rebellion do my body bind,
My king alone can captivate my mind.

Lecture the Twelfth.

DRAMATIC LITERATURE.

THE ORIGIN OF THE ENGLISH DRAMA—JOHN HEYWOOD—RICHARD ODELL—THOMAS RYCHARDES—JOHN STILL—THOMAS SACKVILLE—THOMAS NORTON—RICHARD EDWARDS—JOHN LYLY—GEORGE PEELE—THOMAS KID—THOMAS NASH—ROBERT GREENE—THOMAS LODGE—ANTHONY MUNDAY—HENRY CHATTLE—CHRISTOPHER MARLOW.

TO the dramatic literature of the period of Elizabeth our attention must now be directed, as toward the latter part of her reign that form of composition and its representation, coinciding with the love of magnificence, chivalrous feeling, and romantic adventures, which animated the court, suddenly arose to the highest degree of splendor, and attracted nearly all the poetic genius of the country. But to present this department of English literature clearly before the mind, it will be necessary to notice briefly, the origin and nature of those rude dramatic representations which both remotely and more immediately preceded it, and in which it had its commencement.

At the dawn of modern civilization most countries in Christian Europe possessed a rude kind of theatrical entertainment, consisting, not in those exhibitions of nature, character, and incident which constituted the plays of ancient Greece and Rome, but in representations of the principal supernatural events of the Old and New Testaments, and of the history of the saints, whence they were called *Miracles*, or *Miracle Plays*. Originally, they appear to have been acted by the clergy, or under their immediate management, and they are supposed to have considered them favorable to the diffusion of religious feeling; though from the traces of those *Miracles* which still remain they seem to have been profane and indecorous in the highest degree. A miracle play upon the story of St. Katherine, and in the French language, was acted at Dunstable in 1119, and how long such entertainments may have previously existed in England, is not known. From 1268, a period of more than three hundred years, they were performed almost every year in Chester; and there were few large cities in England which were not then regaled in a similar manner: even in Scotland they were not unknown.

The most sacred personages, not excluding the Deity himself, were introduced into them.

During the reign of Henry the Sixth, persons representing sentiments and abstract ideas, such as *Mercy*, *Justice*, *Truth*, began to be introduced into the 'Miracle plays,' and led to the composition of an improved kind of drama entirely or chiefly composed of such characters, and termed *Moral Plays*, These plays were, certainly, a great advance upon the 'Miracles,' inasmuch as they endeavored to convey sound moral lessons, and at the same time gave occasion to some poetical and dramatic ingenuity, in imaging forth the characters, and assigning appropriate speeches to each. The only Scriptural character retained in them was the devil, who being represented in grotesque habiliments, and perpetually beaten by an attendant character, called the *Vice*, served to enliven what must have been, at the best, a sober, though well-meant entertainment. The *Cradle of Security*, *Hit the Nail on the Head*, *Impatient Poverty*, and the *Marriage of Wisdom and Wit*, are the names of moral plays which enjoyed popularity in the reign of Henry the Eighth. It was about that time that acting first became a distinct profession, both miracles and moral plays having previously been represented by clergymen, school-boys, or the members of trading incorporations; and were only brought forward occasionally, as part of some public or private festivity.

As the introduction of allegorical characters had been an improvement upon those plays which consisted of Scriptural persons only, so was the introduction of historical and actual characters an improvement upon those which employed only a set of impersonated ideas. It was now found that a real human being, with a human name, was better calculated to awaken the sympathies, and keep alive the attention of an audience, and not less so to impress them with moral truths, than a being who only represented a notion of the mind. The substitution of these for the symbolical characters, gradually took place during the earlier part of the sixteenth century; and thus, with some aid from Greek dramatic literature, which now began to be studied, and from the improved theatres of Italy and Spain, the genuine English drama took its rise.

We should, perhaps, here notice the *Interludes* of JOHN HEYWOOD, as occupying a place between the moral plays and the modern drama. Heywood was a native of London, and was partially educated at Oxford; but the severity of academical studies did not suit his gay and sprightly disposition; and he therefore returned to his native city, and soon became familiar with the men of wit about the court, especially with Sir Thomas More, with whom he was on terms of close intimacy. He was particularly noticed and patronized by Henry the Eighth, and was afterward equally a favorite with Queen Mary, whom he is represented to have entertained and amused even on her death-bed. As Heywood was a devoted papist, he left England on the accession of Queen Elizabeth, and retired to Mecklin, in Brabant, where he died in 1565.

Heywood's dramatic compositions, part of which were produced before 1521, generally represented some ludicrous familiar incidents, in a style of the broadest and coarsest farce, but still with no small degree of skill and talent. One of these, called the *Four P's*, turns upon a dispute between a *Palmer*, a *Pardoner*, a *Poticary*, and a *Pedler*, as to which shall tell the grossest falsehood. An accidental assertion of the 'Palmer,' that he never saw a woman out of patience in his life, throws the rest off their guard, all of whom declare it to be the greatest lie they ever heard, and the settlement of the question is thus brought about amid much drollery. There were some less distinguished writers of 'Interludes' than Heywood, and Sir David Lyndsay's *Satire of the Three Estates*, acted in Scotland in 1539, was a play of this kind.

The regular drama, from its very commencement, was divided into comedy and tragedy, the elements of both being found quite distinct in the rude entertainments already described. Of comedy, which was an improvement upon the interludes, the earliest specimen that can now be found bears the singular title of *Ralph Royster Doyster*. It was the production of RICHARD ODELL, master of Westminster school, and is supposed to have been written during the reign of Henry the Eighth, but certainly not later than 1551. The scene is laid in London, and the characters, thirteen in number, exhibit the manners of the middle orders of the people of that day. It is divided into five acts, and the plot is amusing and well constructed. The language is in long and irregularly measured rhyme, of which the following, from a speech of Dame Custance, one of the leading characters, respecting the difficulty of preserving a good reputation, is a specimen :—

—— How necessary it is now-a-days,
That each body live uprightly in all manner ways;
For let never so little a gap be open,
And be sure of this, the worst will be spoken!

THOMAS RYCHARDES, according to Collier, was the author of the second English comedy of which we have now any knowledge. *Mesogonus* is the name of the play here alluded to, and the date of its publication is 1560. The scene is laid in Italy, but the manners are English, and the character of the domestic fool, so important in the old comedy, is fully delineated.

The next English comedy, in the order of time, is *Gammer Gurton's Needle*. This piece was written by JOHN STILL, Master of Arts, and afterward bishop of Bath and Wells, about 1565, or perhaps at an earlier date. 'In this play,' says Hawkins, 'there is a vein of familiar humor, and a kind of grotesque imagery, not unlike some parts of Aristophanes ; but without those graces of language and metre, for which the Greek comedian is so eminently distinguished.' There is certainly much whim and wit in many of the situations ; and the characters, although rudely, are very forcibly delineated. The plot is both simple and coarse, the whole turning upon the loss and recovery of the needle with which Gammer Gurton was mending a pair of breeches belonging to her man Hodge. The following fine old song with which the second act opens is, of itself, sufficient to preserve the whole play from oblivion :—

SONG.

I can not eat but little meat,
  My stomach is not good;
But sure I think that I can drink
  With him that wears a hood.
Though I go bare, take ye no care,
  I nothing am a-cold;
I stuff my skin so full within
  Of jolly good ale and old.
      Back and side go bare, go bare;
        Both foot and hand go cold;
      But belly, God send thee good ale enough,
        Whether it be new or old.

I love no roast but a nut-brown toast,
  And a crab laid in the fire;
And little bread shall do me stead;
  Much bread I nought desire.
No frost, no snow, no wind, I trow,
  Can hurt me if I wold,
I am so wrapp'd, and thoroughly lapp'd,
  Of jolly good ale and old.
      Back and side, &c.

And Tib, my wife, that as her life
  Loveth well good ale to seek,
Full oft drinks she, till ye may see
  The tears run down her cheeks:
Then doth she troul to me the bowl,
  Even as a maltworm should,
And saith, Sweetheart, I took my part
  Of this jolly good ale and old.
      Back and side, &c.

Now let them drink till they nod and wink,
  Even as good fellows should do;
They shall not miss to have the bliss
  Good ale doth bring men to.
And all poor souls that have scour'd bowls,
  Or have them lustily troul'd,
God save the lives of them and their wives,
  Whether they be young or old.
      Back and side, &c.

Tragedy, of later origin than comedy, came directly from the more elevated portions of the moral plays, and from the pure models of Greece and Rome. The earliest known specimen of this kind of composition is the Tragedy of *Ferrex and Porrex*, composed by THOMAS SACKVILLE and THOMAS NORTON, and acted before queen Elizabeth at Whitehall by the members of the Inner Temple, in January, 1561. It is founded on a fabulous incident in early English history, and is full of carnage. It is written, however, in regular blank verse, consists of five acts, and observes some of the more useful rules of the classical drama of antiquity, to which it bears resemblance in the introduction of a chorus—that is, a group of persons whose sole business it is to intersperse the play with moral observations and inferences, expressed in lyrical stanzas. It may occasion some surprise, that the first English tragedy should contain lines like the following:—

Acastus. Your grace should now, in these grave years of yours,
Have found ere this the price of mortal joys;
How short they be, how fading here in earth;
How full of change, how little our estate,
Of nothing sure save only of the death,
To whom both man and all the world doth owe
Their end at last: neither should nature's power
In other sort against your heart prevail,
Than as the naked hand whose stroke assays
The armed breast where force doth light in vain.
Gorboduc. Many can yield right sage and grave advice
Of patient sprite to others wrapp'd in woe,
And can in speech both rule and conquer kind,
Who, if by proof they might feel nature's force,
Would show themselves men as they are indeed,
Which now will needs be gods.

Not long after the appearance of 'Ferrex and Porrex,' both tragedies and comedies had become not uncommon. *Damon and Pythias*, the first English tragedy upon a classical subject, was acted before the queen at Oxford in 1566. It was the composition of Richard Edwards, a learned member of the university, but was inferior to 'Ferrex and Porrex,' in so far as it contained an admixture of vulgar comedy, and was written in rhyme. In the same year two plays, respectively styled *Supposes*, and *Jocasta*, the one a comedy adapted from Ariosto, the other a tragedy from Euripides, were acted in Gray's Inn Hall. A tragedy called *Tancred* and *Gismunda*, composed by five members of the Inner Temple, and presented there before the queen in 1568, was the first English play taken from an Italian novel. Various other dramatic pieces now followed, and between the years 1568, and 1580, no less than fifty-two dramas were acted at court under the superintendence of the *Master of Revels*. Under the date of 1578, the play of *Promos and Cassandra*, by George Whetsone, was produced, on which Shakspeare founded his 'Measure for Measure.' Historical plays were also at this time written, and the *Troublesome Reign of King John*. the *Famous Victories of Henry the Fifth*, and the *Chronicle History of Lear*, *King of England*, formed the quarry from which Shakspeare constructed his dramas on the same events.

As dramatic writing, about this time, began to assume the aspect of a regular profession, buildings for the representation of plays became necessary;

and, accordingly, houses for that purpose were soon erected. The first regular licensed theatre in London was opened at Blackfriar's in 1576; and in ten years from that period, there were, it is estimated, not less than two hundred players in and near the metropolis. When Shakspeare commenced his career, London contained five public theatres, besides several private or select establishments; and curiosity is naturally excited to learn something of the structure and appearance of the buildings in which his immortal dramas first saw the light, and where he unwillingly made himself a 'motley to the view,' in his character of actor. The theatres were constructed of wood, and were of a circular form, open to the weather, excepting over the stage, which was covered with a thatched roof. Outside, on the roof, a flag was hoisted during the time of performance, which commenced at three o'clock, at the third sounding or flourish of trumpets. The courtiers and fair dames of the court of Elizabeth, sat in boxes below the gallery, or were accommodated with stools on the stage, where some of the young gallants also threw themselves at length on the rush-strewn floor, while their pages handed them pipes and tobacco, then a fashionable and highly-prized luxury. The middle classes were crowded in the pit or *yard*, which was destitute of seats, or any other convenience.

Actresses were not introduced upon the stage until after the Restoration, the female parts being played by boys or delicate-looking young men. This may, perhaps, palliate in some degree, the occasional grossness of the language put into the mouths of females in the old plays, while it serves to point out still more clearly the depth of that innate sense of beauty and excellence which prompted the exquisite pictures of loveliness and perfection in Shakspeare's female characters.

Nearly all the dramatic writers preceding Shakspeare, and contemporary with him, were men who had received a learned education at the university of Oxford, or Cambridge. A profusion of classical imagery, therefore, abounds in their plays, but they did not copy the severe and correct taste of the ancient models. They wrote to supply the popular demand for novelty and excitement—for broad farce or superlative tragedy—to introduce the coarse raillery or comic incidents of low life—to dramatize a murder, or embody the vulgar idea of oriental bloodshed and splendid extravagance. 'If we seek for a poetical image,' says Henry Mackenzie, 'a burst of passion, or a beautiful sentiment, a trait of nature, we seek not in vain in the works of our very oldest dramatists. But none of the predecessors of Shakspeare must be thought of along with him, when he appears before us like Prometheus, moulding the figures of men, and breathing into them animation and all the passions of life.' Among the immediate predecessors of the great poet, however, are some worthy of a separate notice; and nearly all of them have touches of that happy poetic diction, free, yet choice and select, which gives a permanent value and interest to these elder masters of English dramatic poetry. To a brief sketch of some of them, therefore, we shall now proceed.

JOHN LYLY, the first to be noticed, was born in Kent in 1553, and educated at Magdalen College, Oxford, where he took his master's degree in 1575. He remained at the university about three years after he had taken his degree, and then removed to London, where he attached himself to the court, and soon became a very great favorite. In 1580 he first appeared as an author, and published his *Euphues*, or the *Anatomy of Wit*, which being excessively affected in style, exercised a very injurious influence on the fashionable literature of the day. Lyly's plays, nine in number, were chiefly written for court entertainments, and the greater part of them were on mythological subjects, such as *Sappho and Phaon*, *Endymion*, and the *Maid's Metamorphosis.* Hazlitt was a very warm admirer of the 'Endymion,' but evidently from the feelings and sentiments which it awakened, rather than from the poetry. 'I know few things more perfect in characteristic painting,' he remarks, 'than the exclamation of the Phrygian shepherds, who, afraid of betraying the secret of Midas's ears, fancy that "the very reeds bow down, as though they listened to their talk;" nor more affecting in sentiment, than the apostrophe addressed by his friend Eumenides to Endymion, on waking from his long sleep, "Behold the twig to which thou laidest down thy head is now become a tree."' There are, however, finer things in the 'Metamorphosis' than these, such as the following passage, where the prince laments Eurymene lost in the woods:—

Adorned with the presence of my love,
The woods I fear such secret power shall prove,
As they'll shut up each path, hide every way,
Because they still would have her go astray,
And in that place would always have her seen,
Only because they would be ever green,
And keep the winged choristers still there,
To banish winter clean out of the year.

Or the song of the fairies—

By the moon we sport and play,
With the night begins our day:
As we dance the dew doth fall,
Trip it, little urchins all.
Lightly as the little bee,
Two by two, and three by three,
And about go we, and about go we.

Lyly's genius was essentially lyrical, and hence the songs in his plays seem to flow forth from the native fountain of his feelings. The following exquisite little pieces are in his drama of *Alexander and Campaspe*, which was written about 1585:—

CUPID AND CAMPASPE.

Cupid and my Campaspe play'd
At cards for kisses; Cupid paid.
He stakes his quiver, bow, and arrows;
His mother's doves and team of sparrows;

Loses them too, and down he throws
The coral of his lip—the rose
Growing on 's cheek, but none knows how;
With these the crystal on his brow,
And then the dimple of his chin;
All these did my Campaspe win;
At last he set her both his eyes;
She won, and Cupid blind did rise.
Oh Love, hath she done this to thee?
What shall, alas, become of me!

SONG.

What bird so sings, yet so does wail?
O 'tis the ravish'd nightingale—
Jug, jug, jug, jug,—tereu—she cries,
And still her woes at midnight rise.
Brave prick-song! who is 't now we hear?
None but the lark so shrill and clear,
Now at heaven's gate, she claps her wings,
The morn not waking till she sings.
Hark, hark! but what a pretty note,
Poor Robin red-breast tunes his throat;
Hark, how the jolly cuckoos sing
'Cuckoo!' to welcome in the spring.

The time of Lyly's death is uncertain; but he is generally supposed to have died about 1600.

George Peele, a contemporary of Lyly, was born about 1556, and was educated at Christ's Church College, Oxford. Immediately after he left the university he repaired to London, and commenced his career as an actor in connection with the same company to which Shakspeare afterward belonged. He also held the situation of city poet, and conductor of pageants for the court; and in 1584, his *Arraignment of Paris*, a court show, was represented before the queen. In 1593, Peele gave an example of an English historical play in his *Edward the First.* The style of this piece is turgid and monotonous; yet in the following allusion to England, we see something of the high-sounding kingly speeches which are found in Shakspeare's historical plays:—

Illustrious England, ancient seat of kings,
Whose chivalry hath royaliz'd thy fame,
That, sounding bravely through terrestrial vale,
Proclaiming conquests, spoils, and victories,
Rings glorious echoes through the farthest world!
What warlike nations, train'd in feats of arms,
What barbarous people, stubborn, or untam'd,
What climate under the meridian signs,
Or frozen zones under his brumal stage,
Erst have not quak'd and trembled at the name
Of Briton and her mighty conquerors?
Her neighbour realms, as Scotland, Denmark, France,

Awed with their deeds, and jealous of her arms,
Have begg'd defensive and offensive leagues.
Thus Europe, rich and mighty in her kings,
Hath fear'd brave England, dreadful in her kings.
And now, to eternize Albion's champions,
Equivalent with Trojan's ancient fame,
Comes lovely Edward from Jerusalem,
Veering before the wind, ploughing the sea;
His stretched sails fill'd with the breath of men,
That through the world admire his manliness.
And lo, at last arrived in Dover road,
Longshank, your king, your glory, and our son,
With troops of conquering lords and warlike knights,
Like bloody-crested Mars, o'erlooks his host,
Higher than all his army by the head,
Marching along as bright as Phœbus' eyes!
And we, his mother, shall behold our Son,
And England's peers shall see their sovereign.

Peele was the author of a number of other dramas, such as *Old Wives' Tale*, and the *Love of King David and Fair Bethsabe;* the former of which written part in prose and part in blank verse, afforded Milton a rude outline of his fable of 'Comus.' The latter, which is Peele's greatest work, with the tragedy of *Absolem*, Campbell terms, 'the earliest fountain of pathos and harmony that can be traced in our dramatic poetry.' This play was not published till 1599, after Shakspeare had written some of his finest comedies, and opened up a fountain compared with which the feeble tricklings of Peele were wholly insignificant. We may, however, allow to Peele the merit of a delicate poetical fancy, and smooth musical versification. The defect in his blank verse is want of variety: the art of varying the pauses and modulating the verse without the aid of rhyme, had not yet been generally adopted. In 'David and Bethsabe' this monotony is less observable, because his lines are smoother, and there is, in some of the scenes, a play of peculiarly rich and luxuriant fancy. We have, however, only space for a single passage from this important work:—

PROLOGUE TO KING DAVID AND FAIR BETHSABE.

Of Israel's sweetest singer now I sing,
His holy style and happy victories;
Whose muse was dipt in that inspiring dew,
Archangels 'stilled from the breath of Jove,
Decking her temples with the glorious flowers
Heaven rain'd on tops of Sion and Mount Sinai.
Upon the bosom of his ivory lute
The cherubim and angels laid their breasts;
And when his consecrated fingers struck
The golden wires of his ravishing harp,
He gave alarum to the host of heaven,
That, wing'd with lightning, brake the clouds, and cast
Their crystal armour at his conquering feet.
Of this sweet poet, Jove's musician,

And of his beauteous son, I press to sing;
Then help, divine Adonai, to conduct
Upon the wings of my well-temper'd verse,
The hearers' minds above the towers of heaven,
And guide them so in this thrice haughty flight,
Their mounting feathers scorch not with the fire
That none can temper but thy holy hand:
To thee for succour flies my feeble muse,
And at thy feet her iron pen doth use.

Peele, like most of his dramatic brethren of that period, led a very irregular life, and died in the midst of poverty, in 1599.

THOMAS KID follows in the order of succession, the dramatists just noticed. He was born about 1560, and apparently liberally educated, but under what circumstances is unknown. In 1588, he produced his play of *Hieronimo* or *Jeronimo*, and a few years afterward a second part under the title of the *Spanish Tragedy*, or *Hieronimo is Mad Again*. The latter tragedy is said to have gone through more editions than any other play of that period. It was revived in 1602, when Ben Jonson is supposed to have improved it by the addition of new scenes. These new scenes are said, by Lamb, to be 'the very salt of the old play,' and so superior to Jonson's acknowledged works that he attributes them to Webster, or even to Shakspeare. The following scene, whoever may have been the author of it, is so exquisite that we can not withhold it. Hieronimo, whose son had been murdered, goes distracted, and he wishes the painter to represent the fatal catastrophe on canvas. He finds that the artist is suffering under a bereavement similar to his own, and the following dialogue ensues:—

'THE PAINTER ENTERS.

Paint. God bless you, Sir!
Hieron. Wherefore? why, thou scornful villain!
How, where, or by what means should I be blest?
Isab. What would you have, good fellow?
Paint. Justice, Madam.
Hieron. Oh! ambitious fellow, would'st thou have that
That lives not in the world?
Why all the undelved minds can not buy
An ounce of justice; 'tis a jewel so inestimable.
I tell thee, God has engrossed all justice in his hand,
And there is none but what comes from him.
Paint. Oh! then I see that God must right me for my murder'd son!
Hieron. How! was thy son murder'd?
Paint. Ay, Sir; no man did hold a son so dear.
Hieron. What! not as thine? That's a lie
As massy as the earth! I had a son,
Whose least unvalued hair did weigh
A thousand of thy sons! and he was murder'd!
Paint. Alas! Sir, I had no more but he.
Hieron. Nor I, nor I; but this same one of mine
Was worth a legion.'

The nature and simplicity of this scene is worth all the ambitious imagery, and rhetorical ornaments, which modern authors lavish upon their dramas, combined. Kid died toward the close of Elizabeth's reign.

Of the dramatic authors who preceded Shakspeare, we have still to notice Nash, Greene, Lodge, Munday, Chettle, and Marlow.

THOMAS NASH was born at Leostoff, Suffolk, in 1562. He was educated at St. John's College, Cambridge, and took orders; but the irregularity of his life preventing his preferment, he repaired to the metropolis, and was soon after known as a professed wit. After indulging his satirical vein for some time against the 'Puritans,' he became a dramatist, and produced, as his first play, a comedy called *Summer's Last Will and Testament*, which was exhibited before Queen Elizabeth in 1592. He next wrote a satirical play under the title of the *Isle of Dogs*, for the severity of which, though the play was never printed, he was, for some time, imprisoned. Another production of Nash's, entitled the *Supplication of Pierce Penniless to the Devil*, was published in 1592, and was followed during the next year by his last important performance, *Christ's Tears over Jerusalem*. He died about 1600, after a 'life spent,' he says, 'in fantastical satirism, in whose veins heretofore I misspent my spirit, and prodigally conspired against good hours.'

The versification of Nash is hard and monotonous, and his style possesses little variety. The following extract is from the comedy of 'Summer's Last Will and Testament,' and is a favorable specimen of his blank verse:—

I never lov'd ambitiously to climb,
Or thrust my hand too far into the fire.
To be in heaven sure is a blessed thing,
But, Atlas-like, to prop heaven on one's back
Can not but be more labour than delight.
Such is the state of men in honour placed:
They are gold vessels made for servile uses;
High trees that keep the weather from low houses,
But can not shield the tempest from themselves.
I love to dwell betwixt the hills and dales,
Neither to be so great as to be envied,
Nor yet so poor the world should pity me.

In his poem of 'Pierce Penniless,' Nash draws the harrowing picture of the despair of a poor scholar:—

Ah, worthless wit! to train me to this woe:
Deceitful arts that nourish discontent:
Ill thrive the folly that bewitch'd me so!
Vain thoughts adieu! for now I will repent—
And yet my wants persuade me to proceed,
For none take pity of a scholar's need.
Forgive me, God, although I curse my birth,

And ban the air wherein I breathe a wretch,
Since misery hath daunted all my mirth,
And I am quite undone through promise breach;
Ah, friends!—no friends that then ungentle frown
When changing fortune casts us headlong down.

Robert Greene was a native of Norfolk, and was educated at Clare-Hall, Cambridge. He early entered into orders, and for a short time held the vicarage of Tollesbury, in Essex, which, however, he lost in 1585. He had, a short time previous to this event, entered upon his career as an author, and in the course of a few years he produced the following plays:—*History of Orlando*, *Friar Bacon and Friar Bungay*, *Alphonsus*, *King of Arragon*, *George-a-Green*, *The Pinner of Wakefield*, *James the Fourth*, and the *Looking-glass for London and England;* the last of which was written in conjunction with Lodge. Besides his plays, Greene was the author of a number of tracts, one of which, *Pandosto*, *the Triumph of Time*, written in 1588, was the source whence Shakspeare derived his 'Winter's Tale.' Some lines contained in this tract, such as the following, are extremely beautiful:—

Ah, were she pitiful as she is fair,
Or but as mild as she is seeming so,
Then were my hopes greater than my despair—
Then all the world were heaven, nothing woe.
Ah, were her heart relenting as her hand,
That seems to melt e'en with the mildest touch,
Then knew I where to seat me in a land
Under the wide heavens, but yet not such.
So as she shows, she seems the budding rose,
Yet sweeter far than is an earthly flower;
Sovereign of beauty, like the spray she grows,
Compass'd she is with thorns and canker'd flower;
Yet, were she willing to be pluck'd and worn,
She would be gather'd though she grew on thorn.

Greene's imagination was lively and discursive, fond of legendary lore, and filled with classical images and illustrations. In his 'Orlando' he thus apostrophizes the evening star:—

Fair queen of love, thou mistress of delight,
Thou gladsome lamp that wait'st on Phœbe's train,
Spreading thy kindness through the jarring orbs,
That in their union praise thy lasting powers;
Thou that hast stay'd the fiery Phlegon's course,
And mad'st the coachman of the glorious wain
To droop in view of Daphne's excellence;
Fair pride of morn, sweet beauty of the even,
Look on Orlando languishing in love.
Sweet solitary groves, whereas the nymphs
With pleasance laugh to see the satyrs play,
Witness Orlando's faith unto his love.
Tread she these lawns?—Kind Flora, boast thy pride:

Seek she for shades?—Spread, cedars, for her sake.
Fair Flora, make her couch amidst thy flowers.
Sweet crystal springs,
Wash ye with roses when she longs to drink.
Ah thought, my heaven! Ah heaven that knows my thought!
Smile, joy in her that my content hath wrought.

Such passages as this prove that Greene succeeds well, as Hallam remarks, 'in that florid and gay style, a little redundant in images, which Shakspeare frequently gives to his princes and courtiers, and which renders some unimpassioned scenes in the historic plays, effective and brilliant.' His comedies contain much boisterous merriment and farcical humor. George-a-Green is a shrewd Yorkshireman, who meets with the kings of Scotland and England, Robin Hood, Maid Marian, and others, and who, after various tricks, receives the pardon of king Edward, accompanied with the following assurance:—

George-a-Green, give me thy hand: there is
None in England that shall do thee wrong.
Even from my court I came to see thyself,
And now I see that fame speaks nought but truth.

The following is a specimen of the simple humor and practical jokes in the play: it is in a scene between George and his servant:—

Jenkin. This fellow comes to me,
And takes me by the bosom: you slave,
Said he, hold my horse, and look
He takes no cold in his feet.
No, marry, shall he, sir, quoth I;
I'll lay my cloak underneath him.
I took my cloak, spread it all along,
And his horse on the midst of it.
George. Thou clown, did'st thou set his horse upon thy cloak?
Jenkin. Ay, but mark how I served him.
Madge and he were no sooner gone down into the ditch,
But I plucked out my knife, cut four holes in my cloak,
And made his horse stand on the bare ground.

But *Friar Bacon and Friar Bungay* is much the best of Greene's comedies. His friars are conjurers, and the piece concludes with one of their pupils being carried off to hell on the back of one of friar Bacon's devils. This was, perhaps, the last time the devil was introduced upon the stage in his proper person. The play was performed for the first time in 1591, but was probably written a year or two earlier.

In some hour of repentance, when death was nigh at hand, Greene wrote a tract called *A Groat's Worth of Wit, Bought with a Million of Repentance*, in which he deplores his fate more feelingly than Nash, and also gives ghostly advice to his acquaintances, 'that spend their wit in making plays.' Marlow he accuses of Atheism; Lodge he designates 'young Juvenal' and 'a sweet boy;' Peele he considers too good for the stage; and he glances thus at Shakspeare, who, in all probability, at that early period began to eclipse all of them:—'For there is an upstart crow beautified with our feathers, that with his tiger's heart wrapt in a player's hide, supposes he is as well able to bombast out a blank verse as the best of you; and being an absolute Johannes Fac-totum, is, in his own conceit, the only Shake-scene in a country.' The punning allusion to Shakspeare is unmistakable: the expressions 'tiger's heart wrapt in a player's hide,' are a parody on the following line in Henry the Sixth:—

O tiger's heart wrapt in a woman's hide.

The 'Groat's Worth of Wit' was published after Greene's death by a brother dramatist, Henry Chettle, who, in the preface to a subsequent work, thus apologizes for the allusion to Shakspeare. 'I am sorry,' he says, 'as if the original fault had been my fault, because myself have seen his demeanor no less civil than he excellent in the quality he professes. Beside, divers of worship have reported his uprightness of dealing, which argues his honesty, and his facetious grace in writing that approves his art.' This apology was published in 1593, and is the more valuable, because it does full justice to Shakspeare's moral worth, and civil deportment, and to his respectability as an actor and author.

The following conclusion of Greene's 'Groat's Worth of Wit,' contains more pathos than all his plays combined. It is, indeed, a harrowing picture of genius debased by vice, and sorrowing in repentance:—

'But now return I again to you three (Marlow, Lodge, and Peele), knowing my misery is to you no news: and let me heartily entreat you to be warned by my harms. Delight not, as I have done, in irreligious oaths; despise drunkenness, fly lust, abhor those epicures, whose loose life hath made religion loathsome to your ears; and when they soothe you with terms of mastership, remember Robert Greene (whom they have often flattered) perishes for want of comfort. Remember, gentlemen, your lives are like so many light tapers that are with care delivered to all of you to maintain; these, with wind-puffed wrath, may be extinguished, with drunkenness put out, with negligence let fall. The fire of my light is now at the last snuff. My hand is tired, and I forced to leave where I would begin; desirous that you should live though himself be dying.—Robert Greene.'

Greene died in September 1592, owing, it is said, to a surfeit of red herring and Rhenish wine! We shall conclude this melancholy picture with his sonnet on *Content*, and the *Song of the Shepherdess.*

CONTENT.

Sweet are the thoughts that savour of content:
The quiet mind is richer than a crown:
Sweet are the nights in careless slumber spent:
The poor estate scorns Fortune's angry frown.
Such sweet content, such minds, such sleep, such bliss,
Beggars enjoy, when princes oft do miss.
The homely house that harbours quiet rest,
The cottage that affords no pride nor care,

The mean, that 'grees with country music best,
The sweet consort of mirth's and music's fare.
Obscured life sets down a type of bliss;
A mind content both crown and kingdom is.

THE SONG OF THE SHEPHERDESS.

Ah! what is love! It is a pretty thing,
As sweet unto a shepherd as a king,
And sweeter too:
For kings have cares that wait upon a crown,
And cares can make the sweetest cares to frown:
Ah then, ah then,
If country loves such sweet desires gain,
What lady would not love a shepherd swain?

His flocks are folded; he comes home at night
As merry as a king in his delight,
And merrier too:
For kings bethink them what the state require,
Where shepherds, careless, carol by the fire:
Ah then, ah then,
If country loves such sweet desires gain
What lady would not love a shepherd swain?

He kisseth first, then sits as blithe to eat
His cream and curd as doth the king his meat,
And blither too:
For kings have often fears when they sup,
Where shepherds dread no poison in their cup:
Ah then, ah then,
If country loves such sweet desires gain,
What lady would not love a shepherd swain?

Upon his couch of straw he sleeps as sound
As doth the king upon his bed of down,
More sounder too:
For cares cause kings full oft their sleep to spill,
Where weary shepherds lie and snort their fill:
Ah then, ah then,
If country loves such sweet desires gain,
What lady would not love a shepherd swain?

Thus with his wife he spends the year as blithe
As doth the king at every tide or syth,
And blither too:
For kings have wars and broils to take in hand,
When shepherds laugh, and love upon the land:
Ah then, ah then,
If country loves such sweet desires gain,
What lady would not love a shepherd swain?

THOMAS LODGE was educated at Trinity College, Oxford, of which he became servitor in, 1573. From Oxford he removed to London, and entered Lincoln's Inn as a student of law; but if he ever followed the legal profession, it must have been for only a short time, as in 1584, he was connected with one of the London theatrical companies as an actor. He soon after retired to the continent, studied medicine, and took his doctor's degree at Avignon, in the south of France. In 1590, he first appeared as an author by the production of a novel under the title of *Rosalind Ephues' Golden Legacy*, in which he recommends the fantastic style of Lyly. From part of the story of 'Rosalind,' Shakspeare constructed his 'As You Like It.' In 1594, Lodge wrote a historical play, the *Wounds of Civil War*, *Lively set forth in the True Tragedies of Marius aud Sylla.* The play, as a whole, is heavy and uninteresting, but the author had the good taste to adopt, as will appear from the following example, the blank verse for which Greene had already become so distinguished:—

Ay, but the milder passions show the man;
For, as the leaf doth beautify the tree,
The pleasant flowers bedeck the painted spring,
Even so in men of greatest reach and power,
A mild and piteous thought augments renown.

The play 'A Looking-glass for London and England,' already alluded to in our notice of Greene, is directed to the defence of the stage. It applies the Scriptural story of Nineveh to the city of London, and amid drunken buffoonery and clownish mirth, contains some powerful satirical writing. Lodge also translated *Josephus* wrote a volume of *Satires*, and other poems, and a serious defence of the drama, in prose. In 1600, he visited the continent in company with Henry Savell, and on his return to London he merged the actor and dramatist in the physician, and soon became prosperous and wealthy. He died in London, of the plague, in 1625.

In Lodge's 'Rosalind' there is a delightful spirit of romantic fancy, and a love of nature that marks the true poet; and some of his minor pieces, such as the following, are truly beautiful:—

ROSALIND'S MADRIGAL.

Love in my bosom, like a bee,
Doth suck his sweet;
Now with his wings he plays with me,
Now with his feet.
Within mine eyes he makes his nest,
His bed amidst my tender breasts;
My kisses are his daily feast,
And yet he robs me of my rest:
Ah, wanton, will ye?

And if I sleep, then percheth he
With pretty flight,
And makes his pillow of my knee,
The live-long night.
Strike I my lute, he tunes the string;
He music plays if so I sing;

He lends me every lovely thing,
Yet cruel he my heart doth sting:
Whist, wanton, still ye?

Else I with roses every day
Will whip you hence,
And bind you, when you long to play,
For your offence;
I'll shut mine eyes to keep you in,
I'll make you fast it for your sin,
I'll count your power not worth a pin;
Alas! what hereby shall I win,
If he gainsay me?

What if I beat the wanton boy
With many a rod?
He will repay me with annoy,
Because a god.
Then sit thou safely on my knee,
And let thy bower my bosom be;
Lurk in mine eyes, I like of thee,
O, Cupid! so thou pity me,
Spare not, but play thee.

BEAUTY.

Like to the clear in highest sphere,
Where all imperial glory shines,
Of self-same colour is her hair,
Whether unfolded or in twines:

Her eyes are sapphires set in snow,
Refining heaven by every wink;
The gods do fear, when as they glow,
And I do tremble when I think.

Her cheeks are like the blushing cloud,
That beautifies Aurora's face;
Or like the silver crimson shroud,
That Phœbus' smiling looks doth grace.

Her lips are like two budded roses,
Whom ranks of lilies neighbour nigh,
Within which bounds she balm incloses,
Apt to entice a deity.

Her neck like to a stately tower,
Where Love himself imprison'd lies,
To watch for glances, every hour,
From her divine and sacred eyes.

With orient pearl, with ruby red,
With marble white, with sapphire blue,
Her body everywhere is fed,
Yet soft in touch, and sweet in view.

Nature herself her shape admires,
The gods are wounded in her sight;
And Love forsakes his heavenly fires,
And at her eyes his brand doth light.

ANTHONY MUNDAY'S name frequently occurs among the dramatic authors of this period, but of his life very little is known. He appeared before the public as a dramatic writer as early as 1579, and was concerned in the production of fourteen plays; and such was the reputation to which he attained that Francis Meres, in 1598, calls him the 'best plotter' among the writers for the stage. One of his dramas, *Sir John Oldcastle*, was written in conjunction with Drayton and others, and was printed in 1600, with the name of Shakspeare on the title-page! *The Death of Robert, Earl of Huntington*, printed in 1601, was Munday's most popular play, and it is said he was assisted in it by Chettle. The pranks of Robin Hood and Maid Marian in merry Sherwood, are thus gayly set forth:—

Wind once more, jolly huntsmen, all your horns,
Whose shrill sound with the echoing woods assist,
Shall ring a sad knell for the fearful deer;
Before our feather'd shafts, death's winged darts,
Bring sudden summons for their fatal ends.
Give me thy hand: now God's curse on me light,
If I forsake not grief in grief's despite.
Much, make a cry, and yeomen stand ye round:
I charge ye never more let woful sound
Be heard among ye; but whatever fall,
Laugh grief to scorn, and so make sorrow small.
Marian, thou seest, though courtly pleasures want,
Yet country sport in Sherwood is not scant.
For the soul-ravishing delicious sound
Of instrumental music, we have found
The winged quiristers, with divers notes,
Sent from their quaint recording pretty throats,
On every branch that compasseth our bower,
Without command contenting us each hour.
For arras hangings, and rich tapestry,
We have sweet nature's best embroidery.
For thy steel glass, wherein thou wont'st to look,
Thy crystal eyes gaze on the crystal brook.
At court, a flower or two did deck thy head,
Now, with whole garlands it is circled;
For what in wealth we want, we have in flowers,
And what we lose in halls, we find in bowers.

HENRY CHETTLE is as little known as Munday. It is supposed by Collier that he had written for the stage before 1592, when he published Greene's posthumous work, 'A Groat's Worth of Wit.' He was a very prolific writer, and was engaged in the composition of no less than thirty-eight plays, during the six years that followed from 1597. Amongst his plays, the names of which have descended to us, is one on the subject of Cardinal Wolsey, which probably was the origin of Shakspeare's 'Henry the Eighth.' The best drama of this author, that we now possess, is a comedy called *Patient Grissell*, taken from the Italian of Boccaccio. The humble charms of the heroine are thus finely described:—

See where my Grissell and her father is,
Methinks her beauty, shining through those weeds,
Seems like a bright star in the sullen night.
How lovely poverty dwells on her back!
Did but the proud world note her as I do,
She would cast off rich robes, forswear rich state,
To clothe her in such poor habiliments.

Our remarks upon the early part of English dramatic literature, have now brought us down to Marlow, who was by far the mightiest of Shakspeare's precursors.

CHRISTOPHER MARLOW was the son of a shoemaker, and was born at Canterbury, Kent, in 1562. He was educated at Bennet College, Cambridge, and took his master's degree in 1587. He had, however, previous to this, commenced his career as a dramatist, and written his tragedy of *Tamberlaine the Great*, which was successfully brought upon the stage, and long continued a favorite. Though there is in the play much rant and fustian, still it has passages of great beauty and wild grandeur, and the versification justifies the compliment afterward paid by Ben Jonson, in the words, 'Marlow's mighty line.' His finely modulated and varied blank verse, observable even in this early play, is one of his most characteristic features. The success of 'Tamberlaine' induced Marlow to commence the profession of an actor; but he was soon incapacitated for the stage by accidentally breaking his leg.

Marlow's second play, the *Life and Death of Dr. Faustus*, exhibits a far wider range of dramatic power than his first. The hero studies necromancy, and makes a solemn disposal of his soul to Lucifer, on condition of having a familiar spirit at his command, and unlimited enjoyment for twenty-four years; during which period Faustus visits different countries, 'calls up spirits from the vasty deep,' and revels in luxury and splendor. At length the time expires, the bond becomes due, and a party of evil spirits enter, amid thunder and lightning, to claim his forfeited life and person. Such a plot afforded scope for deep passion and variety of adventure, and Marlow has constructed from it a powerful though irregular play. Scenes and passages of terrific grandeur, and the most thrilling agony, are intermixed with low humor and preternatural machinery, often ludicrous and grotesque. The ambition of Faustus is a sensual, not a lofty ambition. A feeling of curiosity and wonder is excited by his necromancy and his strange compact with Lucifer; but we do not fairly sympathize till all his disguises are stripped off, and his meretricious splendor is succeeded by horror and despair. Then, when he stands on the brink of everlasting ruin, waiting for the fatal moment, imploring, yet distrusting repentance, a scene of enchaining interest, fervid passion, and overwhelming pathos, carries captive the sternest heart, and proclaims the full triumph of the tragic poet. To illustrate these remarks, we shall here introduce the closing scene of the play. The last fatal midnight approaches, and Faustus is left alone:—

FAUSTUS ALONE.

[*The Clock strikes Eleven.*]

Faust. Oh, Faustus,
Now hast thou but one bare hour to live,
And then thou must be damn'd perpetually.
Stand still, you ever-moving spheres of heaven,
That time may cease and midnight never come.
Fair Nature's eye, rise, rise again, and make
Perpetual day: or let this hour be but
A year, a month, a week, a natural day,
That Faustus may repent and save his soul.
O lente, lente, currite, noctis equi.
The stars move still, time runs, the clock will strike,
The devil will come, and Faustus must be damn'd.
Oh, I will leap to heaven: who pulls me down?
See where Christ's blood streams in the firmament:
One drop of blood will save me: Oh, my Christ,
Rend not my heart for naming of my Christ.
Yet will I call on him: O spare me, Lucifer.
Where is it now? 'tis gone!
And see a threat'ning arm, and angry brow.
Mountains and hills, come, come, and fall on me,
And hide me from the heavy wrath of heaven.
No! then I will headlong run into the earth:
Gape, earth. Oh no, it will not harbour me.
You stars that reign'd at my nativity,
Whose influence have allotted death and hell,
Now draw up Faustus like a foggy mist
Into the entrails of yon labouring cloud;
That when you vomit forth into the air,
My limbs may issue from your smoky mouths,
But let my soul mount and ascend to heaven

[*The Watch strikes.*]

Oh, half the hour is past: 't will all be past anon.
Oh, if my soul must suffer for my sin,
Impose some end to my incessant pain.
Let Faustus live in hell a thousand years,
A hundred thousand, and at last be saved:
No end is limited to damned souls.
Why wert thou not a creature wanting soul?
Or why is this immortal that thou hast?
Oh, Pythagoras, Metempsychosis, were that true,
This soul should fly from me, and I be chang'd
Into some brutish beast.
All beasts are happy, for when they die,
Their souls are soon dissolv'd in elements:
But mine must live still to be plagued in hell.
Curst be the parents that engender'd me:
No, Faustus, curse thyself, curse Lucifer,
That hath depriv'd thee of the joys of heaven.

[*The Clock strikes Twelve.*]

It strikes, it strikes; now, body, turn to air,
Or Lucifer will bear thee quick to hell.

Oh soul, be chang'd into small water drops,
And fall into the ocean: ne'er be found.

[*Thunder, and enter the Devils.*]

Oh mercy, heaven, look not so fierce on me.
Adders and serpents, let me breathe awhile:
Ugly hell gape not, come not Lucifer:
I'll burn my books: Oh, Mephostophilis!

* * * * * * *

[*Enter Scholars.*]

First Sch. Come, gentlemen, let us go visit Faustus,
For such a dreadful night was never seen
Since first the world's creation did begin;
Such fearful shrieks and cries were never heard.
Pray heaven the Doctor have escaped the danger.
Sec. Sch. O help us heavens! see, here are Faustus' limbs
All torn asunder by the hand of death.
Third Sch. The devil whom Faustus serv'd hath torn him thus:
For 'twixt the hours of twelve and one, methought
I heard him shriek and call aloud for help;
At which same time the house seem'd all on fire
With dreadful horror of these damned fiends.
Sec. Sch. Well, gentlemen, though Faustus' end be such
As every Christian heart laments to think on;
Yet, for he was a scholar once admired
For wondrous knowledge in our German schools,
We'll give his mangled limbs due burial:
And all the scholars, cloth'd in mourning black,
Shall wait upon his heavy funeral.
Chorus. Cut is the branch that might have grown full straight,
And burned is Apollo's laurel bough
That sometime grew within this learned man:
Faustus is gone! Regard his hellish fall,
Whose fiendful fortune may exhort the wise
Only to wonder at unlawful things:
Whose deepness doth entice such forward wits
To practice more than heavenly power permits.

The classical taste of Marlow is shown in the fine apostrophe to Helen of Greece, whom the spirit of Mephostophilis conjures up 'between two Cupids' to gratify the sensual gaze of Faustus:—

Was this the face that lanched a thousand ships,
And burn'd the topless towers of Ilium?
Sweet Helen, make me immortal with a kiss!
Her lips suck forth my soul—see where it flies.
Come, Helen, come give me my soul again;
Here will I dwell, for heaven is in these lips,
And all is dross that is not Helena.
O thou art fairer than the evening air,
Clad in the beauty of a thousand stars!
Brighter art thou than flaming Jupiter
When he appeared to hapless Semele;
More lovely than the monarch of the sky
In wanton Arethusa's azure arms;
And none but thou shall be my paramour.

Before 1593, Marlow produced three other dramas, the *Jew of Malta*, the *Massacre of Paris*, and a historical play, *Edward the Second*. The last of these is a noble drama, and contains a number of ably drawn characters and splendid scenes. We subjoin part of the death-scene at the close of the play—a scene which Charles Lamb says, 'moves pity and terror beyond any other scene, ancient or modern.' It may challenge comparison with Shakspeare's death of Richard the Second; but with all his power, Marlow could not interest us in his hero as the great dramatist does in the gentle Richard:—

SCENE,—BERKLEY CASTLE. THE KING IS LEFT ALONE WITH LIGHTBORN, A MURDERER.

Edw. Who's there? what light is that? wherefore com'st thou?
Light. To comfort you, and bring you joyful news.
Edw. Small comfort finds poor Edward in thy looks.
Villain, I know thou com'st to murder me.
Light. To murder you, my most gracious lord!
Far is it from my heart to do you harm.
The queen sent me to see how you were us'd,
For she relents at this your misery:
And what eyes can refrain from shedding tears,
To see a king in this most piteous state.
Edw. Weep'st thou already? list awhile to me,
And then thy heart, were it as Gurney's[1] is
Or as Matrevis,[1] hewn from the Caucasus,
Yet will it melt, ere I have done my tale.
This dungeon where they keep me is a sink,
Wherein the filth of all the castle falls.
Light. O villains!
Edw. And there, in mire and puddle have I stood
This ten days' space; and lest that I should sleep,
One plays continually upon a drum.
They give me bread and water, being a king;
So that, for want of sleep and sustenance,
My mind's distemper'd, and my body's numb'd,
And whether I have limbs or no, I know not.
O would my blood drop out from every vein,
As doth this water from my tattered robes.
Tell Isabel the queen, I looked not thus,
When for her sake I run at tilt in France,
And there unhors'd the Duke of Cleremont.
Light. O speak no more, my lord! this breaks my heart.
Lie on this bed and rest yourself awhile.
Edw. These looks of thine can harbour nought but death:
I see my tragedy written in thy brows.
Yet stay awhile, forbear thy bloody hand,
And let me see the stroke before it comes,
That even then when I shall lose my life,
My mind may be more steadfast on my God.
Light. What means your highness to mistrust me thus?
Edw. What mean'st thou to dissemble with me thus?

[1] His keepers.

Light. These hands were never stain'd with innocent blood,
Nor shall they now be tainted with a king's.
Edw. Forgive my thought, for having such a thought.
One jewel have I left, receive thou this.
Still fear I, and I know not what's the cause,
But every joint shakes as I give it thee.
Oh, if thou harbour'st murder in thy heart,
Let the gift change thy mind, and save thy soul.
Know that I am a king: Oh, at that name
I feel a hell of grief. Where is my crown?
Gone, gone; and do I still remain alive?
Light. You're overwatch'd, my lord; lie down and rest.
Edw. But that grief keeps me waking, I should sleep,
For not these ten days have these eyelids closed.
Now as I speak they fall, and yet with fear
Open again. O wherefore sitt'st thou here?
Light. If you mistrust me, I'll be gone, my lord.
Edw. No, no; for if thou mean'st to murder me,
Thou wilt return again; and therefore stay.
Light. He sleeps.
Edw. O let me not die; yet stay, O stay awhile.
Light. How now, my lord?
Edw. Something still buzzeth in mine ears,
And tells me if I sleep I never wake;
This fear is that which makes me tremble thus.
And therefore tell me, wherefore art thou come?
Light. To rid thee of thy life; Matrevis, come.
Edw. I am too weak and feeble to resist:
Assist me, sweet God, and receive my soul.

In addition to the dramatic productions already mentioned, Marlow assisted Nash in the tragedy of *Dido, Queen of Carthage*, and translated part of *Hero and Leander*, and the *Elegies* of Ovid.

Marlow's life was as wild and irregular as his writings. He was even accused of atheistical opinions; but there is no trace of this in his plays. He came to an early and singularly unhappy end. He was attached to a lady, who favored another lover; and having found them in company together, in a frenzy of rage he attempted to stab the man with his dagger. His antagonist seized him by the wrist, and turned the dagger so that it entered Marlow's own head in such a manner, that, notwithstanding all the means of surgery that could be resorted to, he shortly after died of his wounds. The last words of Greene's address to him, a year or two before, are somewhat ominous:—'Refuse not, with me, till this last point of extremity; for little knowest thou how in the end thou shalt be visited.' Marlow's fatal conflict is supposed to have taken place at Deptford, as he was buried there on the first of June, 1593.

Of the various compliments paid to the genius of this unfortunate poet, the following, by his celebrated contemporary, Michael Drayton, is the finest:—

Next Marlow, bathed in the Thesperian springs,
Had in him those brave translunary things

That the first poets had: his raptures were
All air and fire, which made his verses clear;
For that fine madness still he did retain,
Which rightly should possess a poet's brain.

Besides the dramatists thus far noticed, as the precursors of Shakspeare, we might mention Haughton, Brewer, Porter, Smith, Hathaway, Wilson, and a host of others; for from the diary of Henslowe it appears that, during the seven years following 1591, more than a hundred different plays were performed by *four* only, out of the ten theatrical companies then existing in London. Several good dramas also of this golden age have descended to us, the authors of which are unknown. A few of these possess merit of a very high order; such as the *London Prodigal*, the *Yorkshire Tragedy*, the *Misfortunes of Arthur*, *Lord Cromwell*, *Edward the Third*, and *Arden of Feversham*, the last of which is a domestic tragedy, founded on a murder which took place in 1551. On these, however, our limits will not permit us to dwell: we shall, therefore, at once pass to Shakspeare himself.

Lecture the Thirteenth.

WILLIAM SHAKSPEARE.

THE genius of Greene, of Peele, and of Marlow, had essentially contributed to prepare the way for Shakspeare. These writers had given a more settled and scholastic form to the drama than it had previously possessed, and assigned to it a permanent place in English literature. They adorned the stage also with a greater variety of character and action, with deep passion, and with true poetry; and familiarized the public ear with the sound of blank verse. When Shakspeare, therefore, appeared conspicuously on the dramatic horizon, the scene may be said to have been prepared for his reception. The Genius of the drama had accumulated materials for the use of the great poet, who was destined to extend her empire over limits hitherto unrecognized, and invest it with a degree of splendor surpassing any thing that the world had yet witnessed.

William Shakspeare was of a respectable family, and was born at Stratford-upon-Avon, in Warwickshire, on St. George's day, April the twenty-third, 1564. His father, John Shakspeare, was a wool-comber, and by an early marriage with a rustic heiress, Mary Arden, he not only elevated his social position, but obtained an estate worth nearly seventy pounds a year. The poet's father's fortunes for some years so rapidly advanced that he rose, eventually, to be high bailiff and chief alderman of Stratford; but reverse of fortune compelled him, in 1578, to mortgage his wife's inheritance, and, from the public records of the town, it appears that he had fallen into comparative poverty. William was his eldest son, and was, at this time, at the grammar-school; but the change in his father's circumstances compelled him to return home to assist at his father's business. There is, from this period, a blank of some years in his history; but doubtless he was engaged, whatever might have been his condition or employment, in treasuring up those poetic materials which he afterward expanded with so much splendor. The study of man and of nature, facts in natural history, the country, the fields and the woods, would be gleaned by familiar intercourse and observations among his fellow-townsmen, and in rambling over the beautiful valley of the Avon.

It has been conjectured, and with apparent probability, that he was for some time in a lawyer's office, as his plays abound in technical legal phrases. The London players were also, at that time, in the habit of visiting Stratford; and Burbage, the greatest performer of his day, was originally from Warwickshire. Who can doubt, then, that the high bailiff's son, from the years of twelve to twenty, was a frequent and welcome visitant behind the scenes?—that he there imbibed the tastes and feelings which colored all his future life—and that he there felt the first stirrings of his immortal dramatic genius?

Shakspeare, we are persuaded, had begun to write before he left Stratford, and had, most probably, sketched, if not completed, his *Venus and Adonis*, and the *Lucrece*. These poems were published a few years after his settlement in London, and were both dedicated to the Earl of Southampton in the following modest terms:—'I know not how I shall offend in dedicating my unpolished lines to your lordship, nor how the world will censure me for choosing so strong a prop to support so weak a burthen; only if your honor seem but pleased, I count myself highly praised, and vow to take advantage of all idle hours, till I have honored you with some graver labor. But if the first heir of my invention prove deformed, I shall be sorry it had so noble a god-father, and never after till so barren a land.' As the 'Venus and Adonis' was, in all probability, Shakspeare's first complete poem, we shall here introduce a passage from it in order to exhibit the beginnings of that genius which was destined so soon after to astound the world.

VENUS'S PROPHECY AFTER THE DEATH OF ADONIS.

Since thou art dead, lo! here I prophesy,
Sorrow on love hereafter shall attend;
It shall be waited on with jealousy,
Find sweet beginning, but unsavoury end,
Ne'er settled equally, but high or low:
That all love's pleasure shall not match his woe.

It shall be fickle, false, and full of fraud,
Bud and be blasted in a breathing while,
The bottom poison, and the top o'erstraw'd
With sweets that shall the truest sight beguile.
The strongest body shall it make most weak,
Strike the wise dumb, and teach the fool to speak.

It shall be sparing, and too full of riot,
Teaching decrepit age to tread the measures;
The staring ruffian shall it keep in quiet,
Pluck down the rich, enrich the poor with treasures.
It shall be raging mad, and silly mild,
Make the young old, the old become a child.

It shall suspect, where is no cause of fear,
It shall not fear, where it should most mistrust;
It shall be merciful, and too severe,
And most deceiving when it seems most just:

Perverse it shall be, when it seems most toward,
Put fear to valour, courage to the coward.

It shall be cause of war, and dire events,
And set dissension 'twixt the son and sire:
Subject and servile to all discontents,
As dry combustious matter is to fire.
Sith in his prime, death doth my love destroy,
They that love best, their love shall not enjoy.

The extent to which Shakspeare pursued classical studies at the grammar-school where he received his education, has been made a question of much scrutiny and controversy. Ben Jonson says he had 'little Latin and less Greek;' but this is not denying that he had, at least, some. The choice of the two classical subjects which we have just noticed for his early poems, the Latinized idioms and expressions scattered throughout many of his plays, and his numerous felicitous allusions to the mythology of the ancients, show that he was imbued with the spirit and taste of classical literature, and was a happy student, if not a critical scholar. His mind was too comprehensive to degenerate into pedantry; but when, at the age of twenty-five or twenty-six, he took the field of original dramatic composition, in company with the university-bred authors and wits of the age, he soon distanced them all, in correctness as well as facility, in the intellectual richness of his thoughts and diction, and in the wide range of his acquired knowledge. It may be safely assumed, therefore, that at Stratford he was a hard, though, perhaps, an irregular student.

The precocious maturity of Shakspeare's passions hurried him into a premature marriage. On the twenty-eighth of November, 1582, before he had attained the nineteenth year of his age, he became united to Anne Hathaway, the daughter of a 'substantial yeoman' of the village of Shottery, about a mile from Stratford. He remained in Stratford after his marriage until he became the father of three children, all that he ever had; and having now arrived at early manhood, and feeling the ties of a husband and a father, we may readily suppose that so small a place as his native town did not afford sufficient scope for the ambition of the poet; and he, therefore, removed to London. This important event in his life took place in 1587; and it has been said that his departure was hastened by the effects of a lampoon he had written on a neighboring squire, Sir Thomas Lucy, of Charlecote, in revenge for Sir Thomas prosecuting him for deer-stealing. This story, though inconsistent, is now so intimately associated with the name of Shakspeare, that, from the obscurity which rests, and probably will ever rest, on his history, there seems little likelihood of its ever ceasing to have a place in the public mind.

Shakspeare, on his arrival in London, entered the Blackfriar's Theatrical Company, and in it soon rose to distinction. In the course of two or three years he became one of the shareholders: in 1596, his name is the fifth in a list of only eight proprietors; and in 1603, when a new patent was obtained from King James, he held the second place. Collier has recently discovered that the wardrobe and stage properties also belonged to Shakspeare, and with the shares which he held, were estimated at a sum equal to seven thousand pounds of the present money. He was also proprietor of the Globe Theatre; so that his annual income must, at this time, have been equal to at least fifteen hundred pounds of the present day. As an actor, Shakspeare is said, by Lord Southampton, to have been 'of good account in the company;' but the cause of his unexampled success was his immortal dramas, the delight and wonder of the age. These were thirty-seven in number, and were all produced previous to 1611.

With the nobles, the wits, and the poets of his day, Shakspeare was in constant and familiar intercourse. The 'gentle Shakspeare,' as he was usually styled, was enthroned in all hearts. But notwithstanding his brilliant success in the metropolis, the poet early looked forward to a permanent retirement to the country. He visited Stratford once a year; and when wealth flowed in upon him, he purchased *New Place*, the principal house in the town, together with other property in the vicinity, preparatory to returning thither himself. At what precise period Shakspeare took leave of the city is not known. The latest entry of his name among the king's players is in 1604; but it is certain that he was living in London five or six years after that date. The year 1612, is now generally fixed upon, as the time of his retirement to the country, and is, perhaps, as nearly correct as any that could be selected. In the fullness of his fame, with a handsome competency, and before age had chilled the enjoyment of life, the poet returned to his native town to spend the remainder of his days among the quiet scenes and friends of his youth. His parents were now both dead, but their declining years had been gladdened by the prosperity and fame of their illustrious son. Four years were passed by Shakspeare in this dignified retirement, and the history of literature scarcely presents another such picture of calm felicity and satisfied ambition. He died on the twenty-third of April, 1616, having, on that very day, completed his fifty-second year. His widow survived him seven years. His only son, Hamnet, died in 1596; his two daughters were both married, and one of them had three sons; but they all died without issue, and there is now remaining no lineal representative of the great poet.

Shakspeare began his career as a dramatist by altering old plays and adapting them to the stage. The extract from Greene's 'Groat's Worth of Wit,' which we have given in our sketch of the life of that unhappy author, shows that he had been engaged in this subordinate literary labor previous to 1592. This drudgery he soon, however, abandoned, and relying upon his own internal resources, in a short time eclipsed, by the production of original sketches, all his contemporaries. Some of these sketches, such as *Hamlet*, *Romeo and Juliet*, and the *Merry Wives of Windsor*, he afterward elaborated into their present finished form; and others he abandoned as unworthy of preservation. His plots were nearly all borrowed; some from novels and romances, others from legendary tales, and some from older dramas. His English historical plays are chiefly taken from 'Holinshed's Chronicle;' from which source he also derived the plot of *Macbeth*, perhaps the most transcendant of his works. In his classical subjects, he followed North's translation of *Plutarch's Lives of Illustrious Grecians and Romans.*

Various attempts have been made to determine the chronological order in which Shakspeare's dramas were produced; but we know no other source of information on this subject than that which is discoverable in the works themselves. In *Pericles*, the *Two Gentlemen of Verona*, and the earlier comedies, we see the timidity and immaturity of youthful genius; a half-formed style, bearing frequent traces of that of his predecessors; fantastic quibbles and conceits; only a partial development of character; a romantie and playful fancy; but no great strength of imagination, energy or passion. In *Richard the Second*, and *Richard the Third*, the creative and master mind are visible in the creation of character. In the *Midsummer Night's Dream*, the *Merchant of Venice*, and *Romeo and Juliet*, we find the ripened poetical imagination, prodigality of invention, and a searching meditative spirit. These qualities, with a finer vein of morality and contemplative philosophy, pervade *As You Like It*, and the *Twelfth Night*. In *Henry the Fourth*, the *Merry Wives*, *Measure for Measure*, and *Much Ado About Nothing*, we see the inimitable powers of comedy, full-formed, swelling in an atmosphere of joyous life, and fresh as if from the hand of nature. He took a loftier flight in his classical dramas, and both conceived and finished them with consummate taste and freedom. In his later tragedies, *Lear*, *Hamlet*, *Othello*, *Macbeth*, and the *Tempest*, all his wonderful faculties are combined—his wit, his pathos, his passion and his sublimity—his profound knowledge and observation of mankind, mellowed by a refined humanity and benevolence—his imagination richer from skillful culture and added stories of information—his unrivalled language, like 'light from heaven'—his imagery and versification.

In contemplating the genius of this wonderful dramatist, the mind becomes bewildered amid its compass and variety. From the finest and most delicately spun fibres in the texture of female passion and feeling, he could ascend, without an apparent effort, to the most lofty and terrifically sublime attributes of man—touching all the grades of variety that present themselves in his passage, with unerring fidelity and truth. This power we can ascribe only to the unparalleled *sympathies* of the great poet's nature. To speak of his exquisite delineations of man, in every conceivable grade of life, would be superfluous; for that has been the theme of almost every dramatic critic for the last two hundred years. His excellence in drawing the character of woman has, however, by no means been so generally acknowledged. Even Collins, after eulogizing the female characters of Beaumont and Fletcher, adds —

> But stronger Shakspeare felt for Man alone.

It is true that Shakspeare's females are creations of a very different stamp from those which are apt to be popular on the stage. Their sorrows are not obstreperous and theatrical; but—

The still sad music of Humanity—

as Wordsworth has finely phrased it—is heard throughout all their history. The poet's own description of a lover—

All made of passion, and all made of wishes;
All adoration, duty, and obedience;
All humbleness, all patience, and impatience;
All purity, all trial, all observance;

will apply with equal accuracy to his delineations of woman. Sighs, tears, passion, trial, and humility, are the components of her character; and to whatever extent other dramatic writers may endeavor to 'elevate and surprise' by pursuing a different course, these are the materials which nature, if her dictates be followed, will uniformly furnish.

The general cast of character in Shakspeare's females is tenderness and pathos; but this is not because he was unable to delineate woman in her more dignified and commanding, though less ordinary, attitude. Hence there is nothing more majestic, and, we may say, awful, on the stage than Katherine defending herself against the malice and hypocrisy of Henry; and nothing more fearful and appalling than the whole character of Lady Macbeth, from the first scene in which her ambition is awakened by the perusal of her husband's letter, to the last, in which we discover its bitter fruits, in treason, murder, and insanity. Then there is the Lady Constance—a woman, a mother, and a princess; seen in all the fearful vicissitudes of human life; hoping, exulting, blessing, fearing, weeping, despairing, and, at last, dying. Shall we add the Weird Sisters, those 'foul anomalies,' in whom all that is malignant and base in the female character is exaggerated to an unearthly stature; and those gentler beings, such as Juliet and Desdemona, who, with frailties and imperfections which ally them to earth, yet approximate to those superior and benevolent spirits, of whom we have such exquisite pictures in Ariel, and the Fairies, in the Midsummer Night's Dream? Cleopatra, Volumina, and Isabella, are farther instances of Shakspeare's power of exhibiting the loftier and stronger traits of the female character. His picture of the fascinating Egyptian queen is absolutely a master-piece. In perusing it, we feel no longer astonished that crowns and empires were sacrificed for her. We have many splendid descriptions of her personal charms; but it is her mind, the strength of her passion, the fervor and fury of her love, the bitterness of her hatred, and the desperation of her death, which take so strong a hold upon the imagination. We follow her, we admire her, we sympathize with her; and when the asp has done its fatal work, we are ready to exclaim with Charmion—

Now boast thee, Death! in thy possession lies
A lass unparallel'd.

How different a being from this is the ill-fated fair who slumbers in 'the tomb of the Capulets.' She is all gentleness and mildness, all hidden passion and silent suffering; yet her love is as ardent, her sorrows are as overwhelming, and her death as melancholy. 'The gentle lady wedded to the Moor' is another sweet, still picture, which we contemplate with admiration, until death drops his curtain over it. Imogen and Miranda, Perdita and Ophelia, Cordelia, Helen and Viola, need only to be mentioned to recall to mind the most fascinating pictures of female character that have ever been delineated. The last is, indeed, a mere sketch, but it is a most charming one; and its best description is that exquisite paraphrase, in which the character is so beautifully summed up:—

> ——— She never told her love,
> But let concealment, like a worm i' the bud,
> Feed on her damask cheek. She pined in thought,
> And with a green and yellow melancholy,
> She sat, like Patience on a monument,
> Smiling at Grief.

Of Shakspeare's comic female characters we need mention only Rosalind and Beatrice. In the first we find an admirable compound of wit, gayety, and good-humor, blended, at the same time, with deep and strong passion, with courage and resolution; with unshaken affection to her father, and constant and fervid love for Orlando. How extraordinary and romantic is the character if we contemplate it in the abstract, yet how beautiful and true to nature, if we examine it in all its details. Beatrice is a character of a very different order from Rosalind, and yet she resembles her in some particulars. She has all her wit; but it must be confessed, without her good-humor. Her arrows are not merely piercing, but poisoned. Rosalind's is cheerful raillery, Beatrice's satirical bitterness; Rosalind is not only afraid to strike, but unwilling to wound: Beatrice is careless of the effect of her wit, if she can but find an opportunity to utter it. But we must forbear.

The difficulty of making selections from such a poet as Shakspeare must be obvious to all. His characters are as various and diversified as those in human life; he has exhausted all styles, and has one for each description of poetry and action; his wit, humor, satire, and pathos, are spread throughout his entire works. We have felt our task, therefore, to be something like being deputed to search in some magnificent forest for a handful of the finest leaves or plants, and as if we were diligently exploring the world of woodland beauty to accomplish faithfully this hopeless adventure. Happily Shakspeare is in all hands, and a single leaf will recall the fertile and majestic scenes of his inspiration.

We shall make our selections, as nearly as possible, in the order already indicated, beginning with the much neglected play of Pericles. This was, doubtless, a production of the immortal bard's youth, and therefore contains many imperfections; but the following passages alone, are sufficient to identify its origin:—

PERICLES' SOLILOQUY ON A SHIP AT SEA.

Thou God of the great vast! rebuke these surges
Which wash both heaven and hell; and Thou, that hast
Upon the winds command, bind them in brass,
Having call'd them from the deep! Oh! still thy deaf'ning,
Thy dreadful thunders! gently quench the nimble,
Sulphureous flashes! Thou storm! thou, venomously,
Wilt thou spit all thyself? The seaman's whistle
Is as a whisper in the ears of death,
Unheard.

The following description of the recovery of Thaisa from a state of suspended animation, is also powerfully eloquent:—

——— Nature wakes; a warmth
Breathes out of her; she hath not been entranced
Above five hours. See how she 'gins to blow
Into life's flower again!—She is alone; behold,
Her eyelids, cases to those heavenly jewels
Which Pericles hath lost,
Begin to part their fingers of bright gold,
The diamonds of a most praised water
Appear to make the world twice rich.

Marina, the daughter of Pericles, and heroine of the play, is born at sea, during a storm; and Shakspeare, in this drama, as in the 'Winter's Tale,' leaps over the intervening years, and shows her, in the fourth act, 'on the eve of womanhood;' where her first speech, on the death of her nurse, is sweetly plaintive and poetical:—

No, no; I will rob Tellus of her weed
To strew thy grave with flowers! the yellows, blues,
The purple violets, and marygolds,
Shall as a chaplet hang upon thy grave,
While summer-days do last. Ah me! poor maid,
Born in a tempest, when my mother died,
This world to me is like a lasting storm,
Whirring me from my friends.

In the course of the play Marina undergoes a variety of adventures, in all of which the mingled gentleness and dignity of her character is admirably developed. The interview with her father in the fifth act, is, indeed, one of the most powerful and affecting passages in the whole range of the English drama. The extracts, from other dramas, which follow, are introduced without comment, because they are all well known.

DESCRIPTION OF A MOONLIGHT NIGHT, WITH MUSIC.

Lor. The moon shines bright: in such a night as this,
When the sweet wind did gently kiss the trees,
And they did make no noise; in such a night,
Troilus, methinks, mounted the Trojan's wall,

And sigh'd his soul towards the Grecian tents,
Where Cressid lay that night.
Jes. In such a night
Did Thisbe fearfully o'ertrip the dew;
And saw the lion's shadow ere himself,
And ran dismay'd away.
Lor. In such a night
Stood Dido with a willow in her hand
Upon the wide sea-banks, and waft her love
To come again to Carthage.
Jes. In such a night
Medea gather'd the enchanted herbs
That did renew old Æson.
Lor. In such a night
Did Jessica steal from the wealthy Jew,
And with an unthrift love did run from Venice
As far as Belmont.
Jes. And in such a night
Did young Lorenzo swear he lov'd her well;
Stealing her soul with many vows of faith,
And ne'er a true one.
Lor. And in such a night
Did pretty Jessica, like a little shrew,
Slander her love, and he forgave it her.
* * * * * *
How sweet the moonlight sleeps upon this bank!
Here will we sit, and let the sounds of music
Creep in our ears; soft stillness and the night
Become the touches of sweet harmony.
Sit, Jessica; look how the floor of heaven
Is thick inlaid with patines of bright gold;
There's not the smallest orb which thou behold'st,
But in his motion like an angel sings,
Still quiring to the young-eyed cherubins;
Such harmony is in immortal souls;
But while this muddy vesture of decay
Doth grossly close it in, we can not hear it.
Come, ho, and wake Diana with a hymn:
With sweetest touches pierce your mistress' ear,
And draw her home with music.
Jes. I'm never merry when I hear sweet music.
Lor. The reason is, your spirits are attentive;
For do but note a wild and wanton herd,
Or race of youthful and unhandled colts,
Fetching mad bounds, bellowing and neighing loud,
(Which is the hot condition of their blood;)
If they perchance but hear a trumpet sound,
Or any air of music touch their ears,
You shall perceive them make a mutual stand;
Their savage eyes turn'd to a modest gaze,
By the sweet power of music. Therefore the poet
Did feign that Orpheus drew trees, stones, and floods:
Since nought so stockish, hard, and full of rage,
But music for the time doth change his nature.

The man that hath not music in himself,
Nor is not mov'd with concord of sweet sounds,
Is fit for treasons, stratagems, and spoils;
The motions of his spirit are dull as night,
And his affection dark as Erebus:
Let no such man be trusted

[*Merchant of Venice.*]

THE ATTRIBUTES OF MERCY.

The quality of mercy is not strain'd;
It droppeth as the gentle rain from heaven
Upon the place beneath. It is twice blessed;
It blesseth him that gives, and him that takes.
'Tis mightiest in the mightiest; it becomes
The throned monarch better than his crown:
His sceptre shows the force of temporal pow'r,
The attribute to awe and majesty,
Wherein doth sit the dread and fear of kings.
But mercy is above the sceptred sway;
It is enthroned in the hearts of kings;
It is an attribute to God himself;
And earthly power doth then show likest God's,
When mercy seasons justice. Therefore, Jew,
Though justice be thy plea, consider this—
That in the course of justice none of us
Should see salvation; we do pray for mercy;
And that same prayer doth teach us all to render
The deeds of mercy.

[*Merchant of Venice.*]

LOVE SCENE BY NIGHT IN A GARDEN.

Romeo. He jests at scars, that never felt a wound—
But, soft! what light through yonder window breaks;
It is the east, and Juliet is the sun!

[*Juliet appears above at a window.*]

Arise, fair sun, and kill the envious moon,
Who is already sick and pale with grief
That thou her maid art far more fair than she;
Be not her maid since she is envious;
Her vestal livery is but sick and green,
And none but fools do wear it: cast it off—
It is my lady; O! it is my love;
O that she knew she were!—
She speaks, yet she says nothing. What of that?
Her eye discourses; I will answer it—
I am too bold; 'tis not to me she speaks:
Two of the fairest stars of all the heav'n,
Having some business, do entreat her eyes,
To twinkle in their spheres till they return.
What if her eyes were there, they in her head?
The brightness of her cheek would shame those stars,
As daylight doth a lamp: her eyes in heav'n
Would through the airy region stream so bright,
That birds would sing, and think it were not night.
See how she leans her cheek upon her hand!

O that I were a glove upon that hand,
That I might touch that cheek!
Jul. Ah me!
Rom. She speaks.
Oh, speak again, bright angel! for thou art
As glorious to this sight, being o'er my head,
As is a winged messenger of heav'n,
Unto the white-upturned, wond'ring eyes
Of mortals, that fall back to gaze on him,
When he bestrides the lazy-pacing clouds,
And sails upon the bosom of the air.
Jul. O Romeo, Romeo—wherefore art thou Romeo?
Deny thy father, and refuse thy name:
Or, if thou wilt not, be but sworn my love,
And I'll no longer be a Capulet.
Rom. Shall I hear more, or shall I speak at this?
Jul. 'Tis but thy name that is my enemy:
Thou art thyself, though not a Montague.
What's Montague? It is nor hand, nor foot,
Nor arm, nor face—nor any other part
Belonging to a man. O, be some other name!
What's in a name? That which we call a rose,
By any other name would smell as sweet.
So Romeo would, were he not Romeo call'd,
Retain that dear perfection which he owes,
Without that title. Romeo, doff thy name;
And for that name, which is no part of thee,
Take all myself.
Rom. I take thee at thy word:
Call me but love, and I'll be new baptiz'd;
Henceforth I never will be Romeo.
Jul. What man art thou, that thus, bescreen'd in night,
So stumblest on my counsel?
Rom. By a name
I know not how to tell thee who I am:
My name, dear saint, is hateful to myself,
Because it is an enemy to thee.
Had I it written, I would tear the word.
Jul. My ears have not yet drunk a hundred words
Of that tongue's uttering, yet I know the sound.
Art thou not Romeo, and a Montague?
Rom. Neither, fair saint, if either thee dislike.
Jul. How cam'st thou hither, tell me, and wherefore?
The orchard walls are high, and hard to climb;
And the place death, considering who thou art,
If any of my kinsmen, find thee here.
Rom. With love's light wings did I o'erperch these walls,
For stony limits can not hold love out;
And what love can do, that dares love attempt:
Therefore thy kinsmen are no let to me.
Jul. If they do see thee, they will murder thee.
Rom. Alack! there lies more peril in thine eye
Than twenty of their swords; look thou but sweet,
And I am proof against their enmity.

Jul. I would not for the world they saw thee here.
Rom. I have night's cloak to hide me from their eyes,
And but thou love me, let them find me here;
My life were better ended by their hate,
Than death prorogued, wanting of thy love.
Jul. By whose direction found'st thou out this place?
Rom. By love, that first did prompt me to inquire;
He lent me counsel, and I lent him eyes.
I am no pilot; yet wert thou as far
As that vast shore, wash'd with the farthest sea,
I would adventure for such merchandise.
Jul. Thou know'st the mask of night is on my face,
Else would a maiden blush bepaint my cheek
For that which thou hast heard me speak to-night.
Fain would I dwell on form; fain, fain deny
What I have spoke—but farewell compliment!
Dost thou love me? I know thou wilt say ay;
And I will take thy word. Yet if thou swear'st,
Thou may'st prove false; at lovers' perjuries,
They say, Jove laughs. O, gentle Romeo!
If thou dost love, pronounce it faithfully;
Or, if thou think'st I am too quickly won,
I'll frown and be perverse, and say thee nay,
So thou wilt woo; but else not for the world.
In truth, fair Montague, I am too fond,
And therefore thou may'st think my 'haviour light;
But trust me, gentleman, I'll prove more true
Than those that have more coying to be strange.
I should have been more strange, I must confess,
But that thou over-heard'st, ere I was 'ware,
My true love's passion; therefore pardon me,
And not impute this yielding to light love,
Which the dark night hath so discover'd.
Rom. Lady, by yonder blessed moon I swear,
That tips with silver all these fruit-tree tops—
Jul. O swear not by the moon, th' inconstant moon
That monthly changes in her circled orb:
Lest that thy love prove likewise variable.
Rom. What shall I swear by?
Jul. Do not swear at all;
Or, if thou wilt, swear by thy gracious self,
Which is the god of my idolatry,
And I'll believe thee.
Rom. If my heart's dear love—
Jul. Well, do not swear. Although I joy in thee,
I have no joy of this contract to-night;
It is too rash, too unadvis'd, too sudden,
Too like the lightning, which doth cease to be,
Ere one can say it lightens. Sweet, good night!
This bud of love, by summer's ripening breath,
May prove a beauteous flower, when next we meet.
Good night, good night—as sweet repose and rest
Come to thy heart, as that within my breast.
Rom. O, wilt thou leave me so unsatisfied?

Jul. What satisfaction canst thou have to-night?
Rom. Th' exchange of thy love's faithful vow for mine.
Jul. I gave thee mine before thou didst request it:
And yet I would it were to give again.
Rom. Would'st thou withdraw it? for what purpose, love?
Jul. But to be frank, and give it thee again.
And yet I wish but for the thing I have:
My bounty is as boundless as the sea,
My love as deep; the more I give to thee,
The more I have, for both are infinite.
I hear some noise within. Dear love, adieu!
[*Nurse calls within.*]
Anon, good nurse! Sweet Montague, be true.
Stay but a little, I will come again.
Rom. O, blessed, blessed night! I am afear'd,
Being in night, all this is but a dream;
Too flattering sweet to be substantial.
[*Re-enter Juliet above.*]
Jul. Three words, dear Romeo, and good night indeed.
If that thy bent of love be honourable,
Thy purpose marriage, send me word to-morrow,
By one that I'll procure to come to thee,
Where and what time thou wilt perform the rite;
And all my fortunes at thy foot I'll lay,
And follow thee, my love, throughout the world;
[*Within:* Madam!]
I come, anon—but if thou mean'st not well,
I do beseech thee—[*Within:* Madam!] By-and-by, I come,
To cease thy suit, and leave me to my grief.
To-morrow will I send.
Rom. So thrive my soul—
Jul. A thousand times good night. [*Exit.*]
Rom. A thousand times the worse, to want thy light.
Love goes tow'rd love, as school-boys from their books;
But love from love, tow'rds school with heavy looks.
[*Enter Juliet again.*]
Jul. Hist! Romeo, hist! O for a falconer's voice,
To lure this tassel gentle back again.
Bondage is hoarse, and may not speak aloud;
Else would I tear the cave where echo lies,
And make her airy tongue more hoarse than mine,
With repetition of my Romeo's name.
Rom. It is my soul that calls upon my name.
How silver-sweet sound lovers' tongues by night,
Like softest music to attending ears.
Jul. Romeo!
Rom. My sweet!
Jul. At what o'clock to-morrow
Shall I send to thee?
Rom. At the hour of nine.
Jul. I will not fail; 'tis twenty years till then.
I have forgot why I did call thee back.
Rom. Let me stand here till thou remember it.
Jul. I shall forget, to have thee still stand there;
Rememb'ring how I love thy company.

Rom. And I'll still stay to have thee still forget,
Forgetting any other home but this.
Jul. 'Tis almost morning. I would have thee gone;
And yet no further than a wanton's bird,
Who lets it hop a little from her hand,
Like a poor prisoner in his twisted gyves,
And with a silk thread plucks it back again,
So loving-jealous of his liberty.
Rom. I would I were thy bird.
Jul. Sweet, so would I:
Yet I should kill with much cherishing.
Good night, good night: parting is such sweet sorrow,
That I shall say good night, till it be morrow.
Rom. Sleep dwell upon thine eyes, peace in thy breast!
Would I were sleep and peace, so sweet to rest.
Hence will I to my ghostly friar's close cell,
His help to crave, and my dear hap to tell.

[*Exit Romeo and Juliet.*]

SOLITUDE PREFERRED TO A COURT LIFE, AND THE ADVANTAGES OF ADVERSITY.

Now my co-mates and brothers in exile,
Hath not old custom made this life more sweet
Than that of painted pomp? Are not these woods
More free from peril than the envious court?
Here feel we but the penalty of Adam,
The season's difference; as the icy fang
And churlish chiding of the winter's wind;
Which, when it bites and blows upon my body,
Even till I shrink with cold, I smile and say,
'This is no flattery;' these are counsellors
That feelingly persuade me what I am.
Sweet are the uses of adversity,
Which, like the toad, ugly and venomous,
Wears yet a precious jewel in his head:
And this our life, exempt from public haunt,
Finds tongues in trees, books in the running brooks,
Sermons in stones, and good in every thing.
I would not change it!
Amiens. Happy is your grace,
That can translate the stubbornness of fortune
Into so quiet and so sweet a style!

[*As You Like It.*]

SONG.

Blow, blow, thou winter wind,
Thou art not so unkind,
As man's ingratitude!
Thy tooth is not so keen,
Because thou art not seen,
Although thy breath is rude.
Heigh, ho! sing heigh ho! unto the green holly,
Most friendship is feigning, most loving mere folly.
Then heigh, ho, the holly!
This life is most jolly.

Freeze, freeze, thou bitter sky,
That dost not bite so nigh
  As benefits forgot!
Though thou the waters warp,
Thy sting is not so sharp
  As friend remember'd not.
      Heigh, ho! &c. &c.

[*As You Like It.*]

LIFE AND DEATH WEIGHED.

To be, or not to be, that is the question—
Whether 'tis nobler in the mind to suffer
The slings and arrows of outrageous fortune,
Or to take arms against a sea of troubles,
And, by opposing, end them? To die—to sleep—
No more; and by a sleep to say we end
The heart-ache, and the thousand natural shocks
That flesh is heir to!—'tis a consummation
Devoutly to be wish'd. To die—to sleep—
To sleep!—perchance to dream!—ay, there's the rub;
For in that sleep of death what dreams may come,
When we have shuffled off this mortal coil,
Must give us pause—there's the respect
That makes calamity of so long life:
For who would bear the whips and scorns of time,
The oppressor's wrong, the proud man's contumely,
The pangs of despised love, the law's delay,
The insolence of office, and the spurns
That patient merit of th' unworthy takes,
When he himself might his quietus make
With a bare bodkin? Who would fardels bear,
To groan and sweat under a weary life,
But that the dread of something after death
(That undiscover'd country from whose bourn
No traveller returns) puzzles the will,
And makes us rather bear those ills we have,
Than fly to others that we know not off?
Thus conscience does make cowards of us all;
And thus the native hue of resolution
Is sicklied o'er with the pale cast of thought,
And enterprises of great pith and moment,
With this regard, their currents turn away,
And lose the name of action.

[*Hamlet.*]

FEAR OF DEATH.

Ay, but to die, and go we know not where;
To lie in cold obstruction, and to rot;
This sensible warm motion to become
A kneaded clod; and the delighted spirit
To bathe in fiery floods, or to reside
In thrilling regions of thick-ribbed ice;
To be imprison'd in the viewless winds,

And blown with restless violence round about
The pendant world; or to be worse than worst
Of those, that lawless and incertain thoughts
Imagine howling; 'tis too horrible!
The weariest and most loathed worldly life,
That age, ache, penury, and imprisonment,
Can lay on nature, is a paradise
To what we fear of death.

[*Measure for Measure.*]

END OF ALL EARTHLY GLORIES.

Our revels now are ended: these our actors,
As I foretold you, were all spirits, and
Are melted into air, into thin air;
And, like the baseless fabric of this vision,
The cloud-capt towers, the gorgeous palaces,
The solemn temples, the great globe itself,
Yea, all which it inherit, shall dissolve;
And, like this insubstantial pageant faded,
Leave not a rack behind! We are such stuff
As dreams are made on, and our little life
Is rounded with a sleep.

[*The Tempest.*]

OTHELLO'S RELATION OF HIS COURTSHIP TO THE SENATE.

Most potent, grave, and reverend signiors,
My very noble and approv'd good masters;
That I have ta'en away this old man's daughter,
It is most true; true, I have married her;
The very head and front of my offending
Hath this extent, no more. Rude am I in my speech,
And little blest with the soft phrase of peace;
For since these arms of mine had seven years' pith
Till now, some nine moons wasted, they have us'd
Their dearest action in the tented field;
And little of this great world can I speak,
More than pertains to feats of broil and battle;
And therefore shall I little grace my cause
In speaking for myself. Yet by your gracious patience
I will a round unvarnished tale deliver
Of my whole course of love: what drugs, what charms
What conjuration; and what mighty magic
(For such proceeding I am charg'd withal)
I won his daughter with.
Her father lov'd me, oft invited me;
Still question'd me the story of my life,
From year to year; the battles, sieges, fortunes,
That I have past.
I ran it through, ev'n from my boyish days,
To the very moment that he bade me tell it:
Wherein I spoke of most disastrous chances,
Of moving accidents by flood and field;
Of hair-breadth 'scapes i' th' imminent deadly breach;
Of being taken by the insolent foe,

And sold to slavery; of my redemption thence,
And portance in my travel's history.
Wherein of antres vast and deserts idle,
Rough quarries, rocks, and hills whose heads touch heaven,
It was my lot to speak, such was the process;
And of the cannibals that each other eat,
The Anthropophagi, and men whose heads
Do grow beneath their shoulders. Those things to hear
Would Desdemona seriously incline;
But still the house affairs would draw her thence;
Which ever as she could with haste dispatch,
She'd come again, and with a greedy ear
Devour up my discourse: which I observing,
Took once a pliant hour, and found good means
To draw from her a prayer of earnest heart,
That I would all my pilgrimage dilate,
Whereof by parcels she had something heard,
But not intentively. I did consent,
And often did beguile her of her tears,
When I did speak of some distressful stroke
That my youth suffer'd. My story being done,
She gave me for my pains a world of sighs;
She swore—in faith 'twas strange, 'twas passing strange,
'Twas pitiful, 'twas wondrous pitiful—
She wish'd she had not heard it, yet she wish'd
That heaven had made her such a man:—she thank'd me,
And bade me, if I had a friend that lov'd her,
I should but teach him how to tell my story;
And that would woo her. On this hint I spake;
She lov'd me for the dangers I had pass'd,
And I lov'd her that she did pity them.

DESCRIPTION OF NIGHT IN A CAMP.

From camp to camp, thro' the foul womb of night,
The hum of either army stilly sounds,
That the fix'd sentinels almost receive
The secret whispers of each other's watch.
Fire answers fire; and through their paly flames,
Each battle sees the other's umber'd face.
Steed threatens steed, in high and boastful neighs,
Piercing the night's dull ear; and from the tents,
The armourers, accomplishing the knights,
With busy hammers closing rivets up,
Give dreadful note of preparation.
The country cocks do crow, the clocks do toll,
And the third hour of drowsy morning name.
Proud of their numbers and secure in soul,
The confident and over-lusty French
For the low-rated English play at dice,
And chide the cripple tardy-gaited night,
Who, like a foul and ugly witch, does limp
So tediously away. The poor condemned English,
Like sacrifices, by their watchful fires
Sit patiently, and inly ruminate

The morning's danger: and their gesture sad
(Investing lank lean cheeks, and war-worn coats)
Presenting them unto the gazing moon
So many horrid ghosts. O, now, who will behold
The royal captain of this ruin'd band,
Walking from watch to watch, from tent to tent,
Let him cry praise and glory on his head!
For forth he goes and visits all his host,
Bids them good-morrow with a modest smile,
And calls them brothers, friends, and countrymen.
Upon his royal face there is no note
How dread an army hath enrounded him;
Nor doth he dedicate one jot of colour
Unto the weary and all-watched night;
But freshly looks, and overbears attaint,
With cheerful semblance and sweet majesty;
That every wretch, pining and pale before,
Beholding him, plucks comfort from his looks.
A largess universal, like the sun,
His liberal eye doth give to every one,
Thawing cold fear.

[*Henry the Fifth.*]

THE BLESSINGS OF A SHEPHERD'S LIFE.

O God! methinks it were a happy life
To be no better than a homely swain;
To sit upon a hill, as I do now,
To carve out dials quaintly, point by point,
Thereby to see the minutes how they run:
How many make the hour full complete,
How many hours bring about the day,
How many days will finish up the year,
How many years a mortal man may live.
When this is known, then to divide the times:
So many hours must I tend my flock;
So many hours must I take my rest;
So many hours must I contemplate;
So many hours must I sport myself;
So many days my ewes have been with young;
So many weeks ere the poor fools will yearn;
So many years ere I shall shear the fleece:
So minutes, hours, days, weeks, months, years,
Pass'd over, to the end they were created,
Would bring white hairs unto a quiet grave.
Ah! what a life were this! how sweet! how lovely!
Gives not the hawthorn-bush a sweeter shade
To shepherds looking on their silly sheep,
Than doth a rich embroider'd canopy
To kings that fear their subjects' treachery?
O yes, it doth, a thousandfold it doth.
And to conclude, the shepherd's homely curds,
His cold thin drink out of his leather bottle,
His wonted sleep under a fresh tree's shade,
All which secure and sweetly he enjoys,

Is far beyond a prince's delicates;
His viands sparkling in a golden cup,
His body couched in a curious bed,
When care, mistrust, and treason wait on him.

[*Henry the Sixth.*]

THE VICISSITUDES OF LIFE.

So farewell to the little good you bear me.
Farewell, a long farewell to all my greatness!
This is the state of man: To-day he puts forth,
The tender leaves of hope, to-morrow blossoms,
And bears his blushing honors thick upon him;
The third day comes a frost, a killing frost,
And when he thinks, good easy man, full surely
His greatness is a ripening, nips his root,
And then he falls as I do. I have ventur'd,
Like little wanton boys, that swim on bladders,
These many summers in a sea of glory;
But far beyond my depth: my high-blown pride
At length broke under me; and now has left me,
Weary and old with service, to the mercy
Of a rude stream, that must forever hide me;
Vain pomp and glory of this world, I hate ye!
I feel my heart new open'd. O how wretch'd
Is that poor man that hangs on princes' favours!
There is, betwixt that smile we would aspire to,
That sweet aspect of princes, and their ruin,
More pangs and fears than wars or woman have;
And, when he falls, he falls like Lucifer,
Never to hope again.

[*Henry the Eighth.*]

THE MURDER OF KING DUNCAN.

Macbeth and a Servant.

[MACBETH, PROMPTED BY AMBITION, AND PUSHED ON BY HIS SAVAGE WIFE, RESOLVES TO MURDER THE KING.]

Macb. Go bid thy mistress, when my drink is ready,
She strike upon the bell. Get thee to bed.

[*Exit Servant.*]

Is this a dagger which I see before me,
The handle toward my hand? Come, let me clutch thee.
I have thee not, and yet I see thee still.
Art thou not, fatal vision, sensible
To feeling as to sight?—or art thou but
A dagger of the mind, a false creation
Proceeding from the heat-oppress'd brain?
I see thee yet, in form as palpable
As this which now I draw.
Thou marshal'st me the way that I was going;
And such an instrument I was to use.
Mine eyes are made the fools o' th' other senses,
Or else worth all the rest. I see thee still;
And on thy blade and dudgeon gouts of blood,

Which was not so before. There's no such thing.
It is the bloody business, which informs
Thus to mine eyes. Now, o'er one half the world
Nature seems dead, and wicked dreams abuse
The curtain'd sleep: now witchcraft celebrates
Pale Hecate's offerings; and wither'd Murder,
Alarm'd by his sentinel, the wolf,
Whose howl's his watch, thus with his stealthy pace,
With Tarquin's ravishing strides, tow'rds his design
Moves like a ghost. Thou sound and firm-set earth,
Hear not, my steps, which way they walk, for fear
The very stones prate of my whereabout,
And take the present horror from the time,
Which now suits with it. Whilst I threat, he lives—
Words to the heat of deeds too cold breath gives.

[*A bell rings.*]

I go, and it is done; the bell invites me:
Hear it not Duncan, for it is a knell
That summons thee to heaven or to hell.

[*Enter Lady Macbeth.*]

Lady. That which hath made them drunk, hath made me bold:
What hath quench'd them, hath given me fire. Hark! peace!
It was the owl that shriek'd, the fatal bellman,
Which gives the stern'st good-night—he is about it—
The doors are open; and the surfeited grooms
Do mock their charge with snores. I have drugg'd their possets,
That death and nature do contend about them,
Whether they live or die.

Macb. [*Within.*] Who's there?—what ho!

Lady. Alack! I am afraid they have awak'd;
And 'tis not done. Th' attempt, and not the deed,
Confounds us. Hark! I laid their daggers ready;
He could not miss 'em. Had he not resembled
My father as he slept, I [*Enter Macbeth.*] had done 't. My husband.

Macb. I've done the deed—didst thou not hear a noise?

Lady. I heard the owl scream, and the crickets cry. Did not you speak?

Macb. When?

Lady. Now.

Macb. As I descended?

Lady. Ay.

Macb. Hark!—who lies i' th' second chamber?

Lady. Donalbain.

Macb. This is a sorry sight. [*Looks on his hands.*]

Lady. A foolish thought, to say a sorry sight.

Macb. There's one did laugh in 's sleep, and one cried, Murder!
That they did wake each other; I stood and heard them;
But they did say their prayers, and address'd them
Again to sleep.

Lady. There are two lodg'd together.

Macb. One cried, God bless us! and Amen! the other;
As they had seen me with these hangman's hands,
Listening their fear, I could not say, Amen,
When they did say God bless us.

Lady. Consider it not so deeply.

Macb. But wherefore could not I pronounce Amen!
I had most need of blessing, and Amen
Stuck in my throat.
Lady. These deeds must not be thought,
After these ways; so, it will make us mad.
Macb. Methought I heard a voice cry, Sleep no more!
Macbeth does murder sleep—the innocent sleep—
Sleep that knits up the ravell'd sleeve of care,
The death of each day's life, sore labour's bath,
Balm of hurt minds, great nature's second course,
Chief nourisher in life's feast.
Lady. What do you mean?
Macb. Still it cry'd, Sleep no more, to all the house;
Glamis hath murder'd sleep. And therefore Cawdor
Shall sleep no more; Macbeth shall sleep no more!
Lady. Who was it that thus cry'd? Why, worthy Thane,
You do unbend your noble strength, to think
So brain-sickly of things. Go get some water,
And wash this filthy witness from your hand.
Why did you bring these daggers from the place?
They must lie there. Go, carry them, and smear
The sleepy grooms with blood.
Macb. I'll go no more.
I am afraid to think what I have done;
Look on't again, I dare not.
Lady. Infirm of purpose:
Give me the daggers. The sleeping and the dead
Are but as pictures; 'tis the eye of childhood
That fears a painted devil. If he do bleed,
I'll gild the faces of the grooms withal,
For it must seem their guilt. [*Exit.*]
[*Knocking within.*]
Macb. Whence is that knocking! [*Starting.*]
How is't with me, when every noise appals me?
What hands are here?—ha! they pluck out mine eyes.
Will all great Neptune's ocean wash this blood
Clean from my hand? No; this my hand will rather
The multitudinous seas incarnardine,
Making the green one red——
[*Enter Lady Macbeth.*]
Lady. My hands are of your colour; but I shame
To wear a heart so white. [*Knock.*] I hear a knocking
At the south entry. Retire we to our chamber;
A little water clears us of this deed,
How easy is it then? Your constancy
Hath left you unattended. [*Knocking.*] Hark, more knocking!
Get on your night-gown, lest occasion call us,
And show us to be watchers. Be not lost
So poorly in your thoughts.
Macb. To know my deed, 't were best not know myself. [*Knock.*]
Wake, Duncan, with this knocking. Ay, 'would thou could'st!
[*Exeunt.*]

MARK ANTONY OVER CÆSAR'S BODY.

Ant. Friends, Romans, countrymen, lend me your ears.
I come to bury Cæsar, not to praise him.
The evil that men do lives after them;
The good is oft interred with their bones:
So let it be with Cæsar. Noble Brutus
Hath told you Cæsar was ambitious;
If it were so, it was a grievous fault,
And grievously hath Cæsar answer'd it.
Here, under leave of Brutus, and the rest,
(For Brutus is an honourable man,
So are they all, all honourable men,)
Come I to speak in Cæsar's funeral.
He was my friend, faithful and just to me;
Yet Brutus says he was ambitious;
And Brutus is an honourable man.
He hath brought many captives home to Rome,
Whose ransoms did the general coffers fill.
Did this in Cæsar seem ambitious?
When that the poor have cried, Cæsar hath wept;
Ambition should be made of sterner stuff:
Yet Brutus says he was ambitious;
And Brutus is an honourable man.
You all did see that, on the Lupercal,
I thrice presented him a kingly crown,
Which he did thrice refuse. Was this ambition?
Yet Brutus says he was ambitious;
And, sure, he is an honourable man.
I speak not to disprove what Brutus spoke;
But here I am to speak what I do know.
You all did love him once, not without cause:
What cause withholds you then to mourn for him?
Oh, judgment! thou art fled to brutish beasts,
And men have lost their reason! Bear with me:
My heart is in the coffin there with Cæsar,
And I must pause till it come back to me.
First Cit. Methinks there is much reason in his sayings.
Sec. Cit. If thou consider rightly of the matter,
Cæsar has had great wrong.
Third Cit. Has he, masters? I fear there will a worse come in his place.
Fourth Cit. Mark'd ye his words? He would not take the crown;
Therefore 'tis certain he was not ambitious.
First Cit. If it be found so, some will dear abide it.
Sec. Cit. Poor soul! his eyes are red as fire with weeping.
Third Cit. There's not a nobler man in Rome than Antony.
Fourth Cit. Now, mark him, he begins again to speak.
Ant. But yesterday, the word of Cæsar might
Have stood against the world; now lies he there,
And none so poor to do him reverence.
Oh, masters! If I were dispos'd to stir
Your hearts and minds to mutiny and rage,
I should do Brutus wrong, and Cassius wrong,
Who, you all know, are honourable men.

I will not do them wrong: I rather choose
To wrong the dead, to wrong myself and you,
Than I will wrong such honourable men.
But here's a parchment with the seal of Cæsar:
I found it in his closet; 'tis his will.
Let but the commons hear this testament
(Which, pardon me, I do not mean to read),
And they would go and kiss dead Cæsar's wounds,
And dip their napkins in his sacred blood;
Yea, beg a hair of him for memory,
And dying, mention it within their wills,
Bequeathing it as a rich legacy
Unto their issue.

Fourth Cit. We'll hear the will; read it, Mark Antony.

All. The will! the will! We will hear Cæsar's will!

Ant. Have patience, gentle friends! I must not read it;
It is not meet you know how Cæsar lov'd you.
You are not wood, you are not stones, but men;
And, being men, hearing the will of Cæsar,
It will inflame you, it will make you mad.
'Tis good you know not that you are his heirs;
For if you should, Oh, what would come of it!

Fourth Cit. Read the will; we will hear it, Antony:
You shall read us the will; Cæsar's will!

Ant. Will you be patient? will you stay awhile?
I have o'ershot myself, to tell you of it.
I fear I wrong the honourable men
Whose daggers have stabb'd Cæsar. I do fear it.

Fourth Cit. They were traitors. Honourable men!

All. The will! the testament!

Sec. Cit. They were villains, murderers! The will! Read the will!

Ant. You will compel me, then, to read the will?
Then make a ring about the corpse of Cæsar,
And let me show you him that made the will.
Shall I descend? And will you give me leave?

All. Come down.

Sec. Cit. Descend. [*He comes down from the pulpit.*]

Third Cit. You shall have leave.

Fourth Cit. A ring! Stand round!

First Cit. Stand from the hearse, stand from the body.

Sec. Cit. Room for Antony—most noble Antony!

Ant. Nay, press not so upon me; stand far off.

All. Stand back! room! bear back!

Ant. If you have tears, prepare to shed them now.
You all do know this mantle. I remember
The first time ever Cæsar put it on;
'Twas on a summer's evening in his tent,
That day he overcame the Nervii.
Look! in this place ran Cassius' dagger through;
See, what a rent the envious Casca made!
Through this the well-beloved Brutus stabb'd;
And, as he plucked his cursed steel away,
Mark how the blood of Cæsar followed it!
As rushing out of doors, to be resolv'd

If Brutus so unkindly knock'd or no.
For Brutus, as you know, was Cæsar's angel;
Judge, Oh you gods! how dearly Cæsar lov'd him.
This was the most unkindest cut of all;
For when the noble Cæsar saw him stab,
Ingratitude, more strong than traitors' arms,
Quite vanquish'd him; then burst his mighty heart:
And, in his mantle muffling up his face,
Even at the base of Pompey's statue,
Which all the while ran blood, great Cæsar fell.
Oh, what a fall was there, my countrymen!
Then I, and you, and all of us fell down,
Whilst bloody treason flourish'd over us.
Oh, now you weep; and I perceive you feel
The dint of pity: these are gracious drops.
Kind souls! What! weep you when you but behold
Our Cæsar's vesture wounded! Look you here!
Here is himself, marr'd, as you see, with traitors.

First Cit. O piteous spectacle!
Sec. Cit. O noble Cæsar!
Third Cit. O woful day!
Fourth Cit. O traitors! villains!
First Cit. O most bloody sight!
Sec Cit. We will be reveng'd! Revenge! About—seek—burn—fire—kill—slay! Let not a traitor live!

[*Julius Cæsar.*]

The plays of Shakspeare which we have not had occasion, in the course of our remarks, to notice, and those from which we have made no selections, are the following:—*Comedy of Errors*, *Love's Labour Lost*, *Taming of the Shrew*, *King John*, *All's Well that Ends Well*, *Troilus and Cressida*, *Timon of Athens*, *Cymbeline*, *Coriolanus*, and the *Winter's Tale*. He was the author of numerous *Sonnets* also, many of which are marked by peculiar delicacy and beauty.

Lecture the Fourteenth.

BEN JONSON—FRANCIS BEAUMONT—JOHN FLETCHER.

THE second place in the dramatic literature of this important period, has been usually assigned to Jonson, though some writers may be disposed to claim it for the more Shaksperian genius of Beaumont and Fletcher.

BEN JONSON was descended from Scottish ancestry, and was born at Westminster, in 1574. His early life was full of trials and vicissitudes. His father, a clergyman, died one month before the future poet's birth, and his mother, marrying, some years after, a bricklayer, Ben, who had now been, for some time, at Westminster school, preparing for the university, was taken thence by his step-father, and placed at his own employment. Feeling degraded by this change, and sooner than submit to it, he abandoned his home, and though not fifteen years of age, enlisted in the army then forming for service in Holland. He is reputed to have killed, while abroad, one of the enemy in single combat, in the view of both armies, and to have otherwise distinguished himself by his youthful bravery.

Soon after his return to England, Jonson entered St. John's College, Cambridge; but in consequence of his straitened circumstances, he remained there only a very short time, and in the twentieth year of his age repaired to London, and resorted to the stage. He made his first appearance at a low theatre near Clerkenwell, and, as his opponents afterward reminded him, failed completely as an actor. About the same time he commenced writing for the stage, either by himself, or conjointly with others. He soon after quarreled with another performer, and a duel being the consequence, Jonson had the misfortune to kill his antagonist, and to be severely wounded himself. He was committed to prison on a charge of murder, but was released without being brought to trial. After he regained his liberty, he relinquished the stage, as an actor, and in 1596, when in the twenty-third year of his age, produced his first important drama, *Every Man in his Humour*. The scene of the play was laid in Italy, but the characters and manners which it exhibited were exclusively English. Jonson afterward recast the whole, and transferred the scene itself also to England. In its revised form, 'Every Man in his Humour' was brought out at the Globe Theatre, in 1598, and Shakspeare performed one of the prominent characters. He had himself, previous to this time, produced some of his finest comedies, but Jonson was no imitator of his great rival, who blended a spirit of poetic romance with his comic sketches, and made no attempt to delineate the domestic manners of his countrymen. Jonson opened a new walk in the drama: he felt his strength, and the public cheered him on with its plaudits. Queen Elizabeth patronized the new poet, and ever afterwards he was 'a man of mark and likelihood.' In 1599, appeared his *Every Man out of his Humour*, which was a less able performance than its predecessor. *Cynthia's Revels*, and the *Poetaster*, followed; and the fierce rivalry and contention which clouded Jonson's after-life seem to have begun about this time. He had, in the Poetaster, attacked Marston and Dekker, two of his brother dramatists, with much severity. Dekker replied with spirit in his *Satiromastix*, and Jonson was silent during the following two years, 'living upon one Townsend, and scorning the world,' as is recorded in the diary of a contemporary.

In 1603, Jonson tried 'if tragedy had a more kind aspect,' and produced his classic drama of *Sejanus*. Shortly after the accession of King James, a comedy called *Eastward Hoe*, was written conjointly by Jonson, Chapman, and Marston. Some passages in this play reflected on the Scottish nation, and the matter was represented to the king by Sir James Murray, one of his courtiers, in so strong a light, that the authors were apprehended, thrown into prison, and threatened with the loss of their ears and noses. They were not tried, however; and the presumption is, that what was, at first, regarded as severe satire, was nothing more than playful wit. Jonson's three great comedies, *Volpone, or the Fox*, *Epicene, or the Silent Woman*, and *The Alchemist*, were his next serious performances; and in 1611, appeared *Catiline*, his second classical tragedy. His fame had now reached its highest elevation; but he produced several other comedies, and a vast number of court entertainments, before his star began sensibly to decline. In 1619, he received the appointment of poet laureate, with an annual pension of a hundred marks; and, during the same year, he made a journey on foot to Scotland, where he had many friends. He was well received by the Scottish gentry, and was so much pleased with the country, that he designed a poem on the beauties of Loch-lomond. The last of his visits was made to Drummond, of Hawthornden, with whom he passed three weeks, and Drummond kept notes of his conversation, which, in a subsequent age, were communicated to the world, not much to the credit of either host or guest.

The latter days of Jonson form a striking contrast with those of Shakspeare, being dark and painful in the extreme. Frequent attacks of palsy confined him to his house, and having, by his prodigality, squandered the proceeds of his literary labors as fast as they were received, his necessities compelled him to write for the stage when his pen had lost its vigor, and wanted the charm of novelty. In 1630, he produced his comedy, the *New*

Inn, which was unsuccessful on the stage; and the king, when he heard of this failure, sent him a present of a hundred pounds: he also, soon after, raised his laureate pension to the same sum per annum, adding a tierce of Canary wine yearly. Jonson continued to write to the last. Dryden styled his latter works, his *dotages*, and some of them are certainly unworthy of him; but the *Sad Shepherd*, which he left unfinished, exhibits the poetical fancy of a youthful composition. He died in 1637, in the sixty-fourth year of his age, and was buried in Westminster Abbey, where a square stone, marking the spot where the poet's body was disposed vertically, was long after shown, inscribed only with the words,

"O RARE BEN JONSON."

Jonson founded a style of regular English comedy, massive, well compacted, and fitted to endure; yet not very atractive in its materials. His works, altogether, consist of about fifty dramatic pieces, but by far the greater part of them are *Masques* and *Interludes*. His principal comedies are, *Every Man in his Humour*, *Volpone*, *The Silent Woman*, and *The Alchemist*. The voluptuous 'Volpone' is drawn with great breadth and freedom; and generally his portraitures of eccentric characters—men in whom some peculiarity has grown to an egregious excess—are ludicrous and impressive. His scenes and characters show the labors of the artist, but still an artist possessing rich resources; an acute and vigorous intellect; great knowledge of life from its highest point of elevation down to its lowest descent; wit, lofty declamation, and a power of dramatizing his knowledge and observation, with singular skill and effect. Jonson prided himself immoderately upon his classical attainments, and was apt to slight and condemn his less learned associates; hence his pedantry is often misplaced and ridiculous. His comic theatre is a gallery of strange, original portraits, powerfully drawn, and skillfully disposed, but many of them repulsive in expression, or so exaggerated, as to look like caricatures or libels on humanity. There is little deep passion or winning tenderness to link the beings of his drama with those we love or admire, or to make us sympathize with them as with existing mortals. The charm of reality is generally wanting, or when found, it is not a pleasing reality. When the great artist escapes entirely from his elaborate wit, and personified humors, into the region of fancy, as he does in the lyrical passages of 'Cynthia,' 'Epicene,' and the whole drama of the 'Sad Shepherd,' we are struck with the contrast it exhibits to his ordinary manner. He thus presents two natures; one hard, rugged, gross, and sarcastic—the other, airy, fanciful, and graceful, as if its possessor had never combatted with the world and its bad passions, but nursed his understanding and his fancy in poetical seclusion and contemplation. Indeed, we think, the most delightful, at least, aspect of Jonson's genius is presented in the lyrics found in his dramas, and elsewhere in his writings. *The Forest*, from which the first three of the following poems are taken, was published by Jonson, along with the plays which he had then written, in 1616. It consists of a collection of miscellaneous poems, all of which abound with those delicate touches that form the author's prevailing ·aracteristic.

TO CELIA.

Drink to me only with thine eyes,
  And I will pledge with mine;
Or leave a kiss but in the cup,
  And I'll not look for wine.
The thirst that from the soul doth rise,
  Doth ask a drink divine;
But might I of Jove's nectar sup,
  I would not change for thine.

I sent thee late a rosy wreath,
  Not so much honouring thee,
As giving it a hope, that there
  It could not wither'd be.
But thou thereon didst only breathe,
  And sent'st it back to me;
Since when it grows, and smells, I swear,
  Not of itself, but thee.

SONG.

Oh do not wanton with those eyes,
  Lest I be sick with seeing;
Nor cast them down, but let them rise,
  Lest shame destroy their being.

Oh be not angry with those fires,
  For then their threats will kill me;
Nor look too kind on my desires,
  For then my hopes will spill me.

Oh do not steep them in thy tears
  For so will sorrow slay me;
Nor spread them as distraught with fears;
  Mine own enough betray me.

CELIA'S TRIUMPH.

See the chariot at hand here of love,
  Wherein my lady rideth!
Each that draws is a swan or a dove,
  And well the car love guideth.
As she goes all hearts do duty
    Unto her beauty;
And enamour'd do wish, so they might
    But enjoy such a sight
That they still were to run by her side,
Through swords, through seas, whither she would ride.

Do but look on her eyes, they do light
  All that love's world compriseth!
Do but look on her, she is bright
  As love's star when it riseth!

Do but mark, her forehead's smoother
Than words that soothe her!
And from her arch'd brows, such a grace
Sheds itself through the face,
As alone there triumphs to the life
All the gain, all the good of the elements' strife.

Have you seen but a bright lily grow,
Before rude hands have touch'd it?
Have you mark'd but the fall of the snow
Before the soil hath smutch'd it!
Have you felt the wool of the beaver,
Or swan's down ever?
Or have smell'd of the bud o' the brier?
Or the 'nard in the fire?
Or have tasted the bag of the bee?
O so white! O so soft! O so sweet is she!

HYMN TO DIANA.

Queen and huntress, chaste and fair,
Now the sun is laid to sleep;
Seated in thy silver chair,
State in wonted manner keep.
Hesperus entreats thy light,
Goddess excellently bright!

Earth, let not thy envious shade
Dare itself to interpose;
Cynthia's shining orb was made
Heaven to clear when day did close;
Bless us then with wished sight,
Goddess excellently bright!

Lay thy bow of pearl apart,
And thy crystal shining quiver:
Give unto the flying heart,
Space to breathe, how short soever;
Thou that mak'st a day of night,
Goddess excellently bright!

[*Cynthia's Revels.*]

THE SWEET NEGLECT.

Still to be neat, still to be drest,
As you were going to a feast;
Still to be powder'd, still perfum'd:
Lady, it is to be presum'd,
Though art's hid causes are not found,
All is not sweet, all is not sound.
Give me a look, give me a face,
That makes simplicity a grace;
Robes loosely flowing, hair as free;
Such sweet neglect more taketh me
Than all the adulteries of art:
They strike mine eyes, but not mine heart.

[*The Silent Woman.*]

ADVICE TO A RECKLESS YOUTH.

Knowell. What would I have you do? I'll tell you, kinsman;
Learn to be wise, and practice how to thrive
That would I have you do: and not to spend
Your coin on every bauble that you fancy,
Or every foolish brain that humours you.
I would not have you to invade each place,
Nor thrust yourself on all societies,
Till men's affections, or your own desert,
Should worthily invite you to your rank.
He that is so respectless in his courses,
Oft sells his reputation at cheap market.
Nor would I you should melt away yourself
In flashing bravery, lest, while you affect
To make a blaze of gentry to the world,
A little puff of scorn extinguish it,
And you be left like an unsavoury snuff,
Whose property is only to offend.
I'd ha' you sober, and contain yourself;
Not that your sail be bigger than your boat;
But moderate your expenses now (at first)
As you may keep the same proportion still.
Nor stand so much on your gentility,
Which is an airy, and mere borrow'd thing
From dead men's dust, and bones; and none of yours,
Except you make, or hold it.

[*Every Man in his Humour.*]

LOVE.

Lovell and Hosts of the New Inn.

Lov. There is no life on earth, but being in love!
There are no studies, no delights, no business,
No intercourse, or trade of sense, or soul
But what is love! I was the laziest creature,
The most unprofitable sign of nothing,
The veriest drone, and slept away my life
Beyond the dormouse, till I was in love!
And now I can out-wake the nightingale,
Out-watch an usurer, and out-walk him too,
Stalk like a ghost that haunted 'bout a treasure;
And all that fancied treasure, it is love!
Host. But is your name Love-ill, sir, or Love-well?
I would know that.
Lov. I do not know 't myself,
Whether it is. But it is love hath been
The hereditary passion of our house,
My gentle host, and, as I guess, my friend;
The truth is, I have lov'd this lady long,
And impotently, with desire enough,
But no success: for I have still forborne
To express it in my person to her.
Host. How then?
Lov. I have sent her toys, verses, and anagrams,

Trials of wit, mere trifles, she has commended,
But knew not whence they come, nor could she guess.
Host. This was a pretty riddling way of wooing!
Lov. I oft have been, too, in her company,
And look'd upon her a whole day, admir'd her,
Lov'd her, and did not tell her so; lov'd still,
Look'd still, and lov'd; and lov'd and look'd, and sigh'd;
But as a man neglected, I came off,
And unregarded.
Host. Could you blame her, sir,
When you were silent, and not said a word?
Lov. O, but I lov'd the more; and she might read it
Best in my silence, had she been——
Host. As melancholic
As you are. Pray you, why would you stand mute, sir?
Lov. O thereon hangs a history, mine host.
Did you e'er know or hear of the Lord Beaufort,
Who serv'd so bravely in France? I was his page,
And, ere he died, his friend: I follow'd him
First in the wars, and in the times of peace
I waited on his studies; which were right.
He had no Arthurs, nor no Rosicleers,
No Knights of the Sun, nor Amadis de Gauls,
Primalions, and Pantagruels, public nothings;
Abortives of the fabulous dark cloister,
Sent out to poison courts, and infest manners:
But great Achilles,' Agamemnon's acts,
Sage Nestor's counsels, and Ulysses' slights,
Tydides' fortitude, as Homer wrought them
In his immortal fancy, for examples
Of the heroic virtue. Or, as Virgil,
That master of the Epic poem, limn'd
Pious Æneas, his religious prince,
Bearing his aged parent on his shoulders,
Rapt from the flames of Troy, with his young son.
And these he brought to practice and to use.
He gave me first my breeding, I acknowledge,
Then shower'd his bounties on me, like the Hours,
That open-handed sit upon the clouds,
And pass the liberality of heaven
Down to the laps of thankful men! But then,
The trust committed to me at his death
Was above all, and left so strong a tie
On all my powers, as time shall not dissolve,
Till it dissolve itself, and bury all:
The care of his brave heir, and only son!
Who being a virtuous, sweet, young, hopeful lord,
Hath cast his first affections on this lady.
And though I know, and may presume her such
As out of humour, will return no love,
And therefore might indifferently be made
The courting stock for all to practice on,
As she doth practice on us all to scorn:
Yet out of a religion to my charge,

And debt profess'd, I have made a self-decree
Ne'er to express my person, though my passion
Burn me to cinders.

THE ALCHEMIST.

[*Mammon. Surly, his Friend. The scene Subtle's House.*]

Mam. Come on, sir. Now you set your foot on shore
In *novo orbe*. Here's the rich Peru:
And then within, sir, are the golden mines,
Great Solomon's Ophir! He was sailing to 't
Three years, but we have reach'd it in ten months.
This is the day wherein to all my friends
I will pronounce the happy word, Be rich.
This day you shall be *spectatissimi*.
You shall no more deal with the hollow dye,
Or the frail card. No more be at charge of keeping
The livery punk for the young heir, that must
Seal at all hours in his shirt. No more,
If he deny, ha' him beaten to 't, as he is
That brings him the commodity. No more
Shall thirst of satin, or the covetous hunger
Of velvet entrails for a rude-spun cloak
To be display'd at Madam Agusta's, make
The sons of Sword and Hazard fall before
The golden calf, and on their knees whole nights
Commit idolatry with wine and trumpets;
Or go a-feasting after drum and ensign,
No more of this. You shall start up young viceroys,
And have your punques and punquetees, my Surly:
And unto thee I speak it first, Be rich.
Where is my Subtle there? within ho—

[*Face answers from within.*]

Sir, he'll come to you by and by.
Mam. That's his fire-drake,
His Lungs, his Zephyrus, he that puffs his coals
Till he firk nature up in her own centre.
You are not faithful, sir. This night I'll change
All that is metal in thy house to gold:
And early in the morning will I send
To all the plumbers and the pewterers,
And buy their tin and lead up; and to Lothbury
For all the copper.
Sur. What, and turn that too?
Mam. Yes, and I'll purchase Devonshire and Cornwall,
And make them perfect Indies! You admire now?
Sur. No, faith.
Mam. But when you see the effects of the great medicine!
Of which one part projected on a hundred
Of Mercury, or Venus, or the Moon,
Shall turn it to as many of the Sun;
Nay, to a thousand, so *ad infinitum*:
You will believe me.
Sur. Yes, when I see 't, I will.

Mam. Ha! why,
Do you think I fable with you? I assure you,
He that has once the flower of the Sun,
The perfect Ruby, which we call Elixir,
Not only can do that, but by its virtue
Can confer honour, love, respect, long life,
Give safety, valour, yea, and victory,
To whom he will. In eight and twenty days
I'll make an old man of fourscore a child.
Sur. No doubt; he's that already.
Mam. Nay, I mean,
Restore his years, renew him like an eagle,
To the fifth age; make him get sons and daughters,
Young giants, as our philosophers have done
(The ancient patriarchs afore the flood,)
By taking, once a-week, on a knife's point,
The quantity of a grain of mustard of it,
Become stout Marses, and beget young Cupids.
Sur. The decay'd vestals of Pickt-hatch would thank you,
That keep the fire alive there.
Mem. 'Tis the secret
Of nature naturized 'gainst all infections,
Cures all diseases, coming of all causes;
A month's grief in a day; a year's in twelve;
And of what age soever, in a month:
Past all the doses of your drugging doctors,
I'll undertake withal to fright the plague
Out o' the kingdom in three months.
Sur. And I'll
Be bound the players shall sing your praises, then,
Without their poets.
Mam. Sir, I 'll do 't. Meantime,
I'll give away so much unto my man,
Shall serve the whole city with preservative
Weekly; each house his dose, and at the rate—
Sur. As he that built the water-work does with water!
Mam. You are incredulous.
Sur. Faith I have humour.
I would not willingly be gull'd. Your Stone
Can not transmute me.
Mam. Pertinax Surly,
Will you believe antiquity? Records?
I'll show you a book, where Moses, and his sister,
And Solomon, have written of the Art!
Ay, and a treatise penn'd by Adam.
Sur. How?
Mam. Of the Philosopher's Stone, and in High Dutch.
Sur. Did Adam write, Sir, in High Dutch?
Mam. He did,
Which proves it was the primitive tongue.
Sur. What paper?
Mam. Cedar-board.
Sur. O that, indeed, they say,
Will last 'gainst worms.

Mam. 'Tis like your Irish wood
'Gainst cobwebs. I have a piece of Jason's fleece too,
Which was no other than a book of Alchemy,
Writ in large sheep-skin, a good fat ram-vellum.
Such was Pythagoras' Thigh, Pandora's Tub,
And all that fable of Medea's charms,
The manner of our work: the bulls, our furnace,
Still breathing fire: our *Argent-vive*, the Dragon:
The Dragon's teeth, Mercury sublimate,
That keeps the whiteness, hardness, and the biting:
And they are gather'd into Jason's helm,
(Th' Alembick,) and then sow'd in Mars his field,
And thence sublim'd so often, till they are fix'd.
Both this, the Hesperian Garden, Cadmus' Story,
Jove's Shower, the Boon of Midas, Argus' Eyes,
Boccace his Demogorgon, thousands more,
All abstract riddles of our Stone.

Jonson's Roman tragedies may be considered literal impersonations of classic antiquity 'robust and richly graced,' yet stiff and unnatural in style and construction. They seem to bear about the same resemblance to Shakspeare's classic dramas that sculpture bears to actual life. We think it not, therefore, necessary to introduce more than the following extract from them:—

THE FALL OF CATILINE.

Petreius. The straits and needs of Catiline being such,
As he must fight with one of the two armies
That then had near inclosed him, it pleas'd fate
To make us the object of his desperate choice,
Wherein the danger almost pois'd the honour:
And, as he rose, the day grew black with him,
And fate descended nearer to the earth,
As if she meant to hide the name of things
Under her wings, and make the world her quarry.
At this we roused, lest one small minute's stay
Had left it to be inquired what Rome was;
And (as we ought) arm'd in the confidence
Of our great cause, in form of battle stood,
Whilst Catiline came on, not with the face
Of any man, but of a public ruin:
His countenance was a civil war itself;
And all his host had, standing in their looks,
The paleness of the death that was to come;
Yet cried they out like vultures, and urged on,
As if they would precipitate our fates.
Nor stay'd we longer for 'em, but himself
Struck the first stroke, and with it fled a life,
Which out, it seem'd a narrow neck of land
Had broke between two mighty seas, and either
Flow'd into other; for so did the slaughter;
And whirl'd about, as when two violent tides
Meet and not yield. The furies stood on hills,

Circling the place, and trembling to see men
Do more than they; whilst pity left the field,
Griev'd for that side, that in so bad a cause
They knew not what a crime their valour was.
The sun stood still, and was, behind the cloud
The battle made, seen sweating, to drive up
His frighted horse, whom still the noise drove backward;
And now had fierce Enyo, like a flame
Consum'd all it could reach, and then itself,
Had not the fortune of the commonwealth,
Come, Pallas-like, to every Roman thought;
Which Catiline seeing, and that now his troops,
Cover'd the earth they 'ad fought on with their trunks,
Ambitious of great fame, to crown his ill,
Collected all his fury, and ran in
(Arm'd with a glory high as his despair)
Into our battle, like a Libyan lion
Upon his hunters, scornful of our weapons,
Careless of wounds, plucking down lives about him,
Till he had circled on himself with death:
Then fell he too, t' embrace it where it lay.
And as in that rebellion 'gainst the gods,
Minerva holding forth Medusa's head,
One of the giant brethren felt himself
Grow marble at the killing sight; and now,
Almost made stone, began to inquire what flint,
What rock, it was that crept through all his limbs;
And, ere he could think more, was that he fear'd:
So Catiline, at the sight of Rome in us,
Became his tomb; yet did his look retain
Some of his fierceness, and his hands still mov'd,
As if he labour'd yet to grasp the state
With those rebellious parts.
Cato. A brave bad death!
Had this been honest now, and for his country,
As 't was against it, who had e'er fall'n greater?

In the production of the 'Masque,' a court entertainment very prevalent during the period that we are at present considering, Jonson excelled all his contemporaries. The origin of this species of amusement is to be traced back to the *revels* and *shows* which, during the fourteenth, fifteenth, and sixteenth centuries, were presented, on high festive occasions at court, in the inns of the lawyers, and at the universities, and in those *mysteries* and *moralities* which were the earliest forms of the spoken drama. To illustrate these remarks, we present entire the following masque written by Jonson in 1615, and represented at court, 'by the lords and gentlemen, the king's servants,' as a compliment to James for his love of Justice.

THE GOLDEN AGE RESTORED.

THE COURT BEING SEATED AND IN EXPECTATION.

[*Loud music: Pallas in her chariot descending to a softer music.*]

Look, look! rejoice and wonder
  That you, offending mortals, are
  (For all your crimes) so much the care
Of him that bears the thunder.

Jove can endure no longer,
  Your great ones should your less invade;
  Or that your weak, though bad, be made
A prey unto the stronger,

And therefore means to settle
  Astræa in her seat again
  And let down in his golden chain
An age of better metal.

Which deed he doth the rather,
  That even Envy may behold
  Time not enjoy'd his head of gold
Alone beneath his father,

But that his care conserveth,
  As time, so all time's honours too,
  Regarding still what heaven should do
And not what earth deserveth.

[*A tumult, and clashing of arms heard within.*]

But hark! what tumult from yonder cave is heard?
  What noise, what strife, what earthquake and alarms,
As troubled Nature for her maker fear'd,
  And all the Iron Age were up in arms!

Hide me, soft cloud, from their profaner eyes,
  Till insolent Rebellion take the field;
And as their spirits with their counsels rise
  I frustrate all with showing but my shield.

[*She retires behind a cloud.*]

[*The Iron Age presents itself, calling forth the Evils.*]

I Age. Come forth, come forth, do we not hear
What purpose, and how worth our fear,
  The king of gods hath on us?
He is not of the Iron breed,
That would, though Fate did help the deed,
  Let shame in so upon us.

Rise, rise thou up, thou grandame Vice
Of all my issue, Avarice
  Bring with thee Fraud and Slander,
Corruption with the golden hands,
Or any subtler Ill, that stands
  To be a more commander.

Thy boys, Ambition, Pride, and Scorn,
Force, Rapine, and thy babe last born
  Smooth Treachery, call hither,
Arm Folly forth, and Ignorance,
And teach them all our Pyrrhic dance:
  We may triumph together,

Upon this enemy so great,
Whom, if our forces can defeat,
  And but this once bring under,
We are the masters of the skies,
Where all the wealth, height, power lies,
  The sceptre, and the thunder.

Which of you would not in a war
Attempt the price of any scar,
  To keep your own states even?
But here, which of you is that he,
Would not himself the weapon be,
  To ruin Jove and heaven?

About it then, and let him feel
The Iron Age is turn'd to steel,
  Since he begins to threat her:
And though the bodies here are less
Than were the giants; he'll confess
  Our malice is far greater.

[*The Evils enter for the Antimasque, and dance to two drums, trumpets, and a confusion of martial music. At the end of which Pallas re-appears, showing her shield. The Evils are turned to statues.*]

Pal. So change, and perish, scarcely knowing how,
That 'gainst the gods do take so vain a vow,
And think to equal with your mortal dates,
Their lives that are obnoxious to no fates.
'Twas time to appear, and let their folly see
'Gainst whom they fought, and with what destiny.
Die all that can remain of you, but stone,
And that be seen a while, and then be none!
Now, now descend, you both belov'd of Jove,
And of the good on earth no less the love.

[*The scene changes, and she calls Astræa and the Golden Age.*]

Descend, you long, long wish'd and wanted pair,
And as your softer tunes divide the air,
So shake all clouds off with your golden hair;
For Spite is spent: the Iron Age is fled,
And, with her power on earth, her name is dead.

[*Astræa and the Golden Age descending with a Song.*]

Ast. G. Age. And are we, then,
To live agen,
With men?
Ast. Will Jove such pledges to the earth restore
As justice?
G. Age. Or the purer ore?
Pal. Once more.

G. Age. But do they know,
How much they owe?
Below?
Ast. And will of grace receive it, not as due!
Pal. If not, they harm themselves, not you.
Ast. True.
G. Age. True.
Cho. Let narrow natures, how they will, mistake,
The great should still be good for their own sake.
[*They come forward.*]
Pal. Welcome to earth, and reign.
Ast. G. Age. But how, without a train,
Shall we our state sustain?
Pal. Leave that to Jove: therein you are
No little part of his Minerva's care
Expect awhile.—

You far-famed spirits of this happy isle,
That, for your sacred songs have gain'd the style
Of Phœbus' sons, whose notes the air aspire
Of th' old Egyptian, or the Thracian lyre,
That Chaucer, Gower, Lydgate, Spenser, hight,
Put on your better flames, and larger light,
To wait upon the Age that shall your names now nourish,
Since Virtue press'd shall grow, and buried Arts shall flourish.
Chau. Gow. We come.
Lyd. Spen. We come.
Omnes. Our best of fire
Is that which Pallas doth inspire.
[*They descend.*]

Pal. Then see you yonder souls, set far within the shade,
That in Elysian bowers the blessed seats do keep,
That for their living good, now semi-gods are made,
And went away from earth, as if but tam'd with sleep?
These we must join to make; for these are of the strain,
That justice dare defend, and will the age sustain.

Cho. Awake, awake, for whom these times were kept.
O wake, wake, wake, as you had never slept!
Make haste and put on air, to be their guard,
Whom once but to defend, is still reward.

Pal. Thus Pallas throws a lightning from her shield.
[*The scene of light discovered.*]
Cho. To which let all that doubtful darkness yield.
Ast. Now Peace,
G. Age. And Love,
Ast. Faith,
G. Age. Joys,
Ast. G. Age. All, all increase. [*A pause.*]
Chau. And Strife,
Gow. And Hate,
Lyd. And Fear,
Spen. And Pain,
Omnes. All cease.

Pal. No tumour of an iron vein.
The causes shall not come again.

Cho. But, as of old, all now be gold.
Move, move then to the sounds;
And do not only walk your solemn rounds,
But give those light and airy bounds,
That fit the Genii of these gladder grounds.

[*The first Dance.*]

Pal. Already do not all things smile?
Ast. But when they have enjoy'd awhile
The Age's quickening power:
Age. That every thought a seed doth bring,
And every look a plant doth spring,
And every breath a flower:

Pal. The earth unplough'd shall yield her crop,
Pure honey from the oak shall drop,
The fountain shall run milk:
The thistle shall the lily bear,
And every bramble roses wear,
And every worm make silk.

Cho. The very shrub shall balsam sweet,
And nectar melt the rock with heat,
Till earth have drank her fill:
That she no harmful weed may know,
Nor barren fern, nor mandrake low,
Nor mineral to kill.

[*Here the main Dance. After which,*]

Pal. But here's not all: you must do more,
Or else you do but half restore,
The Age's liberty.
Poe. The male and female us'd to join,
And into all delight did coin
That pure simplicity.

Then Feature did to Form advance,
And Youth call'd Beauty forth to dance,
And every Grace was by:
It was a time of no distrust,
So much of love had nought of lust;
None fear'd a jealous eye.
The language melted in the ear,
Yet all without a blush might hear;
They liv'd with open vow.

Cho. Each touch and kiss was so well plac'd,
They were as sweet as they were chaste,
And such must yours be now.

[*Here they dance with the ladies.*]

Ast. What change is here? I had not more
Desire to leave the earth before,
Than I have now to stay;

My silver feet, like roots, are wreath'd
Into the ground, my wings are sheath'd,
And I can not away.

Of all there seems a second birth;
It is become a heaven on earth,
And Jove is present here.
I feel the godhead; nor will doubt
But he can fill the place throughout,
Whose power is everywhere.

This, this, and only such as this,
The bright Astræa's region is,
Where she would pray to live;
And in the midst of so much gold,
Unbought with grace, or fear unsold,
The law to mortals give.

[*Here they dance the Galliards and Corantos. Pallas ascending, and calling the Poets.*]

'Tis now enough; behold you here,
What Jove hath built to be your sphere,
You hither must retire.
And as his bounty gives you cause,
Be ready still without your pause,
To show the world your fire.

Like lights about Astræa's throne,
You here must shine, and all be one,
In fervour and in flame;
That by your union she may grow,
And, you sustaining her, may know
The Age still by her name.

Who vows, against or heat or cold,
To spin your garments of her gold,
That want may touch you never;
And making garlands ev'ry hour,
To write your names in some new flower,
That you may live forever.

Cho. To Jove, to Jove, be all the honours given.
That thankful hearts can raise from earth to heaven.

Beaumont and Fletcher, in the order of our dramatic investigations, next require our attention. The literary partnerships of the drama which we have had occasion, in the course of our remarks, to notice, were generally brief and incidental, being confined to a few scenes, or a single play. In Beaumont and Fletcher, however, we have the interesting spectacle of two young men of exalted genius, of good birth and connections, living together for ten years, and writing in union a series of dramas, passionate, romantic, and comic, thus blending together their genius and their fame in indissoluble connection. Shakspeare was, beyond a doubt, the inspirer of these kindred spirits. They appeared when his genius was in its meridian splendor, and they were completely subdued by its overpowering influence. They reflected its leading characteristics, not as slavish copyists, but as men of high powers and attainments, proud of borrowing inspiration from a source which they could so well appreciate, and which was at once ennobling and inexhaustible.

Francis Beaumont was descended from the ancient family of Beaumont of Grace-Dieu, in Leicestershire, and was born in 1586. His grandfather, John Beaumont, was master of the rolls, and his father, Francis, one of the judges of the common pleas. Having completed his collegiate studies at Cambridge, young Beaumont entered the Inner Temple, London, as a student of law; but his passion for the muses prevented him from making any great proficiency in his legal studies. He married the daughter and co-heiress of Sir Henry Isley, of Kent, by whom he had two daughters. The tenor of his brief life was even and uninterrupted, and his death occurred on the sixth of March, 1615, before he had attained the thirtieth year of his age. He was buried on the ninth of the same month, at the entrance of St. Benedict's chapel, Westminster Abbey. Thus, in the beautiful language of Hazlitt, was youth, genius, aspiring hope and growing reputation, cut off like a flower in its summer pride, or like the 'lily in its stalk green,' which inclines us to repine at fortune, and almost at nature, that seem to set so little store by their greatest favorites. The life of poets is, or ought to be, if we judge of it from the light it lends to others, a golden drama, full of brightness and sweetness, rapt in Elysium; and it gives one a reluctant pang to see the splendid vision, by which they are attended in their path of glory, fade like a vapor, and their sacred heads laid low in ashes, before the sand of common mortals has half run out.

John Fletcher was of equally distinguished parentage with Beaumont, being the son of Dr. Richard Fletcher, bishop of Bristol, and afterward of Worcester. He was born in Northamptonshire, in 1576, and educated at Bennet College, Cambridge. Though he was ten years older than Beaumont, yet comparatively nothing is known of him from the time at which he left the university, until the thirtieth year of his age, when he seems to have commenced his career of dramatic authorship, conjointly with his youthful and gifted associate. His life was as quiet and as unmarked by striking incidents, as was that of his partner in his early literary labors; and he died of the great plague in 1625, in the fiftieth year of his age. For some reason, not now known, his remains were not honored with a resting-place in Westminster Abbey, but were buried in St. Mary Overy's church, Southwark.

The dramas of Beaumont and Fletcher were fifty-two in number; but as the greater part of them were not published till 1647, it is impossible to ascertain the dates at which they were respectively produced. Dryden remarks that *Philaster* was the first play that brought them into esteem with the public, though they had previously written two or three others. It is improbable in plot, but highly interesting in character and situations. The jealousy of Philaster is forced and unnatural; the character of Euphrasia, disguised as Bellario, the page, is a copy from Viola, yet there is something peculiarly delicate in the following account of her hopeless attachment to Philaster:—

My father oft would speak
Your worth and virtue; and, as I did grow
More and more apprehensive, I did thirst
To see the man so prais'd, but yet all this
Was but a maiden longing, to be lost
As soon as found; till, sitting in my window,
Printing my thoughts in lawn, I saw a god,
I thought (but it was you) enter our gates.
My blood flew out, and back again as fast
As I had puff'd it forth and suck'd it in
Like breath. Then was I called away in haste
To entertain you. Never was a man
Heav'd from a sheep-cote to a sceptre raised
So high in thoughts as I: you left a kiss
Upon these lips then, which I mean to keep
From you forever. I did hear you talk,
Far above singing! After you were gone
I grew acquainted with my heart, and search'd
What stirr'd it so. Alas! I found it love;
Yet far from lust; for could I but have lived
In presence of you, I had had my end.
For this I did delude my noble father
With a feigned pilgrimage, and dress'd myself
In habit of a boy; and for I knew
My birth no match for you, I was past hope
Of having you. And, understanding well
That when I made discovery of my sex,
I could not stay with you, I made a vow,
By all the most religious things a maid
Could call together, never to be known,
Whilst there was hope to hide me from men's eyes,
For other than I seem'd, that I might ever
Abide with you: Then sat I by the fount
Where first you took me up.

Philaster had previously described the circumstances under which he found the disguised maiden by the fount, and the description is highly poetical and picturesque:—

——— Hunting the buck,
I found him sitting by a fountain-side,
Of which he borrow'd some to quench his thirst,
And paid the nymph again as much in tears.
A garland lay him by, made by himself,
Of many several flowers, bred in the bay,
Stuck in that mystic order, that the rareness
Delighted me: But ever when he turn'd
His tender eyes upon them he would weep,
As if he meant to make them grow again.
Seeing such pretty helpless innocence

Dwell in his face, I ask'd him all his story.
He told me that his parents gentle died,
Leaving him to the mercy of the fields,
Which gave him roots; and of the crystal springs,
Which did not stop their courses; and the sun,
Which still, he thank'd him, yielded him his light.
Then took he up his garland, and did show
What every flower, as country people hold,
Did signify; and how all, order'd thus,
Express'd his grief: and to my thoughts did read
The prettiest lecture of his country art
That could be wish'd; so that methought I could
Have studied it. I gladly entertain'd him
Who was as glad to follow.

The *Maid's Tragedy*, supposed to have been written soon after 'Philaster was produced, is a powerful, but unpleasing drama. The purity of female virtue in Amintor and Aspatia, is well contrasted with the guilty boldness of Evadne; and the rough soldier-like bearing and manly feeling of Melantius, render the selfish sensuality of the king, more hateful and disgusting. Unfortunately, there is much licentiousness in this fine play—whole scenes and dialogues are disfigured by this master vice of these authors. Their dramas are 'a rank unweeded garden,' which grew only the more disorderly and vicious as it advanced to maturity.

Besides the plays already mentioned, these writers had produced before Beaumont's death, three tragedies, *King and no King*, *Bonduca*, and *The Laws of Candy;* also five comedies, *The Woman Hater*, *The Knight of the Burning Pestle*, *The Honest Man's Fortune*, *The Coxcomb*, and *The Captain*. Fletcher afterwards wrote three tragic dramas and nine comedies, the best of which are *The Chances*, *The Spanish Curate*, *The Beggar's Bush*, and *Rule a Wife, and Have a Wife*. He also wrote an exquisite pastoral drama, *The Faithful Shepherdess*, which Milton followed pretty closely in the design, and partly in the language and imagery, in his Comus. In *The Two Noble Kinsmen*, another dramatic production of these joint authors, they are represented to have had the aid of Shakspeare; but as the play is not superior to many other of their performances, the statement is, certainly, not sustained by internal evidence.

Of the dramas which Beaumont and Fletcher wrote conjointly, it is impossible to determine what share each took in contriving the plots, and filling up the scenes; but the general impression is, that Beaumont had the greater judgment and the severer taste, and was chiefly employed in retrenching and correcting the luxuriances of Fletcher's wit and fancy. The genius of the former is also said to have leaned more to tragedy than that of the latter. The later works of Fletcher are chiefly of a comic character; and in these the plots are often inartificial and loosely connected, though he is always lively and entertaining. The incidents rapidly succeed each other, and the dialogue is witty, elegant, and amusing. Dryden considered that Fletcher understood and imitated the conversation of gentlemen much better than Shakspeare, and it was, therefore, that he was much more frequently on the stage; and with regard to this, Hallam remarks, 'We can not deny that the depths of Shakspeare's mind were often unfathomable by an audience; the bow was drawn by a matchless hand, but the shaft went out of sight. All might listen to Fletcher's pleasing, though not profound or vigorous language. His thoughts are noble and tinged with the ideality of romance; his metaphors vivid, though sometimes too forced; he possesses the idiom of English without much pedantry, though in many passages he strains it beyond common use; his versification, though studiously irregular, is often rythmical and sweet; yet we are seldom arrested by striking beauties. Good lines occur on every page, fine ones, rarely. We lay down the volume with a sense of admiration of what we have read, but little of it remains distinctly in the memory.' But notwithstanding this may be a correct view of the subject, still the dramas of Beaumont and Fletcher impress us with a high idea of their powers as poets and dramatists. The vast variety and luxuriance of their genius seem to elevate them above Jonson, though they were destitute of his regularity and solidity, and to place them on the borders of the 'magic circle' of Shakspeare. The confidence and buoyancy of youth are visible in all their productions. They had not, like Jonson, tasted of adversity; and they had not the profoundly meditative spirit of their great master, who was cognizant of all human feelings and sympathies. They did not aspire to his more elevated creations, but took as models for their tragedies such of his comedies as the 'Twelfth Night' and 'Winter's Tale.' Life was to them a scene of enjoyment and pleasure, and the exercise of their genius a source of refined delight and ambition. They were gentlemen who wrote for the stage, as gentlemen—had never done before, and have rarely since.

Beaumont and Fletcher 'are,' as Hallam remarks, 'not much quoted, and do not even afford copious materials to those who cull the beauties of ancient lore.' Their dramas are remarkable for the continuous interest they excite, and pleasure they afford, rather than for startling passages, or isolated beauties. Our extracts, therefore, will be few and comparatively limited:—

GRIEF OF ASPATIA FOR THE MARRIAGE OF AMINTOR AND EVADNE.

[*Evadne, Aspatia, Dula, and other Ladies.*]

Evadne. Would thou could'st instill [*To Dula.*]
Some of thy mirth into Aspatia.
Asp. It were a timeless smile should prove my cheek;
It were a fitter hour for me to laugh,
When at the altar the religious priest
Were pacifying the offended powers
With sacrifice, than now. This should have been
My night, and all your hands have been employ'd
In giving me a spotless offering
To young Amintor's bed, as we are now
For you; pardon, Evadne; would my worth

Were great as yours, or that the king, or he,
Or both thought so; perhaps he found me worthless;
But till he did so, in these ears of mine
(These credulous ears) he pour'd the sweetest words
That art or love could frame.

Evad. Nay, leave this sad talk, madam.

Asp. Would I could, then should I leave the cause.
Lay a garland on my hearse of the dismal yew.

Evad. That's one of your sad songs, madam.

Asp. Believe me, 'tis a pretty one.

Evad. How is it, madam?

Asp.
Lay a garland on my hearse
Of the dismal yew;
Maidens, willow branches bear,
Say I died true.
My love was false, but I was firm,
From my hour of birth;
Upon my buried body lie
Lightly, gentle earth!

Madam, good-night; may no discontent
Grow 'twixt your love and you; but if there do,
Inquire of me, and I will guide your moan,
Teach you an artificial way to grieve,
To keep your sorrow waking. Love your lord
No worse than I; but if you love so well,
Alas! you may displease him; so did I.
This is the last time you shall look on me:
Ladies, farewell; as soon as I am dead,
Come all and watch one night about my hearse;
Bring each a mournful story and a tear
To offer at it when I go to earth;
With flattering ivy clasp my coffin round,
Write on my brow my fortune, let my bier
Be borne by virgins that shall sing by course
The truth of maids and perjuries of men.

Evad. Alas! I pity thee. [*Amintor enters.*]

Asp. Go, and be happy in your lady's love; [*To Amintor.*]
May all the wrongs that you have done to me
Be utterly forgotten in my death.
I'll trouble you no more, yet I will take
A parting kiss, and will not be denied.
You'll come, my lord, and see the virgins weep
When I am laid in earth, though you yourself
Can know no pity: thus I wind myself
Into this willow garland, and am prouder
That I was once your love (though now refus'd)
Than to have had another true to me.

[*The Maid's Tragedy.*]

DISINTERESTEDNESS OF BIANCHA.

Enter Cesario and a Servant.

Cesa. Let my friend have entrance.

Serv. Sir, a' shall.

Cesa. Any; I except none.
Serv. We know your mind, sir. [*Exit.*]
Cesa. Pleasures admit no bounds. I'm pitch'd so high
To such a growth of full prosperities,
That to conceal my fortunes were an injury
To gratefulness, and those more liberal favours
By whom my glories prosper. He that flows
In gracious and swoln tides of blest abundance,
Yet will be ignorant of his own fortunes,
Deserves to live contemn'd, and die forgotten:
The harvest of my hopes is now already
Ripen'd and gather'd; I can fatten youth
With choice of plenty, and supplies of comforts;
My fate springs in my own hand, and I'll use it.

[*Enter two Servants and Biancha.*]

First Serv. 'Tis my place.
Sec. Serv. Yours? Here, fair one; I'll acquaint
My lord.
First Serv. He's here; go to him boldly.
Sec. Serv. Please you
To let him understand how readily
I waited on your errand!
First Serv. Saucy fellow!
You must excuse his breeding.
Cesa. What's the matter?
Biancha? my Biancha? To your offices! *Exeunt Serv.*
This visit, sweet, from thee, my pretty dear,
By how much more 't was unexpected, comes
So much the more timely: witness this free welcome
What'er occasion led thee!
Bian. You may guess, sir;
Yet indeed, 'tis a rare one.
Cesa. Prithee, speak it,
My honest virtuous maid.
Bian. Sir, I have heard
Of your misfortunes; and I can not tell you
Whether I have more cause of joy or sadness,
To know they are a truth.
Cesa. What truth, Biancha?
Misfortunes?—how?—wherein?
Bian. You are disclaim'd
For being the lord Alberto's son, and publicly
Acknowledg'd of as mean a birth as mine is:
It can not choose but grieve you.
Cesa. Grieve me? Ha, ha, ha, ha!
Is this all?
Bian. This all?
Cesa. Thou art sorry for 't,
I warrant thee; alas, good soul, Biancha!
That which thou call'st misfortune is my happiness;
My happiness, Biancha!
Bian. If you love me,
It may prove mine too.

Cesa. May it! I will love thee
My good, good maid, if that can make thee happy,
Better and better love thee.
Bian. Without breach then,
Of modesty, I come to claim the interest,
Your protestations, both by vows and letters,
Have made me owner of: from the first hour
I saw you, I confess I wish'd I had been,
Or not so much below your rank and greatness
Or not so much above those humble flames
That should have warm'd my bosom with a temperate
Equality of desires in equal fortunes.
Still, as you utter'd language of affection,
I courted time to pass more slowly on,
That I might turn more full to lend attention
To what I durst not credit, nor yet hope for;
Yet still as more I heard, I wish'd to hear more.
Cesa. Didst thou in troth, wench?
Bian. Willingly betray'd
Myself to hopeless bondage.
Cesa. A good girl!
I thought I should not miss, whate'er thy answer was.
Bian. But as I am a maid, sir, (and i' faith
You may believe me, for I am a maid)
So dearly I respected both your fame
And quality, that I would first have perish'd
In my sick thoughts, than ere have given consent
To have undone your fortunes, by inviting
A marriage with so mean a one as I am:
I should have died sure, and no creature known
The sickness that had kill'd me.
Cesa. Pretty heart!
Good soul, alas, alas!
Bian. Now since I know
There is no difference 'twixt your birth and mine,
Not much 'twixt our estates (if any be,
The advantage is on my side), I come willingly
To tender you the first-fruits of my heart,
And am content t' accept you for my husband,
Now when you are at lowest.
Cesa. For a husband?
Speak sadly; dost thou mean so?
Bian. In good deed, sir,
'Tis pure love makes this proffer.
Cesa. I believe thee.
What counsel urg'd thee on! tell me; thy father?
My worshipful smug host? Was 't not he, wench?
Or mother hostess? ha?
Bian. D' you mock my parentage?
I did not scorn yours: mean folks are as worthy
To be well spoken of, if they deserve well,
As some whose only fame lies in their blood.
Oh, you 're a proud poor man! all your oaths, falsehood,
Your vows, deceit, your letters, forged and wicked!

Cesa. Thoud'st be my wife, I dare swear.
Bian. Had your heart,
Your hand, and tongue, been twins, you had reputed
This courtesy a benefit.
Cesa. Simplicity,
How prettily thou mov'st me! Why, Biancha,
Report has cozen'd thee; I am not fallen
From my expected honours or possessions,
Though from the hope of birthright.
Bian. Are you not?
Then I am lost again! I have a suit too;
You'll grant it, if you be a good man.
Cesa. Any thing.
Bian. Pray do not talk of aught what I have said t' ye.
Cesa. As I wish health, I will not!
Bian. Pity me;
But never love me more!
Cesa. Nay, now you're cruel:
Why all these tears?—Thou shalt not go.
Bian. I'll pray for you,
That you may have a virtuous wife, a fair one;
And when I 'm dead—
Cesa. Fie, fie!
Bian. Think on me sometimes,
With mercy for this trespass!
Cesa. Let us kiss
At parting, as at coming!
Bian. This I have
As a free dower to a virgin's grave;
All goodness dwell with you! [*Exit.*]
Cesa. Harmless Biancha!
Unskill'd! what handsome toys are maids to play with.
[*Fair Maid of the Inn.*]

PASTORAL LOVE.

[*To Clorinda. A Satyr enters.*]

Satyr. Through yon same bending plain,
That flings his arms down to the main,
And through these thick woods have I run,
Whose bottom never kiss'd the sun.
Since the lusty spring began,
All to please my master Pan,
Have I trotted without rest
To get him fruit; for at a feast
He entertains, this coming night,
His paramour the Syrinx bright:
But behold a fairer sight!
By that heavenly form of thine,
Brightest fair, thou art divine,
Sprung from great immortal race
Of the gods, for in thy face
Shines more awful majesty
Than dull weak mortality.

Dare with misty eyes behold,
And live: therefore on this mould
Lowly do I bend my knee
In worship of thy deity.
Deign it, goddess, from my hand
To receive whate'er this land
From her fertile womb doth send
Of her choice fruits; and but lend
Belief to that the Satyr tells,
Fairer by the famous wells
To this present day ne'er grew,
Never better, nor more true.
Here be grapes whose lusty blood
Is the learned poet's good,
Sweeter yet did never crown
The head of Bacchus; nuts more brown
Than the squirrel whose teeth crack them;
Deign, O fairest fair, to take them:
For these, black-eyed Driope
Hath oftentimes commanded me
With my clasped knee to climb.
See how well the lusty time
Hath deck'd their rising cheeks in red,
Such as on your lips is spread.
Here be berries for a queen,
Some be red, some be green;
These are of that luscious meat
The great god Pan himself doth eat:
All these, and what the woods can yield,
The hanging mountain or the field,
I freely offer, and ere long
Will bring you more, more sweet and strong
Till then, humbly leave I take,
Lest the great Pan do awake,
That sleeping lies in a deep glade,
Under a broad beech's shade.
I must go, I must run,
Swifter than the fiery sun. [*Exit.*]

Clor. And all my fears go with thee.
What greatness, or what private hidden power,
Is there in me to draw submission
From this rude man and beast?—Sure I am a mortal;
The daughter of a shepherd; he was mortal,
And she that bore me, mortal; prick my hand
And it will bleed; a fever shakes me, and
The self-same mind that makes the young lambs shrink,
Makes me a-cold: my fear says I am mortal:
Yet I have heard (my mother told it me),
And now I do believe it, if I keep
My virgin flower uncropt, pure, chaste, and fair,
No goblin, wood-god, fairy, elf, or fiend,
Satyr, or other power that haunts the groves,
Shall hurt my body, or by vain illusion

Draw me to wander after idle fires,
Or voices calling me in dead of night
To make me follow, and so tole me on
Through mire and standing pools, to find my ruin.
Else why should this rough thing, who never knew
Manners nor smooth humanity, whose heats
Are rougher than himself, and more misshapen,
Thus mildly kneel to me? Sure there's a power
In that great name of Virgin, that binds fast
All rude uncivil bloods, all appetites
That break their confines. Then, strong chastity,
Be thou my strongest guard; for here I'll dwell
In opposition against fate and hell.

[*Faithful Shepherdess.*]

The lyrical pieces scattered throughout the plays of Beaumont and Fletcher, though not generally equal, are still of much the same character as those with which Jonson's dramas abound. Of these we subjoin the following:—

MELANCHOLY.

Hence, all you vain delights,
As short as are the nights
    Wherein you spend your folly!
There's nought in this life sweet,
If man were wise to see't
    But only melancholy!

Welcome folded arms, and fixed eyes,
A sigh that piercing mortifies,
A look that's fasten'd to the ground,
A tongue chain'd up without a sound!

Fountain heads, and pathless groves,
Places which pale passion loves!
Moonlight walks, when all the fowls
Are warmly hous'd, save bats and owls!
A midnight bell, a parting groan!
These are the sounds we feed upon;
Then stretch our bones in a still gloomy valley:
Nothing's so dainty-sweet as lovely melancholy.

[*Nice Valour.*]

SONG.

Look out, bright eyes, and bless the air!
Even in shadows you are fair.
Shut-up beauty is like fire,
That breaks out clearer still and higher.
Though your beauty be confin'd,
  And soft Love a prisoner bound,
Yet the beauty of your mind
  Neither check nor chain hath found.
Look out nobly, then, and dare
  Ev'n the fetters that you wear!

[*False One.*]

THE POWER OF LOVE.

Hear ye, ladies that despise
  What the mighty Love has done;
Fear examples and be wise:
  Fair Calisto was a nun:
Leda, sailing on the stream,
  To deceive the hopes of man
Love accounted but a dream,
  Doted on a silver swan;
Danae in a brazen tower,
Where no love was, lov'd a shower.

Hear ye, ladies that are coy,
  What the mighty Love can do,
Fear the fierceness of the boy;
  The chaste moon he makes to woo.
Vesta, kindling holy fires
  Circled round about with spies
Never dreaming loose desires,
  Doting at the altar dies;
Ilion in a short hour higher,
He can build, and once more fire.

[*Valentinian.*]

✝ TO PAN, AT THE CONCLUSION OF THE FAITHFUL SHEPHERDESS.

All ye woods, and trees, and bow'rs
All ye virtues and ye pow'rs,
That inhabit in the lakes,
In the pleasant springs or brakes,
    Move your feet
      To our sound,
    Whilst we greet
      All this ground,
With his honour and his name
That defends our flocks from blame.

He is great and he is just,
He is ever good, and must
Thus be honour'd. Daffodilies,
Roses, pinks, and loved lilies,
    Let us fling,
    Whilst we sing
    Ever holy,
    Ever holy,
Ever honour'd, ever young!
Thus great Pan is ever sung.

Lecture the Fifteenth.

GEORGE CHAPMAN—THOMAS DEKKER—JOHN WEBSTER—THOMAS MIDDLETON—JOHN MARSTON—PHILIP MASSINGER—ROBERT TAYLOR—WILLIAM ROWLEY—CYRIL TOURNEUR—GEORGE COOKE—THOMAS NABBES—NATHANIEL FIELD—JOHN DAY—HENRY GLAPTHORNE—THOMAS RANDOLPH—RICHARD BROME—JOHN FORD—THOMAS HEYWOOD—JAMES SHIRLEY.

THE great dramatists with whom we have been engaged during the last two lectures, have absorbed so much of our time and attention, that we shall be constrained to notice much more briefly those of their contemporaries who are still to pass in review before us. Of these, Chapman, Dekker, Webster, Middleton, Marston, and Massinger, first claim our attention.

GEORGE CHAPMAN was born at Hitching Hill, Hertfordshire, in 1557. He commenced his collegiate studies at Oxford, and finished them at Cambridge; but in consequence of devoting himself at both universities to the Latin and Greek classics, to the exclusion of philosophy and logic, he did not succeed in obtaining his degree at either. From Cambridge he repaired to London, when the gracefulness of his manners and the elegance of his taste soon recommended him to the acquaintance, and even intimacy, of Spenser, Sir Philip Sydney, and other leading wits of the age. Chapman commenced his literary career with a translation of the Iliad of Homer. This, with all its faults, is a production of great value and interest. It is written in the cumbrous and unwieldy old English measure of fourteen syllables; but notwithstanding this heavy drawback, such passages as the following description from the thirteenth book, of Neptune and his chariot, exhibit, with great clearness, the force and energy of the translation:—

He took much ruth to see the Greeks from Troy receive such ill,
And mightily incens'd with Jove, stoop'd straight from that steep hill;
That shook as he flew off, so hard his parting press'd the height,
The woods and all the great hills near, trembled beneath the weight
Of his immortal moving feet: three steps he only took,
Before he far off Ægas reach'd; but with the fourth it shook

With his dread entry. In the depth of those seas he did hold
His bright and glorious palace, built of never-rusting gold;
And there arrived, he put in coach his brazen-footed steeds,
All golden-maned, and paced with wings, and all in golden weeds
He clothed himself; the golden scourge, most elegantly done,
He took, and mounted to his seat, and then the God begun
To drive his chariot through the waves. From whirlpits every way
The whales exulted under him, and knew their king; the sea
For joy did open, and his horse so light and swiftly flew,
The under axle-tree of brass no drop of water drew.

The beauty of Chapman's compound Homeric epithets, such as silver-footed Thetis, triple-feathered helm, the fair-haired boy, high-walled Thebes, and the strong-winged lance, bear the impress of a poetical imagination, chaste yet luxuriant.

Chapman's first play, *The Blind Beggar of Alexandria*, was produced in 1598; but as a dramatist, he did not realize the expectations which his translations had excited. He continued to furnish, for the stage, frequent tragedies and comedies for over twenty years, yet of the sixteen that have descended to us, all are heavy and cumbrous, and not one possesses the creative and vivifying power of dramatic genius. In didactic observation and description, he is sometimes happy, and hence he has been praised for possessing 'more thinking' than most of his contemporaries of the dramatic muse. His judgment, however, vanishes in action; for his plots are unnatural, and his style is too hard and artificial to admit of any nice delineation of character. The best of his plays are *Bussy D'Ambois*, *Byron's Conspiracy*, *All Fools*, and *The Gentleman Usher*. Chapman's dramas do not contain many striking passages, but the following invocation for a Spirit of Intelligence, in 'Bussy D'Ambois,' is worthy of very high praise:—

——— I long to know
How my dear mistress fares, and be inform'd
What hand she now holds on the troubled blood
Of her incensed lord. Methought the spirit,
When he had utter'd his perplex'd presage,
Threw his chang'd count'nance headlong into clouds:
His forehead bent, as he would hide his face:
He knock'd his chin against his darken'd breast,
And struck a churlish silence through his powers.
Terror of darkness! O thou king of flames!
That with the music-footed horse dost strike
The clear light out of crystal on dark earth;
And hurl'st instinctive fire about the world;
Wake, wake the drowsy and enchanted night
That sleeps with dead eyes in this heavy riddle.
Or thou, great prince of shades, where never sun
Sticks his far-darted beams; whose eyes are made
To see in darkness, and see ever best
When sense is blindest: open now the heart
Of thy abashed oracle, that, for fear

Of some ill it includes, would fain lie hid:
And rise thou with it in thy greater light.

In addition to his translation of the Iliad, already noticed, Chapman produced a version of Homer's 'Odyssey,' and one of 'The Works and Days' of Hesiod. He also completed a translation of 'Hero and Leander,' which had been begun by Marlow. His life is represented to have been one continuous scene of content and prosperity, thus contrasting remarkably with the lives of the great majority of his dramatic contemporaries. In his personal habits he was temperate and pious, and, according to Oldys, 'preserved in his conduct the true dignity of poetry, which he compared to the flower of the sun, that disdains to open its leaves to the eye of a smoking taper.' The life of this venerable scholar and poet closed in 1634, at the advanced age of seventy-seven years.

Thomas Dekker was, perhaps, a few years younger than Chapman, though he commenced his dramatic career at about the same time. Neither the period nor the place of his birth is now known, nor have we any record of his family or of his early studies. He was evidently, however, a good scholar, and was a very industrious writer, having himself produced, according to Collier, more than twenty entire dramas, besides a number conjointly with other dramatists. He was, for some time, connected with Ben Jonson in writing for the Admiral's theatre; but Jonson and he became, eventually, bitter enemies, and the former, in his 'Poetaster,' satirized Dekker under the character of Crispinus, representing himself as Horace. Jonson's charges against his adversary are, 'his arrogancy and impudence in commending his own things, and for his translating.' To these charges Dekker replied in his *Satiromastix, or the Untrussing the Humorous Poet*, in which Jonson appears as Horace junior. There is more raillery and abuse in Dekker's answer than wit or poetry, but it was well received by the play-going public. Dekker's *Fortunatus, or the Wishing Cap*, unites the simplicity of prose with the graces of poetry, and is, perhaps, his best drama. His poetic diction is choice and elegant, but he often wanders into absurdity. Passages like the following are frequent in his plays, and would do honor to any dramatist:—

PATIENCE.

Patience! why, 'tis the soul of peace:
Of all the virtues, 'tis nearest kin to heaven:
It makes men look like gods. The best of men
That e'er wore earth about him was a sufferer,
A soft, meek, patient, humble, tranquil spirit:
The first true gentleman that ever breath'd.

FEMALE HONOUR AND SHAME CONTRASTED.

Nothing did make me, when I loved them best
To loathe them more than this: when in the street
A fair, young modest damsel I did meet;

She seem'd to all a dove when I pass'd by,
And I to all a raven: every eye
That follow'd her, went with a bashful glance:
At me each bold and jeering countenance
Darted forth scorn: to her, as if she had been
Some tower unvanquish'd, would they all vail:
'Gainst me swoln rumour hoisted every sail;
She, crown'd with reverend praises, pass'd by them;
I, though with face mask'd, could not 'scape the hem:
For, as if heaven had set strange marks on such,
Because they should be pointing-stocks to man,
Drest up in civilest shape, a courtesan.
Let her walk saint-like, noteless, and unknown,
Yet she's betray'd by some trick of her own.

THE PICTURE OF A LADY SEEN BY HER LOVER.

My Infelice's face, her brow, her eye,
The dimple on her cheek: and such sweet skill
Hath from the cunning workman's pencil flown,
These lips look fresh and lively as her own;
Seeming to move and speak. Alas! now I see
The reason why fond women love to buy
Adulterate complexion: here 'tis read;
False colours last after the true be dead.
Of all the roses grafted on her cheeks,
Of all the graces dancing in her eyes,
Of all the music set upon her tongue,
Of all that was past woman's excellence,
In her white bosom; look, a painted board
Circumscribes all! Earth can no bliss afford;
Nothing of her but this! This can not speak;
It has no lap for me to rest upon;
No lip worth tasting. Here the worms will feed,
As in her coffin. Hence, then, idle art,
True love's best pictur'd on a true love's heart.
Here art thou drawn, sweet maid, till this be dead.
So that thou livest twice, twice art buried.
Thou figure of my friend, lie there.

Dekker's life was passed in irregularity and poverty, presenting thus, a striking contrast with that of Chapman. He was, according to Oldys, three years in King's Bench prison; thus reminding us of one of his own beautiful lines:—

We ne'er are angels till our passions die.

He died in want and despair, at an advanced age, in 1638.

JOHN WEBSTER was another of that race of remarkable contemporary dramatists about whose early life scarcely any thing is known. The date of his birth is supposed to have corresponded very nearly with that of Dekker, and it is certain that they both died in the same year. Webster, it has been said, was at one time clerk of St. Andrew's church, Holborn; but Dyce, the editor of his works, searched the register of the parish for his name without success. He commenced his dramatic course of writing conjointly with Dekker—a practice at that time, as we have already had occasion to notice, very common. The dramas which he produced unaided, are, *The Duchess of Malfy*, *Guise, or the Massacre of France*, *The Devil's Law-Case*, *Appius and Virginia*, and *The White Devil, or Vittoria Corombona.*

'The White Devil,' and 'The Duchess of Malfy' have divided the opinion of critics as to their relative merits. They are both powerful dramas, though filled with 'supernumerary horrors.' The former was not successful on the stage, which so incensed the 'noble-minded' author, that in a dedication which accompanied its publication, he introduces the following sarcastic remark:—'Most of the people that come to the play-house resemble those ignorant asses who, visiting stationers' shops, their use is not to inquire for good books, but new books.' Webster was accused of being a slow writer, but he consoled himself with the example of Euripides, and confessed that he did not write with a goose quill winged with two feathers. In this slighted drama there are some exquisite touches of pathos and natural feeling. The grief of a group of mourners over a dead body is thus beautifully described:—

I found them winding of Marcello's corse,
And there is such a solemn melody,
'Tween doleful songs, tears, and sad elegies,
Such as old grandames watching by the dead
Were wont to outwear the nights with; that believe me,
I had no eyes to guide me forth the room,
They were so o'ercharged with water.

The funeral dirge also, for Marcello, sung by his mother, possesses that intenseness of feeling which seems to resolve itself into the elements which it contemplates:—

Call for the robin red-breast, and the wren,
Since o'er shady groves they hover,
And with leaves and flowers do cover
The friendless bodies of unburied men.
Call unto his funeral dole,
The ant, the field-mouse, and the mole,
To raise him hillocks that shall keep him warm,
And, when gray tombs are robb'd, sustain no harm;
But keep the wolf far thence, that's foe to men,
For with his nails he'll dig them up again.

'The Duchess of Malfy' abounds more in the terrible than 'The White Devil.' It turns on the mortal offence which the lady gives to her two proud brothers, Ferdinand, Duke of Calabria, and a cardinal, by indulging in a generous, though infatuated passion, for Antonio, her steward. This passion, a subject always most difficult to treat, is managed in this case with infinite delicacy; and, in a situation of great peril for the author, she condescends, without being degraded, and declares the affection with which her dependant has inspired her, without losing any thing of dignity and respect. The last scene of this play is conceived in a spirit which every attentive student of early English dramatic literature must feel to be peculiar to Webster. By an act of the most refined cruelty Ferdinand, the duke, sends a troop of madmen from the hospital to make a concert round the duchess, who has been seized and cast into prison. This troop is led by Bosola, one of the duke's officers, who, after the lunatics have ended their dancing and singing, enters the prison, and with the following terrific scene the drama closes:—

DEATH OF THE DUCHESS.

Duch. Is he mad too?

Bos. I am come to make thy tomb.

Duch. Ha! my tomb?
Thou speak'st as if I lay upon my death-bed,
Gasping for breath: Dost thou perceive me sick?

Bos. Yes, and the more dangerously, since thy sickness is insensible.

Duch. Thou art not mad sure: dost know me?

Bos. Yes.

Duch. Who am I?

Bos. Thou art a box of wormseed; at best but a salvatory of green mummy. What's this flesh? a little crudded milk, fantastical puff-paste. Our bodies are weaker than those paper-prisons boys use to keep flies in, more contemptible; since ours is to preserve earth-worms. Didst thou ever see a lark in a cage? Such is the soul in the body; this world is like her little turf of grass; and the heavens o'er our heads like her looking-glass, only gives us a miserable knowledge of the small compass of our prison.

Duch. Am not I thy duchess?

Bos. Thou art some great woman, sure, for riot begins to sit on thy forehead (clad in gray hairs) twenty years sooner than on a merry milkmaid's. Thou sleepest worse, than if a mouse should be forced to take up her lodging in a cat's ear: a little infant that breeds its teeth, should it lie with thee, would cry out, as if thou wert the more unquiet bedfellow.

Duch. I am Duchess of Malfy still.

Bos. That makes thy sleeps so broken.
Glories, like glow-worms, afar off shine bright;
But, look'd to near, have neither heat nor light.

Duch. Thou art very plain.

Bos. My trade is to flatter the dead, not the living.
I am a tomb-maker.

Duch. And thou comest to make my tomb?

Bos. Yes.

Duch. Let me be a little merry.
Of what stuff wilt thou make it?

Bos. Nay, resolve me first; of what fashion?

Duch. Why, do we grow fantastical in our death-bed?
Do we affect fashion in the grave?

Bos. Most ambitiously. Princes' images on their tombs do not lie as they were wont, seeming to pray up to heaven: but with their hands under their cheeks (as if they died of the toothache): they are not carved with their eyes fixed upon the stars; but, as their minds were wholly bent upon the world, the self-same way they seem to turn their faces.

Duch. Let me know fully, therefore, the effect
Of this thy dismal preparation,
This talk, fit for a charnel.

Bos. Now I shall.

[*A coffin, cords, and a bell produced.*]

Here is a present from your princely brothers;
And may it arrive welcome, for it brings
Last benefit, last sorrow.

Duch. Let me see it.
I have so much obedience in my blood,
I wish it in their veins to do them good.

Bos. This is your last presence chamber

Car. O, my sweet lady.

Duch. Peace, it affrights not me.

Bos. I am the common bellman,
That usually is sent to condemn'd persons
The night before they suffer.

Duch. Even now thou said'st
Thou wast a tomb-maker.

Bos. 'Twas to bring you
By degrees to mortification; Listen.

DIRGE.

Hark, now every thing is still;
This screech-owl, and the whistle shrill,
Call upon our dame aloud,
And bid her quickly don her shroud.
Much you had of land and rent;
Your length in clay 's now competent.
A long war disturb'd your mind;
Here your perfect peace is sign'd.
Of what is 't fools make such vain keeping?
Sin, their conception; their birth, weeping:
Their life, a general mist of error,
Their death, a hideous storm of terror.
Strew your hair with powders sweet,
Don clean linen, bathe your feet:
And, (the foul fiend more to check,)
A crucifix let bless your neck.
'Tis now full tide 'tween night and day:
End your groan, and come away.

Car. Hence, villains, tyrants, murderers; alas!
What will you do with my lady? Call for help.

Duch. To whom? to our next neighbours? They are mad folks.
Farewell, Cariola,
I pray thee look thou giv'st my little boy
Some syrup for his cold; and let the girl
Say her prayers ere she sleep.—Now what you please;
What death?

Bos. Strangling. Here are your executioners.

Duch. I forgive them.

The apoplexy, catarrh, or cough o' the lungs,
Would do as much as they do.
Bos. Doth not death fright you?
Duch. Who would be afraid on 't,
Knowing to meet such excellent company
In th' other world
Bos. Yet methinks,
The manner of your death should much afflict you:
This cord should terrify you.
Duch. Not a whit.
What would it pleasure me to have my throat cut
With diamonds, or to be smother'd
With cassia? or to be shot to death with pearls?
I know death hath ten thousand several doors
For men to take their exits: and 'tis found
They go on such strange geometrical hinges,
You may open them both ways: any way (for heav'n sake).
So I were out of your whispering: tell my brothers
That I perceive death (now I'm well awake)
Best gift is they can give or I can take.
I would fain put off my last woman's fault;
I'd not be tedious to you.
Pull, and pull strongly, for your able strength
Must pull down heaven upon me.
Yet stay, heaven gates are not so highly arch'd
As princes' palaces: they that enter there
Must go upon their knees. Come, violent death,
Serve for Mandragora to make me sleep.
Go tell my brothers, when I am laid out,
They then may feed in quiet. [*They strangle her, kneeling.*]

[*Ferdinand enters.*]

Ferd. Is she dead?
Bos. She is what you would have her.
Fix your eyes here.
Ferd. Constantly.
Bos. Do you not weep?
Other sins only speak; murder shrieks out,
The element of water moistens the earth,
But blood flies upwards, and bedews the heavens.
Ferd. Cover her face: mine eyes dazzle: she died young.
Bos. I think not so: her infelicity
Seem'd to have years too many.
Ferd. She and I were twins:
And should I die this instant, I had lived
Her time to a minute.

THOMAS MIDDLETON, born about 1560, was, himself, the author of more than twenty plays, and was also frequently engaged with others in the production of dramas and court-pageants. In 1620, he stood so high in public favor, that he was made chronologer, or city poet, of London—an office which Ben Jonson was proud, afterward, to fill. Middleton died in July, 1627, at the age of about sixty-eight.

The dramas of Middleton have no strongly-marked character. Perhaps his best are *Woman Beware of Women*, *The Witch*, and *A Game of Chess*, The following sketch of married happiness, from the first of these plays, is delicate, and finely expressed :—

HAPPINESS OF MARRIED LIFE.

How near am I now to a happiness
That earth exceeds not! not another like it:
The treasures of the deep are not so precious,
As are the conceal'd comforts of a man
Lock'd up in woman's love. I scent the air
Of blessings when I come but near the house.
What a delicious breath marriage sends forth!
The violet bed 's not sweeter. Honest wedlock
Is like a banqueting house built in a garden,
On which the spring's chaste flowers take delight
To cast their modest odours; when base lust,
With all her powders, paintings, and best pride,
Is but a fair house built by a ditch side.
——— Now for a welcome,
Able to draw men's envies upon man;
A kiss now that will hang upon my lip
As sweet as morning dew upon a rose,
And full as long!

'The Witch' of this author is supposed, by many critics, to have supplied the witchcraft scenery, and part of the lyrical incantations of Shakspeare's Macbeth; but the supernatural agents of Middleton are the old witches of legendary story, and not the dim mysterious unearthly beings that accost Macbeth on the blasted heath. The Charm Song is much the same in both plays :—

[*The witches going about the Cauldron.*]

Black spirits and white; red spirits and gray;
Mingle, mingle, mingle, you that mingle may.
Titty, Tiffin, keep it stiff in;
Firedrake, Puckey, make it lucky;
Liard, Robin, you must bob in;
Round, around, around, about, about;
All ill come running in; all good keep out!
First Witch. Here 's the blood of a bat.
Hecate. Put in that; oh put in that.
Sec. Witch. Here 's libbard's bane.
Hecate. Put in again.
First Witch. The juice of toad, the oil of adder.
Sec. Witch. Those will make the younker madder.
All. Round, around, around, &c.

The flight of the witches by moonlight is described with a wild *gusto* and delight, that confer, upon the dramatist, the credit of true poetical imagination. We very much doubt whether the following scene is greatly surpassed by even Shakspeare :—

[*Enter Hecate, Stadlin, Hoppo, and other Witches.*]

Hec. The moon 's a gallant; see how brisk she rides!
Stad. Here 's a rich evening, Hecate.
Hec. Ay, is 't not, wenches,
To take a journey of five thousand miles?
Hop. Ours will be more to-night.
Hec. Oh, it will be precious. Heard you the owl yet?
Stad. Briefly in the copse
As we came through now.
Hec. 'Tis high time for us then.
Stad. There was a bat hung at my lips three times
As we came thro' the woods, and drank her fill:
Old Puckle saw her.
Hec. You are fortunate still.
The very screech-owl lights upon your shoulder,
And woos you like a pigeon. Are you furnished?
Have you your ointments?
Stad. All.
Hec. Prepare to flight then:
I'll overtake you swiftly.
Stad. Hie, then, Hecate:
We shall be up betimes.
Hec. I'll reach you quickly. [*They ascend.*]

[*Enter Firestone.*]

Fire. They are all going a-birding to-night. They talk of fowls i' th' air that fly by day; I'm sure they'll be a company of foul sluts there to-night. If we have not mortality affear'd, I'll be hang'd, for they are able to putrify it to infect a whole region. She spies me now.

Hec. What! Firestone, our sweet son?

Fire. A little sweeter than some of you; or a dunghill were too good for one.

Hec. How much hast there?

Fire. Nineteen, and all brave plump ones; besides six lizards, and three serpentine eggs.

Hec. Dear and sweet boy! What herbs hast thou?

Fire. I have some mar-martin and mandragon.

Hec. Mar-maritin and mandragora thou would'st say.

Fire. Here's pannax too. I thank thee; my pan akes I am sure, with kneeling down to cut 'em.

Hec. And selago.
Hedge Hissop too! How near he goes my cuttings!
Were they all cropt by moonlight?

Fire. Every blade of 'em, or I'm a mooncalf, mother.

Hec. Hie thee home with 'em.
Look well to th' house to-night; I am for aloft.

Fire. Aloft, quoth you? I would you would break your neck once, that I might have all quickly. [*Aside.*] Hark, hark, mother! they are above the steeple already, flying over your head with a noise of musicians.

Hec. They are, indeed; help me! help me! I'm too late else.

SONG.

[*In the air above.*]

Come away, come away,
Hecate, Hecate, come away,

Hec. I come, I come, I come, I come;
With all the speed I may;
With all the speed I may.
Where's Stadlin?
Above. Here.
Hec. Where's Puckle?
Above. Here.
And Hoppo too, and Hellwain too:
We lack but you, we lack but you.
Come away, make up the count.
Hec. I will but 'noint, and then I mount.
[*A Spirit descends in the shape of a cat.*]
Above. There's one come down to fetch his dues;
A kiss, a coll, a sip of blood;
And why thou stay'st so long, I muse, I muse,
Since th' air's so sweet and good.
Hec. Oh, art thou come;
What news, what news?
Spirit. All goes still to our delight.
Either come, or else
Refuse, refuse.
Hec. Now I am furnished for the flight.
Fire. Hark, hark! The cat sings a brave treble
In her own language.
Hec. [*Ascending with the Spirit.*] Now I go, now I fly.
Malkin, my sweet spirit, and I.
Oh, what dainty pleasure 'tis
To ride in the air,
When the moon shines fair,
And sing and dance, and toy and kiss!
Over woods, high rocks, and mountains,
Over seas, our mistress' fountains,
Over steep towers and turrets,
We fly by night, 'mongst troops of spirits.
No ring of bells to our ears sounds;
No howl of wolves, no yelp of hounds;
No, not the noise of waters' breach,
Or cannon's roar our height can reach.
Above. No ring of bells, &c.

John Marston was a rough and vigorous satirist, as well as a dramatic writer. He was, for some time, a student in Corpus Christi College, Oxford, but where he was born, or of what family descended, is not known. His principal dramas are *The Malcontent*, a comedy performed in 1600, *Antonio and Mellida*, a tragedy, in 1602, *The Insatiate Countess*, and *What You Will*. Besides these dramas, Marston wrote, in connection with Jonson and Chapman, the unfortunate comedy of 'Eastward Hoe.' He was the author of a volume of satires also, under the title of *The Scourge of the Villainy*. His death occurred in 1614, and the last literary labor of the great Shakspeare is represented to have been the editing of his plays.

Hazlitt remarks that 'Marston's forte was not sympathy either with the stronger or softer emotions, but an impatient scorn and bitter indignation against the vices and follies of men, which vented itself either in comic irony, or lofty invectives.' The following humorous sketch of a scholar and his dog, is worthy of any poet, however exalted his genius or reputation :—

I was a scholar; seven useful springs
Did I deflower in quotations
Of cross'd opinions 'bout the soul of man:
The more I learnt, the more I learnt to doubt.
Delight, my spaniel, slept, whilst I baus'd leaves,
Toss'd o'er the dunces, pored on the old print
Of titled words: and still my spaniel slept.
While I wasted lamp-oil, baited my flesh,
Shrunk up my veins: and still my spaniel slept.
And still I held converse with Zabarell,
Aquinas, Scotus, the musty saw
Of Antick Donate: still my spaniel slept.
Still on went I; first, *an sit anima;*
Then, an it were mortal. O hold, hold; at that
They're at brain buffets, fell by the ears amain
Pell-mell together; still my spaniel slept.
Then, whether 'twere corporeal, local, fixt,
Ex traduce, but whether 't had free will
Or no, hot philosophers
Stood banding factions, all so strongly propt;
I stagger'd, knew not which was firmer part,
But thought, quoted, read, observ'd, and pried,
Stufft noting-books: and still my spaniel slept.
At length he wak'd, and yawn'd; and by yon sky,
For ought I know, he knew as much as I.

PHILIP MASSINGER was born at Salisbury, in 1584. His father, as appears from the dedication of one of his plays, was in the service of the Earl of Pembroke; and as he was, on one occasion, intrusted with letters to Queen Elizabeth, his situation must have been a confidential one. In 1601, Massinger entered St. Alban's Hall, Oxford; but during the four years which he passed at the university, he applied his mind exclusively to romances and poetry, and, consequently, at the expiration of that time, left without his degree. On quitting Oxford, he repaired to London, there to improve his poetic fancy by intercourse with the men and manners of the metropolis. He soon after began to write for the stage, but for a number of years he had to struggle with poverty, and its usual attendant, distress. In 1614, he made a joint application with Field and Daborne, two brother dramatists, to the manager, Henslowe, for the loan of five pounds, stating that without it *they could not be bailed.* The sequel of Massinger's history is only an enumeration of his plays. He wrote a great many dramas, of which eighteen have been preserved, and his death was sudden and unexpected. On the evening of the eighteenth of March, 1639, he retired to rest in his own house at Bankside, Southwark, in his usual health, and the next morning was found dead in his bed. He was interred at St. Mary Overy's Church, Southwark, in the same grave which had previously received the remains of Fletcher:

and upon the stone that indicated their last resting place, Sir Aston Cockaine incribed the following quaint epitaph :—

In the same grave Fletcher was buried, here
Lies the stage-poet, Philip Massinger.
Plays they did write together, were great friends,
And now one grave includes them at their ends.
So whom on earth nothing did part, beneath
Here in their fames they lie, in spite of death.

Massinger wrote a number of dramas conjointly with Fletcher, Middleton, Rowley, Field, Dekker, and others; and such was his popularity that most of his contemporaries esteemed it an honor to be thus connected with him. Of the dramas exclusively his own, *The Virgin Martyr*, *The Bondman*, *The Fatal Dowry*, *The City Madam*, and *A New Way to Pay Old Debts*, are his best known productions. Massinger's comedy resembles, in its eccentric strength and wayward exhibitions of human nature, that of Ben Jonson. The greediness of avarice, the tyranny of unjust laws, and the miseries of poverty, are drawn with a powerful hand. The luxuries and vices of a city life, also, afforded scope for his indignant and forcible invective. The tragedies of Massinger have a calm and dignified seriousness, and a lofty pride, that impresses the imagination very powerfully. His genius was more eloquent and descriptive than impassioned and inventive; yet his pictures of suffering virtue, its struggles and its trials, are calculated to touch the heart, as well as gratify the taste. The versification is so smooth and mellifluous, as to be second only to that of Shakspeare.

Massinger's dramas afford fine scope for extracts, but our space will allow us to introduce only the following :—

A MIDNIGHT SCENE.

[*Angelo, an Angel, attends Dorothea as a Page.*]

Dor. My book and taper.
Ang. Here, most holy mistress.
Dor. Thy voice sends forth such music, that I never
Was ravish'd with a more celestial sound.
Were every servant in the world like thee,
So full of goodness, angels would come down
To dwell with us: thy name is Angelo,
And like that name thou art. Get thee to rest;
Thy youth with too much watching is opprest.
Ang. No, my dear lady. I could weary stars,
And force the wakeful moon to lose her eyes,
By my late watching, but to wait on you.
When at your prayers you kneel before the altar,
Methinks I'm singing with some quire in heaven,
So blest I hold me in your company.
Therefore my most lov'd mistress, do not bid
Your boy, so serviceable, to get hence;
For then you break his heart.
Dor. Be nigh me still, then.

In golden letters down I'll set that day
Which gave thee to me. Little did I hope
To meet such worlds of comfort in thyself,
This little, pretty body, when I, coming
Forth of the temple, heard my beggar-boy,
My sweet-faced, godly beggar-boy, crave an alms,
Which with glad hand I gave, with lucky hand;
And when I took thee home, my most chaste bosom
Methought, was filled with no hot wanton fire,
But with a holy flame, mounting since higher,
On wings of cherubims, than it did before.
Ang. Proud am I that my lady's modest eye
So likes so poor a servant.
Dor. I have offer'd
Handfuls of gold but to behold thy parents.
I would leave kingdoms, were I queen of some,
To dwell with thy good father; for, the son
Bewitching me so deeply with his presence,
He that begat him must do 't ten times more.
I pray thee, my sweet boy, show me thy parents;
Be not asham'd.
Ang. I am not: I did never
Know who my mother was; but, by yon palace,
Fill'd with bright heav'nly courtiers, I dare assure you,
And pawn these eyes upon it, and this hand,
My father is in heav'n: and, pretty mistress,
If your illustrious hour-glass spend his sand
No worse, than yet it doth, upon my life,
You and I both shall meet my father there,
And he shall bid you welcome.
Dor. A bless'd day.

[*Virgin Martyr.*]

COMPASSION FOR MISFORTUNE.

Luke. No word, sir,
I hope shall give offence; nor let it relish
Of flattery, though I proclaim aloud,
I glory in the bravery of your mind,
To which your wealth 's a servant. Not that riches
Is, or should be, contemn'd, it being a blessing
Deriv'd from heaven, and by your industry
Pull'd down upon you; but in this, dear sir,
You have many equal: such a man's possessions
Extend as far as yours: a second hath
His bags as full; a third in credit flies
As high in the popular voice: but the distinction
And noble difference by which you are
Divided from them, is, that you are styled
Gentle in your abundance, good in plenty;
And that you feel compassion in your bowels
Of others' miseries (I have found it, sir;
Heaven keep me thankful for 'it!), while they are curs'd
As rigid and inexorable * *
Your affability and mildness, clothed

In the garments of your thankful debtors' breath,
Shall everywhere, though you strive to conceal it,
Be seen, and wonder'd at, and in the act
With a prodigal hand rewarded. Whereas, such
As are born only for themselves, and live so,
Though prosperous in worldly understandings,
Are but like beasts of rapine, that, by odds
Of strength, usurp and tyrannize o'er others
Brought under their subjection. * *
Can you think, sir,
In your unquestion'd wisdom, I beseech you,
The goods of this poor man sold at an outcry,
His wife turn'd out of doors, his children forc'd
To beg their bread; this gentleman's estate
By wrong extorted, can advantage you?
Or that the ruin of this once brave merchant,
For such he was esteem'd, though now decay'd,
Will raise your reputation with good men?
But you may urge (pray you, pardon me, my zeal
Makes me thus bold and vehement), in this
You satisfy your anger, and revenge
For being defeated. Suppose this, it will not
Repair your loss, and there was never yet
But shame and scandal in a victory,
When the rebels unto reason, passions, fought it.
Then for revenge, by great souls it was ever
Contemn'd though offer'd; entertain'd by none
But cowards, base and abject spirits, strangers
To moral honesty, and never yet
Acquainted with religion. * *
Sir John. Shall I be
Talk'd out of my money?
Luke. No sir, but intreated
To do yourself a benefit, and preserve
What you possess entire.
Sir John. How, my good brother?
Luke. By making these your beadsmen. When they eat,
Their thanks, next heaven, will be paid to your mercy;
When your ships are at sea, their prayers will swell
The sails with prosperous winds, and guard them from
Tempests and pirates; keep your warehouses
From fire, or quench them with their tears.

[*City Madam.*]

Before we pass on to the writers who close this important dramatic period we must very briefly notice their less eminent contemporaries, Taylor, Rowley, Tourneur, Cooke, Nabbes, Field, Day, Glapthorne, Randolph and Brome.

The public demand for theatrical novelties, called forth, at this time, a succession of writers in this popular, and profitable department of literature, who, though not men of the most exalted genius, still left the rich stamp of the age, both in style and thought, upon many of their pages. Of the personal history of these writers little is known, a few scattered dates usually making up the whole amount of their biography.

Of ROBERT TAYLOR, the author here first mentioned, nothing farther is known than that he wrote an amusing drama under the quaint title, *The Hog hath Lost his Pearl*, and some other pieces of a similar character.

WILLIAM ROWLEY was an actor as well as author. Besides other plays written conjointly with Middleton and Dekker, he produced a tragi-comedy, *The Witch of Edmonton*, in the composition of which Ford also is suspected of having taken a part. His drama embodies, in a striking form, the vulgar superstition respecting witchcraft, which so long debased the popular mind in England. We quote the following passage:—

[*Mother Sawyer alone.*]

Saw. And why on me? why should the envious world
Throw all their scandalous malice upon me?
'Cause I am poor, deform'd, and ignorant,
And like a bow buckled and bent together
By some more strong in mischiefs than myself;
Must I for that be made a common sink
For all the filth and rubbish of men's tongues
To fall and run into? Some call me witch,
And being ignorant of myself, they go
About to teach me how to be one: urging
That my bad tongue (by their bad usage made so)
Forespeaks their cattle, doth bewitch their corn,
Themselves, their servants, and their babes at nurse:
This they enforce upon me; and in part
Make me to credit it.

[*Banks, a Farmer, enters.*]

Banks. Out, out upon thee, witch!
Saw. Dost call me witch?
Banks. I do, witch; I do;
And worse I would, knew I a name more hateful.
What makest thou upon my grounds?
Saw. Gather a few rotten sticks to warm me.
Banks. Down with them when I bid thee, quickly;
I'll make thy bones rattle in thy skin else.
Saw. You won't! churl, cut-throat, miser! there they be. Would they stuck 'cross thy throat, thy bowels, thy maw, thy midriff—
Banks. Say'st thou me so. Hag, out of my ground.
Saw. Dost strike me, slave, curmudgeon? Now thy bones aches, thy joints cramps,
And convulsions stretch and crack thy sinews.
Banks. Cursing, thou hag? take that, and that. [*Exit.*]
Saw. Strike, do: and wither'd may that hand and arm,
Whose blows have lam'd me, drop from the rotten trunk.
Abuse me! beat me! call me hag and witch!
What is the name? where, and by what art learn'd?

What spells, or charms, or invocations,
May the thing call'd Familiar be purchased?
——— I am shunn'd
And hated like a sickness; made a scorn
To all degrees and sexes. I have heard old beldams
Talk of familiars in the shape of mice,
Rats, ferrets, weasels, and I wot not what,
That have appear'd; and suck'd, some say, their blood.
But by what means they came acquainted with them,
I'm now ignorant. Would some powers, good or bad,
Instruct me which way I might be reveng'd
Upon this churl. I'd go out of myself,
And give this fury leave to dwell within
This ruin'd cottage, ready to fall with age:
Abjure all goodness, be at hate with prayer,
And study curses, imprecations,
Blasphemous speeches, oaths, detested oaths,
Or any thing that's ill; so I might work
Revenge upon this miser, this black cur,
That barks, and bites, and sucks the very blood,
Of me, and of my credit. 'Tis all one
To be a witch as to be counted one.

Cyril Tourneur, besides being concerned in the production of many others, wrote, himself, two very good dramas, *The Atheist's Tragedy*, and *The Revenger's Tragedy*. From the former we may select the following characteristic description of a Drowned Soldier :—

——— Walking upon the fatal shore,
Among the slaughter'd bodies of their men,
Which the full-stomach'd sea had cast upon
The sands, it was my unhappy chance to light
Upon a face, whose favour, when it lived,
My astonish'd mind inform'd me I had seen.
He lay in his armour, as if that had been
His coffin; and the weeping sea (like one
Whose milder temper doth lament the death
Of him whom in his rage he slew) runs up
The shore, embraces him, kisses his cheek;
Goes back again, and forces up the sands
To bury him; and every time it parts,
Sheds tears upon him; till at last, (as if
It could no longer endure to see the man
Whom it had slain, yet loath to leave him,)
With a kind of unresolv'd unwilling pace,
Winding her waves one in another, (like
A man that folds his arms, or wrings his hands
For grief,) ebb'd from the body, and descends;
As if it would sink down into the earth,
And hide itself for shame of such a deed.

George Cooke was the author of a lively comedy under the title of *Greene's Tu Quoque*. From the character and finish of this play, we should infer that it was far from being his only dramatic production, though no other has been preserved.

THOMAS NABBES, who died about 1645, was the author of a very successful masque, entitled *Microcosmus.* He also produced several other plays, which were written, either by himself alone, or conjointly with others. In 'Microcosmus' we find the following fine song of love:—

> Welcome, welcome, happy pair,
> To these abodes where spicy air
> Breathes perfumes, and every sense
> Doth find his object's excellence;
> Where 's no heat nor cold extreme,
> No winter's ice, no summer's scorching beam;
> Where 's no sun, yet never night,
> Day always springing from eternal light.
> *Chorus.*—All mortal suffering laid aside,
> Here in endless bliss abide.

NATHANIEL FIELD, who was an actor, and personated one of the characters in Ben Jonson's 'Poetaster,' began to write for the stage about 1609. His principal dramas are *Woman is a Weathercock*, and *Amends for Ladies.* He also had the honor of aiding Massinger in the composition of 'The Fatal Dowry.'

JOHN DAY, in conjunction with Chettle, wrote *The Blind Beggar of Bethnal Green*, a popular comedy, and was also the author of two or three other plays, and some miscellaneous poems.

HENRY GLAPTHORNE was a prolific writer, and is mentioned by his contemporaries as 'one of the chief dramatic poets of the reign of Charles the First.' A number of his plays were published, the principal of which are, *Albertus Wallenstein*, *The Hollander*, *Argalus and Parthenia*, *Wit in a Constable*, and the Lady's Privilege. Glapthorne's plays abound with a certain smoothness and prettiness of expression which is very agreeable, but he is deficient in passion and energy.

THOMAS RANDOLPH, whom we have already noticed among the miscellaneous poets of this period, wrote *The Muses' Looking-glass*, and *The Jealous Lovers.* An anonymous play, *Sweetman, the Woman-hater*, with the production of which Randolph is supposed to have been connected, contains the following happy simile:—

> Justice, like lightning, ever should appear
> To few men's ruin, but to all men's fear.

RICHARD BROME, one of the very best of these secondary dramatists, produced several plays, of which *The Antipodes*, *The City Wit* and *The Court Beggar*, long retained their place upon the stage.

Ford, Heywood, and Shirley close the long and interesting list of dramatic writers who adorned the age of Elizabeth and her two immediate successors.

JOHN FORD was of a good Devonshire family, and was born in 1586. He received a university education, after which he repaired to London, and entered Gray's Inn, as a student of law. Having completed his legal studies and commenced his profession, he turned his attention to the drama as a pastime. His first efforts as a writer for the stage, were made in connection with Webster and Dekker. He also assisted Rowley in the composition of 'The Witch of Edmonton,' already mentioned, the last act of which is supposed to have been written entirely by Ford. In 1628, appeared *The Lover's Melancholy*, dedicated to his friends and associates of the society of Gray's Inn. In 1633, were published his three tragedies, *The Brother and Sister*, *The Broken Heart*, and *Love's Sacrifice*. He next wrote *Perkin Warbeck*, a correct and spirited historical drama. Two other pieces, *Fancies Chaste and Noble*, and *The Lady's Trial*, produced in 1638, complete the list of Ford's works. His death occurred in 1639, in the fifty-fourth year of his age.

A tone of pensive tenderness and pathos, with a peculiarly soft and musical style of blank verse, characterizes all the dramas of this poet. The choice of his subjects was unhappy; yet Coleridge suggests, that the selection of horrible stories for his two best plays, may have been merely an exercise of intellectual power. 'His moral sense was gratified by indignation at the dark possibilities of sin, and by compassion for rare extremes of suffering.' The scenes in his 'Brother and Sister,' describing the criminal loves of Annabella and Giovanni, are painfully interesting, and to the feelings, harrowing in the extreme; and yet they contain his best poetry and finest expression.

The truth is, the old dramatists loved to sport and dally with such forbidden themes, as they tempted the imagination, and thus awoke slumbering fires of pride, passion, and wickedness, that lurk in the recesses of the human heart. They lived in an age of excitement—the newly-awakened intellect warring with the senses—the baser parts of humanity with its noblest qualities. In this struggle, the dramatic poets were plunged; and they depicted forcibly what they saw and felt. Much as they wrote, their time was not spent in shady retirement: they flung themselves into the full tide of the passions, sounded its depths, wrestled with its difficulties and defilements, and were borne onward in headlong career. A few, like poor Marlow and Greene, sunk early in undeplored misery, and nearly all were unhappy. This very recklessness and daring, however, gave a mighty impulse and freedom to their genius. They were emancipated from ordinary restraints; they were strong in their skeptic pride and self-will; they surveyed the whole of life, and gave expression to those wild half-shaped thoughts and unnatural promptings, which wiser conduct and reflection would have instantly repressed and condemned. With them the passion of love was an all-pervading fire, that consumed the decencies of life: sometimes it was gross and sensual, but in other moments, imbued with a wild, preternatural sweetness and fervor. Anger, pity, jealousy, revenge, remorse, and the other primary feelings and elements of our nature, were crowded into their short existence, as they were into their scenes. Nor was the light of religion quenched: there were glimpses of heaven in the midst of the darkest vice and debauchery. Happily the better genius of Shakspeare lifted him above this agitated region.

Ford was apparently of regular deportment, but of morbid diseased imagination. Charles Lamb ranks him with the first order of poets; but this praise is excessive. Admitting his sway over the tender passions, and the occasional beauty of his language and conceptions, still he wants the strength and elevation of great genius. He has, however, the power over tears, and makes his readers sympathize even with his vicious characters. Illustrative of this author's genius and style, we shall present only the following passage:—

CONTENTION OF A BIRD AND A MUSICIAN.

Menaphon and Amethus.

Men. Passing from Italy to Greece, the tales
Which poets of an elder time have feign'd
To glorify their Tempe, bred in me
Desire of visiting that paradise.
To Thessaly I came; and living private,
Without acquaintance of more sweet companions
Than the old inmates to my love, my thoughts,
I day by day frequented silent groves
And solitary walks. One morning early
This accident encounter'd me: I heard
The sweetest and most ravishing contention,
That art (and) nature ever were at strife in.
Amet. I can not yet conceive what you infer
By art and nature.
Men. I shall soon resolve you.
A sound of music touch'd mine ears, or rather,
Indeed, entranced my soul: as I stole nearer,
Invited by the melody, I saw
This youth, this fair-faced youth, upon his lute
With strains of strange variety and harmony,
Proclaiming, as it seem'd, so bold a challenge
To the clear choristers of the woods, the birds,
That, as they flock'd about him, all stood silent,
Wond'ring at what they heard. I wonder'd too.
Amet. And so do I; good! on—
Men. A nightingale,
Nature's best skill'd musician, undertakes
The challenge, and for every several strain
The well-shaped youth could touch, she sung her own;
He could not run division with more art
Upon his quaking instrument, than she,

The nightingale, did with her various notes
Reply to: for a voice, and for a sound,
Amethus, 'tis much easier to believe
That such they were, than hope to hear again.
Amet. How did the rivals part?
Men. You term them rightly;
For they were rivals, and their mistress, harmony.
Some time thus spent, the young man grew at last
In a pretty anger, that a bird
Whom art had never taught clefs, moods, or notes,
Should vie with him for mastery, whose study
Had busied many hours to perfect practice:
To end the controversy, in a rapture
Upon his instrument he plays so swiftly,
So many voluntaries, and so quick,
That there was curiosity and cunning,
Concord in discord, lines of differing method
Meeting in one full centre of delight.
Amet. Now for the bird.
Men. The bird, ordain'd to be
Music's first martyr, strove to imitate
These several sounds: which, when her warbling throat
Failed in, for grief, down dropp'd she on his lute
And broke her heart! It was the quaintest sadness,
To see the conqueror upon her hearse,
To weep a funeral elegy of tears;
That, trust me, my Amethus, I could chide
Mine own unmanly weakness, that made me
A fellow-mourner with him.
Amet. I believe thee.
Men. He look'd upon the trophies of his art,
Then sigh'd, then wiped his eyes, then sigh'd and cried:
'Alas poor creature! I will soon revenge
This cruelty upon the author of it:
Henceforth this lute, guilty of innocent blood,
Shall never more betray a harmless peace
To an untimely end:' and in that sorrow,
As he was pashing it against a tree,
I suddenly stept in.
Amet. Thou hast discours'd
A truth of mirth and pity.

[*Lover's Melancholy.*]

Thomas Heywood was both an actor and poet. Of his life so few particulars have been preserved, that we can ascertain neither the period of his birth, nor the time of his death. He was a native of Lincolnshire, and was a fellow of Peter House College, Cambridge. He commenced writing for the stage as early as 1596, and continued to exercise his ready pen until 1640; during which time he had, as he himself informs us, 'an entire hand, or at least a main finger, in two hundred and twenty plays.' Of this vast number of dramas, only twenty-three have been preserved; the best of which are *A Woman Killed with Kindness*, *The English Traveller*, *A Challenge for Beauty*, *The Royal King and Loyal Subjects*, *The Lancaster*

Witches, *The Rape of Lucrece*, and *Love's Mistress*. In one of his prologues he thus adverts to the various sources of his multifarious labors :—

To give content to this most curious age,
The gods themselves we've brought down to the stage,
And figured them in planets; made even hell
Deliver up the furies, by no spell
(Saving the muse's rapture) further we
Have traffick'd by their help; no history
We have left unrifled; our pens have been dipt
As well in opening each hid manuscript
As tracks more vulgar, whether read or sung
In our domestic or more foreign tongue:
Of fairies, elves, nymphs of the sea and land,
The lawns, the groves, no number can be scann'd
Which we have not given feet to.

These lines were written in 1637, and they show how eager the play-going public were, at that time, for novelties, though they possessed the dramas of Shakspeare and his contemporaries.

As a dramatist, Heywood had a fine poetical fancy and abundance of classical imagery; but his taste was defective, and scenes of low buffoonery, 'merry accidents, intermixed with apt and witty jests,' deform his plays. 'There is a natural repose in his scenes,' says the Edinburgh Review, 'which contrasts pleasingly with the excitement of other writers for the stage at the same period. Middleton looks upon his characters with the feverish anxiety with which we listen to the trial of great criminals, or watch their behaviour upon the scaffold. Webster lays out their corpses in the prison, and sings the dirge over them when they are buried at midnight in unhallowed ground. Heywood leaves his characters before they come into these situations. He walks quietly to and fro among them while they are yet at large as members of society; contenting himself with a sad smile at their follies, or with a frequent warning to them on the consequences of their crimes.' The following description of Psyche, from 'Love's Mistress,' is in his best vein :—

[*Admetus,—Astioche,—Petrea.*]

Adm. Welcome to both in one! Oh, can you tell
What fate your sister hath?
Both. Psyche is well.
Adm. So among mortals it is often said,
Children and friends are well when they are dead.
Ast. But Psyche lives, and on her breath attend
Delights that far surmount all earthly joy;
Music, sweet voices, and ambrosian fare;
Winds, and the light-wing'd creatures of the air;
Clear channell'd rivers, springs, and flowery meads,
Are proud when Psyche wantons on their streams,
When Psyche on their rich embroidery treads,
When Psyche gilds their crystal with her beams.

We have but seen our sister, and, behold!
She sends us with our laps full brimm'd with gold.

There are scattered through Heywood's dramas various songs, some of which, such as the following, flow with peculiar ease and sweetness:—

SONG.

Pack clouds away, and welcome day,
  With night we banish sorrow:
Sweet air blow soft, mount lark aloft,
  To give my love good morrow:
Wings from the wind to please her mind
  Notes from the lark I'll borrow:
Bird, prune thy wing, nightingale sing,
  To give my love good morrow:
    To give my love good morrow,
    Notes from them all I'll borrow.

Wake from thy nest, robin red-breast,
  Sing, birds, in every furrow;
And from each bill let music shrill
  Give my fair love good morrow.
Blackbird and thrush in every bush
  Stare, linnet, and cock-sparrow,
You pretty elves, amongst yourselves,
  Sing my fair love good morrow.
    To give my love good morrow,
    Sing, birds, in every furrow.

Besides his dramatic productions, Heywood published, in 1635, a poem of very considerable pretensions, under the title of *The Hierarchy of Angels.* It is at present, however, little known.

Shirley was the last of these dramatists—'a great race,' says Lamb, 'all of whom spoke nearly the same language, and had a set of moral notions and feelings in common.'

James Shirley was of an ancient family, and was born in the parish of St. Mary, London, in 1595. Early designed for the church, he was sent, for his education, to St. John's College, Oxford; but after he had prepared to take orders, Archbishop Laud refused to ordain him because his left cheek was disfigured by a mole. From Oxford he removed to Cambridge, and having there taken his master's degree, he was soon after ordained, and officiated for a short time as curate at St. Albans, in Hertfordshire. Growing, meantime, unsettled in his religious principles, Shirley finally became a Romanist; in consequence of which he relinquished his curacy, and opened a grammar-school, intending to make teaching his future profession. This self-denying and laborious business soon, however, became irksome to him, and he, therefore, relinquished his school, removed to London, and turned his entire attention to the stage. Thirty-nine plays, proceeded, in a comparatively few years, from his prolific pen, and a modern edition of his works forms six octavo volumes. The moral tone of Shirley's dramas is so comparatively high, that when the Master of the Revels, in 1633, licensed his play of *The Young Admiral*, he entered on his books an expression of admiration of the drama, because it was free from oaths, profanity, and obscureness; trusting that his approbation would encourage the poet 'to pursue this beneficial and cleanly way of poetry.'

When the civil war broke out Shirley exchanged the pen for the sword, and took the field under his patron, the Earl of Newcastle; but after the cessation of that struggle, the theatres being all closed by the prevailing party, he was compelled to return again to his former occupation of teacher. This pursuit he continued to follow until 1660, when the great fire of London drove him and his family from his house in Whitefriars; and shortly after that sad event occurred both he and his wife died on the same day. A life of various labors and reverses thus found a sudden and tragical termination.

Shirley's dramas have less force and dignity than those of Massinger, and less pathos than those of Ford. His comedies have the tone and manner of good society, but no more elevated property. Campbell has praised his 'polished and refined dialect, the airy touches of his expression, the delicacy of his sentiments, and the beauty of his similes.' He admits, however, what every reader *feels*, the want in Shirley's dramas of any strong passion, or engrossing interest. Shirley's best plays are *The Brothers*, *The Grateful Servant*, *The Lady of Pleasure*, and *The Ball*. He produced no play that is stamped, throughout, with a very high order of excellence; but his dramas contain many fine passages, such as the following description which Fernando, in 'The Brothers,' gives of the charms of his mistress:—

Her eye did seem to labour with a tear,
Which suddenly took birth, but overweigh'd
With its own swelling, dropt upon her bosom,
Which, by reflection of her light appear'd
As nature meant her sorrow for an ornament.
After, her looks grew cheerful, and I saw
A smile shoot graceful upward from her eyes,
As if they had gain'd a victory o'er grief;
And with it many beams twisted themselves,
Upon whose golden threads the angels walk
To and again from heaven.

The following passage in 'The Grateful Servant,' where Cleona learns of the existence of Foscari, from her page Dulcino, is in the same vein of delicate fancy and feeling:—

Cleo. The day breaks glorious to my darken'd thoughts
He lives, he lives yet! Cease, ye amorous fears,
More to perplex me. Prithee speak, sweet youth;
How fares my lord? Upon my virgin heart

I'll build a flaming altar, to offer up
A thankful sacrifice for his return
To life and me. Speak, and increase my comforts.
Is he in perfect health ?
Dul. Not perfect, madam,
Until you bless him with the knowledge of
Your constancy.
Cle. O get thee wings and fly then;
Tell him my love doth burn like vestal fire,
Which, with his memory richer than all spices,
Disperses odours round about my soul,
And did refresh it when 't was dull and sad,
With thinking of his absence.
———Yet stay;
Thou goest away too soon; where is he ? speak.
Dul. He gave me no commission for that, lady;
He will soon save that question by his presence.
Cle. Time has no feathers; he walks now on crutches.
Relate his gestures when he gave thee this.
What other words ? Did mirth smile on his brow ?
I would not for the wealth of this great world
He should suspect my faith. What said he, prithee ?
Dul. He said what a warm lover, when desire
Makes eloquent, could speak; he said you were
Both star and pilot.
Cle. The sun's lov'd flower, that shuts his yellow curtain
When he declineth, opens it again
At his fair rising: with my parting lord
I clos'd all my delight; till his approach
It shall not spread itself.

With Shirley we close the first and most splendid period of English dramatic literature; and though our remarks and illustrations have, in their range, been necessarily limited, yet we hope they may awaken an interest in the subject proportioned to its importance. We shall proceed to consider next, the prose writers of this great age of genius and intellect.

Lecture the Sixteenth.

LORD BURLEIGH—SIR WALTER RALEIGH—SIR PHILIP SIDNEY—RICHARD HOOKER.

THE authors who excelled in the various departments of prose during the present period, are confined, chiefly, to the departments of theology, philosophy, and historical and antiquarian information. Hardly any vestige of prose was, as yet, employed with taste in fiction, or even in observations upon manners; though it must not be forgotten that in Elizabeth's reign appeared the once popular romance of 'Arcadia' by Sir Philip Sidney, and in the early part of that of her successor, Thomas Dekker, whom we have already noticed as a dramatist, published a fiction under the title of *The Gull's Hornbook*, which was, at the time, extremely popular. The reign of James, and that of his successor Charles, produced several other acute and humorous describers of human character, which the sequel will develop. The authors whom we are first to notice under the department of literature now to be considered, are Cecil, Raleigh, Sidney, and Hooker.

WILLIAM CECIL, afterward the famous Lord Burleigh, was born at Bourn, Lincolnshire, in 1521. He was educated at St. John's College, Cambridge, and passed thence to Gray's Inn, London, with a view to preparation for the legal profession. The assiduousness with which Cecil applied himself to the study of the law, was such, that he was scarcely admitted at the bar before he became one of its most distinguished ornaments. In the reign of Queen Mary, his abilities were so highly respected that, notwithstanding he had favored the course of Lady Jane Grey, still the queen often consulted him, and he retained throughout her whole reign, the good-will of her ministers. Soon after Elizabeth ascended the throne, Cecil was made secretary of state; and the duties of that arduous and responsible office he continued to discharge with unsullied honor until his death, which occurred in the month of August, 1598. In 1571, Cecil was created by the queen, Lord Burleigh.

As a minister this celebrated man was distinguished for wariness, application, sagacity, calmness, and a degree of closeness, which sometimes degenerated into hypocrisy; and most of these qualities characterize also, what is, properly speaking, his only literary production,—*Precepts or Directions for the Well Ordering and Carriage of a Man's Life.* These precepts were addressed to his son, Robert Cecil, afterward Earl of Salisbury; and a few of them are here subjoined:—

CHOICE OF A WIFE.

When it shall please God to bring thee to man's estate, use great providence and circumspection in choosing thy wife. For from thence will spring all thy future good or evil. And it is an action of life, like unto a stratagem of war; wherein a man can err but once. If thy estate be good, match near home and at leisure; if weak, far off and quickly. Inquire diligently of her disposition, and how her parents have been inclined[1] in their youth. Let her not be poor, how generous soever. For a man can buy nothing in the market with gentility. Nor choose a base and uncomely creature altogether for wealth; for it will cause contempt in others, and loathing in thee. Neither make choice of a dwarf, or a fool; for, by the one thou shalt beget a race of pigmies; the other will be thy continual disgrace, and it will *yirke* thee to hear her talk. For thou shalt find it, to thy great grief, that there is nothing more fulsome than a she-fool.

DOMESTIC ECONOMY.

And touching the guiding of thy house, let thy hospitality be moderate, and, according to the means of thy estate, rather plentiful than sparing, but not costly. For I never knew any man grow poor by keeping an orderly table. But some consume themselves through secret vices, and their hospitality bears the blame. But banish swinish drunkards out of thine house, which is a vice impairing health, consuming much, and makes no show. I never heard praise ascribed to the drunkard, but for the well-bearing of his drink, which is a better commendation for a brewer's horse or a drayman, than for either a gentleman or a serving-man. Beware thou spend not above three of four parts of thy revenues: nor above a third part of that in thy house. For the other two parts will do no more than defray thy extraordinaries, which always surmount the ordinary by much; otherwise thou shalt live like a rich beggar, in continual want. And the needy man can never live happily nor contentedly. For every disaster makes him ready to mortage or sell. And that gentleman, who sells an acre of land, sells an ounce of credit. For gentility, is nothing else but ancient riches. So that if the foundation shall at any time sink, the building must needs follow.

EDUCATION OF CHILDREN.

Bring thy children up in learning and obedience, yet without outward austerity. Praise them openly, reprehend them secretly. Give them good countenance and convenient maintenance according to thy ability, otherwise thy life will seem their bondage, and what portion thou shalt leave them at thy death, they will thank death for it and not thee. And I am persuaded that the foolish cockering of some parents, and the over-stern carriage of others, causeth more men and women to take ill courses, than their own vicious inclinations. Marry thy daughters in time, lest they marry themselves. And suffer not thy sons to pass the Alps; for they shall learn nothing there but pride, blasphemy, and atheism. And if by travel they get a few broken languages, that shall profit them nothing more than to have one meat served in divers dishes. Neither, by my consent, shalt thou train them up in wars; for he that sets up his rest to live by that profession, can hardly be an honest man or a good Christian. Besides, it is a science no longer in request than use; for soldiers in peace are like chimneys in summer.

---

[1] Well-born.

Sir Walter Raleigh was one of the most distinguished of that brilliant constellation of great men that adorned the age of Elizabeth and James. He was of an ancient family, and was born at Hayes Farm, Devonshire, in 1552; and from his youth was distinguished by great intellectual acuteness, but still more by a restless and adventurous disposition. In 1568, he entered Oriel College, Oxford, and soon became eminent for his talents and learning; but his ambition prompted him to pursue the road to fame in an active life, and his residence at the university was, therefore, very brief. When only seventeen years of age, he became a soldier, and as a volunteer fought for the Protestant cause in the civil war of France and the Netherlands; and soon after he accompanied his half-brother, Sir Humphrey Gilbert, on a voyage to Newfoundland. This expedition proved unfortunate; but by familiarizing Raleigh with a maritime life, it probably had great influence in leading him to engage in those subsequent adventures by which he eventually rendered himself so famous. In 1580 he assisted in repressing the Earl of Desmond's rebellion in Ireland, in consequence of which he obtained an estate in that country, and was, for some time, governor of Cork. Having, soon after, occasion to visit London, he attached himself to the court; and with the aid of a handsome person, and winning address, contrived to insinuate himself very thoroughly into the favor of Elizabeth. A well-known anecdote of the time illustrates his gallantry and tact. On one occasion, when he was attending the queen on a walk, she came to a miry part of the road, and for a moment hesitated to proceed. Raleigh perceiving her situation, instantly pulled off his rich plush cloak, and by spreading it before her, enabled her to pass over with unsoiled feet. This mark of attention delighted the queen, from whom, as it was some time after facetiously remarked, his cloak was the means of procuring for him many a good suit.

Not satisfied with the failure of the expedition to Newfoundland, in which he had accompanied his kinsman, Sir Humphrey Gilbert, Raleigh, in 1584, again joined an adventure for the discovery and settlement of unknown countries in the west. With the help of his friends, two ships were sent out in search of gold mines, to that part of North America then known as Wingandacoa, now Virginia. The commodities returned to England by these vessels afforded such ample compensation for the toil and dangers of the voyage, that the owners were induced to fit out, the next year, a fleet of seven ships, under the command of Raleigh's kinsman, Sir Richard Grenville. The design of this second expedition was to colonize America; but the attempt proved an utter failure, and the enterprise was given up. The expedition, however, was important in one particular, as it was the means of introducing tobacco into England, and also of making known the potato, which is a native of Mexico, and was first cultivated in Europe at this time on Raleigh's estate in Ireland.

Raleigh's prosperity at court was meanwhile increasing. He was about this time knighted by the queen, and elected to Parliament from Devonshire. Elizabeth also made very considerable additions to his Irish estate, and conferred upon him other solid marks of her favor. In return for these benefits, he zealously and actively exerted himself for the defence of her dominions against the Spaniards, in 1588; having not only been one of those patriot volunteers who sailed against the formidable Armada in the English Channel, but as a member of her majesty's council of war, contributed, by his advice and experience, to the maturing of those defensive arrangements which led to the discomfiture of the enemy. Elizabeth continued her favors to him for a long time without limit; but at length his troublesome importunities drew from her the pointed question, 'When, Sir Walter, will you cease to be a beggar?' to which, with his usual tact, he replied, 'When your gracious majesty ceases to be a benefactor.' With all his elevated traits of character, it must, however, be confessed that Raleigh was not, at this period of his life, strictly conscientious; and by taking bribes, and otherwise abusing his power and influence at court, he became unpopular with the nation at large, and his fortunes now began, though at first imperceptibly, to wane.

Perceiving the approaching consequences of his unfair practices at court, Raleigh prepared to ward off the blow by attaching to himself the men of science and learning of the day. With this view, he set up an *office of address* intended to serve the purposes now effected chiefly by literary and philosophical societies. The following description of this scheme is given by Sir William Petty: 'It seems to have been a plan by which the wants and desires of all learned men might be made known to each other, where they might know what is already done in the business of learning, what is at present in doing, and what is intended to be done; to the end that by such a general communication of designs and mutual assistance, the wits and endeavours of the world may no longer be as so many scattered coals, which, having no union, are soon quenched, whereas being but laid together, they would have yielded a comfortable light and heat.' Raleigh not only devised this general plan by which to surround himself with literary men, but he also sought the particular friendship of eminent individuals. Accordingly, when on a visit to his Irish estates, he formed an acquaintance with Spenser, which soon ripened into an intimate friendship. He brought the poet over to London, introduced him to Elizabeth, and otherwise benefited him by his encouragement and patronage; in return for which favor Spenser addressed a pastoral to him entitled *Colin Clout's Come Home Again*, where Raleigh is celebrated under the title of the *Shepherd of the Ocean.*

In 1592, Raleigh engaged in one of those predatory expeditions against the enemies of England, which, in Elizabeth's reign, were very common; a fleet of thirteen ships, besides two of her majesty's men-of-war, being intrusted to his command. This armament was destined to attack Panama, and intercept the Spanish plate fleet, but, having been recalled by Elizabeth soon after it set sail, came back with a single prize. Soon after his return Raleigh incurred the deep displeasure of the queen by an amour with one of her maids of honor; in consequence of which, though he married the lady, he suffered imprisonment for some months. While in banishment from the court, he undertook, at his own expense, in 1595, an expedition to Guiana, concerning the riches of which country many wonderful tales were then current. He, however, accomplished nothing farther than to take formal possession of it in the queen's name. The next year after his return to England he published a work entitled *Discovery of the Large, Rich, and Beautiful Empire of Guiana.* This was Sir Walter's first important literary production, and it seems that about the same time he published it, he regained the queen's favor; for we find him holding, in the same year, a command in the expedition against Cadiz, under the Earl of Essex, and Lord Effingham. In the successful attack on that town, his bravery, as well as his prudence, was very conspicuous. In 1597, Raleigh was rear-admiral in the expedition which sailed under Essex to intercept the Spanish West India fleet; and by capturing Fayal, one of the Azores, before the arrival of the commander-in-chief, he gave great offence to the earl, who considered himself robbed of the glory of the action. A temporary reconciliation was, however, soon effected; but Raleigh afterward heartily joined with Cecil in promoting the downfall of Essex, and was a spectator of his execution from a window in the armory.

On the accession of James the First to the English crown, Raleigh's prosperity terminated, hatred toward him having been previously instilled by Cecil into the royal ear. Through the malignant scheming of the same hypocritical minister, he was accused of conspiring to dethrone the king, and place the crown on the head of Arabella Stuart. A trial for high treason ensued, and upon the most paltry evidence conceivable he was, by a servile jury, condemned. Sir Edward Coke, who was at the time attorney-general, abused him on this occasion in violent and disgraceful terms, bestowing upon him freely the lowest and most offensive epithets. Raleigh defended himself with such temper, eloquence, and strength of reasoning, that some, even of his enemies, were convinced of his innocence, and all parties were ashamed of the judgment pronounced against him. He was, however, reprieved, and instead of being executed, was committed to the Tower, in which his wife was permitted to bear him company. During the twelve years of his imprisonment, he wrote most of his works, especially the *History of the World*, of which only a part was finished, comprehending the period from the creation to the downfall of the Macedonian empire, about one hundred and seventy years before Christ.

The learning and genius of Raleigh, who, in the language of Hume, 'being educated amid naval and military enterprises, had surpassed, in the pursuits of literature, even those of the most recluse and sedentary lives,' have excited very general admiration. The style and manner of his celebrated history are vastly superior to any of the English historical productions which had previously appeared. Its style, though partaking of the faults of the age, in being frequently stiff and inverted, has less of these defects than the diction of any other writer of the time. Tytler justly recommends it as 'vigorous, purely English, and possessing an antique richness of ornament, similar to what pleases us when we see some ancient priory or stately manor-house, and compare it with our more modern mansions.'

In 1615, Raleigh was liberated from the Tower, in consequence of having projected a second expedition to Guiana, from which the king expected to receive some advantage. His purpose was to colonize the country, and work gold mines; and with this view, in 1617, a fleet of twelve armed vessels sailed under his command. The whole detail of his intended proceedings, however, were either weakly or treacherously communicated by the king to the Spanish government, by which the scheme was entirely thwarted. Returning to England, he landed at Plymouth, and on his way to London was arrested in the king's name. The projected match between Prince Charles and the Infanta of Spain occupied, just at this period, James's attention; and to propitiate the Spanish government he determined that Raleigh should be sacrificed. After many varied attempts to discover valid grounds of accusation against him, it was found necessary to proceed upon the old sentence, and Raleigh was, accordingly, beheaded on the twenty-ninth of October, 1618. On the scaffold his behaviour was firm and calm. After addressing the people in justification of his character and conduct, he observed to the sheriff, 'This is a sharp medicine, but a sound cure for all diseases.' Having tried how the block fitted his head, he told the executioner that he would give the signal by lifting up his hand: 'and then,' added he, 'fear not, but strike.' He laid himself down, but was requested by the executioner to alter the position of his head. 'So the heart be right,' was his reply, 'it is no matter which way the head lies.' On the signal being given, the executioner failed to act with promptitude, which caused Raleigh to exclaim, 'Why dost thou not strike? Strike, man!' By two strokes, which he then received without shrinking, the head of this intrepid man was severed from his body, and his earthly career thus closed.

While in prison awaiting his execution, Sir Walter addressed the following tender and affectionate valedictory letter to his wife:—

You shall receive, my dear wife, my last words in these my last lines; my love I send you, that you may keep when I am dead, and my counsel, that you may remember it when I am no more. I would not with my will present you sorrows, dear Bess; let them go to the grave with me, and be buried in the dust. And seeing that it is not the will of God that I shall see you any more, bear my destruction patiently, and with a heart like yourself.

First, I send you all the thanks which my heart can conceive, or my words express, for your many travails and cares for me, which, though they have not taken effect as you wished, yet my debt to you is not the less; but pay it I never shall in this world.

Secondly, I beseech you, for the love you bear me living, that you do not hide yourself many days, but by your travails seek to help my miserable fortunes, and the right of your poor child; your mourning can not avail me that am but dust.

* * * * * * * * *

Paylie oweth me a thousand pounds, and Aryan six hundred; in Jersey also, I have much owing me. Dear wife, I beseech you, for my soul's sake, pay all poor men

When I am dead, no doubt you shall be much sought unto; for the world thinks I was very rich; have a care to the fair pretences of men, for no greater misery can befall you in this life than to become a prey unto the world, and after to be despised. I speak, God knows, not to dissuade you from marriage, for it will be best for you, both in respect of God and of the world. As for me, I am no more yours, nor you mine; death hath cut us asunder, and God hath divided me from the world, and you from me. Remember your poor child for his father's sake, who loved you in his happiest estate. I sued for my life, but, God knows, it was for you and yours that I desired it: for know it, my dear wife, your child is the child of a true man, who, in his own respect, despiseth death, and his mis-shapen and ugly forms. I can not write much (God knows how hardly I steal this time when all sleep), and it is also time for me to separate my thoughts from the world. Beg my dead body, which living was denied you, and either lay it in Sherburn or Exeter church, by my father and mother. I can say no more, time and death calleth me away. The everlasting God, powerful, infinite, and inscrutable God Almighty, who is goodness itself, the true light and life, keep you and yours, and have mercy upon me, and forgive my persecutors and false accusers, and send us, to meet in his glorious kingdom. My dear wife, farewell; bless my boy, pray for me, and let my true God hold you both in his arms.

Besides the historical work already mentioned, and from which the first of the following extracts is taken, Raleigh composed a number of political and other pieces, some of which have never been published. Among those best known are his *Maxims of State*, *The Cabinet Council*, *The Skeptic*, and *Advice to his Son;* from the last of which we take the second of the following extracts:—

THE BATTLE OF THERMOPYLÆ.

After such time as Xerxes had transported the army over the Hellespont, and landed in Thrace (leaving the description of his passage alongst that coast, and how the river of Lissus was drunk dry by his multitudes, and the lake near to Pissyrus by his cattle, with other accidents in his marches towards Greece,) I will speak of the encounters he had, and the shameful and incredible overthrows which he received. As first at Thermopylæ, a narrow passage of half an acre of ground, lying between the mountains which divide Thessaly from Greece, where sometimes the Phocians had raised a wall with gates, which was then for the most part ruined. At this entrance, Leonidas, one of the kings of Sparta, with 300 Lacedæmonians, assisted with 1000 Tegeatæ and Mantineans, and 1000 Arcadians, and other Peloponnesians, to the number of 3100 in the whole, besides 100 Phocians, 400 Thebans, 700 Thespians, and all the forces (such as they were) of the bordering Locrians, defended the passage two whole days together against that huge army of the Persians. The valour of the Greeks appeared so excellent in this defence, that, in the first day's fight, Xerxes is said to have three times leaped out of his throne, fearing the destruction of his army by one handful of those men whom not long before he had utterly despised: and when the second day's attempt upon the Greeks had proved vain, he was altogether ignorant how to proceed further, and so might have continued, had not a runagate Grecian taught him a secret way, by which part of his army might ascend the ledge of mountains, and set upon the backs of those who kept the straits. But when the most valiant of the Persian army had almost inclosed the small forces of the Greeks, then did Leonidas, king of the Lacedæmonians, with his 300, and 700 Thespians, which were all that abode by him, refuse to quit the place which they had undertaken to make good, and with admirable courage, not only resist that world of men which charged them on all sides, but, issuing out of their strength, made so great a slaughter of their enemies, that they might well be called vanquishers, though all of them were slain upon the place. Xerxes having lost in this last fight, together with 20,000 other soldiers and captains, two of his own brethren, began to doubt what inconvenience might befall him by the virtue of such as had not been present at these battles, with whom he knew that he shortly was to deal. Especially of the Spartans he stood in great fear, whose manhood had appeared singular in this trial, which caused him very carefully to inquire what numbers they could bring into the field. It is reported of Dieneces the Spartan, that when one thought to have terrified him by saying that the flight of the Persian arrows was so thick as would hide the sun, he answered thus:—'It is very good news, for then shall we fight in the cool shade.'

THREE RULES TO BE OBSERVED FOR THE PRESERVATION OF A MAN'S ESTATE.

Amongst all other things of the world, take care of thy estate, which thou shalt ever preserve if thou observe three things: first, that thou know what thou hast, what every thing is worth that thou hast, and to see that thou art not wasted by thy servants and officers. The second is, that thou never spend anything before thou have it; for borrowing is the canker and death of every man's estate. The third is, that thou suffer not thyself to be wounded for other men's faults, and scourged for other men's offences; which is, the surety for another, for thereby millions of men have been beggared and destroyed, paying the reckoning of other men's riot, and the charge of other men's folly and prodigality; if thou smart, smart for thine own sins; and, above all things, be not made an ass to carry the burdens of other men: if any friend desire thee to be his surety, give him a part of what thou hast to spare; if he press thee farther, he is not thy friend at all, for friendship rather chooseth harm to itself than offereth it. If thou be bound for a stranger, thou art a fool; if for a merchant, thou puttest thy estate to learn to swim; if for a churchman, he hath no inheritance; if for a lawyer, he will find an invasion by a syllable or word to abuse thee; if for a poor man, thou must pay it thyself; if for a rich man, he needs not; therefore, from suretyship, as from a man-slayer or enchanter, bless thyself; for the best profit and return will be this, that if thou force him for whom thou art bound, to pay it himself, he will become thy enemy; if thou use to pay it thyself, thou wilt be a beggar; and believe thy father in this, and print it in thy thought, that what virtue soever thou hast, be it never so manifold, if thou be poor withal, thou and thy qualities shall be despised. Besides, poverty is ofttimes sent as a curse of God: it is a shame amongst men, an imprisonment of the mind, a vexation of every worthy spirit; thou shalt neither help thyself nor others: thou shalt drown thee in all thy virtues, having no means to show them; thou shalt be a burden and an eyesore to thy friends, every man will fear thy company; thou shalt be driven basely to beg and depend on others, to flatter unworthy men, to make dishonest shifts: and, to conclude, poverty provokes a man to do infamous and detested deeds; let no vanity, therefore, or persuasion, draw thee to that worst of worldly miseries.

If thou be rich, it will give thee pleasure in health, comfort in sickness, keep thy mind and body free, save thee from many perils, relieve thee in thy elder years, relieve the poor and thy honest friends, and give means to thy posterity to live, and defend themselves and thine own fame. Where it is said in the Proverbs, 'That he shall be sore vexed that is a surety for a stranger, and he that hateth suretyship is sure;' it is further said, 'The poor is hated even of his own neighbour; but the rich have many friends.' Lend not to him that is mightier than thyself, for if thou lendest him, count it but lost; be not surety above thy power, for if thou be surety, think to pay it.

Sir Philip Sidney, perhaps the most brilliant ornament of the court of queen Elizabeth, was the son of Sir Henry Sidney, and Mary, eldest daughter of John Dudley, duke of Northumberland. He was born at Penshurst in Kent, on the twenty-ninth of November, 1554, and received his Christian name from king Philip of Spain, who had recently married queen Mary. When in the fourteenth year of his age, he was sent to Christ Church College, Oxford, having previously greatly distinguished himself at the grammar-school of Shrewsbury. From Oxford he removed to Cambridge, and at each university displayed remarkable acuteness of intellect, and great thirst for knowledge. At the age of seventeen, without taking a degree, he relinquished his collegiate studies, and left England to make the tour of the continent. He passed three years abroad, and during his absence travelled through the Netherlands, France, Germany, and Italy; and on his return to England, in 1575, was received by queen Elizabeth with marked and distinguished favor. During the following year the queen sent him to Germany on a mission of condolence to the emperor, upon the death of Maximilian. On his return toward his own country, he took occasion to visit Don John of Austria, viceroy in the Netherlands for the king of Spain, and William prince of Orange; the former of whom was so charmed with his youth, wit, and elegance of manners, that he treated him with more attention and respect than he did the ambassadors of great princes at his court.

While Sidney was thus basking in the sunshine of royal favor at home and abroad, and was the idol of the English nation, he, in 1580, unfortunately allowed the impetuosity of his temper so far to overcome his better judgment, that in consequence of a quarrel with the Earl of Oxford, he relinquished the court, and retired to the seat of his brother-in-law, the Earl of Pembroke. Here, in the shades of Wilton, the Earl's seat, he composed his heroic romance, *The Arcadia*, and inscribed it to his sister, the Countess. This production was never finished; and, not having been intended for the press, did not appear till after Sir Philip's death. His next work was a tract entitled *The Defence of Poesy*, the design of which was to repel the objections brought by the Puritans of that age against the poetic art, the possessors of which they contemptuously denominated 'caterpillars of the commonwealth.' This production, though written with the partiality of a poet, is deservedly admired for the beauty of its style, and the general soundness of its reasonings. In 1584, the character of his uncle, the celebrated Earl of Leicester, having been attacked in a publication called *Leicester's Commonwealth*, Sidney wrote a reply, in which, although the heaviest accusations were passed over in silence, he did not scruple to heap upon his opponent the most opprobrious epithets. This performance of Sir Philip seems to have proved unsatisfactory to Leicester and his friends, as it was not published till toward the middle of the eighteenth century.

Sidney was not formed for repose, and his retirement now becoming irksome to him, he contemplated an expedition with Sir Francis Drake, against the Spanish settlements in America; but this design was frustrated by a peremptory mandate from the queen. In 1585, such was his reputation abroad, that he was named as one of the candidates for the crown of Poland, at that time vacant; on which occasion Elizabeth again threw obstacles in his way, being afraid 'to lose the jewel of her times.' He was not, however, permitted to remain long unemployed; for in the same year the queen, having determined to send assistance to the Protestants of the Netherlands, then groaning beneath the oppressive yoke of the Spaniards, he was appointed governor of Flushing, one of the towns ceded to the English in return for this aid. Soon after, the Earl of Leicester, with an army of six thousand men, went over to the Netherlands, where he was joined by Sir Philip, as guard of the horse. The conduct of the Earl in that war was highly imprudent, and such as to call forth repeated expressions of dissatisfaction from his nephew Sir Philip. The military exploits of the latter were, on the contrary, highly honorable to him; in particular, the taking of the town of Axel, in 1586. His career was destined, however, to be short; for having, in September of the same year, accidentally encountered a detachment of the Spanish army at Zutphen, he received a wound, which, in a few weeks, proved mortal. As he was being carried from the field, a well-known incident occurred by which the generosity of his nature was strongly displayed. Overcome with thirst from excessive bleeding and fatigue, he called for water, which was immediately brought to him; but as he was lifting it to his mouth, a poor soldier happened to be carried by, desperately wounded, who at once fixed his eyes eagerly on the cup. Sir Philip, observing this, instantly delivered the beverage to him, with the simple remark, 'Thy necessity is yet greater than mine.' Sidney's death, which occurred on the nineteenth of October, 1586, at the early age of thirty-two, was deeply and extensively lamented. His bravery and chivalrous magnanimity—his grace and polish of manner—the purity of his morals—his learning and refinement of taste—had procured for him love and esteem wherever he was known. By the direction of queen Elizabeth, his remains were conveyed to London, and honored with a public funeral in St. Paul's Cathedral.

To Sir Philip Sidney's poetry we have already alluded; but it is chiefly as a prose writer that he maintains and deserves a prominent place in English literature. In judging of his merits, we should bear in mind the early age at which his career was closed. His 'Arcadia,' on which his fame chiefly rests, was so universally read and admired in the reigns of Elizabeth and her successor, that, in 1633, it had reached the eighth edition. This great work, though the changes which have taken place since it was written, in taste, manners, and opinions, may render it unsuited to modern readers, still must be admitted to contain passages of exquisite beauty—useful observations on life and manners—a variety and accurate discrimination of characters—fine sentiments expressed in strong and adequate terms—animated descriptions, equal to any that occur in the ancient or modern poets—sage lessons of morality, and judicious reflections on government and policy. Sidney was, in reality, the best prose writer of the age, and what Cowper felicitously calls him, a 'warbler of poetic prose.' In personal character, he, like most men of high sensibility and poetical feeling, was strongly inclined to melancholy, and frequently indulged this luxurious feeling to excess. As our extracts from this writer must necessarily be limited, we shall introduce only the following:—

DESCRIPTION OF ARCADIA.

There were hills which garnished their proud heights with stately trees; humble valleys, whose base estate seemed comforted with the refreshing of silver rivers; meadows, enamelled with all sorts of eye-pleasing flowers; thickets, which being lined with most pleasant shade, were witnessed so to, by the cheerful disposition of many well-tuned birds; each pasture stored with sheep, feeding with sober security; while the pretty lambs, with bleating oratory, craved the dam's comfort; here a shepherd's boy piping, as though he should never be old; there a young shepherdess knitting, and withal singing; and it seemed that her voice comforted her hands to work, and her hands kept time to her voice-music.

A TEMPEST.

There arose even with the sun a vail of dark clouds before his face, which shortly, like ink poured into water, had blacked over all the face of heaven, preparing, as it were, a mournful stage for a tragedy to be played on. For, forthwith the winds began to speak louder, and, as in a tumultuous kingdom, to think themselves fittest instruments of commandment; and blowing whole storms of hail and rain upon them, they were sooner in danger than they could almost bethink themselves of change. For then the traitorous sea began to swell in pride against the afflicted navy, under which, while the heaven favoured them, it had lain so calmly; making mountains of itself, over which the tossed and tottering ship should climb, to be straight carried down again to a pit of hellish darkness, with such cruel blows against the sides of the ship, that, which way soever it went, was still in his malice, that there was left neither power to stay nor way to escape. And shortly had it so dissevered the loving company, which the day before had tarried together, that most of them never met again, but were swallowed up in his never-satisfied mouth.

PRAISE OF POETRY.

The philosopher showeth you the way, he informeth you of the particularities, as well of the tediousness of the way, as of the pleasant lodging you shall have when your journey is ended, as of the many bye-turnings that may divert you from your way; but this is to no man, but to him that will read him, and read him with attentive studious painfulness, which constant desire whosoever hath in him, hath already passed half the hardness of the way, and therefore is beholden to the philosopher but for the other half. Nay, truly, learned men have learnedly thought, that where once reason hath so much overmastered passion, as that the mind hath a free desire to do well, the inward light each man hath in itself is as good as a philosopher's book; since in nature we know it is well to do well, and what is well and what is evil, although not in the words of art which philosophers bestow upon us; for out of natural conceit the philosophers drew it. But to be moved to do that which we know, or to be moved with the desire to know, 'hoc opus hic labor est'—(this is the grand difficulty.')

Now, therein, of all sciences (I speak still of human, and according to the human conceit) is our poet the monarch. For he doth not only show the way, but giveth so sweet a prospect into the way, as will entice any man to enter into it. Nay, he doth, as if your journey should lie through a fair vineyard, at the very first, give you a cluster of grapes; that, full of that taste, you may long to pass farther. He beginneth not with obscure definitions; which must blur the margin with interpretations, and load the memory with doubtfulness; but he cometh to you with words set in delightful proportion, either accompanied with, or prepared for, the well enchanting skill of music, and with a tale, forsooth, he cometh unto you, with a tale which holdeth children from play, and old men from the chimney corner; and pretending no more, doth intend the winning of the mind from wickedness to virtue; even as the child is often brought to take most wholesome things, by hiding them in such other as have a pleasant taste; which, if one should begin to tell them the nature of the aloes or rhubarbarum they should receive, would sooner take their physic at their ears than their mouth. So is it in men, (most of whom are childish in the best things, till they be cradled in their graves.) Glad they will be to hear the tales of Hercules, Achilles, Cyrus, Æneas; and hearing them, must needs hear the right description of wisdom, valour, and justice; which, if they had been barely (that is to say, philosophically) set out, they would swear they be brought to school again.

RICHARD HOOKER was one of the most distinguished, as well as one of the earliest prose writers of this period. He was born of poor but respectable parentage, at Heavy-tree, near Exeter, in 1554. His parents, in consequence of the limitedness of their circumstances, designed him for a trade, and accordingly placed him in school at Exeter with a view to prepare for his future employment. His schoolmaster, however, soon discerned his extraordinary genius, and prevailed upon his father to continue him at school, assuring him, 'that his natural endowments and learning were both so remarkable, that God would provide him some patron who would free them from any future care or charge over him.' In consequence of this representation of young Hooker's teacher, his uncle, John Hooker, who was chamberlain of Exeter, felt a deep interest in his future destiny; and being well known to Jewell, bishop of Salisbury, he made him a visit, and 'besought him, for charity's sake, to look favorably upon a poor nephew of his, whom nature had fitted for a scholar; but the estate of his parents was so narrow, that they were unable to give him the advantages of learning; and that the bishop, therefore, would become his patron, and prevent him from being a tradesman, for he was a boy of remarkable hopes.' The bishop, having satisfied himself that this representation was just, took the boy under his care, and obtained admission for him into Corpus-Christi College, Oxford.

At the university Hooker studied with great ardor, and equal success, and soon became much respected for his modesty, prudence, and piety. After Jewell's death, he was patronized by Sandys, bishop of London, who sent his son to Oxford, to enjoy the benefit of Hooker's instructions. He had, at the same time, another pupil, George Cranmer, a grand-nephew of the famous archbishop of the same name; and with both these young men he formed an intimate and lasting friendship. In 1579, Hooker's skill in the oriental languages led to his temporary appointment as deputy-professor of Hebrew; and having held this important position for two years, he, at the expiration of that time, entered into holy orders. Soon after he entered the ministry he had the misfortune to be entrapped into a marriage which proved a constant source of annoyance to him during life. The circumstances of this union, which place, in a strong light, the simple and unsuspecting nature of the man, were as follows:—Having been appointed to preach at St. Paul's Cross, in London, he put up at a house set apart for the reception of the preachers. When he arrived there from Oxford he was wet and weary; but he received so much attention from the hostess, that, according to Walton, in his excess of gratitude, 'he thought himself bound in conscience to believe all that she said. So the good man came to be persuaded by her that he was a man of tender constitution; and that it was best for him to have a wife that might prove a nurse to him—such an one as might both prolong his life and make it more comfortable; and such an one she could and would provide for him, if he thought fit to marry.' Hooker, little apt to suspect in others that guile of which he himself was so entirely free, became the dupe of this woman, authorizing her to select a wife for him, and promising to marry whomsoever she should choose. The wife she provided was her own daughter, described by Walton, as 'a silly, clownish woman, and withal a mere Zantippe,' whom, however, he married according to his promise. With this helpmate Hooker led but an uncomfortable life, though, apparently, in a spirit of resignation. When Sandys and Cranmer visited him at a rectory in Buckinghamshire, to which he had been presented in 1584, they found him reading Horace, and tending sheep in the absence of his servant. In his house they received little entertainment, except from his conversation; and this even, Mrs. Hooker did not fail to disturb, by calling him away to rock the cradle, and by exhibiting such other examples of ill manners, as made them glad to depart on the following morning. In taking leave of his former tutor, Cranmer expressed his regret at the smallness of his income, and the uncomfortable state of his domestic affairs; to which the worthy man replied, 'My dear George, if saints have usually a double share in the miseries of this life, I, that am none, ought not to repine at what my wise Creator hath appointed for me, but labour (as indeed I do daily) to submit mine to his will, and possess my soul in patience and peace.'

On his return to London, Sandys made a strong appeal to his father in behalf of Hooker, the result of which was the appointment of the meek divine, in 1585, to the office of master of the Temple. He, accordingly, removed to London, and commenced his labors as forenoon preacher. At the same period the office of afternoon lecturer at the Temple was filled by Walter Travers, a man of great learning and eloquence, but of high Calvinistical opinions, while the views of Hooker, both in church government and on points of theology, were very moderate. The consequence was, that the doctrines delivered from the pulpit varied in their character, according to the preacher from whom they proceeded. Indeed, the two orators sometimes preached avowedly in opposition to each other—a circumstance which gave occasion to the remark, that 'the forenoon sermons spoke Canterbury, and the afternoon, Geneva.' This disputation, though conducted with good temper, excited so much attention, that Archbishop Whitgift suspended Travers from preaching. A printed controversy ensued between him and Hooker, which, to the latter, was found so disagreeable, that he expressed to the archbishop an earnest desire to retire into the country, where he might be permitted to live in peace, and might have leisure to finish his treatise *Of the Laws of Ecclesiastical Polity*, already begun. A letter which he wrote to the archbishop on this occasion deserves here to be introduced, as it shows, not only the peacefulness of temper which adhered to him through life, but likewise the object that his great work was designed to accomplish. It is as follows :—

My lord,—When I lost the freedom of my cell, which was my college, yet I found some degree of it in my quiet country parsonage. But I am weary of the noise and oppositions of this place; and, indeed, God and nature did not intend me for contentions, but for study and quietness. And, my lord, my particular contests here with Mr. Travers have proved the more unpleasant to me, because I believe him to be a good man; and that belief hath occasioned me to examine mine own conscience concerning his opinions. And to satisfy that, I have consulted the holy Scriptures, and other laws, both human and divine, whether the conscience of him and others of his judgment ought to be so far complied with by us as to alter our frame of church government, our manner of God's worship, our praising and praying to him, aud our established ceremonies, as often as their tender consciences shall require us. And in this examination I have not only satisfied myself, but have begun a treatise in which I intend the satisfaction of others; by a demonstration of the reasonableness of our laws of ecclesiastical polity. But, my lord, I shall never be able to finish what I have begun, unless I be removed into some quiet parsonage, where I may see God's blessings spring out of my mother earth, and eat my own bread in peace and privacy; a place where I may, without disturbance, meditate my approaching mortality, and that great account which all flesh must give at the last day to the God of all spirits.

In consequence of this appeal, Hooker was presented, in 1591, to the rectory of Boscomb, in Wiltshire, where he soon after completed four books of his treatise, which were published in 1594. Queen Elizabeth having, in the following year, presented him to the rectory of Bishop's-Bourne, in Kent, he removed to that place, and there passed the remainder of his life in the faithful discharge of the duties of his office. Here he wrote the fifth book, which was published in 1597; but the remaining three books did not appear until after the author's death, though he had the satisfaction to live long enough to complete them. He died in the month of November, 1600, at the comparatively early age of forty-six. A few days previous to his death, his house was robbed, and when the fact was mentioned to him, he anxiously inquired whether his books and papers were safe. Being answered in the affirmative, he exclaimed, 'Then it matters not, for no other loss can trouble me.'

Hooker's treatise on 'Ecclesiastical Polity,' displays an astonishing amount of learning, sagacity, and industry; and is so excellently written, that, according to the judgment of Bishop Louth, 'the author has, in correctness, propriety, and purity of English style, hardly been surpassed, or even equalled by any of his successors.' His argument against the Puritans is conducted with rare moderation and candor, and certainly the Church of England has never had a more powerful defender. The work is not to be regarded simply as a theological treatise; it is still referred to as a great authority upon the whole range of moral and political principles. It also bears a value as the first publication in the English language that observed a strict methodical arrangement, and presented a train of clear logical reasoning. As specimens of the body of the work, we present the following extracts:—

SCRIPTURE AND THE LAW OF NATURE.

What the Scripture proposeth, the same in all points it doth perform. Howbeit, that here we swerve not in judgment, one thing especially we must observe; namely, that the absolute perfection of Scripture is seen by relation unto that end whereto it tendeth. And even hereby it cometh to pass, that, first, such as imagine the general and main drift of the body of sacred Scripture not to be so large as it is, nor that God did thereby intend to deliver, as in truth he doth, a full instruction in all things unto salvation necessary, the knowledge whereof man by nature could not otherwise in this life attain unto; they are by this very mean induced, either still to look for new revelations from heaven, or else dangerously to add to the word of God uncertain tradition, that so the doctrine of man's salvation may be complete; which doctrine we constantly hold in all respects, without any such things added to be so complete, that we utterly refuse as much as once to acquaint ourselves with any thing further. Whatsoever, to make up the doctrine of man's salvation, is added as in supply of the Scripture's insufficiency, we reject it; Scripture, purposing this, hath perfectly and fully done it. Again, the scope and purpose of God in delivering the holy Scripture, such as do take more largely than behoveth, they, on the contrary, side-racking and stretching it further than by him was meant, are drawn into sundry great inconveniences. They, pretending the Scripture's perfection, infer thereupon, that in Scripture all things lawful to be done must needs be contained. We count those things perfect which want nothing requisite for the end whereto they were instituted. As, therefore, God created every part and particle of man exactly perfect—that is to say, in all points sufficient unto that use for which he appointed it—so the Scripture, yea, every sentence thereof, is perfect, and wanteth nothing requisite unto that purpose for which God delivered the same. So that, if hereupon we conclude, that because the Scripture is perfect, therefore all things lawful to be done are comprehended in the Scripture; we may even as well conclude so of every sentence, as if the whole sum and body thereof, unless we first of all prove that it was the drift, scope, and purpose of Almighty God in holy Scripture to comprise all things which man may practice. But admit this, and mark, I beseech you, what would follow. God, in delivering Scripture to his church, should clean have abrogated among them the Law of Nature, which is an infallible knowledge imprinted in the minds of all the children of men, whereby both general principles for directing of human actions are comprehended, and conclusions derived from them; upon which conclusions groweth in particularity the choice of good and evil in the daily affairs of this life. Admit this, and what shall the Scripture be but a snare and a torment to weak consciences, filling them with infinite perplexities, scrupulosities, doubts insoluble, and extreme despairs? Not that the Scripture itself doth cause any such thing (for it tendeth to the clean contrary, and the fruit thereof is resolute assurance and certainty in that it teacheth); but the necessities of this life urging men to do that which the light of nature, common discretion, and judgment of itself directeth them unto; on the other side, this doctrine teaching them that so to do were to sin against their own souls, and that they put forth their hands to iniquity, whatsoever they go about, and have not first the sacred Scripture of God for direction; how can it choose but bring the simple a thousand times to their wit's end. How can it choose but vex and amaze them? For in every action of common life, to find out some sentence clearly and infallibly setting before our eyes what we ought to do (seem we in Scripture never to expect), would trouble us more than we are aware. In weak and tender minds, we little know what misery this strict opinion would breed, besides the stops it would make in the whole course of men's lives and actions. Make all things sin which we do by direction of nature's light, and by the rule of common discretion, without thinking at all upon Scripture; admit the position, and parents shall cause their children to sin, as oft as they cause them to do any thing, before they come to years of capacity, and be ripe for knowledge in the Scripture. Admit this, and it shall not be with masters as it was with him in the gospel; but servants being commanded to go, shall stand still till they have their errand warranted unto them by Scripture. Which, as it standeth with Christian duty in some cases, so in common affairs to require it were most unfit.

ZEAL AND FEAR IN RELIGION.

Two affections there are, the forces whereof, as they bear the greater or lesser sway in man's heart, frame accordingly to the stamp and character of his religion—the one zeal, the other fear. Zeal, unless it be rightly guided, when it endeavoureth most busily to please God, forceth upon him those unseasonable offices which please him not. For which cause, if they who this way swerve, be compared with such sincere, sound, and discreet as Abraham was in matter of religion, the service of the one is like unto flattery, the other like the faithful sedulity of friendship. Zeal, except it be ordered aright, when it bendeth itself unto conflict with all things either indeed, or but imagined to be, opposite unto religion, useth the razor many times with such eagerness, that the very life of religion itself is thereby hazarded; through hatred of tares the corn in the field of God is plucked up. So that zeal needeth both ways a sober guide. Fear, on the other side, if it have not the light of true understanding concerning God, wherewith to be moderated, breedeth likewise superstition. It is therefore dangerous, that, in things divine, we should work too much upon the spur either of zeal or fear. Fear is a good solicitor to devotion. Howbeit, sith fear in this kind doth grow from an apprehension of Deity endued with irresistible power to hurt, and is, of all affections (anger excepted), the unaptest to admit any conference with reason, for which cause the wise man doth say of fear, that it is a betrayer of the forces of reasonable understanding; therefore, except men know beforehand what manner of service pleaseth God, while they are fearful they try all things which fancy offereth. Many there are who never think on God but when they are in extremity of fear; and then, because what to think or what to do, they are uncertain; perplexity not suffering them to be idle, they think and do, as it were in a phrensy, they know not what. Superstition neither knoweth the right kind, nor observeth the due measure, of actions belonging to the service of God, but is always joined with a wrong opinion touching things divine. Superstition is, when things are either abhorred or observed, with a zealous or fearful, but erroneous relation to God. By means whereof, the superstitious do sometimes serve, though the true God, yet with needless offices, and defraud him of duties necessary, sometimes load others than him with such honours as properly are his.

DEFENCE OF REASON.

But so it is, the name of the light of nature is made hateful with men; the star of reason and learning, and all other such like helps beginneth no otherwise to be thought of, than if it were an unlucky comet; or as if God had so accursed it, that it should never shine or give light in things concerning our duty any way toward him, but be esteemed as that star in the revelation, called Wormwood, which, being fallen from heaven, maketh rivers and waters in which it falleth so bitter, that men tasting them die thereof. A number there are who think they can not admire as they ought the power and authority of the word of God, if in things divine they should attribute any force to man's reason; for which cause they never use reason so willingly as to disgrace reason. Their usual and common discourses are unto this effect. First, 'the natural man perceiveth not the things of the Spirit of God, for they are foolishness unto him; neither can he know them, because they are spiritually discerned,' &c. &c. By these and the like disputes, an opinion hath spread itself very far in the world; as if the way to be ripe in faith, were to be raw in wit and judgment; as if reason were an enemy unto religion, childish simplicity the mother of ghostly and divine wisdom.

* * * * * * * * *

To our purpose, it is sufficient that whosoever doth serve, honour, and obey God, whosoever believeth in him, that man would no more do this than innocents and infants do but for the light of natural reason that shineth in him, and maketh him apt to apprehend those things of God, which being by grace discovered, are effectual to persuade reasonable minds, and none other, that honour, obedience, and credit, belong aright unto God. No man cometh unto God to offer him sacrifice, to pour out supplication and prayers before him, or to do him any service, which doth not first believe him both to be, and to be a rewarder of them who in such sort seek unto him. Let men be taught this, either by revelation from heaven, or by instruction upon earth; by labour, study, and meditation, or by the only secret inspiration of the Holy Ghost; whatsoever the mean be they know it by, if the knowledge thereof were possible without discourse of natural reason, why should none be found capable thereof but only men; nor men till such time as they come unto ripe and full ability to work by reasonable understanding? The whole drift of the Scripture of God, what is it, but only to teach theology? Theology, what is it, but the science of things divine? What science can be attained unto, without the help of natural discourse and reason? Judge you of that which I speak, saith the apostle. In vain it were to speak any thing of God, but that by reason men are able somewhat to judge of what they hear, and by discourse to discern how consonant it is to truth. Scripture, indeed, teacheth things above nature, things which our reason by itself could not reach unto. Yet those also we believe, knowing by reason that the Scripture is the word of God. * * The thing we have handled according to the question moved about it, which question is, whether the light of reason be so pernicious, that, in divising laws for the church, men ought not by it to search what may be fit and convenient? For this cause, therefore, we have endeavored to make it appear, how, in the nature of reason itself, there is no impediment, but that the self-same spirit which revealeth the things that God hath set down in his law, may also be thought to aid and direct men in finding out, by the light of reason, what laws are expedient to be made for the guiding of his church, over and besides them that are in Scripture.

Lecture the Seventeenth.

SIR FRANCIS BACON—RICHARD GRAFTON—JOHN STOW—RAPHAEL HOLINSHED—JOHN HOOKER—FRANCIS BOTEVILLE—WILLIAM HARRISON—RICHARD HAKLUYT—SAMUEL PURCHAS—JOHN DAVIS—GEORGE SANDYS—WILLIAM LITHGOW.

OUR remarks in the last lecture embraced a sketch and illustrations of four very eminent and distinguished men among the early prose writers of the age of Elizabeth. But great as they unquestionably were, they were immeasurably surpassed by the transcendant genius of Bacon, successively made Lord High Chancellor of England, Baron Verulam, and Viscount St. Albans.

FRANCIS BACON was the son of Sir Nicholas Bacon, Lord Keeper of the great seal, and was born in London on the twenty-second of January 1561. In his childhood he had, from his father's position, free access to the court, and he there displayed such vivacity of intellect, and sedateness of conduct, that Queen Elizabeth was accustomed to call him her young lord-keeper. At the age of thirteen he entered Trinity College, Cambridge, where the rapidity and solidity of his literary and scientific attainments, more than realized the brilliant promise of his childhood. Before he was sixteen years of age he became disgusted with the Aristotelian philosophy, which at that time held unquestioned sway in the great English schools of learning. This dislike of the philosophy of Aristotle, Bacon, as he himself declares, 'fell into not for the worthlessness of the author, to whom he would ever ascribe all high attributes, but for the unfruitfulness of the way; being a philosophy only strong for disputations and contentions, but barren of the production of works for the benefit of the life of man.'

After having passed about four years at Cambridge, and when not yet seventeen years of age, Bacon's father called him from the university to attend, into France, the queen's ambassador, Sir Amyas Pawlet. The esteem and confidence of this minister he so thoroughly gained, that he soon after charged him with a mission to the queen, which he executed with the entire approbation of both parties, and then returned again to France to finish his travels. The result of his observation abroad afterward appeared in a work entitled, *Of the State of Europe*, and which was, perhaps, his first literary performance.

The sudden death of his father, which occurred in 1579, compelled Bacon to return hastily to England, and engage in some secular employment. After in vain soliciting his uncle, lord Burleigh, to procure for him such a provision from government as would allow him to devote his time to literature and philosophy, he entered Gray's Inn, where he spent several years in the study of the law. While engaged in practice as a barrister, however, he did not forget philosophy; as it appears that he sketched, at an early period of life, his great work called *The Instauration of the Sciences*. In 1590, Bacon obtained the post of Counsel Extraordinary to the queen; and three years after sat in Parliament for the county of Middlesex. As an orator he is spoken of by Ben Jonson, and other contemporaries in terms of the highest praise. In one of his speeches, he distinguished himself by taking the popular side in a question respecting some large subsidies demanded by the court; but finding that he had given great offence to her majesty, he at once altered his tone, and condescended to apologize with that servility which unhappily appeared in too many of his subsequent actions. To lord Burleigh and his son Robert Cecil, Bacon continued to crouch in the hope of advancement, till at length, finding himself disappointed in that quarter, he attached himself to Burleigh's rival, Essex, who, with the utmost ardor of a generous friendship, endeavored to procure for him, in 1594, the office of attorney general, which was then vacant. In this attempt he was, however, defeated through the influence of the Cecils, who were jealous of both him and his friends; but he, in some degree, soothed Bacon's disappointment by presenting to him an estate at Twickenham, with two thousand pounds. It is painful to relate the manner in which Bacon repaid such benefits. When Essex was brought to trial for a conspiracy against the queen, the friend whom he had so largely obliged, and in whom he had entirely confided, not only deserted him in the hour of need, but unnecessarily appeared as counsel against him, and by every art and distorting ingenuity of a pleader, endeavored to magnify his crimes. He complied, moreover, after the Earl's execution with the queen's request that he would write *A Declaration of the Practices and Treasons Attempted and Committed by Robert, Earl of Essex;* which was published by authority. Into such conduct, which indicates a lamentable want of high moral principle, courage and self-respect, Bacon was, in some measure, led by pecuniary difficulties, into which his improvident and ostentatious habits, coupled with the relative inadequacy of his revenues, had plunged him. By maintaining himself in the good graces of the court, he hoped to secure that professional advancement which would not only fill his empty coffers, but gratify those ambitious longings that had arisen in his mind. But temptations of this sort, though they may palliate, can never excuse such immoralities as those which Bacon, on this, and on several future occasions, showed himself capable.

On the accession of James the First to the crown of England, the fortunes of Bacon began to improve. He was knighted in the first year of that monarch's reign, and, in subsequent years, obtained successively the offices of king's counsel, solicitor-general, judge of the Marshalsea court, and attorney general, the last of which was bestowed upon him in 1613. In the execution of his duties, he did not scruple to lend himself to the most arbitrary measures of the court, and even assisted in an attempt to extort from an aged clergyman named Peacham, a confession of treason, by torturing him on a rack. In 1619, Bacon reached the summit of his ambition, by being created Lord High Chancellor of England, Baron Verulam, and in the following year, Viscount St. Albans. As Chancellor, it can not be concealed that, both in his political and judicial capacities, he grossly deserted his duty. He not only suffered the king's favorite, Villiers, to interfere with his decisions as a judge, but by accepting numerous presents or bribes from suitors, gave occasion, in 1621, to a parliamentary inquiry, which resulted in his condemnation and disgrace. He fully confessed all the articles of corruption laid to his charge—twenty-three in number; and when waited upon by a committee of the House of Lords, appointed to inquire whether the confession was subscribed by himself, he remarked, 'It is my act, my hand, my heart: I beseech your lordships to be merciful to a broken reed.'

Banished by this act from public life, Bacon had now ample leisure to attend to his philosophical aud literary pursuits; though these, even while he was engaged in business, had by no means been neglected. In 1597, he published the first edition of his 'Essays,' which were afterward greatly enlarged. These, as he himself says of them, 'come home to men's business and bosoms; and like the late new half-pence, the pieces are small, and the silver is good.' From the interesting nature of the subjects of these 'Essays,' and the excellence of their style, the work immediately acquired great popularity, and to the present day continues the most generally read of all the author's productions. 'It is also,' to use the language of Dugald Stewart, 'one of those where the superiority of his genius appears to the greatest advantage, the novelty and depth of his reflections often receiving a strong relief from the triteness of his subject. It may be read from beginning to end in a few hours, and, yet after the twentieth perusal, one seldom fails to remark something in it overlooked before. This, indeed, is a characteristic of all Bacon's writings, and is only to be accounted for by the inexhaustible aliment they furnish to our thoughts, and the sympathetic activity they impart to our torpid faculties.'

In 1605, Bacon published another work, which still continues to be extensively perused, under the title, *Of the Proficience and Advancement of Learning, Divine and Human.* This volume constitutes the first part of his great work, called 'The Instauration of the Sciences.' The second part, entitled *Novum Organum*, is that upon which, chiefly, his high reputation, as a philosopher, is based, and on the composition of which he bestowed most labor. It was not published until 1620. The concluding part of the volume relates, exclusively, to revealed religion. In the first part of the *Ad-*

vancement of Learning, after considering the excellencies of knowledge and the means of disseminating it, together with what had already been done for its advancement, and what omitted, Bacon proceeds to divide the subject into the three branches of history, poetry, and philosophy; these having reference to what he considers 'the three parts of man's understanding—memory, imagination, and reasoning.' The second, and most important part of the work, consists of aphorisms, the first of which furnishes a key to the author's leading doctrines. It is as follows:—'Man, who is the servant and interpreter of nature, can act and understand no farther than he has, either in operation or in contemplation, observed of the method and order of nature.' This new method of employing the understanding in adding to human knowledge was designed to effect an entire reformation in the intellectual operations.

The third part of 'The Instauration of the Sciences,' entitled the *History of Nature*, is devoted to the facts and phenomena of natural science, including original observations made by Bacon himself, which, though sometimes incorrect, are useful in exemplifying the inductive method of searching for truth. The fourth, is called *Scala Intellectus*, because it points out a succession of steps by which the understanding may ascend in such investigations. The author projected two other parts to the same general work, but did not live to execute them. He also produced another celebrated work entitled, *Of the Wisdom of the Ancients*, the object of which was to discover secret meanings in the mythological fables of antiquity. He wrote also *Felicities of Queen Elizabeth's Reign*, *a History of King Henry the Eighth*, a philosophical romance called the *New Atlantis*, and several minor productions.

Though ignominiously driven from public life, Bacon devoted himself still with untiring assiduity to philosophical investigations; and one of his experiments was the immediate cause of his death. While travelling in his carriage at a time when there was snow upon the ground, he began to consider whether flesh might not be preserved by snow as well as by salt. In order to make the experiment, he alighted at a cottage near Highgate, bought a hen, and stuffed it with snow. This so chilled him that he was unable to return home, but went to the Earl of Arundel's house, in the neighborhood, where his illness was so much increased by the dampness of the bed into which he was put, that his death soon followed—an event that occurred on the ninth of April, 1626, and in the sixty-third year of his age. Thus died Sir Francis Bacon, who, had the virtues of his heart been equal to his genius, would have been one of the greatest men that any age or country ever produced. His will contains the following strikingly prophetic passage:—'My name and memory I leave to foreign nations, and to mine own country after some time has passed over.'

Bacon, like Sidney, was 'a warbler of poetic prose.' No English writer has surpassed him in fervor and brilliancy of style, in force of expression, or in richness and magnificence of imagery. Keen in discovering analogies where no resemblance is apparent to common eyes, he has sometimes indulged, to excess, in the exercise of this talent. But in general his comparisons are not less clear and apposite than full of imagination and meaning. He has treated of philosophy with all the splendor, yet none of the vagueness, of poetry. Sometimes, too, his style possesses a degree of conciseness very rarely to be found in the compositions of the Elizabethan age. In the subjoined extracts we are aware that we present but a faint view of the genius of this wonderful writer:—

UNIVERSITIES.

As water, whether it be the dew of heaven or the springs of the earth, doth scatter and lose itself in the ground, except it be collected into some receptacle, where it may by union comfort and sustain itself; and, for that cause, the industry of man hath framed and made spring-heads, conduits, cisterns, and pools, which men have accustomed likewise to beautify and adorn with accomplishments of magnificence and state, as well as of use and necessity; so knowledge, whether it descend from divine inspiration or spring from human sense, would soon perish and vanish to oblivion, if it were not preserved in books, traditions, conferences, and places appointed, as universities, colleges, and schools, for the receipt and comforting the same.

USES OF KNOWLEDGE.

Learning taketh away the wildness, barbarism, and fierceness of men's minds though a little of it doth rather work a contrary effect. It taketh away all levity, temerity, and insolency, by copious suggestion of all doubts and difficulties, and acquainting the mind to balance reasons on both sides, and to turn back the first offers and conceits of the kind, and to accept of nothing but [what is] examined and tried. It taketh away all vain admiration of any thing, which is the root of all weakness: for all things are admired, either because they are new, or because they are great. * * If a man meditate upon the universal frame of nature, the earth with men upon it (the divineness of souls excepted) will not seem more than an ant-hill, where some ants carry corn, and some carry their young, and some go empty, and all to and fro a little heap of dust. It taketh away or mitigateth fear of death, or adverse fortune; which is one of the greatest impediments of virtue, and imperfection of manners. * * Virgil did excellently and profoundly couple the knowledge of causes and the conquest of all fears together. It were too long to go over the particular remedies which learning doth minister to all the diseases of the mind—sometimes purging the ill humours, sometimes opening the obstructions, sometimes helping the digestion, sometimes increasing appetite, sometimes healing the wounds and ulcerations thereof, and the like; and I will therefore conclude with the chief reason of all, which is, that it disposeth the constitution of the mind not to be fixed or settled in the defects thereof, but still to be capable and susceptible of reformation. For the unlearned man knoweth not what it is to descend into himself, and call himself to account; nor the pleasure of that most pleasant life, which consists in our daily feeling ourselves become better.[1] The good parts he hath, he will learn to show to the full, and use them dexterously, but not much to increase them: the faults he hath, he will learn how to hide and colour them, but not much to amend them; like an ill mower, that mows on still and never whets his scythe. Whereas, with the learned man it fares otherwise, that he doth ever intermix the correction and amendment of his mind with the use and employment thereof.

---

[1] This expression is given in the original in Latin.

PROSPERITY AND ADVERSITY.

The virtue of prosperity is temperance; the virtue of adversity is fortitude. Prosperity is the blessing of the Old Testament; adversity is the blessing of the New, which carrieth the greater benediction and the clearer revelation of God's favour. Yet even in the Old Testament, if you listen to David's harp, you shall hear as many hearselike airs as carols; and the pencil of the Holy Ghost hath laboured more in describing the afflictions of Job than the felicities of Solomon. Prosperity is not without many fears and distastes; and adversity is not without comforts and hopes. We see in needle-works and embroideries, it is more pleasing to have a lively work upon a sad and solemn ground, than to have a dark and melancholy work upon a lightsome ground; judge, therefore, of the pleasure of the heart by the pleasure of the eye. Certainly virtue is like precious odours, most fragrant where they are incensed or crushed: for prosperity doth best discover vice, but adversity doth best discover virtue.

FRIENDSHIP.

It had been hard for him that spake it, to have put more truth and untruth together in few words, than in that speech, 'Whoever is delighted in solitude, is either a wild beast or a god;' for it is most true, that a natural and secret hatred and aversion towards society, in any man, hath somewhat of the savage beast; but it is most untrue, that it should have any character at all of the divine nature, except it proceed, not out of a pleasure in solitude, but out of a love and desire to sequester a man's self for a higher conversation: such as is found to have been falsely and feignedly in some of the heathens—as Epimenides, the Candian; Numa, the Roman; Empedocles, the Sicilian; and Apollonius, of Tyana; and truly, and really, in divers of the ancient hermits and holy fathers of the church. But little do men perceive what solitude is, and how far it extendeth; for a crowd is not company, and faces are but a gallery of pictures, and talk but a tinkling cymbal where there is no love. The Latin adage meeteth with it a little: 'Magna civitas, magna solitudo,'—['Great city, great solitude;'] because in a great town friends are scattered, so that there is not that fellowship, for the most part, which is in less neighbourhoods; but we may go farther, and affirm most truly, that it is a mere and miserable solitude to want true friends, without which the world is but a wilderness; and, even in this scene also of solitude, whosoever, in the frame of his nature and affections, is unfit for friendship, he taketh it of the beast, and not from humanity.

A principal fruit of friendship is the ease and discharge of the fullness of the heart, which passions of all kinds do cause and induce. We know diseases of stoppings and suffocations are the most dangerous in the body, and it is not much otherwise in the mind: you may take sarza to open the liver, steel to open the spleen, flour of sulphur for the lungs, castoreum for the brain; but no receipt openeth the heart but a true friend, to whom you may impart griefs, joys, fears, hopes, suspicions, counsels, and whatsoever lieth upon the heart to oppress it, in a kind of civil shrift or confession.

It is a strange thing to observe how high a rate great kings and monarchs do set upon this fruit of friendship whereof we speak—so great, as they purchase it many times at the hazard of their own safety and greatness: for princes, in regard of the distance of their fortune from that of their subjects and servants, can not gather this fruit, except, to make themselves capable thereof, they raise some persons to be, as it were, companions, and almost equals to themselves, which many times sorteth to inconvenience. The modern languages give unto such persons the name of favourites, or privadoes, as if it were matter of grace or conversation; but the Roman name attaineth the true use and cause thereof, naming them 'participes curarum,' [participators in cares;] for it is that which tieth the knot: and we see plainly that this hath been done, not by weak and passionate princes only, but by the wisest and most politic that ever reigned, who have oftentimes joined to themselves some of their servants, whom both themselves have called friends, and allowed others likewise to call them in the same manner, using the word which is received between private men.

It is not to be forgotten what Comineus observeth of his first master, Duke Charles the Hardy—namely, that he would communicate his secrets with none; and, least of all, those secrets which troubled him most. Whereupon he goeth on, and saith, that towards his latter time, that closeness did impair and a little perish his understanding. Surely Comineus might have made the same judgment also, if it had pleased him, of his second master, Louis XI., whose closeness was indeed his tormentor. The parable of Pythagoras is dark, but true, 'Cor ne edito,'—['Eat not the heart.'] Certainly if a man would give it a hard phrase, those that want friends to open themselves unto, are cannibals of their own hearts; but one thing is most admirable, (wherewith I will conclude this first fruit of friendship,) which is, that this communicating of a man's self to his friend, works two contrary effects, for it redoubleth joys, and cutteth griefs in halves; for there is no man that imparteth his joys to his friend, but he joyeth the more, and no man that imparteth his griefs to his friend, but he grieveth the less. So that it is, in truth, of operation upon a man's mind of like virtue as the alchymists used to attribute to their stone for man's body, that it worketh all contrary effects, but still to the good and benefit of nature; but yet, without praying in aid of alchymists, there is a manifest image of this in the ordinary course of nature; for, in bodies, union strengtheneth and cherisheth any natural action, and, on the other side, weakeneth and dulleth any violent impression—and even so is it of minds.

The second fruit of friendship is healthful and sovereign for the understanding, as the first is for the affections; for friendship maketh indeed a fair day in the affections from storm and tempests, but it maketh daylight in the understanding, out of darkness and confusion of thoughts. Neither is this to be understood only of faithful counsel, which a man receiveth from his friend; but before you come to that, certain it is, that whosoever hath his mind fraught with many thoughts, his wits and understanding do clarify and break up, in the communicating and discoursing with another; he tosseth his thoughts more easily—he marshalleth them more orderly—he seeth how they look when they are turned into words—finally, he waxeth wiser than himself; and that more by an hour's discourse than by a day's meditation. It was well said by Themistocles to the king of Persia, 'That speech was like cloth of Arras, opened and put abroad'—whereby the imagery doth appear in figure, whereas in thoughts they lie but as in packs. Neither is this second fruit of friendship, in opening the understanding, restrained only to such friends as are able to give a man counsel (they indeed are best,) but even without that a man learneth of himself, and bringeth his own thoughts to light, and whetteth his wits as against a stone, which itself cuts not. In a word, a man were better relate himself to a statue or picture, than to suffer his thoughts to pass in smother.

Add now, to make this second fruit of friendship complete, that other point which lieth more open, and falleth within vulgar observation—which is faithful counsel from a friend. Heraclitus saith well, in one of his enigmas, 'Dry light is ever the best;' and certain it is, that the light that a man receiveth by counsel from another, is drier and purer than that which cometh from his own understanding and judgment, which is ever infused and drenched in his affections and customs So as there is as much difference between the counsel that a friend giveth, and that a man giveth himself, as there is between the counsel of a friend and of a flatterer; for there is no such flatterer as is a man's self, and there is no such remedy against flattery of a man's self as the liberty of a friend. Counsel is of two sorts; the one concerning manners, the other concerning business: for the first, the best preservative to keep the mind in health is the faithful admonition of a friend. The calling of a man's self to a strict account, is a medicine sometimes too piercing and corrosive; reading good books of morality is a little flat and dead; observing our faults in others is sometimes improper for our case; but the best receipt (best, I say, to work, and best to take) is the admonition of a friend. It is a strange thing to behold what gross errors and extreme absurdities many (especially of the greater sort) do commit, for want of a friend to tell them of them, to the great damage both of their fame and fortune: for, as St. James saith, they are as men 'that look sometimes into a glass, and presently forget their own shape and favour:' as for business, a man may think, if he will, that two eyes see no more than one; or that a gamester seeth always more than a looker-on; or, that a man in anger is as wise as he that hath said over the four-and-twenty letters; or, that a musket may be shot off as well upon the arm as upon a rest; and such other fond and high imaginations to think himself all in all: but when all is done, the help of good counsel is that which setteth business straight; and if any man think that he will take counsel, but it shall be by pieces, asking counsel in one business of one man, and in another business of another man; it is as well (that is to say, better, perhaps, than if he asked none at all,) but he runneth two dangers; one, that he shall not be faithfully counselled—for it is a rare thing, except it be from a perfect and entire friend, to have counsel given, but such as shall be bowed and crooked to some ends which he hath that giveth it; the other, that he shall have counsel given, hurtful and unsafe (though with good meaning,) and mixed partly of mischief and partly of remedy—even as if you would call a physician, that is thought good for the cure of the disease you complain of, but is unacquainted with your body—and, therefore, may put you in a way for present cure, but overthroweth your health in some other kind, and so cure the disease, and kill the patient: but a friend, that is wholly acquainted with a man's estate, will beware, by furthering any present business, how he dasheth upon other inconvenience—and, therefore, rest not upon scattered counsels, for they will rather distract and mislead, than settle and direct. After these two noble fruits of friendship (peace in the affections, and support of the judgment,) followeth the last fruit, which is, like the pomegranate, full of many kernels—I mean, aid and bearing a part in all actions and occasions. Here, the best way to represent to life the manifold use of friendship, is to cast and see how many things there are which a man can not do himself; and then it will appear that it was a sparing speech of the ancients to say 'that a friend is another himself.' Men have their time, and die many times in desire of some things which they principally take to heart; the bestowing of a child, the finishing of a work, or the like. If a man have a true friend, he may rest almost secure that the care of those things will continue after him; so that a man hath, as it were, two lives in his desires. A man hath a body, and that body is confined to a place; but where friendship is, all offices of life are, as it were, granted to him and his deputy; for he may exercise them by his friend. How many things are there which a man can not, with any face or comeliness, say or do himself? A man can scarce allege his own merits with modesty, much less extol them; a man can not sometimes brook to supplicate or beg; and a number of the like, but all these things are graceful in a friend's mouth, which are blushing in a man's own. So, again, a man's person hath many proper relations which he can not put off. A man can not speak to his son but as a father; to his wife but as a husband; to his enemy but upon terms: whereas a friend may speak as the case requires, and not as it sorteth with the person. But to enumerate these things were endless: I have given the rule, where a man can not fitly play his own part; if he have not a friend, he may quit the stage.

From the eminent and distinguished prose writers whom we have just noticed, we now revert to a useful, though less brilliant, class of authors—

The English Chroniclers—a continuous succession of whom was kept up during the entire period of which we are now treating. Of these writers, Grafton, Stow, Holinshed, Hooker, Boteville, Harrison, Hakluyt, and Purchas first claim our attention.

Richard Grafton, the first of these writers mentioned, was by trade a printer, and practiced the typographical art in the city of London during the latter part of the reign of Henry the Eighth, through the reigns of that monarch's two immediate successors, and for a number of years after Elizabeth ascended the throne. Being printer to Edward the Sixth, Grafton was employed, after the death of that young king, to prepare the proclamation which declared the succession of Lady Jane Grey to the crown. For this simple professional act, he was deprived of his patent, and afterward, ostensibly for the same reason, committed to prison. While thus removed from his regular calling, he compiled *An Abridgment of the Chronicles of England*, which was published in 1562. The work possesses little merit for originality, and the author, though sometimes referred to as authority by modern compilers, holds but a low rank among English historians. It does not afford any passage that our design requires us to introduce.

John Stow was contemporary with Grafton, and enjoyed a much higher reputation as an accurate and impartial recorder of public events. He was the son of a respectable tailor, and was born in London in 1525. Of his youth nothing is farther known than that he was brought up to his father's trade, and early exhibited a strong inclination for antiquarian research. By industry and perseverance he acquired, while still following his business, a vast amount of historical information; and, in 1560, he formed the design of composing annals of English history. To prepare himself to execute this design successfully, he abandoned his trade, and travelled on foot through a considerable part of England, for the purpose of examining the historical manuscripts preserved in cathedrals and other public establishments. He also enlarged, as far as his pecuniary means would allow him, his collection of old books and manuscripts, of which there were, at that time, many scattered throughout the country, in consequence of the recent suppression of monasteries by Henry the Eighth. He was, however, compelled, through necessity, to resume his trade, and his studies were suspended, till, by the bounty of Parker, archbishop of Canterbury, he was enabled again to prosecute them.

In 1565, Stow published his *Summary of English Chronicles*, embracing the period which elapsed from the coming in of Brutus, until the commencement of the reign of Elizabeth. This work was dedicated to the Earl of Leicester, and was founded on a curious tract written by that nobleman's grandfather while he was confined in the Tower. The original chronicle was entitled *The Tree of the Commonwealth*, and was dedicated to Henry the Eighth, but it never came into that monarch's hands.

The death of bishop Parker, in 1575, materially reduced Stow's income, though he still managed to continue his researches, to which his whole time and energies were now devoted. After many years of laborious research and severe study, appeared, in 1598, his *Survey of London*, the best known of his writings, and the work which has served as the basis of all subsequent histories of that metropolis. He wrote another work, his large *Chronicle*, or *History of England*, on which he bestowed forty years' labor, and which he was very anxious to publish; but no part of it, excepting an extract under the title of *Annals of England*, ever appeared.

In his old age Stow's poverty was such as to compel him to solicit public charity. With this view he made two applications to the mayor and aldermen of London, but with little success. He at length appealed to James the First, and received the royal license 'to repair to churches, or other places, to receive the gratuities and charitable benevolence of well-disposed people.' It is little to the honor of the contemporaries of this worthy and industrious man, that he should have been thus literally reduced to beggary. Under the pressure of want and disease Stow died on the fifth of April, 1605, at the advanced age of eighty years, and was buried in the church of St. Andrew Under Shaft, London, where a suitable monument was afterward erected to his memory by his widow.

The works of this interesting author, though possessing few graces of style, have always been highly esteemed for accuracy and research. He used often to declare that, in composing them he had never allowed himself to be swayed either by fear, favor, or malice; but that he had impartially, and to the best of his knowledge, delivered the truth. So highly was his accuracy esteemed by contemporary authors, that even Bacon and Camden were accustomed to take statements upon his sole authority. We shall conclude these remarks with the following extract, taken from the 'Survey of London.'

SPORTS UPON THE ICE IN ELIZABETH'S REIGN.

When that great moor which washeth Moorfields, at the north wall of the city, is frozen over, great companies of young men go to sport upon the ice; then fetching a run, and setting their feet at a distance, and placing their bodies sidewise, they slide a great way. Others take heaps of ice, as if it were great mill-stones, and make seats; many going before, draw him that sits thereon, holding one another by the hand in going so fast; some slipping with their feet, all fall down together; some are better practiced to the ice, and bind to their shoes bones, as the legs of some beasts, and hold stakes in their hands headed with sharp iron, which sometimes they strike against the ice; and these men go on with speed as doth a bird in the air, or darts shots from some warlike engine: sometimes two men set themselves at a distance, and run one against another, as it were at tilt, with these stakes, wherewith one or both parties are thrown down, not without some hurt to their bodies; and after their fall, by reason of the violent motion, are carried a good distance from one another; and wheresoever the ice doth touch their head, it rubs off all the skin, and lays it bare; and if one fall upon his leg or arm, it is usually broken; but young men, greedy of honour, and desirous of victory, do thus exercise themselves in counterfeit battles, that they may bear the brunt more strongly when they come to it in good earnest.

Raphael Holinshed, to whom we have already had frequent occasion to refer, was one of the most remarkable of these early chroniclers, though of his history, nothing is known farther than that he died about 1580. Toward *The Chronicles* to which Holinshed's name is attached, John Hooker, an uncle of the author of the Ecclesiastical Polity, Francis Boteville, an individual of whom nothing has been recorded, farther than that he was 'a man of great learning and judgment, and a wonderful lover of antiquities,' and William Harrison, contributed. Prefixed to the historical portion of the work is a description of Britain and its inhabitants, by Harrison, which is still highly valued, as affording an interesting picture of the state of the country, and the manners of the people, in the sixteenth century. This is followed by a history of England to the Norman Conquest, by Holinshed; a history and description of Ireland, by one Richard Stanihurst, of whom nothing more is known; additional chronicles of Ireland, translated or written by Holinshed and Hooker; a description and history of Scotland mostly translated from Hector Boece, by Holinshed and Harrison; and a History of England, by Holinshed, from the Norman Conquest to 1577, when the 'Chronicles' were published. It was from the translation of Boece that Shakspeare, as we have already remarked, derived the groundwork of his tragedy of Macbeth.

Among the authors who combined their researches and learning to produce these 'Chronicles,' William Harrison is, perhaps, the most remarkable; and we are tempted to quote from 'The Chronicles,' some of his sarcastic remarks on the degeneracy of his contemporaries, their extravagance in dress, and the growth of luxury among them. But his account of the languages of Britain, being peculiarly suited to the object we have before us in these lectures, and at the same time, from the quaintness and simplicity of the style, highly amusing, is here given in preference to any other extract:—

THE LANGUAGES OF BRITAIN.

The British tongue called Cymric doth yet remain in that part of the island which is now called Wales, whither the Britons were driven after the Saxons had made a full conquest of the other, which we now call England, although the pristine intercourse thereof be not a little diminished by mixture of the Latin and Saxon speeches withal. Howbeit, many poesies and writings (in making whereof that nation hath evermore delighted) are yet extant in my time, whereby some difference between the ancient and present language may easily be discerned, notwithstanding that among all these there is nothing to be found which can set down any sound and full testimony of their own original, in remembrance whereof their bards and cunning men have been most slack and negligent. * *

Next unto the British speech, the Latin tongue was brought in by the Romans, and in manner generally planted through the whole region, as the French was after by the Normans. Of this tongue I will not say much, because there are few which be not skillful in the same. Howbeit, as the speech itself is easy and delectable, so hath it perverted the names of the ancient rivers, regions, and cities of Britain, in such wise, that in these our days their old British denominations are quite grown out of memory, and yet those of the new Latin left as most uncertain. This remaineth, also, unto my time, borrowed from the Romans, that all our deeds, evidences, charters, and writings of record, are set down in the Latin tongue, though now very barbarous, and thereunto the copies and court-rolls, and processes of courts and leets registered in the same.

The third language apparently known is the Scythian,[1] or High Dutch, induced at first by the Saxons (which the Britons call Saysonaec,[2] as they do the speakers Sayson), a hard and rough kind of speech, God wot, when our nation was brought first into acquaintance withal, but now changed with us into a far more fine and easy kind of utterance, and so polished and helped with new and milder words, that it is to be avouched how there is no one speech under the sun spoken in our time, that hath or can have more variety of words, copiousness of phrases, or figures and flowers of eloquence, than hath our English tongue, although some have affirmed us rather to bark as dogs than talk like men, because the most of our words (as they do indeed) incline unto one syllable. This, also, is to be noted as a testimony remaining still of our language, derived from the Saxons, that the general name, for the most part, of every skillful artificer in his trade endeth in *here* with us, albeit the *h* be left out, and *er* only inserted, as scrivenhere, writehere, shiphere, &c.—for scrivener, writer, and shipper, &c.; beside many other relics of that speech never to be abolished.

After the Saxon tongue came the Norman or French language over into our country, and therein were our laws written for a long time. Our children, also, were, by an especial decree, taught first to speak the same, and thereunto enforced to learn their constructions in the French, whensoever they were set to the grammar-school. In like sort, few bishops, abbots, or other clergymen, were admitted unto any ecclesiastical function here among us, but such as came out of religious houses from beyond the seas, to the end they should not use the English tongue in their sermons to the people. In the court, also, it grew into such contempt, that most men thought it no small dishonour to speak any English there; which bravery took its hold at the last likewise in the country with every ploughman, that even the very carters began to wax weary of their mother-tongue, and laboured to speak French, which as then was counted no small token of gentility. And no marvel; for every French rascal, when he came once hither, was taken for a gentleman, only because he was proud, and could use his own language. And all this (I say) to exile the English and British speeches quite out of the country. But in vain; for in the time of King Edward I., to wit, toward the latter end of his reign, the French itself ceased to be spoken generally, but most of all and by law in the midst of Edward III., and then began the English to recover and grow in more estimation than before; notwithstanding that, among our artificers, the most part of their implements, tools, and words of art, retain still their French denominations even to these our days, as the language itself is used likewise in sundry courts, books of record, and matters of law; whereof here is no place to make any particular rehearsal. Afterward, also, by diligent travail of Geoffrey Chaucer and John Gower, in the time of Richard II., and after them of John Scogan and John Lydgate, monk of Bury, our said tongue was brought to an excellent pass, notwithstanding that it never came unto the type of perfection until the time of Queen Elizabeth, wherein John Jewel, bishop of Sarum, John Fox, and sundry learned and excellent writers, have fully accomplished the ornature of the same, to their great praise and immortal commendation; although not a few other do greatly seek to strain the same, by fond affectation of foreign and strange words, presuming that to be the best English which is most corrupted with external terms of eloquence and sound of many syllables. But as this excellency of the English tongue is found in one, and the south part of this island,

---

[1] It is scarcely necessary to remark, that this term is here misapplied.

[2] The Highlanders of Scotland still speak of the English as Sassenach (meaning Saxons).

so in Wales the greatest number (as I said) retain still their own ancient language, that of the north part of the said country being less corrupted than the other, and therefore reputed for the better in their own estimation and judgment. This, also, is proper to us Englishmen, that since ours is a middle or intermediate language, and neither too rough nor too smooth in utterance, we may with much facility learn any other language, beside Hebrew, Greek, and Latin, and speak it naturally, as if we were home-born in those countries; and yet on the other side it falleth out, I wot not by what other means that few foreign nations can rightly pronounce ours, without some and that great note of imperfection, especially the Frenchmen, who also seldom write any thing that savoureth of English truly. But this of all the rest doth breed most admiration with me, that if any stranger doth hit upon some likely pronunciation of our tongue, yet in age he swerveth so much from the same, that he is worse therein than ever he was, and thereto, peradventure, halteth not a little also in his own, as I have seen by experience in Reginald Wolfe, and others, whereof I have justly marvelled.

The Cornish and Devonshire men, whose country the Britons call Cerniw, have a speech in like sort of their own, and such as hath indeed more affinity with the Armorican tongue than I can well discuss of. Yet in mine opinion, they are both but a corrupted kind of British, albeit so far degenerating in these days from the old, that if either of them do meet with a Welshman, they are not able at the first to understand one another, except here and there in some odd words, without the help of interpreters. And no marvel, in mine opinion, that the British of Cornwall is thus corrupted, since the Welsh tongue that is spoken in the north and south part of Wales doth differ so much in itself, as the English used in Scotland doth from that which is spoken among us here in this side of the island, as I have said already.

The Scottish-English hath been much broader and less pleasant in utterance than ours, because that nation hath not, till of late, endeavoured to bring the same to any perfect order, and yet it was such in manner as Englishmen themselves did speak for the most part beyond the Trent, whither any great amendment of our language had not, as then, extended itself. Howbeit, in our time the Scottish language endeavoureth to come near, if not altogether to match, our tongue in fineness of phrase and copiousness of words, and this may in part appear by a history of the Apocrypha translated into Scottish verse by Hudson, dedicated to the king of that country, and containing six books, except my memory do fail me.

Hakluyt is another of the laborious compilers of this period, to whom the world is indebted for the preservation, in an acceptable form, of narratives which would otherwise, in all human probability, have fallen into oblivion. The department of history he chose for his labors was that which is descriptive of the naval adventures and discoveries of his countrymen.

Richard Hakluyt was born in the city of London in 1553, and received his elementary education at Westminster school. From Westminster he entered Christ Church College, Oxford, where, besides the regular studies of the university, he engaged in an extensive course of reading in various languages, on geographical and maritime subjects, toward which he had early evinced a strong inclination. He soon acquired, in these departments of knowledge, such reputation, that he was appointed to lecture at Oxford on cosmography and the collateral sciences; and he carried on, at the same time, a correspondence with the celebrated continental geographers, Ortelius and Mercator. Having taken orders he obtained a desirable parish in Suffolk, but resigned it for the chaplaincy to the English ambassador at Paris, where he continued to reside for five years, during which time he cultivated the acquaintance of all persons there, eminent for their knowledge of geography and maritime history.

On his return from France, in 1588, Hakluyt was appointed by Sir Walter Raleigh one of the society of counsellors, assistants, and adventurers, to whom he assigned his patent for the prosecution of discoveries in America. He had, a few years previously to this appointment, published two small volumes of voyages to America; but these are now included in a much larger work in three volumes, the last of which was published in 1600, and the other two during the two previous years. The title which the whole bears is, *The Principal Navigations, Voyages, Traffiques, and Discoveries of the English Nation, made by Sea or Over Land, to the Remote and Farthest Distant Quarters of the Earth, within the compass of these* 1500 *years.* In the first volume are contained accounts of voyages to the north and north-east; the true state of Iceland; the defeat of the Spanish Armada; and the expedition of the Earl of Essex to Cadiz. In the second, the author relates accounts of voyages to the south and south-east; and in the third he gives the particulars connected with expeditions to North America, the West Indies, and round the world. The work contains narratives of nearly two hundred and twenty voyages, beside many relative documents, such as patents, instructions, and letters. To this collection all the subsequent compilers in this department of history have been largely indebted. In his preface, the author strongly evinces the ardor of his feelings, and presents the following interesting summary of the foreign relations of England at that period. 'Which of the kings of England before Her Majesty,' he remarks, 'displayed their banners in the Caspian Sea? Which of them have traded with the emperor of Persia, and obtained for her merchants numerous and important privileges? Who, at any time before, beheld an English regiment in the stately porch of the Grand Signior at Constantinople? Who ever found English consuls and commercial agents at Tripolis in Syria; at Aleppo, at Babylon, at Balsara: and still more, who, before this period, ever heard of Englishmen at Goa? What English ships did heretofore anchor in the great river Plate, pass and repass the straits of Magellan, range along the coasts of Chili, Peru, and all the western side of New Spain, farther indeed than the vessels of any other nation had ever ventured; traverse the immense surface of the South Sea, land upon the Lazones, in despite of the enemy; enter into alliances, amity, and traffic with the princes of the Moluccas, and the Isle of Java; double the famous Cape of Good Hope, arrive at the isle of St. Helena, and last of all, return home richly laden with the commodities of China.' This work, however, as a whole, embracing five quarto volumes, is too prolix to be interesting.

Hakluyt was the author, also, of translations of two foreign works on Florida; and, when in Paris, he published an enlarged edition of a history in the Latin language, entitled *De Rebus Oceanicis et Orbe Nevo*, by Martyr, an Italian author. This work was afterward translated into English by one Lok, a person of whom no farther mention is made. In 1601, Hakluyt published the *Discoveries of the World, from the First Original to the Year of our Lord* 1555, translated, with additions, from the Portuguese of Antonio Galvano, governor of Ternate, in the East Indies. In 1605, he was made prebendary of Westminster, which, with the rectory of Wetheringset in Suffolk, already alluded to, was the only ecclesiastical promotion that he ever received. Hakluyt died on the twenty-third of November, 1616, and was buried in Westminster Abbey, amid the tombs of other illustrious dead. At his death, his manuscript remains, which were very numerous, fell into the hands of Purchas, a brother clergyman, by whom they were afterward dispersed through his own four volumes of voyages and discoveries.

Samuel Purchas was born at Thaxstead, Essex, in 1577, and was educated at Cambridge; but in what college does not appear. Soon after he left the university he entered into holy orders, and, in 1604, obtained the vicarage of Eastwood in Essex. This, however, he soon resigned in favor of his brother, and removed to London, the better to prosecute his studies. In 1615, he was incorporated at Oxford, bachelor of divinity, having previously received the same honor from the university of Cambridge. He was, at about the same period, made rector of St. Martin's, Ludgate, in London, and chaplain to Abbot, Archbishop of Canterbury.

Though Purchas, during his whole clerical life, strictly fulfilled the sacred functions of his ministry, yet he still devoted much time to the reading of accounts of voyages, and travels, and to the study of the geography of foreign countries. In 1613, before Hakluyt's death, he published a volume under the title of *Purchas his Pilgrimage; or Relations of the World and the Religions Observed in all Ages and Places Discovered from the Creation unt this Present*; and, in 1625, appeared his great work, a history of voyages in four volumes, entitled *Purchas his Pilgrimage.* These two works form a continuation of Hakluyt's collection, but on a more extended plan, and in point of merit they are strikingly similar. Purchas has, however, one trait peculiar to himself,—that of interlarding theological reflections and discussions with his narratives. His death occurred in 1628, not in prison, as has often been asserted, but at his own residence in London, and in the fifty-second year of his age.

Besides his great work, Purchas wrote *Microcosmus, or the History of Man*, and a *Funeral Sermon*, both of which were published in 1619: he also produced the *King's Tower and Triumphant Arch of London*, which appeared in 1623. He was a writer of much ingenuity, of which the following quaint analogy of the sea from his 'Pilgrimage' is certain proof:—

THE SEA.

As God hath combined the sea and land into one globe, so their joint combination and mutual assistance is necessary to secular happiness and glory. The sea covereth one half of this patrimony of man, whereof God set him in possession when he said, 'Replenish the earth, and subdue it, and have dominion over the fish of the sea, and over the fowl of the air, and over every living thing that moveth upon the earth.' Thus should man at once lose half his inheritance, if the art of navigation did not enable him to manage this untamed beast, and with the bridle of the winds and saddle of his shipping, to make him serviceable. Now, for the services of the sea, they are innumerable: it is the great purveyor of the world's commodities to our use; conveyor of the excess of rivers; uniter, by traffic, of all nations: it presents the eye with diversified colours and motions, and is, as it were, with rich brooches, adorned with various islands. It is an open field for merchandise in peace; a pitched field for the most dreadful fights of war; yields diversity of fish and fowl for diet; materials for wealth, medicine for health, simples for medicines, pearls, and other jewels for ornament; amber and ambergrise for delight; 'the wonders of the Lord in the deep' for instruction, variety of creatures for use, multiplicity of natures for contemplation, diversity of accidents for admiration, compendiousness to the way, to full bodies healthful evacuation, to the thirsty earth fertile moisture, to distant friends pleasant meeting, to weary persons delightful refreshing, to studious and religious minds a map of knowledge, mystery of temperance, exercise of continence; school of prayer, meditation, devotion, and sobriety; refuge to the distressed, portage to the merchant, passage to the traveller, customs to the prince; springs, lakes, rivers to the earth; it hath on it tempests and calms to chastise the sins, to exercise the faith, of seamen; manifold affections in itself, to affect and stupify the subtlest philosopher; sustaineth movable fortresses for the soldier; maintaineth (as in our island) a wall of defence and watery garrison to guard the state; entertains the sun with vapours, the moon with obsequiousness, the stars also with a natural looking-glass; the sky with clouds, the air with temperateness, the soil with suppleness, the rivers with tides, the hills with moisture, the valleys with fertility; containeth most diversified matter for meteors, most multiform shapes, most various, numerous kinds, most immense, difformed, deformed, unformed monsters; once (for why should I longer detain you?) the sea yields action to the body, meditation to the mind, the world to the world, all parts thereof to each part, by this art of arts, navigation.

We have still to notice, briefly, before we conclude our present remarks, two very remarkable travellers, the one by sea and the other by land—Davis and Sandys—the former being one of those intrepid navigators of Elizabeth's reign whose adventures are recorded by Hakluyt, and the latter a son of the Archbishop of York, and author of a well-known metrical translation of 'Ovid's Metamorphosis.' We shall allude to Lithgow also, a Scottish contemporary adventurer.

JOHN DAVIS was born in the county of Devonshire, about the middle of the sixteenth century, but of what parentage is unknown. In 1585, and during the two following years, he made three voyages in search of a north-west passage to China, and discovered the straits at the entrance of Hudson's Bay, to which his name still remains attached. In 1595, he himself published a small and now exceedingly rare volume, entitled *The World's Hydrographical Description*, 'wherein,' as the title-page informs us, 'is proued not onely by aucthoritie of writers, but also by late experience of trauellers, and reasons of substantiall probabilitie, that the worlde in all his zones, clymates, and places, is habitable and inhabited, and the seas likewise universally nauigable, without any naturall anoyance to hinder the same; whereby appeares that from England there is a short and speedie passage into the South Seas to China, Molacca, Phillipina, and India, by northerly navigation, to the renowne, honour, and benefit of her maiesties state and communalty.' In corroboration of these positions, he gives a short narrative of his voyages, which, notwithstanding the unsuccessful termination of them all, he considers to afford very strong arguments in favor of the north-west passage. The extract from this narrative, which follows, with its original spelling, forms an interesting specimen of the style in which such relations, in the age of Elizabeth, were written. Davis afterward made five voyages as a pilot to the East Indies, and was killed in 1605, in a skirmish with some Japanese, off the coast of Molucca.

FROM ONE OF DAVIS'S VOYAGES.

Departing from Dartmouth, through God's merciful fauour I ariued to the place of fishing and there according to my direction I left the 2 shipps to follow that busines, taking their faithful promise not to depart vntill my returne vnto them, which shoulde bee in the fine of August, and so in the barke I proceeded for the discouery, but after my departure in sixteen dayes the shippes had finished their voyage, and so presently departed for England, without regard of their promise. My selfe, not distrusting any such hard measure, proceeded in the discouerie and followed my course in the free and open sea, betweene North and Nor west, to the latitude of sixtie seuen degrees, and there I might see America west from me, and Desolation east; then when I saw the land of both sides, I began to distrust that it would prooue but a gulfe. Notwithstanding, desirous to knowe the full certaintye, I proceeded, and in sixtie eight degrees the passage enlarged, so that I could not see the westerne shore; thus I continued to the latitude of seuentie fiue degrees, in a great sea, free from yse, coasting the western shore of Desolation. The people came continually rowing out vnto me in their Canoas, twenty, forty, and one hundred at a time, and would giue me fishe dried, Samon, Samon peale, cod, Caplin, Lumpe, stone base, and such like, besides diuers kindes of birdes, as Partrig, Fesant, Gulls, sea birdes, and other kindes of fleshe. I still laboured by signes to knowe from them what they knew of any sea towards the North. They still made signes of a great sea as we vnderstood them; then I departed from that coast, thinking to discouer the North parts of America, and after I had sayled towards the west neere fortie leages I fell upon a great banke of yse; the wind being North and blewe much, I was constrained to coast the same towardes the South, not seeing any shore West from me, neither was there any yse towards the North, but a great sea, free, large, very salt and blue and of an unsearchable depth. So coasting towardes the South, I came to the place wher I left the shippes to fishe, but found them not. Then being forsaken and left in this distresse referring my selfe to the mercifull prouidence of God, shaped my course for England, and vnhoped for of any, God alone releuing me, I arriued at Dartmouth. By this last discouerie it seemed most manifest that the passage was free and without impediment towards the North, but by reason of the spanish fleete and unfortunate time of master Secretoryes death, the voyage was omitted and neuer sithens attempted.

George Sandys was the youngest son of Sandys, Archbishop of York, and was born at Bishops-Thorpe, Yorkshire, in 1578. His mind developed at so early a period, that he entered Hart-Hall College, Oxford, when only in the eleventh year of his age. He afterward removed to Corpus-Christi College, but whether he took a university degree or not is uncertain. A restless curiosity to visit foreign countries induced him to leave England for this purpose, and in August, 1610, he embarked for the continent. He travelled through the northern European states, thence down to Constantinople and Greece, and from the latter he visited Egypt and Palestine. Returning by the way of Italy, he passed thence through France to his native country, where he was received with strong demonstrations of approbation. King James soon after took him into his confidence, and Charles the First made him one of the members of his privy chamber. Sandys died in March, 1643, at Boxley-Abbey, in Kent, the seat of his niece, Lady Margaret Wyat.

In 1615, Sandys published an account of his travels, entitled *A Relation of a Journey began Anno Domino*, 1610, *Four Books Containing a Description of the Turkish Empire of Egypt, of the Holy Land, of the Remote Parts of Italy, and Islands adjoining*. This work was so popular as to reach a seventh edition in 1673—a distinction not undeserved, since as Kerr in his *Catalogue of Voyages and Travels*, has remarked, 'Sandys was an accomplished gentleman, well prepared by previous study, for his travels; which are distinguished by erudition, sagacity, and a love of truth, and are written in a pleasant style.' He devoted particular attention to the allusions of the ancient poets to the various localities through which he passed; and in his dedication to Prince Charles he thus refers to this subject:—

MODERN STATE OF ANCIENT COUNTRIES.

The parts I speak of are the most renowned countries and kingdoms: once the seats of most glorious and triumphant empires; the theatres of valour and heroical actions; the soils enriched with all earthly felicities; the places where Nature hath produced her wonderful works; where arts and sciences have been invented and perfected; where wisdom, virtue, policy, and civility, have been planted, have flourished; and, lastly, where God himself did place his own commonwealth, gave laws and oracles, inspired his prophets, sent angels to converse with men; above all, where the Son of God descended to become man; where he honored the earth with his beautiful steps, wrought the works of our redemption, triumphed over death, and ascended into glory: which countries, once so glorious and famous for their happy estate, are now, through vice and ingratitude, become the most deplored spectacles of extreme misery; the wild beasts of mankind having broken in upon them, and rooted out all civility, and the pride of a stern and barbarous tyrant possessing the thrones of ancient and just dominions. Who, aiming only at the height of greatness and sensuality, hath in tract of time reduced so great and goodly a part of the world to that lamentable distress and servitude, under which (to the astonishment of the understanding beholder) it now faints and groaneth. Those rich lands, at this present remain waste and overgrown with bushes, receptacles of wild beasts, of thieves and murderers; large territories dispeopled, or thinly inhabited; goodly cities made desolate; sumptuous buildings become ruins; glorious temples either subverted, or prostituted to impiety; true religion discountenanced and oppressed; all nobility extinguished; no light of learning permitted, nor virtue cherished; violence and rapine insulting over all, and leaving no security except to an abject mind, and unlooked-on poverty; which calamities of theirs, so great and deserved, are to the rest of the world as threatening instructions. For assistance wherein, I have not only related what I saw of their present condition, but so far as convenience might permit, presented a brief view of the former estates and first antiquities of those people and countries: thence to draw a right image of the frailty of man, the mutability of whatsoever is worldly, and assurance that, as there is nothing unchangeable saving God, so nothing stable but by his grace and protection.

William Lithgow, a Scotchman, and contemorary with Sandys, traversed on foot, many European, Asiatic, and African countries. He was one of those tourists, now so numerous, who travel from a love of adventure, without having any scientific or literary object in view. According to his own statements, he walked more than thirty-six thousand miles; and so decidedly did he prefer this mode of travelling, that, even when the use of a carriage was offered to him, he declined to avail himself of the accommodation. His narrative was published in London, in 1640, and one of the principal adventures which it contains, occurred at Malaga, in Spain, where he was arrested as an English spy, and committed to prison. The details which he gives of his sufferings while in confinement, and the tortures applied to him in view of extracting a confession, are such as to cause humanity to sicken. Having been at length released by some English residents at Malaga, to whom his situation accidentally became known, he was sent to London by sea, and afterward sent, at the expense of king James, to Bath, where he remained, for more than six months, endeavoring to recruit his shattered frame. Lithgow died in 1640, having previously made several fruitless attempts, through the House of Lords, to obtain redress for his sufferings. As an extract from this writer's travels would not present, in a literary view, any variety, we shall not offer one.

Lecture the Eighteenth.

JAMES HOWELL—THOMAS HERBERT—WILLIAM CAMDEN—JOHN SPEED—SIR HENRY SPELMAN—ROBERT COLTON—THOMAS MAY—JOHN HEYWARD—RICHARD KNOLLES—ARTHUR WILSON—RICHARD BAKER—THOMAS HOBBES—EDWARD HERBERT.

TRAVELLERS' narratives, and descriptions of voyages and other adventures, form so important a part of the literature of the period at present under consideration, that to them we devoted most of the last lecture. To this class of writers Howell and Herbert also, the next authors to be noticed, belong.

JAMES HOWELL, one of the most intelligent travellers and pleasing miscellaneous writers of the early part of the seventeenth century, was the son of the Reverend Thomas Howell, and was born at Abernaut, Carmarthenshire, in 1596. He commenced his education at the free school in Hereford, and after thorough preparation, passed thence to Jesus College, Oxford, where he remained until 1613, when he took his bachelor's degree. Howell's circumstances being now such as to require him to depend upon his own future exertions for success in life, he repaired to London in search of employment. He had not been in London long before Sir Robert Mansel obtained for him the appointment of steward to a patent-glass manufactory, in which capacity he went abroad in 1619, to procure materials, and engage new and skillful workmen. In the course of his travels, which lasted till 1621, he visited many commercial towns in Holland, Flanders, France, Spain, and Italy; and, being of an acute and inquiring mind, laid up a great store of useful observations on men and manners, besides acquiring so extensive a knowledge of modern languages that it was henceforth his boast, 'that he could offer each successive daily prayer during the week in a different language, and on Sunday, pray in seven.' His connection with the glass company ceased soon after his return to England, and he visited France again, in the following year, as travelling companion of a young nobleman.

In the latter part of the year 1622, Howell was sent to Spain, as agent for the recovery of an English vessel which had been seized at Sardinia, on a charge of smuggling; but all hope of obtaining redress being destroyed by the breaking off of the proposed marriage of Prince Charles with the Infanta, he, after two years' absence, returned to England. In 1623, while Howell was abroad on this mission, he was chosen fellow of Jesus College, Oxford, upon the new foundation of Sir Eubule Theloal; and in his letter of thanks to that gentleman, he remarks that he 'will reserve his fellowship, and lay it by as a good warm garment against rough weather, if any fall on him.' Howell's next appointment was that of secretary to lord Scrope, afterward earl of Sunderland, who had been made president of the north. This position brought him to York; and while he resided there, the corporation of Richmond, without any solicitation on his part, and against several competitors, chose him one of their representatives in the parliament of 1627. He next attached himself to the Earl of Leicester, and when that nobleman was sent, in 1632, as English ambassador to the court of Denmark, he accompanied him to Copenhagen as his secretary. After this, Howell's situation was, for some years, uncertain and embarrassed. At length, however, having meantime complimented Charles the First in two small poems, he obtained, in 1640, the clerkship of the council—an important appointment, but of brief continuance, as, three years afterwards, he was imprisoned in the Fleet, by order of a committee of parliament. Here he remained till after the king's death, supporting himself by translating some works, and composing others. At the Restoration he became historiographer-royal, being the first who ever enjoyed that title; and continued his literary avocations till his death, which occurred in the month of November, 1666.

This lively and sensible writer was the author of more than forty publica tions; none of which, however, are now generally read, excepting his Familiar Letters, first published in 1643, and considered to be the earliest specimen of epistolary literature in the language. The letters are dated from various places at home and abroad; and though some of them are supposed to have been compiled from memory while the author was in the Fleet prison, yet the greater number seem to bear sufficient internal evidence of having been written at the times and places indicated. His remarks upon the leading events and characters of that period, as well as the animating accounts given of what he saw in foreign countries, contribute to render the work one of permanent interest and value. Of these letters we present the following specimen:—

TO CAPTAIN THOMAS B.

Noble Captain,—Yours of the 1st of March was delivered me by Sir Richard Scot, and I hold it no profanation of this Sunday evening, considering the quality of my subject, and having (I thank God for it) performed all church duties, to employ some hours to meditate on you, and send you this friendly salute, though I confess in an unusual monitory way. My dear Captain, I love you perfectly well; I love both your person and parts, which are not vulgar; I am in love with your disposition, which is generous, and I verily think that you were never guilty of any pusillanimous act in your life. Nor is this love of mine conferred upon you gratis, but you may challenge it as your due, and by way of correspondence, in regard of those thousand convincing evidences you have given me of yours to me, which ascertain me that you take me for a true friend. Now, I am of the number of those that had rather commend the virtue of an enemy than soothe the vices of a friend; for your own particular, if your parts of virtue and your infirmities were cast into a balance, I know the first would much outpoise the other; yet give me leave to tell you that there is one frailty, or rather ill-favoured custom, that reigns in you, which weighs much; it is a humour of swearing in all your discourses, and they are not slight but deep far-fetched oaths that you are wont to rap out, which you use as flowers of rhetoric to enforce a faith upon the hearers, who believe you never the more; and you use this in cold blood when you are not provoked, which makes the humour far more dangerous. I know many (and I cannot say I myself am free from it, God forgive me), that, being transported with choler, and as it were, made drunk with passion by some sudden provoking accident, or extreme ill-fortune at play, will let fall oaths and deep protestations; but to belch out, and send forth, as it were, whole volleys of oaths and curses in a calm humour, to verify every trivial discourse, is a thing of horror. I knew a king that, being crossed in his game, would amongst his oaths fall on the ground, and bite the very earth in the rough of his passion; I heard of another king, (Henry IV. of France,) that in his highest distemper would swear but 'Ventre de Saint Gris,' ['By the belly of St. Gris;'] I heard of an Italian, that, having been much accustomed to blaspheme, was weaned from it by a pretty wile, for, having been one night at play, and lost all his money, after many execrable oaths, and having offered money to another to go out to face heaven and defy God, he threw himself upon a bed hard by, and there fell asleep. The other gamesters played on still, and finding that he was fast asleep, they put out the candles, and made semblance to play on still; they fell a wrangling, and spoke so loud that he awaked; he hearing them play on still, fell a rubbing his eyes, and his conscience presently prompted him that he was struck blind, and that God's judgment had deservedly fallen down upon him for his blasphemies, and so he fell to sigh and weep pitifully; a ghostly father was sent for, who undertook to do some acts of penance for him, if he would make a vow never to play again or blaspheme, which he did; and so the candles were lighted again, which he thought were burning all the while; so he became a perfect convert. I could wish this letter might produce the same effect in you. There is a strong text, that the curse of heaven hangs always over the dwelling of the swearer, and you have more fearful examples of miraculous judgments in this particular, than of any other sin.

There is a little town in Languedoc, in France, that hath a multitude of the pictures of the Virgin Mary up and down; but she is made to carry Christ in her right arm, contrary to the ordinary custom, and the reason they told me was this, that two gamesters being at play, and one having lost all his money, and bolted out many blasphemies, he gave a deep oath, that that jade upon the wall, meaning the picture of the Blessed Virgin, was the cause of his ill luck; hereupon the child removed imperceptibly from the left arm to the right, and the man fell stark dumb ever after; thus went the tradition there. This makes me think upon the Lady Southwell's news from Utopia, that he who sweareth when he playeth at dice, may challenge his damnation by way of purchase. This infandous custom of swearing, I observe, reigns in England lately, more than anywhere else; though a German in his highest puff of passion swear a hundred thousand sacraments, the Italian, by * * *, the French by God's death, the Spaniard by his flesh, the Welshman by his sweat, the Irishman by his five wounds, though the Scot commonly bids the devil ha'e his soul, yet, for variety of oaths, the English roarers put down all. Consider well what a dangerous thing it is to tear in pieces that dreadful name, which makes the vast fabric of the world to tremble, that holy name wherein the whole hierarchy of heaven doth triumph, that blissful name, wherein consists the fullness of all felicity. I know this custom in you yet is but a light disposition; 'tis no habit, I hope; let me, therefore, conjure you by that power of friendship, by that holy league of love which is between us, that you would suppress it, before it come to that; for I must tell you that those who could find it in their hearts to love you for many other things, do disrespect you for this; they hate your company, and give no credit to whatsoever you say, it being one of the punishments of a swearer, as well as of a liar, not to be believed when he speaks the truth.

Excuse me that I am so free with you; what I write proceeds from the clear current of a pure affection, and I shall heartily thank you, and take it for an argument of love, if you tell me of my weaknesses, which are (God wot) too, too many; for my body is but a Cargazon of corrupt humours, and being not able to overcome them all at once, I do endeavour to do it by degrees, like Sertorius his soldier, who, when he could not cut off the horse's tail at one blow with his sword, fell to pull out the hair one by one. And touching this particular humour from which I dissuade you, it hath raged in me too often by contingent fits, but I thank God for it, I find it much abated and purged. Now, the only physic I used was a precedent fast, and recourse to the holy sacrament the next day, of purpose to implore pardon for what had passed, and power for the future to quell those exorbitant motions, those ravings and feverish fits of the soul; in regard there are no infirmities more dangerous, for at the same instant they have being, they become impieties. And the greatest symptom of amendment I find in me is, because whensoever I hear the holy name of God blasphemed by any other, it makes my heart to tremble within my breast; now, it is a penitential rule, that if sins present do not please thee, sins past will not hurt thee. All other sins have for their object either pleasure or profit, or some aim or satisfaction to body or mind, but this hath none at all; therefore fie upon 't, my dear Captain; try whether you can make a conquest of yourself in subduing this execrable custom. Alexander subdued the world, Cæsar his enemies, Hercules monsters, but he that o'ercomes himself is the true valiant captain.

From another of Howell's works, entitled *Instructions for Foreign Travel*, published in 1642, and which, like his letters, contains many acute and humorous observations on men and things, we extract the following passage on the—

TALES OF TRAVELLERS.

Others have a custom to be always relating strange things and wonders (of the humour of Sir John Mandeville), and they usually present them to the hearers through multiplying-glasses, and thereby cause the thing to appear far greater than it is in itself; they make mountains of mole-hills, like Charenton-Bridge-Echo, which doubles the sound nine times. Such a traveller was he that reported the Indian fly to be as big as a fox; China birds to be as big as some horses, and their mice to be as big as monkeys; but they have the wit to fetch this far enough off, because the hearer may rather believe it than make a voyage so far to disprove it.

Every one knows the tale of him who reported he had seen a cabbage, under whose leaves a regiment of soldiers were sheltered from a shower of rain. Another, who was no traveller (yet the wiser man) said, he had passed by a place where there were 400 braziers making of a cauldron—200 within, and 200 without, beating the nails in; the traveller asking for what use that huge cauldron was? he told him—'Sir, it was to boil your cabbage.'

Such another was the Spanish traveller, who was so habituated to hyperbolize, and relate wonders, that he became ridiculous in all companies, so that he was forced at last to give order to his man, when he fell into any excess this way, and report any thing improbable, he should pull him by the sleeve. The master falling into his wonted hyperboles, spoke of a church in China that was ten thousand yards long; his man, standing behind, and pulling him by the sleeve, made him stop suddenly. The company asking, 'I pray, sir, how broad might that church be?' he replied, 'But a yard broad, and you may thank my man for pulling me by the sleeve, else I had made it four-square for you.'

THOMAS HERBERT, the only other traveller of much celebrity of this period, was born at York about the beginning of the seventeenth century, and commenced his collegiate studies at Jesus College, Oxford; but before he took his degree he removed to Trinity College, Cambridge, where he remained, however, only for a comparatively short time. Immediately after he left the university, he applied to his kinsman, William Herbert, Earl of Pembroke, for aid to enable him to travel abroad to acquire those accomplishments of mind and manners which were then an indispensable part of a gentleman's education. The Earl, being much pleased with his young relative, sent him, in 1626, to the continent, and having hastened to the East, he there spent four years, chiefly in Asia and Africa; after which, returning to England, he waited on his patron at Baynard's castle in London, and communicated to him the result of his travels. From his reception by the Earl his expectations of preferment were of the liveliest kind; but the sudden death of his noble friend blasted all his hopes, and he again left England for the purpose of visiting those parts of Europe which, in his first tour, he had not seen.

On his second return Herbert published, in 1634, *A Relation of some Years' Travels into Africa and the Greater Asia, especially the Territory of the Persian Monarchy, and some parts of the Oriental Indies and Isles Adjacent.* These travels had a great reputation at the time at which they were published, and have since been considered the best that appeared in England previous to the close of the seventeenth century. In the civil wars Herbert sided with the parliament, and when the king was required to dismiss his own servants, was chosen, by his majesty, one of the grooms of the bed-chamber. He then became much attached to the king, served him with great zeal and assiduity, and was on the scaffold when that ill-fated monarch was brought to the block. After the Restoration, Herbert was rewarded by Charles the Second with a baronetcy, and subsequently devoted much of his time to literary pursuits. In 1678, he wrote *Threnodia Carolina, containing an Historical Account of the Two Last Years of the Life of King Charles II.*, which was afterward reprinted in a collection of 'Memoirs' of the same period of that unfortunate monarch's life.

Sir Thomas Herbert died at York on the first of March, 1682. The following is a brief extract from his travels:—

DESCRIPTION OF ST. HELENA.

St. Helena was so denominated by Juan de Nova, the Portugal, in regard he first discovered it on that saint's day. It is doubtful whether it adhere to America or Afric, the vast ocean bellowing on both sides, and almost equally; yet I imagine she inclines more to Afer than Vespusius. 'Tis in circuit thirty English miles, of that ascent and height that 'tis often enveloped with cloudes, from whom she receives moisture to fatten her; and as the land is very high, so the sea at the brink of this isle is excessive deep, and the ascent so immediate, that though the sea beat fiercely on her, yet can no ebb nor flow be well perceived there.

The water is sweet above, but, running down and participating with the salt hills, tastes brackish at his fall into the valleys, which are but two, and those very small, having their appellations from a lemon-tree above, and a ruined chapel placed beneath, built by the Spaniard, and dilapidated by the Dutch. There has been a village about it, lately depopulated from her inhabitants by command from the Spanish king; for that it became an unlawful magazine of seaman's treasure, in turning and returning out of both the Indies, whereby he lost both tribute and prerogative in apparent measure.

Monuments of antique beings nor other rarities can be found here. You see all, if you view the ribs of an old carrick, and some broken pieces of her ordnance left there against the owner's good will or approbation. Goats and hogs are the now dwellers, who multiply in great abundance, and (though unwillingly) afford themselves to hungry and sea-beaten passengers. It has stores of partridge and guinea-hens, all which were brought thither by the honest Portugal; who now dare neither anchor there, nor own their labours, lest the English or Flemings question them.

The isle is very even and delightful above, and gives a large prospect into the ocean. 'Tis a saying with the seaman, a man there has his choice, whether he will break his heart going up, or his neck coming down; either wish bestowing more jocundity than comfort.

From these writers of voyages and travels we now turn our attention to a very different class of authors—those who exerted themselves in the age of Elizabeth to discover and preserve the remains of antiquity which had come down to their times. Of these Camden, Speed, Spelman, and Colton present the first claim to our notice.

William Camden, who, besides being an eminent antiquarian, was one of the best historians of his age, was born in London on the second of May 1551. He received the rudiments of his education at Christ's hospital and St. Paul's school, and at the age of fifteen removed to Magdalen College, Oxford; but completed his studies at Pembroke Hall, in the same univereity. In 1575, he became second master of Westminster school; and while performing the duties of that arduous office, he devoted his leisure hours to the study of the antiquities of Britain—a subject to which, from early years, he had strongly inclined. In order personally to examine ancient remains, he travelled, in 1582, through some of the eastern and northern counties of England; and the fruits of his researches appeared in his most celebrated work entitled, *Britain; or a Chorographical Description of the Most Flourishing Kingdom of England, Scotland, Ireland, and the Adjacent Islands, from Remote Antiquity.* This work, originally written in Latin, was published in 1586, and immediately brought the author into high repute as an antiquarian and man of learning. Anxious to improve and enlarge it, he journeyed at several times into different parts of the country, examined archives and relics of antiquity, and collected, with indefatigable industry, whatever information might contribute to render it more complete. The sixth edition, published in 1607, was that which received Camden's finishing touches; and of this edition an English translation executed, probably with the author's assistance, by Holland, appeared in 1610.

The 'Britannia' has gone through many subsequent editions, and has proved so useful a repository of antiquarian and topographical knowledge, that it was styled, by Bishop Nicholson, 'the common sun, whereat our modern writers have all lighted their little torches.' The last edition of this great work is that of 1789, in two volumes folio, largely augmented by Gough.

In 1593, Camden became head master of Westminster school, and, for the use of his pupils published, four years after, a *Greek grammar*. This work soon became so popular as to be adopted in all the principal grammar-schools in the kingdom. In the same year, 1597, he received the appointment of Clarencieux king-of-arms, an office which allowed him more leisure for his favorite pursuits; and his connection with Westminster school consequently then terminated. The principal works which he subsequently published are, *An Account of the Monuments and Inscriptions in Westminster Abbey; A Collection of Ancient English Histories; A Narrative*, in Latin, *of the Gunpowder Plot;* and *Annals of the Reign of Queen Elizabeth*, also in Latin. The last of these works is praised by Hume as good composition, with respect both to style and matter, and as being 'written with simplicity of expression, very rare in that age, and with strict regard to truth.' Camden died at his own home in Chesselhurst, Kent, on the ninth of November 1623, in his seventy-third year, and was buried in Westminster Abbey. Through his long life he was not less illustrious for his virtues than for his learning. In his writings he was candid and modest, in his conversation, easy and innocent, and under every change of fortune, even and exemplary. From the preface to Holland's translation of the 'Britannia,' we extract the account which Camden gives of his own labors:—

EXTRACT FROM THE PREFACE TO THE BRITANNIA.

I hope it shall be no discredit if I now use again, by way of preface, the same words, with a few more, that I used twenty-four years since in the first edition of this work. Abraham Ortelius, the worthy restorer of ancient geography, arriving here in England about thirty-four years past, dealt earnestly with me that I would illustrate this isle of Britain, or, as he said, that I would restore antiquity to Britain, and Britain to antiquity; which was, (I understood,) that I would renew ancientry, enlighten obscurity, clear doubts, and recall home verity, by way of recovery, which the negligence of writers, and credulity of the common sort, had in a manner proscribed and utterly banished from among us. A painful matter, I assure you, and more than difficult; wherein what toil is to be taken, as no man thinketh, so no man believeth but he who hath made the trial. Nevertheless, how much the difficulty discouraged me from it, so much the glory of my country encouraged me to undertake it. So, while at one and the same time I was fearful to undergo the burden, and yet desirous to do some service to my country, I found two different affections, fear and boldness, I know not how, conjoined in one. Notwithstanding, by the most gracious direction of the Almighty, taking industry for my consort, I adventured upon it, and, with all my study, care, cogitation, continual meditation, pain, and travail, I employed myself thereunto when I had any spare time. I made search after the etymology of Britain and the first inhabitants timorously; neither in so doubtful a matter have I affirmed ought confidently. For I am not ignorant that the first originals of nations are obscure, by reason of their profound antiquity, as things which are seen very deep and far remote; like as the courses, the reaches, the confluences, and the outlets of great rivers are well-known, yet their first fountains and heads lie commonly unknown. I have succinctly run over the Romans' government in Britain, and the inundation of forcing people thereinto, what they were, and from whence they came. I have traced out the ancient divisions of these kingdoms; I have summarily specified the states and judicial courts of the same. In the several counties I have compendiously set down the limits, (and yet not exactly by perch and pole, to breed question,) what is the nature of the soil, which were places of the greatest antiquity, who have been dukes, marquisses, earls, viscounts, barons, and some of the most signal and ancient families therein, (for who can particulate all?) What I have performed, I leave to men of judgment. But time, the most sound and sincere witness, will give the truest information, when envy (which persecuteth the living) shall have her mouth stopped. Thus much give me leave to say—that I have in no wise neglected such things as are material to search and sift out the truth. I have attained to some skill of the most ancient British and Saxon tongues. I have travelled over all England for the most part; I have conferred with most skillful observers in each country; I have studiously read over our own country writers, (old and new,) all Greek and Latin authors which have once made mention of Britain; I have had conference with learned men in the other parts of Christendom; I have been diligent in the records of this realm; I have looked into most libraries, registers, and memorials of churches, cities, and corporations; I have pored over many an old roll and evidence, and produced their testimony (as beyond all exception) when the cause required in their very own words (although barbarous they be) that the honour of verity might in no wise be impeached.

For all this I may be censured as unadvised, and scant modest, who, being but of the lowest form in the school of antiquity, where I might well have lurked in obscurity, have adventured as a scribbler upon the stage in this learned age, amidst the diversities of relishes both in wit and judgment. But to tell the truth unfeignedly, the love of my country, which compriseth all love in it, and hath endeared me to it, the glory of the British name, the advice of some judicious friends, hath overmastered my modesty, and (will'd I, nill'd I) hath enforced me, against mine own judgment, to undergo this burden too heavy for me, and so thrust me forth into the world's view. For I see judgment, prejudices, censures, aspersions, obstructions, detractions, affronts, and confronts as it were, in battle array to environ me on every side; some there are which wholly contemn and avile this study of antiquity as a back-looking curiosity; whose authority as I do not utterly vilify, so I do not overprize or admire their judgment, neither am I destitute of reason whereby I might approve this my purpose to well-bred, well-meaning men, which tender the glory of their native country, and moreover, could give them to understand that, in the study of antiquity, (which is always accompanied with dignity, and hath a certain resemblance with eternity,) there is a sweet food of the mind well befitting such as are of honest and noble disposition. If any there be which are desirous to be strangers in their own soil, and foreigners in their own city, they may so continue, and therein flatter themselves. For such I have not written these lines, nor taken these pains.

JOHN SPEED was born at Farington, Cheshire, in 1555. He was brought up to the business of a tailor, and followed that trade until he rose to such emimence in it as to become one of the principal merchant-tailors in London.

Under what circumstances he abandoned the needle for the pen, is uncertain; but in 1596, he published his first important work under the title of *The Theatre of Great Britain*, which he afterwards enlarged and greatly improved. In 1606, he published maps of Great Britain and Ireland, with the English shires, hundreds, cities, and shire-towns. This work was much superior to any other of the kind that had then appeared. Speed's great work, the *History of Great Britain*, was not published till 1614. Though the author enjoyed few of the advantages of education, yet his history is a highly creditable performance, and was, for a long time, the best in existence. He was the first to reject the fables of preceding chroniclers concerning the origin of the Britons, and to exercise a just discrimination in the selection of authorities. His history commences with the original inhabitants of the island, and extends to the union of England and Scotland under James the First, to whom the work is dedicated. Bishop Nicholson characterizes Speed as 'a person of extraordinary industry and attainments in the study of antiquities.' Besides his histories, Speed published, in 1616, *The Cloud of Witnesses, or Genealogies of Scriptures*, a valuable book of divinity, and often bound up with the Bible. His death occurred on the twenty-eighth of July, 1629, and he was buried in the church of St. Giles, Cripplegate, London, where a monument was erected to his memory.

Henry Spelman was of a respectable family, and was born at Congham, Norfolk, in 1561. He passed two years at Trinity College, Cambridge, and then entered Lincoln's Inn as a student of law. In 1604, he was made Sheriff of Norfolk, and became so well known for his abilities, that the king sent him on three different occasions into Ireland on public business, and afterward appointed him one of the commissioners to inquire into the fees exacted in all the courts and offices in England. He received, soon after, the honor of knighthood from the king, and removing, at the age of fifty, to London, he devoted his life henceforth to historical and antiquarian researches.

Spelman was the intimate friend of Camden, and was a man of remarkably similar tastes. His works are almost exclusively upon legal and ecclesiastical antiquities. Having, in the course of his investigations, found it necessary to study the Saxon language, he embodied the fruits of his labors in his great work called *The Glossary*, the object of which is the explanation of obsolete words occurring in the laws of England. Another of his productions is *A History of the English Councils*, in three parts, the first of which was published in 1639, and the remaining two after the author's death. This is a performance of great learning and research, and embraces an entire history of the church from its first establishment in Britain until the author's own time. Spelman died in London, in 1641, at the advanced age of eighty years, and was buried in Westminster Abbey, near Camden's monument.

The writings of Sir Henry Spelman have furnished valuable materials to

English historians, and he is regarded as the restorer of Saxon literature, both by means of his own studies, and by founding a Saxon professorship at Cambridge.

Robert Colton was descended from a very ancient family, and born at Denton, Huntingdonshire, in 1570. His mind very early developed, and having entered Trinity College, Cambridge, he there took the degree of bachelor of arts before he had passed the fifteenth year of his age. From the university he went to London, where, in his eighteenth year, he became a member of the society of antiquaries, and soon after an industrious collector of records, charters, and writings of every kind relative to the ancient history of England. In the prosecution of his object he enjoyed unusual facilities, the recent suppression of monasteries having thrown many valuable books and written documents into private hands. In 1600, he accompanied Camden on an excursion to Carlisle for the purpose of examining the Picts' wall and other relics of former times. On the accession of James the First, Colton was knighted, and at his suggestion that monarch, in 1611, resorted to the scheme of creating baronets, as a means of supplying the treasury. He died of a fever at Westminster, on the sixth of May, 1631, in his sixty-first year.

Sir Robert Colton was the author of various historical, political, and antiquarian works, which are now of little interest except to men of kindred tastes. His name is remembered chiefly for the benefit which he conferred upon literature, by saving his valuable library of manuscripts from dispersion. After being considerably augmented by his son and grandson, it became, in 1706, the property of the public, and in 1757, was deposited in the British Museum. One hundred and eleven of these manuscripts, many of them highly valuable, had before this time been unfortunately destroyed by fire. From those which remain, historians still continue to extract large stores of information. During his lifetime, materials were drawn from his library by Raleigh, Bacon, and Herbert; and he furnished literary assistance to Camden, Speed, and many other contemporary authors. Colton lived on terms of intimacy with all the literary men of eminence of his own country, and held frequent correspondence with distinguished foreign scholars. The historical writings of the authors last mentioned, do not furnish any examples sufficiently characteristic to require quotation.

Besides the eminent antiquarians and historical writers whom we have already noticed, in connection with this period, we have still to glance at May, Hayward, Knolles, Wilson, and Baker—authors though of less celebrity, yet of sufficient importance to require our attention.

Thomas May was descended from an ancient but declining family of Sussex, and was born at Mayfield, in that county, in 1594. He was early instructed in classical learning in the neighborhood of his home, and afterwards entered a commoner in Sidney Sussex-College, Cambridge, where, in

1612, he took the degree of Bachelor of Arts, but never proceeded any farther in academical advancement. In 1615, he removed to London, and entered Gray's Inn as a student of law; but his taste for belles-lettres studies prevailing over all considerations of permanent advantage from a regular profession, he abandoned his legal pursuits to devote himself to those which were more congenial to his mind. Through association with eminent wits and courtiers, he soon acquired such reputation as to obtain the countenance of Charles the First and his royal consort, under whose particular patronage he published his first volume of poems. From the period of this publication he became a resident at court; and under the same royal favor which countenanced and encouraged his first literary performance, he produced, in succession, five plays; two of which, *The Heir*, and *The Old Couple*, are comedies, and the other three, *Cleopatra*, *Antigone*, and *Agrippiana*, tragedies. May was, however, more successful as a translator of Latin poetry, than as an original writer, and his version of Lucan's Pharsalia is really a meritorious performance. He added to the original poem two books in order to bring the events down to the death of Julius Cæsar. These were written in both the Latin and the English languages.

As most of May's poems were produced at the command of Charles the First, and were dedicated to that monarch, it is natural to infer that a pretty close intimacy must have existed between the king and the poet; yet when the civil wars broke out, the latter joined the parliament, and soon after became their secretary and historiographer. This position imposed upon him the duty of writing *The History of the Parliament of England*, which began November the third, 1640. The work is, in reality, a history of the civil war which arose while that parliament was sitting, rather than of the proceedings of the parliament itself. It gave great offence to the royalists, by whom both the author and his performance were loudly abused. As a composition, it is inelegant, but the candor displayed in it has been pronounced much greater than the royalists were willing to allow; it, therefore, still holds a permanent place in the history of the times. On the thirteenth of November, 1650, May retired to rest in his usual health, and was found, the next morning, dead in his bed. He was buried in Westminster Abbey, near the tomb of Camden, and a monument was erected to his memory.

John Hayward was educated at the university of Cambridge, where he took the degree of doctor of laws; but his birth-place is not known, nor has the time when his birth occurred been preserved. He early became an historian, and in 1599, published *The First Part of the Life and Reign of Henry the Fourth*, which he dedicated to the Earl of Essex. Some passages in this work gave such offence to Queen Elizabeth, that she caused the auth[illegible] undergo a severe and very tedious imprisonment. He was, however[illegible] ronized by James the First, and at the desire of Prince Henry h[illegible] and in 1613, published, *The Lives of the Three Norman Kings of E*[illegible]

William the First, William the Second, and Henry the First. In 1619, Hayward was knighted by James the First, having previously been made historiographer of Chelsea College. At his death, which occurred on the twenty-seventh of June, 1627, he left in manuscript a history of *The Life and Reign of King Edward VI., with The Beginning of the Reign of Queen Elizabeth*, which was published in 1630.

Sir John Hayward wrote with considerable smoothness, but in too dramatic a style, imitating Livy and other ancient historians in the practice of putting speeches into the mouths of the characters. Besides his historical works, he wrote several pieces on religious subjects, which possess very considerable merit.

RICHARD KNOLLES was born in Northamptonshire, and educated at Oxford, but at what college is uncertain. After having taken his degrees he was chosen fellow of Lincoln College, and thence elected master of a free school at Sandwich, in Kent, where he remained until his death, which occurred in 1610.

As a public teacher Knolles was very celebrated, and from year to year sent many pupils to the universities who afterward became eminent scholars; but his genius and literary efforts were by no means restricted to the region of his school. Besides producing *Grammaticæ Latinæ*, *Græcæ*, and *Hebraicæ*, for the especial use of his pupils, he wrote a *History of the Turks*, which Johnson, in the 'Rambler,' praises as exhibiting all the excellencies that narration can admit. 'His style,' says the learned critic, 'though somewhat obscured by time, and sometimes vitiated by false wit, is pure, nervous, elevated, and clear. Nothing could have sunk this author into obscurity but the remoteness and barbarity of the people whose story he relates.' In addition to his history, Knolles wrote the *Lives and Conquests of the Ottoman Kings and Emperors, to the year* 1610, and a brief *Discourse of the Greatness of the Turkish Empire.* From the History of the Turks we select the following passage:—

THE TAKING OF CONSTANTINOPLE BY THE TURKS.

A little before day, the Turks approached the walls and begun the assault, where shot and stones were delivered upon them from the walls as thick as hail, whereof little fell in vain, by reason of the multitude of the Turks, who, pressing fast unto the walls, could not see in the dark how to defend themselves, but were without number wounded or slain; but these were of the common and worst soldiers, of whom the Turkish king made no more reckoning than to abate the first force of the defendants. Upon the first appearance of the day, Mahomet gave the sign appointed for the general assault, whereupon the city was in a moment, and at one instant, on every side most furiously assaulted by the Turks; for Mahomet, the more to distress the defendants, and the better to see the forwardness of the soldiers, had before appointed which part of the city every colonel with his regiment should assail: which they valiantly performed, delivering their arrows and shot upon the defendants so thick, that the light of day was therewith darkened; others in the meantime courageously mounting the scaling-ladders, and coming even to handy-strokes with the defendants upon the wall, where the foremost were for the most part violently borne forward by them which followed after. On the other side, the Christians with no less courage withstood the Turkish fury, beating them down again with great stones and weighty pieces of timber, and so overwhelmed them with shot, darts, and arrows, and other hurtful devices from above, that the Turks dismayed with terror thereof, were ready to retire.

Mahomet, seeing the great slaughter and discomfiture of his men, sent in fresh supplies of his janizaries and best men of war, whom he had for that purpose reserved as his last hope and refuge; by whose coming on his fainting soldiers were again encouraged, and the terrible assault began afresh. At which time the barbarous king ceased not to use all possible means to maintain the assault; by name calling upon this and that captain, promising unto some whom he saw forward golden mountains, and unto others in whom he saw any sign of cowardice, threatening most terrible death; by which means the assault became most dreadful, death there raging in the midst of many thousands. And albeit that the Turks lay dead by heaps upon the ground, yet other fresh men pressed on still in their places over their dead bodies, and with divers event either slew or were slain by their enemies.

In this so terrible a conflict, it chanced Justinianus the general to be wounded in the arm, who, losing much blood, cowardly withdrew himself from the place of his charge, not leaving any to supply his room, and so got into the city by the gate called Romana, which he had caused to be opened in the inner walls; pretending the cause of his departure to be for the binding up of his wound, but being, indeed, a man now altogether discouraged.

The soldiers there present, dismayed with the departure of their general, and sore charged by the janizaries, forsook their stations, and in haste fled to the same gate whereby Justinianus was entered; with the sight whereof the other soldiers, dismayed, ran thither by heaps also. But whilst they violently strive all together to get in at once, they so wedged one another in the entrance of the gate, that few of so great a multitude got in; in which so great a press and confusion of minds, eight hundred persons were there by them that followed trodden under foot, or thrust to death. The emperor himself, for safeguard of his life, flying with the rest in that press as a man not regarded, miserably ended his days, together with the Greek empire. His dead body was shortly after found by the Turks among the slain, and known by his rich apparel, whose head being cut off, was forthwith presented to the Turkish tyrant, by whose commandment it was afterward thrust upon the point of a lance, and in great derision carried about as a trophy of his victory, first in the camp, and afterward up and down the city.

The Turks, encouraged with the flight of the Christians, presently advanced their ensigns upon the top of the uttermost wall, crying Victory; and by the breach entered as if it had been a great flood, which, having once found a breach in the bank, overfloweth, and beareth down all before it; so the Turks, when they had won the utter wall, entered the city by the same gate that was opened for Justinianus, and by a breach which they had before made with their great artillery, and without mercy cutting in pieces all that came in their way, without further resistance became lords of that most famous and imperial city . . . . . In this fury of the barbarians perished many thousands of men, women, and children, without respect of age, sex or condition. Many, for safeguard of their lives, fled into the temple of Sophia, where they were all without pity slain, except some few reserved by the barbarous victors to purposes more grievous than death itself. The rich and beautiful ornaments and jewels of that most sumptuous and magnificent church (the stately building of Justinianus the emperor) were, in the turning of a hand, plucked down and carried away by the Turks; and the church itself, built for God to be honoured in, for the present converted into a stable for their horses, or a place for the execution of their abominable and unspeakable filthiness; the image of the crucifix was also by them taken down, and a Turk's cap put upon the head thereof, and so set up and shot at with their arrows, and afterward, in great derision, carried about in their camp, as it had been in procession, with drums playing before it, railing and spitting at it, and calling it the God of the Christians, which I note not so much done in contempt of the image, as in despite of Christ and the Christian religion.

ARTHUR WILSON was born at Yarmouth, Norfolk, of a genteel family, in 1596. In the fourteenth year of his age he was sent to France to pursue his studies, and after having remained in that country two years he returned to England, and was placed with Sir Henry Spiller, as one of his clerks in the Exchequer office. In Sir Henry's family he remained for some time, but was at length dismissed thence for having written some satirical verses on one of the maid-servants. After his dismissal he devoted a year to reading and poetry, and then, in 1613, entered, as secretary, into the service of Robert, Earl of Essex, whom he attended in various missions upon the continent for many years. Having, through some misunderstanding with the Earl's lady, been dismissed from his services also, he retired, in 1631, to Oxford, and became gentleman commoner of Trinity College, where he remained nearly two years, during which he was scrupulously observant of the orders of the university. He next became steward to the Earl of Warwick, in whose service he died in the month of October, 1652. Wilson's only literary performance of importance is, *The Life and Reign of James the First*, which he left in manuscript, and which was published in 1653, the year after the author's death. He also left, in manuscript, a comedy of some merit, entitled *The Inconstant Lady*.

RICHARD BAKER, with whom we shall conclude our survey of the historical writers of this period, was born at Sissingherst, Kent, in 1568. When in the seventeenth year of his age he entered Hart-hall College, Oxford, and at the end of three years, left the university, went to London, and entered the Inns of Court to study law. He was, however, a man of too considerable quality to follow a profession, and he therefore relinquished his studies in order to travel upon the continent for the improvement of his education. In 1594, he was created master of arts at Oxford, and in the first year of the reign of James the First, was knighted. He married the daughter of Sir George Manwaring of Ightfield, in Shropshire; and having imprudently become security for some of that family's debts, his property, though very considerable, was stripped from him, and to satisfy the balance of the obligation, he was thrown into Fleet prison, where, after lingering for several years, he finally died, on the eighteenth of February, 1645.

While in prison, Sir Richard Baker wrote *Meditations and Disquisitions* on portions of Scripture, translated Balzac's Letters and Malvezzi's Discourses on Tacitus, and composed two pieces in defence of the theatre. His principal work, however, is *A Chronicle of the Kings of England, from the time of the Romans' Government unto the Death of King James*. This work, which appeared in 1641, the author complacently declares to be 'collected with so great care and diligence, that if all other chronicles were lost, this only would be sufficient to inform posterity of all passages memorable or worthy to be known.' Notwithstanding such high pretensions, the 'Chronicle,' *in matter*, must be regarded as an injudicious performance, and not worthy of much reliance. The ***style***, however, is very superior, and is described in a letter written to him by his former college friend, Sir Henry Wotton, as 'full of sweet raptures and of researching conceits; nothing borrowed, nothing vulgar, and yet all flowing from you, I know not how, with a certain equal facility.'

With Hobbes the metaphysician, and Lord Herbert, our present remarks will close.

Thomas Hobbes was the son of a clergyman, and was born at Malmersbury, in Wiltshire, on the fifth of April, 1588. His mother's alarm at the approach of the Spanish Armada, which was then near the coast, is said to have hastened his birth, and was probably the cause of a constitutional timidity with which he was affected through life. Having made considerable progress in the learned languages at school, he entered, in 1603, Magdalen Hall, Oxford, where he spent, in diligent application, five years; and at the expiration of that time he became private tutor to the son of William Cavendish, Earl of Devonshire. In 1610, Hobbes attended Lord Cavendish in his travels through France, Italy, and Germany, and after their return to England he continued to reside with him as his secretary. It was during his residence with the Earl of Devonshire, that he became intimate with Lord Bacon, Lord Herbert of Cherbury, and Ben Jonson. His patron and his pupil both dying, the former, in 1626, and the latter two years after, Hobbes again visited Paris, but in 1631, he undertook to superintend the education of the young Earl of Devonshire, with whom he set off, three years after, on a tour through France, Italy, and Savoy. At Pisa he became intimate with Galileo, the astronomer, and elsewhere held communication with other celebrated characters.

After his return to England in 1637, Hobbes resided in the Earl's family at Chatsworth, in Derbyshire. He now designed to devote himself to study, but he was soon interrupted by the political contentions of the times. Being a zealous royalist, he found it necessary, in 1640, to retire to Paris, where he lived on terms of intimacy with Decartes, and other learned men, whom the patronage of Cardinal de Richelieu had, at that time, drawn together. While at Paris, he engaged in a controversy about the quadrature of the circle, and in 1647, he was appointed mathematical instructor to Charles, Prince of Wales, who then resided in the French capital.

Previously to this time Hobbes had commenced the publication of those works which he sent forth in succession, with the view of curbing the spirit of freedom in England, by showing the philosophical foundation of despotic monarchy. The first of them was originally printed in Latin at Paris, in

1642, under the title of *Elementa Philosophica de Cive;* which when afterward translated into English was entitled *Philosophical Rudiments Concerning Government and Society.* This treatise is regarded as containing the most exact account of the author's political system. With many profound views, it is disfigured by fundamental and dangerous errors. The principles maintained in it were more fully discussed in his larger work, published in 1651, under the title of *Leviathan: or the Matter, Form, and Power of a Commonwealth, Ecclesiastical and Civil.* Man is here represented as a selfish and ferocious animal, requiring the strong hand of despotism to keep him in check; and all notions of right and wrong are made to depend upon views of self-interest alone. Of this latter doctrine, commonly known as the Selfish System of moral philosophy, Hobbes was, indeed, the great champion, both in the 'Leviathan' and more particularly in his small *Treatise on Human Nature*, published in 1650.

In the same year another work from his pen appeared, entitled *De Corpore Politico;* or *Of the Body Politic.* The freedom with which theological subjects were handled in the 'Leviathan,' as well as the offensive political views there maintained, occasioned great outcry against the author, particularly among the clergy. This led Charles to dissolve his connection with the philosopher, who, according to Lord Clarendon, 'was compelled secretly to fly out of Paris, the justice having endeavoured to apprehend him, and soon after escaped into England, where he never received any disturbance.' He again took up his abode with the Devonshire family, and became intimate with Seldon, Cowley, and Dr. Harvey, the discoverer of the circulation of the blood. In 1654, he published a short but admirably clear and comprehensive *Letter upon Liberty and Necessity;* where the doctrine of the self-determining power of the will is opposed with a subtlety and profundity unsurpassed in any subsequent writer on that much agitated question. Indeed, he appears to have been the first who understood and expounded clearly the doctrine of philosophical necessity. On this subject, a long controversy between him and Bishop Bramhall of Londonderry took place. Here he fought with the skill of a master; but in a mathematical dispute with Dr. Wallis, professor of geometry at Oxford, which lasted twenty years, he fairly went beyond his depth, and obtained no increase of reputation. The fact is, that Hobbes did not begin to study mathematics until the age of forty, and, like most late learners, greatly overrated his knowledge. When Charles the Second came to the throne, he conferred upon Hobbes an annual pension of one hundred pounds; but, notwithstanding this and other marks of royal favor, much odium continued to rest both upon him and upon his doctrines. The 'Leviathan' and 'De Cive' were censured in Parliament in 1666, and also drew forth many printed replies.

In 1674, Hobbes entered a new field of literature, and published a metrical version of four books of Homer's Odyssey, which was so well received, that in 1675, when he was eighty-seven years of age, he sent forth a translation of the remainder of that poem, and also the whole of the Iliad. These translations, though very defective, became, nevertheless, so popular, that three large editions of them were required in less than ten years. As a translator in prose he was more successful than in poetry; and his version of the Greek historian Thucydides, one of his early literary performances, is still regarded as one of the best translations of that author ever produced in the English language. Hobbes passed the last five or six years of his life at Chatsworth, and continued to write till his death. His last performance was *Behemoth, or a History of the Civil Wars from* 1640 *to* 1660. His death occurred on the 4th of December, 1679, in the ninety-second year of his age.

In his latter years, Hobbes's growing infirmities and habits of solitude rendered him morose and impatient of contradiction. He was never much inclined to read, and was, consequently, familiar with few books. Homer, Virgil, Thucydides and Euclid, were his favorite authors; and he used to say, that 'if he had read as much as other men, he should have been as ignorant as they.' In consequence of the timidity of his disposition, he was continually apprehensive about his personal safety, insomuch that he could not endure to be left alone in a house. From the same motive, probably, it was that, notwithstanding his notorious heterodoxy, he maintained an external adherence to the established church. Though he has often been stigmatized as an atheist, yet the following passages, particularly the first, would seem to indicate that the charge is groundless:—

GOD.

Forasmuch as God Almighty is incomprehensible, it followeth that we can have no conception or image of the Deity; and, consequently, all his attributes signify our inability and defect of power to conceive any thing concerning his nature, and not any conception of the same, except only this, That there is a God. For the effects, we acknowledge naturally, do include a power of their producing, before they were produced; and that power presupposeth something existent that hath such power: and the thing so existing with power to produce, if it were not eternal must needs have been produced by somewhat before it, and that, again, by something else before that, till we come to an eternal (that is to say, the first) Power of all Powers, and first Cause of all Causes: and this is it which all men conceive by the name of GOD, implying eternity, incomprehensibility, and omnipotency. And thus all that will consider may know that God is, though not *what* he is: even a man that is born blind, though it be not possible for him to have any imagination what kind of thing fire is, yet he can not but know that something there is that men call fire, because it warmeth him.

PITY AND INDIGNATION.

Pity is imagination or fiction of future calamity to ourselves, proceeding from the sense of another man's calamity. But when it lighteth on such as we think have not deserved the same, the compassion is greater, because then there appeareth more probability that the same may happen to us; for the evil that happeneth to an innocent man may happen to every man. But when we see a man suffer for great crimes, which we can not easily think will fall upon ourselves, the pity is the less. And, therefore, men are apt to pity those whom they love; for whom they love they think worthy of good, and therefore not worthy of calamity. Thence it is also, that men pity the vices of some persons at the sight only, out of love to their aspect. The contrary of pity is hardness of heart, proceeding either from slowness of imagination, or some extreme great opinion of their own exemption from the like calamity, or from hatred of all or most men.

Indignation is that grief which consisteth in the conception of good success happening to them whom they think unworthy thereof. Seeing, therefore, men think all those unworthy whom they hate, they think them not only unworthy of the good fortune they have, but also of their own virtues. And of all the passions of the mind, these two, indignation and pity, are the most raised and increased by eloquence; for the aggravation of the calamity, and extenuation of the fault, augmenteth pity; and the extenuation of the worth of the person, together with the magnifying of his success, which are the parts of an orator, are able to turn these two passions into fury.

LOVE OF KNOWLEDGE.

Forasmuch as all knowledge beginneth from experience, therefore also new experience is the beginning of new knowledge, and the increase of experience the beginning of the increase of knowledge. Whatsoever, therefore, happeneth new to man, giveth him matter of hope of knowing somewhat that he knew not before. And this hope and expectation of future knowledge from any thing that happeneth new and strange is that passion which we commonly call admiration; and the same considered as appetite, is called curiosity, which is appetite of knowledge. As in the discerning of faculties, man leaveth all community with beasts at the faculty of imposing names, so also doth he surmount their nature at this passion of curiosity.

For when a beast seeth any thing new and strange to him, he considereth it so far only as to discern whether it be likely to serve his turn or hurt him, and accordingly approacheth nearer to it, or fleeth from it: whereas man, who in most events remembereth in what manner they were caused and begun, looketh for the cause and beginning of every thing that ariseth new unto him. And from this passion of admiration and curiosity, have arisen not only the invention of names, but also suppositions of such causes of all things as they thought might produce them. And from this beginning is derived all philosophy, as astronomy from the admiration of the course of heaven; natural philosophy from the strange effects of the elements and other bodies. And from the degrees of curiosity proceed also the degrees of knowledge amongst men; for, to a man in the chase of riches or authority (which in respect of knowledge are but sensuality), it is a diversity of little pleasure, whether it be the motion of the sun or the earth that maketh the day; or to enter into other contemplations of any strange accident, otherwise than whether it conduce or not to the end he pursueth. Because curiosity is delight, therefore also novelty is so; but especially that novelty from which a man conceiveth an opinion, true or false, of bettering his own estate; for, in such case, they stand affected with the hope that all gamesters have while the cards are shuffling.

'The style of Hobbes,' says Sir James Mackintosh, 'is the very perfection of didactic writing. Short, clear, precise, pithy, his language never has more than one meaning, which never requires a second thought to find. By the help of his exact method, it takes so firm hold on the mind, that it will not allow attention to slacken. His little tract on 'Human Nature' has scarcely an ambiguous or needless word. He has so great a power of always choosing the most significant term, that he never is reduced to the poor expedient of using many in its stead. He had so thoroughly studied the genius of the language, and knew so well to steer between pedantry and vulgarity, that two centuries have not superannuated probably more than a dozen of his words.'

Lord Herbert of Cherbury was an intimate friend of Hobbes, and a brave and high-spirited man, at a time when honorable feeling was rare at the English Court. Like Hobbes he distinguished himself as a free-thinker; and, according to Leland, 'as he was one of the first, so he was confessedly one of the greatest writers that have appeared among us in the deistical cause.'

Edward Herbert was born at Montgomery Castle, in Wales, in 1581. At the age of fourteen he entered a gentleman commoner of University College, Oxford, where he laid the foundation of that admirable learning for which he was afterward so distinguished. From the university he travelled abroad, and applied himself to military exercises in foreign countries, by which he became a most accomplished gentleman. On his return to England, in 1603, he was knighted by King James, and soon after made one of the counsellors of that king for military affairs. In 1616 he was sent ambassador to Paris, and there published, in 1624, his celebrated deistical work, *Of Truth, as it is distinguished from Probable, Possible, and False Revelation.* In this work, the first in which deism was ever reduced to a system, the author maintains the sufficiency, universality, and absolute perfection of natural religion, and the consequent uselessness of supernatural revelation. In reprinting the work in London, in 1645, he added two tracts, the one, *Of the Causes of Error*, and the other, *Of the Religion of a Layman;* and soon afterward he published another book, entitled, *The Ancient Religion of the Gentiles, and Cause of their Errors Considered.*

Lord Herbert died in London on the twentieth of August, 1648; and the next year after his death, appeared his *History of the Life and Reign of King Henry the Eighth.* This work is termed by Lord Orford 'a masterpiece of historic biography;' and in Bishop Nicholson's opinion 'the author has acquitted himself with the like reputation as Lord Chancellor Bacon gained by the life of Henry the Seventh, having in the polite and martial part, been admirably exact, from the best records that remain.' In its style, the work is considered one of the best old specimens of historical composition in the language, being manly and vigorous, and unsullied by the quaintness and pedantry of the age. Lord Herbert is remarkable also as the earliest of English autobiographers. The memoirs which he kept of his own life were first printed in 1764, and have ever since been popular. As a specimen of his historical writing, we present the following passage from his 'Life of Henry the Eighth:'

SIR THOMAS MORE'S RESIGNATION OF THE GREAT SEAL.

Sir Thomas More, Lord Chancellor of England, after divers suits to be discharged of his place, (which he had held two years and a-half,) did at length by the king's good leave resign it. The example whereof being rare, will give me occasion to speak more particularly of him. Sir Thomas More, a person of sharp wit, and en dued besides with excellent parts of learning, (as his works may testify,) was yet (out of I know not what natural facetiousness) given so much to jesting, that it detracted no little from the gravity and importance of his place, which, though generally noted and disliked, I do not think was enough to make him give it over in that merriment we shall find anon, or retire to a private life. Neither can I believe him so much addicted to his private opinions as to detest all other governments but his own Utopia, so that it is probable some vehement desire to follow his book, or secret offence taken against some person or matter, (among which perchance the king's new intended marriage, or the like might be accounted,) occasioned this strange counsel; though, yet, I find no reason pretended for it, but infirmity and want of health. Our king hereupon taking the seal and giving it, together with the order of knighthood, to Thomas Audeley, speaker of the Lower House, Sir Thomas More, without acquainting any body with what he had done, repairs to his family at Chelsea, where, after a mass celebrated the next day in the church, he comes to his lady's pew, with his hat in his hand, (an office formerly done by one of his gentlemen,) and says, 'Madam, my lord is gone.' But she thinking this at first to be but one of his jests, was little moved, till he told her sadly, he had given up the great seal; whereupon she speaking some passionate words, he called his daughters then present to see if they could not spy some fault about their mother's dressing; but they after searching saying they could find none, he replied, 'Do you not perceive that your mother's nose standeth somewhat awry?'—of which jeer the provoked lady was so sensible, that she went from him in a rage. Shortly after, he acquainted his servants with what he had done, dismissing them also to the attendance of some other great personages, to whom he had recommended them. For his fool, he bestowed him on the lord mayor during his office, and afterward on his successors in that charge. And now coming to himself, he began to consider how much he had left, and finding that it was not above one hundred pounds yearly in lands, besides some money, he advised with his daughters how to live together. But the grieved gentlewomen, (who knew not what to reply, or indeed how to take these jests,) remaining astonished, he says, 'We will begin with the slender diet of the students of the law, and if that will not hold out, we will take such commons as they have at Oxford; which yet if our purse will not stretch to maintain, for our last refuge we will go a-begging, and at every man's door sing together a Salve Regina to get alms.' But these jests were thought to have in them more levity, than to be taken everywhere for current; he might have quitted his dignity without using such sarcasms, and betaken himself to a more retired and quiet life, without making them or himself contemptible. And certainly whatsoever he intended hereby, his family so little understood his meaning, that they needed some more serious instructions. So that I can not persuade myself for all this talk, that so excellent a person should omit at fit times to give his family that sober account of his relinquishing this place, which I find he did to the Archbishop Warham, Erasmus, and others.

Lecture the Nineteenth.

TRANSLATION OF THE BIBLE—*ROBERT BURTON*—*JOSEPH HALL*—*THOMAS OVERBURY*—*JOHN SELDEN*—*JAMES USHER*—*JOHN HALES*—*OWEN FELTHAM.*

THE remarkable influence which has resulted to the English language and literature from the translation of the Bible, executed in the commencement of the reign of James the First, and which has now for more than two centuries been the cherished version of the sacred Word with the millions who speak the English tongue, seems to require that, at this period in our remarks, we should notice the circumstances under which that great work was performed. Hazlitt, the accomplished critic, in mentioning the several causes which made the age of Elizabeth and James so distinguished for its great names in literature, assigns to the translation of the Bible the first place. In reference to this subject he observes, in his 'Lectures on the Literature of the age of Elizabeth,' that 'The translation of the Bible was the chief engine in this great work. It threw open, by a secret spring, the rich treasures of religion and morality, which had been there locked up as in a shrine. It revealed the visions of the prophets, and conveyed the lessons of inspired teachers to the meanest of the people. It gave them a common interest in a common cause. Their hearts burnt within them as they read. It gave a mind to the people, by giving them common subjects of thought and feeling. It cemented their union of character and sentiment; it created endless diversity and collision of opinion. They found objects to employ their faculties, and a motive in the magnitude of the consequences attached to them, to exert the utmost eagerness in the pursuit of truth, and the most daring intrepidity in maintaining it.' With such testimony before us respecting the influence which the Bible then exerted, we shall proceed to mention the circumstances under which the present English version was produced; but to do this the more successfully we must notice, briefly, the translations from the sacred volume which were previously made in both the Saxon and the English languages.

The first version of any portion of the Bible into a British tongue, appeared about 727, and was executed by the venerable Bede, who, for the age in which he lived, was a miracle of learning. His translation is supposed to have been made from the Latin Vulgate, and though it embraced only the Gospel of St. John, he himself regarded it as his most important literary performance. From the death of Bede a period of more than one hundred and fifty years elapsed before any other attempt seems to have been made to render any portion of the Scriptures into the vernacular tongue. Alfred the Great, after having succeeded in driving the Danes out of his dominions, and in inducing a state of general peace and prosperity throughout his kingdom, turned his attention toward the moral and spiritual condition of his subjects. For their benefit he, about 895, produced, and rendered popular among them, a translation of the Psalms of David. About a century after, Alfric, Archbishop of Canterbury, with similar views with those which influenced the mind of the great monarch himself toward the common people, translated, for their particular benefit, the first seven books of the Old Testament. The foregoing translations were all made from the Latin into the Saxon language, and were in common use until the Saxon began to give place to the Norman French. This change was gradual, but eventuated, in the course of about three centuries, in forming the basis of the present English tongue.

In 1375, Wickliffe, in order to oppose the more effectually the encroachments and impositions of the Church of Rome, produced an entire translation of the Old and New Testaments from the Latin Vulgate into English, the English language having, at this time, assumed a comparatively permanent form. Nearly two long and dreary centuries, however, followed, during the whole of which the Romish Church waved its iron sceptre over Britain with increasing power, sealing, as it had done from the beginning, for the better effecting of its own wicked purposes, the sacred volume from the common eye. In the commencement of the reign of Henry the Eighth, this power reached its very climax; but a succession of events rapidly followed, which separated the Church of England from the Church of Rome, and prepared the way for the general reception of the Scriptures in the vernacular tongue.

Ten years previously, however, to the withdrawal of Henry the Eighth from the Romish Church, Tyndale, in order to avoid persecution, had retired to the continent, and there prepared, and in 1526, published an English translation of the New Testament out of the original Greek text. This was followed by the publication, in 1530, of a version from the original language, of the first five books of the Old Testament, in which he is said to have been assisted by Coverdale. The translation of Tyndale, when we remember the embarrassing disadvantages under which it was made, must be regarded as a very wonderful performance.

In 1535, Coverdale, having also previously retired from Yorkshire to the continent, produced a translation into English of the entire Bible. The copies of his first edition bear upon their title-page the following inscription:—'Biblia the Bible; that is, the Holy Scriptures of the Old and New Testament, faithfully and newly translated out of the Deutche and Latin.'

To Coverdale, therefore, belongs the honor of having given to the English nation the first translation of the *whole Bible* into their native tongue. Four years after Coverdale's Bible was published, appeared a translation of the Scriptures purporting to be by Thomas Matthewe. The name is generally supposed to be fictitious, and of Matthewe's Bible, John Rogers, who was burned at the stake in the reign of Mary, was the real author.

Cranmer's, or the 'Great Bible,' as it was called, being printed ir a large double folio volume form, appeared in 1539. This was a revision and republication from former translations of the Scriptures, by a number of scholars, but Bishop Cranmer had no farther connection with the work than to write the preface. In the same year appeared Taverner's Bible, the text of which was formed upon Matthewe's, or Rogers's translation, already mentioned.

Cranmer's Bible was now the favorite, and, accordingly, in 1541, Henry the Eighth issued a decree that the 'Great Bible' should be placed in every parish church in England, and all curates not already furnished with a copy of it, were commanded to procure one, and place it in a situation convenient for consultation in their respective churches, and all bishops were required to see that this command was strictly enforced. 'It was wonderful,' says the historian Stripe, 'to see with what joy this book of God was received, not only among the learneder sort, but generally all England over, among all the people; and with what greediness God's Word was read, and what resort to places where the reading of it was.' During the short reign of Edward the Sixth, eleven different impressions of the English Bible was made, but they were merely reprints of some one of the former versions.

In 1560, the 'Geneva Bible' was published. This was a translation, with notes, by Coverdale and others, who, during the reign of queen Mary, had fled for safety from England to Geneva, in Switzerland, and while they resided there they effected this important work. This was long the favorite Bible of the English Puritans and the Scotch Presbyterians; and it is estimated that during the reign of Elizabeth, not less than fifty editions were published. The 'Douay Bible' is the only other version of the Scriptures of any note that preceded the present standard translation. Of this translation the New Testament was printed at Rheims, in 1582, and the Old, at Douay, from which the whole receives its name, in 1609.

Soon after the accession of James the First to the English crown, complaints of discrepancies in the various translations of the English Scriptures then in use, became so common, that on the twenty-fourth of October, 1603, that monarch issued a proclamation, 'Touching a meeting for the hearing and for the determining things pretended to be amiss in the church.' This meeting, known as the 'Conference of the Hampton Court,' was held at that place in the middle of January, 1604, and on the third and last day of the session, Dr. John Rainolds, President of Corpus Christi College, a man of high and unblemished character, and at that time esteemed the most eminent scholar in the kingdom, 'moved,' according to Dr. Barlow, 'his majesty that there might be a new translation of the Bible; because those allowed in the reign of Henry the Eighth and Edward the Sixth were corrupt, and not answerable to the truth of the original.' As the result of the Conference at Hampton, which was composed of the clergy of both the Puritan and the Established Church, fifty-four of the best scholars of the kingdom were designated to carry out the design contemplated. Of these, however, seven either died, or declined to serve before the translation commenced; and the remaining forty-seven were formed into five separate divisions.

The first division met at Westminster, and to them, with Dr. Lancelot Andrews at their head, was assigned that part of the Old Testament which extends from Genesis to the second book of Kings, inclusive.

The second division met at Cambridge, and at their head was placed Dr. Edward Livlie, who, for more than thirty years, was Regius Professor of Hebrew, in Cambridge University. The portion of the Old Testament assigned to this division extended from First Chronicles to Ecclesiastes, inclusive.

The third division met at Oxford, and under the direction of Dr. John Harding, then Regius Professor of Hebrew in the university, and afterward President of Magdelen College, had assigned to them that part of the Old Testament which extends from Isaiah to Malachi, inclusive.

The fourth division also met at Oxford, and with Dr. Thomas Ravis, Dean of Christ's Church, and afterward Bishop of London, at their head, undertook the translation of that part of the New Testament which extends from Matthew to the Acts, inclusive, and the Revelation.

The fifth division, under the guidance of Dr. William Barlow, Dean of Chester, held their sessions at Westminster, and to them was assigned the remaining part of the New Testament, extending from Romans to Jude, inclusive.

In executing their important task, each individual translator was required to translate the entire portion assigned to his division, and when all in any one division had finished, they met together and compared their several translations, decided all differences, and settled upon what they considered the best translation. When the several divisions had finished their labor, they all met together and appointed twelve of their number to revise the whole work. This being done, the new translation was published in 1611, under the following title:—*The Holy Bible containing the Old Testament and the New, newly translated out of the Original Tongues, and with the former Translations diligently compared and revised by his Majesty's Special Commandment.*

As a specimen of the English language, this great work is, in the words of Spenser, emphatically, 'A well of English undefiled;' and as the learned Dr. Adam Clarke remarks:—'The translators have seized the very spirit and soul of the original, and expressed this almost everywhere with pathos and energy: they have not only made a *standard translation*, but have made this translation the standard of our language.' We have little to fear, therefore, from the weak attempts of ephemeral minds to mar its accuracy and beauty.

The importance of a correct view of the English standard translation of the Bible, has led us into a more extended detail of the circumstances under which we came into possession of that invaluable treasure, than the range of these lectures would otherwise have justified. We now proceed to notice those clerical and other writers of the period at present under consideration, to whom we have not hitherto referred. Of these the names of Burton, Hall, Overbury, Selden, Usher, Hales, and Felltham are the first that occur.

Robert Burton was of an ancient family of Leicestershire, and was born at Lindley, in that county, on the eighth of February, 1576. After pursuing the usual preparatory studies at a grammar-school in Warwickshire, he, in 1593, entered Brazen-nose College, Oxford, and six years after was elected student of Christ's Church College, in the same university. Having graduated and taken orders, Burton, in 1616, was preferred to the vicarage of St. Thomas, in the west suburb of Oxford, and received also, a few years after, the rectory of Segrave in Leicestershire, both of which he held, though with some difficulty, till his death, which occurred in January, 1639.

Burton was a man of great benevolence and learning, but of whimsical and melancholy disposition. Though at certain times he was a facetious companion, yet at others, his spirits were very low; and when in this latter condition he would go down to the river near Oxford, and dispel his gloom by listening to the coarse jests and ribaldry of the bargemen, which excited him to violent laughter. To alleviate his mental distress, he wrote a work, entitled *The Anatomy of Melancholy*, which appeared in 1651, and presents, in quaint language, and with many shrewd and amusing remarks, a view of all the modifications of that disease, and the manner of curing it. The erudition displayed in this work is extraordinary, every page abounding with quotations from Latin authors. Its publication was so successful that the publisher realized a fortune by it; and it delighted Dr. Johnson so much, that he said 'it was the only book that ever took him out of bed two hours before he wished to rise.'

Prefixed to the Anatomy of Melancholy, is a poem from which Milton borrowed some of the imagery of 'Il Penseroso.' Of this poem the following are the first six stanzas:—

ABSTRACT OF MELANCHOLY.

When I go musing all alone,
Thinking of divers things foreknown,
When I build castles in the air,
Void of sorrow, void of fear,
Pleasing myself with phantasms sweet,
Methinks the time runs very fleet.
All my joys to this are folly;
Nought so sweet as melancholy.

When I go walking all alone,
Recounting what I have ill-done,
My thoughts on me then tyrannize,
Fear and sorrow me surprise;
Whether I tarry still, or go,
Methinks the time moves very slow.
All my griefs to this are jolly;
Nought so sad as melancholy.

When to myself I act and smile,
With pleasing thoughts the time beguile.
By a brook side or wood so green,
Unheard, unsought for, or unseen,
A thousand pleasures do me bless,
And crown my soul with happiness.
All my joys besides are folly;
None so sweet as melancholy.

When I lie, sit, or walk alone,
I sigh, I grieve, making great moan;
In a dark grove or irksome den,
With discontent and furies then,
A thousand miseries at once
Mine heavy heart and soul esconce.
All my griefs to this are jolly;
Nought so sour as melancholy.

Methinks I hear, methinks I see
Sweet music, wondrous melody,
Towns, palaces, and cities, fine;
Here now, then there, the world is mine.
Rare beauties, gallant ladies shine,
Whate'er is lovely is divine.
All other joys to this are folly;
None so sweet as melancholy.

Methinks I hear, methinks I see
Ghosts, goblins, fiends: my phantasie
Presents a thousand ugly shapes;
Headless bears, black men, and apes;
Doleful outcries and fearful sights
My sad and dismal soul affrights.
All my griefs to this are jolly;
None so damn'd as melancholy.

Of Burton's prose the following brief extract will be a sufficient specimen:—

MELANCHOLY AND CONTEMPLATION.

Voluntary solitariness is that which is familiar with melancholy, and gently brings on, like a Siren, a shooing-horn, or some sphinx, to this irrevocable gulf; a primary cause Piso calls it: most pleasant it is at first, to such as are melancholy given, to lie in bed whole days, and keep their chambers; to walk alone in some solitary grove, betwixt wood and water, by a brook side; to meditate upon some delightsome and pleasant subject, which shall affect them most; 'amabilis insania,' and 'mentis gratissimus error.' A most incomparable delight it is to melancholize, and build castles in the air; to go smiling to themselves, acting an infinite variety of parts, which they suppose and strongly imagine they represent, or that they see acted or done. 'Blanda quidem ab initio,' ('pleasant, indeed, it is at first,') saith Lemnius, to conceive and meditate of such pleasant things sometimes, *present, past,* or *to come,* as Rhasis speaks. So delightsome these toys are at first, they could spend whole days and nights without sleep, even whole years alone in such contemplations and fantastical meditations which are like unto dreams; and they will hardly be drawn from them, or willingly interrupt. So pleasant their vain conceits are, that they hinder their ordinary tasks and necessary business; they can not address themselves to them, or almost to any study or employment: these fantastical and bewitching thoughts so covertly, so feelingly, so urgently, so continually set upon, creep in, insinuate, possess, overcome, distract and detain them; they can not, I say, go about their more necessary business, stave off or extricate themselves, but are ever musing, melancholizing, and carried along, as he (they say) that is led round about an heath with a puck in the night. They run earnestly on in this labyrinth of anxious and solicitous melancholy meditations, and can not well or willingly refrain, or easily leave off winding and unwinding themselves as so many clocks, and still pleasing their humours, until at last the scene is turned upon a sudden, by some bad object; and they, being now habituated to such vain meditation and solitary places, can endure no company, can ruminate of nothing but harsh and distasteful subjects. Fear, sorrow, suspicion, 'subrusticus pudor,'—['clownish bashfulness,'] discontent cares, and weariness of life, surprise them, in a moment; and they can think of nothing else; continually suspecting, no sooner their eyes open, but this infernal plague of melancholy seizeth upon them, and terrifies their souls, representing some dismal object to their minds, which now, by no means, no labour, no persuasions, they can avoid.

JOSEPH HALL, whom we have briefly noticed as a poetical satirist, was born in Bristow Park, Leicestershire, on the first of July, 1574. At the age of fifteen he was sent to Emanuel College, Cambridge, of which, after taking his degrees, he became a fellow. After remaining six years at College, Hall took orders, and was soon after presented to the rectory of Halsted, in Suffolk. In 1605 he accompanied Sir Edward Bacon to the Spa, and while residing there composed his *Century Meditations*, the most popular of his works. Hall's 'Meditations' greatly pleased Prince Henry, in consequence of which he selected him for his chaplain, and, in 1612, caused the degree of doctor of Divinity to be conferred upon him. The Prince would have retained his chaplain near his person, but about this time Hall received, from the Earl of Norwich, the vicarage of Waltham, in Essex, with the quiet retirement of which he was so much delighted that no prospect of preferment had any influence with him. In the delightful relations of a country parson he remained at Waltham for many years. In 1618 he was sent, by King James, to the synod of Dordt. Indisposition, however, soon compelled him to return to England; but before his departure he preached a Latin sermon to that famous assembly, with which they were so much pleased that they soon after sent him a gold medal, having upon it a portraiture of the synod.

In 1624 Hall was offered the bishopric of Gloucester, which he declined; but three years after he accepted that of Exeter, from which, in 1641, he was transferred to the see of Norwich In December of the same year, having joined with other bishops in protesting against the validity of all laws made during their compulsory absence from the parliament, he was, with others, committed to the Tower, in January, 1642. In the following June, having obtained his release, he returned to Norwich, where he passed a few months without molestation; but the sequestration of his revenues by parliament, in April, 1643, so embarrassed his relations to his see, that a few years after he retired to a small estate, which he rented at Higham, near Norwich, where he died, on the eighth of September, 1656.

Bishop Hall is universally allowed to have been a man of great wit and learning, and of equal meekness, modesty, and piety. He was a very zealous opposer of popery, and was equally severe upon those protestants who separated from the Established Church without extreme necessity. His writings are voluminous; and from the pithy and sententious quality of his style, he has been called 'the English Seneca.' Many parts of his prose writings have the thought, feeling, and melody of the finest poetry. The most popular of his works is his 'Meditations,' a few extracts from which follow:—

UPON THE SIGHT OF A TREE FULL-BLOSSOMED.

Here is a tree overlaid with blossoms; it is not possible that all these should prosper; one of them must needs rob the other of moisture and growth; I do not love to see an infancy over-hopeful; in these pregnant beginnings one faculty starves another, and at last leaves the mind sapless and barren: as, therefore, we are wont to pull off some of the too frequent blossoms, that the rest may thrive, so, it is good wisdom to moderate the early excess of the parts, or progress of over-forward childhood. Neither is it otherwise in our Christian profession; a sudden and lavish ostentation of grace may fill the eye with wonder, and the mouth with talk, but will not at the last fill the lap with fruit.

Let me not promise too much, nor raise too high expectations of my undertakings; I had rather men should complain of my small hopes than of my short performances.

UPON OCCASION OF A RED-BREAST COMING INTO HIS CHAMBER.

Pretty bird, how cheerfully dost thou sit and sing, and yet knowest not where thou art, nor where thou shalt make thy next meal; and at night must shroud thyself in a bush for lodging! What a shame is it for me, that see before me so liberal provisions of my God, and find myself sit warm under my own roof, yet am ready to droop under a distrustful and unthankful dullness. Had I so little certainty of my harbour and purveyance, how heartless should I be, how careful; how little should I have to make music to thee or myself! Surely thou comest not hither without a providence. God sent thee not so much to delight, as to shame me, but all in a conviction of my sullen unbelief, who, under more apparent means, am less cheerful and confident; reason and faith have not done so much in me, as in thee mere instinct of nature; want of foresight makes thee more merry if not more happy here, than the foresight of better things maketh me.

O God, thy providence is not impaired by those powers thou hast given me above these brute things; let not my greater helps hinder me from a holy security, and comfortable reliance on thee.

UPON HEARING OF MUSIC BY NIGHT.

How sweetly doth this music sound in this dead season! In the day-time it would not, it could not, so much affect the ear. All harmonious sounds are advanced by a silent darkness; thus it is with the glad tidings of salvation; the gospel never sounds so sweet as in the night of preservation, or of our own private affliction; it is ever the same, the difference is in our disposition to receive it. O God, whose praise it is to give songs in the night, make my prosperity conscionable, and my crosses cheerful.

The sermons of Bishop Hall display an uncommonly rapid and vehement species of eloquence, well fitted to arouse and impress even the most listless audience. As a specimen, we present the following extract from a discourse on the text, 'It is finished:'—

CHRIST CRUCIFIED AFRESH BY SINNERS.

Behold, this storm, wherewith all the powers of the world were shaken, is now over. The elders, Pharisees, Judas, the soldiers, priests, witnesses, judges, thieves, executioners, devils, have all tired themselves in vain with their own malice; and he triumphs over all, upon the throne of his cross: his enemies are vanquished, his Father satisfied, his soul with this world at rest and glory; 'It is finished.' Now there is no more betraying, agonies, arraignments, scourgings, scoffings, crucifying, conflicts, terrors; all 'is finished.' Alas! beloved, and will we not let the Son of God be at rest? Do we now again go about to fetch him out of his glory, to scorn and crucify him? I fear to say it: God's spirit dare and doth; 'They crucify again to themselves the Son of God, and make a mock of him:' to themselves, not in himself; that they can not, it is no thanks to them; they would do it. See and consider: the notoriously sinful conversations of those that should be Christians, offer violence unto our glorified Saviour; they stretch their hand to heaven, and pull him down from his throne to his cross; they tear him with thorns, pierce him with nails, load him with reproaches. Thou hatest the Jews, spittest at the name of Judas, railest on Pilate, condemnest the cruel butchers of Christ; yet thou canst blaspheme, swear him quite over, curse, swagger, lie, oppress, boil with lust, scoff, riot, and livest like a debauched man; yea, like a human beast, yea, like an unclean devil. Cry Hosanna as long as thou wilt; thou art a Pilate, a Jew, a Judas, an executioner of the Lord of life; and so much greater shall thy judgment be, by how much thy light and his glory is more. Oh, beloved, is it not enough that he died once for us? Were those pains so light that we should every day redouble them? Is this the entertainment that so gracious a Saviour hath deserved of us by dying? Is this the recompense of that infinite love of his that thou shouldest thus cruelly vex and wound him with thy sins? Every of our sins is a thorn, and nail, and spear to him; while thou pourest down thy drunken carouses, thou givest thy Saviour a portion of gall; while thou despisest his poor servants, thou spittest on thy proud dresses, and liftest up thy vain heart with high conceits, thou settest a crown of thorns on his head, while thou wringest and oppressest his poor children, thou whippest him, and drawest blood of his hands and feet. Thou hypocrite, how darest thou offer to receive the sacrament of God with that hand which is thus imbrued with the blood of him whom thou receivest? In every ordinary thy profane tongue walks, in the disgrace of the religious and conscionable. Thou makest no scruple of thine own sins, and scornest those that do: not to be wicked, is crime enough. Hear him that saith, 'Saul, Saul, why persecutest thou me?' Saul strikes at Damascus; Christ suffers in heaven. Thou strikest; Christ Jesus smarteth, and will revenge. These are the afterings of Christ's sufferings. In himself it is 'finished;' in his members it is not, till the world be finished. We must toil, and groan, and bleed, that we may reign;

if he had not done so, 'It had not been finished.' This is our warfare; this is the religion of our sorrow and death. Now are we set upon the sandy pavement of our theatre, and are matched with all sorts of evils; evil men, evil spirits, evil accidents, and, which is worst, our own evil hearts; temptations, crosses, persecutions, sicknesses, wants, infamies, death; all these must in our courses be encountered by the law of our profession. What should we do but strive and suffer, as our general hath done, that we may reign as he doth, and once triumph in our consummatum est?[1] God and his angels sit upon the scaffolds of heaven, and behold us: our crown is ready; our day of deliverance shall come; yea, our redemption is near, when all tears shall be wiped from our eyes, and we that have sown in tears shall reap in joy. In the mean time, let us possess our souls not in patience only, but in comfort; let us adore and magnify our Saviour in his sufferings, and imitate him in our own. Our sorrows shall have an end; our joys shall not: our pains shall soon be finished; our glory shall be finished, but never ended.

THOMAS OVERBURY, memorable chiefly for his tragical end, was of an ancient family, and born in Warwickshire, in 1581. At the age of fourteen he was entered a gentleman commoner of Queen's College, Oxford, where he applied himself to his studies with such diligence, that when but seventeen years of age he received the degree of bachelor of arts. His father designing him for the legal profession, he entered the Middle Temple as a student of law; but his genius most inclined him to polite literature, and the elegancies of a court life impelled him to push his fortunes in that direction. Accordingly, soon after the coronation of James the First, he commenced an acquaintance with the famous Robert Car, afterward Earl of Somerset; and that gentleman, finding that Overbury's accomplishments would be very serviceable to him in furthering his ambitious views, entered into the most intimate connection with him. Car becoming, in a few years, a very great favorite of the king, used his influence, in 1608, to obtain for Overbury the honor of knighthood, and at the same time had his father appointed one of the judges for Wales. The year following, Sir Thomas made a tour through Holland, Flanders, and France, and on his return to England, published his observations abroad in a large quarto volume.

In 1612, Overbury assisted his friend, who had meantime become Viscount Rochester, in an amour with the notorious Countess of Essex; but being afterward displeased with his lordship's design of marrying that worthless lady, he remonstrated with him with the same liberty that he had been accustomed to use on other subjects. The courtier was offended, and made no scruple of sacrificing his friend to his purpose. Disclosing, therefore, the interview with Sir Thomas, to Lady Essex, it was immediately resolved, that the successful issue of their intrigue necessarily required the removal of Overbury out of the way. With this view, the minion first obtained for him from his majesty, the offer of an embassy to Russia; and then prevailing on him to refuse it, easily procured his imprisonment for a contempt of the king's command. He was, accordingly, apprehended, and on the twenty-first of August, 1613, sent to the Tower, where his death was soon after compassed by poison.

[1] It is finished.

Sir Thomas Overbury was a witty and ingenious describer of characters. He had also some pretensions to poetry, and early wrote two didactic poems, called *The Wife* and *The Choice of a Wife;* but though popular at the time, they are now held in little estimation. Some of his prose *Characters, or Witty Descriptions of the Properties of Sundry Persons*, are, however, excellent, though, like many other productions of James's reign, disfigured by far-fetched conceits. Of these, the following is a fair specimen :-

THE FAIR AND HAPPY MILKMAID

Is a country wench, that is so far from making herself beautiful by art, that one look of hers is able to put all face-physic out of countenance. She knows a fair look is but a dumb orator to command virtue, therefore minds it not. All her excellences stand in her so silently, as if they had stolen upon her without her knowledge. The lining of her apparel, which is herself, is far better than outsides of tissue; for though she be not arrayed in the spoils of the silk-worm, she is decked in innocence, a far better wearing. She doth not, with lying long in bed, spoil both her complexion and conditions: nature hath taught her, too immoderate sleep is rust to the soul; she rises, therefore, with Chanticleer, her dame's cock, and at night makes the lamb her curfue. In milking a cow, and straining the teats through her fingers, it seems that so sweet a milk-press makes the milk whiter or sweeter; for never came almond-glore or aromatic ointment on her palm to taint it. The golden ears of corn fall and kiss her feet when she reaps them, as if they wished to be bound and led prisoners by the same hand that felled them. Her breath is her own, which scents all the year long of June, like a new-made hay-cock. She makes her hand hard with labour, and her heart soft with pity; and when winter evenings fall early, sitting at her merry wheel, she sings defiance to the giddy wheel of fortune. She doth all things with so sweet a grace, it seems ignorance will not suffer her to do ill, being her mind is to do well. She bestows her year's wages at next fair, and in choosing her garments, counts no bravery in the world like decency. The garden and bee-hive are all her physic and surgery, and she lives the longer for it. She dares go alone, and unfold sheep in the night, and fears no manner of ill, because she means none; yet to say truth, she is never alone, but is still accompanied with old songs, honest thoughts, and prayers, but short ones; yet they have their efficacy, in that they are not palled with ensuing idle cogitations. Lastly, her dreams are so chaste, that she dare tell them; only a Friday's dream is all her superstition; that she conceals for fear of anger. Thus lives she, and all her care is, she may die in the spring-time, to have store of flowers stuck upon her winding-sheet.

JOHN SELDEN, a man of extensive knowledge and vast learning, was of a respectable family, and was born at Salvington, in Sussex, on the sixteenth of December, 1584. He commenced his classical education at the free-school in Chichester, and at sixteen years of age was sent to Hart-Hall College, Oxford, where he remained three years. He then went to London and entered Clifford's Inn, as a student of law; but at the expiration of two years he removed to the Inner Temple, where he soon acquired great reputation for his learning. Though he designed to make the law his profession, yet he by no means confined himself to its dry details, but gave much of his time and attention to subjects more purely literary. Between 1607, and 1610, he published, in the Latin language, several historical and antiquarian works relative to his native country. These acquired for him, besides considerable reputation, the esteem and friendship of Camden, Spelman, Colton, Browne, and also of Drayton, to whose 'Polyolbion' he furnished notes. By Milton he is afterward mentioned as 'the chief of learned men reputed in this land.'

Selden's largest English work, *A Treatise on Titles of Honour*, was published in 1614, and still continues to be a standard authority respecting the degrees of nobility and gentry in England, and the origin of such distinctions in other countries. In 1617 his fame was greatly extended, both at home and on the continent, by the publication of a Latin work on the idolatry of the Syrians, and more especially on the heathen deities mentioned in the Old Testament. In his next performance, *A History of Tithes*, published in 1618, he, by leaning to the side of those who question the divine right of the church to that fund, gave great offence to the clergy, at whose instigation the king summoned the author to his presence, and reprimanded him. He was also called before several members of the formidable high commission court, who extracted from him a written declaration of sorrow for what he had done, without, however, any retraction of his opinions. To this great work several replies appeared, but to these he was not allowed to publish a rejoinder.

During the subsequent part of his life, Selden showed but little respect for his clerical contemporaries, whose conduct he deemed arrogant and oppressive. Nor did he long want an opportunity of showing that civil tyranny was as little to his taste as ecclesiastical; for being consulted by the parliament in 1621, on the occasion of the dispute with James concerning their powers and privileges, he spoke so freely on the popular side, and took so prominent a part in drawing up the spirited protestation of parliament, that he suffered a short confinement in consequence of the king's displeasure. As a member of parliament, both in this and the subsequent reign, he continued to defend the liberty of the people, for which, upon one occasion, he was committed to the Tower, on a charge of sedition. In 1640, when the Long Parliament met, Selden was unanimously elected one of the representatives of Oxford university; but though he still opposed the abuses and oppressions of which the people complained, he was averse to extreme measures, and desirous to prevent the power of the sword from falling into the hands of either party. Finding his exertions to ward off a civil war unavailing, he seems to have withdrawn himself as much as possible from public life. While in parliament he constantly exerted his influence in behalf of learning and of learned men, and performed great services to both universities. In 1643, he was appointed keeper of the records of the Tower; but his political occupations were not suffered to divert his mind altogether from literary pursuits. Besides an account published in 1628, of the celebrated Arundelian marbles, which had been brought from Greece during the previous year, and which, by furnishing the dates of many events in ancient history, proved of very great use in chronological investigations, he gave to the world various works on legal and ecclesiastical antiquities; particularly those of the Jewish nation. He also wrote, in 1635, an elaborate Latin treatise in support of the right of British dominion over the circumjacent seas. This work found great favor with all parties, and a defence of it against a Dutch writer, was his last literary performance. Selden died on the thirtieth of November, 1654, at the residence of Elizabeth, countess of Kent, with whom he had long lived on terms of very close intimacy. His funeral sermon was preached by his friend, Archbishop Usher, and his valuable library was added, by his executors, to the Bodleian library, at Oxford.

After Selden's death, a collection of his sayings, entitled *Table Talk*, was published by his amanuensis, who states that he enjoyed, for twenty years, the opportunity of hearing his employer's discourse, and was in the habit of committing faithfully to writing, 'the excellent things that usually fell from him.' It is more by his 'Table Talk' than by the works published during his life-time, that Selden is now generally known as a writer; for though he was a man of great talent and learning, his style was deficient in ease and grace, and the class of subjects upon which he employed his pen, was little suited to the popular taste. Many of the apophthegms to be found in his 'Table Talk,' are exceedingly acute; many of them are harmonious; while some embody propositions, which, though uttered in familiar conversation, he probably would not have seriously entertained. As might be expected, satirical remarks on the clergy of the Establishment abound, and there are displays also of that cautious spirit which distinguished him throughout his whole career. Marriage, for example, he characterizes as 'a desperate thing: the frogs in Æsop were extreme wise; they had a great mind to some water, but they would not leap into the well, because they could not get out again.' The following are farther extracts from the 'Table Talk:'

EVIL SPEAKING.

1. He that speaks ill of another, commonly before he is aware, makes himself such a one as he speaks against; for, if he had civility or breeding, he would forbear such kind of language.

2. A gallant man is above ill words. An example we have in the old lord of Salisbury, who was a great wise man. Stone had called some lord about court, fool; the lord complains, and has Stone whipped; Stone cries, 'I might have called my lord of Salisbury fool often enough, before he would have had me whipped.'

3. Speak not ill of a great enemy, but rather give him good words, that he may use you the better, if you chance to fall into his hands. The Spaniard did this when he was dying; his confessor told him, to work him to repentance, how the devil tormented the wicked that went to hell; the Spaniard replying, called the devil, my lord: 'I hope my lord the devil is not so cruel.' His confessor reproved him. 'Excuse me,' said the Don, 'for calling him so; I know not into what hands I may fall; and if I happen into his I hope he will use me the better for giving him good words.'

HUMILITY.

1. Humility is a virtue all preach, none practice, and yet every body is content to hear. The master thinks it good doctrine for his servant, the laity for the clergy, and the clergy for the laity.

2. There is humilitas quædam in vitio.[1] If a man does not take notice of that ex-

cellency and perfection that is in himself, how can he be thankful to God, who is the author of all excellency and perfection? Nay, if a man hath too mean an opinion of himself, it will render him unserviceable both to God and man.

3. Pride may be allowed to this or that degree, else a man can not keep up his dignity. In gluttons there must be eating, in drunkenness there must be drinking; it is not the eating, nor it is not the drinking, that is to be blamed, but the excess. So in pride.

We select the following fine passage from the preface to Selden's 'History of Tithes.'

FREE INQUIRY.

For the old skeptics that never would profess that they had found a truth, yet showed the best way to search for any, when they doubted as well of what those of the dogmatical sects too credulously received for infallible principles, as they did of the newest conclusions. They were, indeed, questionless, too nice, and deceived themselves with the nimbleness of their own sophisms, that permitted no kind of established truth. But, plainly, he that avoids their disputing levity, yet being able, takes to himself their liberty of inquiry, is in the only way that in all kinds of studies leads and lies open even to the sanctuary of truth; while others that are servile to common opinion and vulgar suppositions, can rarely hope to be admitted nearer than into the base court of her temple, which too speciously often counterfeits her inmost sanctuary.

JAMES USHER, archbishop of Armagh, in Ireland, a prelate equally illustrious for his piety and other virtues, as for his great abilities and profound learning, was descended from a very ancient family, and was born in Dublin, on the fourth of January, 1580. His father was one of the clerks in chancery, and is memorable for having been the first to move Queen Elizabeth to found and endow Trinity College, in his native city. James discovered unusual talents, and a strong passion for books, even from his childhood; and having been taught to read by two blind aunts, he was placed, when only eight years of age, under the care of a young Scotch gentleman, named Hamilton, who had settled in Dublin to follow the profession of schoolmaster. In 1593, at the age of thirteen, he entered Trinity College, being one of the first three students that were admitted, the college having been completed that same year. Hamilton, meantime, becoming one of the professors in the new college, Usher continued to enjoy the advantages of his instructions. During his studies at college, he became a fine classical scholar, though his chief attention was devoted to history and chronology. At that early period he collected and arranged most of those materials which he afterward elaborated in his *Annals*. He was early designed for the law, but the death of his father, whose wishes inclined to that profession, allowed him to follow his own inclinations for theology. He succeeded to his father's estate, but wishing to devote himself uninterruptedly to study, he gave it up to his brother, reserving for himself only a sufficiency for his maintenance at college, and the purchase of books. He early displayed great zeal against the Roman Catholics; and notwithstanding the mildness

[1] Such a thing as a faulty excess of humility.

of his personal character, continued, throughout his life, to manifest a highly intolerant spirit toward them. In 1606, he visited England, and became acquainted with Camden and Sir Robert Colton, to the former of whom he communicated many valuable particulars about the ancient state of Ireland, and the history of Dublin; which were afterward inserted by Camden in his 'Britannia.'

For thirteen years subsequent to 1607, Usher filled the chair of divinity in the university of Dublin, in performing the duties of which he confined his attention chiefly to the controversies between the Protestants and Romanists. At the convocation of the Irish clergy, in 1615, when they determined to assert their independence as a national church, the articles drawn up on the occasion emanated chiefly from his pen; and by asserting in them the Calvinistic doctrines of election and reprobation in their broadest aspect as well as by his advocacy of the rigorous observance of the Sabbath, and his known opinion, that bishops were not a distinct order in the church, but only superior in degree to presbyters, he exposed himself to the charge of being a favorer of Puritanism. Having been accused as such to the king he went over to England, in 1619, and in a conference with his majesty, so fully cleared himself, that he was soon after appointed to the see of Meath, and, in 1624, to the archbishopric of Armagh. Bishop Usher had scarcely reached his elevated position before he gave evidence of his intolerant spirit toward the Romanists, by acting as the leading man at the drawing up of a protestation commencing as follows:—'The religion of the Papists is superstitious and idolatrous; their faith and doctrines erroneous and heretical; their Church, in respect of both, apostatical. To give them, therefore, a toleration, or to consent that they may freely exercise their religion, and possess their faith and doctrine, is a grievous sin.'* At a later period, Usher's zeal showed itself in a more creditable shape on the occasion of a letter from the king to the Irish archbishops, complaining of the increase of Popery in Ireland. He invited persons of the Romish persuasion to his house, and endeavored to convert them by friendly argument, in which attempt his great skill in disputation is said to have given him considerable success.

During the political convulsions of Charles's reign, Usher, in a treatise entitled *The Power of the Prince, and Obedience of the Subject*, maintained the absolute unlawfulness of taking up arms against the king. The Irish rebellion, in 1641, drove him to England, where he was well received by King Charles, whose residence was, at that time, at Oxford. Here Usher settled; but the civil war which soon followed, compelled him frequently to change his abode, until it at last became fixed at the Countess of Peterborough's seat at Ryegate, where he died, on the twenty-first of March, 1656, and was buried, by order of Cromwell, the Protector, with great pomp and magnificence, in Westminster Abbey.

Most of the writings of Archbishop Usher relate to ecclesiastical history, and antiquities, and were mainly intended to furnish arguments against the Romanists; but the production for which he is chiefly celebrated is a great chronological work entitled *Annales*, or *Annals*, the first part of which was published in 1650, and the second, in 1654. It is a chronological digest of universal history, from the creation of the world to the destruction of Jerusalem by Titus, in the seventieth year of the Christian era. In this work, which was received with great applause by the learned throughout Europe, and has been several times reprinted on the continent, the author, by fixing the three epochs of the deluge, the departure of the Israelites from Egypt, and their return from Babylon, has reconciled the chronologies of sacred and profane history; and down to the present time, his chronological system is the one which is most generally received. A posthumous work, which he left unfinished, was published in 1660, under the title of *Chronologia Sacra*. It shows the grounds and calculations of the principal epochs of the 'Annals,' and as a guide to the study of sacred history, is a very valuable production. Usher and Selden contributed more, perhaps, than any other scholars of the age, to extend the reputation of English learning on the continent of Europe.

The following letter, the only specimen of Usher's style that we shall present, was written when he was not yet twenty years of age, and has reference to a public disputation between him and one Fitz-Symonds, a prominent Jesuit of that day:—

'I was not purposed, Mr. Fitz-Symonds, to write unto you, before you had first written to me, concerning some chief points of your religion, as at our last meeting you promised; but seeing you have deferred the same, for reasons best known to yourself, I thought it not amiss to inquire further of your mind, concerning the continuation of the conference began betwixt us. And to this I am the rather moved, because I am credibly informed of certain reports, which I could hardly be persuaded should proceed from him, who in my presence pretended so great love and affection unto me. If I am a boy, as it hath pleased you very contemptuously to name me, I give thanks to the Lord that my carriage toward you hath been such, as could minister unto you no just occasion to despise my youth. Your spear belike is in your own conceit a weaver's beam, and your abilities such, that you desire to encounter with the stoutest champion in the host of Israel; and therefore like the Philistine, you contemn me as being a boy. Yet this I would fain have you know, that I neither came then, nor now do come unto you, in any confidence of any learning that is in me; in which respect notwithstanding I thank God, I am what I am: but I come in the name of the Lord of hosts, whose companies you have reproached, being certainly persuaded, that even out of the mouths of babes and sucklings he was able to show forth his own praises. For the farther manifestation thereof, I do again earnestly request you, that, setting aside all vain comparisons of persons, we may go plainly forward, in examining the matters that rest in controversy between us; otherwise I hope you will not be displeased, if, as for your part you have began, so I also for my own part may be bold, for the clearing of myself and the truth which I possess, freely to make known what hath already passed concerning this matter. Thus entreating you in a few lines to make known unto me your purpose in this behalf, I end; praying the Lord, that both this and all other enterprises that we take in hand may be so ordered, as may most make for the advancement of his own glory, and the kingdom of his son Jesus Christ.

Tuus ad Aras usque

JAMES USHER.'

John Hales, usually called the Ever Memorable, was born at Bath, Somersetshire, in 1584. At thirteen years of age he was sent to Corpus Christi College, Oxford; and in 1605, was chosen fellow of Merton, through the interest of the warden of that college, Sir Henry Saville. His knowledge of the Greek language was so consummate, that, in 1612, he was appointed professor of Greek in the university. Sir Thomas Bodley, founder of the Bodleian library, at Oxford, dying in 1613, Hales was chosen by the university to deliver his funeral oration; and the same year he was admitted a fellow of Eton College. In 1618, he accompanied Sir Dudley Carleton, the king's ambassador to the Hague, in the quality of chaplain, and by this means he obtained admission to the synod of Dort, then in session there. Witnessing all their proceedings and transactions, he gave Sir Dudley an account of them in a series of letters afterward published among his *Golden Remains.* Farinden, his friend, tells us, in a letter prefixed to this collection, that Hales 'in his younger days was a Calvinist; but the arguments of the Armenian champion, Episcopius, urged before the synod, made him 'bid John Calvin good night.'' His letters from Dort are characterized by Lord Clarendon as 'the best memorial of the ignorance, and passion, and animosity and injustice of that convention.'

The eminent learning and abilities of Hales would, certainly, on his return to England, have led to high preferment in the church; but he chose rather to live in studious retirement, and accordingly withdrew to Eton College, where he enjoyed the fellowship to which we have already alluded. Of this, after the defeat of the royal party, he was deprived, for refusing to take the oath of fidelity to the Commonwealth of England, as then established without a king or a house of lords. His ejection, by cutting off the means of subsistence, reduced him to such straits, that he was at length under the necessity of selling the greater part of his library for less than one third of its original cost. This event and his death are touchingly noticed by his intimate friend Farinden, in the following extract from one of his letters:—'Paying him a visit, a few months before his death, I found him in very mean lodgings at Eton, but in a temper gravely cheerful, and well becoming a good man under such circumstances. After a very slight and homely dinner, some discourse passed between us concerning our old friends, and the black and dismal aspect of the times; and at last he asked me to walk out with him into the churchyard. There his necessities compelled him to tell me that he had been forced to sell his whole library, save a few books, which he had given away, and six or eight little volumes of devotion which lay in his chamber; and that for money he had no more than seven or eight shillings which he then showed me: 'and besides,' said he, 'I doubt I am indebted for my lodging. When I die,' he proceeded, 'which I hope is not far off, for I am weary of this uncharitable world, I desire you to see me buried in that place of the churchyard,' pointing to a particular spot. 'But why not in the church,' said I, 'with the provost, Sir Henry Saville, Sir Henry Wotton, and the rest of your friends and predecessors?' 'Because,' said he, 'I am neither the founder of it, nor have I been a benefactor to it.' ' Hales died on the nineteenth of May, 1656, and the day following he was buried, in accordance with his own desire, in Eton College churchyard. He is reported to have said in his former days, that he 'thought he should never die a martyr;' but he suffered more than many martyrs have suffered, and certainly died little less than a martyr to unwavering integrity and principle.

Besides sermons and miscellanies, the former of which compose the chief portion of his works, Hales wrote a famous *Tract concerning Schism and Schismatics*, in which the causes of religious disunion, and, in particular, the bad effects of Episcopal ambition, are freely discussed. The style of his sermons is clear, simple, and correct; and the subjects are frequently illustrated with quotations from the ancient philosophers and Christian fathers. The following extract is from a sermon, *Of Inquiry and Private Judgment in Religion*:—

PRIVATE JUDGMENT IN RELIGION.

It were a thing worth looking into, to know the reason why men are so generally willing, in point of religion, to cast themselves into other men's arms, and, leaving their own reason, rely so much upon another man's. Is it because it is modesty and humility to think another man's reason better than our own? Indeed, I know not how it comes to pass, we account it a vice, a part of envy, to think another man's goods, or another man's fortunes, to be better than our own, and yet we account it a singular virtue to esteem our reason and wit meaner than other men's. Let us not mistake ourselves; to contemn the advice and help of others, in love and admiration to our own conceits, to depress and disgrace other men's, this is the foul vice of pride: on the contrary, thankfully to entertain the advice of others, to give it its due, and ingenuously to prefer it before our own if it deserve it, this is that gracious virtue of modesty: but altogether to mistrust and relinquish our own faculties, and commend ourselves to others, this is nothing but poverty of spirit and indiscretion. I will not forbear to open unto you what I conceive to be the causes of this so general an error amongst men. First peradventure the dregs of the church of Rome are not yet sufficiently washed from the hearts of many men. We know it is the principal stay and supporter of that church, to suffer nothing to be inquired into which is once concluded by them. Look through Spain and Italy; they are not men, but beasts, and Issachar-like, patiently couch down under every burden their superiors lay upon them.

Secondly, a fault or two may be in our own ministry; thus, to advise men, (as I have done,) to search into the reasons and grounds of religion, opens a way to dispute and quarrel, and this might breed us some trouble and disquiet in our cures, more than we are willing to undergo; therefore, to purchase our own quiet, and to banish all contention, we are content to nourish this still humour in our hearers; as the Sibarites, to procure their ease, banished the smiths, because their trade was full of noise. In the mean time we do not see that peace, which ariseth out of ignorance, is but a kind of sloth, or moral lethargy, seeming quiet because it hath no power to move. Again, maybe the portion of knowledge in the minister himself is not over great; it may be, therefore, good policy for him to suppress all busy inquiry in his auditory, that so increase of knowledge in them might not at length discover some ignorance in him. Last of all, the fault may be in the people themselves, who, because they are loath to take pains (and search into the grounds of knowledge is evermore painful), are well content to take their ease, to gild their vices with goodly names, and to call their sloth modesty, and their neglect of inquiry filial obedience. These reasons, beloved, or some of kin to these, may be the motives unto this easiness of the people, of entertaining their religion upon trust, and of the neglect of the inquiry into the grounds of it.

To return, therefore, and proceed in the refutation of this gross neglect in men of their own reason, and casting themselves upon their wits. Hath God given you eyes to see, and legs to support you, that so yourselves might lie still, or sleep, and require the use of other men's eyes and legs? That faculty of reason which is in every one of you, even in the meanest that hears me this day, next to the help of God, is your eyes to direct you, and your legs to support you, in your course of integrity and sanctity; you may no more refuse or neglect the use of it, and rest yourselves upon the use of other men's reason, than neglect your own and call for the use of other men's eyes and legs. The man in the gospel, who had bought a farm, excuses himself from going to the marriage supper, because himself would go and see it: but we have taken an easier course; we can buy our farm, and go to supper too, and that only by saving our pains to see it; we profess ourselves to have made a great purchase of heavenly doctrine, yet we refuse to see it and survey it ourselves, but trust to other men's eyes, and our surveyors: and wot you to what end? I know not, except it be, that so we may with the better leisure go to the marriage supper; that, with Haman, we may the more merrily go in to the banquet provided for us; that so we may the more freely betake ourselves to our pleasures, to our profits, to our trades, to our preferments and ambition.

Would you see how ridiculously we abuse ourselves when we thus neglect our own knowledge, and securely hazard ourselves upon other's skill? Give me leave, then, to show you a perfect pattern of it, and to report to you what I find in Seneca the philosopher, recorded of a gentleman in Rome, who, being purely ignorant, yet greatly desirous to seem learned, procured himself many servants, of which some he caused to study the poets, some the orators, some the historians, some the philosophers, and, in a strange kind of fancy, all their learning he verily thought to be his own, and persuaded himself that he verily knew all that his servants understood; yea, he grew to that height of madness in this kind, that, being weak in body and diseased in his feet, he provided himself of wrestlers and runners, and proclaimed games and races, and performed them by his servants; still applauding himself, as if himself had done them. Beloved, you are this man: when you neglect to try the spirits, to study the means of salvation yourselves, but content yourselves to take them upon trust, and repose yourselves altogether on the wit and knowledge of us that are your teachers, what is this in a manner but to account with yourselves, that our knowledge is yours, that you know all we know, who are but your servants in Jesus Christ?

OWEN FELLTHAM, another deeply interesting writer of this period, was a native of Suffolk, where his family had resided for several generations; but of his own personal history little farther is known. His learning and virtues appear to have recommended him to the notice of the earl of Themond, in whose family he, for some years, lived in easy and honorable dependence. During his residence in the family of the earl, Fellthain produced a work of very great merit, under the title of *Resolves; Divine, Moral, and Political.* The date of the first publication of this interesting production is uncertain, but the second edition appeared in 1628, and so popular did the book continue during the seventeenth century, that in 1709, it had reached the twelfth edition.

The 'Resolves' consists of essays on religious and moral subjects, and seems to derive its name from the circumstance, that the author, who evidently wrote for his own improvement, generally forms resolutions at the end of each essay. Both in substance and in manner, the work, in many places, bears a considerable resemblance to the essays of Bacon. Felltham's style is, for the most part, vigorous, harmonious, and well adapted to the subjects; sometimes imaginative and eloquent, but occasionally chargeable with prolixity, superabundance of illustration, and too great familiarity of expression. His sentiments are distinguished by good sense, and great purity of religious and moral principle. The following passages will illustrate these remarks :—

LIMITATION OF HUMAN KNOWLEDGE.

Learning is like a river, whose head being far in the land, is, at first rising, little, and easily viewed; but, still as you go, it gapeth with a wider bank; not without pleasure and delightful winding, while it is on both sides set with trees, and the beauties of various flowers. But still the further you follow it the deeper and the broader 'tis; till at last, it inwaves itself in the unfathomed ocean; there you see more water, but no shore—no end of that liquid fluid vastness. In many things we may sound Nature, in the shallows of her revelations. We may trace her to her second causes; but, beyond them, we meet with nothing but the puzzle of the soul, and the dazzle of the mind's dim eyes. While we speak of things that are, that we may dissect, and have power and means to find the causes, there is some pleasure, some certainty. But when we come to metaphysics, to long-buried antiquity, and unto unrevealed divinity, we are in a sea, which is deeper than the short reach of the line of man. Much may be gained by studious inquisition; but more will ever rest, which man can not discover.

OF NEGLECT.

There is the same difference between diligence and neglect, that there is between a garden properly cultivated and the sluggard's field which fell under Solomon's view, when overgrown with nettles and thorns. The one is clothed with beauty, the other is unpleasant and disgusting to the sight. Negligence is the rust of the soul, that corrodes through all her best resolutions. What nature made for use, for strength, and ornament, neglect alone converts to trouble, weakness, and deformity. We need only sit still, and diseases will arise from the mere want of exercise.

How fair soever the soul may be, yet while connected with our fleshy nature, it requires continual care and vigilance to prevent its being soiled and discoloured. Take the weeders from the Floralium[1] and a very little time will change it to a wilderness, and turn that which was before recreation for men into a habitation for vermin. Our life is a warfare; and we ought not, while passing through it, to sleep without a sentinel, or march without a scout. He who neglects either of these precautions, exposes himself to surprise, and to becoming a prey to the diligence and perseverance of his adversary. The mounds of life and virtue, as well as those of pastures, will decay; and if we do not repair them, all the beasts of the field will enter, and tear up every thing good which grows within them. With the religious and well-disposed, a slight deviation from wisdom's laws will disturb the mind's fair peace.

Macarius did penance for only killing a gnat in anger. Like the Jewish touch of

[1] Flower-garden.

things unclean, the east miscarriage requires purification. Man is like a watch; if evening and morning he be not wound up with prayer and circumspection, he is unprofitable and false, or serves to mislead. If the instrument be not truly set, it will be harsh and out of tune; the diapason dies, when every string does not perform his part. Surely, without a union to God, we can not be secure or well. Can he be happy who from happiness is divided? To be united to God, we must be influenced by his goodness, and strive to imitate his perfections. Diligence alone is a good patrimony; but neglect will waste the fairest fortune. One perseveres and gathers; the other, like death, is the dissolution of all. The industrious bee, by her sedulity in summer, lives on honey all the winter. But the drone is not only cast out from the hive, but beaten and punished.

MEDITATION.

Meditation is the soul's perspective glass; whereby, in her long remove, she discerneth God, as if he were nearer hand. I persuade no man to make it his whole life's business. We have bodies as well as souls; and even this world, while we are in it, ought somewhat to be cared for. As those states are likely to flourish where execution follows sound advisements; so is man, when contemplation is seconded by action. Contemplation generates; action propagates. Without the first, the latter is defective; without the last the first is abortive, and embryous. Saint Bernard compares contemplation to Rachel, which was the more fair; but action to Leah, which was the more fruitful. I will neither always be busy, and doing; nor ever shut up in nothing but thought. Yet that which some would call idleness, I will call the sweetest part of my life, and that is, my thinking.

Lecture the Twentieth.

JOHN EARLE — PETER HEYLIN — WILLIAM CHILLINGWORTH — JOHN GAUDEN— JEREMY TAYLOR — THOMAS BROWNE — JOHN KNOX — DAVID CALDERWOOD— SIR JAMES MELVIL—JOHN LESLEY—JOHN SPOTISWOOD.

THE present lecture will close our remarks upon the literature of the age of Queen Elizabeth and King James; and though we may be thought to have dwelt too long and too minutely upon this period, yet its varied intellectual richness would not permit us to make our investigations less thorough, or less extensive. 'There were giants in the land in those days,' and the impress of their mighty minds upon their still living and breathing pages, throws round their productions a halo of splendor from which we instinctively draw back with awe. Their works are the offspring of that creative mental power which moulds every thing with which it comes in contact into its own likeness; and though occasional defects may be found in their writings, they are uniformly the defects incident to the highest order of genius. Of these writers we have still to notice Earle, Heylin, Chillingworth, Gauden, Taylor, and Browne.

JOHN EARLE was born at York, in 1601, and educated at Merton College, Oxford. He was a man of extensive learning and great eloquence, extremely agreeable and facetious in conversation, and of such excellent moral and religious qualities, that in the language of Walton, there had lived, since the death of Richard Hooker, no man 'whom God had blessed with more innocent wisdom, more sanctified learning, or a more pious, peaceable, primative temper.' He was at one period chaplain and tutor to Prince Charles, and went with him into exile during the civil wars, after having been deprived of his whole property for his adherence to the royal cause. At the Restoration his fidelity was amply rewarded, being first made dean of Windsor, then Bishop of Worcester, and, in 1663, Bishop of Salisbury, where he died two years after this last honor was conferred upon him.

Bishop Earle was a very successful writer, and extremely happy in the drawing of characters. His principal literary performance is entitled *Micro-*

cosmography, or a Piece of the World Discovered, in Essays and Characters. This was published in 1628, and is a valuable storehouse of particulars illustrative of the manners of the times. Among the characters drawn are those of an Antiquary, a Carrier, a Player, a Pot-poet, a University Dun, and a Clown. The last of these we here present:—

THE CLOWN.

The plain country fellow is one that manures his ground well, but lets himself lie fallow and untilled. He has reason enough to do his business, and not enough to be idle or melancholy. He seems to have the punishment of Nebuchadnezzar, for his conversation is among beasts, and his talons none of the shortest, only he eats not grass, because he loves not sallets. His hand guides the plough, and the plough his thoughts, and his ditch and land-mark is the very mound of his meditations. He expostulates with oxen very understandingly, and speaks gee, and ree, better than English. His mind is not much distracted with objects; but if a good fat cow come in his way, he stands dumb and astonished, though his haste be never so great, will fix here half an hour's contemplation. His habitation is some poor thatched roof, distinguished from his barn by the loop-holes that let out smoke, which the rain had long since washed through, but for the double ceiling of bacon on the inside, which has hung there from his grandsire's time, and is yet to make rashers for posterity. His dinner is his other work, for he sweats at it as much as at his labour; he is a terrible fastener on a piece of beef, and you may hope to stave the guard off sooner. His religion is a part of his copyhold, which he takes from his landlord, and refers it wholly to his discretion: yet if he give him leave he is a good Christian, to his power (that is), comes to church in his best clothes, and sits there with his neighbours, where he is capable only of two prayers, for rain and fair weather. He apprehends God's blessings only in a good year, or a fat pasture, and never praises him but on good ground. Sunday he esteems a day to make merry in, and thinks a bagpipe as essential to it as evening prayer, where he walks very solemnly after service with his hands coupled behind him, and censures the dancing of his parish. His compliment with his neighbour is a good thump on the back, and his salutation commonly some blunt curse. He thinks nothing to be vices but pride and ill husbandry, from which he will gravely dissuade the youth, and has some thrifty hobnail proverbs to clout his discourse. He is a niggard all the week, except only market-day, where, if his corn sell well, he thinks he may be drunk with a good conscience. He is sensible of no calamity but the burning a stack of corn, or the overflowing of a meadow, and thinks Noah's flood the greatest plague that ever was, not because it drowned the world, but spoiled the grass. For death he is never troubled, and if he get in but his harvest before, let it come when it will, he cares not.

PETER HEYLIN was another of those clerical adherents of the king, who, like Bishop Earle, were despoiled of their goods by the Parliament. Descended from an ancient family, and born at Burford, in Oxfordshire, on the twenty-ninth of November, 1600, he, in the fourteenth year of his age, entered Hart-Hall College, Oxford, and two years after passed to Magdalen College, in the same university. While at school Heylin had given a specimen of his genius for dramatic poetry, in the production of a tragedy on the war of Troy; and during his third collegiate year he wrote a drama entitled *Spurious*, with which the president of the college was so much pleased that he ordered it to be performed in his presence. Heylin, however early abandoned poetry, and turned his attention to more solid pursuits. In 1619, he became lecturer to his college on cosmography, and two years after published his *Microcosmus, or Description of the Great World.* This publication acquired, for its author, so great celebrity, as to attract royal attention, and, accordingly, in 1629, he was made chaplain to his majesty, and in the course of the two following years, received the rectory of Hemmingford, the prebendary of Westminster, and the living of Houghton, in Durham. In 1633, the degree of doctor of divinity was conferred upon him, and in 1637, he was made rector of Islip, in Oxfordshire; but while he was expecting higher preferments, he found his hopes at once shattered by the violence of civil war, and he was, therefore, not only stripped of his benefices and property, but declared, by parliament, a delinquent. He fled from the fury of his persecutors, and concealed himself, for some time, first at Winchester, then at Minster Lovel, in Oxfordshire, and afterward at Abingdon, where he remained, for a number of years, in comparative repose, and devoted himself exclusively to literature. At the Restoration he was reinstated in all his ecclesiastical honors, but while he expected, in higher dignities, the reward of his faithful services in favor of royalty, he sunk under a disease brought on, or at least aggravated by disappointment, and died on the eighth of May, 1662. The king, who had refused Heylin's ecclesiastical promotion, ordered him, at his death, a burial in Westminster Abbey.

This able and indefatigable writer, whom Wood declares to have been endowed with 'singular gifts, and a sharp and pregnant wit,' was the author of no less than thirty-seven different publications, of which the 'Microcosmus,' already mentioned, is the most celebrated. As an historian, he displays too much of the spirit of a partisan and bigot, and must be ranged among the defenders of civil and ecclesiastical tyranny. His works, though now almost forgotten, were much read in the seventeenth century, and portions of them may still be perused with pleasure. In a narrative of a six weeks' tour in France, which he published in 1620, he gives the following humorous description of that people:—

THE FRENCH.

The present French is nothing but an old Gaul, moulded into a new name: as rash he is, as headstrong, and as hair-brained. A nation whom you shall win with a feather, and lose with a straw; upon the first sight of him, you shall have him as familiar as your sleep, or the necessity of breathing. In one hour's conference you may endear him to you, in the second unbutton him, the third pumps him dry of all his secrets, and he gives them you as faithfully as if you were his ghostly father, and bound to conceal them 'sub sigillo confessionis,' (' under the seal of confession;') when you have learned this, you may lay him aside, for he is no longer serviceable. If you have any humour in holding him in further acquaintance (a favour which he confesseth, and I believe him, he is worthy of), himself will make the first separation: he hath said over his lesson now unto you, and now must find somebody else to whom to repeat it. Fare him well; he is a garment whom I should be loath to wear above two days together, for in that time he will be threadbare. 'Familiare est hominis omnia sibi remittere,'—('it is usual for men to overlook their own faults,') saith Velleius of all; it holdeth most properly in this people. He is very kind-hearted to himself, and thinketh himself as free from wants as he is full; so much he hath in him the nature of a Chinese, that he thinketh all men blind but himself. In this private self-conceitedness he hateth the Spaniard, loveth not the English, and contemneth the German; himself is the only courtier and complete gentleman, but it is his own glass which he seeth in. Out of this conceit of his own excellency, and partly out of a shallowness of brain, he is very liable to exceptions; the least distaste that can be draweth his sword, and a minute's pause sheatheth it to your hand; afterward, if you beat him into better manners, he shall take it kindly, and cry, serviteur. In this one thing they are wonderfully like the devil; meekness or submission makes them insolent; a little resistance putteth them to their heels, or makes them your spaniels. In a word (for I have held him too long), he is a walking vanity in a new fashion.

I will give you now a taste of his table, which you shall find in a measure furnished (I speak not of the peasant), but not with so full a manner as with us. Their beef they cut out into such chops, that that which goeth there for a laudable dish, would be thought here a university commons, new served from the hatch. A loin of mutton serves amongst them three roastings, besides the hazard of making pottage with the rump. Fowl, also, they have in good plenty, especially such as the king found in Scotland; to say truth, that which they have is sufficient for nature and a friend, were it not for the mistress or the kitchen wench. I have heard much fame of French cooks, but their skill lieth not in the neat handling of beef and mutton. They have (as generally have all this nation) good fancies, and are special fellows for the making of puff-pastes, and the ordering of banquets. Their trade is not to feed the belly, but the palate. It is now time you were set down, where the first thing you must do is to say your grace; private graces are as ordinary there as private masses, and from thence I think they learned them. That done, fall to where you like best; they observe no method in their eating, and if you look for a carver, you may rise fasting. When you are risen, if you can digest the sluttishness of the cookery (which is most abominable at first sight), I dare trust you in a garrison. Follow him to church, and there he will show himself most irreligious and irreverent: I speak not of all, but the general. At a mass, in Cordeliers' church in Paris, I saw two French papists, even when the most sacred mystery of their faith was celebrating, break out into such a blasphemous and atheistical laughter, that even an Ethnic would have hated it; it was well they were Catholics, otherwise some French hothead or other would have sent them laughing to Pluto.

The French language is, indeed, very sweet and delectable: it is cleared of all harshness, by the cutting and leaving out the consonants, which maketh it fall off the tongue very volubly; yet, in my opinion, it is rather elegant than copious; and, therefore, is much troubled for want of words to find out paraphrases. It expresseth very much of itself in the action; the head, body, and shoulders, concur all in the pronouncing of it; and he that hopeth to speak it with good grace, must have something in him of a mimic. It is enriched with a full number of significant proverbs, which is a great help to the French humour in scoffing; and very full of courtship, which maketh all the people complimental. The poorest cobbler in the village hath his court cringes, and his eau benite de cour; his court holy-water as perfectly as the prince of Condé.

WILLIAM CHILLINGWORTH, like his contemporary Usher, was one of those pillars of the Church of England, whose opposition to Romanism was uncompromising. He was born at Oxford, in October, 1602, and having, until the sixteenth year of his age, pursued preparatory studies at a private grammar-school in his native place, he then entered Trinity College, in Oxford university, whence he took both of his degrees, and of which he eventually became a fellow. He was early destined for the clerical office, and his studies, therefore, were chiefly directed to preparation for its sacred duties; but he, at the same time, gave sufficient attention to other branches of learning, to become a respectable poet, and an accomplished mathematician. Having resolved to take orders, his fellowship enabled him to remain at Oxford, and there prosecute his studies in divinity without embarrassment. There were, through the indulgence of the king, residing at this period, in the vicinity of Oxford, many Romanists of extensive literary attainments, among whom John Perse, or, as he is usually called, Fisher, a Jesuit, was the most conspicuous. This cunning priest took every opportunity of coming in contact with university students, and as Chillingworth had early acquired a love of disputation, and great skill in argument, he was the frequent object of Perse's attacks. Long practice in disputation eventually induced a habit of doubting to such an extent, that his opinions became unsettled on almost all subjects, insomuch that the Jesuit succeeded in arguing him into a belief of the doctrines of Popery. The main argument that led to this result was that which maintained the necessity of an infallible living guide in matters of faith, to which character the Romish church appeared to him to be best entitled. In consequence of the effect thus wrought upon his mind, Chillingworth left Oxford and repaired to the Jesuit's College at Douay, in France; where he continued his theological studies, until induced, by the correspondence of Laud, his godfather, and now bishop of London, to return to England. On his return he re-entered the university of Oxford, where, after additional study of the points of difference, he declared in favor of the Protestant faith. This necessarily drew him into severe controversies, in which he employed the arguments that were afterward methodically arranged and exhibited in his famous work entitled *The Religion of the Protestants a Safe Way to Salvation*, published in 1637. This treatise, which has placed its author in the first rank of religious controversialists, is a model of perspicuous reasoning, and one of the ablest defences of the Protestant cause ever produced. In it the writer maintains that the Scriptures are the only rule to which appeal ought to be made in theological disputes; and that the Apostles' Creed embraces all the necessary points of faith.

The latitudinarianism of Chillingworth brought upon him the appellation of Arian, and Socinian; and his character of orthodoxy was still farther shaken by his refusal to accept of preferment on condition of subscribing to the thirty-nine articles. His scruples having, however, at length been overcome, he was promoted, in 1638, to the chancellorship of Salisbury. During the civil war, he zealously adhered to the royal party, and even at the siege of Gloucester, in 1643, called his mathematical knowledge into requisition, and acted as engineer. Soon after, having accompanied Lord Hopton, general of the king's forces in the west, to Arundel Castle, in Sussex, he was there taken prisoner on the ninth of December, 1643, by the parliamentary forces under the command of Sir William Waller, who obliged the forces of the castle to surrender. Being much out of health, and not able to accompany the garrison to London, Chillingworth was permitted to retire to Chichester, where he was lodged in the bishop's palace, and soon after died, at the early age of forty-two.

Lord Clarendon, who was one of his intimate friends, has drawn the following character of this eminent divine:—'He was a man of so great subtilty of understanding, and so rare a temper in debate, that, as it was impossible to provoke him to any passion, so it was very difficult to keep a man's self from being a little discomposed by his sharpness and quickness of argument, and instances, in which he had a rare facility, and a great advantage over all the men I ever knew.' Writing to a Romanist, in allusion to the changes of his own faith, Chillingworth says:—'I know a man, that of a moderate Protestant turned a Papist, and the day that he did so, was convicted in his conscience that his yesterday's opinion was an error. The same man afterward, upon better consideration, became a doubting Papist, and of a doubting Papist to a confirmed Protestant. And yet this man thinks himself no more to blame for all these changes, than a traveller, who, using all diligence to find the right way to some remote city, did yet mistake it, and after find his error and amend it. Nay, he stands upon his justification so far, as to maintain that his alterations, not only to you, but also from you, by God's mercy, were the most satisfactory actions to himself that ever he did, and the greatest victories that ever he obtained over himself, and his affections, in those things which in this world are most precious.' In the same liberal spirit is the whole of Chillingworth's great work written.

Besides 'The Religion of the Protestants a Safe Way to Salvation,' Chillingworth published a collection of nine sermons preached before Charles the First, many of which are of unusual merit. From one of these sermons we extract the following animated expostulation with his noble hearers upon a very delicate subject. The text upon which the discourse is founded is the following:—'The fool hath said in his heart there is no God.'

AGAINST DUELLING.

But how is this doctrine (of the forgiveness of injuries) received in the world? What counsel would men, and those none of the worst sort, give thee in such a case? How would the soberest, discreetest, well-bred Christian advise thee? Why, thus: If thy brother or thy neighbour have offered thee an injury, or an affront, forgive him? By no means; thou art utterly undone, and lost in reputation with the world, if thou dost forgive him. What is to be done, then? Why, let not thy heart take rest, let all other business and employment be laid aside, till thou hast his blood. How? A man's blood for an injurious, passionate speech—for a disdainful look? Nay, that is not all: that thou mayst gain among men the reputation of a discreet, well-tempered murderer, be sure thou killest him not in passion, when thy blood is hot and boiling with the provocation; but proceed with as great temper and settledness of reason, with as much discretion and preparedness as thou wouldst to the communion: after several days' respite, that it may appear it is thy reason guides thee, and not thy passion, invite him kindly and courteously into some retired place, and there let it be determined whether his blood or thine shall satisfy the injury.

Oh, thou holy Christian religion! Whence is it that thy children have sucked this inhuman poisonous blood, these raging fiery spirits? For if we shall inquire of the heathen, they will say, They have not learned this from us; or of the Mohammedans, they will answer, We are not guilty of it. Blessed God! that it should become a most sure settled course for a man to run into danger and disgrace with the world, if he shall dare to perform a commandment of Christ, which is as necessary for him to do, if he have any hopes of attaining heaven, as meat and drink is for the maintaining of life! That ever it should enter into Christian hearts to walk so curiously and exactly contrary unto the ways of God! That whereas he sees himself every day and hour almost, contemned and despised by thee, who art his servant, his creature, upon whom he might, without all possible imputation of unrighteousness, pour down all the vials of his wrath and indignation; yet he, notwithstanding, is patient and long-suffering toward thee, hoping that his long-suffering may lead thee to repentance, and beseeching thee daily by his ministers to be reconciled unto him; and yet thou, on the other side, for a distempered passionate speech or less, should take upon thee to send thy neighbour's soul, or thine own, or likely both, clogged and oppressed with all your sins unrepented of, (for how can repentance possibly consist with such a resolution?) before the tribunal seat of God, to expect your final sentence; utterly depriving yourself of all blessed means which God has contrived for thy salvation, and putting thyself in such an estate, that it shall not be in God's power almost to do thee any good. Pardon, I beseech you, my earnestness, almost intemperateness, seeing that it hath proceeded from so just, and warrantable a ground, and since it is in your power to give rules of honour and refutation to the whole kingdom, do you not teach others to be ashamed of this inseparable badge of your religion—charity and forgiving of offences: give men leave to be Christians without danger or dishonour; or if religion will not work with you, yet let the laws of that state wherein you live, the earnest desires and care of your righteous prince prevail with you.

John Gauden was a theologian of a far more worldly and ambitious character than either of the three preceding divines. He was the son of the vicar of Mayfield, in Essex, and was born in 1605. Having prepared for the university at a grammar-school in Suffolk, at sixteen years of age, he entered St. John's College, Cambridge, where he soon became distinguished for his scholarship, and at the usual time took his successive degrees. In 1630, he married the daughter of Sir William Russel, of Chippenhamme in Cambridgeshire, and was immediately after presented to the vicarage of that place. He also obtained the rectory of Brightwell, in Berkshire; and as this was near Oxford, he entered Wadham College of that university, and became tutor to two of his father-in-law's sons: several other young gentlemen, and some noblemen were also placed under his care. In this situation he passed about five years, faithfully regarding those under his care, and at the same time devoting his leisure hours with such untiring industry to his studies, that, in 1635, he took the degree of bachelor of divinity, and five years after, that of doctor.

When about thirty years of age, Gauden added to his other duties, the chaplaincy to the earl of Warwick, one of the Presbyterian leaders of that period; and being of a temporizing disposition, he not only professed the opinions current with the earl's party, but, in 1640, preached before the house of commons a sermon which gave so much satisfaction, that the members gave him a vote of thanks, and also presented him with a silver tankard. Next year the rich deanery of Bocking, in Essex, was added to his preferments; all of which, when the Presbyterian form of church government and worship was substituted for the Episcopal, he kept by conforming to the new order of things, though not without apparent reluctance.

When the army resolved to impeach and try the king, in 1648, Gauden published *A Religious and Loyal Protestation* against their purposes and proceedings. This tract was followed in subsequent years by various other pieces, in defence of the cause of the royalists. But his grand service to that party consisted in writing the famous *Ikon Basilikê; or the Portraiture of his Most Sacred Majesty in his Solitude and Sufferings*—a work professing to emanate from the pen of Charles the First himself, and to contain the devout meditations of his latter days. It was the intention of Gauden to publish the 'Portraiture,' before the execution of the king, as an attempt to save his life, by working upon the feelings of the people; but either from the difficulty of getting it printed, or some other cause, it did not appear till several days after his majesty's death. The sensation which it produced in the unfortunate monarch's favor was extraordinary. 'It is not easy,' says Hume, 'to conceive the general compassion excited toward the king by the publishing, at so critical a juncture, a work so full of piety, meekness, and humanity. Many have not scrupled to ascribe to that book the subsequent restoration of the royal family. Milton compares its effects to those which were wrought on the tumultuous Romans by Antony's reading to them the will of Cæsar.' So eagerly and universally was the book perused by the nation, that it passed through fifty editions in a single year; and probably through its influence the title of Royal Martyr was applied to the king. As a sample of the 'Ikon,' we present the following meditations upon *The Various Events of the Civil War*:—

"The various successes of this unhappy war have at least afforded me variety of good meditations. Sometimes God was pleased to try me with victory, by worsting my enemies, that I might know how with moderation and thanks to own and use his power, who is only the true Lord of Hosts, able, when he pleases, to repress the confidence of those that fought against me with so great advantages for power and number.

From small beginnings on my part, he let me see that I was not wholly forsaken by my people's love or his protection.

Other times God was pleased to exercise my patience, and teach me not to trust in the arm of flesh, but in the living God.

My sins sometimes prevailed against the justice of my cause; and those that were with me wanted not matter and occasion for his just chastisement, both of them and me. Nor were my enemies less punished by that prosperity, which hardened them to continue that injustice by open hostility, which was begun by most riotous and unparliamentary tumults.

There is no doubt but personal and private sins may ofttimes overbalance the justice of public engagements; nor doth God account every gallant man (in the world's esteem) a fit instrument to assert in the way of war a righteous cause. The more men are prone to arrogate to their own skill, valour, and strength, the less doth God ordinarily work by them for his own glory.

I am sure the event or success can never state the justice of any cause, nor the peace of men's consciences, nor the eternal fate of their souls.

Those with me had, I think, clearly and undoubtedly for their justification the word of God and the laws of the land, together with their own oaths; all requiring obedience to my just commands; but to none other under heaven without me, or against me, in the point of raising arms.

Those on the other side are forced to fly to the shifts of some pretended fears, and wild fundamentals of state, as they call them, which actually overthrow the present fabric both of church and state; being such imaginary reasons for self-defence as are most impertinent for those men to allege, who, being my subjects, were manifestly the first assaulters of me and the laws, first by unsuppressed tumults, after by listed forces. The same allegations they use, will fit any faction that hath but power and confidence enough to second with the sword all their demands against the present laws and governors, which can never be such as some side or other will not find fault with, so as to urge what they call a reformation of them to a rebellion against them."

In 1662, soon after the Restoration, Gauden was promoted to the bishopric of Worcester; a dignity, however, of which he did not long enjoy the fruits, as he died on the twentieth of September in the same year, through disappointment at not having received the richer see of Winchester, which he had solicited of the king.

Of the numerous profound theologians who, at this time, adorned the English Church, by far the most eloquent and imaginative was Jeremy Taylor. He has been styled by some, the Shakspeare, and by others, with more propriety, the Spenser, of English theological literature; and in the complexion of his taste and genius he is certainly closely allied to the author of the 'Faery Queen.' In his prolific fancy and diction, in a certain musical arrangement and sweetness of expression, in prolonged description, and in delicious musings and reveries, suggested by some favorite image or metaphor on which he dwells with the fondness of a young poet, his resemblance to Spenser is very apparent. He writes like an orator, and produces his effect by reiterated strokes and multiplied impressions. His picture of the Resurrection, in one of his sermons, is in the highest style of poetry, but generally he deals with the gentle and familiar; and his allusions to natural objects—as trees, birds, and flowers, the rising and setting sun, the charms of youthful innocence and beauty, the helplessness of infancy and childhood—possess an almost angelic purity of feeling and delicacy of fancy. When presenting rules for morning meditation and prayer, he often stops to indulge his love of nature. 'Sometimes,' he says, 'be curious to see the preparation which the sun makes when he is coming forth from his chambers of the east.' He compares a young man to a dancing bubble, 'empty and gay, and shining like a dove's neck, or the image of a rainbow, which hath no substance, and whose very imagery and colors are fantastical.' The fulfillment of our duties he calls, 'presenting a rosmary or chaplet of good works to our Maker,' and he dresses even the *grave* with the flowers of fancy. This freshness of feeling and imagination remained with him to the last, amidst all the strife and violence of the civil war, and the still more deadening effects of polemical controversy and systems of casuistry and metaphysics. The stormy vicissitudes of his life seem only to have taught him greater gentleness, resignation, toleration for human failings, and a more ardent love of humanity.

JEREMY TAYLOR was of gentle, and even heroic blood, and was born at Cambridge about the first of August, 1613. He was the lineal representative of Dr. Rowland Taylor, who suffered martyrdom in the reign of Queen Mary; and his family had formerly been distinguished in the county of Gloucester. The Taylors, however, had 'fallen into the portion of needs and out-worn faces,' to use an expression of their most illustrious member, and Jeremy's father followed the humble occupation of a barber, in Cambridge. He was, however, a man of ambition far above his circumstances, and resolved, therefore, to raise, if possible, through his son, the family to their former position. With this view, he had him carefully instructed in his preparatory learning, and at the early age of thirteen entered him in Caius College, Cambridge, where he successfully prosecuted his studies, until he took his master's degree.

In 1631 Taylor entered into sacred orders, and soon after went to London to deliver some lectures for a college friend, in St. Paul's Cathedral. His eloquent discourses, aided by what a contemporary calls 'his florid and youthful beauty, and pleasant air,' entranced all hearers, and procured him the patronage of Archbishop Laud, the friend of learning, if not of liberty. By Laud's assistance, Taylor obtained a fellowship in All Souls College, Oxford, became chaplain to the archbishop, and rector of Uppingham, in Rutlandshire. In 1639 he married Phœbe Langdale, of whom we know nothing but her musical name, and soon after, in consequence of the decline of the king's cause, he retired into Wales, where, under the protection of the earl of Carberry, he was permitted to officiate in Carmarthenshire, as a minister, and to teach school for the maintenance of his wife and children. Death, however, removed his wife from him about three years after his marriage, and to this calamity with others of a more public nature, he thus feelingly alludes:—'In the great storm which dashed the vessel of the church all in pieces, I had been cast on the coast of Wales, and in a little boat, thought to have enjoyed that rest and quietness which in England, in a far greater, I could not hope for. Here I cast anchor, and thinking to ride safely, the storm followed me with so impetuous violence, that it broke a cable, and I lost my anchor. And here again I was exposed to the mercy of the sea, and the gentleness of an element that could neither distinguish things nor persons; and, but that He that stilleth the raging of the sea, and the noise of his waves, and the madness of his people, had provided a plank for me, I had been lost to all the opportunities of content or study; and I know not whether I have been more preserved by the courtesies of my friends, or the gentleness and mercies of a noble enemy.' This fine passage is found in the dedication to Taylor's *Liberty of Prophesying*, a work published in 1647, *Showing the Unreasonableness of Prescribing to other Men's Faith, and the Iniquity of Persecuting Different Opinions.* By 'prophesying' the author means preaching or expounding the gospel. This work has been justly described as 'perhaps of all Taylor's writings, that which shows him farthest in advance of the age in which he lived, and of the ecclesiastical system in which he had been reared—as the first distinct and avowed defence of toleration which had been ventured on in England, perhaps in Christendom.' He builds the right of private judgment upon the difficulty of expounding Scripture—the insufficiency and uncertainty of tradition—the fallibility of councils, the pope, ecclesiastical writers, and the church as a body, as arbiters of controverted points—and the consequent necessity of letting every man choose his own guide, or judge of the meaning of Scripture for himself.'

The style of this masterly 'Discourse' is more argumentative and less ornate than that of his sermons and devotional treatises; but his enlightened zeal often breaks forth in striking condemnation of those who are 'curiously busy about trifles and impertinences, while they reject those glorious precepts of Christianity and holy life which are the glories of our religion, and would enable us to gain a happy eternity.' He closes the work with the following interesting and instructive apologue, which he had found in the Jew's books:—

'When Abraham sat at his tent door, according to his custom, waiting to entertain strangers, he espied an old man stopping and leaning on his staff, weary with age and travel, coming toward him, who was a hundred years of age. He received him kindly, washed his feet, provided supper, and caused him to sit down; but observing that the old man ate and prayed not, nor begged for a blessing on his meat, asked him why he did not worship the God of heaven? The old man told him that he worshiped the fire only, and acknowledged no other God; at which answer Abraham grew so zealously angry, that he thrust the old man out of his tent, and exposed him to all the evils of the night and an unguarded condition. When the old man was gone, God called to Abraham, and asked him where the stranger was? He replied, I thrust him away because he did not worship Thee: God answered him, I have suffered him these hundred years, although he dishonoured me, and couldst thou not endure him one night, when he gave thee no trouble? Upon this, saith the story, Abraham fetched him back again, and gave him hospitable entertainment and wise instruction. Go thou and do likewise, and thy charity will be rewarded by the God of Abraham.'

Before Taylor retired into Wales, he had, by virtue of the king's mandate, been made a doctor of divinity; and at the command of Charles, he wrote, soon after, a defence of Episcopacy, to which he was in principle, strongly attached. By a second marriage to a Welch lady of some fortune, he was released from the irksome duties of a schoolmaster, and thenceforth, during his stay in that country, he devoted all his leisure time to writing. Besides the 'Liberty of Prophesying,' he produced an *Apology for Authorized and Set Forms of Liturgy*, and in 1648, *The Life of Christ*, or *The Great Exemplar*, a valuable and highly popular work. These were followed by his treatises of *Holy Living* and *Holy Dying*, *Twenty-seven Sermons for the Summer Half-Year*, and various other minor productions. He wrote also an excellent little manual of devotion, entitled *The Golden Grove*, in honor of his patron, the Earl of Carberry, whose estates bore that name. He next completed his *Course of Sermons for the Year*, and published some controversial tracts on the doctrine of *Original Sin*, respecting which his opinions were thought to be rather latitudinarian.

In 1657, Taylor removed to London, and officiated in a private congregation of Episcopalians, till an offer was made to him by the Earl of Conway to accompany him to Ireland, and act as lecturer to a church at Lisburn. Thither he accordingly repaired, fixing his residence at Portmore, on the banks of Lough Neagh, about eight miles from Lisburn. Two years were passed in this happy retirement, at the expiration of which, in 1660, Taylor went to London to publish his *Cases of Conscience*, the most elaborate but least successful of all his works. His journey, however, was made at an auspicious period; for soon after his arrival, Charles the Second entered London, May the twenty-ninth, in triumphal procession, and in August following Taylor was appointed Bishop of Down and Connor. He was afterward made chancellor of the university of Dublin, and a member of the Irish privy council. The see of Dromore was also annexed to his other bishopric, 'on account of his virtue, wisdom, and industry.' The duties of his Episcopal functions were discharged with zeal, mingled with charity, and the few sermons which we possess, delivered by him in Ireland, are truly apostolic, both in spirit and language. His well-deserved honors, however, he continued to enjoy for but the brief space of six years, at the expiration of which he died of a fever at Lisburn, on the thirteenth of August, 1667, and in the fifty-fifth year of his age.

A finer pattern of a Christian divine never, perhaps, since the days of the apostles, lived, than Jeremy Taylor. His learning dignified the high station to which he at last attained; his gentleness and courtesy shed a grace over his whole conduct and demeanor; while his commanding genius and energy in the cause of truth and virtue, render him worthy of everlasting affection and veneration. From his numerous volumes we select the following characteristic and beautiful passages:—

THE AGE OF REASON AND DISCRETION.

We must not think that the life of a man begins when he can feed himself or walk alone, when he can fight or beget his like, for so he is contemporary with a camel or a cow; but he is first a man when he comes to a certain steady use of reason, according to his proportion; and when that is, all the world of men can not tell precisely. Some are called at age at fourteen, some at one-and-twenty, some never; but all men late enough; for the life of a man comes upon him slowly and insensibly. But, as when the sun approaching toward the gates of the morning, he first opens a little eye of heaven, and sends away the spirits of darkness, and gives light to a cock, and calls up the lark to matins, and by and by gilds the fringes of a cloud, and peeps over the eastern hills, thrusting out his golden horns like those which decked the brows of Moses, when he was forced to wear a vail, because himself had seen the face of God; and still, while a man tells the story, the sun gets up higher, till he shows a fair face and a full light, and then he shines one whole day, under a cloud often, and sometimes weeping great and little showers, and sets quickly: so is a man's reason and his life. He first begins to perceive himself, to see or taste, making little reflections upon his actions of sense, and can discourse of flies and dogs, shells and play, horses and liberty; but when he is strong enough to enter into arts and little institutions, he is at first entertained with trifles and impertinent things, not because he needs them, but because his understanding is no bigger, and little images of things are laid before him, like a cock-boat to a whale, only to play withal: but, before a man comes to be wise, he is half dead with gouts and consumption, with catarrhs and aches, with sore eyes and worn-out body. So that, if we must not reckon the life of a man but by accounts of his reason, he is long before his soul be dressed, and he is not to be called a man without a wise and an adorned soul, a soul at least furnished with what is necessary toward his well-being.

And now let us consider what that thing is which we call years of discretion. The young man is passed his tutors, and arrived at the bondage of a caitiff spirit; he is to run from discipline, and is let loose to passion. The man by this time hath wit enough to choose his vice, to act his lust, to court his mistress, to talk confidently, and ignorantly, and perpetually; to despise his betters, to deny nothing to his appetite, to do things that, when he is indeed a man, he must forever be ashamed of; for this is all the discretion that most men show in the first stage of their manhood. They can discern good from evil; and they prove their skill by leaving all that is good, and wallowing in the evils of folly and an unbridled appetite. And by this time the young man hath contracted vicious habits, and is a beast in manners, and therefore it will not be fitting to reckon the beginning of his life; he is a fool in his understanding, and that is a sad death.

USEFUL STUDIES.

Spend not your time in that which profits not; for your labour and your health, your time and your studies, are very valuable; and it is a thousand pities to see a diligent and hopeful person spend himself in gathering cockle-shells and little pebbles, in telling sands upon the shores and making garlands of useless daisies. Study that which is profitable, that which will make you useful to churches and commonwealths, that which will make you desirable and wise. Only I shall add this to you, that in learning there are variety of things as well as in religion: there is mint and cummin, and there are the weighty things of the law; so there are studies more and less useful, and every thing that is useful will be required in its time; and I may in this also use the words of our blessed Saviour, 'These things ought you to look after, and not to leave the other unregarded.' But your great care is to be in the things of God and of religion, in holiness and true wisdom, remembering the saying of Origen, 'That the knowledge that arises from goodness is something that is more certain and more divine than all demonstrations,' than all other learnings of the world.

REAL AND APPARENT HAPPINESS.

If we should look under the skirts of the prosperous and prevailing tyrant, we should find, even in the days of his joys, such allays, and abatements of his pleasure, as may serve to represent him presently miserable, besides his final infelicities. For I have seen a young and healthful person warm and ruddy under a poor and a thin garment; when at the same time an old rich person hath been cold and paralytic under a load of sables, and the skins of foxes. It is the body that makes the clothes warm, not the clothes the body; and the spirits of a man makes felicity and content, not any spoils of a rich fortune wrapt about a sickly and uneasy soul. Apollodorus was a traitor and a tyrant, and the world wondered to see a bad man have so good a fortune, but knew not that he nourished scorpions in his breast, and that his liver and his heart were eaten up with spectres and images of death; his thoughts were full of interruptions, his dreams of illusions; his fancy was abused with real troubles and fantastic images, imagining that he saw the Scythians flaying him alive, his daughters like pillars of fire, dancing round about a cauldron in which himself was boiling, and that his heart accused itself to be the cause of all these evils.

Does he not drink more sweetly that takes his beverage in an earthen vessel, than he that looks and searches into his golden chalices, for fear of poison, and looks pale at every sudden noise, and sleeps in armour, and trusts nobody, and does not trust God for his safety?

Can a man bind a thought in chains, or carry imaginations in the palm of his hand? can the beauty of the peacock's train, or the ostrich plume, be delicious to the palate and the throat? does the hand intermeddle with the joys of the heart? or darkness that hides the naked, make him warm? does the body live, as does the spirit? or can the body of Christ be like common food? Indeed, the sun shines upon the good and bad; and the vines give wine to the drunkard, as well as to the sober man; pirates have fair winds and a calm sea, at the same time when the just and fearful merchantman hath them. But, although the things of this world are common to good and bad, yet sacraments and spiritual joys, the food of the soul, and the blessing of Christ, are the peculiar right of saints.

PRAYER.

Prayer is an action of likeness to the Holy Ghost, the spirit of gentleness and dove-like simplicity; an imitation of the Holy Jesus, whose spirit is meek, up to the greatness of the biggest example, and a conformity to God; whose anger is always just, and marches slowly, and is without transportation, and often hindered, and never hasty, and is full of mercy: prayer is the peace of our spirit, the stillness of our thoughts, the evenness of recollection, the seat of meditation, the rest of our cares, and the calm of our tempest: prayer is the issue of a quiet mind, of untroubled thoughts; it is the daughter of charity, and the sister of meekness; and he that prays to God with an angry, that is, with a troubled and discomposed spirit, is like him that retires into a battle to meditate, and set up his closet in the out-quarters of an army, and chooses a frontier-garrison to be wise in. Anger is a perfect alienation of the mind from prayer, and therefore is contrary to that attention which presents our prayers in a right line to God. For so have I seen a lark rising from his bed of grass, and soaring upward, singing as he rises, and hopes to get to heaven, and climb above the clouds; but the poor bird was beaten back with the loud sighings of an eastern wind, and his motion made irregular and inconstant, descending more at every breath of the tempest, than it could recover by the libration and frequent weighing of his wings, till the little creature was forced to sit down and pant, and stay till the storm was over; and then it made a prosperous flight, and did rise and sing, as if it had learned music and motion from an angel, as he passed sometimes through the air, about his ministries here below. So is the prayer of a good man: when his affairs have required business, and his business was matter of discipline, and his discipline was to pass upon a sinning person, or had a design of charity, his duty met with the infirmities of a man, and anger was his instrument, and the instrument became stronger than the prime agent, and raised a tempest, and overruled the man, and then his prayer was broken, and his thoughts were troubled, and his words went up toward a cloud; and his thoughts pulled them back again, and made them without intention; and the good man sighs for his infirmities, but must be content to lose that prayer, and he must recover it, when his anger is removed, and his spirits is becalmed, made even as the brow of Jesus, and smooth like the heart of God; and then it ascends to heaven upon the wings of the holy dove, and dwells with God, till it returns, like the useful bee, loaden with a blessing and the dew of heaven.

ON DEATH.

Nature calls us to meditate of death by those things which are the instruments of acting it; and God, by all the variety of his providence, makes us see death everywhere, in all variety of circumstances, and dressed up for all the fancies, and the expectations of every single person. Nature hath given us one harvest every year, but death hath two; and the spring and the autumn send throngs of men and women to charnel-houses; and all the summer long, men are recovering from their evils of the spring, till the dog-days come, and then the Sirian star makes the summer deadly; and the fruits of autumn are laid up for all the year's provision, and the man that gathers them eats and surfeits, and dies and needs them not, and himself is laid up for eternity; and he that escapes till winter, only stays for another opportunity, which the distempers of that quarter minister to him with great variety. Thus death reigns in all the portions of our time. The autumn with its fruits provides disorders for us, and the winter's cold turns them into sharp diseases, and the spring brings flowers to strew our hearse, and the summer gives green turf and brambles to bind upon our graves. Calentures and surfeit, cold and agues, and the four quarters of the year; and you can go no whither, but you tread upon a dead man's bones.

The wild fellow in Petronius, that escaped upon a broken table from the furies of a shipwreck, as he was sunning himself upon the rocky shore, espied a man rolled upon his floating bed of waves, ballasted with sand in the folds of his garment, and carried by his civil enemy, the sea, toward the shore to find a grave. And it cast him into some sad thoughts, that peradventure this man's wife, in some part of the continent, safe and warm, looks next month for the good man's return; or, it may be, his son knows nothing of the tempest; or his father thinks of that affectionate kiss which still is warm upon the good old man's cheek, ever since he took a kind farewell, and he weeps with joy to think how blessed he shall be when his beloved boy returns into the circle of his father's arms. These are the thoughts of mortals; this is the end and sum of all their designs. A dark night and an ill guide, a boisterous sea and a broken cable, a hard rock and a rough wind, dashed in pieces the fortune of a whole family; and they that shall weep loudest for the accident are not yet entered into the storm, and yet have suffered shipwreck. Then, looking upon the carcass, he knew it, and found it to be the master of the ship, who, the day before, cast up the accounts of his patrimony and his trade, and named the day when he thought to be at home. See how the man swims, who was so angry two days since! His passions are becalmed with the storm, his accounts cast up, his cares at an end, his voyage done, and his gains are the strange events of death, which whether they be good or evil, the men that are alive seldom trouble themselves concerning the interest of the dead.

It is a mighty change that is made by the death of every person, and it is visible to us who are alive. Reckon but from the sprightfulness of youth, and the fair cheeks and full eyes of childhood; from the vigorousness and strong flexure of the joints of five-and-twenty, to the hollowness and deadly paleness, to the loathsomeness and horror of a three days' burial, and we shall perceive the distance to be very great and very strange. But so have I seen a rose newly springing from the clefts of its hood, and, at first, it was fair as the morning, and full with the dew of heaven, as a lamb's fleece, but when a ruder breath had forced open its virgin modesty, and dismantled its too youthful and unripe retirements, it began to put on darkness, and to decline to softness and the symptoms of a sickly age; it bowed the head, and broke its stalk; and at night, having lost some of its leaves, and all its beauty, it fell into the portion of weeds and outworn faces. The same is the portion of every man and every woman; the heritage of worms and serpents, rottenness and cold dishonour, and our beauty so changed, that our acquaintance quickly knew us not; and that change mingled with so much horror, or else meets so with our fears and weak discoursings, that they who, six hours ago, tended upon us either with charitable or ambitious services, can not, without some regret, stay in the room alone, where the body lies stripped of its life and honour. I have read of a fair young German gentleman, who, living, often refused to be pictured, but put off the importunity of his friends' desire by giving way, that, after a few days' burial, they might send a painter to his vault, and, if they saw cause for it, draw the image of his death unto the life. They did so, and found his face half eaten, and his midriff and back-bone full of serpents; and so he stands pictured among his armed ancestors. So does the fairest beauty change; and it will be as bad with you and me; and then what servants shall we have to wait upon us in the grave? what friends to visit us? what officious people to cleanse away the moist and unwholesome cloud reflected upon our faces from the sides of the weeping vaults, which are the longest weepers for our funeral.

A man may read a sermon, the best and most passionate that ever man preached, if he shall but enter into the sepulchres of kings. In the same Escurial where the Spanish princes live in greatness and power, and decree war or peace, they have wisely placed a cemetery, where their ashes and their glory shall sleep till time shall be no more; and where our kings have been crowned their ancestors lie interred, and they must walk over their grandsire's head to take his crown. There is an acre sown with royal seed, the copy of the greatest change, from rich to naked, from ceiled roofs to arched coffins, from living like gods to die like men. There is enough to cool the flames of lust, to abate the heights of pride, to appease the itch of covetous desires, to sully and dash out the dissembling colours of a lustful, artificial, and imaginary beauty. There the warlike and the peaceful, the fortunate and the miserable, the beloved and the despised princes mingle their dust, and pay down symbol of mortality, and tell all the world that, when we die, our ashes shall be equal to kings, and our accounts easier, and our pains for our crowns shall be less.

THOMAS BROWNE, the last of the eloquent writers of this great literary era, whom we shall particularly notice, was descended from an ancient family of Cheshire, and born in London, on the nineteenth of October, 1605. His father died during his childhood, and his mother soon after marrying Sir Thomas Dutton, a gentleman who held a post under government in Ireland, accompanied her husband into that country, leaving her son under the care of an unprincipled guardian, who spoiled him of much of his fortune. Browne received the rudiments of his education at Westminster school, and thence passed to Pembroke College, Oxford, where he successfully completed his collegiate studies, and then entered upon preparation for the medical profession. To effect his object the more thoroughly, he resolved to travel abroad; and after having visited Ireland, he passed over to the continent, and travelled extensively in France, Italy, and Holland. At Leyden he obtained the degree of doctor of medicine, and on his return to his own country settled, as a practitioner, at Norwich.

In 1642, Browne published his first work, entitled *Religio Medici*, or *The Religion of a Physician*, which immediately rendered him famous as a literary man. In this singular production, he gives a minute account of his opinions, not only on religious, but also on a variety of fanciful points, besides affording the reader many glimpses into the eccentricities of his personal character. The language of the work is bold and poetical, adorned with picturesque imagery, but frequently pedantic and obscure. His next publication, entitled *Pseudodoxia Epidemica* or *Treatises on Vulgar Errors*, appeared in 1640. It is much more philosophical in its character than the 'Religio Medici,' and is, perhaps, the most solid and useful of all his productions. The title of the work sufficiently indicates its topics. In 1658 he published his *Hydriotaphia*, or *Urn Burial; a Discourse on the Sepulchral Urns Lately Found in Norfolk*, a work not inferior, in ideality of style, to the 'Religio Medici.' Here the author's learning appears in the details which he gives concerning the modes in which the bodies of the dead have been disposed of in different ages and countries; while his reflections on death, oblivion, and immortality, are, for solemnity and grandeur, probably unsurpassed in English literature. The occasion which called forth this work was the following:—

In a field at Walsingham were dug up between forty and fifty urns, containing the remains of human bones, some small brass instruments, boxes, and other fragmentary relics. Coals and burnt substances were found near the same plot of ground, and hence it was conjectured that this was the *Ustrina*, or the place of burning, or the spot whereon the Druidical sacrifices were made. Furnished with such a theme for his philosophical musings, he comments, first on that vast charnel-house, the earth, and then successively describes and comments upon the different modes of interment and decomposition observed by various nations at different periods. Among the beauties of expression with which this work abounds may be noticed the following eloquent definition: 'Nature is not at variance with art, nor art with nature—they being both servants of his providence. Art is the perfection of nature. Were the world now as it was the sixth day, there were yet a chaos. Nature hath made one world, art another. In belief, all things are artificial, for nature is the art of God.'

To the 'Hydriotaphia' Browne appended a small treatise, called *The Garden of Cyrus; or the Quincunical Lozenge, or Network Plantations of the Ancients, Artificially and Mystically Considered.* This is written in a similar style, and displays much of the author's whimsical fancy and propensity to laborious trifling. One of the most striking of these fancies, though often quoted, we can but repeat. Wishing to denote that it is late, or that he was writing at a late hour, he says, that 'the Hyades (the quincunx of heaven) run low—that we are unwilling to spin out our awaking thoughts into the phantasms of sleep—that to keep our eyes open longer were but to act our antipodes—that the huntsmen are up in America—and that they are already past their first sleep in Persia.' This is fantastic, but it is still the offspring of genius. Browne lived in a world of ideal contemplation, but before he surrendered himself up to his reveries, he had stored his mind with vast and multifarious learning. Among his posthumous pieces is a collection of aphorisms entitled *Christian Morals*, to which Dr. Johnson prefixed a life of the author. He left also various essays on antiquarian and other subjects. In 1671, he was knighted by Charles the Second at Norwich, and died on his birthday, October the nineteenth, 1682, having just completed the seventy seventh year of his age.

In the writings of Sir Thomas Browne, the practice of employing Latin words with English terminations, is carried to such excess, that, to persons acquainted with their native tongue only, many of his sentences must be nearly unintelligible. Thus, speaking in his 'Vulgar Errors' of the nature of ice, he remarks: 'Ice is only water congealed by the frigidity of the air, whereby it acquireth no new form, but rather a consistence or determination of its diffluency, and emitteth not its essence, but condition of fluidity. Neither doth there any thing properly conglaciate but water, or watery humidity; for the determination of quicksilver is properly fixation, that of milk coagulation, and that of oil and unctious bodies only incrassation.' Such words as delucidate, ampliate, manuduction, indigitate, reminiscential, evocation, farraginous, advenient, ariolation, and lapifidical, occur on almost every page of his writings; and all who are acquained with Dr. Johnson's style, will at once perceive the resemblance, particularly in respect to the abundance of Latin words, which it bears to that of Sir Thomas Browne. Indeed there can be no doubt that the author of the 'Rambler' acquired much of his fondness for pompous and high-sounding expressions from the writings of the learned knight of Norwich. From this interesting author we have only space for the following brief extracts:—

OF MYSELF.

For my life it is a miracle of thirty years, which to relate were not a history, but a piece of poetry, and would sound to common ears like a fable. For the world I count it not an inn but a hospital, and a place not to live but to die in. The world that I regard is myself; it is the microcosm of my own frame that I can cast mine eye on—for the other I use it but like my globe, and turn it round sometimes for my recreation. * * The earth is a point not only in respect of the heavens above us, but of that heavenly and celestial part within us. That mass of flesh that circumscribes me, limits not my mind. That surface that tells the heavens it hath an end, can not persuade me I have any. * * Whilst I study to find how I am a microcosm or little world, I find myself something more than the great. There is surely a piece of divinity in us—something that was before the heavens, and owes no homage to the sun. Nature tells me I am the image of God as well as Scripture. He that understands not thus much, hath not his introduction or first lesson, and hath yet to begin the alphabet of men.

STUDY OF GOD'S WORKS.

The world was made to be inhabited by beasts, but studied and contemplated by man; it is the debt of our reason we owe unto God, and the homage we pay for not being beasts; without this, the world is still as though it had not been, or as it was before the sixth day, when as yet there was not a creature that could conceive or say there was a world. The wisdom of God receives small honour from those vulgar heads that rudely stare about, and with a gross rusticity admire his works; those highly magnify him whose judicious inquiry into his acts, and deliberate research into his creatures, return the duty of a devout and learned admiration.

CHARITY.

But to return from philosophy to charity: I hold not so narrow a conceit of this virtue, as to conceive that to give alms is only to be charitable, or think a piece of liberality can comprehend the total of charity. Divinity hath wisely divided the acts thereof into many branches, and hath taught us in this narrow way many paths unto goodness: as many ways as we may do good, so many ways we may be charitable; there are infirmities, not only of body, but of soul and fortunes, which do require the merciful hand of our abilities. I can not contemn a man for ignorance, but behold him with as much pity as I do Lazarus. It is no greater charity to clothe his body, than apparel the nakedness of his soul. It is an honourable object to see the reasons of other men wear our liveries, and their borrowed understandings do homage to the bounty of ours. It is the cheapest way of beneficence, and like the natural charity of the sun, illuminates another without obscuring itself. To be reserved and caitiff in this part of goodness, is the sordidest piece of covetousness, and more contemptible than pecuniary avarice. To this (as calling myself a scholar) I am obliged by the duty of my condition: I make not, therefore, my head a grave, but a treasure of knowledge; I intend no monopoly, but a community in learning; I study not for my own sake only, but for theirs that study not for themselves. I envy no man that knows more than myself, but pity them that know less. I instruct no man as an exercise of my knowledge, or with an intent rather to nourish and keep it alive in mine own head, than beget and propagate it in his; and in the midst of all my endeavours, there is but one thought that dejects me, that my acquired parts must perish with myself, nor can be legacied among my honoured friends. I can not fall out, or contemn a man for an error, or conceive why a difference in opinion should divide an affection: for controversies, disputes, and argumentations, both in philosophy and in divinity, if they meet with discreet and peaceable natures, do not infringe the laws of charity. In all disputes, so much as there is of passion, so much there is of nothing to the purpose; for then reason, like a bad hound, spends upon a false scent, and forsakes the question first started. And this is one reason why controversies are never determined; for though they be amply proposed, they are scarce at all handled, they do so swell with unnecessary digressions; and the parenthesis on the party is often as large as the main discourse upon the subject.

We have now brought our remarks upon the literary era of Elizabeth and James to a close; but before we entirely dismiss the subject, we must briefly notice the few Scottish prose writers which this period produced. The principal of these were Knox, Calderwood, Melvil, Lesley, and Spotiswood.

John Knox, the celebrated reformer, was born at Haddington, in 1505. Though educated at the university of St. Andrews, and bred a friar, still he early embraced the doctrines of the Reformation, and while disseminating them, was, in 1547, carried prisoner to France as a punishment for his offence. Being set at liberty two years afterward, he returned to England, and there continued to preach till the accession of Mary, in 1553, when he retired to the continent, and, for some time, resided alternately at Geneva, and Frankfort. In 1555, he visited Scotland, and by his exertions in Edinburgh, greatly strengthened the Protestant cause; but at the earnest solicitation of the English congregation at Geneva, he, in 1556, once more took up his abode in that city. At Geneva he published *The First Blast of the Trumpet against the Monstrous Regiment of Women*, directed chiefly against Mary of England, and the Queen-regent of Scotland. In 1559, Knox returned to Scotland, and continued his exertions in behalf of Protestantism, which, by the aid of an English army, triumphed in the following year. He died on the twenty-fourth of November, 1572, and when laid in his grave, was characterized by the Earl of Morton, as one 'who never feared the face of man.'

The theological works of Knox are numerous; but his most important literary production is a *History of the Reformation of Religion within the Realm of Scotland*, published after his death. Although, from having been written at intervals, and amid the distractions of a busy life, much of the work is in a confused and ill-digested state, yet it still maintains its value as a chief source of information in the ecclesiastical history of the eventful period during which the author lived; and though sometimes inaccurate, and the production of a partisan, its statements have, in the main, been confirmed by the researches of later historians.

DAVID CALDERWOOD, another zealous Presbyterian divine, wrote in the early part of the reign of James the Sixth, a work similar to that of Knox, but on a much more extensive scale, more minute, and involving many important public documents. The original production, in six folio volumes of manuscript, reposes in the library of Glasgow, but an abridgment has been printed under the title of *The True History of the Church of Scotland.* Thy style of this performance deserves little commendation; but, though deeply tinged with party feeling, it has always been highly valued as a repertory of historical facts. The date of Calderwood's birth is not known, but his death occurred in 1657.

SIR JAMES MELVIL, privy councillor and gentleman of the bed-chamber to Mary Queen of Scots, was born at Hall-hill, Fifeshire, in 1530, and died in 1606. He left in manuscript an historical work, which for a considerable time lay unknown in the castle of Edinburgh, but having at length been discovered, was published in 1683, under the title of *Memoirs of Sir James Melvil of Hall-hill, containing an Impartial Account of the Most Remarkable Affairs of State during the Last Age, not mentioned by other Historians; more particularly Relating to the Kingdoms of England and Scotland under the Reigns of Queen Elizabeth, Mary Queen of Scots, and King James. In all which Transactions the Author was Personally and Publicly Concerned.* This work, for the simplicity of its style, and as the sole authority for the history of many important events, is very highly esteemed.

JOHN LESLEY, bishop of Ross, was born in 1527, and educated at the university of Aberdeen. He was a zealous partisan of Queen Mary, and actively exerted himself in her behalf during her imprisonment in England. In consequence of being identified with various conspiracies against the life of Elizabeth, he was obliged to flee to the continent, where he was made, in 1593, bishop of Constance, and in that situation employed his wealth and influence in founding three colleges for the instruction of his countrymen—one at Rome, one at Paris, and one at Douay. Being, however, far advanced in life, he soon after resigned the mitre, and retired to a monastery in the Netherlands, where he died on the thirty-first of May, 1596.

Lesley's principal works are a *Treatise in Defence of Queen Mary, and Her Title to the English Crown;* a *Description of Scotland and the Scottish Isles;* and a work on the *Origin, Manners, and Exploits of the Scotch.* All these are in Latin; the last two forming a volume which he published at Rome, in 1578. He wrote also, in the Scottish language, a *History of Scotland from* 1436, *to* 1561, of which a Latin translation was published by himself; the original, however, was published in Edinburgh in 1830. In 1842 a work appeared entitled *Vestiarium Scoticum*, the body of which consisted of a catalogue of the tartans peculiar to Scottish families, composed by Bishop Lesley in the Scottish language, and which had long been preserved in manuscript in the college of Douay.

John Spotiswood, the last of these writers whom we shall notice, and who was successively archbishop of Glasgow, and of St. Andrews, was born in 1565. A strenuous and active promoter of the schemes of James the First of England to establish Episcopacy in Scotland, he stood high in the favor of that king, as well as of Charles the First, by whom he was made chancellor of Scotland, in 1635. His death occurred in 1639, in London, whither the popular commotions had obliged him to retire.

Spotiswood wrote, at the command of James, a *History of the Church of Scotland, from* 203 *to* 1625. When the king, in expressing his desire for the composition of that work, was told that some passages might possibly bear too hard upon the memory of his mother, he desired Spotiswood to 'write and spare not.' The history was published in London, in 1655, and is considered to be, on the whole, a faithful and impartial narrative of the events of which it treats.

Lecture the Twenty-First.

JOHN MILTON.

IN the last lecture we closed our remarks upon the writers of the age of Elizabeth and James, and in the present we shall speak of Milton, the great connecting link between the school of Elizabeth and that of Anne—uniting, in himself, all the genius of the former, with the delicacy, the polish, and the elegance of the latter.

JOHN MILTON was born in the city of London on the ninth of December, 1608. He was descended from the ancient and honorable family of Milton, in Oxfordshire—his grandfather being an underranger to the king. In his religious sentiments, Milton's grandfather was a decided Papist, but his father early embraced the Protestant faith, in consequence of which he was disinherited, and turned from his home. Having, however, received a good education, he went to London, where he thought the means of acquiring a livelihood would be more readily found than at any other place. Soon after his arrival in that city, he engaged in the business of a scrivener, which, at that period, was not only a respectable, but even an honorable calling; and he soon after married a lady of rank and fortune. This lady was also of the Protestant faith, and was devotedly pious, in consequence of which John, who was their eldest child, was trained up with the greatest care, even from his infancy, in piety and virtue. When yet a mere child, his parents placed him under the care of Mr. Young, who was at that time one of the most devoted and successful teachers in London, and by whom Milton was carefully instructed in those rudiments of classical learning which laid the foundation for his future eminence as a scholar; and the grateful expression of Milton's recollection of Mr. Young's careful attention to his studies, forms one of those delightful pictures which are so sweet a relief to the instructor's laborious avocation.

When sufficiently advanced in his studies, Milton was placed at St. Paul's School, with a view of immediate preparation for the university; and at twelve years of age, such was his devotion to learning, that, not considering the day of sufficient length to afford the time which study required, he devoted half the night also to that purpose. His constitution was naturally weak, and at this early period, the vigor and energy of his mind, together with his unwearied attention to study, laid the foundation of those infirmities of body which attended him during the remainder of his life, and which eventuated, long before his death, in total blindness. Even at this early period of life, he gave evidence, in the production of some minor poems, of the possession of those extraordinary poetic and intellectual powers which afterward immortalized his name.

Having made thorough preparation for the university, Milton, at the age of seventeen, entered Christ's College, Cambridge; and, during his whole collegiate course, though poetry was his passion, he devoted himself unremittingly to the various other studies of the institution. In 1628, in the twentieth year of his age, he took his Bachelor's degree; and as, from his infancy, he had been designed by his parents for the church, his mind was now turned to such subjects, and to such inquiries as were immediately connected with the Christian ministry. The result, however, of his inquiries, was unfavorable to his parents' most ardent wishes; for he soon perceived that the condition of the clergy of that period was such as to prevent any man of a thoughtful and independent spirit from officially entering upon the service of the church; and he, therefore, remained at the university till 1632, when he took his Master's degree, immediately after which he retired to his father's country-seat at Horton, in Buckinghamshire. Here, the circumstances of the family being easy and independent, he passed five successive years in that delightful ease and retirement which is so grateful to the studious mind; and stored his memory, meantime, with all that is interesting and valuable in classical learning. It was during Milton's residence at Horton that he composed those minor poems—*Comus*, *Il Penseroso*, *L'Allegro*, and *Lycidas*, which alone would have been sufficient to immortalize any other name than his own. 'Comus' was written at the request of the Earl of Bridgewater, and was first privately performed at the residence of that nobleman; and 'Lycidas' was elicited by the death of Edward King, one of Milton's classmates at the university, and who was accidentally drowned while crossing the Irish Sea, to visit his parents in Dublin.

In 1638, when Milton was in the thirty-first year of his age, he had the misfortune to lose his mother, and though his father was a kind and affectionate parent, yet by this irreparable loss, his home, hitherto endeared by so many interesting considerations, lost, comparatively, all its attractions for him; and he accordingly desired his father to permit him to visit the continent. This desire was readily gratified, and he therefore, with this view, attended by a single servant, left his native country, and soon after arrived in Paris. Hugo Grotius, whose fame was at that time greater than that of any other scholar on the continent, was then in that city, and the effect of the introduction of these two men to each other, can better be conceived than expressed. After having spent about two months in Paris, Milton passed through Nice, Genoa, Leghorn, and Pisa, to Florence, where he also remained two months; and there he so remarkably distinguished himself in Italian poetry, as to be admired by all ranks and conditions of men, in that city of taste and refinement. It was during his residence in Florence that that extraordinary compliment was paid him by Salvaggi, an eminent Italian poet, which is little more than translated in the following lines of Dryden :—

> Three poets in three different ages born;
> Greece, Italy, and England did adorn.
> The first in majesty of thought surpassed,
> The next in gracefulness; in both, the last.
> The force of nature could no farther go,
> To make a third, she joined the other two.

From Florence, Milton passed through Sierra, to Rome, and remained two months also in the imperial city. Here, in a short space of time, he formed a close intimacy with all the great men of Rome, and every facility was, accordingly, afforded him for acquiring all the information that he desired there to obtain. From Rome, he passed down to Naples with the intention of visiting Sicily and Greece; but while at Naples, he received intelligence of the disastrous conflict into which his own country, about that time, became involved; and his patriotism and love of home triumphing over his curiosity and desire for knowledge, he determined to return at once to England; and, therefore, passing through Florence and Lucca, he crossed the Apeninnes, hastily visited Bologna, Ferrara, Venice, Verona and Milan, and thence he passed over Lake Leman to Geneva, in Switzerland, whence, through France, he eventually reached England, after an absence of fifteen months.

When Milton arrived in England, he found his father had left his residence at Horton, and had gone to reside with a younger brother; and as his sense of propriety and duty would no longer permit him to depend upon his father's bounty and kindness, he resolved to adopt such means for his future subsistence as might most readily offer. He, therefore, took, at the solicitation of his sister, Mrs. Phillips, a small house in London, for the purpose of conducting the education of her two sons, Edward and John. The success which attended the instruction of these two lads soon attracted the attention of other friends, and he was, therefore, induced, at their solicitation, to take a larger house, and open a regular academy. In this arduous, but delightful profession, Milton passed nearly eight years of his life. Meanwhile, however, he was very actively engaged in defending the principles of liberty, for which the Parliamentary party to which he had now attached himself, was then contending.

In 1641, he published his minor poems, which at once contributed to place him in the first rank of English poets; and from that period till he wrote *Paradise Lost*, his mind was constantly brooding over the production of some great work, which according to his own remark, 'his countrymen would not willingly let die.'

In 1643, Milton married the daughter of Richard Powell, a gentleman of Oxford. This union, however, was the source of great vexation and disquiet to him; for Mr. Powell, being a devoted royalist, his daughter, perhaps through her father's influence, left Milton's house in less than a month after her marriage; and though he frequently solicited her to return, yet she positively resisted all his endeavors to induce her to do so. Both irritated and mortified at the conduct of his wife, he immediately turned his attention toward the divine institution of marriage, and the law of divorce; and so fully did he become convinced that divorce was not only lawful, but even advisable, when, between the married parties there existed an incongruity of constitutional habit and temperament, which would forever mar their happiness, especially if there were no children to bind the parties together, that to prove his sincerity in the opinions he now advanced, he at once commenced paying his addresses to another young lady, of great wit and beauty, with the apparent prospect of a speedy union. His friends now interposed their offices of reconciliation, and his wife having meantime relented, they succeeded in introducing her into the house of a mutual acquaintance, where he was expected soon to arrive; and on his entrance she prostrated herself at his feet with such submission, and such apparent contrition, that he at once raised her to his arms, and a permanent reconciliation immediately followed. This incident is supposed to have suggested that exquisite scene in Paradise Lost, of the reconciliation of Adam and Eve after her transgression—

——— Soon his heart relented
Towards her—his life so late, and sole delight
Now at his feet, submissive in distress.

In 1643, Milton commenced a history of England, the principal design of which was, or seems to have been, to exhibit the principles of Ancient British freedom, and to warn the nation against the arbitrary oppressions of royalty. This important work, however, he never completed. In Kennett's *History of England* are to be found the first six books, and such other parts as he finished.

On the death of Charles the First, Milton was made Latin Secretary to the council of State, and the next ten years of his life were devoted to state affairs, and to the writing of his political works. In 1652, while engaged in the composition of one of these works, *Pro populo Anglicano defensio, contra Claudie Salmasii defensionem regiam*, he lost his sight, which had, indeed, been, for many years previous, exceedingly weak.

On the elevation of Charles the Second to the crown, Milton, though one of the most strenuous, and perhaps most effective opponents of royalty in England, was, through his great eminence, solicited by that monarch to retain the office of Latin Secretary—an office which he had so eminently honored for so many years. He chose, however, to relinquish the honors of court, and to retire into private life; for he now felt, more powerfully than ever, the influence of that impulse, which had, for many years, indicated his power to produce some work of immortality. Accordingly, after having repeatedly removed from place to place, he finally settled in a house in Artillery-walk, leading to Burnhill fields, where he passed the remainder of his eventful life.

In 1665, Milton finished *Paradise Lost*, and having placed it into the hands of Mr. Ellwood, a quaker gentleman, who was in the habit of visiting him, in order to obtain his opinion of the work, the latter, when he returned it, kindly said, 'Thou hast said much of 'Paradise Lost,' what hast thou to say of 'Paradise Found?'' This hint led to the composition of *Paradise Regained*, which was soon after followed by *Sampson Agonistes*, the last of his poetic performances.

Milton died in the month of November, 1674, in the sixty-sixth year of his age, and was buried, at his own request, by the side of his father. A monument was afterward erected for him in Westminster Abbey.

Milton is represented to have been symmetrically beautiful, so that while at the university, he was called 'the lady of Cambridge.' His picture of Adam, some have therefore supposed, was drawn from himself.

In contemplating the genius of Milton, one of the first thoughts that occurs to the mind, is the remarkable circumstances under which it was matured. The stormy and turbulent times in which he lived, while they would have oppressed ordinary powers, were such as only contributed to give additional energy to an order of mind like his own. Indeed it is evident that such times are more favorable to poetry, than those which are more quiet and peaceful. The muse catches fire and inspiration from the storm, and genius rides upon the whirlwind, while, perhaps, it would only slumber during the calm. Chaucer wrote amid the irritation and fury excited by the progress of the Reformation—Spenser and Shakspeare, while the nation was contending for its very existence against the power of Spain; and it was during the political and religious frenzy of the 'Revolution,' that Milton stored his mind with those sublime imaginings which afterwards expanded into that vast masterpiece of human genius—'Paradise Lost.'

There can, indeed, be but little doubt, that when this illustrious poet, a man so accomplished both in mind and manners, joined the Parliamentary party, he made many sacrifices of both taste and feeling, for what he considered the cause of civil and religious liberty.

We have already noticed the circumstances under which 'L'Allegro,' 'Il Penseroso,' 'Comus,' and 'Lycidas' were written, and have also mentioned their peculiar character, and the height to which they would have raised the poet's celebrity, had he written nothing else. We have also alluded to the manner in which his mind was occupied during the time he served as Latin Secretary to the council of state; and perhaps the very intensity with which his mind dwelt upon the one great object that he was then contemplating, may account for that apparent want of variety and versatility with which some critics have been inclined to charge him; but while in these particulars, some other poets may have surpassed him, in intensity of style and thought, in unity of purpose, and in the power and grandeur with which he piles up the single monument of genius, to which his mind is, for the time, devoted, he has been by no other poet, even approached. His harp may, indeed, have but one string, but that is such an one as none but his own fingers know how to touch.

'Paradise Lost' has few inequalities, and fewer blemishes—it seems like a work not taken up and continued at intervals, but one continuous effort, lasting perhaps for years, but never remitted, elaborated with the highest degree of polish, yet with all the marks of ease and simplicity in its composition, conceivable.

To begin with the least of Milton's merits—what author ever knew how to

> Untwist all the links that tie
> The hidden soul of harmony,

as he did? Whence came this knowledge? Upon what rules or system did he proceed in building up his magnificent stanza?—and what has become of the discovery which he made?—for it has evidently not been preserved by any of his successors.

There is comparatively no blank verse in the language worthy of the name—real verse, not measured prose, but the legitimate medium for the expression of the thoughts and feelings of poetry, beyond the volumes of Milton.

With all his varied excellencies, however, the peculiar and distinguishing feature of his poetry, is its sublimity. The sublime is reached by other poets, when they excel themselves, and hover amid unusual brightness, but it is Milton's native reign:—when he descends, he descends to meet the greatness of others; when he soars, it is to reach heights unattainable by any but himself. The first two books of Paradise Lost, are one continuous effort of unmitigated sublimity—no spot—no blemish—no inequality—no falling off from beginning to end; and then how wonderfully fine is the contrast when the third book opens with that inimitable pathetic address to Light, in which the poet alludes, with a pardonable egotism to the calamity, under which he himself is suffering—

> Hail, holy light! offspring of Heaven first-born,
> Or of the Eternal, co-eternal beam,
> May I express thee unblamed! since God is light,
> And never but in unapproached light
> Dwelt from Eternity, dwelt then in thee,
> Bright effluence of bright essence increate.

But because Milton is universally admitted to excel in sublimity, therefore some critics have chosen to deny him pathos. This, however, we feel bound to regard as that cant of criticism which will insist that the faults of every writer must balance his excellencies, and which delights in nothing but antithesis. Thus Shakspeare, we are gravely told, is a great but an irregular genius, Jonson is a powerful but rough and coarse writer—and Milton is a sublime, but not a pathetic poet; whereas the plain truth, obvious to all who take the time to examine, is, that Shakspeare is *not* an irregular genius, that Jonson is not a rough or coarse writer, that Milton is a pathetic poet, and a writer of powerful, and even tremendous pathos.

To sustain this last assertion, we need only direct our attention to Adam's lament after the fall—to Eve's farewell to Paradise, or to Satan, when about to address his adherents, and endeavoring to assume the tone and aspect of a God, bursting involuntarily into tears—

'Tears such as angels weep,'

as the remembrance of the height from which he has fallen, forces itself upon his memory, and compels this evidence of his weakness.

Milton's descriptive powers, also, are of the highest order. Whether he paints landscape or history, the pencil of a master is equally exhibited. The burning lake—the bowers of Paradise—angels and demons—humanity and Deity, are portrayed with unerring fidelity and truth. We need but to instance his description of Death, to justify this remark.

——— The other shape
If shape it might be called, that shape had none,
Distinguishable in member, joint, or limb;
Or substance might be called, that shadow seemed,
For each seemed either; black it stood as night,
Fierce as ten furies, terrible as Hell;
And shook a deadly dart. What seemed his head
The likeness of a kingly crown had on.

Indeed such is the genius of Milton, that we can scarcely find a fitting comparison for it. When he sets the Deity in arms, when he marshals myriads of indignant spirits in battle array against Omnipotence; when he paints the bliss of Heaven, and the horrors of Hell, he reminds us of the power and sublimity of Michael Angelo. When he shows us our first parents, sinless, artless, and endowed with God-like beauty—

Adam the goodliest man of men since born,
His sons; the fairest of her daughters, Eve,

he exhibits all the grace and beauty of Raphael. When he paints the happy fields of Paradise, where nature played at will, her virgin fancies, he seems to have caught the pencil of Claude Lorraine; and when we listen to the solemn and majestic flow of his verse, and the ear dwells upon the rich harmony of his periods, we are reminded of another art, and feel that neither Mozart nor Handel could produce music so soul-stirring as that of Milton. But we must here forbear; for this wondrous genius is like Niagara's mighty cataract—the more we contemplate it, the more overwhelming the contemplation becomes.

To select suitable illustrations, therefore, from the writings of such a poet, is an exceedingly difficult task; for where every thing is of the first order of excellence, it is almost impossible to say which shall be preferred. We would for this reason recommend to all who may hear or read these remarks, not to rest satisfied with the scanty specimens which our limited space will here allow us to introduce, but for their own satisfaction and instruction, to have immediate recourse to the entire poems themselves.

The following beautiful extract is from the *Hymn on the Nativity*—a poem which we have not hitherto noticed:—

HYMN ON THE NATIVITY.

It was the winter wild,
While the heaven-born child
  All meanly wrapt in the rude manger lies;
Nature, in awe to him,
Had doff'd her gaudy trim,
  With her great Master so to sympathize:
It was no season then for her
To wanton with the sun, her lusty paramour.

Only with speeches fair
She woos the gentle air,
  To hide her guilty front with innocent snow;
And on her naked shame,
Pollute with sinful blame,
  The saintly vail of maiden white to throw;
Confounded, that her Maker's eyes
Should look so near upon her foul deformities.

But he, her fears to cease,
Sent down the meek-ey'd Peace;
  She, crown'd with olive green, came softly sliding
Down through the turning sphere,
His ready harbinger,
  With turtle wing the amorous clouds dividing;
And, waving wide her myrtle wand,
She strikes a universal peace through sea and land.

No war or battle sound,
Was heard the world around:
  The idle spear and shield were high up hung;
The hooked chariot stood
Unstain'd with hostile blood;
  The trumpet spake not to the armed throng;
And kings sat still with awful eye,
As if they surely knew their sov'reign lord was by.

But peaceful was the night,
Wherein the Prince of Light
  His reign of peace on earth began:
The winds, with wonder whist,
Smoothly the waters kiss'd,
  Whispering new joys to the mild Ocean,
Who now hath quite forgot to rave,
While birds of calm sit brooding on the charmed wave.

The stars, with deep amaze,
Stand fix'd in steadfast gaze,
  Bending one way their precious influence;
And will not take their flight,
For all the morning light,
  Or Lucifer that often warn'd them thence;
But in their glimmering orbs did glow,
Until their Lord himself bespake, and bid them go.

And the shady gloom
Had given day her room,
  The sun himself withheld his wonted speed,
And hid his head for shame.
As his inferior flame
  The new-enlightened world no more should need;
He saw a greater sun appear
Than his bright throne, or burning axletree could bear.

The shepherds on the lawn
Or ere the point of dawn,
  Sat simply chatting in a rustic row;
Full little thought they then
That the mighty Pan
  Was kindly come to live with them below;
Perhaps their loves, or else their sheep,
Was all that did their silly thoughts so busy keep.

When such music sweet
Their hearts and ears did greet,
  As never was by mortal finger strook,
Divinely-warbled voice
Answering the stringed noise,
  As all their souls in blissful rapture took:
The air, such pleasure loath to lose,
With thousand echoes still prolongs each heavenly close.

Nature that heard such sound,
Beneath the hollow round
  Of Cynthia's seat, the airy region thrilling,
Now was almost won,
To think her part was done,
  And that her reign had here its last fulfilling;
She knew such harmony alone
Could hold all Heaven and Earth in happier union.

At last surrounds their sight
A globe of circular light,
  That with long beams the shamefac'd night array'd;
The helm'd cherubim
And sworded seraphim,
  Are seen in glittering ranks with wings display'd,
Harping in loud and solemn choir,
With unexpressive notes, to Heaven's new-born heir.

Such music, as 'tis said,
Before was never made,
  But when of old the sons of morning sung,

While the Creator great
His constellations set,
  And the well-balanced world on hinges hung,
And cast the dark foundations deep,
And bid the weltering waves their oozy channel keep.

Ring out, ye crystal spheres,
Once bless our human ears,
  If ye have power to touch our senses so;
And let your silver chime
Move in melodious time;
  And let the base of Heaven's deep organ blow;
And with your ninefold harmony,
Make up full concert to the angelic symphony.

For, if such holy song
Enwrap our fancy long,
  Time will run back, and fetch the age of gold;
And speckled Vanity
Will sicken soon and die,
  And leprous Sin will melt from earthly mould;
And Hell itself will pass away,
And leave her dolorous mansions to the peering day.

Yea, Truth and Justice then
Will down return to men,
  Orb'd in a rainbow; and, like glories wearing,
Mercy will sit between,
Thron'd in celestial sheen,
  With radiant feet the tissued clouds down steering;
And Heaven, as at some festival,
Will open wide the gates of her high palace hall.

Perhaps no poems in the English language contain more perfect specimens of versification, or surpass, in descriptive ease and elegance, 'L'Allegro' and 'Il Penseroso.' From these beautiful poems, however, we can offer only the following brief extracts:—

FROM 'L'ALLEGRO.'

  Haste thee, nymph, and bring with thee
Jest, and youthful Jollity,
Quips, and cranks, and wanton wiles,
Nods, and becks, and wreathed smiles,
Such as hang on Hebe's cheek,
And love to live in dimple sleek;
Sport that wrinkled Care derides,
And Laughter holding both his sides.
Come and trip it as you go
On the light fantastic toe;
And in thy right-hand lead with thee
The mountain-nymph, sweet Liberty:
And, if I give the honour due,
Mirth, admit me of thy crew,

To live with her, and live with thee,
In unreproved pleasures free:
To hear the lark begin his flight,
And singing startle the dull night,
From his watch-tower in the skies,
Till the dappled dawn doth rise;
Then to come, in spite of sorrow
And at my window bid good-morrow,
Through the sweet-brier, or the vine,
Or the twisted eglantine;
While the cock with lively din,
Scatters the rear of darkness thin,
And to the stack, or the barn door,
Stoutly struts his dames before:
Oft list'ning how the hounds and horn
Cheerly rouse the slumbering morn,
From the side of some hoar hill,
Through the high wood echoing shrill:
Sometimes walking not unseen
By hedge-row elms, on hillocks green,
Right against the eastern gate,
Where the great sun begins his state,
Robed in flames, and amber light,
The clouds in thousand liveries dight,
While the ploughman near at hand
Whistles o'er the furrow'd land,
And the milk-maid singeth blithe,
And the mower whets his scythe,
And every shepherd tells his tale,
Under the hawthorn in the dale.

* * * * *

And ever against eating cares,
Lap me in soft Lydian airs,
Married to immortal verse,
Such as the meeting soul may pierce,
In notes, with many a winding bout
Of linked sweetness long drawn out,
With wanton heed, and giddy cunning,
The melting voice through mazes running;
Untwisting all the chains that tie
The hidden soul of harmony;
That Orpheus' self may heave his head
From golden slumbers on a bed
Of heap'd Elysian flowers, and hear
Such strains as would have rung the ear
Of Pluto, to have quite set free
His half-regain'd Eurydice.
These delights, if thou canst give,
Mirth, with thee I mean to live.

FROM 'IL PENSEROSO.'

Sweet bird, that shunn'st the noise of folly,
Most musical, most melancholy!

Thee, chantress, oft the woods among
I woo, to hear thy evening song;
And missing thee, I walk unseen
On the dry smooth-shaven green,
To behold the wand'ring moon,
Riding near her highest noon,
Like one that had been led astray
Through the heavens' wide pathless way;
And oft, as if her head she bowed,
Stooping through a fleecy cloud.
Oft on a plat of rising ground,
I hear the far-off curfew sound,
Over some wide water'd shore
Singing slow with sullen roar.
Or if the air will not permit,
Some still removed place will fit,
Where glowing embers through the room
Teach light to counterfeit a gloom;
Far from all resort of mirth,
Save the cricket on the hearth,
Or the bellman's drowsy charm,
To bless the doors from nightly harm.
Or let my lamp, at midnight hour,
Be seen in some high lonely tow'r,
Where I may oft out-watch the Bear,
With thrice-great Hermes; or unsphere
The spirit of Plato, to unfold
What worlds, or what vast regions, hold
The immortal mind that hath forsook
Her mansion in this fleshly nook:
And of those demons that are found
In fire, air, flood, or under ground,
Whose power hath a true consent
With planet, or with element.

* * * * * *

And let my due feet never fail
To walk the studious cloisters pale,
And love the high embowed roof,
With antic pillars massy proof,
And storied windows richly dight,
Casting a dim religious light.
There let the pealing organ blow
To the full-voic'd quire below,
In service high, and anthems clear,
As may with sweetness, through mine ear,
Dissolve me into ecstacies,
And bring all heav'n before mine eyes.
And may at last my weary age
Find out the peaceful hermitage,
The hairy gown and mossy cell,
Where I may sit and rightly spell
Of ev'ry star that heav'n doth shew,
And ev'ry herb that sips the dew:

Till old experience do attain
To something like prophetic strain.
  These pleasures, Melancholy give,
And I with thee will choose to live.

From *Comus*, we have selected the 'Praise of Chastity,' and 'The Spirit's Epilogue;' not that we consider these passages superior to the rest of the drama, but because they are best suited to our purpose.

PRAISE OF CHASTITY.

'Tis Chastity, my brother, Chastity;
She that has that is clad in complete steel,
And like a quiver'd nymph with arrows keen,
May trace huge forests, and unharbour'd heaths,
Infamous hills, and sandy perilous wilds,
Where, through the sacred rays of Chastity,
No savage fierce, bandit, or mountaineer,
Will dare to soil her virgin purity:
Yea, there, where very desolation dwells,
By grots and caverns shagg'd with horrid shades,
She may pass on with unblench'd majesty,
Be it not done in pride, or in presumption.
Some say no evil thing that walks by night
In fog or fire, by lake or moorish fen,
Blue meagre hag, or stubborn unlaid ghost,
That breaks his magic chains at curfew time,
No goblin or swart fairy of the mine,
Hath hurtful power o'er true virginity.
Do ye believe me yet, or shall I call
Antiquity from the old schools of Greece
To testify the arms of Chastity?
Hence had the huntress Dian her dread bow,
Fair silver-shafted queen, forever chaste,
Wherewith she tamed the brinded lioness
And spotted mountain-pard, but set at nought
The frivolous bolt of Cupid; gods and men
Fear'd her stern frown, and she was queen o' th' woods.
What was that snaky-headed Gorgon shield
That wise Minerva wore, unconquered virgin,
Wherewith she freez'd her foes to congeal'd stone,
But rigid looks of chaste austerity,
And noble grace that dash'd brute violence
With sudden adoration and blank awe?
So dear to heav'n is saintly Chastity,
That when a soul is found sincerely so,
A thousand liveried angels lacquey her,
Driving far off each thing of sin and guilt,
And in clear dream and solemn vision
Tell her of things that no gross ear can hear,
Till oft converse with heavenly habitants
Begin to cast a beam on th' outward shape,
The unpolluted temple of the mind,
And turns it by degrees to the soul's essence,
Till all be made immortal.

THE SPIRIT'S EPILOGUE.

To the ocean now I fly,
And those happy climes that lie
Where day never shuts his eye,
Up in the broad fields of the sky:
There I suck the liquid air
All amidst the gardens fair
Of Hesperus, and his daughters three
That sing about the golden tree:
Along the crisped shades and bowers
Revels the spruce and jocund spring;
The Graces, and the rosy-bosomed hours,
Thither all their bounties bring;
There eternal summer dwells,
And west-winds with musky wing,
About the cedar'n alleys fling
Nard and Cassia's balmy smells.
Iris there with humid bow
Waters the odorous banks, that blow
Flowers of more mingled hue
Than her purpled scarf can shew;
And drenches with Elysian dew
(List, mortals, if your ears be true)
Beds of hyacinth and roses,
Where young Adonis oft reposes,
Waxing well of his deep wound
In slumber soft, and on the ground
Sadly sits the Assyrian queen.
But far above in spangled sheen
Celestial Cupid, her fam'd son, advanc'd,
Holds his dear Psyche sweet entranced.
After her wandering labours long,
Till free consent the gods among
Make her his eternal bride,
And from her fair unspotted side
Two blissful twins are to be born,
Youth and Joy; so Jove hath sworn.
  But now my task is smoothly done,
I can fly, or I can run,
Quickly to the green earth's end,
Where the bow'd welkin slow doth bend;
And from thence can soar as soon
To the corners of the moon.
  Mortals, that would follow me,
Love Virtue; she alone is free:
She can teach thee how to climb
Higher than the sphery chime;
Or if Virtue feeble were,
Heaven itself would stoop to her.

From 'Paradise Lost,' perhaps the great masterpiece of human genius, we find more difficulty in making suitable selections than from any other poem with which we are familiar; for should we aim at the *sublime*, it prevails continuously throughout the whole of the first and second books; and the *beautiful* equally abounds in other parts of the poem. As, however, the necessity of making a choice is imposed upon us, we venture, though with much diffidence, to select the following passages:—

SATAN CAST FROM HEAVEN.

* * * * * * Him the Almighty Power
Hurl'd headlong flaming from th' ethereal sky,
With hideous ruin and combustion, down
To bottomless perdition; there to dwell
In adamantine chains and penal fire,
Who durst defy th' Omnipotent to arms.
Nine times the space that measures day and night
To mortal men, he with his horrid crew
Lay vanquished, rolling in the fiery gulf,
Confounded though immortal: But his doom
Reserv'd him to more wrath; for now the thought
Both of lost happiness and lasting pain
Torments him; round he throws his baleful eyes,
That witness'd huge affliction and dismay,
Mix'd with obdurate pride and steadfast hate:
At once, as far as angels' ken, he views
The dismal situation waste and wild:
A dungeon horrible on all sides round,
As one great furnace flam'd; yet from those flames
No light, but rather darkness visible
Serv'd only to discover sights of woe,
Regions of sorrow, doleful shades, where peace
And rest can never dwell: hope never comes
That comes to all: but torture without end
Still urges, and a fiery deluge, fed
With ever-burning sulphur unconsum'd:
Such place eternal justice had prepar'd
For those rebellious; here their pris'n ordain'd
In utter darkness, and their portion set
As far removed from God and light of heaven,
As from the centre thrice to th' utmost pole.
Oh how unlike the place from whence they fell!
There the companions of his fall, o'erwhelm'd
With floods and whirlwinds of tempestuous fire,
He soon discerns, and weltering by his side
One next himself in power, and next in crime,
Long after known in Palestine, and nam'd
Beelzebub.

THE ASSEMBLING OF THE FALLEN ANGELS.

All these and more came flocking; but with looks
Downcast and damp, yet such wherein appear'd
Obscure some glimpse of joy, t' have found their chief
Not in despair, t' have found themselves not lost
In loss itself; which on his countenance cast
Like doubtful hue: but he, his wonted pride

Soon recollecting, with high words that bore
Semblance of worth, not substance, gently raised
Their fainting courage, and dispell'd their fears.
Then straight commands that, at the warlike sound
Of trumpets loud and clarions, be uprear'd
His mighty standard; that proud honour claim'd
Azazel at his right, a cherub tall;
Who forthwith from the glittering staff unfurl'd
Th' imperial ensign, which full high advanc'd,
Shone like a meteor streaming to the wind,
With gems and golden lustre rich emblaz'd
Seraphic arms and trophies, all the while
Sonorous metal blowing martial sounds:
At which the universal host upsent
A shout, that tore Hell's concave, and beyond
Frighted the reign of Chaos and old Night.
All in a moment through the gloom were seen
Ten thousand banners rise into the air
With orient colours waving: with them rose
A forest huge of spears; and thronging helms
Appear'd, and serried shields in thick array,
Of depth unmeasurable: anon they move
In perfect phalanx to the Dorian mood
Or flutes and soft recorders; such as rais'd
To height of noblest temper heroes old
Arming to battle; and, instead of rage,
Deliberate valour breathed, firm and unmov'd,
With dread of death, to flight or foul retreat;
Nor wanting power to mitigate and 'suage,
With solemn touches, troubled thoughts, and chase
Anguish, and doubt, and fear, and sorrow, and pain,
From mortal or immortal minds. Thus they
Breathing united force, with fixed thought
Mov'd on in silence to soft pipes, that charm'd
Their painful steps o'er the burnt soil; and now
Advanc'd in view, they stand, a horrid front
Of dreadful length, and dazzling arms, in guise
Of warriors old with order'd spear, and shield
Awaiting what command their mighty chief
Had to impose: he through the armed files
Darts his experienc'd eye, and soon traverse
The whole battalion, views their order due,
Their visages and statures as of Gods;
Their number last he sums. And now his heart
Distends with pride, and hard'ning in his strength
Glories; for never since created man
Met such embodied force as, nam'd with these,
Could merit more than that small infantry
Warr'd on by cranes, through all the giant brood
Of Phlegra with th' heroic race were join'd,
That fought at Thebes, and Ilium on each side
Mix'd with auxiliar gods; and what resounds
In fable or romance of Uther's son,
Begirt with British and Armoric knights;

And all who since, baptiz'd or infidel,
Jousted in Aspramont or Montalban,
Damasco or Morocco, or Trebisond;
Or whom Biserta sent from Afric shore,
When Charlemain with all his peerage fell
By Fontarabia. Thus far these beyond
Compare of mortal prowess, yet observed
Their dread commander; he above the rest
In shape and gesture proudly eminent,
Stood like a tower; his form had not yet lost
All her original brightness, nor appear'd
Less than Archangel ruin'd, and th' excess
Of glory obscur'd: as when the sun new risen
Looks through the horizontal misty air,
Shorn of his beams; or from behind the moon
In dim eclipse, disastrous twilight sheds
On half the nations, and with fear of change
Perplexes monarchs. Darken'd so, yet shone
Above them all th' Archangel: but his face
Deep scars of thunder had intrench'd, and care
Sat on his faded cheek, but under brows
Of dauntless courage and considerate pride,
Waiting revenge: cruel his eye, but cast
Signs of remorse and passion to behold
The fellows of his crime, the followers rather,
(Far other once beheld in bliss) condemn'd
Forever now to have their lot in pain;
Millions of spirits for his fault amerc'd
Of Heav'n, and from eternal splendours flung
For his revolt, yet faithful how they stood,
Their glory wither'd: as when Heav'ns fire
Hath scath'd the forest oaks, or mountain pines,
With singed top their stately growth, though bare,
Stands on the blasted heath. He now prepar'd
To speak: whereat their doubled ranks they bend
From wing to wing, and half inclose him round
With all his peers: attention held them mute.
Thrice he essay'd; and thrice, in spite of scorn,
Tears such as angels weep, burst forth; at last
Words interwove with sighs, found out their w

THE GARDEN OF EDEN.

So on he fares, and to the border comes
Of Eden, where delicious Paradise.
Now nearer, crowns with her inclosure green,
As with a rural mound, the champaign head
Of a steep wilderness, whose hairy sides
With thicket overgrown, grotesque and wild,
Access denied, and overhead upgrew
Insuperable height of loftiest shade,
Cedar and pine, and fir and branching palm,
A sylvan scene, and as the ranks ascend,
Shade above shade, a woody theatre
Of stateliest view. Yet higher than their tops

The verd'rous wall of Paradise up-sprung:
Which to our general sire gave prospect large
Into his nether empire neighb'ring round.
And higher than that wall a circling row
Of goodliest trees, loaden with fairest fruit,
Blossoms and fruits at once of golden hue,
Appear'd, with gay enamell'd colours mix'd;
Of which the sun more glad impress'd his beams
Than in fair evening cloud, or humid bow,
When God hath shower'd the earth; so lovely seem'd
That landscape; and of pure, now purer air
Meets his approach, and to the heart inspires
Vernal delight and joy, able to drive
All sadness but despair; now gentle gales
Fanning their odoriferous wings, dispense
Native perfumes, and whisper whence they stole
Those balmy spoils: as when to them who sail
Beyond the Cape of Hope, and now are past
Mozambic, off at sea north-west winds blow
Sabean odours from the spicy shore
Of Araby the blest; with such delay
Well pleas'd they slack their course, and many a league,
Cheer'd with the grateful smell, old Ocean smiles.

EVE'S ACCOUNT OF HER CREATION.

I first awak'd, and found myself repos'd
Under a shade of flow'rs, much wond'ring where
And what I was, whence thither brought, and how.
Not distant far from thence a murmur'ing sound
Of waters issued from a cave, and spread
Into a liquid plain, then stood unmov'd,
Pure as the expanse of Heaven; I thither went
With inexperienced thought, and laid me down
On the green bank, to look into the clear
Smooth lake, that to me seem'd another sky.
As I bent down to look, just opposite,
A shape within the watery gleam appear'd,
Bending to look on me; I started back,
It started back: but pleas'd I soon return'd,
Pleas'd it return'd as soon with answ'ring looks
Of sympathy and love: there I had fix'd
Mine eyes till now, and pin'd with vain desire,
Had not a voice thus warn'd me: 'What thou seest,
What there thou seest, fair creature, is thyself:
With thee it came and goes; but follow me,
And I will bring thee where no shadow stays
Thy coming and thy soft embraces; he
Whose image thou art; him thou shalt enjoy,
Inseparably thine; to him shalt bear
Multitudes like thyself, and thence be call'd
Mother of human race.' What could I do,
But follow straight, invisibly thus led?
Till I espied thee, fair indeed and tall,

Under a plantain; yet methought less fair,
Less winning soft, less amiably mild,
Than that smooth watery image: back I turn'd;
Thou following cry'st aloud, 'Return, fair Eve,
Whom fly'st thou? whom thou fly'st of him thou art,
His flesh, his bone: to give thee being I lent,
Out of my side to thee, nearest my heart,
Substantial life to have thee by my side
Henceforth an individual solace dear;
Part of my soul I seek thee, and thee claim
My other half.' With that thy gentle hand
Seiz'd mine; I yielded, and from that time see
How beauty is excell'd by manly grace
And wisdom, which alone is truly fair.
So spake our general mother, and with eyes
Of conjugal attraction, unreprov'd,
And meek surrender, half embracing lean'd
On our first father; half her swelling breast
Naked met his under the flowing gold
Of her loose tresses hid; he in delight
Both of her beauty and submissive charms,
Smil'd with superior love, as Jupiter
On Juno smiles; when he impregns the clouds
That shed May flowers, and press'd her matron lip
With kisses pure.

ADAM'S MORNING PRAYER.

These are thy glorious works, Parent of good,
Almighty, thine this universal frame,
Thus wondrous fair; thyself how wondrous then!
Unspeakable, who sitt'st above the heav'ns
To us invisible, or dimly seen
In these thy lowest works; yet these declare
Thy goodness beyond thought, and power divine.
Speak ye who best can tell, ye sons of light,
Angels! for ye behold Him, and with songs,
And choral symphonies, day without night,
Circle His throne rejoicing; ye in heav'n:
On earth join all ye creatures, to extol
Him first, Him last, Him midst, and without end!
Fairest of stars, last in the train of night,
If better thou belong not to the dawn,
Sure pledge of day; that crown'st the smiling morn,
With thy bright circlet, praise Him in thy sphere
While day arises, that sweet hour of prime.
Thou sun! of this world both eye and soul,
Acknowledge Him thy greater; sound His praise
In thy eternal course, both when thou climb'st,
And when high noon has gain'd, and when thou fall'st.
Moon! that now meet'st the orient sun, now fly'st
With the fix'd stars, fix'd in their orb that flies;
And ye five other wand'ring fires! that move
In mystic dance not without song, resound

His praise, who out of darkness call'd up light.
Air, and ye elements! the eldest birth
Of nature's womb, that in quaternian run
Perpetual circle, multiform, and mix,
And nourish all things; let your ceaseless change
Vary to our great Maker still new praise.
Ye mists, and exhalations! that now rise
From hill, or streaming lake, dusky or gray,
Till the sun paint your fleecy skirts with gold,
In honour to the world's great Author rise:
Whether to deck with clouds the uncolour'd sky,
Or wet the thirsty earth with falling showers,
Raising or falling, still advance his praise.
His praise, ye winds! that from four quarters blow,
Breathe soft or loud; and wave your tops, ye pines!
With every plant, in sign of worship wave.
Fountains, and ye that warble as ye flow,
Melodious murmurs, warbling tune his praise.
Join voices all, ye living souls: ye birds
That singing up to Heaven gate ascend,
Bear on your wings and in your notes His praise.
Ye that in waters glide, and ye that walk
The earth, and stately tread, or lowly creep,
Witness if I be silent morn or even,
To hill, or valley, fountain or fresh shade,
Made vocal by my song, and taught his praise.
Hail, universal Lord! be bounteous still
To give us only good; and, if the night
Have gather'd aught of evil or conceal'd,
Disperse it, as now light dispels the dark.

THE EXPULSION FROM PARADISE.

He ended; and the Archangel soon drew nigh,
Not in his shape celestial, but as man
Clad to meet man. * *
* * * * * *
Adam bow'd low; he kingly, from his state
Inclined not, but his coming thus declared:—
'Adam, Heaven's high behest no preface needs:
Sufficient that thy pray'rs are heard, and death
Then due by sentence when thou didst transgress,
Defeated of his seizure many days,
Giv'n thee of grace, wherein thou may'st repent,
And one bad act with many deeds well done
May'st cover: well may then thy Lord appeas'd
Redeem thee quite from Death's rapacious claim:
But longer in this Paradise to dwell
Permits not; to remove thee I am come,
And send thee from the garden forth to till
The ground whence thou wast taken, fitter soil.'
He added not, for Adam at the news
Heart-struck with chilling gripe of sorrow stood,
That all his senses bound; Eve, who unseen,

Yet all had heard, with audible lament
Discover'd soon the place of her retire.
'O unexpected stroke; worse than of death!
Must I thus leave thee, Paradise? thus leave
Thee, native soil, these happy walks and shades,
Fit haunt of gods? where I had hoped to spend,
Quiet, though sad, the respite of that day
That must be mortal to us both. O flowers!
That never will in other climate grow,
My early visitation, and my last
At even, which I bred up with tender hand
From the first opening bud, and gave ye names!
Who now shall rear ye to the sun, or rank
Your tribes, and water from the ambrosial fount?
Thee lastly, nuptial bower, by me adorn'd
With what to sight or smell was sweet, from thee
How shall I part, and whither wander down
Into a lower world, to this obscure
And wild? how shall we breathe in other air
Less pure, accustom'd to immortal fruits?'
Whom thus the Angel interrupted mild:—
'Lament not, Eve, but patiently resign
What justly thou hast lost; nor set thy heart,
Thus over-fond, on that which is not thine:
Thy going is not lonely; with thee goes
Thy husband; him to follow thou art bound;
Where he abides, think there thy native soil.'
Adam by this from the cold sudden damp
Recovering, and his scatter'd spirits return'd,
To Michael thus his humble words address'd:—
'Celestial, whether among the thrones, or nam'd
Of them the highest, for such of shape may seem
Prince above princes, gently hast thou told
Thy message, which might else in telling wound
And in performing end us; what besides
Of sorrow, and dejection, and despair
Our frailty can sustain, thy tidings bring;
Departure from that happy place, our sweet
Recess, and only consolation left
Familiar, to our eyes, all places else
Inhospitable appear and desolate,
Nor knowing us, nor known: and if by prayer
Incessant, I could hope to change the will
Of him who all things can, I would not cease
To weary him with my assiduous cries:
But prayer against his absolute decree
No more avails than breath against the wind,
Blown stifling back on him that breathes it forth:
Therefore to his great bidding I submit
* * * * * * * *
* * * * Now too nigh
Th' Archangel stood, and from the other hill
To their fixed station, all in bright array,
The cherubim descended; on the ground

Gliding meteorous, as evening mist
Ris'n from a river o'er the marish glides,
And gathers ground fast at the lab'rer's heel
Homeward returning. High in front advanc'd,
The brandish'd sword of God before them blaz'd,
Fierce as a comet; which with torrid heat,
And vapours as the Libyan air adust,
Began to parch that temp'rate clime: whereat
In either hand the hast'ning angel caught
Our ling'ring parents, and to the eastern gate
Led them direct, and down the cliff as fast
To the subjected plain; then disappear'd.
They, looking back, all the eastern side beheld
Of Paradise, so late their happy seat,
Wav'd over by the flaming brand, the gate
With dreadful faces throng'd and fiery arms:
Some natural tears they dropt, but wip'd them soon
The world was all before them, where to choose
Their place of rest, and Providence their guide.
They hand in hand, with wand'ring steps and slow,
Through Eden took their solitary way.

We forbear to prolong these extracts by the introduction of any passages from Milton's *Sonnets*, *Lycidas*, *Paradise Regained*, or *Sampson Agonistes:* not that suitable ones might not from these poems with great felicity be drawn, but because we feel confident that our estimation, exalted as it is, of his genius, is abundantly sustained by the passages already introduced from his other works. We shall, therefore, close this extended, though we hope, not tedious lecture, by a very brief notice of him as a writer in prose.

Though, as an author, Milton's celebrity rests mainly upon his poetry, yet in prose his style is lofty, clear, vigorous, expressive, and frequently adorned with profuse and glowing imagery. Like that of many other productions of the age, it is, however, deficient in simplicity and smoothness; which is doubtless attributable to his fondness for the Latin idiom in the construction of his sentences. Yet a recent critic in the Edinburgh Review remarks, that 'it is to be regretted that the prose writings of Milton should, in our time, be so little read. As compositions, they deserve the attention of every man who wishes to become acquainted with the full power of the English language. They abound with passages, compared with which the finest declamations of Burke sink into insignificance. They are a perfect field of cloth of gold. The style is stiff with gorgeous embroidery. Not even in the earlier books of Paradise Lost has he ever risen higher, than in those parts of his controversial works in which his feelings, excited by conflict, find a vent in bursts of devotional and lyric rapture. It is, to borrow his own majestic language, 'a sevenfold chorus of hallelujahs and harping symphonies.'

Milton's principal works in prose are the *History of England*, already alluded to, *A Speech for the Liberty of Unlicensed Printing*, *A Tractate of Education*, *A Treatise on Christian Doctrine*, *Three Tracts on Divorce*, and the *Areopagitica*. Our time will not, however, permit us longer to linger with this interesting author: we shall therefore close our present remarks with the following extract, entitled his *Literary Musings*, as it shadows forth his Divine Poem, 'Paradise Lost.'

LITERARY MUSINGS.

After I had, from my first years, by the ceaseless diligence and care of my father, whom God recompense, been exercised to the tongues, and some sciences, as my age would suffer, by sundry masters and teachers, both at home and at the schools, it was found that whether aught was imposed me by them that had the overlooking, or betaken to of my own choice in English, or other tongue, prosing or versing, but chiefly the latter, the style, by certain vital signs it had, was likely to live. But much latelier, in the private academies of Italy, whither I was favoured to resort, perceiving that some trifles which I had in memory, composed at under twenty or thereabout (for the manner is, that every one must give some proof of his wit and reading there), met with acceptance above what was looked for; and other things which I had shifted, in scarcity of books and conveniences, to patch up among them, were received with written encomiums, which the Italian is not forward to bestow on men of this side the Alps, I began thus far to assent both to them and divers of my friends here at home; and not less to an inward prompting, which now grew daily upon me, that by labour and intent study (which I take to be my portion in this life), joined to the strong propensity of nature, I might perhaps leave something so written, to after-times, as they should not willingly let it die. These thoughts at once possessed me, and these other, that if I were certain to write as men buy leases, for three lives and downward, there ought no regard be sooner had than to God's glory, by the honour and instruction of my country.

For which cause, and not only for that I knew it would be hard to arrive at the second rank among the Latins, I applied myself to that resolution which Ariosto followed against the persuasions of Bembo, to fix all the industry and art I could unite to the adorning of my native tongue; not to make verbal curiosities the end, that were a toilsome vanity; but to be an interpreter, and relater of the best and safest things among mine own citizens, throughout this island, in the mother dialect. That what the greatest and choicest wits of Athens, Rome, or modern Italy, and those Hebrews of old did for their country, I in my proportion, with this over and above, of being a Christian, might do for mine, not caring to be once named abroad, though perhaps I could attain to that, but content with these British islands as my world, whose fortune hath hitherto been, that if the Athenians, as some say, made their small deeds great and renowned by their eloquent writers, England hath had her noble achievements made small by the unskillful handling of monks and mechanics.

Time serves not now, and perhaps I might seem too profuse, to give any certain account of what the mind at home, in the spacious circuits of her musing, hath liberty to propose to herself, though of highest hope and hardest attempting. Whether that epic form, whereof the two poems of Homer, and those other two of Virgil and Tasso are a diffuse, and the book of Job a brief model; or whether the rules of Aristotle herein are strictly to be kept, or nature to be followed, which in them that know art and use judgment, is no transgression, but an enriching of art. And lastly, what king or knight before the conquest might be chosen, in whom to lay the pattern of a Christian hero. And as Tasso gave to a prince of Italy his choice, whether he would command him to write of Godfrey's expedition against the infidels, or Belisarius against the Goths, or Charlemagne against the Lombards, if to the instinct of nature and the emboldening of art aught may be trusted, and that there be nothing adverse in our climate, or the fate of this age, it haply would be no rashness, from an equal diligence and inclination, to present the like offer in our own ancient stories. Or whether those dramatic constitutions, wherein Sophocles and Euripides reign, shall be found more doctrinal and exemplary to a nation. The Scripture also affords us a fine pastoral drama in the Song of Solomon, consisting of two persons, and a double chorus, as Origen rightly judges, and the Apocalypse of St. John is the majestic image of a high and stately tragedy, shutting up and intermingling her solemn scenes and acts with a seven-fold chorus of hallelujahs and harping symphonies. And this my opinion, the grave authority of Pareus, commenting that book, is sufficient to confirm. Or if occasion shall lead, to imitate those magnific odes and hymns, wherein Pindarus and Callimachus are in most things worthy, some others in their frame judicious, in their matter most, and end faulty. But those frequent songs throughout the law and prophets, beyond all these, not in their divine argument alone, but in the very critical art of composition, may be easily made appear, over all the kinds of lyric poesy, to be incomparable. These abilities, wheresoever they be found, are the inspired gift of God, rarely bestowed, but yet to some (though most abuse) in every nation: and are of power, besides the office of a pulpit, to inbreed and cherish in a great people the seeds of virtue and public civility; to allay the perturbations of the mind, and set the affections in right tune; to celebrate in glorious and lofty hymns the throne and equipage of God's almightiness, and what he suffers to be wrought with high providence in his church; to sing victorious agonies of martyrs and saints, the deeds and triumphs of just and pious nations, doing valiantly through faith against the enemies of Christ; to deplore the general relapses of kingdoms and states from justice and God's true worship.

Lastly, whatsoever in religion is holy and sublime, in virtue amiable or grave, whatsoever hath passion or admiration in all the changes of that life which is called fortune from without, or the wily subtleties and refluxes of man's thoughts from within; all these things, with a solid and treatable smoothness, to paint out and describe. Teaching over the whole book of sanctity and virtue, through all the instances of example, with such delight to those, especially of soft and delicious temper, who will not so much as look upon truth herself, unless they see her elegantly dressed; that whereas the paths of honesty and good life appear now rugged and difficult indeed. And what a benefit would this be to our youth and gentry, may be soon guessed by what we know of the corruption and bane which they suck in daily from the writings and interludes of libidinous and ignorant poetasters, who, having scarce ever heard of that which is the main consistence of a true poem, the choice of such persons as they ought to introduce, and what is moral and decent to each one, do for the most part lay up vicious principles in sweet pills, to be swallowed down, and make the taste of virtuous documents harsh and sour. But because the spirit of man can not demean itself lively in this body without some repeating intermission of labour and serious things, it were happy for the commonwealth if our magistrates, as in those famous governments of old, would take into their care not only the deciding of our contentious law cases and brawls, but the managing of our public sports and festival pastimes, that they might be not such as were authorized awhile since, the provocations of drunkenness and lust, but such as may inure and harden our bodies, by martial exercises, to all warlike skill and performances; and may civilize, adorn, and make discreet our minds, by the learned and affable meeting of frequent academies, and the procurement of wise and artful recitations, sweetened with eloquent and graceful enticements to the love and practice of justice, temperance, and fortitude; instructing and bettering the nation at all opportunities, that the call of wisdom and virtue may be heard everywhere, as Solomon saith: 'She crieth without, she uttereth her voice in the streets, in the top of high places, in the chief concourse, and in the openings of the gates.' Whether this may be not only in pulpits, but after another persuasive method, at set and solemn paneguries, in theatres, porches, or what other place or way may win most upon the people, to receive at once both recreation and instruction, let them in authority consult. The thing which I had to say and those intentions which have lived within me ever since I could conceive myself any thing worth to my country, I return to crave excuse, that urgent reason hath plucked from me, by an abortive and foredated discovery. And the accomplishment of them lies not but in a power above man's to promise; but that none hath by more studious ways endeavoured, and with more unwearied spirit that none shall, that I dare almost aver of myself, as far as life and free leisure will extend; and that the land had once enfranchised herself from this impertinent yoke of prelacy, under whose inquisitorious and tyrannical duncery no free and splendid wit can flourish. Neither do I think it shame to covenant with any knowing reader, that for some years yet I may go on trust with him toward the payment of what I am now indebted, as being a work not to be raised from the heat of youth or the vapours of wine; like that which flows at waste from the pen of some vulgar amorist, or the trencher-fury of a rhyming parasite; nor to be obtained by the invocation of dame memory and her syren daughters; but by devout prayer to that eternal Spirit, who can enrich with all utterance and knowledge, and sends out his seraphim with the hallowed fire of his altar, to touch and purify the lips of whom he pleases. To this must be added industrious and select reading, steady observation, insight into all seemly arts and affairs; till which in some measure be compassed, at mine own peril and cost, I refuse not to sustain this expectation from as many as are not loath to hazard so much credulity upon the best pledges that I can give them. Although it nothing content me to have disclosed thus much beforehand, but that I trust hereby to make it manifest with what small willingness I endure to interrupt the pursuit of no less hopes than these, and leave a calm and pleasing solitariness, fed cheerful and confident thoughts, to embark in a troubled sea of noises and hoarse disputes; from beholding the bright countenance of truth in the quiet and still air of delightful studies, to come into the dim reflection of hollow antiquities sold by the seeming bulk, and there be fain to club quotations with men whose learning and belief lies in marginal stuffings; who when they have, like good sumpters, laid you down their horse-load of citations and fathers at your door, with a raphsody of who and who were bishops here or there, you may take off their pack-saddles, their day's work is done, and episcopacy, as they think, stoutly vindicated. Let any gentle apprehension that can distinguish learned pains from unlearned drudgery, imagine what pleasure or profoundness can be in this, or what honour to deal against such adversaries.

Lecture the Twenty-Second.

EDMUND WALLER—SAMUEL BUTLER—HENRY VAUGHAN—SIR JOHN DENHAM—WILLIAM CHAMBERLAYNE—ANDREW MARVELL.

THE exalted position which Milton occupies in English Literature, has induced us to afford to the history of his life, and the examination of his genius and writings, a much larger space than we shall be permitted to extend to any of his contemporaries or successors.

EDMUND WALLER, the poet whom we shall next notice, was the son of John Waller, a gentleman of large estates, and Anne, sister of the celebrated John Hampden. He was born at Coleshill, Hertfordshire, in 1605, and received his education, preparatory for the university, under the supervision of the Reverend Mr. Dobson, minister of the parish of Great Wycombe He early entered King's College, Cambridge, where he remained about three years, and then left without taking his degree, being elected, when he had scarcely attained the seventeenth year of his age, to a seat in the last parliament of King James the First. His father, at his death, which occurred during the infancy of the future poet, had left him in the possession of the ample fortune of three thousand pounds a year, and through the means of his wealth, Waller found easy access to familiar intercourse with the court and the nobility of the country.

Soon after he entered parliament, and when but eighteen years of age, he published his first poem; and at the age of twenty-five he married a rich heiress of London, whom, however, he had the misfortune to lose within the following year. He then became a suitor to Lady Dorathea Sidney, eldest daughter of the Earl of Leicester; and to this proud and peerless fair one, he dedicated the better portion of his poetry, making the groves of Penshurst echo to the praises of his Sacharissa. Lady Dorathea, however, was inexorable, and bestowed her hand on the Earl of Sunderland. It is said that, meeting her many years after, when she was far advanced in life, the lady asked him when he would again write such verses upon her. 'When you are as young, madam, and as handsome as you were then,' replied the ungallant poet. This incident is the more important, as it affords a key to

Waller's whole character. He was easy, witty, and accomplished, but cold and selfish in the extreme; and entirely destitute of both high principle and deep feeling.

In parliament Waller was either a friend or opponent of the royal party, as his own interest seemed to require, and throughout his long life the same want of principle prevailed. He, at one period of his parliamentary career greatly distinguished himself on the popular side, and was chosen to conduct the prosecution against Judge Crawley for his opinion in favor of levying ship-money. His speech on delivering the impeachment, was printed, and twenty thousand copies of it sold in one day. Shortly afterward, however, he joined in a plot to surprise the city militia, and let the king's forces into the city of London, for which he was tried and sentenced to one year's imprisonment, and to pay a fine of ten thousand pounds. His conduct upon this occasion was mean and abject in the extreme; and at the expiration of his imprisonment, he went abroad, and resided, for some years, amid much splendor, in France.

Waller returned to England during the Protectorate, and when Cromwell died he celebrated the event in one of his most vigorous and impressive poems. The image of the commonwealth, though reared by no common hands, soon fell to pieces under Richard Cromwell, and Waller was ready with a congratulatory address to welcome Charles the Second to the crown. The royal offering was considered inferior to the panegyric on Cromwell, and the king himself, who was in the habit of admitting the poet to terms of courtly intimacy, took occasion to point out the disparity to him. 'Poets, sire,' replied the witty, self-possessed Waller, 'always succeed better in fiction than in truth!'

In the first parliament summoned by Charles the Second, Waller sat for the town of Hastings, and he served for different places in all the succeeding parliaments of that reign. At the accession of James the Second, in 1685, the venerable poet, at that time eighty years of age, was elected representative for a borough in Cornwall. The mad career of James, in seeking to subvert the national church and constitution, was foreseen by this wary and sagacious observer: 'he will be left,' said he, 'like a whale upon the strand.,' Feeling his long-protracted life drawing to a close, Waller purchased a small property at Coleshill, remarking that, 'he would be glad to die like the stag, where he was roused.' His desire was not, however, gratified, as he died at Beaconsfield, on the twenty-first of October, 1687, and was buried in the churchyard of that place, where a monument was afterward erected to his memory.

The poems of Waller have all the smoothness and polish of modern verse, and hence a high rank has been assigned to him as one of the first reformers and improvers of our versification. One cause of his refinement was, doubtless, his early and familiar intercourse with the court and nobility, and the bright conversational nature of most of his productions. He wrote for the world of fashion and taste—consigning

The noon of manhood to a myrtle shade;

and he wrote in the same strain till just before the close of his long and eventful life. The first collection of his poems was made by himself, and published in 1664. It passed through numerous editions in his lifetime; and in 1690, a second collection was made of such pieces as he had produced in his latter years. In a poetical dedication to Lady Harley, prefixed to this edition, and written by Elijah Fenton, Waller is styled the

Maker and model of melodious verse.

This eulogium seems to embody the opinion of Waller's contemporaries, and it was afterward confirmed by Dryden and Pope, neither of whom had, however, sufficiently studied the excellent models of versification furnished by the old poets, as well as their rich poetical diction. The playfulness of his fancy, the smoothness of his numbers, his good sense, and uniform elegance, rendered him as popular with critics as with the multitude; while his prominence as a public man would naturally increase curiosity with regard to his works. His poems are chiefly short and incidental effusions, though toward the close of his life, he produced, in six cantos, a more elaborate work, the subject of which was, *Divine Love.* But though such employments of his talents was graceful and becoming in advanced life, yet in this new and higher walk of the muse, he did not succeed; his fame, therefore, must ever rest on his light, airy, and fanciful performances.

In the following selections from this author, we have aimed to illustrate and sustain the preceding remarks, and to exhibit all the varieties of his style:

GO, LOVELY ROSE.

Go, lovely rose!
Tell her that wastes her time and me,
That now she knows,
When I resemble her to thee,
How sweet and fair she seems to be.

Tell her, that's young,
And shuns to have her graces spied,
That, hadst thou sprung
In deserts, where no men abide,
Thou must have uncommended died.

Small is the worth
Of beauty from the light retir'd;
Bid her come forth,
Suffer herself to be desired,
And not blush so to be admir'd.

Then die! that she
The common fate of all things rare
May read in thee,
How small a part of time they share
That are so wondrous sweet and fair.

SAY, LOVELY DREAM.

Say, lovely dream! where could'st thou find
  Shades to counterfeit that face?
Colours of this glorious kind
  Come not from any mortal place.

In heav'n itself thou sure wert dress'd
  With that angel-like disguise;
Thus deluded, am I blest,
  And see my joy with closed eyes.

But, ah! this image is too kind
  To be other than a dream;
Cruel Sacharissa's mind
  Ne'er put on that sweet extreme.

Fair dream! if thou intend'st me grace,
  Change that heavenly face of thine;
Paint despised love in thy face,
  And make it t' appear like mine.

Pale, wan, and meagre, let it look,
  With a pity-moving shape,
Such as wander by the brook
  Of Lethe, or from graves escape.

Then to that matchless nymph appear,
  In whose shape thou shinest so;
Softly in her sleeping ear
  With humble words express my woe.

Perhaps from greatness, state, and pride,
  Thus surprised, she may fall;
Sleep does disproportion hide,
  And, death resembling, equals all.

OLD AGE AND DEATH.

The seas are quiet when the winds give o'er;
So calm are we when passions are no more:
For then we know how vain it was to boast
Of fleeting things, too certain to be lost.
Clouds of affection from our younger eyes
Conceal that emptiness which age descries.

The soul's dark cottage, batter'd and decay'd,
Lets in new light through chinks that time has made:
Stronger by weakness, wiser men become,
As they draw near to their eternal home.
Leaving the old both worlds at once they view,
That stand upon the threshold of the new.

A PANEGYRIC TO THE LORD PROTECTOR.

While with a strong and yet a gentle hand,
You bridle faction, and our hearts command,
Protect us from ourselves, and from the foe,
Make us unite, and make us conquer too;

Let partial spirits still aloud complain,
Think themselves injured that they can not reign,
And own no liberty, but where they may
Without control upon their fellows prey.

Above the waves as Neptune show'd his face,
To chide the winds, and save the Trojan race,
So has your Highness, raised above the rest,
Storms of ambition tossing us repress'd.

Your drooping country, torn with civil hate,
Restor'd by you, is made a glorious state,
The seat of empire, where the Irish come,
And the unwilling Scots, to fetch their doom.

The sea 's our own; and now all nations greet,
With bending sails, each vessel of our fleet;
Your power extends as far as winds can blow,
Or swelling sails upon the globe may go.

Heav'n, that hath plac'd this island to give law,
To balance Europe, and its states to awe;
In this conjunction doth on Britain smile,
The greatest leader, and the greatest isle!

Whether this portion of the world were rent
By the rude ocean from the continent,
Or thus created, it was sure design'd
To be the sacred refuge of mankind.

Hither the oppressed shall henceforth resort,
Justice to crave, and succour at your court;
And then your Highness, not for our's alone,
But for the world's Protector shall be known.

* * * * * * *

Still as you rise, the state exalted too,
Finds no distemper while 'tis chang'd by you;
Chang'd like the world's great scene! when, without noise,
The rising sun night's vulgar lights destroys.

Had you, some ages past, this race of glory
Run, with amazement we should read your story;
But living virtue all achievements past,
Meets envy still to grapple with at last.

This Cæsar found; and that ungrateful age,
With losing him, went back to blood and rage;
Mistaken Brutus thought to break their yoke,
But cut the bond of union with that stroke.

That sun once set, a thousand meaner stars
Give a dim light to violence and wars;
To such a tempest as now threatens all,
Did not your mighty arm prevent the fall?

If Rome's great senate could not wield that sword,
Which of the conquer'd world had made them lord,
What hope had ours, while yet their power was new,
To rule victorious armies, but by you?

You, that had taught them to subdue their foes;
Could order teach, and their high sp'rits compose;
To every duty could their minds engage,
Provoke their courage, and command their rage.

So when a lion shakes his dreadful mane,
And angry grows, if he that first took pain
To tame his youth approach the haughty beast,
He bends to him, but frights away the rest.

As the vex'd world, to find repose, at last
Itself into Augustus' arms did cast;
So England now does, with like toil opprest,
Her weary head upon your bosom rest.

Then let the Muses, with such notes as these,
Instruct us what belongs unto our peace.
Your battles they hereafter shall indite,
And draw the image of our Mars in fight.

Samuel Butler, the poet of this period who follows Waller in the order of time, was the son of a respectable English yeoman, and was born at Stresham, in Worcestershire, about the first of February, 1612. Having early discovered an inclination for learning, his father placed him at the free school of Worcester, under the care of Mr. Henry Bright, a very able master; and after there passing through the several classes, he removed to Cambridge, but in consequence of his limited resources was never matriculated in the university. From Cambridge, after a residence in that city of six or seven years, he returned to his native county, and became clerk to justice Jefferys of that district, with whom he remained for several years, during which he passed his time in easy and respectable circumstances, devoting his leisure hours to poetry, history, and, as an amusement, to painting. From the justice's office, through the recommendation and influence of some friends, whose favor the propriety of his conduct had secured, he entered into the service of the Countess of Kent, and there enjoyed not only the advantages of a good library, but frequent and even familiar intercourse with the celebrated Selden. Thus passed the years of Butler's youth and early manhood, and so far he can not be considered as unfortunate, if we are to suppose that he found his chief enjoyment, as scholars usually do, in opportunities for study and intellectual improvement.

From the family of the Countess of Kent, Butler removed to that of Sir Samuel Luke, in which he officiated as tutor to that gentleman's children. Luke was one of Cromwell's principal officers, and was probably marked, to an unusual degree, by the well-known peculiarities of his party. The situation could not have been a very agreeable one to a man whose disposition was so much inclined toward wit and humor, even though those qualities had not made their possessor a royalist, which, in such an age, they could scarcely fail to do. Daily exposed to association with persons whose character, from contrast with his own, he could not but loathe, it is not surprising that his muse, which had now become mature, should have conceived the design of a general satire on the sectarian party. The matchless fiction of Cervantes supplied him with a model, in which he had only to substitute the extravagances of a political and religious fanaticism for those of chivalry. Luke himself is understood to be exhibited in Sir Hudibras, and for this Butler has been accused of a breach of the laws of hospitality; but as we are not acquainted with the circumstances attending their separation, this is a question that we are not prepared to decide.

The 'Restoration' faintly lighted up Butler's future path with hope. He was appointed secretary to the Earl of Carbury, President of the principality of Wales; and when the wardenship of the Marshes was revived, the earl made his secretary steward of Ludlow Castle. The poet, now fifty years of age, seemed to add to his security for the future by marrying a widow named Herbert, who was of good family, and possessed a very considerable fortune; but this prospect proved delusive, in consequence of the failure of the parties with whom the lady's fortune was invested.

Butler is supposed to have commenced his *Hudibras*, the burlesque poem upon which his reputation exclusively rests, before he left the family of Sir Samuel Luke, but the first part of that extraordinary work was not published until 1663. Its popularity immediately became extraordinary. Its wit, so appropriate to the taste of that period, and the breadth of the satiric pictures which it presented, each of which had hundreds of prototypes within the recollection of all men then living, could not fail to give it extensive currency. By the Earl of Dorset, an accomplished friend of letters, it was introduced to the notice of the court; and the king was afterward in the habit of quoting many of its most pointed passages. In 1664, the second part was presented to the public; and the third and last part appeared in 1678. But though the poet and his work were the praise of all ranks, from royalty down to the common laborer, yet he was himself little benefited by it. What emoluments he derived from his stewardship, or whether he derived any emoluments from it at all, is entirely uncertain; but it is a melancholy truth that the latter part of his life was spent in needy and struggling circumstances, in London. The Earl of Clarendon promised him a place at court, but he never obtained it; and the king presented him with three hundred pounds, but that sum was not sufficient to discharge the debts pressing upon him at the time. Such are the circumstances which chequered the last twenty years of the life of the most brilliant comic genius that England ever, perhaps, produced. Butler died in an obscure street near Covent Garden, on the twenty-fifth of September, 1680, and was privately buried in an adjacent churchyard, at the expense of a Mr. Longueville.

'Hudibras' is a cavalier burlesque of the extravagant ideas and rigid manners of the Puritans of the civil war and commonwealth. It is a production of matchless wit and fancy; but the construction of the story, and the delineation of the characters, have often been praised far beyond their merit. In these particulars it has very slender claims to originality. Cervantes is evidently the model which Butler followed; and Hudibras is Don Quixote turned puritan. He has exchanged the helmet of Malbrino for the close cap of Geneva. Instead of encountering giants and enchanters, he wages war with papists and prelatists. Instead of couching his lance at tilts and tournaments, he mounts the pulpit, and harangues the 'long-eared' multitude. He is not quite so unsophisticated a lunatic as Quixote. When his own interest is concerned, his apprehension becomes wonderfully keen. Ralpho, also, is but a conventical edition of Sancho; but that Butler should have failed in copying from such models as these, is not at all surprising. The work in which the adventures of the Knight of La Mancha are recorded, is, perhaps, as nearly perfect as any work of human genius could be made: it is matchless and inimitable.

It is, however, possible to be a great and powerful genius, and yet be inferior to Cervantes; and such is Butler. The poem of the latter can not be expected to be so fascinating as the work of the former, for its subject is far more repulsive. The Knight's greatest weaknesses are amiable, and of vices he has none. We sympathize in all his misfortunes, and almost wish him success in his wildest enterprises. We can hardly help quarrelling with the windmills for resisting his attack; and feel inclined to tilt a lance in support of his chivalrous assault upon the flock of sheep. Butler certainly might have made the fanaticism of Hudibras more amiable, and more sincere, without at all weakening either the truth or the comic force of the picture. As it is, we rather turn from it with disgust, than gaze upon it with admiration. These observations, however, apply only to our author's delineation of character, and not to the fine touches of satire, and to the keen and profound observations on morals and manners, in which his work is so remarkably rich. Butler's genius was eminently didactic. He was not an inventor, but an observer. His satire is keen and caustic; his wit brilliant and delightful. His knowledge of the arts and sciences appears to have been both extensive and profound; and he has brought a wonderful variety of attainment and research to the embellishment of his poem. He has also enriched it with many beauties of thought and diction, which form a strong contrast to its general ludicrous cast and character. Nothing, for instance, can be finer than the following lines:—

> The moon put off her vail of light
> Which hides her by the day from sight:
> Mysterious vail! of brightness made,
> That's both her lustre and her shade.

This passage, besides being poetically beautiful, is philosophically true—the rays of the sun causing us to see the moon by night, and preventing us from seeing it during the day. Without, however, pausing to introduce farther instances of this peculiar trait of the author's genius, we shall close this notice by exhibiting the personal appearance, the accomplishments, and the religious sentiments of the hero of the poem, Hudibras himself:—

THE PERSONAL APPEARANCE OF HUDIBRAS.

His tawny beard was th' equal grace
Both of his wisdom and his face;
In cut and dye so like a tile,
A sudden view it would beguile;
The upper part thereof was whey,
The nether, orange, mix'd with gray.
This hairy meteor did denounce
The fall of sceptres and of crowns;
With grisly type did represent
Declining age of government;
And tell, with hieroglyphic spade
Its own grave and the state's were made.
Like Samson's heart-breakers, it grew
In time to make a nation rue;
Though it contributed its own fall,
To wait upon the public downfall;
It was monastic, and did grow
In holy orders by strict vow;
Of rule as sullen and severe,
As that of rigid Cordelier;
'Twas bound to suffer persecution
And martyrdom with resolution;
T' oppose itself against the hate
And vengeance of th' incensed state,
In whose defiance it was worn,
Still ready to be pull'd and torn;
With red-hot irons to be tortur'd,
Revil'd, and spit upon, and martyr'd;
Maugre all which 'twas to stand fast
As long as monarchy should last;
But when the state should hap to reel,
'Twas to submit to fatal steel,
And fall, as it was consecrate,
A sacrifice to fall of state;
Whose thread of life the fatal sisters
Did twist together with its whiskers,
And twine so close, that Time should never,
In life or death, their fortunes sever;
But with his rusty sickle mow
Both down together at a blow.
His doublet was of sturdy buff,
And though not sword, yet cudgel proof;
Whereby 'twas fitter for his use,
Who fear'd no blows but such as bruise.
His breeches were of rugged woollen,
And had been at the siege of Bullen;
To old king Harry so well-known,
Some writers held they were his own;
Though they were lin'd with many a piece
Of ammunition, bread and cheese,
And fat black puddings, proper food
For warriors that delight in blood;

For, as we said, he always chose
To carry victual in his hose,
That often tempted rats and mice
Th' ammunition to surprise;
And when he put a hand but in
The one or t' other magazine,
They stoutly on defence on 't stood
And from the wounded foe drew blood;
And till they were storm'd and beaten out,
Ne'er left the fortified redoubt;
And though knights-errant, as some think,
Of old did neither eat nor drink,
Because when thorough deserts vast,
And regions desolate they pass'd,
When belly-timber above ground,
Or under, was not to be found,
Unless they graz'd, there's not one word
Of their provision on record;
Which made some confidently write
They had no stomachs but to fight.
'Tis false; for Arthur wore in hall
Round table like a farthingal;
On which, with shirt puff'd out behind,
And eke before, his good knights din'd;
Though 'twas no table some suppose,
But a huge pair of round trunk hose,
In which he carried as much meat
As he and all the knights could eat;
When laying by their swords and truncheons,
They took their breakfasts or their luncheons.
But let that pass at present, lest
We should forget where we digress'd,
As learned authors use, to whom
We leave it, and to the purpose come.
His puissant sword unto his side,
Near his undaunted heart, was tied,
With basket hilt that would hold broth,
And serve for fight and dinner both;
In it he melted lead for bullets
To shoot at foes, and sometimes pullets,
To whom he bore so fell a grutch,
He ne'er gave quarter t' any such.
The trenchant blade, Toledo trusty,
For want of fighting, was grown rusty,
And ate into itself, for lack
Of some body to hew and hack:
The peaceful scabbard where it dwelt,
The rancour of its edge had felt;
For of the lower end two handful
It had devoured, it was so manful,
And so much scorn'd to lurk in case,
As if it durst not show its face.
In many desperate attempts
Of warrants, exigents, contempts,

It had appear'd with courage bolder
Than Serjeant Bum invading shoulder:
Oft had it ta'en possession,
And prisoners too, or made them run.
This sword a dagger had his page,
That was but little for his age;
And therefore waited on him so
As dwarfs upon knights-errant do:
It was a serviceable dudgeon,
Either for fighting, or for drudging:
When it had stabb'd or broke a head,
It would scrape trenches, or chip bread;
Toast cheese or bacon, though it were
To bait a mouse trap, would not care:
'Twould make clean shoes, and in the earth
Set leeks and onions, and so forth:
It had been 'prentice to a brewer,
Where this and more it did endure,
But left the trade as many more
Have lately done on the same score.

THE ACCOMPLISHMENTS OF HUDIBRAS.

When civil dudgeon first grew high
And men fell out, they knew not why:
When hard words, jealousies, and fears,
Set folks together by the ears,
And made them fight, like mad or drunk,
For Dame Religion as for punk;
Whose honesty they all durst swear for,
Though not a man of them knew wherefore:
When gospel-trumpeter, surrounded
With long-ear'd rout, to battle sounded,
And pulpit, drum ecclesiastic,
Was beat with fist, instead of a stick:
Then did Sir Knight abandon dwelling,
And out he rode a-colonelling.
A wight he was, whose very sight would
Entitle him, mirror of knighthood;
That never bow'd his stubborn knee
To any thing but chivalry;
Nor put up blow, but that which laid
Right-worshipful on shoulder blade:
Chief of domestic knights and errant,
Either for chartel or for warrant:
Great on the bench, great on the saddle,
That could as well bind o'er, as swaddle:
Mighty he was at both of these,
And styl'd of war as well as peace.
(So some rats of amphibious nature,
Are either for the land or water.)
But here our authors make a doubt,
Whether he were more wise or stout;
Some hold the one, and some the other:
But howsoe'er they make a pother,

The diff'rence was so small, his brain
Outweigh'd his rage but half a grain:
Which made some take him for a tool
That knaves do work with, called a fool.
For 't has been held by many, that
As Montaigne, playing with his cat,
Complains she thought him but an ass,
Much more she would Sir Hudibras.
(For that's the name our valiant knight
To all his challenges did write.)
But they 're mistaken very much;
'Tis plain enough he was no such:
We grant, although he had much wit,
He was very shy of using it;
As being loath to wear it out,
And, therefore, bore it not about;
Unless on holydays or so,
As men their best apparel do;
Beside, 'tis known he could speak Greek
As naturally as pigs squeak;
That Latin was no more difficile,
Than for a blackbird 'tis to whistle:
Being rich in both, he never scanted
His bounty unto such as wanted,
But much of either would afford
To many, that had not one word.

* * * * * *

He was in logic a great critic,
Profoundly skill'd in analytic;
He could distinguish, and divide
A hair 'twixt south and south-west side;
On either which he would dispute,
Confute, change hands, and still confute;
He'd undertake to prove by force
Of argument, a man 's no horse;
He'd prove a buzzard is no fowl,
And that a lord may be an owl,
A calf an alderman, a goose a justice,
And rooks committee-men and trustees.
He'd run in debt by disputation,
And pay with ratiocination:
All this by syllogism, true
In mood and figure, he would do.
For rhetoric, he could not ope
His mouth, but out there flew a trope;
And when he happen'd to break off
I' the middle of his speech, or cough,
H' had hard words, ready to show why,
And tell what rules he did it by:
Else, when with greatest art he spoke,
You'd think he talk'd like other folk;
For all a rhetorician's rules
Teach nothing but to name his tools.

But, when he pleas'd to show 't, his speech
In loftiness of sound was rich;
A Babylonish dialect,
Which learned pedants much affect:
It was a party-colour'd dress
Of patch'd and piebald languages;
'T was English cut on Greek and Latin,
Like fustian heretofore on satin.
It had an odd promiscuous tone,
As if he had talk'd three parts in one;
Which made some think, when he did gabble,
Th' had heard three labourers of Babel;
Or Cerberus himself pronounce
A leash of languages at once.
This he as volubly would vent
As if his stock would ne'er be spent;
And truly to support that charge,
He had supplies as vast and large:
For he would coin or counterfeit
New words with little or no wit:
Words so debas'd and hard, no stone
Was hard enough to touch them on:
And when with hasty noise he spoke 'em,
The ignorant for current took 'em;
That had the orator, who once
Did fill his mouth with pebble-stones
When he harangu'd, but known his phrse,
He would have us'd no other ways.

RELIGION OF HUDIBRAS.

For his religion, it was fit
To match his learning and his wit.
'T was Presbyterian true blue;
For he was of that stubborn crew
Of errant saints—whom all men grant
To be the true church militant;
Such as do build their faith upon
The holy text of pike and gun;
Decide all controversies by
Infallible artillery;
And prove their doctrine orthodox
By apostolic blows and knocks;
Call fire, and sword, and desolation,
A godly thorough reformation,
Which always must be carried on,
And still be doing, never done;
As if religion were intended
For nothing else but to be mended;
A sect whose chief devotion lies
In odd perverse antipathies;
In falling out with that or this,
And finding somewhat still amiss;

More peevish, cross, and splenetic,
Than dog distraught or monkey sick;
That with more care keep holyday
The wrong, than others the right way;
Compound for sins they are inclined to,
By damning those they have no mind to.
Still so perverse and opposite,
As if they worship'd God for spite;
The self-same thing they will abhor
One way, and long another for;
Free will they one way disavow,
Another nothing else allow;
All piety consists therein
In them, in other men all sin;
Rather than fail, they will defy
That which they love most tenderly;
Quarrel with minc'd-pies, and disparage
Their best and dearest friend, plum-porridge;
Fat pig and goose itself oppose,
And blaspheme custard through the nose.
Th' apostles of this fierce religion,
Like Mahomet, were ass and widgeon,
To whom our knight, by fast instinct
Of wit and temper, was so link'd,
As if hypocrisy and nonsense
Had got th' advowson of his conscience.

As conspicuous as is Butler's wit in his poetry, it shines with no less brilliancy in some of his prose works, the manuscripts of which were left, at his death, with his friend Longueville, but were not presented to the public in printed form, until 1759. The most interesting of these works, is the one from which we select the following extract. It is entitled *Characters;* and it closely resembles, in style, those of Overbury, Earle, and Hall.

A SMALL POET

Is one that would fain make himself that which nature never meant him; like a fanatic that inspires himself with his own whimsies. He sets up haberdasher of small poetry, with a very small stock, and no credit. He believes it is invention enough to find out other men's wit; and whatsoever he lights upon, either in books or company, he makes bold with as his own. This he puts together so untowardly, that you may perceive his own wit has the rickets, by the swelling disproportion of the joints. You may know his wit not to be natural, 'tis so unquiet and troublesome in him: for as those that have money but seldom, are always shaking their pockets when they have it, so does he, when he thinks he has got something that will make him appear. He is a perpetual talker, and you may know by the freedom of his discourse that he came lightly by it, as thieves spend freely what they get. He is like an Italian thief, that never robs but he murders, to prevent discovery; so sure is he to cry down the man from whom he purloins, that his petty larceny of wit may pass unsuspected. He appears so over-concerned in all men's wits, as if they were but disparagements of his own; and cries down all they do, as if they were encroachments upon him. He takes jests from the owners and breaks them, as justices do false weights, and pots that want measure. When he meets with any thing that is very good, he changes it into small money, like three groats for a shilling, to serve several occasions. He disclaims study, pretends to take things in motion, and to shoot flying, which appears to be very true, by his often missing of his mark. As for epithets, he always avoids those that are near akin to the sense. Such matches are unlawful, and not fit to be made by a Christian poet; and therefore all his care is to choose out such as will serve, like a wooden leg, to piece out a maimed verse that wants a foot or two, and if they will but rhyme now and then into the bargain, or run upon a letter, it is a work of supererogation. For similitudes, he likes the hardest and most obscure best; for as ladies wear black patches to make their complexion seem fairer than they are, so when an illustration is more obscure than the sense that went before it, it must of necessity make it appear clearer than it did; for contraries are best set off with contraries. He has found out a new sort of poetical Georgics—a trick of sowing wit like clover-grass on barren subjects, which would yield nothing before. This is very useful for the times, wherein, some men say, there is no room left for invention. He will take three grains of wit, like the elixir, and, projecting it upon the iron age, turn it immediately into gold. All the business of mankind has presently vanished, the whole world has kept holyday; there has been no men but heroes and poets, no women but nymphs and shepherdesses: trees have borne fritters, and rivers flowed plum-porridge. When he writes, he commonly steers the sense of his lines by the rhyme that is at the end of them, as butchers do calves by the tail. For when he has made one line which is easy enough, and has found out some sturdy hard word that will but rhyme, he will hammer the sense upon it, like a piece of hot iron upon an anvil, into what form he pleases. There is no art in the world so rich in terms as poetry; a whole dictionary is scarcely able to contain them; for there is hardly a pond, a sheep-walk, or a gravel-pit in all Greece, but the ancient name of it is become a term of art in poetry. By this means, small poets have such a stock of able hard words lying by them, as dryades, hamadryades, aönides, fauni, nymphæ, sylvani, &c., that signify nothing at all; and such a world of pedantic terms of the same kind, as may serve to furnish all the new inventions and 'thorough reformations' that can happen between this and Plato's great year.

From Waller and Butler we pass to notice Vaughan, Denham, Chamberlayne, and Marvell, with the last of whom our present remarks will close.

Henry Vaughan was born on the banks of the river Usk, in Brecknockshire, in 1614, and at the age of seventeen entered the university of Oxford. His parents designed him for the legal profession, but after he had completed his collegiate studies he resolved to turn his attention to medicine. With this view he repaired to London, and after there perfecting himself in the healing art, he retired, at the commencement of the civil wars, to his home, and there, for many years, practiced as a physician, with very considerable success. Much of his time, however, he devoted to the muses; and in 1651, he published a volume of miscellaneous poems, evincing considerable strength and originality of thought and copious imagery, though tinged with a gloomy sectarianism, and marred by crabbed rhymes. But Campbell scarcely does justice to him when he styles him 'one of the harshest even, of the inferior order of the school of conceit,' though he admits that he has 'some few scattered thoughts that meet our eye amid his harsh pages, like wild flowers on a barren heath.'

In his latter days Vaughan became deeply serious and devout, and published a volume of religious poems, containing his happiest effusions. As a sacred poet he evinces an intensity of feeling inferior only to Crashaw. From these poems we select the following specimens:—

EARLY RISING AND PRAYER.

When first thy eyes unvail, give thy soul leave
To do the like; our bodies but forerun
The spirit's duty: true hearts spread and heave
Unto their God, as flowers do to the sun;
Give him thy first thoughts then, so shalt thou keep
His company all day, and in him sleep.

Yet never sleep the sun up; prayer should
Dawn with the day: there are set awful hours
'Twixt heaven and us; the manna was not good
After sun-rising; far day sullies flowers:
Rise to prevent the sun; sleep doth sin glut
And heaven's gate opens when the world's is shut.

Walk with thy fellow-creatures; note the hush
And whisperings amongst them. Not a spring
Or leaf but hath his morning hymn; each bush
And oak doth know I AM. Canst thou not sing!
O leave thy cares and follies! Go this way
And thou art sure to prosper all the day.

Serve God before the world; let him not go
Until thou hast a blessing; then resign
The whole unto him, and remember who
Prevail'd by wrestling ere the sun did shine;
Pour oil upon the stones, weep for thy sin,
Then journey on, and have an eye to heaven.

Mornings are mysteries; the first, the world's youth,
Man's resurrection, and the future's bud,
Shroud in their births; the crown of life, light, truth,
Is styled their star; the stone and hidden food:
Three blessings wait upon them, one of which
Should move—they make us holy, happy, rich.

When the world 's up, and every swarm abroad,
Keep well thy temper, mix not with each clay;
Dispatch necessities; life hath a load
Which must be carried on, and safely may;
Yet keep those cares without thee; let the heart
Be God's alone, and choose the better part.

THE RAINBOW.

Still young and fine, but what is still in view
We slight as old and soil'd, though fresh and new.
How bright wert thou when Shem's admiring eye
Thy burnish'd flaming arch did first descry:

When Zerah, Nahor, Haran, Abram, Lot,
The youthful world's gray fathers, in one knot
Did with inventive looks watch every hour
For thy new light and trembled at each shower!
When thou dost shine, darkness looks white and fair;
Forms turn to music, clouds to smiles and air;
Rain gently spends his honey-drops, and pours
Balm on the cleft earth, milk on grass and flowers.
Bright pledge of peace and sunshine, the sure tie
Of thy Lord's hand, the object of his eye!
When I behold thee, though my light be dim,
Distinct, and low, I can in thine see him,
Who looks upon thee from his glorious throne,
And minds the covenant betwixt all and One.

Vaughan wrote some pieces in prose also, but they are such as not to require any particular notice. He died in his native place, in 1695, and in the eighty-second year of his age.

John Denham was the only son of Sir John Denham, knight, of Little Horseley, in Essex, and was born in the city of Dublin, in 1615. His father, at the time of the future poet's birth, was chief baron of the exchequer of Ireland, and one of the lords commissioners of that kingdom; but being created, in 1617, one of the barons of the exchequer of England, he removed to London, and in that city young Denham pursued his preparatory collegiate studies. In 1631, he entered Trinity College, Oxford, as a gentleman commoner; 'but being looked upon,' says Wood, 'as a slow and dreaming young man by his seniors and contemporaries, and given more to cards and dice than his study, they could never then imagine that he could ever enrich the world with his fancy or issue of his brain, as he afterward did.'

Notwithstanding these unfavorable auspices, Denham, at the expiration of three years, took his master's degree, immediately after which he repaired to London, and entered Lincoln's Inn, as a student of law. Surrounded now with new facilities for indulging his favorite vice, he devoted, to gaming, his entire time, and all the revenues that he could command; and intelligence of his evil habits finally reaching the ear of his father, the knight threatened to disinherit him if he did not immediately relinquish his vicious practices. Artfully, or sincerely, Denham, upon this occasion, produced his fine *Essay upon Gaming*, which he presented to his father as an evidence of his reformation. But upon the death of the old gentleman, which soon after occurred, he again returned to the gaming table; and his losses so rapidly succeeded each other, that the large fortune which he had recently inherited, became in the course of a few months, sensibly impaired.

Meantime, with all his irregularities, Denham was not idle; and accordingly, in 1641, he produced a tragedy entitled *The Sophy*, the merits of which were such as to call forth the admiration of the most competent judges of the dramatic art; and induce Waller to observe, that the author 'broke out like the Irish rebellion, threescore thousand strong, when nobody was aware, or in the least expected it!' The 'Sophy' must, however, upon critical examination, be acknowledged not to rise, in intrinsic merit, above mediocrity. Soon after the publication of his tragedy, Denham was made sheriff of Surrey, and governor of Farnham Castle for the king; but not being skilled in military affairs, he relinquished that post, and retired to Oxford, where his majesty then held his court. At Oxford, in 1643, he wrote *Cooper's Hill*—the poem upon which his poetic reputation mainly rests—'A poem,' says Dryden, 'which for majesty of style, is, and ever will be, the standard of good writing.'

In 1648, Denham conveyed James, Duke of York, to France, and in consequence of his connection with the royal family, his estate was sold, during his absence, by order of Parliament; but the Restoration revived his fallen dignity and fortunes. He was made surveyor of the king's buildings, and at the coronation of Charles the Second, created Knight of the Bath. He had freed himself from his early excesses and follies, but an unfortunate marriage darkened his closing years, which were also unhappily visited by insanity. He, however, sufficiently recovered to receive the congratulations of Butler, his fellow poet, and to commemorate the recent death of Cowley, in one of his happiest effusions. Denham died on the nineteenth of March, 1668, and was buried on the twenty-third of the same month, in Westminster Abbey, near the graves of Chaucer and Spenser.

'Cooper's Hill,' the poem by which Sir John Denham is now best known, consists of between three and four hundred lines, written in the heroic couplet. The descriptions are interspersed with sentimental digressions, suggested by surrounding objects—the river Thames, a ruined Abbey, Windsor forest, and the field of Runnymede. The view from Cooper's Hill is represented to be rich and luxuriant, but the muse of Denham was more reflective than descriptive. Dr. Johnson assigns to this poet the praise of 'being the author of a species of composition that may be denominated local poetry, of which the fundamental subject is some particular landscape, to be poetically described, with the addition of such embellishments as may be supplied by historical retrospection or incidental meditation.' The versification of Denham is generally smooth and flowing, but he wanted both depth and delicacy of feeling. In reading his poetry, therefore, we must be satisfied with smoothness, regularity, and order, without the higher attributes of genius. The following extract is from 'Cooper's Hill', and the four lines in Italics have been praised by every critic from Dryden down to the present time:—

THE THAMES AND WINDSOR FOREST.

Mine eye, descending from the hill, surveys
Where Thames among the wanton valleys strays;
Thames, the most lov'd of all the ocean's sons
By his old sire, to his embraces runs,
Hasting to pay his tribute to the sea,

Like mortal life to meet eternity.
Though with those streams he no remembrance hold,
Whose foam is amber and their gravel gold,
His genuine and less guilty wealth to explore,
Search not his bottom, but survey his shore,
O'er which he kindly spreads his spacious wing,
And hatches plenty for th' ensuing spring,
And then destroys it with too fond a stay,
Like mothers which their infants overlay;
Nor with a sudden and impetuous wave,
Like profuse kings, resumes the wealth he gave.
No unexpected inundations spoil
The mower's hopes, nor mock the ploughman's toil,
But Godlike his unwearied bounty flows;
First loves to do, then loves the good he does.
Nor are his blessings to his banks confin'd,
But free and common, as the sea or wind.
When he to boast or to disperse his stores,
Full of the tributes of his grateful shores,
Visits the world, and in his flying towers
Brings home to us, and makes both Indies ours:
Finds wealth where 't is, bestows it where it wants,
Cities in deserts, woods in cities plants;
So that to us no thing, no place is strange,
While his fair bosom is the world's exchange.
O, could I flow like thee, and make thy stream
My great example, as it is my theme!
Though deep yet clear, though gentle yet not dull,
Strong without rage, without overflowing full.
* * * * * *
But his proud head the airy mountain hides
Among the clouds: his shoulders and his sides
A shady mantle clothes; his curled brows
Frown on the gentle stream, which calmly flows
While winds and storms his lofty forehead beat,
The common fate of all that 's high or great.
Low at his foot a spacious plain is plac'd,
Between the mountain and the stream embrac'd,
Which shade and shelter from the hill derives,
While the kind river wealth and beauty gives;
And in the mixture of all these appears
Variety, which all the rest endears.
This scene had some bold Greek or British bard
Beheld of old, what stories had we heard
Of fairies, satyrs, and the nymphs their dames,
Their feasts, their revels, and their amorous flames!
'Tis still the same, although their airy shape
All but a quick poetic sight escape.

We subjoin an extract also from Denham's *Elegy*, in which it will appear, however, that the poet seems to have forgotten, that Shakspeare was buried on the banks of his own native Avon, not in Westminster Abbey, and that both he and Fletcher died long ere time had 'blasted their bays.'

ON THE DEATH OF MR. ABRAHAM COWLEY.

Old Chaucer, like the morning star,
To us discovers day from far.
His light those mists and clouds dissolv'd
Which our dark nation long involv'd;
But he, descending to the shades,
Darkness again the age invades;
Next (like Aurora) Spenser rose
Whose purple blush the day foreshows;
The other three with his own fires
Phœbus, the poet's god, inspires:
By Shakspeare's, Jonson's, Fletcher's lines,
Our stage's lustre Rome's outshines.
These poets near our princes sleep,
And in one grave their mansion keep.
They lived to see so many days,
Till time had blasted all their bays;
But cursed be the fatal hour
That pluck'd the fairest sweetest flower
That in the Muses' garden grew,
And amongst wither'd laurels threw.
Time, which made them their fame outlive,
To Cowley scarce did ripeness give.
Old mother wit and nature gave
Shakspeare and Fletcher all they have:
In Spenser and in Jonson, art
Of slower nature got the start;
But both in him so equal are,
None knows which bears the happiest share;
To him no author was unknown,
Yet what he wrote was all his own;
He melted not the ancient gold,
Nor with Ben Johnson did make bold
To plunder all the Roman stores
Of poets and of orators:
Horace his wit and Virgil's state
He did not steal, but emulate;
And when he would like them appear,
Their garb, but not their clothes, did wear:
He not from Rome alone, but Greece
Like Jason bought the golden fleece;
To him that language (though to none
Of th' others) as his own was known.
On a stiff gale, as Flaccus sings,
The Theban swan extends his wings,
When through th' ethereal clouds he flies
To the same pitch our swan doth rise;
Old Pindar's heights by him are reach'd,
When on that gale his wings are stretch'd;
His fancy and his judgment such,
Each to th' other seem'd too much;
His severe judgment giving law,
His modest fancy kept in awe.

Contemporary with Denham was the comparatively unknown poet, Chamberlayne—an author whose genius was imbued with a depth of poetical spirit to which the former was an entire stranger. Denham could reason fluently in verse, without any glaring faults of style; but such a description of a summer morning as the following, from Chamberlayne, was altogether beyond his powers:—

> The morning hath not lost her virgin blush,
> Nor step, but mine, soil'd the earth's tinsell'd robe.
> How full of heaven this solitude appears,
> This healthful comfort of the happy swain;
> Who from his hard but peaceful bed roused up,
> In 's morning exercise saluted is
> By a full quire of feather'd choristers,
> Wedding their notes to the enamour'd air!
> Here nature in her unaffected dress
> Plaited with valleys, and emboss'd with hills
> Enchas'd with silver streams, and fring'd with woods,
> Sits lovely in her native russet.

William Chamberlayne was born at Shaftesbury, Dorsetshire, in 1619. Of his family, and of his early education, nothing is now definitely known. He studied the medical profession, and afterward practiced as a physician in his native place; but he appears to have wielded the sword as well as the lancet, as he was present, and took part with the royalists, in the famous battle of Newbury. His circumstances, like those of Vaughan, seem to have been, during his whole life, far from flourishing; and he bitterly complains that his continuous poverty debarred him from the society of the congenial wits of the age. The latter part of his life was passed in the toils of his laborious profession, and his death occurred in 1688, the memorable year that witnessed the downfall of James the Second.

The principal works of Chamberlayne are *Love's Victory*, a tragic-comedy, published in 1658; and *Pharonnida, a Heroic Poem*, which appeared in the following year. The scene of the first is laid in the island of Sicily, and that of 'Pharonnida,' partly in Sicily and partly in Greece. With no court connection, no light or witty copies of verses to float him into popularity, relying solely on his too long and comparatively unattractive works—to appreciate which, through all the windings of romantic love, plots, escapes, and adventures, more time is required than the author's busy age could afford—we should not be surprised that Chamberlayne was an unsuccessful poet. His works were, indeed, almost entirely forgotten, till Campbell, in his 'Specimens of the Poets,' published in 1819, by quoting largely from 'Pharonnida,' and pointing out the 'rich breadth and variety of its scenes,' and the power and pathos of its characters and situations, drew attention to the passion, the imagery, the purity of sentiment, and the tenderness of description, which lay, 'like metals in the mine' in the neglected volume of this author. We do not, however, think that the works of Chamberlayne can ever be popular;

for though his genius is of a very high order, his beauties are constantly marred by infelicities of execution. But fine passages, like the description of morning already quoted, and that which follows, abound in every part of his works:—

——— Where every bough
Maintain'd a feather'd chorister to sing
Soft panegyrics, and the rude wings bring
Into a murmuring slumber, whilst the calm
Morn on each leaf did hang her liquid balm,
With an intent before the next sun's birth,
To drop it in those wounds, which the cleft earth
Receiv'd from last day's beams.

Of virgin purity, he says, with singular beauty of expression—

——— The morning pearls,
Dropt in the lily's spotless bosom, are
Less chastely cool, ere the meridian sun
Hath kiss'd them into heat.

In a grave narrative passage of 'Pharonnida,' the beauties of morning, of which, like Milton, he seems to have been peculiarly fond, are thus sweetlv touched off—

——— The glad birds had sung
A lullaby to-night, the lark was fled,
On dropping wings, up from his dewy bed
To fan them in the rising sunbeams.

We shall close these brief extracts with the following finely executed description of a dream:—

——— A strong prophetic dream,
Diverting by enigmas nature's stream,
Long hovering through the portals of her mind
On vain fantastic wings, at length did find
The glimmerings of obstructed reason, by
A brighter beam of pure divinity
Led into supernatural light, whose rays
As much transcended reason's, as the days
Dull mortal fires, faith apprehends to be
Beneath the glimmerings of divinity.
Her unimprison'd soul, disrob'd of all
Terrestrial thoughts (like its original
In heaven, pure and immaculate), a fit
Companion for those bright angels' wit
Which the gods made their messengers, to bear
This sacred truth, seeming transported where
Fix'd in the flaming centre of the world,
The heart o' th' microcosm, about which is hurl'd
The spangled curtains of the sky, within
Whose boundless orbs the circling planets spin
Those threads of time upon whose strength rely
The pond'rous burdens of mortality.

An adamantine world she sees, more pure,
More glorious far than this—fram'd to endure
The shock of doomsday's darts.

This passage so strikingly resembles the splendid opening lines of Dryden's *Religio Laici*, as to leave the impression that it must have suggested them.

Andrew Marvell, the assistant of Milton as Latin secretary under the protectorate of Cromwell, was the son of a clergyman, and was born at Kingston, upon Hull, where his father officiated, in 1620. He early evinced great aptness for learning, and such was his proficiency in his studies that before he reached the thirteenth year of his age he was admitted into Trinity College, Cambridge. Some monks, however, of the Jesuit order, who resided near the university, prevailed upon him to relinquish his studies and repair to London, where they placed him, as a clerk, in a bookstore. Here his father found him, and having convinced him of his error, easily persuaded him to return to Cambridge and resume his studies.

In 1638, Marvell took the degree of bachelor of arts; and about the same time he had the misfortune to lose his excellent father, who was unfortunately drowned, while crossing the Humber, in attendance upon the daughter of an intimate female friend, to her marriage in Lincolnshire. The lady, thus rendered childless, sent for young Marvell, and in order to render him all the return in her power for his sad bereavement, conferred upon him a very considerable fortune. Possessed thus of ample means for the purpose, he resolved to enlarge his information by foreign travel; and he accordingly visited, in succession, all the polite countries of the continent. At Rome he passed some time in close and severe study, and thence went to Constantinople, as secretary to the English embassy at that court.

Marvell's expenses abroad had drawn so very considerably upon his fortune, that, on his return to England, in 1653, he accepted the situation of tutor in languages to the daughter of General Fairfax; and four years after he became assistant to Milton, the Latin secretary of state, upon the recommendation of that great poet himself. Shortly before the Restoration, Marvell was elected member of parliament for his native city; and though not like Waller, an eloquent speaker, yet his consistency and integrity caused him to be highly esteemed and greatly respected. He is supposed to have been the last English member of parliament who was remunerated by his constituents for his services in the house. Charles the Second delighted in his society, and believing that every man had his price, he resolved to win Marvell over to his interest. With this view he sent his treasurer, Lord Danby, to wait upon him, with an offer of a place at court, and an immediate present of a thousand pounds. But the inflexible patriot resisted his offers, and it is said humorously illustrated his independence by calling his servant to witness that he had dined for three days successively on a shoulder of mutton! Marvell preserved his integrity to the last, and till his death, continued to satirize, with great wit and pungency, the profligacy and arbitrary measures of the court. He died on the sixteenth of August, 1678, without any previous illness or visible decay, which gave rise to a report that he had been poisoned. The town of Hull voted an appropriate sum to erect a monument to his memory; but the court interfered, and forbade the votive tribute.

As an author, Marvell's reputation rested, in his day, much more upon his prose than upon his poetry. As his prosaic works were, however, chiefly written for temporary purposes, they have passed out of mind with the circumstances that produced them. In 1672, he attacked the future Bishop Parker, in a piece entitled *The Rehearsal Transposed*, and with great force of argument vindicated the fair fame of Milton, who he says, 'was and is a man of as great learning and sharpness of wit as any man living.' One of Marvell's treatises, *An Account of the Growth of Popery and Arbitrary Government in England*, was considered so formidable that a reward was offered for the discovery of the author and printer. Among the first, if not the very first traces of that vein of sportive humor and raillery on national manners and absurdities, which was afterward carried to perfection by Addison, Steele, and others, may be found in Marvell. He wrote with great liveliness, point and vigor, though he was often too coarse and personal. His poetry is easy and elegant, rather than elevated and forcible: it was an embellishment to his character of patriot and controversialist, but not a 'substantive ground of honor and distinction.' Yet none but a good and amiable man could have written verses so full of tenderness and pathos as the following:—

THE EMIGRANTS IN BERMUDAS.

Where the remote Bermudas ride
In th' ocean's bosom unespied,
From a small boat that row'd along
The list'ning winds received their song.
'What should we do but sing His praise
That led us through the watery maze
Unto an isle so long unknown,
And yet far kinder than our own?
Where He the huge sea monsters racks,
That left the deep upon their backs;
He lands us on a grassy stage,
Safe from the storms and prelates, rage.
He gave us this eternal spring
Which here enamels every thing,
And sends the fowls to us in care,
On daily visits through the air.
He hangs in shades the orange bright,
Like golden lamps in a green night,
And does in the pomegranates close
Jewels more rich than Ormus shows.
He makes the figs our mouths to meet.
And throws the melons at our feet.

But apples, plants of such a price,
No tree could ever bear them twice.
With cedars, chosen by his hand,
From Lebanon he stores the land;
And makes the hollow seas that roar,
Proclaim the ambergris on shore.
He cast (of which we rather boast)
The Gospel's pearl upon our coast;
And in these rocks for us did frame
A temple where to sound his name.
Oh let our voice his praise exalt,
Till we arrive at Heaven's vault,
Which then perhaps rebounding may
Echo beyond the Mexic bay.'
Thus sang they in the English boat,
A holy and a cheerful note,
And all the way to guide their chime
With falling oars they kept the time.

Lecture the Twenty-Third.

ABRAHAM COWLEY—THOMAS STANLEY—THE DUCHESS OF NEWCASTLE—KATHERINE PHILIPS—CHARLES COTTON—JOHN DRYDEN.

WE are now in the midst of the poets of the Commonwealth, and of the Restoration. Authors were still a select class, and literature, the delight of the learned and the ingenious, had not yet become food for the multitude. The chivalrous and romantic spirit which prevailed in the age of Elizabeth, had even, before her death, begun to yield to more sober and practical views of human life and society; and a spirit of inquiry was fast spreading among the people. The long period of peace under James the First, and the progress of commerce, gave scope to domestic improvement, and fostered the reasoning faculties, rather than the imagination. The reign of Charles the First, a prince of taste and accomplishments, partially revived the style of the Elizabethan era, but its lustre extended little beyond the court and the nobility. During the civil war, and the protectorate, poetry and the drama were buried under the strife and anxiety of contending factions. Cromwell, with a just and generous spirit, boasted that he would make the name of an Englishman, as great as ever that of a Roman had been; and he realized the fulfillment of this declaration in Blake's naval triumphs, and the unquestioned supremacy of England abroad; but neither the time nor the inclination of the Protector allowed him to be a patron of literature. Charles the Second was, by natural powers, birth, and education, better fitted for such a task; but he had imbibed a false taste, which, added to his indolent and sensual disposition, was as injurious to art and literature as to the public morals. Poetry now declined, and was degraded from a high and noble art, to a mere courtly amusement, a pander to immorality. Happily, to this general truth, there were a few brilliant exceptions; and among these, Cowley, after Milton, is, perhaps, the most conspicuous.

ABRAHAM COWLEY, was born in the city of London in 1618, and was the posthumous son of a respectable grocer. His mother, through the influence of some powerful friends, procured admission for him as a king's scholar into Westminster school; and in his eighteenth year he was elected a member of Trinity College, Cambridge. Cowley 'lisped in numbers;' and in 1633, before he had attained the sixteenth year of his age, and while yet at Westminster, he published a volume of poems under the appropriate title of *Poetical Blossoms.* According to his own statement, a copy of Spenser's poems used to lie in his mother's parlor, with the reading of which he was so much delighted, that to its influence he attributes his first poetical impulses. The intensity of his youthful ambition may be seen from the two first lines in his miscellanies—

What shall I do to be forever known,
And make the age to come mine own?

In 1643, Cowley, having previously taken his master's degree, was ejected from Cambridge for being a royalist; upon which he entered St. John's College, Oxford, and there prosecuted his studies, until his affection for the royal family induced him to enter into the service of the king. Here he became intimately acquainted with Lord Falkland and many other eminent men, whom the fortune of the war had drawn together. During the heat of the civil strife, he was settled in the family of the Earl of St. Albans; and when the queen mother was forced to retire, for safety, into France, he attended her thither, and remained in that country twelve years, the whole of which were passed, either in bearing a share in the distresses of the royal family, or in exertions to promote their interest. He was sent on various embassies, and deciphered the correspondence of Charles and his queen, which, for years, occupied his exclusive time.

At length, the Restoration came, with all its hopes and fears. England anticipated happy days, and loyalty ample reward for its devotion to the royal cause; but both were sadly disappointed. Cowley expected to be made master of the Savoy, or to receive some other appointment equally advantageous; but his claims were entirely disregarded. In his youth he had written an *Ode to Brutus*, which was now remembered to his disadvantage; and a dramatic production, *The Cutter of Coleman Street*, which he brought out soon after the Restoration, and in which the jollity and debauchery of the cavaliers are painted in strong colors, was misrepresented, or misconstrued, at court. This disappointment Cowley felt so keenly, that he at once resolved to retire into the country. He had only just passed his fortieth year, but the most important part of his life had been spent in incessant labor, amid dangers and suspense. 'He always professed,' says his biographer Sprat, 'that he went off the world as it was man's, into the same world as it was nature's, and as it was God's. The whole compass of the creation, and all the wonderful effects of the divine wisdom, were the constant prospect of his senses and his thoughts. And, indeed, he entered with great advantage on the studies of nature, even as the first great men of antiquity did, who were generally both poets and philosophers.'

Though disappointed, Cowley was not, however, altogether neglected; for he obtained, through the influence of Lord St. Albans, and the Duke of

Buckingham, the lease of some lands belonging to the queen, worth about three hundred pounds per annum—a decent pension, at least, for his retirement. He finally settled at Chertsey, on the banks of the Thames, where his house may still be seen. Here he cultivated his fields, his garden, and his plants; he wrote of solitude and obscurity, of the perils of greatness, and the happiness of liberty. He renewed his acquaintance with the beloved poets of antiquity, whom, in ease and elegance, and in commemorating the charms of a country life, he sometimes rivalled; and here also he composed his fine prose discourses, so full of gentle thoughts, and well-digested knowledge, heightened by a delightful bonhommie and communicativeness worthy of even a Horace or a Montaigne. Cowley was not, however, happy in his retirement. Solitude, that had so long wooed him to her arms, was a phantom that vanished in his embrace. He had, it is true, attained the long-wished-for object of his studious youth and busy manhood—the woods and the fields at length inclosed the 'melancholy Cowley' in their shades; but happiness was still distant. He had quitted the 'monster London;' he had gone out from Sodom, but had not found the little Zoar of his dreams. The place of his retreat was ill selected, and the change of situation materially affected his health. The people of the country, he soon found, were no better, or more innocent, than those of the town. He could not collect his rents, and the grass of his meadows was nightly eaten up by cattle let into them by his neighbors. From this harassing situation this amiable and accomplished man of genius was at length released by his death, which occurred on the twenty-eighth of July, 1667. His remains were interred, with great pomp, in the poet's corner in Westminster Abbey, and the king, when he received intelligence of the bereavement which the nation had sustained, graciously remarked that, 'Cowley had not left a better man behind him.'

The poems of Cowley are *Miscellanies*, *The Mistress*, or *Love Verses*, *Pindaric Odes*, and the *Davideis, a heroic poem of the Troubles of David.* The peculiar character of his genius is happily expressed by Pope in the following lines:—

Who now reads Cowley? If he pleases yet,
His moral pleases, not his pointed wit:
Forget his epic, nay Pindaric art,
But still I love the language of his heart.

Cowley's 'Love Poems' are generally fantastic and sickly, and it is evident that heart had no share in them; but his 'Anacreontics' are easy, lively, and full of spirit. They are redolent of joy and youth, and of images of natural and poetic beauty, that touch the feeling as well as the fancy. His 'Pindaric Odes,' though deformed by metaphysical conceits, though they do not roll the full flood of Pindar's unnavigable song, though we admit that even the art of Gray was higher, yet contain some noble lines and illustrations. The 'Davideis' is, as a whole, a tedious and unfinished poem, but the extract which follows, containing an account of the Creation, is full of eloquence and poetry, and shows how well Cowley was capable of writing in the heroic couplet:—

THE CREATION.

They sung how God spoke-out the World's vast ball,
From nothing; and from nowhere call'd forth all.
No Nature yet, or place for 't to possess,
But an unbottom'd gulf of emptiness;
Full of himself, th' Almighty sate, his own
Palace, and without solitude alone.
But he was goodness whole, and all things will'd;
Which ere they were, his active word fulfill'd:
And their astonished heads o' th' sudden rear'd;
An unshaped kind of something first appear'd,
Confessing its new being, and undrest,
As if it stepp'd in haste before the rest;
Yet, buried in this matter's darksome womb,
Lay the rich seeds of every thing to come;
From hence the cheerful flame leap'd up so high,
Close at its heels the nimble air did fly;
Dull Earth with his own weight did downwards pierce
To the fix'd navel of the Universe,
And was quite lost in waters; till God said
To the proud Sea, 'Shrink in your insolent head;
See how the gaping Earth has made you place!'
That durst not murmur, but shrunk in apace:
Since when, his bounds are set; at which in vain
He foams and rages, and turns back again.
With richer stuff he bade Heaven's fabric shine,
And from him a quick spring of light divine
Swell'd up the Sun, from whence his cherishing flame
Fills the whole world, like him from whom it came.
He smooth'd the rough-cast Moon's imperfect mould,
And comb'd her beamy locks with sacred gold:
'Be thou,' said he, 'Queen of the mournful night!'
And as he spake, she rose, clad o'er in light,
With thousand Stars attending in her train,
With her they rise, with her they set again.
Then Herbs peep'd forth, now Trees admiring stood,
And smelling flowers painted the infant wood;
Then flocks of Birds through the glad air did flee,
Joyful, and safe before Man's luxury,
Singing their Maker in their untaught lays:
Nay the mute Fish witness no less his praise;
For those he made, and clothed with silver scales,
From Minnows to those living islands, Whales,
Beasts, too, were his command; what could he more?
Yes, Man he could, the bond of all before;
In him he all things with strange order hurl'd,
In him that full abridgment of the World!

The following lyric, also from the same poem, in which David speaks of his love for Saul's daughter, is a perfect gem:—

Awake, awake my Lyre!
And tell thy silent master's humble tale,
In sounds that may prevail;
Sounds that gentle thoughts inspire:
Though so exalted she,
And I so lowly be,
Tell her, such different notes make all thy harmony!

Hark! how the strings awake!
And though the moving hand approach not near,
Themselves with awful fear
A kind of numerous trembling make:
Now all thy forces try,
Now all thy charms apply,
Revenge upon her ear the conquests of her eye.

Weak Lyre! thy virtue sure
Is useless here, since thou art only found
To cure, but not to wound;
And she to wound but not to cure:
Too weak too wilt thou prove
My passion to remove
Physic to other ills, thou 'rt nourishment to Love.

Sleep, sleep again my Lyre!
For thou canst never tell my humble tale
In sounds that will prevail;
Nor gentle thoughts in her inspire;
All thy vain mirth lay by,
Bid thy strings silent lie;
Sleep, sleep again, my Lyre! and let thy master die!

The following ode on the death of Cowley's college companion, Harvey, is highly imaginative, and abounds in tenderness:—

It was a dismal and a fearful night,
Scarce could the morn drive on th' unwilling light,
When sleep, death's image, left my troubled breast,
By something liker death possest.
My eyes with tears did uncommanded flow,
And on my soul hung the dull weight
Of some intolerable fate.
What bell was that? Ah me! too much I know.

My sweet companion, and my gentle peer,
Why hast thou left me thus unkindly here,
Thy end forever, and my life to moan?
O thou hast left me all alone!
Thy soul and body when death's agony
Besieged around thy noble heart,
Did not with more reluctance part
Than I, my dearest friend, do part from thee.

My dearest friend, would I had died for thee!
Life and this world henceforth will tedious be.
Nor shall I know hereafter what to do,
    If once my griefs prove tedious too.
Silent and sad I walk about all day,
    As sullen ghosts stalk speechless by
    Where their hid treasures lie;
Alas, my treasure's gone! why do I stay?

He was my friend, the truest friend on earth;
A strong and mighty influence join'd our birth.
Nor did we envy the most sounding name.
    By friendship given of old to fame,
None but his brethren he, and sisters, knew,
    Whom the kind youth preferred to me;
    And ev'n in that we did agree,
For much above myself I loved them too.

Say, for you saw us, ye immortal lights,
How oft unwearied have we spent the nights?
Till the Ledæan stars, so fam'd for love,
    Wonder'd at us from above.
We spent them not in toys, in lusts, or wine,
    But search of deep philosophy,
    Wit, eloquence, and poetry;
Arts which I lov'd, for they, my friend, were thine.

Ye fields of Cambridge, our dear Cambridge, say,
Have ye not seen us walking every day?
Was there a tree about, which did not know
    The love betwixt us two?
Henceforth, ye gentle trees, forever fade;
    Or your sad branches thicker join
    And into darksome shades combine;
Dark as the grave wherein my friend is laid.

* * * * *

To him my muse made haste with every strain,
Whilst it was new, and warm yet from the brain.
He lov'd my worthless rhymes, and like a friend
    Would find out something to commend.
Hence now, my muse, thou canst not me delight;
    Be this my latest verse,
    With which I now adorn his hearse;
And this my grief, without thy help shall write.

* * * * * *

His mirth was the pure spirits of various wit,
Yet never did his God or friends forget,
And, when deep talk and wisdom came in view,
    Retir'd and gave to them their due.
For the rich help of books he always took,
    Though his own searching mind before
    Was so with notions written o'er,
As if wise nature had made that her book.

* * * * *

With as much zeal, devotion, piety,
He always liv'd as other saints do die;
Still with his soul severe account he kept,
Weeping all debts out ere he slept.
Then down in peace and innocence he lay
Like the sun's laborious light,
Which still in water sets at night,
Unsullied with his journey of the day.

Wondrous young man, why wert thou made so good,
To be snatcht hence ere better understood?
Snatcht before half enough of thee was seen!
Thou ripe, and yet thy life but green!
Nor could thy friends take their last sad farewell
But danger and infectious death,
Maliciously seized on that breath
Where life, spirit, pleasure, always used to dwell.

EPITAPH ON THE LIVING AUTHOR.

Here, stranger, in this humble nest,
Here Cowley sleeps; here lies,
Scaped all the toils that life molest,
And its superfluous joys.

Here, in no sordid poverty,
And no inglorious ease,
He braves the world, and can defy
Its frowns and flatteries.

The little earth, he asks, survey:
Is he not dead indeed?
'Light lie that earth,' good stranger, pray,
'Nor thorn upon it breed!'

With flowers, fit emblem of his fame,
Compass your poet round;
With flowers of every fragrant name,
Be his warm ashes crown'd!

As Cowley holds a distinguished position among the prose writers of this age, and has ever been placed at the head of those who first cultivated that clear, easy, and natural style which was afterward brought so nearly to perfection by Addison, we shall here introduce, as an appropriate specimen, the following account of himself:—

OF MYSELF.

It is a hard and nice subject for a man to write of himself; it grates his own heart to say any thing of disparagement, and the reader's ears to hear any thing of praise from him. There is no danger from me of offending him in this kind; neither my mind, nor my body, nor my fortune, allow me any materials for that vanity. It is sufficient, for my own contentment, that they have preserved me from being scandalous, or remarkable on the defective side. But besides that, I shall here speak of myself only in relation to the subject of these precedent discourses, and shall be likelier thereby to fall into the contempt, than rise up to the estimation of most people. As far as my memory can return back into my past life, before I knew or was capable of guessing what the world, or glories, or business of it were, the natural affections of my soul gave a secret bent of aversion from them, as some plants are said to turn away from others, by an antipathy imperceptible to themselves, and inscrutable to man's understanding. Even when I was a very young boy at school, instead of running about on holydays, and playing with my fellows, I was wont to steal from them, and walk into the fields, either alone with a book, or with some one companion, if I could find any of the same temper. I was then, too, so much an enemy to constraint, that my masters could never prevail on me, by any persuasions or encouragements, to learn, without book, the common rules of grammar, in which they dispensed with me alone, because they found I made a shift to do the usual exercise out of my own reading and observation. That I was then of the same mind that I am now (which, I confess, I wonder at myself), may appear at the latter end of an ode which I made when I was but thirteen years old, and which was then printed, with many other verses. The beginning of it is boyish; but of this part which I here set down (if a very little were corrected), I should hardly now be much ashamed.

This only grant me, that my means may lie
Too low for envy, for contempt too high.
    Some honour I would have,
Not from great deeds, but good alone;
Th' unknown are better than ill-known.
    Rumour can ope the grave:
Acquaintance I would have; but when 't depends
Not on the number, but the choice of friends.

Books should, not business, entertain the light,
And sleep, as undisturb'd as death, the night.
    My house a cottage, more
Than palace, and should fitting be
For all my use, no luxury.
    My garden painted o'er
With Nature's hand, not Art's; and pleasures yield,
Horace might envy in his Sabine field.

Thus would I double my life's fading space,
For he that runs it well, twice runs his race.
    And in this true delight,
These unbought sports, that happy state,
I would not fear nor wish my fate,
    But boldly say each night,
To-morrow let my sun his beams display,
Or in clouds hide them; I have liv'd to-day.

You may see by it I was even then acquainted with the poets (for the conclusion is taken out of Horace); and perhaps it was the immature and immoderate love of them which stamped first, or rather engraved, the characters in me. They were like letters cut in the bark of a young tree, which, with the tree, still grow proportionably. But how this love came to be produced in me so early, is a hard question: I believe I can tell the particular little chance that filled my head first with such chimes of verse, as have never since left ringing there: for I remember when I began to read, and take some pleasure in it, there was wont to lie in my mother's parlour (I know not by what accident, for she herself never in her life read any book but of devotion); but there was wont to lie Spenser's works; this I happened to fall upon, and was infinitely delighted with the stories of the knights, and giants, and monsters, and brave houses, which I found everywhere there (though my understanding had little to do with all this); and by degrees, with the tinkling of the rhyme, and dance of the numbers; so that I think I had read him all over before I was twelve years old. With these affections of mind, and my heart wholly set upon letters, I went to the university; but was soon torn from thence by that public violent storm, which would suffer nothing to stand where it did, but rooted up every plant, even from the princely cedars, to me, the hyssop. Yet I had as good fortune as could have befallen me in such a tempest; for I was cast by it into the family of one of the best persons, and into the court of one of the best princesses in the world. Now, though I was here engaged in ways most contrary to the original design of my life; that is, into much company, and no small business, and into a daily sight of greatness, both militant and triumphant (for that was the state then of the English and the French courts); yet all this was so far from altering my opinion, that it only added the confirmation of reason to that which was before but natural inclination. I saw plainly all the paint of that kind of life, the nearer I came to it; and that beauty which I did not fall in love with, when, for aught I knew, it was real, was not like to bewitch or entice me when I saw it was adulterate. I met with several great persons, whom I liked very well, but could not perceive that any part of their greatness was to be liked or desired, no more than I would be glad or content to be in a storm, though I saw many ships which rid safely and bravely in it. A storm would not agree with my stomach, if it did with my courage; though I was in a crowd of as good company as could be found anywhere, though I was in business of great and honourable trust, though I eat at the best table, and enjoyed the best conveniences for present subsistence that ought to be desired by a man of my condition, in banishment and public distresses; yet I could not abstain from renewing my old school-boy's wish in a copy of verses to the same effect:

> Well, then, I now do plainly see
> This busy world and I shall ne'er agree, &c.

And I never then proposed to myself any other advantage from his majesty's happy restoration, but the getting into some moderately convenient retreat in the country, which I thought in that case I might easily have compassed, as well as some others, who, with no greater probabilities or pretences, have arrived to extraordinary fortunes. But I had before written a shrewd prophecy against myself, and I think Apollo inspired me in the truth, though not in the elegance of it:

> Thou neither great at court, nor in the war,
> Nor at the Exchange shall be, nor at the wrangling bar;
> Content thyself with the small barren praise
> Which thy neglected verse does raise, &c.

However, by the failing of the forces which I had expected, I did not quit the design which I had resolved on; I cast myself into it a *corpus perditum*, without making capitulations, or taking counsel of fortune. But God laughs at man, who says to his soul, Take thy ease: I met presently not only with many little incumbrances and impediments, but with so much sickness (a new misfortune to me) as would have spoiled the happiness of an emperor as well as mine. Yet I do neither repent nor alter my course; *Non ego perfidum dixi sacramentum.*[1] Nothing shall separate me from a mistress which I have loved so long, and have now at last married; though she neither has brought me a rich portion, nor lived yet so quietly with me as I hoped from her.

---

[1] I have not falsely sworn.

——— Nec vos, dulcissima mundi
Nomina, vos musæ, libertas, otia, libri,
Hortique, sylvæque, animâ remanente relinquam.

——— Nor by me e'er shall you,
You of all names the sweetest and the best,
You muses, books, and liberty, and rest;
You gardens, fields, and woods forsaken be,
As long as life itself forsakes not me.

From Cowley, who has occupied our attention longer than we had designed, we pass to notice very briefly, Thomas Stanley, the Duchess of Newcastle, Katherine Philips, and Charles Cotton; and shall then close our present remarks with the justly celebrated John Dryden.

THOMAS STANLEY, the learned editor of Æschylus, was the son of Sir Thomas Stanley, knight, of Camberlow-Green, in Hertfordshire, and was born in 1625. In the fourteenth year of his age he entered Pembroke Hall, Cambridge, and soon distinguished himself as a linguist and philosopher. Having successfully pursued his studies at Cambridge, and taken his degrees, he afterward became incorporated into the university of Oxford, and thence passed to the continent, making the tour of France, Italy, and Spain, and remaining in each of these countries a sufficient length of time to perfect himself in its language. On his return to England he entered the Middle Temple as a student of law, and while residing there, married the daughter of Sir James Engan, of Flower, in the county of Northampton. He did not, however, suffer this change in his condition to interfere, in the least degree, with his application to study, but persevered with such untiring industry, that, while yet a comparatively young man, he became one of the most accomplished scholars of the age.

Stanley's first serious literary performance was a *History of Philosophy*, 'containing the lives, opinions, actions, and discourses of the philosophers of every sect.' This work being very popular, passed through four editions in English in comparatively rapid succession, and was then translated into the Latin tongue, and published at Leipsic in 1711. The account of the Oriental learning and philosophy with which it concludes, is both curious and interesting, and has often received the commendation of learned foreigners. He next published his Æschylus, the text of which he restored, and illustrated it with so much learning as to excite the admiration of all who are able to appreciate the labor he bestowed upon it. The remainder of his life was chiefly spent in editing other Greek poets, among whom were Sophocles, and Euripides; and his death occurred in 1678.

The greater number of the original poems of Stanley were written while he was at the university; and they are remarkable for richness of style, of thought, and of expression, though somewhat tinctured with the conceits of the age. The following are among the happiest of his effusions:—

THE TOMB.

When, cruel fair one, I am slain
By thy disdain,
And, as a trophy of thy scorn,
To some old tomb am borne,
Thy fetters must their power bequeath
To those of Death;
Nor can thy flame immortal burn,
Like monumental fires within an urn:
Thus freed from thy proud empire, I shall prove
There is more liberty in Death than Love.

And when forsaken lovers come
To see my tomb,
Take heed thou mix not with the crowd,
And (as a victor) proud,
To view the spoils thy beauty made,
Press near my shade,
Lest thy too cruel breath or name
Should fan my ashes back into a flame,
And thou, devour'd by this revengeful fire,
His sacrifice, who died as thine, expire.

But if cold earth, or marble, must
Conceal my dust,
Whilst hid in some dark ruins, I,
Dumb and forgotten, lie,
The pride of all thy victory
Will sleep with me;
And they who should attest thy glory,
Will, or forget, or not believe this story.
Then to increase thy triumph, let me rest,
Since by thine eye slain, buried in thy breast.

THE LOSS.

Yet ere I go,
Disdainful Beauty, thou shalt be
So wretched as to know
What joys thou fling'st away with me.

A faith so bright,
As Time or Fortune could not rust;
So firm, that lovers might
Have read thy story in my dust,

And crown'd thy name
With laurel verdant as thy youth,
Whilst the shrill voice of Fame
Spread wide thy beauty and my truth.

This thou hast lost,
For all true lovers, when they find
That my just aims were crost,
Will speak thee lighter than the wind.

And none will lay
Any oblation on thy shrine,
But such as would betray
Thy faith to faiths as false as thine.

Yet, if thou choose
On such thy freedom to bestow,
Affection may excuse,
For love from sympathy doth flow.

MARGARET, Duchess of Newcastle, was the daughter of Sir Charles Lucas, and was born about 1622. She early evinced a fondness for literary pursuits, and was educated with the greatest care. Having been appointed one of the maids of honor to Henrietta Maria, consort of Charles the First, she accompanied the queen to France, and at Paris married the Marquis of Newcastle, in 1645. The marquis, soon after their marriage, took up his residence at Antwerp, and there his lady wrote and published, in 1653, a volume entitled *Poems and Fancies.* The marquis assisted her in her compositions, and so indefatigable were the noble pair, that they filled nearly twelve volumes folio, with plays, poems, orations and philosophical discourses. On the restoration of Charles the Second, the marquis and his lady returned to England, and lived in domestic happiness and devoted loyalty until her death, which occurred in 1673.

As a poetess, the Duchess possessed invention, knowledge, and imagination, but wanted energy and taste. *The Pastime and Recreation of the Queen of Fairies in Fairy Land*, is her most popular work. The following description of the elvish queen is extremely fine:—

She on a dewy leaf doth bathe,
And as she sits, the leaf doth wave;
There like a new-fallen flake of snow,
Doth her white limbs in beauty show.
Her garments fair her maids put on,
Made of the pure light from the sun.

Mirth and Melancholy are also very fancifully personified. The former woos the poetess to dwell with her, promising sport and pleasure, and drawing the following gloomy but forcible and poetical sketch of her rival Melancholy:—

Her voice is low, and gives a hollow sound;
She hates the light, and is in darkness found;
Or sits with blinking lamps, or tapers small,
Which various shadows make against the wall.
She loves naught else but noise which discord makes,
As croaking frogs whose dwelling is in lakes;
The raven's hoarse, the mandrake's hollow groan,
And shrieking owls which fly i' the night alone;
The tolling bell, which for the dead rings out;
A mill, where rushing waters run about;

The roaring winds, which shake the cedars tall,
Plough up the seas, and beat the rocks withal.
She loves to walk in the still moonshine night,
And in a thick dark grove she takes delight;
In hollow caves, thatch'd houses, and low cells,
She loves to live, and there alone she dwells.

To this passage we add the picture of Melancholy's dwellings, as drawn by herself:—

I dwell in groves that gilt are with the sun;
Sit on the banks by which clear waters run;
In summer's hot down in a shade I lie;
My music is the buzzing of a fly;
I walk in meadows, where grows fresh green grass;
In fields, where corn is high, I often pass;
Walk up the hills, where round I prospects see,
Some bushy woods, and some all champaigns be;
Returning back, I in fresh pastures go,
To hear how sheep do bleat, and cows do low;
In winter cold, when nipping frosts come on,
Then I do live in a small house alone;
Although 'tis plain, yet cleanly 'tis within,
Like to a soul that's pure, and clear from sin;
And there I dwell in quiet and still peace,
Not fill'd with cares how riches to increase;
I wish nor seek for vain and fruitless pleasures;
No riches are, but what the mind intreasures.
Thus am I solitary, live alone,
Yet better lov'd, the more that I am known;
And though my face ill-favour'd at first sight,
After acquaintance, it will give delight.
Refuse me not, for I shall constant be;
Maintain your credit and your dignity.

Katherine Philips, born in 1631, was a worthy contemporary of the Duchess of Newcastle. She was honored with the praise of Cowley and Dryden, and Jeremy Taylor addressed to her a Discourse on Friendship. This amiable lady was the wife of James Philips of the Priory, Cardigan, and died of the small-pox, in the year 1664. Her poetical name of 'Orinda' was very popular with her contemporaries; but her effusions are said to have been published without her consent. The following lines *On a Country Life* offer a fair specimen of the productions of her delicate muse:—

A COUNTRY LIFE.

How sacred and how innocent
  A country-life appears,
How free from tumult, discontent,
  From flattery or fears!

This was the first and happiest life,
  When man enjoy'd himself,

Till pride exchanged peace for strife,
And happiness for pelf.

'Twas here the poets were inspir'd,
Here taught the multitude;
The brave they here with honour fir'd,
And civiliz'd the rude.

The golden age did entertain
No passion but of love:
The thoughts of ruling and of gain
Did ne'er their fancies move.

Them that do covet only rest,
A cottage will suffice:
It is not brave to be possess'd
Of earth, but to despise.

Opinion is the rate of things,
From hence our peace doth flow;
I have a better fate than kings,
Because I think it so.

When all the stormy world doth roar,
How unconcerned am I!
I can not fear to tumble lower,
Who never could be high.

Secure in these unenvied walls,
I think not on the state,
And pity no man's ease that falls
From his ambition's height.

Silence and innocence are safe;
A heart that's nobly true,
At all these little arts can laugh,
That do the world subdue.

The name of Charles Cotton calls up a number of pleasing associations. It is best known from its piscatory and affectionate union with that of good old Izaak Walton, but Cotton was a cheerful, witty, accomplished gentleman, and only wanted prudence to have made him one of the leading characters of his day. He was the son of Sir George Cotton, and was born in Staffordshire, in 1630. His father, at his death, which occurred in 1658, left him an estate at Ashbourne, in Derbyshire, near the river Dove, so celebrated in the annals of trout-fishing. The property at the time was greatly encumbered, and the poet soon added to its burdens. As a means of procuring relief, therefore, as well as recreation, Cotton translated several works from the French and the Italian, with both of which languages he seems to have been critically familiar. Of these translations, that of the Essays of Montaigne was dedicated to the Marquis of Halifax, and was of such rare excellence as to receive the unqualified approbation of that learned and accomplished nobleman.

In 1670, when forty years of age, Cotton obtained a captain's commission in the army; and soon after made a fortunate marriage with the Countess Dowager of Ardglass, who possessed an annual income of fifteen hundred pounds. The lady's fortune was, however, secured from his mismanagement, and his embarrassments were still unrelieved; but amidst them all, his happy, careless disposition seems to have enabled him to study, to angle, and to afford delight to his friends. His death occurred in 1687, and in the fifty-eighth year of his age.

Besides his numerous translations, Cotton published several burlesques and travesties, the principal of which was *Lucian burlesqued; or the Scoffer Scoffed.* He wrote, also, some copies of verses full of genuine poetry, and as a poet, he may properly be ranked with Marvell. The following beautiful stanzas were addressed to Izaak Walton as an invitation to him to visit the poet, and angle with him in the Dove. Though Walton was at that time in the eighty-third year of his age, yet the invitation seems to have been accepted:—

INVITATION TO IZAAK WALTON.

Whilst in this cold and blustering clime,
  Where bleak winds howl, and tempests roar,
We pass away the roughest time
  Has been of many years before;

Whilst from the most tempestuous nooks
  The chillest blasts our peace invade,
And by great rains our smallest brooks
  Are almost navigable made;

Whilst all the ills are so improv'd
  Of this dead quarter of the year,
That even you, so much belov'd,
  We would not now wish with us here:

In this estate, I say, it is
  Some comfort to us to suppose,
That in a better clime than this,
  You, our dear friend, have more repose;

And some delight to me the while,
  Though nature now does weep in rain,
To think that I have seen her smile,
  And happy may I do again.

If the all-ruling Power please
  We live to see another May,
We 'll recompense an age of these
  Foul days in one fine fishing day.

We then shall have a day or two,
  Perhaps a week, wherein to try
What the best master's hand can do
  With the most deadly killing fly.

A day with not too bright a beam;
  A warm, but not a scorching sun;
A southern gale to curl the stream;
  And, master, half our work is done.

Then, whilst behind some bush we wait
  The scaly people to betray,
We 'll prove it just, with treacherous bait,
  To make the preying trout our prey;

And think ourselves in such an hour,
  Happier than those, though not so high,
Who, like leviathans, devour
  Of meaner men the smaller fry.

This, my best friend, at my poor home,
  Shall be our pastime and our theme;
But then—should you not deign to come,
  You make all this a flattering dream.

JOHN DRYDEN, one of the most voluminous writers of the language, ana the most popular poet of the age of Charles the Second, was the son of Erasmus Dryden, of Tichmersh, in Northamptonshire, and was born at Aldwincle, in that county, on the ninth of August, 1631. His early studies were pursued as king's scholar at Westminster school, where his attainments seem to have been rather solid, than brilliant, as he did not leave that school until the nineteenth year of his age, when he was elected to Trinity College, Cambridge. Dryden, both at school and at college, had occasionally indulged his poetic vein, and on one occasion translated 'The third satire of Persius,' as an evening exercise; but his first important poetical production did not appear until 1658, and was then drawn forth in the form of heroic stanzas on the death of Oliver Cromwell. The ripeness of style and versification of these stanzas, indicated the future excellence of the author; and in all Waller's poems on the same subject, there is nothing equal to such verses as the following:—

His grandeur he deriv'd from heaven alone,
  For he was great ere Fortune made him so;
And wars, like mists that rise against the sun,
  Made him but greater seem, not greater grow.

Nor was he like those stars which only shine
  When to pale mariners they storms portend;
He had his calmer influence, and his mien
  Did love and majesty together blend.

Dryden's father was a strict Puritan, and he himself had been educated in that faith; but when monarchy was restored, he went over with the tuneful throng who welcomed Charles the Second to England. He had now done with the Puritans, and was prepared to write poetical addresses to the king and the lord chancellor. The amusements of the drama, which had been suppressed during the commonwealth and the administration of Cromwell, were revived after the Restoration, and Dryden became a candidate for theatrical laurels. In 1662, and the two following years, he produced *The Wild Gallant*, *The Rival Ladies*, and *The Indian Emperor*, the last of which was very popular. Dryden's name was now conspicuous; and in 1665 he married the Lady Elizabeth Howard, daughter of the Earl of Berkshire. The marriage, however, added neither to his wealth nor his happiness; and the poet afterward revenged himself by constantly inveighing against matrimony. The probability is that his literary habits deprived his wife of his society to an extent to which ladies are not inclined quietly to submit; and, accordingly, when she petulantly 'wished to be a book, that she might enjoy more of his company,' he is represented to have ungallantly replied, 'Be an almanac then, my dear, that I may change you once a year.' As a farther expression of his contempt for the female sex, he, in his play of the *Spanish Friar*, most impolitely states, that, 'woman was made from the dross and refuse of a man.' Indeed, all Dryden's plays, being twenty-five in number, are marked with the indelicacy and gross licentiousness of the age—vices which he fostered rather than attempted to check.

In 1667, Dryden published a long poem, *Annus Mirabilis*, being an account of the important events of the year 1666. The style and versification seem to have been copied from Davenant; but Dryden's performance fully sustained his previous reputation. About the same time he wrote an *Essay on Dramatic Poesy*, in which he vindicates the use of rhyme in tragedy. The style of his prose is easy, natural, and graceful; and his thoughts seem to have flown forth without an apparent effort. He next undertook to write for the king's players no less than three dramas a year, for which he was to receive annually three hundred pounds. During his engagement with the king's players, he was made poet-laureate and royal historiographer, with a salary of two hundred pounds. These were golden days for the poet; but they did not last long. His irritable temper and arrogant disposition involved him in controversies and quarrels; and the Earl of Rochester, in order to mortify him, set up a miserable rhymster by the name of Settle, as his opponent. Dryden was also successfully ridiculed by Buckingham, in his 'Rehearsal.'

These instances of opposition drew forth the first of those masterly satires which have immortalized Dryden's genius, and placed his name among the names of the great poets of the language. In 1681, he published the satire of *Absalom and Achitophel*, written in the style of a Scriptural narrative, the names and situations of personages in the holy text being applied to those contemporaries to whom the author assigned places in his poem. The Duke of Monmouth was Absalom, and the Earl of Shaftesbury, Achitophel; while the Duke of Buckingham was drawn under the character of Zimri. The success of this bold political satire—the most vigorous and elastic, the most finely versified, varied, and beautiful, that the English language can boast—was almost unprecedented. Dryden was now placed above all his poetical contemporaries; and he soon after prolonged the feeling excited against Shaftesbury in a poem called *The Medal, a Satire against Sedition.* The attacks of Shadwell, a rival poet, drew from Dryden *Mac-Flecknoe*, another satire, even more vigorous than the former, but not so refined and delicate. A second part of 'Absalom and Achitophel' was published in 1684, but the body of the poem was written by Tate—Dryden contributing only about two hundred lines, containing highly wrought characters of Settle and Shadwell, under the names of Doeg and Og.

In the same year that witnessed the appearance of the second part of 'Absalom and Achitophel,' Dryden published his *Religio Laici*, a poem written to defend the Church of England against the dissenters; yet with regard to revealed religion, evincing a decided skeptical spirit. The opening of this poem is singularly solemn and majestic:—

Dim as the borrow'd beams of moon and stars
To lonely, weary, wandering travellers,
Is Reason to the soul; and as on high
Those rolling fires discover but the sky,
Not light us here; so Reason's glimmering ray
Was lent; not to assure our doubtful way,
But guide us upward to a better day.
And as those nightly tapers disappear,
When day's bright lord ascends our hemisphere;
So pale grows Reason at Religion's sight,
So dies, and so dissolves, in supernatural light.

Soon after the publication of this important poem, Dryden's religious doubts, according to his own statement, were dispelled; and that he might, in future, be under the influence of what he considered an unerring guide, he embraced the Roman Catholic faith; this change of his religious views occurring at a time when his interests would be likely to be promoted by his becoming a Catholic, was regarded with much suspicion. His conduct upon this important occasion is, however, in the judgment of Dr. Johnson and Sir Walter Scott, not fairly open to the charge, so often preferred against him, of sordid and unprincipled selfishness. The first public fruits of his change of creed was his allegorical poem of the *Hind and Panther*, in which the main argument of the Romish Church, all that has or can be said for tradition and authority, is fully stated. 'The wit in the Hind and Panther,' says Hallam, 'is sharp, ready, and pleasant; the reasoning is sometimes admirably close and strong; it is the energy of Bossuet in verse.' The Hind is the Church of Rome, the Panther, the Church of England, while the Independents, the Quakers, the Baptists and other sects, are represented as bears, hares, boars, and other animals. The obloquy and censure which Dryden's change of religion entailed upon him, are alluded to in the following lines of this poem, with more depth of feeling than he usually evinced:—

If joys hereafter must be purchased here
With loss of all that mortals hold so dear,

Then welcome infamy and public shame,
And last, a long farewell to worldly fame!
'Tis said with ease, but, oh, how hardly tried
By haughty souls to human honour tied!
O sharp convulsive pangs of agonizing pride!
Down, then, thou rebel, never more to rise,
And what thou didst, and dost so dearly prize,
That fame, that darling fame, make that thy sacrifice;
'T is nothing thou hast given, then add thy tears
For a long race of unrepenting years:
'T is nothing yet, yet all thou hast to give;
Then add those may-be years thou hast to live:
Yet nothing still; then poor and naked come,
Thy Father will receive his unthrift home,
And thy blest Saviour's blood discharge the mighty sum.

The Revolution, in 1688, deprived Dryden of his laureate; but the want of an independent income seems only to have stimulated his faculties, and his latter unendowed years produced the noblest of his works. Besides several of his best plays, he now gave to the world his versions of Juvenal and Persius, and a still weightier task—a translation of Virgil. The latter, however, must be considered the least happy of all his great performances. Dryden's want of sensibility unfitted him to translate an author who abounds, like Virgil, in tenderness, and in calm and serene dignity. This laborious work brought the poet about twelve hundred pounds; and had he complied with the wishes of Tonson, his publisher, and dedicated it to King William, he would doubtless have received a much larger sum.

The immortal ode to St. Cecilia, commonly called *Alexander's Feast*, was Dryden's next work; and it is the loftiest and most imaginative of all his compositions. 'No man,' says a learned and accomplished critic, 'has ever qualified his admiration of this noble poem.' In 1699, he published his *Fables*, for which he received three hundred pounds. The poet was now in his sixty-eighth year, but his fancy was brighter and more prolific than it had been at any earlier period of his life; it was like a brilliant sunset, or a river that expands in breadth, and fertilizes a wider tract of country, ere it is finally engulfed in the ocean. The 'Fables' are imitations of Boccacio and Chaucer, and afford the finest specimens of the author's happy versification. No narrative poems in the language have been more generally read and admired than these finished productions. They shed a glory on the last days of the poet, and sweetly embalm the remembrance of his genius. Dryden died on the first of May, 1700, and his remains, after being embalmed, and lying in state twelve days, were interred, with great pomp, in Westminster Abbey.

The range of Dryden's muse embraced almost every variety of poetical composition. He was not, however, in all equally successful. His dramas, though we occasionally find in them redeeming passages, are, as a whole, essentially and utterly bad. For character, passion, action, or interest, we search through them in vain; and it is only surprising that so superior a mind as his confessedly was, should not have perceived its total want of dramatic sympathy. In lyric, in didactic, and in narrative poetry, his genius shines forth with almost unparalleled splendor. His odes are as nearly perfect as any odes in the language; and amongst English satirists he occupies the foremost place in the foremost ranks. The satire, notwithstanding its extreme polish and splendor, is appalling, and tremendous. It excites our indignation against its objects, not only on account of the follies, or faults, which it imputes to them, but also on account of their writhing beneath the infliction of so splendid a weapon. We forget the offender in the awfulness and majesty of the power by which he is crushed. Instead of shrinking at the horror of the carnage, we are lost in admiration of the brilliancy of the victory. Like the lightning of heaven, the satire of Dryden throws a splendor around the object which it destroys. He has immortalized the persons whom he branded with contempt; for who would have remembered Shadwell, if he had not been handed down to everlasting fame, as MacFlecknoe. The energy, the beauty, the power, the majesty, and the delicacy of his style, in poetic narration, are unrivalled. His versification is even now, notwithstanding the efforts of Pope, and his other successors, the noblest and the most perfect in the language. As Milton in blank verse, so Dryden in the heroic rhymed measure, is without a competitor or even an approximator.

Waller was smooth, but Dryden taught to join
The varying verse, the full resounding line,
The long majestic march, and energy divine.

The following extracts are introduced in the order in which we have noticed the author's various poems. We shall not, however, present an entire scene from any one of his dramas, but shall content ourselves with selecting a few striking passages from different plays.

Love is that madness which all lovers have;
But yet 'tis sweet and pleasing so to rave.
'T is an enchantment where the reason 's bound;
But Paradise is in th' enchanted ground.
A palace void of envy, cares, and strife;
Where gentle hours delude so much of life.
To take those charms away, and set me free,
Is but to send me into misery.
And prudence, of whose cure so much you boast,
Restores those pains which that sweet folly lost.

[*Conquest of Grenada.*]

LOVE AND BEAUTY.

A change so swift what heart did ever feel!
It rushed upon me like a mighty stream,
And bore me in a moment far from shore.
I've loved away myself; in one short hour
Already am I gone an age of passion.

Was it his youth, his valour, or success?
These might perhaps be found in other men.
'T was that respect, that awful homage paid me;
That fearful love which trembled in his eyes,
And with a silent earthquake shook his soul.
But when he spoke, what tender words he said
So softly, that like flakes of feather'd snow,
They melted as they fell.

[*Spanish Friar.*]

MIDNIGHT REPOSE.

All things are hush'd, as Nature's self lay dead;
The mountains seem to nod their drowsy head,
The little birds in dreams their songs repeat,
And sleeping flowers beneath the night-dew sweat;
Even lust and envy sleep, yet love denies
Rest to my soul and slumber to my eyes.
Three days I promis'd to attend my doom,
And two long days and nights are yet to come,
'Tis sure the noise of a tumultuous fight; [*Noise within.*]
They break the truce and sally out by night.

[*Indian Emperor.*]

FEAR OF DEATH.

Berenice. Saint Catherine.

Ber. Now death draws near, a strange perplexity
Creeps coldly on me, like a fear to die:
Courage uncertain dangers may abate,
But who can bear th' approach of certain fate?
St. Cath. The wisest and the best some fear may show,
And wish to stay, though they resolve to go.
Ber. As some faint pilgrim, standing on the shore,
First views the torrent he would venture o'er,
And then his inn upon the farther ground,
Loath to wade through, and loather to go round:
Then dipping in his staff, does trial make
How deep it is, and, sighing, pulls it back:
Sometimes resolved to fetch his leap; and then
Runs to the bank, but there stops short again:
So I at once
Both heavenly faith and human fear obey;
And feel before me in an unknown way.
For this blest voyage I with joy prepare,
Yet am asham'd to be a stranger there.

[*Tyrannic Love.*]

ADAM AFTER THE FALL.

Adam. Raphael. Eve.

Adam. Heaven is all mercy; labour I would choose;
And could sustain this Paradise to lose:
The bliss; but not the place. 'Here,' could I say,
'Heaven's winged messenger did pass the day;

Under this pine the glorious angel stay'd:'
Then show my wondering progeny the shade.
In woods and lawns, where'er thou didst appear,
Each place some monument of thee should bear.
I, with green turfs, would grateful altars raise,
And heaven, with gums and offer'd incense, praise.
Raph. Where'er thou art, He is, th' eternal mind
Acts through all places; is to none confined:
Fills ocean, earth, and air, and all above,
And through the universal mass does move.
Thou canst be nowhere distant; yet this place
Had been thy kingly seat, and here thy race,
From all the ends of peopled earth, had come
To reverence thee, and see their native home.
Immortal then, now sickness, care, and age,
And war, and luxury's more direful rage,
Thy crimes have brought, to shorten mortal breath,
With all the numerous family of death.
* * * * * * *
Adam. The deaths thou show'st are forced and full of strife,
Cast headlong from the precipice of life.
Is there no smooth descent—no painless way
Of kindly mixing with our native clay?
Raph. There is—but rarely shall that path be trod,
Which, without horror, leads to death's abode.
Some few, by temperance taught, approaching slow,
So distant fate by easy journeys go;
Gently they lay them down, as evening sheep
On their own woolly fleeces softly sleep.
Adam. So noiseless would I live, such death to find,
Like timely fruit, not shaken by the wind,
But ripely dropping from the sapless bough,
And, dying, nothing to myself would owe.
Eve. Thus daily changing, with a duller taste
Of lessening joys, I, by degrees, would waste:
Still quitting ground, by unperceived decay,
And steal myself from life, and melt away.

[*State of Innocence.*

ALEXANDER'S FEAST.

'T was at the royal feast, for Persia won,
By Philip's warlike son:
Aloft in awful state
The godlike hero sate
On his imperial throne:
His valiant peers were plac'd around,
Their brows with roses and with myrtle bound;
So should desert in arms be crown'd.
The lovely Thais by his side
Sat, like a blooming Eastern bride,
In flower of youth and beauty's pride.
Happy, happy, happy pair;
None but the brave,
None but the brave,
None but the brave deserves the fair.

Timotheus, plac'd on high
Amid the tuneful choir
With flying fingers touch'd the lyre:
The trembling notes ascend the sky,
And heavenly joys inspire.
The song began from Jove,
Who left his blissful seats above,
Such is the power of mighty Love!
A dragon's fiery form belied the god:
Sublime on radiant spheres he rode,
When he to fair Olympia press'd;
And while he sought her snowy breast,
Then round her slender waist he curl'd,
And stamp'd an image of himself, a sov'reign of the world.
The list'ning crowd admire the lofty sound;
A present deity, they shout around;
A present deity, the vaulted roofs rebound:
With ravish'd ears
The monarch hears,
Assumes the god,
Affects to nod,
And seems to shake the spheres.

The praise of Bacchus then the sweet musician sung,
Of Bacchus ever fair, and ever young:
The jolly god in triumph comes:
Sound the trumpets, beat the drums;
Flush'd with a purple grace
He shows his honest face.
Now, give the hautboys breath! he comes! he comes!
Bacchus, ever fair and young,
Drinking joys did first ordain:
Bacchus' blessings are a treasure;
Drinking is the soldier's pleasure:
Rich the treasure
Sweet the pleasure
Sweet is pleasure after pain.

Sooth'd with the sound, the king grew vain:
Fought all his battles o'er again:
And thrice he routed all his foes, and thrice he slew the slain.
The master saw the madness rise;
His glowing cheeks, his ardent eyes;
And, while he heav'n and earth defied,
Chang'd his head, and check'd his pride.
He chose a mournful muse.
Soft pity to infuse:
He sang Darius great and good,
By too severe a fate
Fall'n, fall'n, fall'n, fall'n,
Fall'n from his high estate,
And welt'ring in his blood:
Deserted at his utmost need
By those his former bounty fed,

On the bare earth expos'd he lies,
With not a friend to close his eyes.
With downcast look the joyless victor sate,
Revolving in his alter'd soul
The various turns of fate below;
And now and then a sigh he stole,
And tears began to flow.

The mighty master smil'd to see
That love was in the next degree;
'Twas but a kindred sound to move;
For pity melts the mind to love.
Softly sweet in Lydian measures,
Soon he sooth'd his soul to pleasures;
War, he sung, is toil and trouble;
Honour but an empty bubble;
Never ending, still beginning,
Fighting still, and still destroying;
If the world be worth thy winning,
Think, O think it worth enjoying!
Lovely Thais sits beside thee,
Take the good the gods provide thee.
The many rend the skies with loud applause;
So love was crown'd, but music won the cause.
The prince, unable to conceal his pain.
Gazed on the fair
Who caus'd his care,
And sigh'd and look'd, sigh'd and look'd,
Sigh'd and look'd, and sigh'd again.
At length with love and wine at once oppress'd,
The vanquish'd victor sunk upon her breast.

Now strike the golden lyre again;
A louder yet, and yet a louder strain.
Break his bands of sleep asunder,
And rouse him like a rattling peal of thunder.
Hark! hark! the horrid sound
Has rais'd up his head,
As awak'd from the dead,
And, amazed, he stares around.
Revenge, revenge, Timotheus cries;
See the Furies arise;
See the snakes that they rear!
How they hiss in the air,
And the sparkles that flash from their eyes!
Behold a ghastly band,
Each a torch in his hand!
These are Grecian ghosts, that in battle were slain,
And unburied remain
Inglorious on the plain;
Give the vengeance due
To the valiant crew:
Behold how they toss their torches on high!
How they point to the Persian abodes,
And glitt'ring temples of their hostile gods!

The princes applaud, with a furious joy;
And the king seiz'd a flambeau, with zeal to destroy;
Thais led the way,
To light him to his prey,
And, like another Helen, fir'd another Troy.

Thus long ago,
Ere heaving billows learn'd to blow,
While organs yet were mute,
Timotheus to his breathing flute
And sounding lyre,
Could swell the soul to rage, or kindle soft desire.
At last divine Cecilia came,
Inventress of the vocal flame;
The sweet enthusiast, from her sacred store,
Enlarg'd the former narrow bounds,
And added length to solemn sounds,
With Nature's mother-wit and arts unknown before.
Let old Timotheus yield the prize,
Or both divide the crown:
He rais'd a mortal to the skies;
She drew an angel down.

CHARACTER OF SHAFTESBURY.

Of these the false Achitophel was first;
A name to all succeeding ages curst:
For close designs and crooked counsels fit;
Sagacious, bold, and turbulent of wit;
Restless, unfix'd in principles and place;
In power unpleas'd, impatient of disgrace:
A fiery soul, which, working out its way,
Fretted the pigmy body to decay,
And o'er-informed the tenement of clay.
A daring pilot in extremity;
Pleas'd with the danger, when the waves went]
He sought the storms; but, for a calm unfit,
Would steer too nigh the sands to boast his wi
Great wits are sure to madness near allied,
And thin partitions do their bounds divide;
Else why should he, with wealth and honour b!
Refuse his age the needful hours of rest?
Punish a body which he could not please;
Bankrupt of life, yet prodigal of ease?
And all to leave what with his toil he won,
To that unfeather'd two-legged thing, a son;
Got, while his soul did huddled notions try,
And born a shapeless lump, like anarchy.
In friendship false, implacable in hate;
Resolv'd to ruin or to rule the state:
To compass this, the triple bond he broke,
The pillars of the public safety shook,
And fitted Israel for a foreign yoke:
Then, seiz'd with fear, yet still affecting fame,
Usurp'd a patriot's all-atoning name.

So easy still it proves, in factious times,
With public zeal to cancel private crimes;
How safe is treason, and how sacred ill
Where none can sin against the people's will!
Where crowds can wink, and no offence be known,
Since in another's guilt they find their own!
Yet fame deserv'd no enemy can grudge;
The statesman we abhor, yet praise the judge.
In Israel's court ne'er sat an Abethdin
With more discerning eyes, or hands more clean,
Unbrib'd, unsought, the wretched to redress,
Swift of dispatch, and easy of access.
Oh! had he been content to serve the crown
With virtues only proper for the gown;
Or had the rankness of the soil been freed
From cockle, that oppress'd the noble seed;
David for him his tuneful harp had strung,
And heaven had wanted one immortal song.
But wild ambition loves to slide, not stand;
And fortune's ice prefers to virtue's land.
Achitophel, grown weary to possess
A lawful fame, and lazy happiness,
Disdain'd the golden fruit to gather free,
And lent the crowd his arm to shake the tree.

CHARACTER OF BUCKINGHAM.

Some of their chiefs were princes of the land:
In the first rank of these did Zimri stand;
A man so various that he seem'd to be,
Not one, but all mankind's epitome:
Stiff in opinions, always in the wrong,
Was ev'ry thing by starts, and nothing long,
But, in the course of one revolving moon,
Was chemist, fiddler, statesman, and buffoon;
Then all for women, painting, rhyming, drinking,
Besides ten thousand freaks that died in thinking.
Blest madman! who could every hour employ
With something new to wish, or to enjoy,
Railing and praising were his usual themes;
And both, to show his judgment, in extremes;
So over-violent, so over-civil,
That every man with him was God or devil.
In squandering wealth was his peculiar art;
Nothing went unrewarded but desert:
Beggar'd by fools, whom still he found too late,
He had his jest, and they had his estate;
He laugh'd himself from court, then sought relief
By forming parties, but could ne'er be chief;
For, spite of him, the weight of business fell
On Absalom and wise Achitophel;
Thus, wicked but in will, of means bereft,
He left not faction, but of that was left.

THE HIND AND PANTHER.

A milk-white hind, immortal and unchang'd,
Fed on the lawns, and in the forest rang'd;
Without, unspotted; innocent, within;
She fear'd no danger, for she knew no sin:
Yet had she oft been chased with horns and hounds,
And Scythian shafts and many winged wounds
Aim'd at her heart; was often forced to fly,
And doom'd to death, though fated not to die.
Panting and pensive, now she ranged alone,
And wander'd in the kingdoms once her own:
The common hunt, though from their rage restrain'd
By sovereign power, her company disdain'd,
Grinn'd as they pass'd, and with a glaring eye
Gave gloomy signs of secret enmity.
'Tis true she bounded by, and tripp'd so light,
They had not time to take a steady sight:
For truth had such a face and such a mien,
As to be lov'd, needs only to be seen.
*   *   *   *   *   *   *
The Panther, sure the noblest next the Hind,
And fairest creature of the spotted kind;
Oh, could her in-born stains be wash'd away,
She were too good to be a beast of prey!
How can I praise, or blame, and not offend,
Or how divide the frailty from the friend?
Her faults and virtues lie so mix'd, that she
Nor wholly stands condemn'd nor wholly free;
Then like her injur'd lion, let me speak;
He can not bend her, and he would not break.
Unkind already, and estrang'd in part,
The wolf begins to share her wandering heart:
Though unpolluted yet with actual ill,
She half commits who sins but in her will.
If, as our dreaming Platonists report,
There could be spirits of a middle sort,
Too black for heaven, and yet too white for hell,
Who just dropt half-way down, nor lower fell;
So pois'd, so gently, she descends from high,
It seems a soft dismission from the sky.

THEODORE AND HONORIA.

The spring was in the prime; the neighbouring grove
Supplied with birds, the choristers of love:
Music unbought, that minister'd delight
To morning walks, and lull'd his cares by night:
There he discharg'd his friends, but not th' expense
Of frequent treats and proud magnificence.
He liv'd as kings retire, though more at large
From public business, yet with equal charge;
With house and heart still open to receive;
As well content as love would give him leave:

He would have liv'd more free; but many a guest,
Who could forsake the friend, pursu'd the feast.
 It hapt one morning, as his fancy led,
Before his usual hour he left his bed;
To walk within a lonely lawn, that stood
On every side surrounded by a wood:
Alone he walk'd, to please his pensive mind,
And sought the deepest solitude to find;
'T was in a grove of spreading pines he stray'd;
The winds within the quivering branches play'd,
And dancing trees a mournful music made.
The place itself was suiting to his care,
Uncouth and savage, as the cruel fair.
He wander'd on, unknowing where he went,
Lost in the wood, and all on love intent:
The day already half his race had run,
And summon'd him to due repast at noon,
But love could feel no hunger but his own.
 Whilst listening to the murmuring leaves he stood,
More than a mile immers'd within the wood,
At once the wind was laid, the whispering sound
Was dumb; a rising earthquake rock'd the ground;
With deeper brown the grove was overspread;
A sudden horror seiz'd his giddy head,
And his ears tinkled, and his colour fled;
Nature was in alarm; some danger nigh
Seem'd threaten'd, though unseen to mortal eye.
Unus'd to fear he summon'd all his soul,
And stood collected in himself, and whole;
Not long: for soon a whirlwind rose around,
And from afar he heard a screaming sound,
As of a dame distress'd, who cried for aid,
And fill'd with loud laments the secret shade.

Besides contributing more, perhaps, than any other English writer to improve the poetical diction of his native tongue, Dryden performed also essential service of the same kind with respect to the quality of English prose. Throwing off, still more than Cowley had done, those inversions and other forms of Latin idiom which abound in the pages of his most distinguished predecessors, he speaks in the language of one addressing, in easy yet dignified conversational phraseology, an assemblage of polite and well-educated men. Strength, ease, copiousness, variety, and animation, a the predominant qualities of his style; but the haste with which he posed often betrayed him into negligence, and even carelessness in th struction of his sentences. Notwithstanding this defect, however, t prose of Dryden may be assigned the foremost place among the spec which can be furnished of vigorous and genuine idiomatic English. following brief specimen, though far from being one of his happiest p productions, is sufficient to justify these remarks:—

LAMPOON.

In a word, that former sort of satire, which is known in England by the name of lampoon, is a dangerous sort of weapon, and for the most part unlawful. We have no moral right on the reputation of other men. It is taking from them what we can not restore to them. There are only two reasons for which we may be permitted to write lampoons; and I will not promise that they can always justify us. The first is revenge, when we have been affronted in the same nature, or have been any ways notoriously abused, and can make ourselves no other reparation. And yet we know, that, in christian charity, all offences are to be forgiven, as we expect the like pardon for those which we daily commit against Almighty God. And this consideration has often made me tremble when I was saying our Saviour's prayer; for the plain condition of the forgiveness which we beg, is the pardoning of others the offences they have done to us; for which reason I have many times avoided the commission of that fault, even when I have been notoriously provoked. Let not this, my lord, pass for vanity in me, for it is truth. More libels have been written against me than almost any man now living; and I had reason on my side to have defended my own innocence. I speak not of my poetry, which I have wholly given up to the critics: let them use it as they please: posterity, perhaps, may be more favourable to me; for interest and passion will lie buried in another age, and partiality and prejudice be forgotten. I speak of my morals, which have been sufficiently aspersed: that only sort of reputation ought to be dear to every honest man, and is to me. But let the world witness for me, that I have been often wanting to myself in that particular: I have seldom answered any scurrilous lampoon, when it was in my power to have exposed my enemies: and, being naturally vindictive, have suffered in silence, and possessed my soul in quiet.

Any thing, though never so little, which a man speaks of himself, in my opinion, is still too much; and therefore I will waive this subject, and proceed to give the second reason which may justify a poet when he writes against a particular person; and that is, when he is become a public nuisance. All those, whom Horace in his Satires, and Persius and Juvenal have mentioned in theirs, with a brand of infamy, are wholly such. It is an action of virtue to make examples of vicious men. They may and ought to be upbraided with their crimes and follies, both for their amendment, if they are not yet incorrigible, and for the terror of others, to hinder them from falling into those enormities, which they see are so severely punished in the persons of others. The first reason was only an excuse for revenge; but this second is absolutely of a poet's office to perform: but how few lampooners are now living who are capable of this duty! When they come in my way, it is impossible sometimes to avoid reading them. But, good God! how remote they are, in common justice, from the choice of such persons as are the proper subject of satire! And how little wit they bring for the support of their injustice! The weaker sex is their most ordinary theme; and the best and fairest are sure to be the most severely handled. Amongst men, those who are prosperously unjust are entitled to pangyric; but afflicted virtue is insolently stabbed with all manner of reproaches; no decency is considered, no fulsomeness is omitted; no venom is wanting, as far as dullness can supply it; for there is a perpetual dearth of wit; a barrenness of good sense and entertainment. The neglect of the readers will soon put an end to this sort of scribbling. There can be no pleasantry where there is no wit; no impression can be made where there is no truth for the foundation. To conclude: they are like the fruits of the earth in this unnatural season; the corn which held up its head is spoiled with rankness; but the greater part of the harvest is laid along, and little of good income and wholesome nourishment is received into the barns. This is almost a digression, I confess to your lordship; but a just indignation forced it from me.

Lecture the Twenty-Fourth.

THE EARL OF ROSCOMMON—THE EARL OF DORSET—SIR CHARLES SEDLEY—THE EARL OF ROCHESTER—THE DUKE OF BUCKINGHAM—MATTHEW PRIOR—JOHN POMFRET—JONATHAN SWIFT.

THE reign of Charles the Second was a period fraught with evil and danger to all the sober restraints, the decencies, and the domestic virtues of life. It was natural, therefore, that poetry should suffer in the general deterioration; and we find, accordingly, that some of the most eminent wits of the age prostrated the noble attribute of poetic genius to the base purposes of vice and licentiousness. Unfortunately, too, many of the most prominent members of the 'Merry Monarch's' court, were noblemen whose influence over the literature of the age was such as to enable them to control, in a great measure, its entire tone and spirit. Of these, Roscommon, Dorset, Sedley, Rochester, and Buckingham occupy the foremost rank.

WENTWORTH DILLON, Earl of Roscommon, was born in Ireland, in 1633. He was the nephew of the celebrated Earl of Stratford, and after having passed the years of his childhood in his native country, was removed to the Earl's seat in Yorkshire, and placed under the tuition of Dr. Hall, afterward bishop of Norwich, by whom he was so thoroughly instructed in the Latin tongue, as to be able to write in that language with classical accuracy and elegance. When the cloud of civil strife began to gather over England, and the Earl of Stratford was singled out for an impeachment, young Dillon was, by the advice of the lord primate Usher, sent to finish his education at Caen, in Normandy, under the care and direction of the learned Bochart. He afterwards travelled over much of the continent, and at Rome remained until he had acquired so complete a knowledge of the Italian language, that he was frequently taken for a native of Italy.

Soon after the Restoration, Roscommon returned to England, and was received by Charles the Second, who made him captain of the band of pensioners, in the most gracious manner. Unfortunately, in the gayeties of that corrupt age, he was tempted to indulge a violent passion for gaming;

in consequence of which he frequently hazarded his life in duels, and exceeded the bounds of his moderate fortune. A dispute with the Lord Privy Seal, about part of his estate, compelled him to revisit his native country, where he had designed to remain; but the pleasures of the English court, and the friendships which he had there contracted, finally induced him to return to London. Soon after his arrival he was made master of the horse to the Duchess of York, and married the lady Frances, eldest daughter of the Earl of Burlington. Roscommon was now settled in life; and though still addicted to the vice of gambling, yet he found time to cultivate his taste for literature, and to produce a poetical *Essay on Translated Verse*, a translation of Horace's 'Art of Poetry,' and some minor poems. He also planned, in conjunction with Dryden, a scheme for refining the English language, and fixing its standard. But while he was meditating on this and similar topics connected with literature, the arbitrary measures of James the Second, threw the whole nation into a state of alarm; and Roscommon, dreading the result, prepared to retire to Rome, saying,—'It was best to sit near the chimney when the chamber smoked.' An attack of the gout, however, prevented his departure, and he died on the seventeenth of January, 1684, in the fifty-second year of his age. 'At the moment in which he expired,' says Johnson, 'he uttered, with an energy of voice that expressed the most fervent devotion, two lines of his own version of 'Dies Iræ':—

My God, my Father, and my Friend,
Do not forsake me in my end!

Roscommon's 'Essay on Translated Verse,' is his only production which may be said to elevate him above mediocrity. In it he inculcates, in didactic poetry, the rational principles of translation previously laid down by Cowley and Denham; and it is worthy of remark, that though Milton's 'Paradise Lost' had then been published only four years, Roscommon notices the sixth book of that great poem for its sublimity. Dryden has heaped on this poet the most lavish praise, and Pope has said that 'every author's merit was his own;' but posterity has not confirmed these judgments. Roscommon stands on the same ground with Denham—elegant and sensible, but cold and unimpassioned. We subjoin a single passage from his 'Essay on Translated Verse,' and his version of the 'Dies Iræ.'

CAUTION AGAINST FALSE PRIDE.

On sure foundations let your fabric rise,
And with attractive majesty surprise;
Not by affected meretricious arts,
But strict harmonious symmetry of parts;
Which through the whole insensibly must pass
With vital heat, to animate the mass.
A pure, an active, an auspicious flame,
And bright as heaven, from whence the blessing came.

But few—O few! souls free-ordain'd by fate,
The race of gods have reach'd that envied height
No rebel Titan's sacrilegious crime,
By heaping hills on hills, can hither climb:
The grisly ferryman of hell denied
Æneas entrance, till he knew his guide.
How justly then will impious mortals fall,
Whose pride would soar to heaven without a call.
  Pride (of all others the most dangerous fault)
Proceeds from want of sense, or want of thought.
The men who labour and digest things most,
Will be much apter to despond than boast;
For if your author be profoundly good,
'T will cost you dear before he 's understood.
How many ages since has Virgil writ!
How few are they who understand him yet!
Approach his altars with religious fear:
No vulgar deity inhabits there.
Heaven shakes not more at Jove's imperial nod
Than poets should before their Mantuan god.
Hail mighty Maro! may that sacred name
Kindle my breast with thy celestial flame,
Sublime ideas and apt words infuse:
The Muse instructs my voice, and thou inspire the Muse.

ON THE DAY OF JUDGMENT.

That day of wrath, that dreadful day.
Shall the whole world in ashes lay,
As David and the Sibyls say.

What horror will invade the mind,
When the strict Judge, who would be kind,
Shall have few venial faults to find!

The last loud trumpet's wondrous sound,
Shall through the rending tombs rebound,
And wake the nations under ground.

Nature and Death shall, with surprise,
Behold the pale offender rise,
And view the Judge with conscious eyes.

Then shall, with universal dread,
The sacred mystic book be read,
To try the living and the dead.

The Judge ascends his awful throne;
He makes each secret sin be known,
And all with shame confess their own.

O then, what interest shall I make
To save my last important stake,
When the most just have cause to quake?

Thou mighty formidable King,
Thou mercy's unexhausted spring,
Some comfortable pity bring.

Forget not what my ransom cost,
Nor let my dear-bought soul be lost
In storms of guilty terror tost.

* * * *

Prostrate my contrite heart I rend,
My God, my Father, and my Friend,
Do not forsake me in my end!

Well may they curse their second breath,
Who rise to a reviving death.
Thou great Creator of mankind,
Let guilty man compassion find.

CHARLES SACKVILLE, Earl of Dorset, was a direct descendant from Thomas Sackville, Lord Buckhurst, and was born on the twenty-fourth of January, 1637. He received his education under the guidance and instruction of a private tutor, after which he travelled upon the continent, passing most of his time in Italy, whence he returned to England just before the Restoration. He soon after entered the House of Commons, where he might have shone conspicuously, had he devoted himself to the politics of the times; but he unfortunately lived in an age when pleasure was more in fashion than business, and he applied his talents rather to looks, conversation, gallantry, and the fashionable excesses of Charles's court, than to the more important pursuits of a statesman. In the first Dutch war, he went a volunteer under the Duke of York; and the night before the naval engagement, in which Opdam, the Dutch admiral, was, with all his crew, blown up, he wrote a song, which is his best composition, and which Prior pronounced, 'one of the prettiest songs that ever was made.' On his return from the war, Dorset was made a lord of the bedchamber to Charles the Second; and on account of his rare accomplishments and distinguished politeness, was frequently, sent by that monarch, on embassies of compliment into France. When William and Mary came into power, Dorset was made lord chamberlain of the household; and as his office obliged him to take the king's pension from Dryden, it is said that he allowed him an equivalent out of his own estate.

Dorset was a very liberal patron of the wits of that age, and took great pleasure in promoting their interest. He introduced Butler's 'Hudibras' to the notice of the court, was consulted by Waller, and almost idolized by Dryden. Hospitable, generous, and refined, we need not wonder at the incense which was heaped upon him by his contemporaries. His works are trifling, a few satires and songs making up the catalogue. They are eloquent, and sometimes forcible; but when a man like Prior writes of them, that 'there is a lustre ln his verses like that of the sun in Claude Lorraine's landscapes,' it is impossible not to be struck with that gross adulation of rank and fashion which disgraced the literature of the age. Dorset died at Bath, on the nineteenth of January, 1706, in his seventieth year. To the following song we have already alluded, and we introduce it as his best performance:—

SONG.

(*Written at sea*, 1665, *the night before an engagement in the first Dutch war.*)

To all you ladies now at land,
  We men at sea indite;
But first would have you understand
  How hard it is to write;
The Muses now, and Neptune too,
We must implore to write to you.
    With a fa la, la, la, la.

For though the Muses should prove kind,
  And fill our empty brain;
Yet if rough Neptune rouse the wind,
  To wave the azure main,
Our paper, pen, and ink, and we,
Roll up and down our ships at sea.
    With a fa, &c.

Then, if we write not by each post,
  Think not we are unkind:
Nor yet conclude our ships are lost
  By Dutchmen or by wind:
Our tears we 'll send a speedier way;
The tide shall bring them twice a-day.
    With a fa, &c.

The king with wonder and surprise,
  Will swear the seas grow bold;
Because the tides will higher rise
  Than e'er they did of old:
But let hlm know it is our tears
Bring floods of grief to Whitehall stairs.
    With a fa, &c.

Should foggy Opdam chance to know
  Our sad and dismal story,
The Dutch would scorn so weak a foe.
  And quit their fort at Goree:
For what resistance can they find
From men who 've left their hearts behind?
    With a fa, &c.

Let wind and weather do its worst,
  Be you to us but kind;
Let Dutchmen vapour, Spaniards curse,
  No sorrow we shall find:
'Tis then no matter how things go,
Or who 's our friend, or who 's our foe.
    With a fa, &c.

To pass our tedious hours away,
  We throw a merry main;
Or else at serious ombre play;
  But why should we in vain

Each other's ruin thus pursue?
We were undone when we left you.
With a fa, &c.

But now our fears tempestuous grow,
And cast our hopes away;
While you, regardless of our woe,
Sit careless at a play:
Perhaps permit some happier man
To kiss your hand, or flirt your fan.
With a fa, &c.

When any mournful tune you hear,
That dies in every note,
As if it sigh'd with each man's care
For being so remote:
Think then how often love we've made
To you, when all those tunes were played.
With a fa, &c.

In justice, you can not refuse
To think of our distress,
When we for hopes of honour lose
Our certain happiness:
All those designs are but to prove
Ourselves more worthy of your love.
With a fa, &c.

And now we've told you all our loves,
And likewise all our fears,
In hopes this declaration moves
Some pity for our tears;
Let 's hear of no inconstancy,
We have too much of that at sea.
With a fa la, la, la, la.

Sir CHARLES SEDLEY, one of the brightest satellites of the court of Charles the Second, was the son of Sir John Sedley, and was born at Aylesford, Kent, in 1639. At seventeen years of age he became a fellow-commoner of Wadham College, Oxford; but becoming dissatisfied with college life, he retired, after passing a year or two at his studies, without a degree, to his native county, where he remained, apparently unoccupied, until the Restoration. As soon, however, as that important event occurred he went to London in order to join the general jubilee; and at once commenced wit, courtier, poet, and gallant. He was so much admired for his taste and elegance, that he became a kind of oracle among the poets; and no performance was either applauded or condemned till Sir Charles Sedley had given judgment upon it. His popularity and influence induced the king to ask him, jestingly, 'if he had not obtained from Nature a patent to be Apollo's viceroy?'

Sedley's career at court was, for some years, brilliant almost without a parallel; but it cost him the sacrifice of his estate, his time, and his morals.

In more advanced years, however, he thoroughly reformed; obtained a seat in parliament, and actively assisted to bring about the Revolution. King James had had an intrigue with Sedley's daughter, and created her Countess of Dorchester—a circumstance which greatly exasperated the poet against the court. 'I hate ingratitude,' said he, 'and as the king has made my daughter a countess, I will endeavor to make his daughter a queen'—alluding to the Princess Mary, wife of the Prince of Orange. Sedley's conversation was highly prized, and he lived to delight his friends with it till nearly the sixty-third year of his age. His death occurred in 1701.

Sir Charles Sedley was a much more voluminous writer than any other of his noble contemporary wits. His works comprise two octavo volumes, and consist of plays, translations, songs, and occasional poems. His songs are light and graceful, with a more studied and felicitous diction than is seen in any other of the court poets. One of his best, 'Ah, Chloris! could I now but sit,' is found in his play, *The Mulberry Garden*, and has often been published as the composition of the Scottish patriot, Duncan Forbes, of Culloden. It is as follows:—

SONG.

Ah, Chloris! could I now but sit
  As unconcern'd as when
Your infant beauty could beget
  No happiness or pain.
When I this dawning did admire,
  And praised the coming day,
I little thought the rising fire
  Would take my rest away.

Your charms in harmless childhood lay
  Like metals in a mine;
Age from no face takes more away,
  Than youth conceal'd in thine.
But as your charms insensibly
  To their perfection prest,
So love as unperceiv'd did fly,
  And center'd in my breast.

My passion with your beauty grew-
  While Cupid at my heart,
Still as his mother favour'd you,
  Threw a new flaming dart.
Each gloried in their wanton part;
  To make a lover, he
Employ'd the utmost of his art—
  To make a beauty, she.

John Wilmot, Earl of Rochester, was the son of Henry, Earl of Rochester, and was born on the ninth of April, 1647. He was educated in classical literature at Burford free-school, and there acquired the Latin language to such perfection, that till his death he retained the keenest relish for its beauties. In 1659, he was admitted a nobleman of Wadham College, Oxford, and in 1661, was, by special dispensation, created master of arts in convocation. Rochester, after he left the university, travelled through France and Italy, and on his return to England became connected with the court, and soon, in the figurative language of Dr. Johnson, 'blazed out his youth and his health in lavish voluptuousness,' and died from physical exhaustion and decay, on the twenty-sixth of July, 1680, before he had reached the thirty-third year of his age.

In the profligate court of Charles the Second, Rochester was the most profligate. His intrigues, his low amours, and disguises, his erecting a stage and playing the mountebank on Tower-hill, and his having been five years in a state of inebriety, are circumstances well known, and even admitted by himself. It is remarkable, however, that his domestic letters, which were recently published, show him in a totally different light—tender, playful, and alive to all the affections of a husband, a father, and a son. His repentance itself says much for the natural character of the unfortunate profligate. If we may judge from the memoir left by Dr. Burnet, who was his lordship's spiritual guide on his death-bed, it was sincere and unreserved. We may therefore, without hesitation, regard Rochester as one of those unfortunate men whose vices are less the effect of an inborn tendency, than of external corrupting circumstances. It may, with great propriety, be said of him, that 'nothing in his life became him like the leaving it.'

Rochester's poems consist chiefly of light effusions, thrown off without apparent labor. Many of them are so very licentious as to be unfit for publication; but in one of these, he has, *in one line*, happily hit off the character of Charles the Second:—

A merry monarch, scandalous, and poor.

Rochester's songs, of which the two that follow are but fair specimens, are exceedingly sweet and musical:—

SONG.

While on those lovely looks I gaze,
  To see a wretch pursuing,
In raptures of a bless'd amaze,
  His pleasing happy ruin;
'Tis not for pity that I move;
  His fate is too aspiring,
Whose heart, broke with a load of love,
  Dies wishing and admiring.

But if this murder you'd forego,
  Your slave from death removing,
Let me your art of charming know,
  Or learn you mine of loving.
But whether life or death betide,
  In love 'tis equal measure;
The victor lives with empty pride,
  The vanquish'd die with pleasure.

CONSTANCY.

I can not change as others do,
  Though you unjustly scorn;
Since that poor swain that sighs for you,
  For you alone was born.
No, Phillis, no; your heart to move
  A surer way I'll try;
And, to revenge my slighted love,
  Will still love on, will still love on, and die.

When kill'd with grief Amyntas lies,
  And you to mind shall call
The sighs that now unpitied rise,
  The tears that vainly fall;
That welcome hour that ends this smart
  Will then begin your pain,
For such a faithful, tender heart
  Can never break, can never break in vain.

The following letters, the one to his wife, and the other to his son, will ever be read with deep interest; as confirmatory of the tenderness of his domestic relations:—

I am very glad to hear news from you, and I think it very good when I hear you are well; pray be pleased to send me word what you are apt to be pleased with, that I may show you how good a husband I can be; I would not have you so formal as to judge of the kindness of a letter by the length of it, but believe of every thing that it is as you would have it.

'Tis not an easy thing to be entirely happy; but to be kind is very easy, and that is the greatest measure of happiness. I say not this to put you in mind of being kind to me; you have practiced that so long, that I have a joyful confidence you will never forget it; but to show that I myself have a sense of what the methods of my life seem so utterly to contradict, I must not be too wise about my own follies, or else this letter had been a book dictated to you, and published to the world. It will be more pertinent to tell you, that very shortly the king goes to Newmarket, and then I shall wait on you at Adderbury; in the mean time, think of any thing you would have me do, and I shall thank you for the occasion of pleasing you.

Mr. Morgan I have sent in this errand, because he plays the rogue here in town so extremely, that he is not to be endured; pray, if he behaves himself so at Adderbury, send me word, and let him stay till I send for him. Pray, let Ned come up to town; I have a little business with him, and he shall be back in a week.

Wonder not that I have not written to you all this while, for it was hard for me to know what to write upon several accounts; but in this I will only desire you not to be too much amazed at the thoughts my mother has of you, since, being mere imaginations, they will as easily vanish, as they were groundlessly erected; for my own part, I will make it my endeavour they may. What you desired of me in your other letters, shall punctually have performed. You must, I think, obey my mother in her commands to wait on her at Aylesbury, as I told you in my last letter. I am very dull at this time, and therefore think it pity in this humour to testify myself to you any farther; only, dear wife, I am your humble servant,

ROCHESTER.

Run away like a rascal, without taking leave, dear wife; it is an impolite way of proceeding, which a modest man ought to be ashamed of. I have left you a prey to your own imaginations, amongst my relations—the worst of damnations; but there will come an hour of deliverance, till when may my mother be merciful to you; so I commit you to what shall ensue, woman to woman, wife to mother, in hopes of a future appearance in glory. The small share I could spare you out of my pocket, I have sent as a debt to Mrs. Rowse. Within a week or ten days I will return you more: pray, write as often as you have leisure to your

ROCHESTER.

I hope, Charles, when you receive this, and know that I have sent this gentleman to be your tutor, you will be very glad to see I take such care of you, and be very grateful, which is best shown in being obedient and diligent. You are now grown big enough to be a man, and you can be wise enough; for the way to be truly wise is to serve God, learn your book, and observe the instructions of your parents first, and next your tutor, to whom I have entirely resigned you for this seven years, and, according as you employ that time, you are to be happy or unhappy forever; but I have so good an opinion of you, that I am glad to think you will never deceive me; dear child, learn your book and be obedient, and you shall see what a father I will be to you. You shall want no pleasure while you are good, and that you may be so are my constant prayers.

ROCHESTER.

JOHN SHEFFIELD, Duke of Buckingham, was descended from a long series of illustrious ancestors, and was born in 1649. His father, the Earl of Mulgrave, died in 1658, when Sheffield was only nine years of age; and the young lord was placed under the care of a governor to be brought up and educated. He, however, was so little satisfied with this arrangement, that he soon relieved his tutor of his charge, and at an age not exceeding twelve years, resolved to educate himself. Such a purpose formed at so early an age, is, in itself, extraordinary; and being successfully prosecuted, it imparts a lesson of sound instruction. Through his own personal efforts, Sheffield early became an accomplished scholar; and his literary acquisitions are the more wonderful, as they were made during the tumult of a military life, or the gayety of a court. He accompanied Prince Rupert, as a volunteer, in the second Dutch war; and in order to become an accomplished soldier he afterward served a campaign in the French army, under Marshal Turenne. Having signalized himself in various commands abroad, Sheffield, on his return to England, was made one of the lords of the bed-chamber to Charles the Second; and on the accession of James the Second to the crown, he became a member of that monarch's privy council. He, however, acquiesced in the Revolution, and was afterward a member of the cabinet council of William and Mary, with an annual pension of three thousand pounds. Sheffield was a distinguished favorite with Queen Anne, who, after she ascended the throne, heaped favors upon him with a very lavish hand. Opposed to the accession of George the First, he continued actively engaged in public affairs till his death, which occurred on the twenty-fourth of February, 1721.

Sheffield was the author of several poems, among which are an *Essay on Satire*, and an *Essay on Poetry*, the latter of which should, perhaps, be regarded as his principal performance. It is written in the heroic couplet, and in all probability suggested Pope's 'Essay on Criticism.' It is of the style and order of merit of Denham and Roscommon—plain, perspicuous, and sensible, but contains little of true poetry. We subjoin the following extract:—

Of all those arts in which the wise excel,
Nature's chief master-piece is writing well;
No writing lifts exalted man so high,
As sacred and soul-moving poesy:
No kind of work requires so nice a touch,
And if well finish'd, nothing shines so much.
But heaven forbid we should be so profane
To grace the vulgar with that noble name.
'Tis not a flash of fancy, which, sometimes
Dazzling our minds, sets off the slightest rhymes;
Bright as a blaze, but in a moment done:
True wit is everlasting like the sun,
Which, though sometimes behind a cloud retir'd,
Breaks out again, and is by all admir'd.
Number and rhyme, and that harmonious sound
Which not the nicest ear with harshness wound,
Are necessary, yet but vulgar arts;
And all in vain these superficial parts
Contribute to the structure of the whole;
Without a genius, too, for that's the soul:
A spirit which inspires the work throughout,
As that of nature moves the world about;
A flame that glows amidst conceptions fit,
Even something of divine, and more than wit;
Itself unseen, yet all things by it shown,
Describing all men, but describ'd by none.
Where dost thou dwell? what caverns of the brain
Can such a vast and mighty thing contain?
When I at vacant hours in vain thy absence mourn,
O where dost thou retire? and why dost thou return,
Sometimes with powerful charms, to hurry me away
From pleasures of the night and business of the day?
Ev'n now too far transported, I am fain
To check thy course, and use the needful rein,
As all is dullness when the fancy's bad,
So without judgment fancy is but mad:
And judgment has a boundless influence,
Not only in the choice of words or sense,
But on the world, on manners, and on men:
Fancy is but the feather of the pen;
Reason is that substantial useful part
Which gains the head, while t' other wins the heart.

From the noble poets who have thus far occupied our attention during the present remarks, we proceed to notice Prior, Pomfret, and Swift, by whom we shall be fairly introduced to the literary age of Queen Anne.

Matthew Prior belongs to that extraordinary class of men whose menta energy is sufficient to triumph over the disadvantages of an obscure origin, and finally to rise to eminence. He was the son of a joiner, and was born at Wimborne, in Middlesex, on the twenty-first of July, 1664. His father, at his death, which occurred during the childhood of the future poet and statesman, left him in the care of an uncle who was a vintner, near Charing Cross, and who discharged the trust reposed in him with a tenderness truly paternal. At a proper age he sent him to Westminster school, then under the care of the celebrated Dr. Busby; but not being in circumstances to extend his education beyond that of the school, he took him, after he had become well advanced in literature, to his own home to aid him in the business of the inn. Here he was accidentally found by the Earl of Dorset, that celebrated patron of genius, reading Horace; and with his proficiency the nobleman was so much delighted, that he at once undertook the care, and assumed the expense, of his academical education. Prior, in the eighteenth year of his age, entered St. John's College, Cambridge. and soon became distinguished for his classical attainments. He was made a bachelor of arts in 1686, and soon after produced, in conjunction with Charles Montague, the *City Mouse and Country Mouse*, in ridicule of Dryden's 'Hind and Panther.' The Earl of Dorset did not, as is too often the case, forget the poet that he had snatched from obscurity; but invited him to London, and obtained for him an appointment as secretary to the Earl of Berkeley, ambassador to the Hague. In this capacity he had the good fortune to obtain the approbation of King William, who appointed him one of the gentlemen of his bed-chamber. In 1697, Prior was appointed secretary to the embassy on the treaty of Ryswick, at the conclusion of which he was presented with a considerable amount of money by the lords justices. During the following year he was sent ambassador to the court of Versailles; and after some other temporary honors and appointments, was made a commissioner of trade. In 1701, Prior entered the House of Commons as representative for the borough of East-Grimstead, and abandoning his former friends, the Whigs, joined the Tories in impeaching Lord Somers. This came with a peculiarly bad grace from Prior; for the charge against Somers was, that he had advised the partition treaty, in which treaty the poet himself had acted as agent. He evinced his patriotism, however, by afterward celebrating, in verse, the battles of Blenheim and Ramillies. When the Whig government was at length overturned, Prior became attached to Harley's administration, and went with Lord Bolingbroke to France, in 1711, to negotiate a treaty of peace. He lived in Paris in great splendor, was a favorite of the French monarch, and enjoyed all the honors of ambassador.

Prior returned to London in 1715, and the Whigs being again in office, he was committed to prison on a charge of high treason. The accusation against him was, that he had held clandestine conferences with the French plenipotentiary, though, as he justly replied, no treaty was ever made without private interviews and preliminaries. The Whigs were indignant at the disgraceful treaty of Utrecht; but Prior only shared in the culpability of the government. The able but profligate Bolingbroke was the master-spirit that prompted the humiliating concession to France. After being kept in confinement during two tedious years, the poet was at length released without even the form of a trial. He had, in the interval, written his poem of *Alma;* and being now left without any other support than that which he derived from his fellowship of St. John's College, he continued his studies, and produced his *Solomon*, the most elaborate of his works. He had also recourse to the publication of a collected edition of his poems, from which he realized the handsome sum of four thousand pounds. An equal amount was presented to him by the Earl of Oxford, and his old age was thus amply provided for. He was now ambitious only of comfort and private enjoyment. These, however, he did not long possess; as his death, which occurred on the eighteenth of September, 1721, soon followed his retirement.

The works of Prior embrace odes, songs, epistles, epigrams, and tales, and exhibit a great variety of style and subject. His largest poem, 'Solomon,' is of a serious character, and was regarded by the author as his best production. It is certainly the most moral, and perhaps the most correctly written; but the tales and lighter pieces of Prior, are, in our judgment, his happiest efforts. In these he displays that 'charming ease' with which he embellishes all his poems, added to the lively illustration and colloquial humor of his great model, Horace. No poet, perhaps, ever possessed, in greater perfection, the art of graceful and fluent versification, than Prior. His narratives flow on like a clear stream, without a single fall, and interest us by their perpetual good-humor and vivacity, even when they wander into metaphysics, as in 'Alma,' or into licentiousness, as in his *Tales*. His expression is choice and studied, abounding in classical allusions and images, but without any air of pedantry or constraint. Like Swift, he loved to versify the common occurrences of life, and relate his personal feelings and adventures; but he had none of the dean's bitterness or misanthropy, and employed no stronger weapons of satire than raillery and arch allusion. He sported on the surface of existence, noting its foibles, its pleasures, and its eccentricities, but without the power of penetrating into its recesses, or evoking the higher passions of our nature. He was the most natural of artificial poets—a seeming paradox, yet as true as the old maxim, that 'the perfection of art is the concealment of art.' The following specimens sufficiently exemplify all the peculiar characteristics of this author to which we have alluded:—

THE GARLAND.

The pride of every grove I chose,
The violet sweet and lily fair,
The dappled pink and blushing rose,
To deck my charming Chloe's hair.

At morn the nymph vouchsaf'd to place
Upon her brow the various wreath;
The flowers less blooming than her face,
The scent less fragrant than her breath.

The flowers she wore along the day,
And every nymph and shepherd said,
That in her head they look'd more gay
Than glowing in their native bed.

Undress'd at evening, when she found
Their odours lost, their colours past,
She chang'd her look, and on the ground
Her garland and her eyes she cast.

That eye dropp'd sense distinct and clear,
As any muse's tongue could speak,
When from its lid a pearly tear
Ran trickling down her beauteous cheek.

Dissembling what I knew too well,
My love, my life, said I, explain
This change of humour; prithee tell—
That falling tear—what does it mean?

She sigh'd, she smil'd; and to the flowers
Pointing, the lovely mor'list said,
See, friend, in some few fleeting hours,
See yonder, what a change is made.

Ah me! the blooming pride of May
And that of beauty are but one;
At morn both flourish bright and gay,
Both fade at evening, pale, and gone.

AN EPITAPH.

Interr'd beneath this marble stone,
Lie sauntering Jack and idle Joan.
While rolling threescore years and one
Did round this globe their courses run;
If human things went ill or well,
If changing empires rose or fell,
The morning past, the evening came,
And found this couple just the same.
They walk'd and ate, good folks: What then?
Why, then they walk'd and ate again;
They soundly slept the night away;
They did just nothing all the day.
Nor sister either had nor brother;
They seem'd just tallied for each other.
Their Moral and Economy
Most perfectly they made agree;
Each virtue kept its proper bound,
Nor trespass'd on the other's ground.
Nor fame nor censure they regarded;
They neither punish'd nor rewarded.

He cared not what the footman did;
Her maids she neither prais'd nor chid:
So every servant took his course,
And, bad at first, they all grew worse.
Slothful disorder fill'd his stable,
And sluttish plenty deck'd her table.
Their beer was strong, their wine was port;
Their meal was large, their grace was short.
They gave the poor the remnant meat,
Just when it grew not fit to eat.
They paid the church and parish rate,
And took, but read not, the receipt;
For which they claim'd their Sunday's due,
Of slumbering in an upper pew.
No man's defects sought they to know,
So never made themselves a foe,
No man's good deeds did they commend,
So never rais'd themselves a friend.
Nor cherish'd they relations poor,
That might decrease their present store;
Nor barn nor house did they repair,
That might oblige their future heir.
They neither added nor confounded;
They neither wanted nor abounded.
Nor tear nor smile did they employ
At news of public grief or joy,
When bells were rung and bonfires made,
If ask'd, they ne'er denied their aid;
Their jug was to the ringers carried,
Whoever either died or married.
Their billet at the fire was found,
Whoever was depos'd or crown'd.
Nor good, nor bad, nor fools, nor wise,
They would not learn, nor could advise;
Without love, hatred, joy, or fear,
They led—a kind of—as it were;
Nor wish'd, nor car'd, nor laugh'd, nor cried;
And so they liv'd, and so they died.

FOR MY OWN MONUMENT.

As doctors give physic by way of prevention,
Matt, alive and in health, of his tombstone took care:
For delays are unsafe, and his pious intention
May haply be never fulfilled by his heir.

Then take Matt's word for it, the sculptor is paid;
That the figure is fine, pray believe your own eye;
Yet credit but lightly what more may be said,
For we flatter ourselves, and teach marble to lie.

Yet counting as far as to fifty his years,
His virtues and vices were as other men's are;
High hopes he conceiv'd, and he smother'd great fears,
In a life party-colour'd, half pleasure, half care.

Nor to business a drudge, nor to faction a slave,
He strove to make int'rest and freedom agree;
In public employments industrious and grave,
And alone with his friends, Lord! how merry was he.

Now in equipage stately, now humbly on foot,
Both fortunes he tried, but to neither would trust;
And whirl'd in the round as the wheel turn'd about,
He found riches had wings, and knew man was but dust.

This verse, little polish'd, though mighty sincere,
Sets neither his titles nor merit to view;
It says that his relics collected lie here,
And no mortal yet knows if this may be true.

Fierce robbers there are that infest the highway,
So Matt may be kill'd and his bones never found;
False witness at court, and fierce tempests at sea,
So Matt may yet chance to be hang'd or be drown'd.

If his bones lie in earth, roll in sea, fly in air,
To Fate we must yield, and the thing is the same;
And if passing thou giv'st him a smile or a tear,
He cares not—yet prithee, be kind to his fame.

EPITAPH EXTEMPORE.

Nobles and heralds, by your leave,
  Here lies what once was Matthew Prior,
The son of Adam and of Eve;
  Can Stuart or Nassau claim higher.

John Pomfret, of whom very little is known, was the son of a clergyman, and was born at Luton, Bedfordshire, in 1667. He was educated at Queen's College, Cambridge, where he took his bachelor's degree in 1684, but did not proceed to the degree of master of arts, until 1698. On leaving the university he entered into orders, and became rector of Malden, in Bedfordshire, with an immediate prospect of preferment; but Compton, bishop of London, had conceived unjustly the idea that Pomfret's poem, *The Choice*, conveyed an immoral sentiment, and refused, therefore, to institute him into a living of considerable value to which he had been presented. Detained for a long time in London by the circumstances connected with this unfortunate affair, Pomfret, in 1703, took the small-pox, and soon after died.

The works of this amiable ill-fated author consist of occasional poems, and some *Pindaric Essays;* but his only production now popular is 'The Choice.' This has always been a favourite with that class of readers whose literary pursuits have no higher object than their own amusement. It exhibits a system of life adapted to common notions and equal to common expectations; and 'The Choice' has, therefore, been perhaps, as frequently read as any other poem in the language. To these brief remarks we add the following extract:—

FROM THE CHOICE.

If Heaven the grateful liberty would give
That I might choose my method how to live ;
And all those hours propitious fate should lend.
In blissful ease and satisfaction spend ;
Near some fair town I'd have a private seat,
Built uniform, not little, nor too great ;
Better if on a rising ground it stood ;
On this side fields, on that a neighbouring wood.
It should within no other things contain
But what are useful, necessary, plain.
Methinks 'tis nauseous ; and I'd ne'er endure
The needless pomp of gaudy furniture.
A little garden grateful to the eye,
And a cool rivulet run murmuring by ;
On whose delicious banks a stately row
Of shady limes or sycamores should grow.
At th' end of which a silent study plac'd
Should be with all the noblest authors grac'd :
Horace and Virgil, in whose mighty lines
Immortal wit and solid learning shines ;
Sharp Juvenal, and amorous Ovid too,
Who all the turns of love's soft passion knew :
He that with judgment reads his charming lines,
In which strong art with stronger nature joins,
Must grant his fancy does the best excel ;
His thoughts so tender, and express'd so well :
With all those moderns, men of steady sense,
Esteem'd for learning and for eloquence.
In some of these as fancy should advise,
I'd always take my morning exercise ;
For sure no minutes bring us more content
Than those in pleasing useful studies spent.
I'd have a clear and competent estate,
That I might live genteelly, but not great ;
As much as I could moderately spend ;
A little more, sometimes t' oblige a friend.
Nor should the sons of poverty repine
Too much at fortune ; they should taste of mine ;
And all that objects of true pity were,
Should be reliev'd with what my wants could spare ;
For that our Maker has too largely given
Should be return'd in gratitude to Heaven.
A frugal plenty should my table spread ;
With healthy, not luxurious, dishes spread ;
Enough to satisfy, and something more,
To feed the stranger, and the neighbouring poor.
Strong meat indulges vice, and pampering food
Creates diseases, and inflames the blood.
But what 's sufficient to make nature strong,
And the bright lamp of life continue long,
I'd freely take, and, as I did possess,
The bounteous Author of my plenty bless.

JONATHAN SWIFT, one of the most remarkable men of his age, was descended from a very ancient family, and was born in the city of Dublin on the thirtieth of November, 1667. His father was steward to the society of the King's Inns, but died in abject poverty before the birth of his distinguished son. His mother, a lady of Leicestershire, possessed no other fortune than a trifling annuity of twenty pounds a year; and the future poet was, therefore, from his infancy, thrown upon the bounty of his uncle, who, though kind and benevolent, had little to bestow upon his destitute nephew. The circumstances of want and dependence with which Swift was early familiar, seemed to have sunk deep into his haughty soul, and contributed much toward the formation of his future character. 'Born a posthumous child,' says Sir Walter Scott, 'and bred up an object of charity, he early adopted the custom of observing his birthday as a term, not of joy, but of sorrow, and of reading, when it annually occurred, the striking passage of Scripture in which Job laments and execrates the day upon which it was said in his father's house 'that a man child was born."

When six years of age Swift was sent to the grammar-school of Kilkenney, and in his fourteenth year was admitted a student of Trinity College, Dublin. His mind had now become somewhat awakened to the beauties of history and poetry, and to those objects he devoted himself to the neglect of academic learning, in consequence of which he was, at the expiration of four years, refused his bachelor's degree. Stung with this disgrace, he resolved from that time to study eight hours a day, and he persevered in this resolution for seven years. In 1688, when in the twenty-first year of his age, Swift was, by the death of his uncle Godwin, deprived of the meagre support which that kind uncle had been able to extend to him; in consequence of which he repaired to Leicester, where his mother then resided, to consult her respecting the future course of his life. She recommended him to seek the advice and patronage of Sir William Temple, as that nobleman had married one of her distant relatives. Temple received him with much kindness, and ultimately became so much pleased with his conversation that he detained him in his house two years. Here Swift met King William, and from the kindness and familiarity of the monarch's treatment of him, he was led to indulge hopes of preferment; the fulfillment of which, however, was never realized.

In 1692, Swift repaired to Oxford for the purpose of taking his master's degree; and having obtained this distinction, he resolved to quit the establishment of Sir William, and take orders in the Irish Church. He procured the prebend of Kilroot, in the diocess of Connor, but soon became disgusted with the life of an obscure country clergyman with an income of a hundred pounds a year. He therefore relinquished his living at Kilroot, and returned to the residence of Sir William Temple, at Moor-park. Temple died in 1699, and Swift embraced an opportunity which soon after offered, of accompanying Lord Berkeley into Ireland in the capacity of chaplain. From this nobleman he obtained the rectory of Aghar, and the vicarages of Laracor and Rathveggan; to which was afterward added the prebend of Dunlavin; all of which however, made his income only about two hundred pounds per annum. In 1701, Swift became a political writer on the side of the Whigs; and on his subsequent visit to England, he associated intimately with Addison, Steele, and Arbuthnot. In 1710, conceiving, and perhaps justly that he was neglected by the ministry, he quarrelled with the Whigs, and united with Harley and the Tory administration. He was, of course, received with open arms; for he carried with him strong weapons for party warfare—irresistible and unscrupulous satire, steady hate, and a dauntless spirit. From his new allies, he received, in 1713, the deanery of St. Patrick's, in Ireland, which was the highest point in church dignity that he ever attained.

With the return of Swift to Ireland is connected the development of some of the most extraordinary events of his life. During his residence at Moor-park, he had contracted an intimacy with Hester Johnson, daughter of Sir William Temple's steward; and on his settlement in Ireland, that lady, accompanied by another female of middle age, went to reside in his neighborhood. Her future life became, from that period, intimately connected with that of Swift, and he has immortalized her under the name of *Stella*. All this is poetic, and so far pardonable; but, unfortunately, while residing in London, he had engaged the affections of another young lady, Esther Vanhomrigh, who, under the name of *Vanessa*, rivalled Stella in poetical celebrity, and in personal misfortune. After the death of her father, this young lady and her sister retired to Ireland where they possessed a small property near Dublin. Human nature has, perhaps, never before or since presented the spectacle of a man of such transcendant powers involved in such a pitiable labyrinth of the affections. His pride or ambition led him to postpone indefinitely his marriage with Stella, to whom he was early and ardently attached; and he dared not afterward, with manly sincerity, declare his situation to Vanessa, when this second victim avowed her passion. He was flattered that a girl of eighteen, of beauty and accomplishments, sighed for 'a gown of forty-four,' and he did not stop to weigh the consequences. The removal of Vanessa to Ireland, as Stella had done before, to be near the presence of Swift—her irrepressible passion, which no coldness or neglect could extinguish—her life of deep seclusion, only chequered by his occasional visits, each of which she commemorated by planting, with her own hand, a laurel in the garden where they met—her agonizing remonstrances, when all her devotion and offerings had failed, are touching beyond expression. 'The reason I write to you,' she says, 'is because I can not tell it to you, should I see you. For when I begin to complain, then you are angry; and there is something in your looks so awful, that it strikes me dumb. O! that you may have so much regard for me left, that this complaint may touch your soul with pity. I say as little as ever I can. Did you but know what I thought, I am sure it would move you to forgive me, and believe that I can not help telling you this, and live.'

To a lady thus agitated and engrossed with the strongest passion, how cruel must have seemed the following return of Swift:—

Cadenus, common forms apart,
In every scene had kept his heart;
Had sighed and languished, vowed and writ
For pastime, or to show his wit;
But books, and time, and state affairs,
Had spoiled his fashionable airs;
He now could praise, esteem, approve,
But understood not what was love:
His conduct might have made him styled
A father, and the nymph his child.
That innocent delight he took
To see the virgin mind her book,
Was but the master's secret joy
In school to hear the finest boy.

The tragedy continued to deepen as it approached its close. Eight years had Vanessa nursed in solitude the hopeless attachment. At length she wrote to Stella, to ascertain the nature of the connection between her and Swift; and the latter, obtaining the fatal letter, rode instantly over to Marley abbey, the residence of the unhappy Vanessa. 'As he entered the apartment,' to adopt the picturesque language of Scott used in recording the scene, 'the sternness of his countenance, which was peculiarly formed to express the stronger passions, struck the unfortunate Vanessa with such terror that she could scarce ask whether he would not sit down. He answered by flinging a letter on the table; and instantly leaving the house, mounted his horse, and returned to Dublin. When Vanessa opened the packet, she only found her own letter to Stella. It was her death-warrant. She sunk at once under the disappointment of the delayed yet cherished hopes which had so long sickened her heart, and beneath the unrestrained wrath of him for whose sake she had indulged them. How long she survived this last interview is uncertain, but the time does not seem to have exceeded a few weeks.' Even Stella, though ultimately united to Swift, dropped into the grave without any public recognition of the tie, the marriage being secretly performed in the garden of the deanery, when on her part all but life had faded away. In the subsequent life and melancholy death of Swift, the fair sufferers were deeply avenged.

To interpret Swift's conduct toward Stella and Vanessa, is extremely difficult. The only charitable—perhaps the just—interpretation is, that the malady which at length overwhelmed his reason might then have been lurking in his frame: the heart might have felt its ravages before they reached the intellect. From the time of Stella's death, which occurred in January, 1727, Swift habituated himself much to retirement, and the austerity of his temper increased: he would no more participate in public entertainments, and he sometimes avoided the company of his most intimate friends. At length, even retirement itself wearied him, and the absence of former associates and associations preyed upon his restless spirit till it produced intensest anguish. In a letter to Gay, written in 1732, he says, 'he had a large house, and should hardly find one visitor, if he was not able to hire him with a bottle of wine;' and in another to Pope he exclaims, 'all my friends have forsaken me.' He realized, when too late, that he who spurns the world, will invariably find the world quite ready to spurn him in return. Old age was now rapidly approaching, deafness and giddiness his constant attendants, his temper ungovernable, and his reason giving way. Truly and beautifully has Scott said, 'the stage darkened ere the curtain fell.' The almost total silence that pervaded the last three years of his life absolutely appals and overawes the imagination. His death occurred on the nineteenth of October, 1745, and he was buried in St. Patrick's cathedral, amid the tears and prayers of his countrymen.

Notwithstanding all Swift's moral delinquencies, he was still a devoted patriot. When he first settled in Ireland he was greatly disliked, but the *Drapier's Letters*, and other similar works soon gave him unbounded popularity. His wish to serve his country was one of his ruling passions; yet it was something like the instinct of inferior animals toward their offspring—waywardness, contempt, and abuse were strangely mingled with affectionate attachment and ardent zeal. Kisses and curses were alternately on his lips. Ireland, however, gave him her whole heart—of the rabble he was more than king; hence the tears and prayers that attended his death. His fortune, which amounted to nearly twelve thousand pounds, he left chiefly to found a hospital for lunatics in Dublin.

Swift's poetry is a perfect model of its kind. He never attempted to rise above the visible earth. He was content to lash the frivolities of the age, and to depict its absurdities. In his too faithful representations, there is much to condemn and much to admire. Who has not felt the truth and humor of his *City Shower*, and his description of *Morning*. Or the liveliness of his *Grand Question Debated*, in which the knight, his lady, and the chambermaid, are so admirably drawn. His most ambitious flight is his *Rhapsody on Poetry*; and even this is pitched on a rather low key. The best lines in it are the following:—

Not empire to the rising sun,
By valour, conduct, fortune won;
Not highest wisdom in debates
For framing laws to govern states;
Not skill in sciences profound,
So large to grasp the circle round,
Such heavenly influence require,
As how to strike the muses' lyre.

Swift's verses on his own death are the finest example of his peculiar poetical vein that his poems afford. He predicts what his friends will say of his illness, his death, and his reputation; varying the style and the topics to suit each of the parties. The versification is easy and flowing, with nothing but the most familiar and common-place expressions. There are some little touches of homely pathos, which are felt like trickling tears, and the effect of the piece altogether, is electrical: it carries with it the strongest conviction of its sincerity and truth; and we see and feel how faithful a delineator of human nature, in its frailty and weakness, was the misanthropic dean of St. Patrick's. From this poem we select the following extract:—

ON HIS OWN DEATH.

Suppose me dead; and then suppose
A club assembled at the Rose,
Where, from discourse of this and that,
I grew the subject of their chat.
'The dean, if we believe report
Was never ill-received at court.
Although ironically grave,
He shamed the fool, and lashed the knave.
To steal a hint was never known,
But what he writ was all his own.'
'Sir, I have heard another story;
He was a most confounded Tory,
And grew, or he is much belied,
Extremely dull, before he died.'
'Can we the Drapier then forget?
Is not our nation in his debt?
'T was he that writ the Drapier's letters!'
'He should have left them for his betters;
We had a hundred abler men,
Nor need depend upon his pen.
Say what you will about his reading,
You never can defend his breeding;
Who, in his satires running riot,
Could never leave the world in quiet;
Attacking, when he took the whim,
Court, city, camp—all one to him.
But why would he, except he slobbered,
Offend our patriot, great Sir Robert,
Whose counsels aid the sovereign power
To save the nation every hour?
What scenes of evil he unravels,
In satires, libels, lying travels!
Not sparing his own clergy-cloth,
But eats into it like a moth!'
'Perhaps I may allow, the dean
Had too much satire in his vein,
And seemed determined not to starve it
Because no age could more deserve it.
Vice, if it e'er can be abashed,
Must be or ridiculed or lashed.
If you resent it who 's to blame?
He neither knew you, nor your name:

Should vice expect to 'scape rebuke,
Because its owner is a duke?
His friendships, still to few confined,
Were always of the middling kind;
No fools of rank or mongrel breed,
Who fain would pass for lords indeed,
Where titles give no right or power,
And peerage is a withered flower.
He would have deemed it a disgrace,
If such a wretch had known his face.
He never thought an honour done him,
Because a peer was proud to own him;
Would rather slip aside, and choose
To talk with wits in dirty shoes;
And scorn the tools with stars and garters,
So often seen caressing Charteris.
He kept with princes due decorum,
Yet never stood in awe before 'em.
He followed David's lesson just;
In princes never put his trust:
And, would you make him truly sour,
Provoke him with a slave in power.'
'Alas, poor dean! his only scope
Was to be held a misanthrope.
This into general odium drew him,
Which, if he liked, much good may 't do him.
His zeal was not to lash our crimes,
But discontent against the times:
For, had we made him timely offers
To raise his post, or fill his coffers,
Perhaps he might have truckled down,
Like other brethren of his gown.
For party he would scarce have bled:
I say no more—because he 's dead.
What writings has he left behind?
I hear they 're of a different kind:
A few in verse; but most in prose:
Some high-flown pamphlets, I suppose:
All scribbled in the worst of times,
To palliate his friend Oxford's crimes;
To praise Queen Anne, nay more, defend her,
As never favouring the Pretender:
Or libels yet concealed from sight,
Against the court, to show his spite:
Perhaps his travels, part the third;
A lie at every second word—
Offensive to a loyal ear:
But—not one sermon, you may swear.'
'As for his works in verse or prose,
I own myself no judge of those.
Nor can I tell what critics thought 'em;
But this I know all people bought 'em,
As with a moral view designed,
To please, and to reform mankind:

And, if he often missed his aim,
The world must own it to their shame,
The praise is his, and theirs the blame.
He gave the little wealth he had
To build a house for fools and mad;
To show, by one satiric touch,
No nation wanted it so much.
That kingdom he hath left his debtor;
I wish it soon may have a better.
And since you dread no further lashes,
Methinks you may forgive his ashes.'

To these lines we add the following :—

DESCRIPTION OF MORNING.

Now hardly here and there a hackney-coach
Appearing showed the ruddy morn's approach.
The slipshod 'prentice from his master's door
Had pared the dirt, and sprinkled round the floor.
Now Moll had whirled her mop with dextrous airs,
Prepared to scrub the entry and the stairs.
The youth with broomy stumps began to trace
The kennel's edge, where wheels had worn the place.
The small-coal man was heard with cadence deep,
Till drown'd in shriller notes of chimney-sweep:
Duns at his lordship's gate began to meet;
And brick-dust Moll had screamed through half the street.
The turnkey now his flock returning sees,
Duly let out a-nights to steal for fees;
The watchful bailiffs take their silent stands,
And school-boys lag with satchels in their hands.

Swift's poetry, however, formed only a sort of interlude to the strangely mixed drama of his life. None of his works were written for mere fame or solitary gratification. His restless and insatiable ambtion prompted him to wield his pen as a means of advancing his interests, or expressing his personal feelings, caprices, or resentments. Though perhaps, the most powerful and original prose writer of the age, we find little in his works with which we can sympathize. His satires, such as the *Battle of the Books*, and *Argument against the Abolition of Christianity*, are, doubtless, written with much talent; and *Gulliver's Travels*, and the *Tale of a Tub* display much original genius: but how any clergyman could write and publish in such a strain is, to us, inconceivable. We shall, however, no longer dwell upon this author, but with the following paper from the 'Tatler' close our present remarks :—

OVERSTRAINED POLITENESS, OR VULGAR HOSPITALITY.

Those inferior duties of life, which the French call *les petites morales*, or the smaller morals, are with us distinguished by the name of good manners or breeding. This I look upon, in the general notion of it, to be a sort of artificial good sense, adapted to the meanest capacities, and introduced to make mankind easy in their commerce with each other. Low and little understandings, without some rules of this kind, would be perpetually wandering into a thousand indecencies and irregularities in behaviour; and in their ordinary conversation, fall into the same boisterous familiarities that one observeth amongst them when a debauch hath quite taken away the use of their reason. In other instances, it is odd to consider, that for want of common discretion the very end of good breeding is wholly perverted; and civility, intended to make us easy, is employed in laying chains and fetters upon us, in debarring us of our wishes, and in crossing our most reasonable desires and inclinations. This abuse reigneth chiefly in the country, as I found to my vexation, when I was last there, in a visit I made to a neighbour about two miles from my cousin. As soon as I entered the parlour, they put me into the great chair that stood close by a huge fire, and kept me there by force, until I was almost stifled. Then a boy came in great hurry to pull off my boots, which I in vain opposed, urging, that I must return soon after dinner. In the mean time, the good lady whispered to her eldest daughter, and slipped a key into her hand. The girl returned instantly with a beer-glass half full of aqua mirabilis and syrop of gilly-flowers. I took as much as I had a mind for; but madam vowed I should drink it off (for she was sure it would do me good after coming out of the cold air), and I was forced to obey; which absolutely took away my stomach. When dinner came in I had a mind to sit at a distance from the fire; but they told me it was as much as my life was worth, and set me with my back just against it. Although my appetite were quite gone, I resolved to force down as much as I could; and desired the leg of a pullet. Indeed, Mr. Bickerstaff, says the lady, you must eat a wing to oblige me; and so put a couple upon my plate. I was persecuted at this rate during the whole meal. As often as I called for small beer, the master tipped the wink, and the servant brought me a brimmer of October. Some time after dinner, I ordered my cousin's man, who came with me, to get ready the horses, but it was resolved I should not stir that night; and when I seemed pretty much bent upon going, they ordered the stable-door to be locked; and the children hid my cloak and boots. The next question was, what I would have for supper? I said I never eat any thing at night; but was at last, in my own defence, obliged to name the first thing that came into my head. After three hours spent chiefly in apologies for my entertainment, insinuating to me, 'That this was the worst time of the year for provisions; that they were at a great distance from any market; that they were afraid I should be starved; and that they knew they kept me to my loss,' the lady went and left me to her husband (for they took special care I should never be alone). As soon as her back was turned, the little misses ran backward and forward every moment; and constantly as they came in or went out, made a curtsy directly at me, which in good manners I was forced to return with a bow, and, your humble servant, pretty miss. Exactly at eight the mother came up, and discovered by the redness of her face that supper was not far off. It was twice as large as the dinner, and my persecution doubled in proportion. I desired at my usual hour to go to my repose, and was conducted to my chamber by the gentleman, his lady, and the whole train of children. They importuned me to drink something before I went to bed; and upon my refusing, at last left a bottle of stingo, as they called it, for fear I should wake and be thirsty in the night. I was forced in the morning to rise and dress myself in the dark, because they would not suffer my kinsman's servant to disturb me at the hour I desired to be called. I was now resolved to break through all measures to get away; and after sitting down to a monstrous breakfast of cold beef, mutton, neat's-tongues, venison pastry, and stale beer, took leave of the family. But the gentleman would needs see me part of my way, and carry me a short cut through his own grounds, which he told me would save half a mile's riding. This last piece of civility had like to have cost me dear, being once or twice in danger of my neck, by leaping over his ditches, and at last forced to alight in the dirt; when my horse, having slipped his bridle, ran away, and took us up more than an hour to recover him again. It is evident, that none of the absurdities I met with in this visit proceeded from an ill intention, but from a wrong judgment of complaisance, and a misapplication in the rules of it.

END OF VOLUME THE FIRST.

www.ingramcontent.com/pod-product-compliance
Lightning Source LLC
LaVergne TN
LVHW021228110826
845150LV00002B/274